■ Heaven on Earth

Heaven on Earth

*The Varieties of the Millennial
Experience*

Richard Landes

OXFORD
UNIVERSITY PRESS

OXFORD
UNIVERSITY PRESS

Oxford University Press, Inc., publishes works that further
Oxford University's objective of excellence
in research, scholarship, and education.

Oxford   New York
Auckland   Cape Town   Dar es Salaam   Hong Kong   Karachi
Kuala Lumpur   Madrid   Melbourne   Mexico City   Nairobi
New Delhi   Shanghai   Taipei   Toronto

With offices in
Argentina   Austria   Brazil   Chile Czech   Republic France   Greece
Guatemala   Hungary   Italy   Japan   Poland   Portugal   Singapore
South Korea   Switzerland   Thailand   Turkey   Ukraine   Vietnam

Copyright © 2011 by Oxford University Press, Inc.

Published by Oxford University Press, Inc.
198 Madison Avenue, New York, New York 10016

www.oup.com

Oxford is a registered trademark of Oxford University Press

Library of Congress Cataloging-in-Publication Data

Landes, Richard Allen.
  Heaven on earth: the varieties of the millennial experience / Richard Landes.
    p.   cm.
  ISBN 978-0-19-975359-8 (hardcover: alk. paper)   1. Millennialism—
History.   I. Title.

  BL503.2.L36 2011
  202'.3—dc22   2010039766

1   3   5   7   9   8   6   4   2

Printed in the United States of America
on acid-free paper

■ *To my mother who taught me how to read, my father who taught me how to think, and my daughters who taught me how to explain myself.*

The stone that the builders rejected became the cornerstone.
—Psalms 118:22

If the fool would persist in his folly, he would become wise.
—William Blake, *Proverbs of Hell*

CONTENTS

PART V: ■ Postmodern Millennialism

The work on this book has, with multiple interruptions, taken place over more than a decade. In the process it has changed shape numerous times, and relegated many completed chapters to subsequent volumes. The idea for this particular assembly of studies of millennial movements first occurred to me in the years around 2000 when I was struggling with both the (ultimately unsuccessful) effort to launch the Center for Millennial Studies in the pseudo-apocalyptic time of millennium's turn, and my own partially incorrect and unfortunately too-correct predictions of what might happen in the new millennium.

At the time, the first three (originally four) chapters of introduction led to a discussion of demotic millennialism from its Jewish origins to the Peace Movements of the turn of the first Christian millennium. These historical chapters, now awaiting revision, will hopefully appear in shorter order under the provisional title of *While God Tarried: Millennialism from Jesus to the Peace of God* (33–1033). In the meantime, I wanted to write a more introductory and general work on millennialism that would take my conceptual chapters as an introduction to a series of studies of millennial movements the world over. I selected them to illustrate the varieties of the phenomenon as it manifests in tribal, agrarian, industrial, and (post-) modern societies. The idea was to take two examples of each type.

Guiding my specific choices was a conceptual conceit borrowed loosely from Georges Perec. Perec, whose parents "disappeared" in the Holocaust, wrote an entire book, *La Disparition*, without using the letter *e*, a letter even more common in French than in English.[1] To illustrate the near universality of millennialism, to cut against the grain that assumes a Judeo-Christian origin for all millennialism, I selected for treatment here only *non*-Jewish and *non*-Christian movements.

My two tribal cases constitute classic examples of a widespread phenomenon: the apocalyptic millennial response of tribal cultures to the advent of imperialist conquest. Here the choices were almost limitless: the native Indian Ghost Dance, the Mau Mau, the Rastafarians. In the specific case of the Xhosa, the Cattle-Slaying came after several military messianic uprisings; in the case of the cargo cults, various individual cargo movements came and went for nearly a century. I chose the Xhosa specifically because it illustrates a case of cataclysmic

---

[1] Georges Perec, *La Disparition* (Paris: Gallimard, 1990). The letter "e" appears 12.7 percent of the time in English versus 14.7 percent in French: M. S. Mayzner and M.E. Tresselt, *Tables of Single-Letter and Diagram Frequency Counts for Various Word-Length and Letter-Position Combinations*, Psychonomic Monograph Supplements 1(1965): 13–32.

millennialism turned against the "self," a phenomenon we may be witnessing in the West right now. I chose the cargo cults because they have a postmodern analog in some UFO cults.

Several millennia separate the two agrarian cases I've chosen—Akhenaten in the fourteenth century BCE and the Taiping in the nineteenth century CE. On the one hand, we have the bizarre and inexplicable case of the "heretic Pharaoh" Akhenaten, which illustrates possibly the earliest example of the hierarchical formula (One God, One King) and the case of a millennial movement arising not from catastrophe and despair, but from heady success. On the other hand, the Taiping illustrates how even a demotic movement predicated on radical egalitarianism can, once power achieved, become hierarchical and imperial. For the sake of my conceit, I probably should have treated the Boxer Rebellion (1900), which, unlike the Taiping, has no trace of Christian influence. But unlike the Boxers, the Taiping succeeded in taking power, and the results—the shift to imperialism and the death of over 20 *million* in fourteen years of millennial warfare against the Qing dynasty—illustrate the tendency of some millennial movements toward mega-death.

Initially, for the section on industrial societies, I intended only to treat Communist (demotic) and Nazi (hierarchical) millennialism. But the overwhelming resistance I got from modern historians to the identification of these allegedly "secular" "revolutionary" movements meant that the range of objections I needed to address, and the material I found, got out of hand. So two chapters became four. These four chapters will surely be the most controversial, since they challenge positivist notions about the clear division between secular and religious phenomena. These positivist notions have surprising inertial force when it comes to analyzing apocalyptic thinking, even in postmodern circles. They are also the most relevant for understanding our current dilemmas.

Finally, for the postmodern, or contemporary cases, I selected UFO beliefs (despite the fact that with one partial exception, none of them have generated substantive movements) because they illustrate how key millennial tropes—apocalyptic scenarios filled with both outrageous hopes and fears and paranoid conspiracy thinking—continue to work on allegedly modern, enlightened minds. The final chapter treats global jihad, the first major worldwide apocalyptic movement of the third millennium, riding on a wave of unprecedented globalization, population mobility, and instant communication systems. It constitutes potentially the largest, most powerful—and, as an "active cataclysmic" apocalyptic movement,the most problematic—movement in the long and convulsive history of millennialism.

■ TO THE SCHOLARS

As a result of my choices, I have been forced to work in fields where I am not a specialist, even where the primary sources are in languages I cannot read. I am fully aware that, despite my efforts to read the secondary literature, I venture generalizations and observations that may strike specialists in any of the fields into which I blunder as either crude or obvious; and I apologize in advance for my sins of commission and omission.

Certainly, specialists, above all the fearsome "splitters,"[2] can pick apart my presentations and find reasons to undermine any of my comparisons or analogies. And given my implicit reproach to them, that they have neglected the millennial dimension, I can imagine no small number will want to object that I have not read the latest literature; that I ignored a whole range of allegedly contradictory evidence; that I made no mention of some critical debate; that others, whom I do not cite, have already made the same arguments. My fondest hope is that I get accused of "smashing in open doors."

That is all possibly true. In my defense, each of these chapters is five times longer than intended, and at least twice as long as they should be, and every time I have investigated an objection by a colleague who read a chapter, I have found more millennial material, including in the material presented to me as contradictory. Just in scratching the surface, one finds such a wealth of material that it suggests a hidden treasure trove to those who would persist.

For example, I initially planned neither a chapter on the French Revolution nor on Marx (who would be part of the chapter on Communism). But in trying to present Marx, I found it necessary to back up to the previous apocalyptic wave that produced him and to whose disappointment he is one of the next generation's responses. A chapter on Hegel is missing here, as is one on the American Revolution, but certainly not because they cannot be written (and in the case of the American Revolution, such studies already exists).[3] The problem here is not so much establishing the link between any given phenomenon, like modern revolutions, to millennialism; it is how to then follow through on what that connection means. Most historians will grant the former, but demur on the latter or demur on the former lest they need to confront the latter.

Indeed, presented with a millennial analysis, some scholars respond with the curious ploy of banality. Position 1: nothing apocalyptic about x (e.g., the year 1000). Response: look at this and this and this. Position 2: "Oh that, that's as common as lice."[4] End of discussion. From nonexistent to banal: in any case, *irrelevant*.

Similarly, once the case made for relevance, the criticism shifts to over-relevance. When I presented the material I had uncovered on the sabbatical millennium

---

[2] On the debate between Hexter (the splitter) and Hill (the lumper), see William G. Palmer, "The Burden of Proof: J.H. Hexter and Christopher Hill," *Journal of British Studies* 19, no. 1 (1979): 122–29, online: http://www.jstor.org/stable/175685, August 26, 2010.

[3] Ruth Bloch, *Visionary Republic: Millennial Themes in American Thought, 1756–1800* (Cambridge: Cambridge University Press, 1985); Stephen Marini, "Uncertain Dawn: Millennialism and Political Theology in Revolutionary America," in *Anglo-American Millennialism from Milton to the Millerites*, edited by Richard Conners and Andrew Colin Gow (Leiden: Brill, 2004), 159–78.

[4] See Janet Nelson, "Review of *The Peace of God,*" *Speculum* 69 (1994): 165.

(i.e., Apocalypse in the year 6000 from creation[5]) to a seminar at the University of Chicago, one participant asked ironically, "What does this *not* explain?" Several interlocutors have restated the quip as an epistemological challenge: "What evidence can falsify your claims?"

This grasps the issue at the wrong end of the stick. I am not proposing a scientific explanation for either millennialism or its impact on society; disconfirmation procedures are, at the very least, premature. Even my "laws" of apocalyptic dynamics are not laws. On the contrary, they are guidelines to thinking. The cases where, for example, one person's messiah is *not* another person's Antichrist, are precisely interesting because they defy a strong tendency, not because they disprove the existence of that tendency. As for those who still think the epistemological challenge is relevant, I pose the counter-challenge: What evidence can disprove that millennialism is *not* a causal factor? Recall that the actual "fallacy of the argument *ex silentio*" states that absence of documentary evidence does *not* prove absence, not, as historians often invoke it, to claim that one cannot "prove" presence from silence.

Given the almost instinctive hostility most historians feel toward millennialism, I can imagine historians finding no end of "contradictions" in whatever generalizations I offer. Nothing is easier to do, and it can even become something of an irresistible urge.[6] This is not to dismiss these criticisms in advance. I have no doubt that a volume of this size has many flaws, particularly since I am a specialist in none of the subjects. I welcome, therefore, the response of those who know the material better than I do. In any case, despite the size of this book, I have had to cut extensive sections from almost every chapter. For those who wish to consult further, I make the additional material available at my website, either in the form of appendices, or in the form of extended footnotes (many with URLs) indicated in the text by an asterisk (*).[7] Additionally, to cut down the references, I have put the books I cite in several chapters in a select bibliography at the end of the book.

My only request is that, before specialists assume that the material I have not mentioned contradicts my argument, or that I contradict myself or misapply my own categories—again, all serious possibilities—could they at least try and see how the analysis I suggest might actually help understand the material they have in mind? In so doing, I recommend reexamining every zero-sum argument: "this, not that," and ask if it might not be both.[8] If I had a scholarly tome for every time

---

[5] R. Landes, "Lest the Millennium be Fulfilled: Apocalyptic Expectations and the Pattern of Western Chronography, 100–800 CE," *The Use and Abuse of Eschatology in the Middle Ages*, edited by W. Verbeke, D. Verhelst, and A. Welkenhuysen (Leuven: Leuven University Press,1988), 137–211.

[6] Sylvain Goughenheim dedicted an entire, very bad book to this endeavor: *Les fausses terreurs de l'an mil: Peur de la fin des temps, ou aproffondissement de la foi*? (Paris: Picard, 1999).

[7] Website for book: www.richardlandes.com/hoe/.

[8] Simon McLean concludes that Bede's criticism of "rustics" who disagreed with him referred to "...the politicized accusations of his rivals he sought to undermine by calling them vulgar [*rustici*], *not* the weight of 'popular opinion,'" ("Apocalypse and Revolution: Europe around the Year 1000," *Early Medieval Europe* 15, no. 1 [2007]: 86–106 at n. 62), as if he could not have wanted to smear his rivals by lumping them with "popular" millennial opinion.

someone has said, "No," in response to an argument I made about millennialism, and then proceeded to restate the argument, I would have a handsome library today.

■ TO THE PUBLIC

If there were one salient feature of the nonspecialists' reactions—academic and larger public—to the subject of millennialism, it is their determination to identify it as something to do with a date—the year 2000 or 1000. "So what are you doing, now that the millennium's over?" was the single most frequent question I have been asked since January 1, 2000. And if I tried to explain that the millennium, the thousand years, was not about a date, but about the length of the messianic era, it was as if I were speaking in a foreign tongue: incomprehension and indifference mingled in copious quantities.

This response goes far beyond a popular response. I expected this from people who had not had discussions with me beforehand, even from people with little familiarity with the issues. But colleagues, academics who specialize in such obviously related fields such as religion, people with whom I had had extensive conversations about what scholars mean by "millennialism," asked the same question. Indeed, days after 9-11, a colleague introduced me as a scholar of millennialism "who has nothing to do for the next 999 years."

Why, I have asked myself, would intelligent people, prefer so restricted a definition of millennialism that it rendered the topic irrelevant—especially after 2000—just when millennial matters took a serious turn for the worst (as in, 9-11)? Why would they insist on a trivial meaning, even after exposure to another, far more substantive (and, I think, far more interesting) definition? Why prefer a constricting definition to one that offers an analytic tool for examining major historical dynamics?

In the end, I suspect that some would rather not think about the issues, and dismissing them as a silly mistake helps. If the subject ceases to have import when the "End" came neither in 1000 nor 2000, then we need no longer think about the role of apocalyptic in matters of social change. Like their predecessors, for example, the opponents of apocalyptic in the fourth century CE, who "stopped up the mouths of those who prattled inanely on the advent of Antichrist or of our Lord,"[9] these historians wish people like me would stop bringing up such matters. After publishing an two-part article in *Le Moyen Age* entitled *Millenarismus absconditus* in 1992–93,[10]

---

[9] Jacob of Nisibe, described by Gennadius, *De viris illustribus* 1, *Patrologia Latina* 58:1059. Online: http://books.google.com/books?vid=OCLC12663742&id=2uMVhREYv7MC&pg=PP9&lpg=PP9&dq =%22in+hoc+tomo+LVIII#v=onepage&q&f=false.

[10] Richard Landes, "*Millenarismus absconditus*: L'historiographie augustinienne et l'An Mil," *Le Moyen Age* 98, no. 3–4 (1992): 355–77; "Sur les traces du Millennium: La *via negativa*," *Le Moyen Age* 99, no. 1–2 (1993): 5–26.

a senior medievalist offered well-meaning (and, in terms of the field, quite accurate) advice: make this your last word on millennialism, and move on to other subjects. If, as Michel de Certeau has written, historiography is a burial rite, a mourning process for an irretrievably lost past,[11] then many—historians and layfolk—have tended to pass unceremoniously by the burial sites of apocalyptic hopes and fears.

Even scholars who have focused on apocalyptic find it hard to stay tuned. Although Leon Festinger discovered (and coined the term) "cognitive dissonance," as a result of studying the responses of an apocalyptic UFO cult to disappointment, his subsequent systematic study of the phenomenon, *Cognitive Dissonance*, scarcely treats apocalyptic expectations.[12] Historians of Christianity who will grant that Jesus and Paul may have entertained apocalyptic beliefs rapidly lose track of the phenomenon once they move to the early church. A number of scholars have written about a major historical event as millennial, without ever returning to the subject.[13] One of the ironies of my subtitle, taken from William James's *The Varieties of Religious Experience*, is that millennialism does not appear in his book.[14] He has, like so many of the observers of our past and present, written a *Disparition*: a survey of religiosity without millennialism is like a text without the letter "e," a twice-untold tale.

Thus, only three chapters in this book constitute millennial movements according to the scholarly consensus—the Xhosa Cattle-Killing, Micronesian Cargo Cults, and the Chinese Taiping. No one, as far as I know, has ever suggested that we consider the Egyptian pharaoh Akhenaten a millennial "thinker," and despite some efforts to place secular revolutions in a millennial framework, most scholars do not think of the French Revolution, Communism, or even Nazism as millennial phenomena. *Tausendjähriges Reich?*—mere rhetoric. As for UFOs and global jihad, some scholars acknowledge, even work with, the connection; but they remain a minority. In the crucial case of global jihad, if anything, the consensus has tended to avoid millennial analysis.

■ A MENTAL EXERCISE: WORKING HYPOTHESES

As a result, allow me to do some special pleading. I hope the specialists in the fields I so rudely blunder into will forgive my intrusion, my rough knowledge, and at

[11] Michel de Certeau, "Making History: Problems of Method and Problems of Meaning," in *The Writing of History*, trans. Tom Conley (New York: Columbia University Press, 1984), 46.

[12] Leon Festinger, *A Theory of Cognitive Dissonance* (Palo Alto, Calif.: Stanford University Press, 1957), 247–51.

[13] Bloch, Visionary Republic; James Rhodes, *The Hitler Movement: A Modern Millenarian Revolution* (Stanford: Hoover Institute Press, 1984).

[14] "Now in these lectures I propose to ignore the institutional branch entirely, to say nothing of the ecclesiastical organization, to consider as little as possible the systematic theology and the ideas about the gods themselves, and to confine myself as far as I can to personal religion pure and simple," William James, *Varieties of Religious Experience* (New York: Simon & Schuster, [1902]1997), 33. Surely there is a "personal" dimension to participating in a millennial movement.

least "try on" as a purely theoretical exercise, the working hypotheses I suggest in this book.

And those working hypotheses run as follows:

- That the emotional drives that underlie perfectionist social thinking, whether secular or religious, whether monotheist or polytheist or a-theist, share important dynamics.
- That these common emotions play an important role in the shape taken by *movements* dedicated to bring about that social perfection.
- That these movements, over the course of their sometimes magnificent, but always doomed efforts, span an "apocalyptic curve" of inebriating acceleration out of, and disorienting free-fall back into, "normal time."
- That the key moment for all those (rare) cases where believers have ridden their apocalyptic surge to positions of prominence and power is the terrible disappointment in realizing that their expectations had failed.
- That the dynamics of how various millennial movements deal with this disappointment produce some of the prominent historical phenomena that we seek to understand—"new" religions, empires, revolutions, even modernity.
- And, finally, that the documentation we have inherited from the authors, editors, and archivists of our past represents, always already, the product of people working *ex post defectu*—from after/out of the failure of apocalyptic hopes, and therefore cannot be taken at face value, as transparent on the "reality" they describe.

The stakes involved in this suggested revision of our own view of our history are considerable, as my final chapter on global jihad suggests. *Historians* can mistake the sparse *written* record as so much flotsam and jetsam, rather than the tips of massive oral icebergs of millennial discourse, and thereby sink their ships of historical reconstruction without realizing it. But we who have to deal with a millennial movement *before* it has spent its energy cannot afford such blissful ignorance. If we make the same errors in the present, *we*, not some scholar's narrative about the past, may sink. We may find that we have not merely ignored movements of mega-death as they "took," but even, once we realize we have a problem, end up throwing oil on the fire in our attempts to put it out.

■ METHODOLOGY

I make no effort here to offer a predictive "social science" model of apocalyptic millennialism—when it will break out? what course it will run? Because people in thrall to apocalyptic time behave so unusually, historians and sociologists have often attempted causal and predictive models for millennialism. But what leads one movement to "take" and many another to fizzle seems more appropriate for chaos theory, than historical and social "logic" alone; and anything more "scientific" is just hindsight. So I have no discussions in this book on why any given movement "takes" other than describing the conditions of combustion. Even that, however, fails to appreciate the unanticipated currents that produce a really raging forest fire.

What most concerns me in this book is what happens once the movement does "take":

- What are the characteristics of millennialists who manage to "break into" the public sphere and change the conversation, winning adherents, converts, and activists, gaining momentum toward taking power?
- What happens when they take power and "try out" their millennial experiment of *Paradise Now*?
- And, of course, what happens when they are, inevitably, disappointed, when their millennial presuppositions about the nature of evil or the key to perfection prove false?

The most striking and horrifying of these movements respond badly to disappointment: they deny, they rage, they grow paranoid, they lash out; they turn the passion of their followers into rivers of blood and mountains of skulls; they go down in flames.

But actually, even within any specific movement, the moment of disappointment acts like a prism, sending individuals and groups hurtling off in different trajectories, some toward (self-induced) cataclysm, others toward more transformative scenarios. At the critical moment, in the chaotic early stages of cognitive dissonance, a wide variety of voices arise—from self-reflective and transformational, to paranoid and violent. The crucial question is: how does the larger movement respond to the voices and which tendencies do they favor? Which "scenario" gains momentum, and what happens to it as it "takes over" the movement/revolution?

For despite how much the mega-death option might seem inevitable, nothing millennial, beyond disappointment, is fated. These movements all begin as voluntary, and once liberated from the certain vision by time's inexorable chariot plodding onward, believers must, once again, make choices. In some cases, like the American Revolution or, possibly, in the transition from the Peace of God to the urban and rural communes of the eleventh century, leaders of millennially inspired movements may actually admit that the extravagant hopes were mistaken, and that settling for something less, but far better than before, is a worthy path to take. We have yet to write the history of these moments and their dynamics. Millennialism is an immensely important topic that we ignore at our own cost, and in some cases, at our own peril.

* * *

It is, of course, impossible to thank all the people who have helped in the creation of a book whose composition spans fifteen years, and so many conversations. Some people, however, stand out: Stephen O'Leary, who helped me conceive of how to even think about these movements; Brenda Brasher, who, whatever new direction I headed down, had already been there and could guide me through the maze; Al Baumgarten, master of historical analogy; Michael Barkun, the dean of millennial studies in the United States; Oded Irshai and Paula Fredriksen, who taught me about Christian millennialism and "retrospective narratives"; Garry Trompf, master of disparate millennial fields; Andrew Gow, who has combined rigorous training with an imaginative mind; David Cook, who introduced me to and guided me through the painful realities of Muslim apocalyptic; David Van Meter, who, in a brief but brilliant career in academia, did some of the most valuable work on millennialism around the year 1000, and who taught me much about my own specialty; Eli Sagan, whose books and conversation were an endless inspiration; Jan Assmann and Edward Bleiberg, who helped me with the most recondite of all subjects, Akhenaten; and, finally, Arthur Mendel, whom I never met, but whose book, discovered by accident in the library, remains the single most profound meditation on millennialism I know.[15]

These scholars helped inspire and create the Center for Millennial Studies (1996–2003), which was so ably managed despite the circumstances by Beth Forrest and David Kessler. My thanks to the many "regulars" and other participants, who came to our annual conferences and contributed to the dazzling array of insights that that ongoing discussion generated. In some ways, this book is one of the receptacles for those many conversations with (in no particular order) David Redles, Glenn McGhee, Chip Berlet, Ted Daniels, Lee Quinby, Charles Strozier, Robert Jay Lifton, Moshe Idel, Johannes Fried, Guy Lobrichon, Wilhelm Brandes, Gary Dickson, Paul Magdalino, Daniel Noel, Charles Cameron, Ted Daniels, John Reilly, Damian Thompson, Alan Dechert, Gershom Gorenberg, Cathy Gutierrez, Steve Marini, David Eddy, Clifford Backman, Rosalind Hackett, Daniel Wojcik, Chris King (one of the first to declare himself the Messiah in cyberspace), Jay Gary, Catherine Wessinger, Hillel Schwartz, Tom Doyle, Aaron Katz, Bob McLenon, David Kydd, Michael Shermer, and Victor Balaban.

Personally, I would like to thank my family and friends, for putting up with my obsessions which, given the scope of millennialism, have run the gamut from honor-shame cultures, to envy, to communications revolutions, to conspiracy theories, to weird movies, to militant Islam, and on and on: Steven Antler, Fred Paxton, and Mark Spero for keeping me grounded with their good humor and constantly stimulating conversations; Eric Frieden, who found me more bibliographical references than I imagined possible and whose challenging conversation kept me on track; Isi Liebler, whose magnificent library made it possible for me to complete my final chapter while in Jerusalem; to my editor, Cynthia Read and all the staff at Oxford University Press; and above all, to my parents and daughters, who talked with me constantly, asked good questions, and gave me a hard time when I needed it (even if it did not seem like I was listening), and especially my wife Esther, who stepped effortlessly into the whirlwind and calmly guided me out.

RICHARD LANDES
Jerusalem, Summer 2010

[15] Arthur Mendel, *Vision and Violence* (Ann Arbor: Michigan University Press, 2000).

■ PART ONE

Introduction: Roosters, Owls, Bats

1 The Varieties of the Millennial Experience

An old Jewish tale tells of a traveler who passes by a little village in Eastern Europe (Chelm) and finds a solitary watchman looking out. Thinking that this village hardly had the wealth either to make such a guard necessary or even to pay him, the traveler asked him why he was there.

"I am here to watch for the messiah," he responded.

Years later, passing through the same region, the traveler went back to see if the man was still there. And he was.

"Nu, doesn't this get a bit boring?" he asked.

"Yes," replied the messianic watchman, "but think of the job security."

Now, this joke actually has two points to make about messianic expectations. The source of the watchman's job security comes from the messiah's interminable delay. But it also, and more tellingly, derives from the willingness of this poor village to continue to pay their fellow to keep watch, however long the messiah tarry. This irrational expenditure of resources, as a modern economist might put it, on something so predictably wrong as messianic expectations, represents one of the central conundrums of social history, and especially the history of the "Western world."

Take an example: around 200 CE, a Roman theologian wrote the first Christian commentary on a biblical book, the book of Daniel, in which he told the following tale about a nearby Christian community:

There was a leader of a church of Pontus, a pious and modest man *who did not have a solid understanding of the scriptures,* and gave more credence to his own visions. After three dreams, he started *preaching to his brothers like a prophet*... "Know, brothers, that *in one year the Judgment will take place... The day of the Lord has come.*" The brothers prayed to the Lord day and night with tears and sighs, for they had before their eyes the imminence of Judgment. This man had provoked so great a fear and astonishment that *they left their lands fallow, did not go out to work their fields, and almost all of them sold their possessions.* And this man said to them: "If things do not come to pass as I have foretold, then do not believe in scriptures and do what you please." But when the year had passed and nothing happened as he had predicted, he harvested only lies and confusion. As for Scriptures, they lost none of their authority, but all the brethren were scandalized to the point where *their virgins got married and their men went back to the fields.* And those foolish enough to have sold their goods, went begging.[1]

[1] Hippolytus, *In Danielem* 4:26, Hippolyte, *Commentaire Sur Daniel*, trans. Maurice Lefèvre, Sources Chrétiennes 14 (Paris: Éditions du Cerf, 1947), 193; italics mine.

Many of the key elements of what I will term "apocalyptic expectations" appear in this paragraph: the inspired "prophet"; the receptive community that, in the expectation of an imminent and radical transformation of the world, "burns bridges" to the "normal" future and "goes for broke"; the disastrous results of the error; and the retrospective and disapproving voice of the narrator writing after the failure of the expectations.

As bizarre as this behavior may seem, it has continued to manifest itself in many cultures, including even, rather *especially*, the "modern." In 1666, Jews the world over plunged into the apocalyptic vortex of messianic expectation around the preaching of Sabbatai Zvi.[2] In 1843, tens if not hundreds of thousands of literate American Christians, their crops and businesses neglected, flocked to the hills to greet the returning Jesus.[3] And of course, in some cases as we shall see, the neglect of future concerns like crops can become active destruction of an entire people's livelihood or even (so far unsuccessfully) the whole world.[4]

The question people commonly ask when they find out about apocalyptic beliefs is: Why do they keep on happening? Without exception, every expectation that "soon," "in our days," the end of the world will happen [or] the messianic era will arrive," has produced an unbroken string of failures—traumatic, humiliating, catastrophic. How many times have foolish peasants, their fields abandoned, or townsfolk, their possessions sold, gathered on hilltops and rooftops, waiting for the chariot to swing low? How many times have waves of pilgrims broken on the rocky shores of the "Promised" Land, the Pure Land, the Land of Cockaigne, coming to participate in the glorious End of History or savor the delights of the messianic era? How many waves of warriors have thrown themselves into the bullets of the enemy, believing that their shirts magically rendered them invisible or their skin invulnerable? How many times will people destroy what possessions they have in the hopes that the ancestors or the space ships will bring them new and better "cargo"?

How many times, in other words, must apocalyptic prophecy fail, before it loses its promise?

And yet, like Charlie Brown always ready to kick the football that his "friend" Lucy holds and will, at the last second, pull away, people continue to believe that somehow, this time it will be different, this time will really bring *The End*. In the West, to take a pointed example, millennial promises and apocalyptic prophecies go back at least three thousand years, probably more. Still unfulfilled, they

---

[2] The classic study of the movement is by GershomScholem, *Sabbatai Sevi: The Mystical Messiah, 1626–76*, trans. R. J. ZviWerblowski (Princeton, N.J.: Princeton University Press, 1973); for a more recent discussion, see Moshe Idel, *Messianic Mystics* (New Haven, Conn,: Yale University Press, 1998), 183–211.

[3] There is an immense literature on the Millerites and their most successful post-apocalyptic product, the Seventh Day Adventists. For one of the more interesting analyses from the point of view of this discussion, see O'Leary, *Arguing the Apocalypse*, 93–133.

[4] See below, chapter 4, on the Xhosa; Robert Jay Lifton, *Destroying the World to Save It: AumShinrikyo, Apocalyptic Violence, and the New Global Terrorism* (New York: Metropolitan Books, 1999).

continued to show vigor, even after the colossal and widely publicized failure of the American Millerite prophecy in 1843–44. Over a century and a half later, America, the most "cutting-edge" nation on the planet, continues to have one of the world's more apocalyptic cultures.[5] At the approach of 2000, both secular and religious forms intensified across Western culture, but nowhere more visibly than in the United States. Here we find the origins of the first techno-apocalyptic prophecy to spread bottom-up across the world (Y2K), a vast new popular literature of "Left Behind" fantasy series,[6] a "New Age" industry that teems with millennial themes including mainstream fantasies like *The X-Files, Armageddon, Avatar, Book of Eli.* And now, after a hiatus of several years since 2000, a new date has appeared on the horizon: 2012.[7]

"But," you say, "we weathered that, we got past 2000 with no serious Y2K problems.[8] Isn't the 'millennium' over?"

The question is badly posed on two counts: first, the *millennium* is not about a date but about the period of the messianic era (1000 years long), whereas the year 2000 (or 1000, or 6000) is an *apocalyptic* date at which that millennium might begin; and second, disappointment represents a critical stage in the apocalyptic process, not its dissolution. While the spectacular expectations for a Y2K disaster, or the "tribulation" and "rapture," or peace in the Middle East and global harmony, did not materialize, those expectations did not just vanish, and in some cases they became more dangerous. For example, some of the worst kind of apocalyptic thinking—conspiracy thinking—not only flourished with unprecedented vigor in the final decade of the millennium, West and East, but has only intensified since

---

[5] Lee Quimby deconstructed the millennial narrative she saw gaining strength in the 1990s in *Anti-Apocalypse: Exercises in Genealogical Criticism* (Minneapolis: University of Minnesota Press, 1984).*

[6] On the "surprising" success of the "Left Behind" series, see Thomas Doyle, "Competing Fictions: The Uses of Christian Apocalyptic Imagery in Contemporary Popular Fictional Works, Part 1: Premillennialist Apocalyptic Fictions," *Journal of Millennial Studies* (2001); online: http://www.mille. org/publications/winter2001/Newone.pdf, January 24, 2010; Jennie Chapman, "Selling Faith without Selling Out: Reading the Left Behind Novels in the Context of Popular Culture," in Walliss and Newport, *End All Around Us* (London: Equinox Press, 2009) Crawford Gribben, *Rapture Fiction and the Evangelical Crisis* (Peabody, Mass.: Evangelical Press, 2006).

[7] See Lee Quinby, "'The Days are Numbered': The Romance of Death, Doom, and Deferral in Contemporary Apocalypse Films," in Walliss and Newport, *End All Around Us.* There is a website dedicated to "world-ending" movies, Apocalyptic Movies.com, online: http://www.apocalypticmovies. com/movie-index/, January 26, 2010; on 2012, see *2012 endofdays*, online: http://www.2012endofdays. org/general/resources.php, April 19, 2010.

[8] In the interests of disclosure, I confess to having thought Y2K would create significantly greater problems than it did. For my 1999 reflections, which sought the optimal win-win approach, whatever happened, with a post-2000 addendum, see my "Millennialism Now and Then," in *Calling Time: Religion and Change at the Turn of the Millennium*, ed. Martyn Percy (Sheffield: Sheffield Academic Press, 2000), 233–61. See also Charles Cameron, "Y2ko To Y2ok," in *The End that Does: Art, Science and Millennial Accomplishment*, ed. Cathy Gutierrez and Hillel Schwartz (London: Equinox Press, 2006), 215–34.

then.[9] Our third chronological millennium is off to a very bad start, blighted by the specter of suicide terror, and many of its unfortunate dynamics the world over make all too much sense from the perspective of millennial studies.[10]

But why? Why is this folly such an enduring cultural trait? How many times can the boy cry *Wolf!* the knave, madman, and fool, *Apocalypse! Judgment! Vindication!*? How many times before significant numbers of people stop dropping everything and running out, breathless, to see what's happening?

Such rhetorical questions come from the rationalists, those who believe they have renounced these impulses. But in so renouncing, they seem to have not only given up the (absurd) hope for perfection, but also an ability to empathize with those who prefer the clean clear air of apocalyptic righteousness. Postmodernists can declare the end to all "grand narratives."[11] But millennial grand narratives carry an elating coherence that skeptical dismissals cannot hope to touch, and which even postmodernism does not escape. Indeed, millennial world histories are the mother of all grand narratives (and, I would argue, mother to many of the West's grand narratives).

To understand the perennial appeal, however, one must enter into the world of the apocalyptic hopefuls.

■ HIDDEN TRANSCRIPTS AND THE APPEAL OF APOCALYPTIC MILLENNIALISM

The Augustinian Perception of Normal Time

Most of us are governed—largely unconsciously—by one of the most enduring intellectual paradigms in European history: Augustine's teaching on the secular nature of history.[12] Ironically, despite Augustine's enormous popularity in the Middle Ages, it was only as modern thinking emerged that Western intellectuals first began to understand Augustine's anti-millennial teachings on the nature of history and its end.[13] Now his influence so permeates our thought we, including Augustinian scholars, do not realize how pervasive it is.[14]

---

[9] For a study of the transformation of conspiracy thinking in the last decade of the last millennium, see Michael Barkun, *The Culture of Conspiracy: UFOs, the "New World Order," and the Rise of Improvisational Millennialism* (Berkeley and Los Angeles: University of California Press, 2002) and R. Landes, "Jews as Contested Ground in Post-Modern Conspiracy Theory," *Jewish Political Studies Review* 19, no. 3–4 (2007): 9–34. For further discussion, see below, chapter 14.

[10] See chapter 14 on global jihad.

[11] On "end of grand narrative," see the fundamental work of Jean-François Lyotard, *La condition postmoderne: Rapport sur le savoir* (Paris: Edition de Minuit, 1979).

[12] For the best analysis of this issue, see Robert Markus, *Saeculum: History and Society in the Theology of St Augustine* (Cambridge: Cambridge University Press, 1989).

[13] The irony here is quite exceptional: historians who self-consciously adopted Augustinian theology, like Orosius and Otto of Freising, actually fell prey to what one French historian called "augustinisme politique," or the systematic *mis*-understanding of Augustine; see Arquillère, *L' augustinismepolitique* (Paris:Vrin, 1933).*

[14] See reflections on this theme in R. Landes, "The Historiographical Fear of an Apocalyptic Year 1000: Augustinian History Medieval and Modern," *Speculum* 75 (2000): 97–145.

This book attempts to free us from Augustine's thrall, not because I think he was wrong about how we should think about apocalyptic expectation, or even about the nature of this *saeculum*. His radical agnostic solution to the still extant question of the End of Time is the most intellectually responsible for an eschatological believer: *no one can know when; it could happen at any time.* My quarrel with Augustine comes not with how he wants us to read the apocalyptic future, but how he and those who accept his approach read the Apocalypse-driven past.[15]

Most of us—especially intellectuals—live in a gray zone where matters, both moral and intellectual, are complex, multifaceted, open-ended, where years and generations come and go, bringing their share of fortunes and misfortunes, where we learn to suspend our judgments and avoid simple morality tales. According to Augustine, we live in the *saeculum*, the world of time and space, of history and its sufferings, in which all incarnate human existence takes place. And this *saeculum* is a *corpus permixtum*, a messy world where good and evil inextricably mingle, where even so salvific an institution as the Church, has its full share of both. The *saeculum* is a world of immense weight, like an olive press: it is inherently crushing.[16] Everywhere one looks, one finds the workings of envy, of *libido dominandi* (the lust to dominate), of intimate betrayals, condemning us all to a life of misery and bitter disappointment at the hand of our fellow inhabitants of the *saeculum*. As crushed olives under this immense pressure, our only choice is whether we render sweet or bitter oil.

This teaching fundamentally nullifies the millennial vision, the belief that at some point in history, peoples everywhere will turn to each other in good will and live in a transformed world, a world of fellowship, abundance, sharing... "peace on earth, good will toward men." Indeed, if the last two centuries have told us anything, it is how dangerous those who would perfect the world become when they seize power. This does not mean that we cannot improve matters, cannot add small and even large pieces of justice and fairness to human interactions, but at some fundamental level, as this disquieting twentieth century has passed into a still-more-disquieting twenty-first, we have to admit that the social world—the blank human slate—is far less malleable than we would like. We cannot attain perfection; and, as the Augustinian Pascal lamented, "the more we try to be angels, the more we become beasts."[17]

---

[15] For a good example of the mistaken application of Augustine to the historical record, see Sylvain Goughenheim, *Les fausses terreurs de l'an mille: Attente de la fin du monde ou approfondissement de la foi?* (Paris: Picard, 1999), 56–63.

[16] On Augustine and the "olive press" as metaphor for the *saeculum*, see Peter Brown, *Augustine of Hippo* (Berkeley and Los Angeles: University of California Press, 2000), 291–96; Robert Kirschner, "Two Responses to Epochal Change: Augustine and the Rabbis on Ps. 137 (136)," *Vigiliae Christianae* 44, no. 3 (1990): 254.

[17] "L'homme n'est ni ange ni bête, et le malheur veut que qui veut faire l'Ange fait la bête," Blaise Pascal, *Pensées de M. Pascale sur la religion* (Paris: Guillaume Desprez, 1669) 6: 358; online: http://gallica.bnf.fr/ark:/12148/btv1b8606964f.image.r=Pens%C3%A9es+de+M+Pascal.f9.langFR. See the gloomy reflections of Bernard-Henry Levy, *Left in Dark Times: A Stand against the New Barbarism* (New York: Random House, 2008).

We must, in other words, learn to live with evil, violence, injustice. (Of course, this is easier for those who are not directly the object of the most crushing malevolence.) To those of us reasonably comfortable in the modern world, theodicy tends to stay on the back burner where Augustine put it. To the question "Why, if God is both good and omnipotent, do the evil flourish and the good suffer?" the contemporary answer: "There is no God, certainly not a good and omnipotent one." Or, those who prefer the modesty of agnosticism might say: "If there is such a being, God does not intervene in history."

And if God does not intervene in history, then a fortiori we believe his self-proclaimed representatives have no business exercising political power. The "separation of church and state" outlaws theocracy. This issue of theocracy underlines the degree to which we moderns, especially Americans, are true Augustinians, even more rigorous, at least on this subject, than the good bishop himself. The fundamental secular accommodation with religion involves the issue of coercion. Civil polities make any use of religious coercion illegal; they banish any notion of "real" theocracy. Even as they innovate dramatically by allowing freedom of (religious) assembly, they insist that all religious activity be voluntary. In this sense, they solve the Augustinian problem and disarm the millennial impulse more than he did in the late Roman Empire.[18]

Apocalyptic Millennialism as a "Full-Throated Hidden Transcript"

And yet, even in an advanced civil polity where church and state are formally sundered, apocalyptic ideas continue to have immense appeal. In order to understand the difference between "normal" and "apocalyptic" time, it helps to understand James C. Scott's distinction between the "public transcript" and "hidden transcripts." Most people operate in a world of the "public transcript"—a world dominated by mimetic public gestures and formulas that indicate our acceptance of the prevailing order.[19] We make these gestures of obeisance—whether kowtowing to an emperor, averting one's gaze and bowing one's head in the presence of an aristocrat, or laughing at a boss's joke—in order to win approval and avoid the unpleasant consequences when we openly defy those who have more power and authority than we.

---

[18] On the strange relationship of Augustine to tolerance—he shifted toward persecution even as he articulated a theology that should lead to tolerance (God will decide in the end), see Peter Brown, "Saint Augustine's Attitude towards Religious Coercion," *Journal of Roman Studies* 54 (1964): 107–16; Herbert Deane, *The Political and Social Ideas of St. Augustine* (New York: Columbia University Press, 1966); Markus, *Saeculum*, chap. 6. For a critique of the "ironic" school, one that targets "liberal" priorities and reads Augustine's justification of religious coercion more favorably, see John R. Bowlin, "Augustine on Justifying Coercion," *Annual of the Society of Christian Ethics* 17 (1997): 49–70.

[19] The notion of public and private transcript, which I will use often in this book, I learned from James C. Scott, *Domination and the Arts of Resistance*.

But beneath the surface of the public, official, well-documented transcript of approved, socially stable interactions, lies a world of hidden transcripts. Here we find whispered, anonymous, secretive narratives of resentment and hatred. Here, as the Ethiopian proverb runs, "When the great lord passes, the wise peasant bows low and silently farts." As long as those who suffer keep their suffering to themselves, and do not openly challenge authorities, they can continue to grumble. Only totalitarian societies seek to change hidden transcripts; other, less intrusive authoritarian systems view them as an escape valve.[20] And the key to keeping them down is the certain knowledge that breaches will bring on sure reprisal. The peasant must fart silently lest there be an address for retaliation.

In an authoritarian society, those negative consequences may be quite severe, from off-stage eliminations to public massacres of unarmed restive populations.

And as long as these public acts of defiance remain anonymous, they remain individual, scattered, impotent. Thus, throughout history, small, sometimes tiny minorities, can dominate, abuse, even crush much larger majorities. Only rarely does the voice of protest reach a critical mass, and hidden transcripts breach the public sphere loudly, with force.[21] These moments are transformative, and much modern political "science" addresses under what conditions and with what consequences such collective breaches occur. To use the language of evolutionary epidemiology, millennialism is a *meme* programmed to spread as rapidly and pervasively as possible.[22] Under the right—apocalyptic—conditions, that meme can spread at epidemic speeds and breach the public transcript with explosive force. Scott calls the millennial narrative a "full throated hidden transcript."[23]

The Muting of Hidden Transcripts in Modern Polities

Granted, we moderns inhabit a world far more open and flexible than that inhabited by our predecessors in "traditional societies," and as a result we suffer far softer retaliation for making private transcripts public. Some of this seems distinctly positive, such as freedom of speech. But freedom of speech, it turns out, demands discipline and discrimination. Like knowledge of good and evil (morality), free

---

[20] The "Festival of Fools" and Carnival even offer brief moments when the hierarchy is reversed, and the hidden transcripts can surface, but only to return to obscurity the next day. For the now-classic treatment of this issue, see Mikhail Bakhtin, *Rabelais and his World* (Bloomington: Indiana University Press, 1984); for the link between these moments and latemedieval and earlymodern revolts, see Emmanuel Le Roy Ladurie, *Le carnaval de Romans. De la Chandeleur au mercredi des Cendres 1579–1580* (Paris: Gallimard, 1986).

[21] See below, chapter 8 on "prime divider societies."

[22] Aaron Lynch, *Thought Contagion: How Belief Spreads Through Society* (New York: Basic Books, 1999); Susan J. Blackmore, *The meme machine* (Oxford: Oxford University Press, 1999).

[23] Scott, *Domination*, 38.

speech can serve good as well as bad purposes: hypocrisy, to mention the least of verbal sins, is the compliment that vice pays to virtue. And no matter how much we welcome free speech in principle, its practice inevitably brings on some kind of retaliation. No one in a position of authority likes criticism, and certainly no one, short of the proverbial saint, welcomes public humiliation.

Thus, even in modern cultures, where egalitarian principles allegedly govern our behavior, there are public and hidden transcripts.[24] Even when only persuasive and not coercive, the "public transcript" of conformity and mimetic desire has a powerful grip on our lives. It means we get entangled in a world of good *and* bad, integrity *and* guilt, honor *and* shame. Basic civics teaches the fundamental positive-sum lesson that "the essence of democracy is compromise."[25]

These compromises demanded by the *saeculum* are at once reassuring and depressing. The secular world, as its proponents conceive it, is one in which, now grownups, we cast off childish and neurotic beliefs in God and courageously confront a meaningless, indifferent universe, unimpeded by religious zealots who would compel us to adhere to their irrational dogmas.[26] No matter how convinced we feel that something is "true"—scientifically, religiously—we must maintain sufficient exegetical and epistemological modesty to allow the possibility that we are wrong. Not surprisingly, some of the most difficult conceptual reorientations come from evolutionary thinkers who challenge any notion of some "overarching director" to our existence. As Stephen Jay Gould insisted above all, there is no "crown" to creation—and certainly not *you*—no matter how deep and convincing Gracie Slick makes it sound.[27]

If we discard even "secular" grand narratives like "the edge of objectivity," or "the inexorable advance of freedom and enlightenment," how much the more should we avoid totalistic apocalyptic fantasies, whose adepts so often tend toward inconceivably destructive even self-destructive madness.[28] Just as there is a virus that reproduces best in a cow's stomach but keeps getting excreted, and so has evolved to infect ants with the irresistible urge to climb to the top of the grass blades so that cows can eat them, just so the apocalyptic meme seizes

---

[24] See the rich analysis of Arlene Saxonhouse, *Free Speech and Democracy in Ancient Athens* (New York: Cambridge University Press, 2006).

[25] On these issues, see below, chapter 8.

[26] For recent reassertions of the atheistic position: Sam Harris, *The End of Faith: Religion, Terror, and the Future of Reason* (New York: W.W. Norton and Co., 2004). On the crisis of meaninglessness brought on by a modern scientific worldview and its consequences for the emergence of "secular religions," see Paul Zawadsky, "'Jewish World Conspiracy' and the Question of Secular Religions: An Interpretative Perspective," in *The Paranoid Apocalypse*, chap. 8.*

[27] Stephen J. Gould, *Wonderful Life: The Burgess Shale and Nature of History* (New York: W.W. Norton, 1989), 28–31; Jefferson Airplane *Crown of Creation*. Lyrics by Paul Katner. RCA LSP-4058. Originally released in 1968.

[28] Lee Quinby, *Anti-Apocalypse: Exercises in Genealogical Criticism* (Minneapolis: University of Minnesota Press, 1994).

people—rides them—to destinations and for purposes not theirs, indeed harm-ful to them.[29]

The material successes of this messy, agnostic, sober, anti-apocalyptic, modern world offer us a well-tuned Epicurean treadmill of work and play that takes rea-sonably good care of our needs. If we crave spirituality, or mental stimulation, there are marketplaces for that too. As for evil and good, we are all guilty and all innocent, all too compromised to be saints, all too "challenged" to be really evil. At best we're "the Diet Coke of evil."[30] The cynics get the most nods when they say, "everyone's like that."

All this disorientation comes, ironically, at a time when we have developed our powers with technology to such a degree that, by and large, we have "taken the wheel" in driving our own destiny and may well crash. We humans at the turn of the second millennium CE are a social entity in self-transformation... but, appar-ently, with nowhere to go. The "best" we can imagine is *more*—more democracies, more "vibrant" civil societies, more industrial societies, more trade, more and higher numbers, and *less*—less pollution, less poverty and hunger, less misery. We moderns (along with our "postmodern" offspring) live rather in the care of an invisible commercial hand, to which we have entrusted our earthly success. This hand, unlike the stern and demanding God of the Hebrew Bible, asks little of us. We can be as selfish as we like (no inner conditions demanded), as long as we play by the rules, and if we do, success will come to us and our society.

And yet, in that success we have sidelined both moral concerns (private greed is public good) and our religious concerns (private not public devotions), or, in Bowlin's phrase, we have substituted "sincerity for truth."[31] Thus we see stresses and failures appear around the world in both nature and societies, indeed in our own back yards—toxic wake, churning behind the sleek and powerful ship of modernity.

These anomalies, these problems of technology "biting back," are, we hope, best handled with social and material technologies. When the stock market is booming and the spigots are flowing, it all seems like a good deal. We muddle through with varying but considerable success. Granted, technological and social developments threaten to get out of hand, making inhuman demands on our and the earth's ability to adapt to rapid and radical change. But, argues the anti-apocalyptic thinker, we have always managed before, and we will continue to muddle through it all. Indeed, according to some optimists, we are doing better all the time. Particularly as scholars and public figures, our training urges skepticism of sweeping claims, of dramatic and alarming scenarios.

---

[29] On the ants, see Dennet, *Breaking the Spell: Religion as a Natural Phenomenon* (New York: Viking, 2006) 3. (Note the metaphor does not actually support atheism so much as it warns against being duped and "used" against one's own personal self-interest.)

[30] "You're semi-evil. You're quasi-evil. You're the margarine of evil. You're the Diet Coke of evil. Just one calorie, not evil enough." *Austin Powers: The Spy Who Shagged Me*, 1999 http://www.imdb.com/title/tt0145660/quotes, April 6, 2010.

[31] Bowlin, "Augustine on Justifying Coercion," 69.

The Apocalyptic Perception of Time

Apocalyptic believers behold a dramatically different world. They pay close attention to human suffering, and its causes—evil, injustice, oppression, the looming payback of bad karma.[32] The religious among them believe that a benevolent and omnipotent God, or gods, or ancestors do exist and intervene in the *saeculum*. To the challenge of theodicy, of why God allows evil to flourish in this world, they answer: "He is testing us now and will judge us later."

Monotheists await God's Day of Judgment. They believe he allows evil to flourish in this world as a test, whose term comes either at death, or more dramatically, at a vast, collective, *Apocalypse*: the final *Revelation* of his Justice. For believers, the unhappy anomalies that most of us sweep under our mental rugs—the greed and immorality that are the price of democratic tolerance—lie at the heart of the matter. God's unwillingness to intervene in history stems not from nonexistence, or indifference, or impotence—but from a desire to see what we do "on our own." He does not punish the bad and reward the good on an ongoing basis. Instead God shows remarkable restraint in the face of the victory of the bad, who thus flourish everywhere. But at last, on that great and terrible Judgment Day, on Doomsday, evil will get its just punishment and good, its just reward. The last shall be first and the first shall get it in the neck.

Indeed, so great and dramatic a transformation will take place on this day, that millennialists believe the world will then enter a wondrous period (conventionally 1000 years—*mille anni, millennium*) of justice, joy, fellowship, and abundance. Here the rapacious social world will turn upside down. Here the lamb shall lie down with the lion *and* get a good night's sleep.[33] Here the weapons of elite dominion—sword and spear—become the tools of honest labor—plowshare and pruning hook. Here people enjoy and share the fruits of their honest labor undisturbed. Here nations live at peace and no longer study war.

Millennialists have a passion for justice. They think they know good and evil well. When they look at humanity, many see not a wide and nuanced spectrum of people, but a few saints and a vast sea of sinners, some redeemable, some (most) not. They are quite clear on who will suffer punishment, and who will gain reward at the final Revelation. And when they believe the moment has come, they do not believe in compromise.

They anticipate the absolute eradication of evil—corruption, violence, oppression—and the wondrous bliss of the just kingdom for the good. The Angel of the Endtime despises fence-sitters: "I know your works, you are neither cold nor hot.

---

[32] Margaret Atwood, *Payback: Debt and the Shadow Side of Wealth* (Toronto: House of Anansi Press, 2008). On "empirically justified" apocalyptic fears, see below, Conclusion.

[33] The joke tells of a zoo-keeper who had a fabulous "messianic" exhibit where a lion and a lamb shared the same cage. "How do you do it?" asked an amazed observer. "Easy," he replied, "Lots of lambs."

Would that you were cold or hot! So, because you are lukewarm, and neither cold nor hot, I will spew you out of my mouth. For you say, I am rich, I have prospered, and I need nothing; not knowing that you are wretched, pitiable, poor, blind, and naked" (Rev. 3:15–17).[34] For millennialists, the gray world of the *corpus permixtum* is an illusion in which the "bad guys" are only first for the time being; it will—it *must*—pass away. Then the last, the meek, the humble, the powerless, will be first.

All millennialists hope that commitment to their beliefs will spread far and wide enough to bring about a transformation of the social and the political universe. That is the very essence of millennialism, as opposed to other forms of eschatology: *the just will live free in this world.* It is a collective salvation, a social mysticism. It might come by and by, but such a promise is no pie in the sky. It imagines a transformation of humanity, an evolutionary leap to a different way of human interaction that can have enormous emotional appeal. To use the language of political science, millennialism is a (perhaps the first) revolutionary ideology.[35]

Revolutionary ideologies only begin to appeal to large numbers (i.e., the *meme* only spreads widely) when people feel themselves close to the moment of transformation. Indeed, while many of us are millennialists in some way (i.e., we hope that eventually humankind will enter a new stage of peace and justice), very few of us are apocalyptic millennialists (i.e., believe that this world-historical event is about to happen). Only in those relatively rare moments when large numbers are convinced and mobilized by the conviction that at last *the time has come*, does millennialism become a movement that has entered the apocalyptic vortex.

The historian rarely gets to see millennialism unless apocalyptic time activates it. But long before we set our document-trained sights on the written accounts that such apocalyptic movements produce in their wake, the inhabitants of an entire town, a region, even a whole generation of people, have gone into a world where anything has become possible, where grown men can cry, where lifelong enemies can forgive and embrace, where unimaginable forgiveness and revenge can be taken, where the supernatural forces of the universe come to the aid of those who long for salvation.

Many things come to people who believe themselves in the midst of apocalyptic time; many things become possible. Such people bring us saintly men wandering through Europe preaching peace, and warriors with crosses wading in blood up to their horses' bridles, both believing that *this* was the Day our Lord promised, to rejoice therein. And those of us who read descriptions of their deeds so many years later must realize that *we* should not have happened. To the future they believed in, and acted upon, it was unthinkable that, after they died, so long after, denizens of the *saeculum* like us would still exist.

[34] Islam began with a similar message (see below, chapter 14).
[35] Karl Mannheim, *Ideology and Utopia* (London: Routledge, 1936): Norman Cohn, *The Pursuit of the Millennium* (Fairlawn, N.J.: Essential Books, 1957). See below, chapter 8.

And although they were quite wrong in thinking as they did, that hardly means they had no impact on the world in which they played out their mistaken fantasies. The first "law" of apocalyptic dynamics states: *Wrong does not mean inconsequential.* On the contrary, the more energetically wrong, the more consequential. The history of apocalyptic millennialism is a tale of unintended consequences.

For people who have entered apocalyptic time, everything quickens, enlivens, coheres. They become semiotically aroused—everything has meaning, patterns. The smallest incident can have immense importance and open the way to an entirely new vision of the world, one in which forces unseen by other mortals operate.[36] If the warrior lives with death at his shoulder, then apocalyptic warriors live with cosmic salvation before them, just beyond their grasp.[37]

Sometimes the apocalyptic pattern they detect is frighteningly nefarious—an international conspiracy by the forces of evil to enslave humankind; sometimes benevolent—the dawn of a new age. In any case, for them, whereas once the apocalyptic pattern lay only in the shadows, scarcely discernable, the signs of its advent become now legible, visible, clear to anyone with discernment. As one such believer described the approach of the Rapture in the year 2000 using an image the new millennium's technology would render obsolete: "It's like the final moments before a Polaroid picture takes shape...."

Such semiotic arousal fires the imagination, loosening tongue, hand, body to write, speak, sing, paint, dance the visions, to communicate the good news to as many as possible—those with eyes to see and ears to hear. Thus, those in apocalyptic semiosis become the *vocationally aroused*, stepping out of their closets, and into the public arena, burning with enough fervor and conviction that they are ready to forsake the safety of convention, the anonymity of consensus, the protection of obeying the public transcript. Believers who have received this calling burn bridges to their past lives: they give away their wealth, they leave their homes, forsake spouses and families, friendships, jobs and professions. As Jesus preached in a highly controversial passage: "If any one comes to me and does not hate his own father and mother and wife and children and brothers and sisters, yes, and even his own life, he cannot be my disciple" (Luke 14:26).[38]

And all the signs apocalyptic believers read point in one direction: *now is the time!* Believers commit themselves to this world of transformation, convinced of

---

[36] Jung called this synchronicity (Carl Jung, *Synchronicity—An Acausal Connecting Principle* (New York: Routledge and Kegan Paul, 1972). Whether, how, or why it happens is not clear; that people think it does happen, unquestionably occurs often.

[37] "When a man knows he is to be hanged in a fortnight, it concentrates his mind wonderfully...." Samuel Johnson, quoted by James Boswell, *Life of Johnson*, ed. G.B. Hill, revised by L.F. Powell September 19, 1777 (Oxford: Clarendon Press, 1934–64), 3:167.

[38] Even as hyperbole, the passage clearly articulates the radical break required; cf. a milder variant in Matthew 10:37. Other passages have Jesus renouncing his family—"what have I to do with thee?" (John 2:4)—and claiming that those who follow the Lord are his true family, not his birth family. The break with family that the hyperbole suggests seems of a pair with the hostility to the parent religion, Judaism, in the same sources.

the superiority of their perceptions, convinced that the uncomprehending masses (including the old elites about to pass away) will either soon join them or get shredded in the coming cosmic upheaval. The tendency of apocalyptic belief to render everything in dualistic terms, to spew out the tepid, means that their good will toward nonbelievers has a limited term: as long as the apocalyptic "other" has not had a chance to take sides, he or she is a neutral, even, potentially, a positive figure. But once the apocalyptic message rejected, the "other" joins the forces of darkness. This explains the second law of apocalyptic dynamics: *One person's messiah is another's antichrist.* In extreme cases, we find the negative-sum formula: *My enemy's enemy is my enemy.*

Apocalyptic believers will say things that deliberately offend the powerful and influential. They are capable of both sacred joy and sacred violence. In all acute cases, however, such behavior is radical, whether it benefits others or harms them. In all cases, believers have broken with the past by making a leap of faith into a future whose advent they *see* coming. Henri Desroches described the apocalyptic movement as akin to the fakir's rope trick: believers climb up on something anchored only in hope.[39]

Apocalyptic zealots leave old, organic communities, ones they inherited by birth, and join voluntary communities. At their outset, all apocalyptic millennial movements are voluntary. *Ana*-baptism means to be baptized again as a conscious adult—because the first time, as an infant, was a meaningless ceremony. Adherence is a movement of the soul: *metanoia.* Only the "called," only those capable of a self-conscious voluntarily engagement in the process of transformation (repentance and return) can become members of an apocalyptic community. That is why so many movements demand such great sacrifices to enter, as with the Xhosa killing their cattle.[40]

These voluntary apocalyptic communities are temporal hothouses, brief moments when a self-selecting group of strangers comes together in circumstances where all "normal existence" ceases and a series of interlocking and energizing paradoxes come to life.

- The loss of one's "organic" community precedes entry into a still-more-intensely intimate voluntary community. The sense of spiritual connection, mutual purpose, cosmic commitments, that believers feel in these groups is perhaps the single most powerful motivator behind both the formation of millennial groups and of their persistence after prophecy fails.[41]

[39] Henri Desroche, *The Sociology of Hope,* trans. Carol Martin-Sperry (London: Routledge and Kegan Paul, 1979).

[40] See below, chapter 4.

[41] Leon Festinger et al., *When Prophecy Fails* (New York: Harper & Row, 1956); see also the application of this to the earliest extensive documentation, that of Israelite prophets by Robert P. Carroll, *When Prophecy Failed* (New York: Seabury Press, 1979).

- The radical act of individualism that leads believers to break with their past can turn into a radical act of submission and ego-renunciation to the cause, to the new group, to the leader. The kinds of mental vulnerabilities—especially at the hands of trusted spiritual leaders—that members of apocalyptic groups necessarily experience leads those on the outside to attribute it to a weak-minded and brain-washed lack of will.[42]
- The shorter the temporal horizon, the more intense the apocalyptic expectations become. Every apocalyptic episode is a game of chicken with the approaching end as the crack-up. The trade-off is between caution and passion. What seems irrational, if not insane, from the outside, fuels ardor and gets the adrenaline flowing on the inside. Hence, we find the tendency to up the ante in the face of disappointment.
- The apocalyptic moment induces extreme behavior of wildly opposing types, from radical asceticism to extravagant generosity to sometimes-violent antinomianism (sexual license, breaking taboos, even murder). The same wild swings hold for apocalyptic "social structures." All movements are profoundly antiauthoritarian (at least where older authorities are concerned) and often begin in radical egalitarianism (communal property). But they can, in certain circumstances, develop into still-more-intense forms of authoritarianism with equally radical inequalities.[43]

Living in such a world carries obvious advantages. Believers are cosmic warriors in the battle with evil: the adrenaline runs, every fiber of their being engaged in their navigation of every last precious moment. No longer bound by customary rules, no longer prisoners of conventional expectations, millennialists can explore the world of human possibilities and experiment radically with their lives and the lives of others.

Their imaginations unfettered, they can make connections and intuit relations at levels of that escape most of us with pedestrian minds. In his brilliant and fanciful "Proverbs of Hell," enumerated in the *Marriage of Heaven and Hell* (1796), William Blake articulates an assertive millennial mindset, uninhibited by conventional "wisdom":[44]

- Prudence is a rich ugly old maid, courted by incapacity.
- The tigers of wrath are more valuable than the horses of instruction.
- He who desires but acts not, breeds pestilence.

---

[42] See the controversy around "cult mind control": Steve Hassan, *Combating Cult Mind Control* (Rochester, Vt.: Park Street Press, 1990).

[43] Following Lord Acton's principle, this is especially true of millennial movements that take power, whether briefly (Münster, 1533–35; Taiping, China, 1840–54; Nazi Germany, 1933–45), or more lastingly (Ming and Maoist China, Soviet Russia).

[44] William Blake, *The Marriage of Heaven and Hell*, Facsimile edition (New York: Oxford University Press, 1975), xvii ff; on the millennial aspects of his thought and the time, see E.P. Thompson *Witness against the Beast: William Blake and the Moral Law* (New York: Cambridge University Press, 1993).

- What is now proved was once only imagined.
- Energy is Eternal Delight.
- Exuberance is Beauty.

Millennialists are prolific in what they do. They live in an enchanted and exciting world, and they want nothing more than to bring the rest of us into it. Or, if we refuse, they will bring it to us. And if we still resist, alas too often, they will strike us down as the apocalyptic enemy or force us to strike them down.

Believers have varied careers. Apocalyptic time is always in the offing, although disasters certainly encourage it. But rarely do they give birth to millennial movements, still more rarely do those movements make a lasting mark on the public consciousness, and still more rarely do millennial movements, like most of those under study in this volume, take power.

Moreover, no movement that takes power can sustain the hallucination that the new world is indeed messianic for more than a short while. Most burn out quickly, in months or years; in rare cases, in a decade or two. We historians, therefore, have a decided disadvantage in trying to understand what we deal with, precisely because the record of such ephemeral moments is written by people deeply hostile to the millennial actors, or, if not to the actors, to their (incorrect) apocalyptic expectation.[45]

Understanding what has happened demands that we fill in many blanks, from the millennial ideology in its quiescent state, to the galvanizing effects of apocalyptic time as it turns believers into a movement, prompting them to burn their bridges to normal time with abandon, embracing the elating freedom of infinite possibilities, peaking, then, inevitably, entering into the terrifying disorientation of failure, the descent back into "normal time." How do such believers reenter a world they had never imagined would still be there? How do they deal with their shame in front of people they had only recently dismissed with contempt? How do they handle the cognitive dissonance of having embraced a prophecy that failed spectacularly?[46]

■ THE VARIETIES OF MILLENNIAL EXPERIENCE: TERMINOLOGY

In order to understand millennial beliefs and their apocalyptic movements, we must become familiar with their fundamental tensions. The following terminological discussion offers definitions that may or may not be conventionally accepted, but, in my opinion, work particularly well in understanding and discussing the dynamics of apocalyptic millennialism, the topic of this book. The key terms are *apocalyptic, eschatology*, and *millennialism*.

---

[45] See below, chapter 3.
[46] See below, chapter 2.

Apocalyptic: My most idiosyncratic usage is the term "apocalyptic," which most often refers to "revelatory" literature, often about the end time. In this book, it refers to two related issues: a sense *imminence* about the great upheaval and the scenario whereby we now go from this evil and corrupt world to the redeemed one. The key element is, therefore, timing. Millennial or eschatological thinkers who anticipate a distant date for these events—six billion years till the sun goes nova, centuries before the advent of the millennium—tend to adopt passive postures. *Apocalyptic* believers, on the other hand, tend toward hyperactivity. Indeed, the more impending the end, the more frenetic their behavior. Like the followers of the bishop of Pontus, who ceased to work and sold all their goods, or the Xhosa who killed all their cattle and stopped planting, such believers will burn every bridge to prove their faith. So timing lies at the center of all apocalyptic rhetoric.[47]

All apocalyptic believers have scenarios: what is to come, and how we get from here to there. Some are violent and envision cosmic destruction (e.g., the book of Revelation), some transformative and call for a change of the heart (e.g., Isaiah's and Micah's vision of nations voluntarily "beating sword into plowshare..."). Some involve active human participation, some predict a supernatural event for which humans should prepare. But even in the case of the most passive forms of apocalyptic thinking, the demands can be radical, like Jesus' demand that we love our enemies and forgive seven times seventy. Apocalypse thinking is, by nature, totalistic.

The central role of apocalyptic expectations in *activating* millennialism, and therefore making it "visible," has obscured the distinction between apocalyptic and millennial. Indeed most definitions of millennialism, including Norman Cohn's, include the apocalyptic component.[48] Separating millennial from apocalyptic as descriptive terms, however, permits us to identify non-apocalyptic millennialism and track its presence through (sometimes long) periods of quiescence.[49] But before delving deeper into the phenomenon, we must consider the goal of the anticipated transformation and distinguish between *eschatology* and *millennialism*.

Eschatology anticipates a complete end to history, to the *saeculum*. This can take both religious and secular forms. In the secular, some "extinction-level event" (comets, nuclear war) will occur that will wipe out all humankind.[50] In the religious scenarios (mostly monotheist), God holds court at a Last Judgment where he will

---

[47] O'Leary, *Arguing the Millennium*, 195–206.

[48] Cohn, *Pursuit of the Millennium*; Jacob Talmon, *The Origins of Totalitarian Democracy* (New York: Praeger, 1960); Brian Wilson, *The Social Dimensions of Sectarianism: Sects and New Religious Movements in Contemporary Society* (Oxford: Clarendon Press, 1990).

[49] Landes, "Lest the Millennium," (traces the sabbatical millennium more than seven centuries (200–800 CE); "Historiographical Fear," another two centuries (800–1033).

[50] The role of "apocalyptic time" in activating eschatological concerns comes out in the famous anecdote of the astronomer who, after lecturing on how the sun will eventually *nova*, burning the earth up, had one of the audience query him on how long until that happened. "Five billion years," he replied. "Oh," said the questioner, "thank goodness. I thought you said five million."

judge the quick and the dead in the sight of all. In religious eschatological thought the conclusion is final and decisive. The messiness of earthly existence itself burns up in the process. This vision of an ultimate solution welcomes zero-sum (dualistic) thinking, imagining a closed form of redemption: the good in heaven, the evil in hell; the body, and all its messy delights and suffering, disappears permanently.

Tertullian's vision of a heaven where the saved get to watch the torments of the damned in all their locations in Hell (which also inspired Dante to visionary poetry) may well represent, as Nietzsche pointed out, a high-water mark in *ressentiment*,[51] but it also illustrates the workings of closed images of redemption. When the body and soul are separated, the very drama of moral existence has been resolved... a *final solution*. There is no future, no more tests, no more hopes. Future generations, and the open-ended dramas in which people might repent or harden their hearts, no longer have a say in the redemptive process. For the apocalyptic believers, when the *Eschaton* arrives, *les jeux sont fait*.

While apocalyptic eschatological beliefs can have a powerful impact, they tend to be short-lived. Like all apocalyptic beliefs, they prove wrong, and do so quite rapidly when the destruction fails to come. Thus while a whole town may get swept up in an eschatological fear—be it of the imminence of God's wrath or invading aliens—such panics last for a few hours, or days at most.

Eschatological variants map on two axes: The first concerns the split between secular (annihilationist) and religious (redemptive) forms. In most secular and cyclical apocalyptic scenarios, the end of the world or age results in the complete destruction of the physical world and the annihilation of even nonphysical life (i.e., souls). This can happen through a nuclear holocaust or an alien race "plowing the earth under," or the built-in cycles of the cosmos, as it can through God's "rolling up the heavens like a scroll." As an object of fear, most "secular versions" can only inspire horror of oblivion. In the religious scenarios, the Apocalypse consists of a Last Judgment where an omniscient God judges the (resurrected) "quick and the dead." The good go to heaven; the wicked go to hell.[52] In a cosmic swoop, God answers Job's agony, and makes his theodicy public.

This religious notion of a "Last Judgment" occupies most of the range in the other axis: denominational versus moral eschatology. On this axis, we find one pole in which redemption comes to those who believe a specific doctrine and follow an identifiable practice, or even just believe in a specific apocalyptic date.[53]

---

[51] See Nietzsche on Tertullian, *Genealogy of Morals*, 2:17. Tertullian's eschatological scenario's emphasis on the joy of the saints in watching the suffering of sinners is the opposite of Origen's heretical notion that even Satan himself, a fortiori all people, will eventually be saved.

[52] Purgatory appears in the twelfth century to help make this stark event more palatable as a popular theodicy. Jacques Le Goff, *The Birth of Purgatory*, trans. A. Goldhammer (Chicago: University of Chicago Press, 1986).

[53] If the story is true, at the approach of 1988, in response to Edgar Wisenant's tract *88 Reasons Why the Rapture Will Happen in 1988*, one believer actually ran up a large credit card bill. If he did so, he assumed that, at the Last Judgment, God would forgive him for cheating because he believed in the date.

On the other pole redemption comes to those who behave morally, whose inter-personal deeds are weighed in the balance and found worthy.

Denominational eschatology focuses on orthodoxy and the ritual monopoly of the mechanisms of salvation. In the case of turn of the first millennium reliccults, one gets the sense that adopting a particularly powerful patron—Sainte Foy, Saint Martial—could even assure one's chances at Judgment.[54] This approach draws strong lines between religious communities—us versus them—and makes claims to a monopoly on salvation: *extra ecclesiam nulla salus* [outside the Church there is no salvation]. Such claims may have room for a moral dimension. But even if moral behavior is necessary, it is not sufficient for salvation. The most moral person in the world cannot attain salvation *extra ecclesiam*.

Moral eschatology reverses this emphasis by drawing the fundamental line at moral behavior: a denomination may, with its teaching, help believers to lead moral lives, help prepare them for redemption, but it cannot be decisive. Adherents of any religion will not go to heaven if they behave badly toward their fellows; and similarly, will go to heaven no matter what their religion is if they behave well. Moral eschatology therefore tends toward ecumenism and has important demotic appeal. After all, manual laborers, living at the margins of subsistence, tend to care less whether those with whom they deal in this world are of a certain denomina-tion, than they do whether they are honest men and women.

Intellectual elites, on the other hand, especially clerics, tend to care more about religious boundaries. For example, two late Carolingian bishops com-plained bitterly about the undue influence of Jewish rabbis on Christian com-moners, who not only asked these rabbis to bless their fields, but attended their services "because the sermons are better."[55] Indeed, the later Carolingian period offers a dense body of evidence about the intersection of apocalyptic politics, Judeophobic tropes, and the application of "the specifics of corpse and blood pollution to an argument for legal restrictions [on Jews] to be promulgated across the empire."[56]

Millennialism: The second possible goal for the apocalyptic transformation focuses here on earth. Hence *millennialism* (also *chiliasm* from the Greek for 1000) designates the belief that at some point in the future *the world that we live in will be radically transformed* into one of perfection—of peace, justice, fellowship, and plenty. This definition of millennialism, unlike the one offered for apocalypticism above, is the accepted one in scholarly discourse. Both the church fathers, who

---

[54] "Un problème de cultures ou de culture? La statue-reliquaire et les *joca* de Sainte Foy de Conques dans le *Liber miraculorum* de Bernard d'Angers," *Cahiers de Civilisation Médiévale* 33 (1990): 351–79; R. Landes, *Relics, Apocalypse and the Deceits of History* (Cambridge Mass.: Harvard University Press), 52–72.

[55] Cited in Abigail Firey, *A Contrite Heart: Prosecution and Redemption in the Carolingian Empire* (Leiden: Brill, 2005), 139 and n. 79.

[56] Ibid., 84; see her note 58 for a reference to the "especially intriguing parallel" with the Muslim legal jurists (Maliki) attempt to do the same with Christians.

despised precisely this "earthly" element, and modern anthropologists, who study it in its active forms, call these beliefs millennialism.[57]

And, since millennialism anticipates the destruction of the current "world order" before the new world can begin, it is profoundly subversive notion: the world that passes is not the natural world, but the political world that now exists. Such beliefs can, but need not, entail a belief in God. The *secular*[58] dimension of millennialism—its insistence that redemption occurs in the world of time and history, in the *saeculum*—makes it possible for non-theistic versions to emerge, like utopianism and communism. Our civilization's current technological prowess has made it possible to turn even the most unlikely apocalyptic scenario into something that true believers can bring about through their own exertions.

Apocalyptic millennial beliefs thus have a far greater direct impact on history than eschatological ones since they call for active participation in revolutionizing history. They can last years, even decades; and when they fail, they leave a far deeper mark on the society in which they occurred. Millennial scenarios and movements can include *messianic* leaders who lead the faithful to the Promised Land, or arise from a movement without a specific leader.

Nor should we limit millennialism to violent radical social change.[59] Individual millennial believers or groups can change from one extreme to the other of their various options of dealing with others in apocalyptic time—peace, violence, reconciliation, extermination—and however radically different they may seem to us, as reported in the documents, they do share significant traits. Millennial messiahs include both the most elevated souls and the most violent psychotics.

Some historians object to maintaining so capacious a definition for millennialism that it includes virtually every radical movement in history.[60] My suggestion is that we are far too early in our research to decide what relevance millennial studies has for these various topics or not. Given that most people have never thought about Nazism as a millennial movement—and this includes scholars who

---

[57] For a sense of the full range of millennial beliefs and the various disciplines that contribute to this field of study, see Ted Daniels, *Millennialism: An International Bibliography* (New York: Garland, 1992); for a discussion of the anthropological dimensions, see "Millennial Countdown in New Guinea," ed. Pamela Stewart and Andrew Strathern, *Ethnohistory* 47, no. 1 (Winter 2000), and below, chapter. 5. One of the most astute students of both anthropological and theological dimensions of millennialism is Garry Trompf, *Early Christian Historiography: Narratives of Retributive Justice* (London: Continuum, 2000) and *Payback: the Logic of Retribution in Melanesian Religions* (New York: Cambridge University Press, 1994).

[58] Here I use the term in Augustine's sense of the time-space continuum, the embodied, and hence the historical.

[59] For Charles Hill, the socially disruptive dimension is key: *Regnum Caelorum: Patterns of Future Hope in Early Christianity* (Clarendon: Oxford, 1992), p. 1 n. 1. This seems to be a widespread tendency among historians, drawn largely from a (possibly superficial reading) of Cohn's *Pursuit of the Millennium*. See further discussion throughout this volume.

[60] Often historians, especially historians of theology, use a more restrictive term for millennialism, as, for example, recently Charles Hill, *Regnum Caelorum*, 1–8.*

know that the Nazis claimed to inaugurate the *tausandjähriges Reich*, it seems a bit early to decide how useful or bloated the term might be.[61]

My contention is that by understanding movements that share the simple combination of *a millennial vision of the world transformed, and an apocalyptic belief in that transformation's imminence*, one can make sense of these movements in significant ways. They participate in an unusual and characteristic dynamic that is well worth understanding. These movements form a natural grouping of socio-cultural phenomena that cut across all cultures and regions and periods of history. They are still with us. We are in their current.

Hierarchical, Imperial, Iconic Millennialism

One pole of millennial thinking works from a top-down model of the "perfect" society. Here the cosmic battle for humanity pits chaos (evil) against order (good) and calls for the establishment of justice and peace imposed by a hierarchy on earth that mirrors the hierarchy in heaven.[62] Some tradition of a messianic "world conqueror" who inaugurates the golden age appears in many world historical traditions, and one finds current expressions in both Maitreya Buddhism and Hinduism.[63] Perhaps the earliest manifestation of this form of millennialism came under the rule of the "heretic" pharaoh, Akhenaten.[64]

Among the many characteristic products of imperial millennialism, we find a wide range of monumental sculptural programs, including the iconic depiction of the emperor (and the empress).[65] The advent of the imperial Roman style in the first century BCE generated at once a massive iconic program featuring a salvific ruler and his relationship to the forces of the universe.[66] This kind of thinking also has an affinity with bee imagery and sun-king imagery, the divinization as it were, of Hobbes' *Leviathan*, as the all-nurturing center. Akhenaten believed that God was the sun, and that he, the pharaoh, was his incarnation on earth who poured the rays of his beneficence out upon all his subjects. Almost all great *empires* with a demotic program "for all"—Hellenistic, Roman, Christian, Buddhist—bring

---

[61] See below, chapter 15.

[62] Norman Cohn, *Cosmos, Chaos, and the World to Come: The Ancient Roots of Apocalyptic Faith* (New Haven, Conn.: Yale University Press, 1993).

[63] For Buddhism, see Takashi James Kodera's "Nichiren and His Nationalistic Eschatology," *Religious Studies* 15 (1979): 41–53; Hue-Tam Ho Tai, *Millenarianism and Peasant Politics in Vietnam* (Cambridge: Harvard University Press, 1993). On Hinduism, see Robert F. Maher, "Tommy Kabu Movement of the Purari Delta," *Oceania* 29 (1958): 75–90.

[64] See below, chapter 6.

[65] Garth Fowden, *Empire to Commonwealth* (Princeton, N.J.: Princeton University Press, 1994), chap. 6; see also Efraim Karsh, *Islamic Imperialism: A History* (New Haven, Conn.: Yale University Press, 2006), pp. 37–38, 50–52; and see below, chapter 5.

[66] Paul Zanker, *The Power of Images in the Age of Augustus* (Ann Arbor: University of Michigan Press, 1990).

with them massive public campaigns of visual art aimed at establishing the *icon* of the ruler in the social imagination.

Alone, Islam has succeeded in breaking this matrix between empire and icon, between, on the one hand, a world salvific conquest and empire (which it undoubtedly pursued), and, on the other, a fairly strict adherence to the prohibition on images imbedded in Muslim scriptures.[67] Indeed, this significant exception aside, one might single out as the distinguishing feature of hierarchical millennialism, the "feedback" between the megalomanic sense of a messianic king—one who brings salvation to his people and the world—and the iconic program of monotheism, in which he sees his own divine image reflected.

Monotheistic variants of this theory favor the political formula: *One God, one emperor*, and, quite often, *one religion*. The emperor-messiah represents God on earth and constitutes the image or icon of God on earth.[68] Hence, *iconic millennialism*. Here heaven's order becomes a model for that of earth, and just as the one God rules in heaven, so on earth, the one king rules over a numerous, obedient, and grateful population of people, saved by the beneficent conqueror's *pax*.

Such an idea has particular attraction for clerical elites who believe that the particular liturgies they conduct assure the harmonious alignment between celestial and terrestrial forces and who, in return, receive the generous support of the emperor. Thus, temple-based cities whose very architecture replicates heavenly symmetries often stand at the center of a great imperial tradition.[69] The rituals of the central temple create the capital of the empire, where court and cult become monumental. Such projects often involve large amounts of forced, slave labor, and therefore the radical subjection of large numbers of people to such projects.[70] They also create a strong market for the arts and trades, channeling

---

[67] Fowden, *Empire to Commonwealth*, chap. 6; see also Karsh, *Islamic Imperialism*, chap. 1–2.

[68] Eric Peterson argues that monotheism's central political corollary is "one God, one king," *Monotheismus als politisches Problem. Ein Beitrag zur Geschichte der politischen Theologie im Imperium Romanum* (Leipzig: Hegner, 1935). This argument has found considerable echo in recent arguments that monotheism is "inherently" violent: Barrington Moore Jr., *Moral Purity and Persecution in History* (Princeton, N.J.: Princeton University Press, 2000); Rodney Stark, *One True God: Historical Consequences of Monotheism* (Princeton, N.J.: Princeton University Press, 2000). Garth Fowden also assumes that this is the central political meaning of monotheism in *From Empire to Commonwealth*. For critiques of this position, see below.

[69] This is not to say that these forms of government may arise without any identifiable millennialism as their ideological basis, but hierarchical millennialism *produces* this kind of configuration quite consistently.

[70] In the Babylonian myth, *Enumah Elish*, the defeated gods created humankind so that someone else would build the temples of their divine conqueror Marduk (see Cohn, *Cosmos*, 45–49). Obviously, the pyramids and other great temple complexes illustrate the dynamic (in particular, those built during the reigns of Amenhotep III, the "Sun King," and Akhenaten, the "monotheist pharoah" in fourteenth-century-BCE Egypt; see below, chapter 6). One finds similar tendencies toward hierarchical centralization and the crushing weight of conscripted labor for massive building projects in the Davidic monarchy, especially under Solomon; see I Kings 5:27–12:4; see also Israel Knohl, *The Sanctuary of Silence: The Priestly Torah and the Holiness School* (Augsburg: Fortress Publications, 1994).

talented cultural energy and resources into these publicly funded projects dedicated to the glory of the elites and the gods they serve.

In the millennial variants of such an ideal hierarchical order, we find a world conqueror who brings all peoples under his messianic wing, who, with a new "law," inaugurates the new world, the new dispensation. In Islam, for example, the great Muslim empires used millennial rhetoric extensively in the early stages of their development.[71] In Christianity, despite the strongly *anti*-imperialistic apocalyptic tradition it had inherited from Judaism, the tradition of the messianic emperor first appears with Eusebius' writings on Constantine in the fourth century.

Eusebius hails Constantine as the first Christian emperor, the savior who inaugurated the "peace" the prophets had promised.[72] Of course Eusebius was wrong about Constantine: the *pax christiana romana* he inaugurated hardly fulfilled the expectations of the millennialists in the Church. On the contrary, most Christian millennialists saw Rome's entry into the Church as a moment of apocalyptic catastrophe—the Whore of Babylon had ridden the Beast into the heart of the sanctuary.[73] But the fantasy Eusebius and Constantine had aroused proved astoundingly durable, and, in an imperial parallel to the "Second Coming," Christendom developed beliefs about a once-and-future "Last Emperor" who had already come and would return to conquer the world and bring all within the just confines of true Christianity.[74]

On one level, this kind of millennialism has a great deal in common with normative aristocratic ideologies. The evil forces that hierarchical millennialists target come from "below" (the unruly masses) and from "without" (foreigners). Among the apocalyptic signs of oncoming chaos—the world turned upside down[75]—they identify commoners who do not know their place, women who talk back, aristocrats treated as slaves, rulers thrown out of their cities.[76] Alone a strong king can

---

[71] Moshe Sharon, *Black Banners from the East: The Establishment of the 'Abbāsid State* (Jerusalem: Magnes Press, 1983); Karsh, *Islamic Imperialism*; Timothy Furnish, *Holiest Wars: Islamic Mahdis, Their Jihads, and Osama bin Laden* (Westport, Conn.: Praeger, 2005), 30–71.

[72] Nicely articulated by Edward Cranz, "Kingdom and Polity," *Harvard Theological Review* 44 (1951): 47–66. Church historians are not fond of the analysis, and point to Eusebius' hostility to chiliasm. In the terminology of this book, Eusebius opposed demotic (egalitarian) millennialism, even as (because) he represented the opposite variety. For an analysis that comes close to this perception, see Harold A. Drake, *In Praise of Constantine: A Historical Study and New Translation of Eusebius' Tricennial Orations* (Berkeley and Los Angeles: University of California Press, 1976). I will address this issue at length in *While God Tarried: Millennialism from Jesus to the Peace of God (33–1033)* (forthcoming).

[73] On the millennialism of the Donatists and their anti-imperialism, see Markus, *Saeculum*, 55.

[74] Paul Alexander, *The Byzantine Apocalyptic Tradition*, ed. Dorothy deF. Abrahamse (Berkeley and Los Angeles: University of California Press, 1985); Hannes Möhring, *Der Weltkaiser der Endzeit* (Stuttgart: Thorbeke, 2000).

[75] Christopher Hill, *The World Turned Upside-Down* (London: Penguin, 1991).

[76] On the *Prophecies of Neferti* and the *Admonitions of Ipuwer*, see Miriam Lichtheim, *Ancient Egyptian Literature: A Book of Readings* (Berkeley and Los Angeles: University of California Press, 1975), 134–61; on these images of a social order inverted as a reflection of "the anxieties of the privileged, their sense of living on a tiny island of order and civilization amidst a sea of disorder and barbarism," see Cohn, *Cosmos*, 20.

keep chaos at bay, and in relegating his immense task to his officers, he serves both his subjects and his aristocracy.[77] Here we encounter again the firm belief of most premodern "political" thinkers (including Eusebius) that democracy was a recipe for anarchy and social disaster.[78]

The overlap between this hierarchical vision of the ideal society and the stratified structures of premodern polities made it the most attractive form of millennial belief to elites. And it found special favor among "reformers."[79] In apocalyptic time, they permitted one to rally support for a conqueror among the populace, to present the conqueror as their true friend, as the anointed messenger of God sent to free commoners from the tyranny of their aristocracies.[80]

At the same time, they deployed the forces of warrior aristocracies in the service of the highest principles. After all, forward-looking (millennial) myths structured on the order/chaos duality tend toward the cataclysmic: the world has succumbed to evil, and the (vast) majority of humankind is irredeemably corrupted. In order for the world to be as it should be—as God or Allah, or the dialectic, or the race wills it—then the forces of order must annihilate those of evil. The hierarchical perfect world will only come when the messianic conqueror has destroyed forever the mad passions that drive men to civil war and violence and submitted men to God's will.[81] Not surprisingly, then, elites prefer hierarchical millennialism. And, of course, given its easy tendency to slip from (failed) millennial promise to normative empire, this form of millennialism has the longest lasting consequences, but leaves the weakest millennial signature in the wake of its failures.[82]

---

[77] Reinhard Bendix, *Kings or People* (Berkeley and Los Angeles: University of California Press, 1978), 118–28.

[78] "Monarchy far transcends every other constitution and form of government: for that democratic equality of power, which is its opposite, may rather be described as anarchy and disorder," Eusebius, *Praise of Constantine*, Nicene and Post-Nicene Fathers, ed. Phillip Schaff and Henry Wace (Edinburgh: T & T Clark, 1890), vol. 1, chap. 3, p. 584, http://www.ccel.org/ccel/schaff/npnf201.iv.viii.iv.html, July 6, 2008.

[79] On the link between millennialism and reform in the early Church, see Gerhard Ladner, *The Idea of Reform: Its Impact on Christian Thought and Action in the Age of the Fathers* (Cambridge, Mass.: Harvard University Press, 1959), 27–32. For an astute analysis of the working of a radical "reforming elite" in eleventh-century Western Europe (without reference to millennial currents), see R.I. Moore, *Formation of a Persecuting Society: Power and Deviance in Western Europe, 950–1250* (Oxford: Blackwell, 1987).

[80] See the Maccabees' vision of themselves (1 and 2 Maccabees); on Napoleon, see chapter 9; on Islamic expansion, see chapter 14.

[81] Many imperial ideologies insist on the role of the emperor in putting an end to civil war and the unconquerable passions of men (e.g., Rome, China).

[82] Indeed, Norman Cohn, despite having done a great deal of work on demotic millennialism in *Pursuit of the Millennium*, identified this ur-millennial myth of a battle between good/order and evil/chaos as the primary form of millennialism (*Cosmos, Chaos and the World to Come*). Most of Greek Orthodox millennial thought is of this variety: Alexander, *Byzantine Apocalyptic Tradition*; Francis Dvornik, *Early Christian and Byzantine Political Philosophy: Origins and Background* (Washington, D.C.: Dumbarton Oaks, 1966).

Demotic, Egalitarian, Iconoclastic Millennialism

Demotic millennialism embraces the opposite conception of the universe to the iconic one: where the latter sees chaos and popular movements as the problem, the former sees imposed order and elites as the problem; where the latter seeks to perfect dominion, the former wants to replace top-down order with holy anarchy (see figure 1.1.[83] For these visionaries, freedom and justice in the messianic age will abolish all dominion of people over each other; the "saved" behave justly not from fear but from love. "*No king but God!*" was the political formula of monotheism according the apocalyptic millennial Zealots of Jesus' time, and the rabbinical tradition that survived them enshrined that formula in its prayers.[84] Marx appealed to the same vision with his "withering away of the state."

Demotic millennialism emphasizes voluntarism: the inhabitants of the messianic world act justly not from fear but *by choice*, and thus there will be no need for government, *anarchy*. Here the sword and spear, weapons of predatory aristocratic dominion, become plow and pruning hook, tools of honest labor; here commoners enjoy the fruits of their labor and share freely with their neighbors (Micah 4:4): *Liberté, égalité, fraternité.*

Demotic millennialism can take a variety of actual forms, from particularistic to universalistic. Some forms "unify" a given population of believers—tribe, denomination, religious community, nation, race. Others imagine a multicultural world, where "*nation* does not lift up sword against *nation*," but each finds their own style of worshipping a deity that defies definition. Some, like the Enlightenment notion of historical progress, imagine a cosmopolitan world of peace.[85]

Aniconic monotheism maintains the formula: *No King but God; and God is too great for any one religion.* It has a powerful antinomian strain that views laws in stratified societies, with their built-in favor to elites, as part of the evil world. Part of their iconoclasm involves shattering taboos, in particular about sex. The antinomian claim that the believers stand above the law represents the view of those who believe they have already, proleptically, reached the other side of the apocalyptic transformation. Looking back at the laws governing behavior on the unjust side of the apocalyptic divide, such restraints are useless or worse. Laws of adultery do not apply since the new humans stand so far above the petty jealousies that make free love so destructive.

---

[83] See Christopher Hill, *Antichrist in Seventeenth-Century England* (London: Oxford University Press, 1971).

[84] Josephus, *Antiquities of the Jews*, book 18, chap. 1.6: "These men agree in all other things with the Pharisaic notions; but they have an invisible attachment to liberty; and they say that God is to be their only Ruler and Lord." Josephus, *Josephus: The Complete Works*, trans. William Whiston (Grand Rapids, Mich.: Kregel Publications, 1978), 377. For examples in the rabbinic prayers, see the *Avinu Malkenu* [Our Father, Our King] and the Nishmatcol chai [Let the soul of every living thing], see *The Koren Siddur*, trans. Rabbi Jonathan Sacks (Jerusalem: Koren Publishing, 2009), pp. 138, 444. Further discussed below, chapter 8, n. 109.

[85] On the Enlightenment as a secularization of demotic millennialism and the French Revolution as a secular apocalyptic movement, see below, chapters 8 and 9.

As the millennial antinomian Blake put it in his *Proverbs of Hell*: "Prisons are built with stones of law and brothels with bricks of religion."[86] Laws and prohibitions impede the flow of energy and therefore of delight. They throttle the abundance that by nature wishes to burst forth in the messianic age. Elites, with their zero-sum commitments to a social order that replicates itself and their place above the prime divider, strangle human resources, impoverish commoners, and produce cultures of poverty.[87] Such rules beg to be broken; and transgressing them offers the most elating form of millennial behavior.[88]

Where do we find such demotic millennialism? Virtually everywhere. Indeed, all mass millennial movements, even eventually hierarchical ones like Islamic, Napoleonic, and Soviet imperialism begin as demotic: how else do they get their first recruits, the ones that come *before* the movement becomes a "strong horse" and attracts those who want to be on the side of the eventual winner?

Restorative versus Innovative Millennialism

The other major axis of millennial varieties concerns whether the imagined messianic era will constitute a return to a primeval Eden or the creation of a new, never-before-seen form of social organization. The restorative variety appeals to conservative sentiments and relies largely on magical thinking.[89] The Ghost Dancers in the American northwest believed that their dancing would lead the earth to shed the whites and their technology like a snake sheds its skin and return the world to its pristine condition, when the buffalo roamed free; the Xhosa believed that if they killed their cattle, the ancestors would bring new, healthy cattle and sweep the white man away like a broom sweeps dust. The most powerful current form of restorative millennialism today is Salafism, the drive to return to the original purity of Islam, to join the seventh-century followers of Muhammad and restore the Sharia law they established.[90]

Innovative millennialism favors a progressive vision of the future, one featured prominently by technologically enhanced forms of "postmillennialism"—the Christian belief that the millennium will be inaugurated first by (divinely inspired) humans, and only then (*after* the millennium) will Jesus return. Most

---

[86] Blake, *Marriage of Heaven Hell,* plate 8.

[87] On economic development, see William Russell Easterly, "Inequality Does Cause Underdevelopments: Insights from a New Instrument," *Journal of Developmental Economics* 84, no. 2 (Nov. 2007): 755–66; also by the same author, *The White Man's Burden: Why the West's Efforts to Aid the Rest Have Done So Much Ill and So Little Good* (New York: Penguin Press, 2006). On the cultural dimensions of wealth production, see David S. Landes, *The Wealth and Poverty of Nations.*

[88] This antinomianism lay at the heart of numerous Christian groups like the Taborites and the Ranters, as well as Jewish groups like the Sabbatians and the Frankists.

[89] Bryan R. Wilson, *Magic and the Millennium.*

[90] Roel Meije, ed., *Global Salafism: Islam's New Religious Movement* (New York: Columbia University Press, 2009).

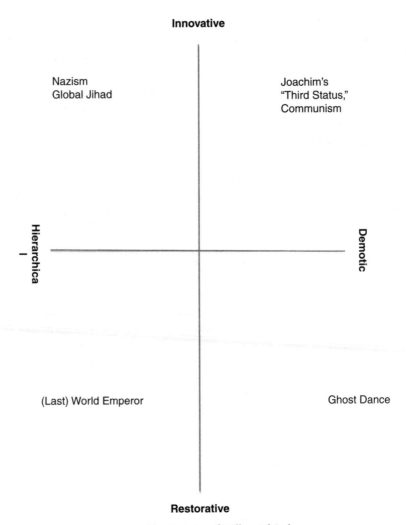

Figure 1.1 The Varieties of Millennial Styles

forms of secular millennialism—especially communism—anticipate a world of perfection never before realized, indeed never before possible. In many such cases, the advent of new technology, often communications technology, marks the dawn of the new era.

Innovative millennialism has, for obvious reasons, become all the more prominent over the last several centuries, and at this point permeates virtually every current form of millennialism, including some of the most "restorative."[91] Salafism, for example, rides on the wings of cyberspace, and its adherents view the technology of the modern world as the vehicle for their success.[92] Indeed, all of the varieties I have described do not represent fixed entities, but often blend various elements, which then surface at times in the career of a millennial movement. But in order to understand those dynamics, we must return to the question of the dynamics of apocalyptic time.

▪ APOCALYPTIC SCENARIOS AND DYNAMICS

Apocalyptic Timing: A Time Neither to Sow nor Reap

I have defined apocalyptic as a sense of imminence. But there are all kinds of intensities to that feeling, from immediate to "within my lifetime," and along that spectrum run a large gamut of emotions, from quiet determination to delirium, exalted or panicked. For prophets, this creates a quintessential problem: the greater the sense of imminence the more motivated the believer...*and* the more acute the disappointment. People who believe that the end will come sometime in their lifetime operate in a tepid zone; they tend not to burn bridges, but rather to build longer term projects.

According to Stephen O'Leary, a prophecy of apocalypse some twenty to thirty years away offers an excellent period in which to spread the message. As in the case of the Millerites (1820–43), the appeal of such a well-seeded message can accelerate rapidly in the final years. As the movement enters the "hot zone," urgency drives people to more dramatic deeds like not planting or sowing. And in their aftermath, such moments bring bitter disappointment. Thus, preachers of apocalyptic prophecies are caught in a trap: the more powerful their claims, the more imminently disprovable.

Medieval texts reveal a wide range of strategies adopted by ecclesiastical leaders who at once seek to impress their congregations with the salutary fear of God's omniscient judgment looming, and yet cannot become so explicit that their predictions prove false. Augustine wrote an extensive discussion on apocalyptic expectation entitled "On the Three Opinions about the End." He rejects the two most common options: neither say *soon*, for it can lead to disappointment and loss of faith; nor say *later*, for it discourages the faithful. Augustine's solution: it can happen any time, and we cannot know when; live with the apocalypse at your shoulder.

But this radical agnosticism held virtually everyone to too high a standard. On the contrary, for centuries before and centuries after—indeed to this day—believers have alternated between the two options Augustine rejected. One can read the

---

[91] For a provocative interpretation of technology as a form of millennial activity and its consequences for both millennialism and for science, see David Noble, *The Religion of Technology: The Divinity of Man and the Spirit of Invention* (New York: Alfred A. Knopf, 1998); and Gutierrez and Schwartz, *End that Does*.

[92] See below, chapter 14.

record of this battle going on over almost a thousand years in the history of changing dating systems used by early Christian authorities, who preferred *later*, and
found it necessary to shift their chronologies every time the apocalyptic date
approached, particularly the approach of the year 6000 *anno mundi*.[93]

Take, for example, the famous letter of Pope Gregory the Great to Æthelbert, the
newly converted ruler of Kent, in 601. It shows the importance of apocalyptic
rhetoric as a motivator, as well as the necessary distance any responsible public
figure needs to take from a foolish and easily disprovable stance. Gregory instructs
the Æthelbert to destroy the pagan shrines and convert his people to Christianity.

> Suppress the worship of idols; overthrow the structures of the temples; establish the
> manners of your subjects by much cleanness of life, exhorting, terrifying, winning, cor-
> recting, and showing forth an example of good works, that you may obtain your reward
> in Heaven from Him, Whose Name and the knowledge of Whom you have spread
> abroad upon earth.[94]

He then adds the following highly ambiguous remarks, meant on the one hand to
give urgency to the demand, and on the other, to avoid committing to a disprovable claim:

> Besides, we would have your Highness know that, as we find in Holy Scripture from the
> words of the Almighty Lord, the end of this present world, and the kingdom of the saints,
> which will never come to an end, *is at hand*. But as the end of the world draws near, many
> things are about to come upon us which were not before, to wit, changes in the air, and
> terrors from heaven, and tempests out of the order of the seasons, wars, famines, pesti-
> lences, earthquakes in divers places; which things will not, nevertheless, all happen in
> our days, but will all follow after our days.

Normally "at hand" means imminent, that is, by my definition "apocalyptic," and
therefore the exact opposite of "after we are dead." And there is considerable evidence that Gregory the Great, like his Gallican contemporary Gregory of Tours,
indeed thought he lived at the end of time.[95] Moreover, in this context, the comment seems clearly part of an effort to impress on Æthelbert the urgency of the
task at hand, given his reluctance to force conversion.[96]

But Gregory knew his Augustine, and had to include indefiniteness in his letter.
Thus we have what one might call an "apocalyptic buffer" at the end of the sentence:
"not all happen in our day." With that codicil, Gregory saved himself from causing

---

[93] Landes, "Lest the Millennium."

[94] Bede, *Ecclesiastical History of the English Nation*, 1:32. Note that one of the most central themes in
Christian apocalyptic discourse centers around the spreading of the Gospel before the Second Coming.

[95] Robert Markus, *Gregory the Great and His World* (Cambridge: Cambridge University Press,
1997), 51–67.

[96] "For he had learned from his teachers and authors of his salvation that the services of Christ
ought to be voluntary not compulsory," Bede, *Ecclesiastical History of the English Nation* 1: 26.

that which Augustine had warned against, when prophetic failure leads to loss of faith.[97] How can one disprove a prophecy that will only happen after one's death?

Having made such an indiscretion and then retracted it, Gregory concludes with remarks that speak implicitly to those who understand, and concludes with the important agenda:

> If, therefore, you perceive that any of these things come to pass in your country, let not your mind be in any way disturbed; for these signs of the end of the world are sent before, for this reason, that we may take heed to our souls, and be watchful for the hour of death, and may be found prepared with good works to meet our Judge. Thus much, my illustrious son, I have said in few words, with intent—that when the Christian faith is spread abroad in your kingdom, our discourse to you may also be more copious, and we may desire to say the more, as joy for the full conversion of your nation is increased in our mind.

In other words, signs of the end should not panic you but increase your determination to convert your whole people. All apocalyptic discourse must walk this fine line between now and later.

Apocalyptic Scenarios

Once a believer embraces the imminence, the key to understanding his or her behavior concerns the apocalyptic scenario whereby this world will be transformed into the perfect one. In the same manner that we can map millennialism on two axes, we can do so for apocalyptic scenarios: on one axis, we find a tension between violent, even cataclysmic, scenarios and more peaceful transformative ones. On the other axis, we find a tension between an active or passive role for humankind (see figure 1.2)

Cataclysmic apocalyptic scenarios foresee enormous destruction preceding the advent of God's kingdom (or just total annihilation). These scenarios tend to emphasize the depravity of humankind—most people are damned and must perish before any truly just society can come about. This is true even for many "secular" scenarios like the more radical versions of global warming, which identify human failings (greed, irresponsibility) as the source of the problem.

Cataclysmic apocalyptic scenarios often involve staggering levels of violence and destruction—rivers of blood, plagues, earthquakes, floods, famines, the devastation of war, and natural calamities. Religious forms of cataclysmic apocalyptic belief, like modern "premillennial dispensationalism" among American Protestants, tend to emphasize the central role of God and divine agents in bringing about the millennium.[98] In these scenarios, evil forces control the world either openly or, in many Christian and antimodern versions, secretly in the form of a worldwide

---

[97] "Gregory also professed not to know the time of the end, but his sense of its nearness is unequalled since the fading of the early Christian eschatological expectations," Markus, *Gregory the Great*, 51.

[98] Mal Couch, ed., *Dictionary of Premillennial Theology* (Grand Rapids, Mich.: Kregel Publications, 1996).

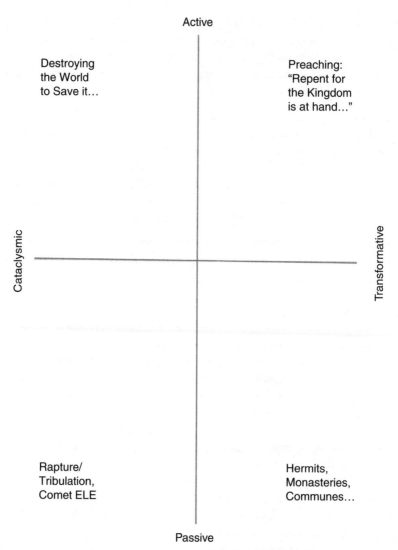

Figure 1.2 The Varieties of Apocalyptic Styles

conspiracy that will soon—at the apocalyptic moment—spring its trap and attempt to enslave the whole world.

The most widespread current form of this paranoid cataclysmic belief in a totalitarian cabal concerns the *New World Order*.[99] Modern Protestant "premillennialism"

---

[99] The locus classicus of this is the *Protocols of the Elders of Zion* (Chulmleigh: Britons, 1968 or New York: Beckwith, 1920); also Landes and Katz, *The Paranoid Apocalypse.* For more recent avatars, see UFO narratives: Keith Thompson, *Angels and Aliens: UFO's and the Mythic Imagination* (Reading, Mass.: Addison Wesley Longman, 1991); Christian fundamentalist versions: Pat Robertson, *The New World Order* (Dallas: Word Publications,1991); New World Order conspiracies: Franklin Allen Leib, *Behold a Pale Horse* (New York: Forge, 2000).

expects Jesus to return *before* the millennium to destroy the Antichrist and his agents in the battle of Armageddon, and then to found the kingdom of the saints (millennium). Here humanity has a passive role, largely limited to penitence and preaching: "Repent, for the kingdom of heaven is at hand." Heaven's Gate, and many other gnostic apocalyptic approaches, view this physical world as a prison from which we all need to be released, this planet as something that will be "plowed under" at the great transformation.[100] When we imagine "apocalyptic" as disastrous and speak of "doomsday" as a day of terror, we are referring primarily to various manifestations of the cataclysmic scenario.

Transformational Apocalyptic Scenarios emphasize people's voluntary and peaceful change. A massive collective change of heart, perhaps divinely inspired, brings on the messianic age: "I will give them a new heart and put a new spirit in you…" (Ezekiel 36:26). Transformational scenarios assume that large numbers of people can transcend their current social paradigms ("heart of stone") and move into a messianic mode voluntarily—lions lie down with lambs, aristocrats beat their swords into plowshares and their spears into pruning hooks. Transformational apocalyptic tends to foster programs of radical—often unrealistic—social change (peace movements, temperance drives, emancipation, utopian communities) and places great emphasis on educational reforms that create "new" people (citizens, comrades, believers).

Currently, one of the more prominent form of transformational millennialism comes from the "new age" movements set in motion by the millennial wave of the '60s—environmentally harmonized communes.[101] In Protestant circles, transformational millennialism is known as "postmillennialism" (that is, Jesus comes back *after* his faithful create the millennium on earth), although there are cataclysmic variants of postmillennialism.[102] Historically, transformational (post-)millennialism has contributed to a number of typically American "reformist" developments—the Great Awakenings, Emancipation, utopian farming, and industrial communities (from the Shakers and Amish to the Oneida and Fourier communities), the profession of social work, the civil rights movement, and so on.[103]

Active versus Passive Apocalyptic Scenarios: Both these scenarios vary internally according to the various roles they assign to God and humans in bringing about the transformation. The most passive eschatological scenarios are non-millennial (nothing to change on earth) and cataclysmic (only superhuman forces can effect the necessary destruction). Such scenarios relegate a passive

---

[100] See below, chapter 13.

[101] Arthur Mendel, *Vision and Violence*, 223–64; John R. Hall, *The Ways Out: Utopian Communal Groups in an Age of Babylon* (London: Routledge & Kegan Paul, 1978).

[102] For example, consider the postmillennial Reconstructionists, whose cataclysmic scenario made Y2K so attractive to some (Gary North). Chip Berlet has described these groups as "Calvinism on crack," "Millennialist and Apocalyptic Influences on Dominionism," *Lapis Magazine*, http://www.lapismagazine.org/index.php?option=com_content&task=view&id=76&Itemid=2.

[103] See, for example, Daniel Walker Howe, *What Hath God Wrought: The Transformation of America (1815–1848)* (New York: Oxford University Press, 2007).

role to humans: they must await God's "appointed" time, and their message calls for repentance not for social transformation.

Paul apparently embraced such a notion when he called on slaves to remain in their place (1 Corinthians 7:17–24) and Christian subjects to accept the rule of the "powers that be" (Romans 13:1–7). Paul did not anticipate slavery and the rule of unjust pagans (especially those of the Roman Empire) as a feature of the coming kingdom. But nor should apocalyptic believers expend their final efforts, just before the return of Christ in power and glory, to resisting a doomed system: "For you know what hour it is, how it is full time now for you to wake from sleep. For salvation is nearer to us now than when we first believed; the night is far gone, the day is at hand" (Romans 13:11–12).

Active scenarios, on the other hand, place agency in human hands: humankind, perhaps inspired by God, brings about the dramatic events. Most active apocalyptic scenarios at least start out as transformative—human beings, transfigured by God's grace (or that of the historical dialectic), inaugurate the millennial world; subsequently, as a result of the frustration of their expectation, some turn more violent. All *secular* scenarios (at least the millennial ones) are activist. There is no God to await. But so are many religious ones. The messianic vision of Isaiah and Micah places the key in the actions of the nations, but that action is to accept the yoke of God's justice, to voluntarily submit to God's kingship (and, hence, his rebuke).

Passive non-millennial (eschatological) scenarios, even cataclysmic ones, are largely apolitical, and tend, therefore, to be more "respectable" to the adepts of "normal time":[104] as long as they are not apocalyptic, they actually encourage conservative behavior: "pie in the sky by and by." Active apocalyptic scenarios aiming at a millennial transformation of this world, however, are almost by definition subversive. Only by emphasizing an almost invisible, individual transformation that will eventually and almost imperceptibly bring on the millennium, can active apocalyptic rhetoric not arouse violent opposition in most cultures. Joachim of Fiore's "third status" of the Church, which he articulated in the final decades of the twelfth century, managed to make it under the Augustinian radar of Church officials, much to the consternation of subsequent generations of ecclesiastics faced with the violently active millennial movements his beliefs spawned in the thirteenth century.[105]

Millennial movements adopt active cataclysmic apocalyptic scenarios in part because they want to transform this world. But even eschatological expectations can involve active variants, especially with the advent of serious technological empowerment. In particular, the feverish apocalyptic visions induced by nuclear weapons offer us a growing array of cataclysmic apocalyptic thinking that is

---

[104] Wilson calls these "introverted," *Magic and the Millennium*, 348–449.
[105] Marjorie Reeves, *Joachim of Fiore and the Prophetic Future* (New York: Harper & Row, 1977), 29–58.

vigorously activist.[106] Such groups, starting out small, tend to view the social world as if it were a set of high-pressured tectonic plates where a small but well-aimed explosion can trigger a massive quake. Aum Shinrikyo attempted mass murder in the Tokyo subway system as a prelude to world destruction: destroying the world to save it.[107] What they lack in strength, they make up for in enhanced technology and the true (gnostic) understanding of who is good and who evil.[108]

Now, while all these apocalyptic and millennial variants appear to have mutually exclusive traits, this is only the deception of a categorical approach that tries to define a movement by a single set of beliefs. On the contrary, millennialism is a dynamic phenomenon, and in the course of an apocalyptic episode, a movement can literally flip from one extreme to the other. Among the classic cases, we find the Anabaptists who, in the course of their failed millennium at Münster from 1533–35, went from the most radically pacifist and egalitarian of the new "Protestant" groups to a violent and authoritarian group (from transformational demotic to cataclysmic hierarchical).[109] Inversely, a violently revolutionary group like the Baha'i could transform into a radically demotic, transformative millennial religion.[110]

The key issue, which this book intends to explore in all of its case studies, concerns the inevitable dimension of all apocalyptic belief: the failure of those expectations. Indeed, one might venture a preliminary possibility that the inevitable disappointment of any apocalyptic group's hopes will act as a toggle-switch to flip back and forth between active and passive, demotic and hierarchic, cataclysmic and transformational. And in this paradoxical volatility we may find some of the keys to the strange relationship between millennial vision and violence.[111]

Thus, the apocalyptic and millennial variants presented above should be taken not as categories, but as a map of terrain over which millennial groups, in the course of an apocalyptic episode, may travel extensively. So in order to understand

---

[106] Paul Boyer, *When Time Shall Be No More: Prophecy Belief in Modern American Culture* (Cambridge, Mass.: Harvard University Press, 1992).

[107] Lifton, *Destroying the World*.

[108] Hence Eric Vogelin identified what we are here calling the millennial, as "gnostic," because of the power of the knowledge in defining the course of action. Of course, all of Vogelin's examples are aggressive, activist forms of Gnosticism that represent only a minor dimension of Gnosticism as discussed by ancient historians: compare Hans Jonas' definition of Gnosticism (*The Gnostic Religion: The Message of the Alien God and the Beginnings of Christianity* [Boston: Beacon Press, 2001]), which is in principle a-millennial (this world is unredeemable), with Voegelin's *The New Science of Politics* (Chicago: University of Chicago Press, 1986). In the language of this book, Vogelin's "Gnostic" groups are millennial projects (based on esoteric knowledge), triggered by apocalyptic time (we have "finally understood"). Laurent Murawiec makes the same terminological move in his study of apocalyptic and millennial dimensions of current Islam in *The Mind of Jihad* (Cicero, Ind.: Hudson Institute, 2005), 169–208. See also Stefan Rossbach, *Gnostic Wars: The Cold War in the Context of the History of Western Spirituality* (Edinburgh: Edinburgh University Press, 1999).

[109] Erik Middlefort, "Madness and the Millennium of Münster, 1534–1535."

[110] Abbas Amanat, *Resurrection and Renewal: The Making of the Babi Movement in Iran, 1844–1850* (Ithaca, N.Y.: Cornell University Press, 1989).

[111] Mendel, *Vision and Violence*.

the phenomenon in practice, rather than conceptually, we must turn to the great "activator" of millennial hopes—apocalyptic expectations. These convictions of the imminence of the transformation drive millennialists out of the closet and into the public arena. Once successful in the public sphere, millennial movements have a life of their own, one that traces out an apocalyptic curve from early high hopes and dizzying trajectories, to the inevitable pull of gravity that draws them back into "normal time." The next chapter will trace this "apocalyptic curve."

2 Roosters and Owls

On the Dynamics of the Apocalyptic Curve

> A rooster and a bat were waiting for the light.
> The rooster said to the bat, I await the dawn.
> But you, why do you want the light?
> —Talmud Sanhedrin, 98a

Shortly after the year 847–48, a prominent monastic chronicler named Rodulf of Fulda wrote about an unusual development.

> At that time a certain woman from Allemania, by the name of Thiota the *pseudo-prophetess*, came to Mainz where, in no small way, she disturbed the parish of Bishop Solomon with her prophecies. For she claimed that, as if by divine revelation, she knew the very day of the End of the world and many other matters which are known only to God, and she predicted that the Last Day would fall that very year. Whence many commoners (*plebs*) of both sexes, terror-struck, flocked to her, bearing gifts, and offered themselves up to her with their prayers. And what is still worse, men from the holy orders, *setting aside ecclesiastical doctrine*, followed her as if she were *a master sent from heaven*.
>
> This woman was taken before the presence of the bishops at Saint-Albans and questioned about her claims, and she admitted that a certain priest had suggested these things to her, and that she had said these things *for the sake of personal gain*. Therefore, by the judgment of the synod, she was publicly whipped, and *she* shamefully lost the ministry of preaching, which she had rashly and unreasonably appropriated and presumed to claim for herself against the custom of the church. At last confounded, she put an end to her prophesying.[1]

This short, dense paragraph offers a good example of an "apocalyptic moment," a discrete period of time during which large numbers of people join together publicly in the common belief that the End (or the millennium) was about to occur, and their behavior changes radically. Indeed, it illustrates a classic "world-turned-upside-down" event, in which a common woman becomes a figure of supreme authority.

But the text offers only a glimpse of what happened. It stands alone; indeed it only appears in one manuscript. Neither the author, nor any other writer from Mainz and the surrounding area tells us anything about previous apocalyptic

---

[1] *Annales Fuldenses* ad. an. 847; *Monumenta Germaniae Historica, Scriptores (MGH SS)* vol. 1, p. 365 (my translation); cf. *Annals of Fulda*, trans. Timothy Reuter (Manchester: University of Manchester Press, 1992), 26.*

expectations, commoner women who play significant public roles, or any subsequent consequence to Thiota's fifteen minutes of fame. And we have nothing written by one of her many literate (clerical) supporters.

How can we interpret this passage, both in terms of what it says and what it does not (e.g., the "many other matters known only to God")? Just what did "the end of the world" mean? Last Judgment or Millennium? What did she exhort her followers to do in preparation for this awesome event? How much can we rely on Rudolf's account? Did the "Church" handle Thiota with the ease and finality the story suggests? Did her followers go quietly back to their lives as Rudolf's silence implies? And if not, how, and with what authority, can we correct and fill in the gaps?[2]

Even though the story only raises questions, some of which we may never answer even in terms of likely probabilities, without this text we would be completely in the dark. We could not even assert for certain that the population of Mainz was familiar with Christian eschatology—much less, receptive to an apocalyptic call. After all, historians of Carolingian religiosity can carry on extensive discussions without a reference to such beliefs.[3] How much more improbable would be the claim that they were susceptible to mass apocalyptic excitement, and even more so, that believers—clerics included—would then throw themselves at the feet of a common-born woman claiming powers of prophecy? Granted, those familiar with the prominent role of women in Christian millennialism from the earliest centuries,[4] and with the details of Christian eschatology, its centrality in Christian thought, particularly as it informed elite-commoner discourse,[5] might not find this so surprising. Indeed, such background knowledge might help us interpret the text more amply.

What, for example, does the phrase "master (fem.) sent from heaven" [magistra coelitus destinatam] mean? That Thiota presented herself as a religious authority, probably an exegetical authority in the sense that she was interpreting biblical text to make/prove her prophecies. In so doing, she violated Augustine's central anti-apocalyptic rule: you cannot interpret scripture in light of current events to make apocalyptic predictions. Gog and Magog, for example, may not be identified as the

---

[2] A Russian once reported that her father used to sit her down with *Pravda*, read an article, and say, "Okay, now tell me what really happened." The medieval scholar might equally say, "Okay, now that you've read Rudolf of Fulda, tell me what you think really happened."

[3] This is as true of conventional histories like the various chapters in *The New Cambridge Medieval History*, vol. 2 (c.700–c.900), ed. Rosamond McKitterick (Cambridge: Cambridge University Press, 1995), as well as for studies that advertise themselves as deliberately iconoclastic, for example James C. Russell, *The Germanization of Early Medieval Christianity* (New York: Oxford University Press, 1994). For a discussion of millennialism in the Carolingian period, see R. Landes, "Lest the Millennium be Fulfilled"; Brandes, "'Tempora periculosa sunt.'"*

[4] The most famous case, of course being the Montanist movement of the mid-secondcentury, Trevett, *Montanism*, 151–97.

[5] That it does inform, possibly constitute a central focus of, Church-commoner discourse seems highly likely. See, for example, Bishop Hesychius' comments to Augustine cited below, n. 12.

Goths and the Visigoths.[6] That certainly accounts for Rodulfus' remark about clerics "abandoning their ecclesiastical doctrines"—in following Thiota, they violated Augustine's formal prohibition to the clergy.

On one level, this passage reflects the horror of Carolingian churchmen at the utterly inappropriate behavior of a woman—and a commoner at that!—engaging in public preaching and acquiring clerical (i.e., literate) followers. But the key here, what makes Thiota capable of breaking the gender and class barrier and establishing herself as an independent preacher/teacher in mid-ninth-century Mainz, derives not from her learning, but from her *apocalyptic* message: it was the power of her apocalyptic rhetoric that mobilized the population and the clergy, that made her challenge to the clerical elites *effective*.

But does her offense stop there? What, for example, did she do with all the gifts the populace showered her with? Rudolf, in claiming that she admitted having concocted the fraud with a priest "for personal gain," may imply that she hoarded her newfound wealth. Certainly, the annals of apocalyptic preaching offer many cases of outright fraud.

But this is not a hoarding economy; it is a gift economy: for Thiota to receive and not distribute would undermine her charisma. Indeed, to distribute generously was one of the classic ways in which apocalyptic prophets recruited and retained followers. Here Gregory of Tours describes a millennial messiah in the late sixth century whose career shows many of the same characteristics as Thiota's:

> A multitude of people flocked to him bringing the sick, whom he touched and restored to health. They who came to him brought him also gold and silver and garments. *These he distributed among the poor to deceive them the more easily*…A great multitude of people was led astray by him, *not only the common ilk but priests in orders*. More than three thousand people followed him.[7]

The gifts, the adherence even of clerics, the huge popularity among the commoners, all characterize both Thiota and the "False Christ's" career, and which often led to an escalation of their claims, from holy preachers, to apostles, to messianic pretenders, a phenomenon that had occurred and would recur in almost every century.[8] Thus, *magistra* means more than teacher here. It means that she was, in some senses, a *judge*, a rival ruler of the city to both the bishop and to the count.

---

[6] Landes, "Lest the millennium," 156–60; for a more complete discussion of all these issues, see below, chapter 3.

[7] Gregory of Tours, *History of the Franks*, 10.25, 584–86.

[8] See the case of Adalbert, Boniface's "bête noire," Jeffrey B. Russell, Boniface and the Eccentrics," *Church History: Studies in Christianity and Culture* 33 (1964): 235–247; and the characters featured in Norman Cohn, *Pursuit of the Millennium*, 41–52, including his discussion of the Zulu messiah, Isaiah Shembe (51–52).

What was Thiota's apocalyptic promise to her followers? Was it eschatological—the Day of Judgment and the end of the world are at hand? Or was it also millennial—that after the Judgment, the meek (those who flocked to her side) would inherit the earth? And what relationship existed between these promises and her position as *magistra*? How do we assess its significance in terms of understanding the later ninth and tenth centuries? After all, Western Christianity was on the verge of its great mutation that, among other things, involves transformations in the relations between elites and commoners?[9]

Of course, my argument—that disturbing the public order was the key to the problem, that apocalyptic preaching lay at the core of this "breach" in public order, and that the ecclesiastics had serious problems with a woman who rivaled their authority not only in matters of teaching, but also justice and distribution of wealth—is also conjecture. I only contend that my reconstruction is at least as plausible as the more conventional reading, that it constitutes a legitimate working hypothesis. Indeed, in terms of the dynamics of apocalyptic time, including the cases we know from the Middle Ages, it is at least plausible, possibly more likely than the "plain" meaning of Rudolf's text.

We have every reason to be wary of the "plain meaning" of narratives about apocalyptic moments. The literary elites who indirectly inform us about these matters *ex post defectu*, men trained in the style of Augustine, like Rudolf of Fulda, or Gregory of Tours, or Radulfus Glaber, work hard to give the impression that their ecclesiastical party dominated these problems. And the hard *retrospective* "fact"—that all these apocalyptic prophecies failed—reinforces that impression among modern historians. But adopting such a perspective *ab initio* does not help us understand how the people of Mainz experienced her prophetic career, and, therefore, keeps us from gaining any insight into both the sources and strengths of her popularity, on the one hand, and her impact on the culture in which she emerged, on the other.

■ APOCALYPTIC ROOSTERS: THE DISINHIBITING ANTICIPATION

It may help conceptualize the problems presented to historians by such texts by contrasting apocalyptic "roosters" with anti-apocalyptic "owls." The rooster crows: "Dawn breaks, arise for the Day of the Lord!" The owl hoots: "Quiet! It's still the middle of the night; the master sleeps; the foxes are out; and you can only do damage by awakening the barnyard prematurely." The cautionary tale of *Chicken Little* illustrates the point nicely: Chicken Little, convinced that the sky was falling

---

[9] Rachel Fulton, *From Judgment to Passion: Devotion to Christ and the Virgin Mary, 800–1200* (New York: Columbia University Press, 2002), 60–141; R. Landes, "Economic Development and Demotic Religiosity." For more on the turn of the millennium, see below, chapter 3, and appendix at website.

because she got hit by a falling acorn, feels she must tell the king, and enlists a half dozen other fowls from the barnyard to join her. They end up becoming Foxy Loxy's dinner. Chaucer's "Miller's Tale" presents a similar story of foolish belief in apocalyptic prophecies and, in this case, with humiliating consequences for the cuckolded carpenter.

But despite the ridicule with which cautionary tales treat roosters, the list of those who fit the definition offered here include a wide range of major historical figures, including many of the founders of major monotheistic religions and sects. The irony of millennial historiography arises from this extraordinary contrast between the contempt with which our normative sources treat so many roosters, and the uncomfortable observation that both Jesus and Muhammad were roosters. But then again, so were Hitler and Hong Xiuquan, masters of death.[10] Thus, on one level, all apocalyptic historiography has to find its way between the rhetoric of these two diametrically opposing voices.

Most of the time, roosters do not dare crow. To do so would risk swift reaction: ridicule, retaliation, repression. Only on rare occasions do roosters crow loudly, and even more rarely, as in the case of Thiota above, do they gain a large following as a result. When they do so, they can launch a millennial movement. This book is largely the study of those doubly rare occasions when apocalyptic discourse *goes public*, and *wins over* the public.

Most of the time, however, apocalyptic beliefs remain either dormant or concealed. They reside in the realm of "hidden transcripts," and most of us do not even notice the non-apocalyptic millennialists in our very midst. Indeed, millennial believers can operate invisibly, adapting to our secular world, even as they nurture their outrageous hopes. China has a long tradition of "secret societies" whose centuries-long, possibly millennia-long, history is punctuated by apocalyptic outbursts, revolts, and revolutions.[11] These believers have accepted the current rules "under protest" even if that protest is, provisionally, silent. They await eagerly the moment when the rules will change, and change dramatically.

In the early fifth century, a rooster bishop named Hesychius wrote to Augustine, in a veiled reproach for his opposition to the widespread apocalyptic expectation of the day, that he felt the bishop's job was precisely to offer this hope to his flock: "... by noticing and believing the existing signs of the Coming, it befits me to hope for it *and to distribute this food to believers, that they may hope for and love the coming of Him* who said: 'When you shall see all these things, now ye that it is nigh, even at the doors.'"[12] In the mid-nineteenth century, Aggy, an African-American slave woman, spoke more vehemently, if more privately, to a trusted governess

---

[10] See below, chapters 7 and 12.

[11] Susan Naquin, *Millenarian Rebellion in China: The Eight Trigrams Rebellion* (New Haven, Conn.: Yale University Press, 1976).

[12] Augustine, *Epistolae*, 198 [418 CE], trans. W. Parsons, *Letters* (New York: Fathers of the Church, 1955), 4:353. For more on this correspondence, see below, chapter 3.

from New England: "There's a day a-coming! I hear the rumbling of the chariots, I see...white folks' blood a-running on the ground like a river and the dead heaped up that high! O Lord! Hasten the day when the blows and the bruises and the aches and the pains shall come to the white folks.... *O Lord! Give me the pleasure of living to that day.*"[13]

James C. Scott has called these sentiments a "full-throated hidden transcript," the most elaborate and all-encompassing of the resentments that people, forced to pretend to like what they hate, tell themselves and their trusted friends in times of unguarded candor.[14] The fact that Aggy had a rich Christian apocalyptic imagination despite the fact that the slaves' access to Christian texts was, in principle, severely restricted, underlines the radical split between public and private discourse. Aggy, like so many other commoners, who do not normally "count," had access to an oral biblical tradition, far more radical than the one taught in the schools she could not attend.[15] Rather than the public Christian transcript of Southern slave-owner—Slaves obey your masters (Ephesians 6:5; Colossians 3:22)—it was the exact opposite—cruel masters will have burning coals heaped on their head in the day of Judgment (Romans 12:20).

And although Scott does not say so explicitly, it seems implicit in his thesis that the more violence goes into enforcing the "public transcript" and its *prime divider* between elites and commoners, the more violence fills the apocalyptic visions of its disappearance.[16] The powerful—the *potentes*—often know well that such transcripts exist and seek to suppress them, as did the clerics of Thiota's Mainz. But as we can see from the mention of clerics who sided with the prophetess, the clergy was of mixed mind about the object of divine wrath: was it the "heretics" like Thiota, or the cruel elite (including, perhaps, members of the ecclesiastical aristocracy)? An early eleventh-century Anglo-Saxon text targets the lay aristocracy: "For then will end the tyranny of kings and the injustice and rapine of reeves and their cunning and unjust judgments and wiles. Then shall those who rejoiced and were glad in this life groan and lament. Then shall their mead, wine and beer be turned into thirst for them."[17] These are the proleptic rejoicings of people who truly hate their ruling elites and eagerly anticipate their demise.

The elites know about hidden transcripts, but they generally consider such expressions of ill-will as acceptable pressure-valve releases... *as long as they remain*

---

[13] Words of Aggy, a Southern slave cook quoted in Mary Livermore, *My Story of the War* (Hartford, 1889), cited in Scott, *Domination*, 5; italics mine.

[14] Scott, *Domination*, chap. 1. He points out how Aggy had said this not in front of her master (who had just whipped her daughter for a theft she had not committed), but after he had left, in the presence of the governess from New England whom she apparently trusted not to tell the master.

[15] Timothy E. Fulop and Albert J. Raboteau, eds., *African-American Religion: Interpretive Essays in History and Culture* (New York: Routledge, 1997).

[16] On the prime divider, see below, chapter 8.

[17] *Byrhtferth's Manual*, ed. S. J. Crawford, Early English Text Society, Original Series177 (London, Humphrey Milford, 1972), p. 242, lines 3–9.

private or, at least, anonymous.[18] The danger comes when such hidden transcripts go public, when the status quo and its rules are openly challenged. These are moments of great emotion, when public discourse can change dramatically, challenging and even overthrowing the prevailing power structure.[19] And roosters are, at heart, people who hope and dream of this day. For them, it is a Day of *pleasure*.

Apocalyptic expectations—the imminence of the Day—provide one of the most powerful dynamics for bringing hidden transcript, to the surface. The whole point of public transcripts is that they get *everyone* to pretend that they *voluntarily* accept the current situation. Violence, almost by definition, should not play a visible role in their maintenance, except in specific, often ritually defined conditions (e.g., sacrifice, execution). The public transcript is the very quintessence of *self*-imposed inhibition. And it is the threat of *future* punishment for transgressions that keeps people in line. We, denizens of society, learn to inhibit ourselves out of *fear* of this predictable future retaliation.[20] "And the most intense hatred is that rooted in fear, which compels to silence and drives vehemence into constructive vindictiveness, an imaginary annihilation of the detested object, something like the hidden rites of vengeance with which the persecuted have a dark vent for their rage."[21]

But when people believe that in the near future, everything will change and the dominant will lose their power to harm, such apocalyptic enthusiasts become radically uninhibited, at least in terms of the current public transcript. None of the "normal" threats work to intimidate someone who, to those on the outside, appears literally "mad." These people burn bridges to a "normal" future; they welcome death—martyrdom. They are beyond the reach of normal controls.

Nothing frightens the guardians of the public transcript more than such a rogue voice "with nothing to lose." Indeed, at the dawn of the twenty-first century, that rogue voice has taken on the terrifying form of suicidal terrorism.[22] Of all hidden transcripts, the most dangerous are the apocalyptic voices of prophetic vengeance. And, historically, most elites generally have responded by exterminating any manifestation of it.

However frightening to the guardians of order, apocalyptic time means deliverance for millennialists. Convinced that the moment for the great transformation is at hand, they step into a dramatically different universe, one where the final, cosmic revelation, the final resolution of good and evil, now enters the public sphere. Here

[18] Scott calls these anonymous expressions of resistance "infra-politics" (*Domination*, 183–84, 199–201).

[19] The term "hegemonic discourse" refers to the prevailing public transcript. Scott has a good discussion, *Domination*, 70–107.

[20] Scott notes astutely that the public transcript not only constrains those below, but also those in the elite whose behavior must conform to expectations in order for them to maintain their position of authority (he analyzes Orwell's "The Elephant Hunter" in this connection), Scott, *Domination*, 10–11.

[21] George Eliot, *Daniel Deronda*, vol. 10 in *Works by George Eliot* (London: W. Blackwood, 1903), 413; cited in Scott, *Domination*, 1.

[22] See below, chapter 14.

the "powers" that rule this world will soon receive their just humiliation, if not eternal punishment. Here "saints" who have suffered—at least humiliation, at most real pain and even death—at last have their day of vindication. Here all earlier suffering, all the turned cheeks, the humiliations, the crushing burdens, becomes meaningful. Here, at last, the apocalyptic hopeful gets to say a resounding, a cosmic "I told you so!" Like real roosters, apocalyptic believers crow to signal that the long night has passed, and the dawn of the great and terrible "Day of Rejoicing" is at hand.

This enthusiasm becomes problematic when the millennialist's expectations are disappointed or frustrated: the failure, *defectum*. Here we find a frequent tendency to "up the ante," like addicts increasing their doses and the potency of the drugs they use to keep themselves "up."[23] In the case of the Xhosa cattle-killing, the failure of a publicly awaited date—the August moon of 1856—led not to a reappraisal of the credibility of the fifteen-year-old girl "prophetess" who told her people to kill all their cattle so that the ancestors could come with new and healthier cattle, but to an even greater wave of cattle-killing.

Semiotic arousal becomes semiotic promiscuity—anything means something and free association becomes a convincing system of meaning. Vocational arousal becomes megalomania, in which one stands not merely near or on the stage, but at the very center of the entire cosmic drama of good and evil. In such apocalyptic conditions, not just opposition, but even tepidity becomes an affront, a willful obstacle to the glorious salvation on its way. Because you are lukewarm, and neither cold nor hot, I will spew you out of my mouth (Revelation 3:16). And so, megalomania often leads to paranoia, whence the elaborate conspiracy theories that so often populate the minds of millennialists. After all, what is paranoia but the megalomanic belief that most of the people in the world have nothing better to do with their time than to plot against you? The history of millennialism is littered with the wreckage of groups with leaders who, unable to tolerate the world's enduring imperfection (including their own), preferred to destroy everything they could.[24]

Of course, the idea that one can fill such an emotional void with a fantasy of a situation in which one is already and will soon be visibly the center of the cosmos has profound conceptual flaws, not the least of which is the inevitable disappointment. Roosters believe that, in the very near future, either God or some cosmic

---

[23] Al Baumgarten notes, "... there are moments when millennial movements need to 'up the ante,' by forcing their members to accept risks which will increase solidarity and loyalty. At the simplest level, movements 'up the ante' in order to take advantage of the bonds established between those who share dangers... The risk binds those who will share in the imminent blessings, unlike the apostates doomed to perdition. Designating and expelling these apostates also contributes to the sense of solidarity among those who endure," from *Apocalyptic Time*, ed. Albert I. Baumgarten (Leiden: Brill, 2000), x–xi.

[24] On Hitler, see below, chapter 13. For a contemporary example of a rural/tribal adoption of the Ten Commandments in a new religious movement in Africa, see the Movement for the Restoration of the Ten Commandments of God in Uganda, on which see Massimo Introvigne, "Tragedy in Uganda: The Restoration of the Ten Commandments of God, a Post-Catholic Movement." Online: http://www. cesnur.org/testi/uganda_002.htm, April 13, 2010; and below, n. 65.*

force (extraterrestrials, the dialectic of history, technological breakthroughs) will *publicly* intervene *on their side*, punishing those who scoffed and opposed them, rewarding them and their faithful companions. Muhammad's initial prophecy proclaimed the imminence of judgment, and, when he was greeted with derision, he promised the imminent humiliation and suffering of those who mocked his message.[25] The popular "Left Behind" series of novels, based on the Christian evangelical premillennial scenario, affords the reader ample passages depicting the regret of unbelievers when comes the awesome *tribulation* (based on the book of Revelation), a seven-year period of staggering punishment for the billions of sinners (nonbelievers) on the planet.[26]

There is historical irony behind all such thinking. Historians can safely say that in the past, the coming tribulation was not that of the owls, the outsiders who clung pitifully to their antiquated notions of a world that goes on tomorrow much as it has today, who scoffed at the news and mocked the prophet. No, the tribulation will strike the true apocalyptic believers, the roosters, who must confront their own failed expectation and endure the humiliations heaped upon them by the skeptics. In some cases, this can be violent—death, or, as Thiota experienced, whipping... what Melanesian Cargo cultists call "eating the cane."[27] This is true, moreover, whether the rooster successfully produces a radical change in this world or not. However much power men like Robespierre, Lenin, Hitler, Mao, Khoumeini, or any other "successful" roosters wield, they always find that humans fail them, that the new citizen, comrade, Aryan, or Muslim, who in principle should emerge from the ruin of the forces of evil, fails to materialize. Because roosters are perfectionists—at once their strength and weakness—they cannot be satisfied with partial transformations: they must confront failure.

Thus, in a profound sense, the study of millennialism as a historical force is the study of disappointment (even in cases where a more generous soul might see success), and a study of how extravagant optimists have come to terms with their failed hopes. As we shall see in the course of this study, the results are as extravagant as the hopes, ranging from the formation of new religions, to totalitarianism and total war, to civil polities.

The key paradox here is that although millennialism has *always* proven wrong in its apocalyptic expectations, it has rarely proven inconsequential or unproductive. Studies have shown that while pessimists are more often right in predicting the future, optimists accomplish more.[28] Partly that is due to the willingness to take risks; partly to the enthusiasm that optimism brings to a task; partly to a willingness to learn from mistakes. The history of millennialism reflects such a dynamic—a range of fruitful mistakes, however nourishing or poisonous. And the history of

---

[25] See below, chapter 14.
[26] See above, chapter 1, n. 6.
[27] See below, chapter 5, n. 63.
[28] Lionel Tiger, *Optimism: The Biology of Hope* (New York: Simon and Schuster, 1979).

the most millennial culture in world history—the West—is that of a long series of interlocking and unintended consequences that we, retrospectively, like to call progress. In matters apocalyptic, *wrong does not mean inconsequential.*

Although I have presented roosters here as apocalyptic prophets calling for the Day of the Lord, there are both modified and secularized versions of these prophecies. When Jonah prophesied destruction, he was not "apocalyptic" in my sense— only the city of Ninevah was threatened—nor did he call for a preparation for the inevitable "Day of Wrath and Justice." He offered the classic prophetic warning: change or else. His is the language of reform, not revolution; and the consequences of his prophecy (especially when they lead to repentance) have a secular dimension—they change the way people interact in this world. Thus successful prophecy can play (and has played) a major role in social change.

The distinction between prophetic and apocalyptic, however, has only limited value. They are kissing cousins and spend so much time together that they share the same wardrobe and address the same audiences. Prophets with unexpected success eagerly expand the range of their mission;[29] less successful ones reduce their scope as seamlessly as possible.[30] Reformers can often sound apocalyptic alarms and promise nearly millennial results just to motivate people. After all, apocalyptic rhetoric may be the hardest to sell, but once it "takes," no motivation is more powerful.

Environmentalists are the most obvious current case of roosters crowing warnings that range from the prophetic to the apocalyptic, using the stick of cataclysmic destruction if we do not change, and the carrot of millennial harmony with both nature and technology as the reward for repenting of our greedy, wasteful ways. Few millennial discourses seem worthier at the dawn of the twenty-first century, though global climate–change zealots may unfortunately cling tenaciously to the road of excess long after the palace of wisdom has been passed.[31] Thus roosters, by my definition, need not be "apocalyptic" in the cosmic or religious sense, although any apocalyptic believer is by definition a rooster or a rooster's disciple. And any truly successful rooster must struggle with the demons of apocalyptic megalomania.[32]

■ ANTI-APOCALYPTIC OWLS: THE NOCTURNAL WISDOM OF THE PUBLIC TRANSCRIPT

Every force has its contrary. Not surprisingly, a force as volatile and uncompromisingly hostile to the status quo as apocalyptic expectations has its implacable enemies. For every rooster crowing on his dunghill that the great and terrible Day has

[29] The Xhosa; see below, chapter 4.

[30] Handsome Lake. Arthur C. Parker, "The Code of Handsome Lake, the Seneca Prophet" in *Parker on the Iroquois*, ed. William N. Fenton (Syracuse: Syracuse University Press, 1968).

[31] See below, concluding chapter.

[32] See Dostoyevski's masterful handling of the key passage in the New Testament on this issue, the "Temptations of Jesus" (Matthew 4:1–11); Dostoyevsky's "The Parable of the Grand Inquisitor" in *The Brothers Karamazov*, trans. Richard Pevear and Larissa Volokhonsky (New York: Knopf, 1992).

dawned, there are a dozen owls hooting from their lecterns that the night is still long, the foxes abroad, the master asleep, and only damage can come from prematurely awakening the barnyard. To roosters, owls seem, at best, like a cross between ostriches with their heads in the sand and bats blinded by daybreak. At worst, they are the agents of the evil empire. But the historian must acknowledge that they have a certain wisdom. Minerva's owl looks backward; it flies, *ex post defectu*, at dusk.

There are different kinds of owls: (1) millennial owls—who believe the millennium will come, but, for a variety of reasons, believe that now is not the time (quiet optimists); (2) reluctant owls—who do not believe the millennium will come, although they do not like the world as it is (quiet pessimists); and (3) aggressive owls—who like or accept the world as it is, and will resist any effort to change it, unless it be to their advantage.

True owls are, by nature, conservative creatures, anxious of if not hostile to rapid change, suspicious of radical new ideas and approaches. Obviously, most people in the established elite of any culture tend to be owls. The process is self-selecting. But that is never true of all of the cultural elite; and societies where the dominant religion promises an apocalyptic resolution to the current world—Judaism, Christianity, Islam—tend to produce an unusually high number of roosters *within their own elites*. One might argue that therein lies one key to understanding the exceptional nature of the "modern West."

Normally, and especially in premodern societies, owls dominate public discourse, and one of their jobs is to make sure that roosters do not breach the public transcript. Indeed, so profoundly do they dominate, that most roosters, unlike Thiota, never even appear on our documentary screens. Writing is generally an owl's medium, a retrospective act, almost inherently hostile to apocalyptic discourse. Owls are powerful and influential precisely because they have played the extant rules to their own advantage (true of both aristocrats born into positions of power and meritocrats who achieve them).

Owls symbolize wisdom, and in most cases of apocalyptic prophecy, that reputation is well deserved.[33] The vast majority of roosters have, in fact, proposed ludicrous scenarios and equally implausible rule sets. Nongqawuse, who promised that the ancestors would reward the Xhosa if they killed every last one of their cattle, stands as a poster-child of rooster's folly. The owls' steady grip on public discourse, therefore, provides important stability. After all, any culture whose elite runs after even a small fraction of apocalyptic rumors circulating will not long endure. True, what is now proved was once only imagined, and roosters excel in imagination; but most of what is imagined does not get proven. So owls are cautious, and counsel against hasty enthusiasms.

---

[33] I took the imagery of the rooster from the Talmudic discussion cited as an epigraph to this chapter; but rather than use the bat as its antithesis, I preferred the imagery of the "wise" owl as my nocturnal animal because bat as a symbol seems too invidious, and whether the proud roosters like Reb Simlai like it or not, the historian has to admit that the owls have consistently gotten it right.

Some of the earliest recorded "owl" sayings come, appropriately, from the first messianic religious culture for which we have extensive literature, rabbinic Judaism. As Yochanan ben Zakkai, a man who had seen the devastating impact of the millennial revolt of the Zealots (67–73 CE) on his people and engineered the "re-entry" of Judaism into "normal time" after the destruction of the Temple, put it: "If you have a tree shoot in your hand and someone says to you, 'Here is the Messiah'—go and plant the tree, and afterwards go and greet him."[34] Ironically, in the Christian tradition, the proverb has been attributed not to an owl, but to Martin Luther,[35] one of the more prominent Christian "roosters."[36] Still more sharply, a colleague of Rabbi Akiva, the man who disastrously identified Bar Kochba (132–35 CE) as the long-awaited messiah, rebuked him by noting: "Grass will grow between your cheeks [i.e., you will be long dead] before the messiah comes."[37]

The great horned owl of the Christian tradition is Augustine. He founded the great school of anti-millennial, anti-apocalyptic discourse that dominated the thinking of the Latin Christian writers to this day. Never say that the Apocalypse is imminent, Augustine warned his fellow Churchmen, lest, if you are wrong, your flocks loose faith. Do not interpret current events as the fulfillment of biblical apocalyptic prophecy: you may not "read" the Goths and the Visigoths as Gog and Magog.[38]

In the Middle Ages, Augustinian scribes called owls the *saniores mentis*—those sounder of mind—as in the following passage, composed in the early twelfth century about the traumatic destruction of the Holy Sepulcher in Jerusalem a century earlier:

---

[34] Avot de Rabi Natan B 31; *The Fathers according to Rabbi Nathan*, trans. Anthony J. Saldarini, Studies in Judaism in late antiquity, 11 (Leiden: Brill Archive, 1975), 182.*

[35] The attribution to Luther, is late but it played a role in reassuring the German population at the end of World War II. "Und wenn morgen die Welt unterginge, so wollen wir heute unser Apfelbaeumchen flanzen [And if in the morning the world will go under, still we will today plant our appletree shoots]," internal circular letter from Minister Karl Lotz, October 5, 1944 to his congregation (Kirche von Kurhessen-Waldeck). This represents the first certain attribution to Luther of that expression. See Martin Schloemann, *Luthers Apfelbaeumchen? Ein Kapitel deutscher Mentalitätsgeschichte seit dem Zweiten Weltkrieg* (Goettingen: Vandenhoeck Rupprecht, 1994).

[36] Luther was one of the most prominent articulators of apocalyptic rhetoric in the early sixteenth century; see Andrew Colin Gow, *The Red Jews: Antisemitism in an Apocalyptic Age, 1200–1600* (Leiden: Brill,1995); Heiko Oberman, *The Roots of Anti-Semitism*, trans. J. Porter (Philadelphia: Fortress Press, 1984). Yochanan ben Zakkai, on the other hand, was a survivor of the disastrous messianic war against Rome (66–73 CE), the founder of an owl's rabbinical school.

[37] Comment to Akiva, *Jerusalem Talmud*, Taanit chapter 4:5, p. 68d. The passage makes clear the terrible impact of the Bar Kochba rebellion, including the massive slaughter. See Gerbern S. Oegema, *The Anointed and His People: Messianic Expectations from the Maccabees to Bar Kochba*, JPS Supplements (Sheffield: Sheffield Academic Press, 1998), esp. 28–29 for a discussion of this text.*

[38] On Augustine's teachings about the End, see his classic and oft-copied *De fine saeculi* (Letter to Hesychius, 419 CE), Epist. 199, CSEL 57, pp. 279–92, copied verbatim by Bede at the end of his *De temporum ratione*, [724 CE] chap. 67–71, ed. Jones, CCSL t. 123 B, pp. 536–44. For further discussion of this theme, see Robert Markus, *Saeculum*; and R. Landes, "The Historiographical Fear of an Apocalyptic Year 1000: Augustinian History Medieval and Modern," *Speculum* 75 (2000): 97–145.

In the year 1009, the land of Jerusalem was invaded, with God's permission, by unclean Turks, and Jerusalem seized and the glorious Sepulcher of the Lord Christ was taken over by them.... And in that year, many Jews converted to Christianity for fear of their lives. In the year 1010, in many places throughout the World, a rumor spread that frightened and saddened many hearts, that the End of the World approached. But those sounder of mind (*saniores mentis*) turned themselves to correcting their own lives.[39]

This is a revealing account. It was composed about a century after the events in question—plenty of time for people to realize and absorb the failure of those apocalyptic expectations. And it alludes to the brief public prominence of roosters, before pronouncing the victory of wiser owls. Note that even the owls in this case preached self-criticism and repentance. And so it should be: in a relatively sane culture, elites *should* follow Augustine's advice. Societies cannot afford to believe apocalyptic prophecies.

But what *should* happen and what *did* happen do not always coincide. In the case of the destruction of the Holy Sepulcher in 1009, the memory over a century later reports on an apocalyptic moment where those "frightened and saddened" by the rumors of the End, among other zealous deeds, gave the Jews the classic apocalyptic choice of conversion or death, and when they did not convert, massacred them.[40] But like Rudolf in his account of Thiota's brief career, the author prefers to reformulate the chronology, euphemize their reaction, and then emphasize the teachings they *should have* heeded. As the next chapter will examine in greater detail, Augustinian owls may be right about the future, right to insist that apocalyptic expectations will prove false, but they often distort the past in the service of that insistence.

Thus, just as roosters have both their strengths and their weaknesses, so do owls. Their main failure inverts the rooster's great strength, that is, they lack imagination and they cling to the current order of things even after it has become dysfunctional. Owls have an almost instinctual response to sweeping ideas or predictions of social mutation—they dismiss them, often with scorn and ridicule, if necessary with violent repression.

But behind this reflexive response often lies an unwillingness to question the prevailing paradigm. As Kuhn puts it in speaking about scientific challenges to the status quo, "normal scientists" are problem solvers; they know the rules, and they pose their problems and seek their solutions according to them.[41] To question the rules disrupts an orderly world and undermines predictable rewards for diligence, for mimetic discourse. Northrop Frye, in discussing one of the most brilliant

---

[39] B.N.lat.4893, f.56v; Martin Bouquet, *Recueil des historiens de la France* (Paris: Victor Palmé, 1869–1904), 10:262; Landes, *Relics*, 45, n. 122.

[40] R. Landes, "The Massacres of 1010."

[41] Thomas Kuhn, *Structure of Scientific Revolutions* (Chicago: University of Chicago Press, 1962), chap. 3.

roosters of all time, William Blake, points out the drawbacks of the owls' mini-malism, their lack of imagination, or, in Blake's terms, the relation between the "prolific" and the "devourers":

> [P]edantry means…that kind of contact with culture which consists in belittling the size and scope of the conceptions of genius, the "nothing but" principle of reading everything on the minimum imaginative level.…Imaginative intensity applied to a wrong or inadequate object can be corrected; a deficiency in intensity never can be.[42]

Of course, these observations may serve well in literary criticism, but when the unbridled apocalyptic imagination takes off, millions may die before the "correction."

And just as the rooster's danger is to pass from exhilaration to megalomania, so the owl's danger is to move from skepticism into negativity, from critical reasoning to clinging to "reason" as a defense against any challenging information. Overall, these seem like venial sins when compared with the colossal crimes of maniacal messiahs. But as we will see, even these can contribute to serious and perhaps unnecessary culture wars.

■ OWLS AND ROOSTERS INTERACT: CHICKEN LITTLES VERSUS OSTRICHES

When owls hear roosters crow, they consider them "Chicken Littles"—alarmists whose excessive imaginations have cooked up panic from nothing. Roosters, of course, tend to set off such responses because they, almost from the start of their missions, articulate their insights with the intention of shocking, of knocking their listeners loose from their complacent attachment to what the roosters know is a fast fading world. Roosters want and need rapid and energetic responses—for the good of their listeners. They thus have little patience with the slow deliberation and reasoned skepticism of their owlish interlocutors.

Thus, just as owls tend to see roosters as Chicken Littles, roosters tend to see owls as ostriches, their heads in the sand, blissfully and tragically unaware of the oncoming dangers. Roosters hear the Doppler sound of oncoming Apocalypse; owls seem deaf. And of course, if one would make oneself heard by someone whose head is in the sand, obviously one must speak louder. Yet, the louder one speaks, the more incomprehensible and unreliable seems the resulting speech. So the shriller the Chicken Little roosters…the more unresponsive, the farther down in the sand, do the ostrich owls bury their ears.

What we have here is a failure to communicate, something that has often led to tragic consequences in the course of millennial history. But it is more than just a well-intentioned failure. It is a lack of understanding on both sides to imagine

---

[42] Northrop Frye, *Fearful Symmetry* (Princeton, N.J.: Princeton University Press, 1965), 422.*

anything but a zero-sum relationship between roosters and owls. Each sees the other as its nemesis, each works toward eliminating the other. Behind the exuberant embrace of the rooster lies a profound fanaticism and a deeply worrisome capacity for violent intolerance. Behind the seeming deafness and ridicule of the owls lies a more aggressive defensiveness which, should the rooster persist, can shift from impolite dismissal to violent objection.[43] The owls, as do the roosters, know full well that were the new message successful, it would spell the end of the old hegemony—cultural, social, political. Owls do not stand poised between listening and ignoring. Most of the time, and throughout most of human history, owls have maneuvered between ignoring and exterminating. Louder rarely means more success when roosters try to reach owls. Most often it just further enrages both sides.

The most dangerous situations occur when the rooster crows loudly and attracts an enthusiastic audience of people who, eagerly consuming a heady diet of resentful private transcripts now become public, grow progressively hostile to the authorities. The apocalyptic community bathes in the charisma of openly speaking what so many hearts for so long kept locked away. The prophet "externalizes and articulates what it is that others can as yet only feel, strive towards and imagine but cannot put into words or translate explicitly into action."[44]

As long as roosters crow to unresponsive barnyards, owls can mock and ignore. But when the rooster's rhetoric resonates among a significant public, a contagion affect can develop that turns owls into their own kind of hostile roosters. One of the main "laws" of apocalyptic dynamics holds that *one person's messiah is another's antichrist*. As a result, roosters can not only sharpen the hostility of owls, but also awaken forces diametrically opposed to them. This contagion of apocalyptic beliefs and discourses further undermines any "sober" discourse, and, under some rare conditions, can cause the conflict to metastasize far beyond its initial cultural matrix.

Thus, when roosters gather a large and enthusiastic following, when their claims begin to gain currency strong and wide, the situation becomes intolerable. The royal priest Amaziah expresses the owl's reaction to the rooster Amos when speaking to the king: "Amos has conspired against you in the midst of the house of Israel. The land is not able to bear all his words..." (Amos 7:10). When owls see a real threat from roosters, they shift from ostrich to hawk, confining roosters to monasteries, prisons and mental hospitals where possible, where necessary executing them and massacring their followers. That was certainly the Roman imperial

---

[43] The classic case here is the Canudos community in the backlands of Brazil at the end of the nineteenth century—around 14,000 men, women, and children wiped out for having the temerity to drop out of a society where they occupied the bottom rungs. See Robert Levine, *Vale of Tears: Revisiting the Canudos Massacre in Northeastern Brazil, 1893–1897* (Berkeley and Los Angeles: University of California Press, 1992).

[44] Burridge, *New Heaven, New Earth*, 155; Scott, *Domination*, 19–20.

policy with apocalyptic Jews: Jesus, no matter how apolitical and pacifist he might have been, proved intolerable to the Romans merely because of the excitement he aroused. Messiahs, in the premodern period, rarely die of natural causes.

The reason why audience becomes so important is that, unlike a political candidate whose 20 percent following may at most shake up the electoral calculus, apocalyptic leaders with even a fraction of a percent of an audience, have a weapon of enormous potency. Messiahs exercise immense influence over their followers. Charismatic leaders demand total response, and the rewards of apocalyptic belief are commensurate with the intensity of the commitment.[45] If we do not understand millennialism, we do not understand a critical element of one of our own culture's greatest passions.

■ ANATOMY OF AN APOCALYPTIC WAVE

In order to get a better sense of what happens during such apocalyptic episodes, it helps to conceive of them as operating according the dynamics of a wave. The ocean wave model applies best for the activist millennial movements (the primary focus of this book) insofar as they achieve significant levels of power and authority (e.g., revolutionary movements or new religions). These "successful" ones gain momentum, build to a critical mass and, with time's passage acting like the rising ocean floor, break upon the social shore, churning forward with a powerful momentum. The other model, the Doppler effect, works best with more passive eschatological movements that primarily await a moment of complete overturning, a cosmic intervention that never comes. These lesser ones, like sirens, bring electrifying excitement (and anxiety) rising in sometimes dramatic intensity at their approach, and drop off rapidly with the passage of their apocalyptic "moment."

In the following schema, I will lay out the general characteristics that mark the four major stages of apocalyptic episodes:

1. a **waxing wave** of roosters, a crescendo of passionate conviction that breaks into public discourse and gains social mass and speed;
2. a **breaking wave**, when the Doppler sound hits the peak of its power and provokes the greatest turmoil, when roosters for a brief moment dominate public life;
3. a **churning wave**, when the impetus of the movement carries it beyond the failure of expectations, when the members of the group have lost a major element of their credibility and must confront the failure of their expectations, when the millennial movement must mutate to survive as it spreads over the shoreline; and

---

[45] Robert Tucker, "The Theory of Charismatic Leadership," *Daedalus* 97:3 (1968): 731–56; see also O'Leary, *Arguing the Apocalypse*.

4. a **receding wave,** when the Doppler drops off the instrument panels, when owls regain the ascendant and the wise rooster has learned either to become an owl or fake it. (It does not do to peddle last month's apocalyptic prophecy.)

All millennial movements—cosmic or more localized—go through some form of these phases that we can best conceive of as a curve of apocalyptic intensity (see figure 2.1).

Normal Time refers to Augustine's *saeculum,* that period when people plan on tomorrow, next year, next generation, following the same cycles that previous days and years have, since time out of mind, when farmers save their grain for next year's crop and plant fruit trees for coming decades, women have children, and students go to school so that, at the end of their education, they can have professional careers. Normal time predominates among most people, most of the time. Here owls dominate discourse and roosters must bite their tongues and bide their time.

Stage 1: Apocalyptic Time, the Waxing Wave

A number of things can set off a widespread apocalyptic perception that time is about to end. These can include many combinations of the following:

- Natural catastrophes, especially those that destroy large numbers of people and homes, making normal life impossible, and those that constitute rare demonstrations of nature's power (earthquakes, volcanoes, devastating storms, tsunamis.)[46]

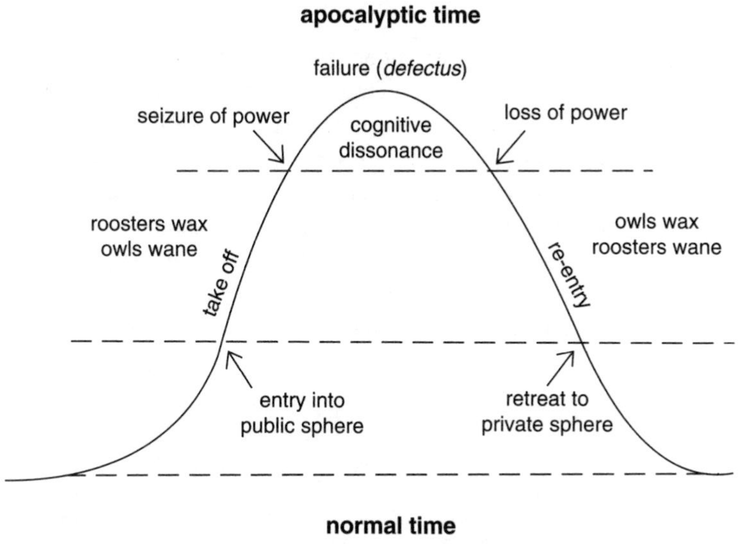

apocalyptic time

failure (*defectus*)

seizure of power   cognitive dissonance   loss of power

roosters wax owls wane   owls wax roosters wane

take off   re-entry

entry into public sphere   retreat to private sphere

normal time

Figure 2.1 The Apocalyptic Wave

[46] Michael Barkun, *Disaster and the Millennium* (New Haven, Conn.: Yale University Press, 1974).

- Celestial signs and wonders—comets, meteors, novas, eclipses, apparitions.
- Cultural upheaval, especially when one culture finds itself overwhelmed by another, or a new technology (like communications), which dramatically changes social relations (e.g., between generations). The advent of modernity (itself arguably a product of multiple millennial waves) with its pervasive penetration and domination of less developed cultures often brings on such responses in indigenous cultures.[47]
- Charismatic leaders, apocalyptic prophets, capable of articulating in the most electrifying terms not only an apocalyptic scenario, but appropriate action.
- Dates, especially ones that have circulated widely for long periods of time, and political developments that appear to fulfill published apocalyptic prophecies.[48]

Apocalyptic discourse generally starts soft, a constant (endemic) background murmuring for a small audience, shy of the public spotlight, confidential, nonconfrontational. Moving too soon, openly displaying an apocalyptic agenda early on, can endanger success from the outset. But under favorable circumstances the movement grows, gathering numbers and confidence, developing communities that begin to withdraw both (physically) from the surrounding culture and (psychologically) from "secular" (normal) time. These communities at once spread the word and, in their own lives and groups, proleptically live the saved life that will soon come for all who have ears to hear.

Stage 2: The Breaking Wave

The key event in a successful movement occurs when apocalyptic language breaks into public discourse with enough momentum to overcome the built-in resistances of the guardians of "normal time." When enough strong apocalyptic preconditions come together, roosters—like Thiota, or Gregory of Tours' "False Christ" of Bourges[49]—grow to prominence by appealing to large, enthusiastic audiences and are capable of taking over entire towns, regions, even governments.

And as roosters wax, owls wane, finding, much to their surprise, that what normally works—reasoned words of caution, belittling scorn—carries little weight. When a rooster like Hitler can gather rallies of a million people shouting *Heil*

---

[47] Weston La Barre, *Ghost Dance* (Prospect Heights, Ill.: Waveland Press, 1972); Michael Adas, *Prophets of Rebellion: Millenarian Protest Movements against the European Colonial Order* (Cambridge: Cambridge University Press, 1979); Wilson, *Magic and the Millennium.* Many of the movements studied in this book, especially the Xhosa (chapter 4), Cargo cults (chapter 5), the Taiping (chapter 7), and global Jihad (chap. 14) represent the response of cultures threatened by Western imperialism.

[48] O'Leary, *Arguing the Apocalypse*, 172–93.

[49] See above, n. 7.

Hitler! with tears running down their cheeks because they have at last found their savior, there is little the voice of reason can hope to accomplish.[50]

The period of time that a millennial movement holds its own in public discourse, or even dominates it, constitutes an *apocalyptic moment*. In such moments, both believers and their opponents reach feverish pitches of emotional intensity. Public discourse moves to an all-out struggle between good and evil. During this period, apocalyptic movements have a much broader impact than merely among the true believers (who burn bridges to get to the millennial kingdom). All of society becomes susceptible. The owls must now fight with the roosters for popularity, and the roosters have momentum on their side, if only, but crucially, for the moment.

Successful millennial movements, those with growing numbers of disciples and supporters, take their success as proof of the validity of their apocalyptic beliefs. Apocalyptic intensity feeds on itself, thrilling to the sense of continuing acceleration, anticipating the glorious process whereby the entire world will either be saved (converted) or damned (destroyed). The infectiousness of apocalyptic beliefs during such a time can become overwhelming, drawing in people who would normally not succumb to the siren call of millennial fervor.

The recent suggestion by evolutionary theorists that *memes* (idea genes) play a key role in cultural evolution and mutation, includes the important idea that these memes are programmed to spread. Apocalyptic memes are the hardest to set in motion, but programmed to spread as far and wide as they can: "Ye shall be witnesses unto me [and the apocalyptic message of repentance before the Day] ... unto the ends of the earth" (Acts 1:8).[51] If we imagine every individual as having an owl shell that prevents the rooster from emerging, then the hotter the ambient temperature, the weaker the shell; and each time one shell melts and a rooster emerges, the hotter the ambient temperature. At a certain point, the critical temperature is reached and shells melt rapidly. In some particularly intense cases, a collective apocalyptic moment can send people who had previously heard and ignored the call to convert running in panic and clamoring enter churches.[52] Desroche describes apocalyptic movements as "taking" the way a forestfire takes, igniting, spreading,

---

[50] See below, chapter 12.

[51] See Richard Dawkins, *The Selfish Gene* (New York: Oxford University Press, 1999); Robert Wright, *Non-Zero: The Logic of Human Destiny* (New York: Vintage, 2001). Aaron Lynch argues that the "continued nonoccurrence of the apocalypse tends to provoke cognitive immune reactions against the meme." And yet, no matter how often it fails, the apocalyptic meme continues to return with such force, perhaps because once it gets going, no other meme has the power to replicate as powerfully; *Thought Contagion: How Belief Spreads Through Society* (New York: Basic Books, 1996), 110.

[52] See, for example, the incident in 351 in Jerusalem (*Patrologia Graeca*, vol. 33, col. 1165–76; *The Works of Saint Cyril of Jerusalem*, trans. Leo P. McCauley and Anthony A. Stephenson, *The Fathers of the Church*, 64 (Washington, DC: Catholic University of America Press, 2000), 232–33; analyzed by Oded Irshai, "Cyril of Jerusalem: The Apparition of the Cross and the Jews," in *Contra Iudaeos: Ancient and Medieval Polemics between Christians and Jews*, ed. Ora Limor and Guy G. Stroumsa (Tübingen: Mohr Siebeck, 1996), 85–104.

sometimes consuming whole regions, nations, and cultures before passing from the scene.[53] All the precautions in the world cannot prevent all forest fires.

But such hopes cannot effectively hold their own in public for long—perhaps hours,[54] days,[55] months,[56] years,[57] and, in extremely rare cases and with peaks and troughs, for the better part of a generation.[58] Once a forest fire has started, the best one can hope for is to contain it and wait till it burns out.

Stage 3: Cognitive Dissonance and the Broken Wave

Eventually, the apocalyptic booster rocket burns out—the signs cease to appear with ever-intensifying regularity, the number of converts starts to fall, and personality politics in the charismatic circles (messiah and intimates) produces discordant behavior, even defections. Sometimes there is a defining moment—often, a specific prophecy fails (The Great Disappointment), in other cases the messiah or antichrist figure dies (Frederick II),[59] is murdered/executed (Jesus), or converts (Sabbatai Zvi).[60] Apocalyptic failure has, at least so far, been a universal feature of all such expectations. Rarely can any respectable historian say so categorically about any phenomenon, much more about a religious one, "In every case, this belief has been wrong."

This is true not only for the passive movements that await the intervention of supra-terrestrial powers—whether divine or, lately, extraterrestrial—like the one Augustine described as happening that day in 398 in Constantinople.[61] It also holds true for even the most successful of activist movements striving to *bring about* the millennial kingdom. For these active millennialists, these revolutionaries who actually seize the reins of power, the very act of succeeding marks the beginning of their failure.

Political "reality" invariably spoils millennial work. Constantine's turn to Christianity in the early fourth century did not transform pagans into true Christians and the oppressive empire of Diocletian into a salvific *pax ecclesiae romana*. Zhu Yuanzhang, whose millennial revolt ousted the Mongol dynasty, did not produce the Pure Land (1368), but rather another Chinese dynasty, which

---

[53] Desroche, *The Sociology of Hope*, 145–59.

[54] Above, n. 52.

[55] Constantinople 398 (three days of public penitence); discussed below.

[56] Northern Italian "Great Allelulia of 1233 (8 months)"; see Augustine Thompson, *Revival Preachers and Politics in Thirteenth-Century Italy: The Great Devotion of 1233* (Oxford: Clarendon Press, 1992).

[57] Fall of Rome (a decade, at least from 410–19); see website.

[58] From John the Baptist to the destruction of the Temple (ca. 25–70 CE), Peace of God (980s–1030s).

[59] Robert Lerner, "Frederick II: Alive, Aloft and Allayed, in Franciscan-Joachite Theology," in Verbeke, Verhelst, and Welkenhuysen, *Use and Abuse of Eschatology*, 349–80.

[60] Scholem, *Sabbatai Sevi*.

[61] For an extensive treatment of this account of an apocalyptic moment illustrating the Doppler effect, described by Augustine in his "Sermon on the fall of the city" (Rome), see Appendix at website.

burned the sacred books of the millennial movement that had brought him to power.[62] The revolutionary seizure of the French government did not bring on the "new citizen,"[63] any more than the seizure of the Russian or Chinese governments created a "new comrade." Even in success, every millennial movement is in for failure.

The more the believer has invested in the vision of the coming world, the more overwhelming the disappointment. Indeed, the mere act of acknowledging the disappointment, that the vision has failed, is so staggering that most commonly and persistently believers respond to negative developments with denial, followed by redoubled efforts.[64] Believers have wagered their all on this moment and movement—they have blown up their bridges behind them—and they will maintain and intensify momentum in any way they can. Among other responses intended to sustain apocalyptic time, we get

- *redating* (we miscalculated; the apocalyptic scenario was right, the timing wrong)
- a *second coming* of the messiah (our dead prophet or emperor will return, soon)
- *proselytizing* (we have to spread the word before he or she returns)
- *withdrawal* (we must maintain our solidarity despite the hostility of the world)
- *coercive purity* (use our recently acquired strength to carry out God's unfulfilled punishment for the wicked, and to enforce our millennium/ eschaton)
- *spiritualization* (the kingdom of heaven is within)

One of the key crises at these times of increasing cognitive dissonance concerns the relationship of the leadership, especially of a prophetic messiah who claims to speak directly to and for God, and his or her following.[65] Failed prophecy feels like betrayal, and once having failed, prophets must, for the first time, explain themselves to their apocalyptic followers. This they do in a variety of ways which,

---

[62] Edward Farmer, *Zhu Yuanzhang and Early Ming Legislation: The Reordering of Chinese Society Following the Era of Mongol Rule*, Sinica Leidensia 34 (Leiden: Brill, 1995).

[63] See below, chapter 8.

[64] The classic study of this, the one that first coined the term *cognitive dissonance*, is Leon Festinger, et al., *When Prophecy Fails*; for a critique, see Stephen O'Leary, "When Prophecy Fails and When It Succeeds: Apocalyptic Prediction and the Re-entry into Ordinary Time," in *Apocalyptic Time*, ed. Al Baumgarten (Leiden: Brill 2000), 341–62, with further bibliography.

[65] For a recent and particularly horrifying case, see the murder of the faithful by the leaders of the Movement for the Ten Commandments in Africa in 2000; Ian Fisher, "Uganda's Trauma: A Deadly Cult Stirs Lively Questions About a Nation's Soul," *New York Times*, April 9, 2000. A decade later, the "Lord's Resistance Army" continued to massacre civilians by the hundreds and thousands; see Xan Rice, "'Stench of Death' in Congo Confirms Resurgence of Lord's Resistance Army," *The Guardian*, March 28, 2010, online: http://www.guardian.co.uk/world/2010/mar/28/lra-congo-uganda-un, April 6, 2010.

unfortunately, tend to favor the paranoid and megalomanic tendencies inherent in messianic claims,[66] systematically "upping the ante"[67] to the breaking point and adopting the politics of coercive purity. If the liberated citizen fails to respond appropriately, the enlightened vanguard may just have to "force him to be free."[68] The permanent irony of apocalyptic expectations is that the tribulation the believers imagine assuredly coming will be theirs, and not that of their enemies.

Even in the mildest cases, where public ridicule alone is the cost of failure, recognition comes slowly. One's own failures of course are bad enough, but to give victory to the owls is particularly galling. And the owls, now back in control, are in no mood to sympathize. So apocalyptic roosters, once out of the closet and publicly committed to the "playing out" of their scenarios, will do whatever they can to sustain promise and hope and avoid admitting failure. Thus, they try to prolong the period of denial by whatever means, by an apocalyptic improvisation, a kind of apocalyptic jazz in which they discard their preformulated scenario for any set of developments to which they can plausibly attribute cosmic status. And, more ominously, if they have the means, they use violence. New dates, new signs, new sequences of events, new tasks to accomplish, new leaders keep the faith alive.[69]

The dynamics of apocalyptic denial, provocation, and crisis at the climactic moment of expectation—the height of the Doppler, the breaking point of the wave—are at once deeply psychological and enormously consequential. One might even argue, for example, that the greater the violence in the apocalyptic rooster's initial scenario, in his or her emotional imagination, the more painful his or her own tribulation in disappointment. The worst of the dialectical turns to negative-sum and can become, at such moments, self-fulfilling prophecies of auto-destruction.

Here we find the world of coercive purity coming to replace a failed "voluntarism," a world where humans anoint themselves agents of a just and vengeful God and seek to effect those promises that He has failed to deliver. In such cases, the "breaking points" can be disastrous—self-inflicted, like the Xhosa, or Heaven's Gate's quiet suicide of 1997; inflicted by enemies, like the Canudos massacre of 1896;[70] martyrdom sought and provoked, like the Boxers of 1900[71] and the suicide

---

[66] For a good recent analysis of this in Freudian terms, see Ted Daniels, *Millennialism: An International Bibliography*, xiii–xxxiii; for a Jungian analysis, see David Redles, *Hitler and the Apocalypse Complex: Salvation and the Spiritual Power of Nazism* (New York: New York University Press, 2004). Both are excellent descriptions of the psychological dynamics.

[67] Al Baumgarten, "Introduction," in *Apocalyptic Time* (Leiden: Brill, 2000), x–xiii.

[68] Rousseau's unfortunate phrase has earned him, via the French Revolutionary Terror, a place in the annals of totalitarian thought. Talmon, *Rise of Totalitarian Democracy*, 38–49; Isaiah Berlin, *Freedom and Its Betrayal: Six Enemies of Human Liberty*, ed. Henry Hardy (London: Chatto & Windus, 2002).

[69] One of the more stunning examples—because it involves faithful who had previously been radical pacifists—concerns the case of the Anabaptists at Münster; see Middelfort, "Madness and the Millennium at Münster"; Anthony Arthur, *The Tailor-King: The Rise and Fall of the Anabaptist Kingdom of Münster* (New York: Saint Martin's Press, 1999).

[70] Levine, *Vale of Tears*.

[71] Paul Townsend, *History in Three Keys: The Boxer as Event, Experience and Myth* (New York: Columbia, 1998).

terrorists of the Islamic Jihad after 2000.[72] In the worst-case scenarios, megalo-manic messiahs seize power and create a cauldron of totalitarian paranoia and exterminationist violence, as in the French, Russian, German, and Chinese revolu-tions of modern times. And recently we have seen, in both Aum Shinrikyo and some aspects of Jihadist thinking, the rise of an active cataclysmic apocalyptic vision that seeks to "save the world by destroying it."[73]

And yet, alternative, less violent and totalistic paths out of apocalyptic time do exist. The profoundly irenic nature of many millennial visions can encourage a radically different, productive and pacific dénouement. Here the disappointed believers focus on preserving what is best of the voluntarist vision of an egalitarian and just society and use the social flexibility, moral discipline, and commitment to manual labor of the millennial group to create viable and constructive post-apocalyptic communities. The Shakers, the Amish, and the Oneida communities all reflect what Arthur Mendel has called "tautological" millennialism, which stays loyal to principles of peace and voluntarism no matter how bitter and deep the disappointment.[74] As Stephen O'Leary points out, instead of the tragic pride of the apocalyptic believer who would rather destroy everything than admit fault, we find the comic humility of those who would rather admit error so that they can build at least part of their vision.[75] This alternative direction characterizes what we might call transformative apocalyptic. Generally speaking, cataclysmic apocalypti-cism produces, in disappointment, totalitarianism; transformative produces a civil polities.

These vastly differing directions suggest how vital it is to understand the dynamics of the period of cognitive dissonance—that period from the time the apocalyptic scenario deviates from expectations, to the time that the believer acknowledges, in deed if not in fact, that the End is not imminent. This is the great black box of millennial studies. To understand it unlocks secrets and riches of the millennial vision and illuminates the various roles that millennial dreams and actions have played in the unfolding of our past.

Stage 4: Return to Normal Time: The Ultimate Victory of the Owls

With millennial movements, this process of ultimate defeat can have spectacular, often violent, results, but they can also have more subtle resolutions. Roosters can and do become respectable owls.[76] Sometimes, by the end of the day, the rooster's

---

[72] See below, chapter 14.

[73] Lifton, *Destroying the World to Save It*.

[74] Mendel, *Vision and Violence*, 82.

[75] O'Leary, *Arguing the Apocalypse*, 200–01.

[76] To propose a variant to the famous expression: "Whoever is twenty and not a rooster has no heart, whoever is forty and still a rooster, has no head." And whoever is sixty and has not learned to get the head and heart to cooperate, has no learning curve.

team has lost all its players to the owls, even its leadership. The question, then, when dealing with religious movements of such intensity and complexity, especially when their belief had spread, however momentarily, throughout much of the culture, is what kinds of processes mark the ultimate victory of the owl. What kind of "invisible" transformations have accompanied "reentry"?

Inexorable time gives victory to the owls. Apocalyptic battles resemble those between Lancelot and Gawain—Gawain's strength waxed till noon and then waned.[77] By the end of the day, Lancelot had reclaimed dominance. Karl Morrison commented that trying to decipher the meaning of twelfth-century interpretations of the *Apocalypse* puts us in the position of "spectators who arrive at a field after the game is over."[78] The teams have left; the final score, posted; and the clean-up crews are busy removing any remaining mess. Indeed, as we shall see, some are busy removing any remaining evidence that a contest even took place.

Above all, we must understand cognitive dissonance: how the psyche, in a state of profound disorientation, unconsciously compensates for a reality that consciousness cannot acknowledge (the radical denial that the prophetic hope has failed). Without grasping the intensity of the problem and the extraordinarily inventive nature of the process of solving it, one cannot understand the impact of millennial movements on a culture. Without a sense of the workings of cognitive dissonance, one cannot follow a millennial movement forward beyond its inaugurating apocalyptic stage through the mutations that permit it to survive in "normal time," nor can one track linearly backward from the mutated form and identify its earlier manifestations in apocalyptic time. Indeed, for lack of this understanding, most historians have systematically missed both the trace and the influence of millennialism.

Of course, this was more than just a cognitive error—a great deal of political investment in the "current order" lies behind the hostility of the guardians of that order. And their hostility to millennial roosters is never more ferocious than in the immediate aftermath of an apocalyptic episode, a moment when the pain and embarrassment of losing control of public discourse is still fresh in the owl's mind. The dominant voice at such times overwhelmingly rejects the use of apocalyptic discourse.

In response to the same cultural forces, (former) roosters, in order to salvage a modified version of their original vision, disguise their origins, deny incorrect dates, propose future alternatives, reformulate and articulate their vision in ways that eliminate the mistaken hopes. Thus, what the apocalyptic moment had so starkly revealed—who the roosters, who the owls—the post-apocalyptic moment,

---

[77] Keith Busby, "Gawain," in *The New Arthurian Encyclopedia*, ed. Norris J. Lacy (New York: Garland, 1991).

[78] This metaphor of "clean-up crews after the game is over" comes from Karl Morrison's remarkable essay, "The Exercise of Thoughtful Minds: The Apocalypse in Some German Historical Writings," in *The Apocalypse in Medieval Culture*, ed. R. Emmerson and B. McGinn (Ithaca, N.Y.: Cornell University Press, 1992), 352–73; see esp. p. 354; below, chapter 3, n. 9.

and especially the formal, public, official, written discourse of the aftermath, intentionally obscures. The owls do not want to talk of their period of disorientation (when Thiota was *magistra*); the roosters deny it (what happened to her ecclesiastical followers?).[79] The record, most often, goes silent. And if a writer does try his hand at describing a millennial movement, he writes in the retrospective perfect, most often, with the contempt of his *ex post defectu* certainty. Thus, at the end of such a narrative, written after the failure, Radulfus of Fulda shows us a humiliated and chastised Thiota, slinking away in disgrace.

The documentation thus preserves the "end" of the story, the ignominious failure, the ridiculous folly, and repaints it by bleaching out apocalypticism.[80] Up until quite recently, the historical record of millennial activities has been primarily the propaganda of the victorious owls, whether they had previously been roosters or owls. It is filled with accounts of *pseudo*-prophetesses and *false* messiahs, with knaves and fools and mad, bad fanatics capable of great damage to themselves and others. And where our sources leave us some small scraps of this discourse scattered through their literate verbiage, we have no lack of historians quick to tell us to ignore them. It becomes a simple tale, stark in its rights (correct) and wrongs (mistaken), the cautionary tale of imprudent Chicken Little and the fools who followed her into Foxy-Loxy's den, of the attention-starved boy who cried wolf, of the duped and naked emperor in public denial. Such a perspective hardly encourages us, the inheritors of some three thousand years of consistently disappointed apocalyptic expectation, to take millennialism seriously.

Given this relationship between roosters and owls, the literary remains their temporally volatile interactions leave in the documentation need careful analysis. As with subatomic particles, we can only read the traces of their passage on the written page. So now, let us turn to how historians have, and can, read those traces.

---

[79] See, for example, the case of the rabbinical authorities after the failure of Sabbatai Sevi in 1666; Scholem, *Sabbatai Sevi*, 687–820.

[80] Frank Kermode, *The Sense of an Ending: Studies in the Theory of Fiction* (Oxford: Oxford University Press, 2000).

3 Bats and Turkeys

Historians and Recovering the Millennial Past

> A drunk was wandering under a lamppost looking for his keys.
> After helping look a while, a good Samaritan asked,
> "Are you sure you lost them here?"
> "Oh, no," replied the drunk. "I lost them in the bushes.
> But this is where the light is."

Let us return to a series of questions posed about the aftermath of Thiota's brief tenure as *magistra* of Mainz circa 848. With her trial, whipping, and dismissal in disgrace, our chronicler Rudolf of Fulda would apparently like us to think the story was appropriately finished. He certainly never mentions it again despite reporting a series of incidents over the next decade that might have interested her audience considerably: the condemnation by the same court of the "arch-heretic" of the period (Gottschalk) the following year (849); the devastating famine that drove people to cannibalism and Bishop Rabanus to feeding hundreds of paupers daily (850); the series of prodigies that terrified the populace of the entire region for the next decade, culminating, on January 1, 858, in an earthquake that badly damaged the church where Thiota and Gottschalk were condemned.

Should we treat Rudolf's silence about the reactions of the public that so admired Thiota to these events as a reflection of the finality of Thiota's defeat in 848, and more broadly of the plebs' general indifference to further apocalyptic prophecies? Should we stop our inquiry with the written version, under the assumption that whatever they thought, these commoners "do not count"? Or should we try to imagine what kinds of rumors might be circulating among that same plebs that flocked to Thiota? Most historians answer these questions tacitly but definitively by ignoring them. With the partial exception of Paul Dutton, no significant discussion of Thiota exists,[1] and few historians consider her role, or that of any other "charismatic" messiahs in the history of the "conversion" of the populace to Christianity in the early medieval period.[2]

---

[1] See brief mentions in: Paul Dutton, *The Politics of Dreaming in the Carolingian Empire* (Lincoln: University of Nebraska Press, 1994), 127–31; Janet Nelson, "Women and the Word in the Earlier Middle Ages," in *Women in the Church*, ed. W. J. Sheilsand D. Wood, Studies in Church History 27 (Cambridge: Blackwell, 1991), 73–74. On Abigail Firey's work, see below, n. 33.*

[2] For example, there is no mention of either Thiota or other apocalyptic prophets in Richard Fletcher's *The Barbarian Conversion* (Berkeley and Los Angeles: University of California Press, 1997), or *The Cross Goes North: Processes of Conversion in Northern Europe, AD 300–1000*, ed. Martin Carver (York: York Medieval Press, 2003), or any other major work on the "conversion" of Europe.*

■ VESPERIAN HISTORIOGRAPHY: BATS WORKING WITH OWLS' DOCUMENTS

Thiota's historiographical obscurity illustrates a larger and multifaceted problem: by and large historians do not like treating millennial movements. While some very few make it a focus of their work—Norman Cohn most famously—the vast majority prefer to marginalize the phenomenon. In a sense, the less historically significant a movement, the more readily historians might acknowledge a millennial dimension, whereas the more important, the more reluctantly do they do so. Indeed, among the case studies in this book, scholarly consensus recognizes only three as millennial movements—the Xhosa Cattle-Slaying, the Melanesian Cargo Cults and the Chinese Taiping. With Akhenaten, scholars have never considered a millennial dimension. In the case of UFOs and jihad, some scholars recognize the millennial dimension, but most specialists ignore it. And in the case of the French Revolution, Communism, and Nazism, most scholars resist any effort to argue a millennial element. This chapter explores the reasons for this neglect, which have to do both with the nature of the documentation and with historians' predispositions.

Let us begin just by documenting the historiographical phenomenon, with examples from medieval historiography, starting with an incident already cited.[3] At the end of his tale of the "False Christ of Bourges," Gregory of Tours comments that the false messiah's assassination by men sent by the Bishop of Clermont and the torture of his "Mary" failed to dissuade his followers from believing he was divine (thus making the Church guilty of deicide in the eyes of his followers):

> Quite a number of men now came forward in various parts of Gaul and by their trickery, gathered round them foolish women who, in their frenzy put it about that they were saints. These men acquired great influence over the common people. I saw quite a few of them myself. I did my best to argue with them and to make them give up their inane pretensions.[4]

Now, Gregory rarely misses an occasion to vaunt his debating skills, which suggests that he failed to gain much ground in these encounters, leaving much of Gaul "prey" to these apocalyptic charismatics, and Gregory deeply concerned about the approaching end.[5]

---

[3] Above, chapter 2, n. 7.

[4] Gregory of Tours, *History of the Franks* 10.25, 586. See above, discussion at chap. 2, n. 7.

[5] See Giselle de Nie, *Views from a Many-Windowed Tower: Studies of Imagination in the Works of Gregory of Tours* (Amsterdam: Rodopi, 1987), who depicts Gregory's deeply gloomy and apocalyptic mood at the end of his work, citing both the chronology with which he framed his account and his invocation of apocalyptic biblical passages to describe the present (10.23–25), a violation of Augustinian anti-apocalyptic teachings (only mitigated by his use of Matthew 24, rather than Revelation), and his final coda (10.31) in which he uses language redolent of Revelation 22:18–19. See my treatment of Gregory as well, "Lest," 166–68.

And yet one prominent historian dismissed the whole incident as no more than a "local nuisance," and characterized the profoundly apocalyptic tone of Gregory's final writings as "mere rhetoric."[6] Such an approach characterizes what I would call "vesperian historiography"—bats citing owls, or, in this case, mis-citing "should-be" Augustinian owls who, faced with pervasive calamity, had become roosters despite their training. And of course, since after Gregory we have no historical narration for over a century, how one views the situation at the end of the sixth century in Gaul has a good deal to do with how one reads Gregory's last writings, and the sparse but suggestive dossier of material hinting at widespread apocalyptic expectation, even in Gregory the Great's Rome.[7] Such examples of vesperian historiography can be multiplied at will,[8] as we shall see repeatedly throughout this book.

These historical "analyses"—really dismissals—represent an extraordinary spectacle. The historian who tries to figure out what happened during an apocalyptic episode is in the position, to use Karl Morrison's image, of "spectators who arrive at a field after the game is over."[9] And yet, by and large, rather than act as forensic detectives arriving at a crime scene looking for clues, many historians hasten to join the owls' clean-up crews, underplaying the significance of apocalyptic and millennial evidence that might have survived, discounting, dismissing, and even concealing evidence.[10]

■ EX POST DEFECTU: VESPERIAN HISTORIOGRAPHY AND THE CONTOURS OF ARCHIVAL REMNANTS

Unlike the way they behave in so many other matters, where the rare and the complex *attract* their attention, many historians, unfamiliar with the dynamics of millennialism, and perhaps disagreeably struck by the anomalous power of such ludicrous and repeatedly disproven beliefs, turn away from the subject. After all, among the religious beliefs historians study, apocalyptic prophecy is one of the few that one can safely claim has been *wrong*. No serious historian can legitimately claim that the "Trinity" or the existence of an afterlife is false; but we can claim that every prophecy

---

[6] Walther Goffart, *The Narrators of Barbarian History* (A.D. 550–800): *Jordanes, Gregory of Tours, Bede and Paul the Deacon* (Princeton, N.J.: Princeton University Press, 1988), 187 nn. 323–24.

[7] The generation following the end of Gregory's history is notoriously under-documented, but Michel Rouche put together a dossier of documents suggesting a major and sustained crisis of apocalyptic proportions; see Rouche, *L' Aquitaine des Wisigothsaux Arabes* (Paris: Touzot, 1979), 405–22. Goffart targets both Rouche and De Nie (above, n. 6) in his dismissive remarks.

[8] For another example of a modern historian reinterpreting a medieval one so as to align him with the Augustinian imperative, see the handling of Radulfus Glaber by Sylvain Gouguenheim discussed in Landes, "Introduction," *The Apocalyptic Year 1000: Religious Expectation and Social Change, 950–1050*, ed. R. Landes, A. Gow, and D. Van Meter (New York: Oxford University Press, 2003), 4 and n. 6.*

[9] Morrison, "Exercise of Thoughtful Minds," 354; discussed above, chapter 2, n. 78.

[10] For an extensive discussion of these matters seen in the historiography of the year 1000, see appendix at website.

of an imminent apocalyptic transformation, either to a millennial kingdom or to the eschatological annihilation of this world, has most definitively proven false.

And in a culture that highly prizes "being right," many scholars seem to find apocalyptic beliefs distasteful. Medieval historians working on the year 1000, for example, might grant that some marginal few, maybe even many, fell dupe to such an idea, but not the whole generation, and certainly not the great men and women who shaped the age. That would be unthinkable, or worse, "unjust, indeed an outrage to human dignity."[11] In a sense, it is as if the dysfunctional relationship between roosters and owls has a second life in the realm of historiography, where most historians favor and replicate the claims of the owls, whose initial opposition the passage of time had verified.

But this assumes that in matters apocalyptic, *wrong means inconsequential*. On the contrary, because of the passions they arouse and, in the case of millennialism, because of their determination to transform *this* world, apocalyptic beliefs prove remarkably resilient and influential even after their inevitable disappointment. I insist on this point here, not because this book explores these long-term effects, but to explain why historians generally do not, and yet should, pay attention to the central focus of this book: the dynamics of millennial movements activated by apocalyptic beliefs. As wrong as roosters may be at the time of their millennial movement, so may vesperian historians be misguided in their retrospective dismissal of these roosters' role in history.

The Lamplight: Owls Compose, Edit, and Archive the Documentation

Before any more specific discussion, however, we must examine closely the ways in which dysfunctional communication in apocalyptic time translates into retrospective memory and affects the crucial issue of evidence, of documentation. What survives of these apocalyptic moments? Who decides to "tell" the story in writing, and when? What relationship does it have to events and experiences at the time of the events described? Which narratives survive and where? And what can we do to recover the erasures of memory, both active and passive?

Here the modern historian must confront a very difficult problem: owls compose most and preserve *all* the accounts that survive. Their imprint marks the documentation everywhere, both its articulations and its silences. Our surviving documentation, for example, features three immediately post-apocalyptic voices:

- the emphatic *"I told you so"* of the owls, which appears primarily in the rare, explicit accounts of an apocalyptic episode (Rudolf on Thiota and the people of Mainz; Augustine on those of Constantinople);

---

[11] Plaine, "Les prétenduest erreurs de l'an mille," *Revue des questions historiques* 13 (1873): 164. This seems to be an early example of "liberal cognitive egocentrism": "we enlightened, rational ones have liberated ourselves from superstition, and it is offensive to suggest that those we admire in the past had not." See below, chapter 5, n. 79, 80.

- the discretely allusive *"I knew that"* of those who had wavered during the crescendo (those who had clamored at the doors of the churches to convert and now want to revert);
- and the passionate *"I (or he) never said that"* of the rooster turned owl; she always claimed that "The kingdom of heaven is within" (Luke 17:21).

Thus, even if clerics well trained in Augustine's teaching did at some time give in to apocalyptic enthusiasm, the documents we have access to were composed and preserved by men who knew that such temptations had proven false. They have no interest in recording and preserving the trace of such humiliating errors.

Thus, at first reading, any surviving record strongly supports a thesis that although on occasion crazy people thought and did foolish, even dangerous and (self-) destructive things, those of sound mind (like us) prevailed. Once enough time has passed, people can claim that even when the Doppler was loudest they did not flinch. (How many people who stocked goods in their basements for Y2K admit it?) But such an undoubtedly hasty conclusion surely has a good deal less to do with "reality" back when the panic spread, than it does with the way "reality" turned out. No historian of these phenomena can understand the documentation with which he or she works without realizing that the aggressive and retrospective triumph of the owls of post-apocalyptic time dominates our sources.

Historical "analyses" that take this documentation at face value, and, when necessary, dismiss evidence that might suggest the contrary, constitute a serious methodological lapse. For them, apparently, the traces of oral apocalyptic discourse that appear in our texts are so much flotsam and jetsam of a ship that Augustine, with his anti-apocalyptic theology, sank in Late Antiquity. Thus they think they can sail their ships of historiographical reconstruction safely through such waters without concern for those small floating objects.

But a closer look suggests we should treat the rare documented cases, the ones that managed to dent the systemic hostility of the written medium, as the tip of an oral iceberg of millennial discourse that only occasionally bursts into apocalyptic time and even (much) more rarely into written narrative. Thiota's message activated a set of eschatological/millennial beliefs that had to have existed before she came with her apocalyptic message about which we historians have no explicit documentary indications. Her reception—including the enthusiasm of clerics trained in Augustinian strictures—gives us unexpected insights into the relations between elites and commoners at this time, a submerged iceberg of apocalyptic discourse.

Here we find the exact opposite of the normal imposition from above downward. Did any of those clerics who followed her or the False Christ of Bourges write in the aftermath? And if they did, what happened to their documents? Did these "false prophets" have a school after them, like the Israelite prophets?[12] Or did

---

[12] Carroll, *When Prophecy Failed* (above chap. 1, n. 42) discusses the role of a scribal school that reworked the prophetic works after "prophecy failed," preserving *ex post defectu* both the redemptive vision and the radical critique of society.

the school of Amatzia prevail in the archival culture of early seventh-century Gaul, in which those who believed that "the land cannot bear all the [apocalyptic prophets'] words" controlled the public record, if not the public discourse?[13] In the case of the "False" Christ of Bourges, the surviving record is akin to what we would have were only Jewish/Roman documents to survive about Jesus.[14]

Modern historians, however, inevitably share with the owls who produced and preserved our archives the same retrospective perspective, and often enough they also share their psychological attitudes. They therefore almost instinctively end up confirming their sources' prejudices. They show limited interest in what apocalyptic discourse might circulate orally, and take the lack of documentation as sufficient reason to look in the lamplight of explicit documentation. For many of them, textual silence indicates real absence—a particularly problematic case of *argumentum ex silentio*.[15] And since, unlike experimental scientists, historians can only be contradicted by existing hard evidence on such matters, their ships can have sunk on these apocalyptic icebergs without their even knowing it...especially if their colleagues agree. The result risks becoming what Franklin Ankersmit called a "spectral illusion...created by the historical profession itself."[16] And, alas, the dead cannot shout out "the historian is naked."

■ GETTING THE STORY CROOKED: ON MOTIVATIONS AND CAUSES

In a now famous incident, two groups of historians, the empirical traditionalists and the theoretical deconstructionists, concluded a meeting at which they tried to communicate across the postmodern divide with the following exchange: "After all, what counts is to get the story straight..." said one old-timer who believed in

---

[13] Cf. Amos 7:10, in which the royal priest Amatzia chases Amos from the king's territory. The remarkable thing about ancient Israelite culture was not that "they killed their prophets," (all premodern cultures kill persistent and radical dissenters, certainly Latin Christendom did) but that Israel's canonical scriptures preserved these prophets' voices and told *their* story, not those of the tyrannical kings who tried to kill them.

[14] And unlike the case of Jesus, where the accusation of deicide against the Jews comes from the followers of Jesus, in the case of the False Christ, Bishop Gregory openly admits the Church killed him. His followers' continued belief in his divinity means that for them, the Church was a deicide.

[15] This is not what historians normally mean by an argument *ex silentio*, which they typically conceive of as a conspiratorial argument—the lack of the evidence is proof of the conspiracy (something dismissive historians use about my own arguments). As David Hackett Fischer points out, however, this is only one form of the fallacy. The argument of a *lack* in reality (e.g., no apocalyptic discourse), based on the lack of evidence, also constitutes an argument *ex silentio*. See Fischer, *Historian's Fallacies: Toward a Logic of Historical Thought* (New York: Harper & Row, 1970), 47. For an example of such a fallacy, see how Dominique Barthélemy interprets silence as absence, and uses it to "silence" the commoners in Barthélemy, *L'An mil et la paix de Dieu: La France chrétienne et féodale 980–1060* (Paris: Fayard, 1999), 366, 370.

[16] Franklin R. Ankersmit, "Hayden White's Appeal to the Historians," *History and Theory* 37 (1998): 87.

"facts" and "objectivity." To which another replied, "Oh, but you see, the point is precisely to get the story crooked."

> Around the table, the facial responses... seemed (in my view) to divide the international gathering in half: on the one hand were the smiles of those who had a sense that they had just heard something as true as it was clever, even if they were not quite in agreement as to how "getting the story crooked" was the point; on the other hand, the exasperated grimaces of those who, even if they could accept a fundamentally rhetorical description of the processes of historical representation, could not accept the playfulness of this response, its apparent abdication of epistemological responsibility and perhaps of reality itself.[17]

Every historian who believes the task is to "get the story crooked" has his or her own notions of how to do it. But I do wish to contribute to the task, perhaps rephrased as "getting the crooked story straight." That is, to understand the products of apocalyptic movements, we have to trace the long winding path that leads from the bushes of apocalyptic discourse into the lamplight of written testimony. And in order to do so, we have to understand that the believers who tread that path, driven by inevitable and repeated disappointment, improvise constantly with unintended consequences. And some of those improvisations, whose genealogy we may not know, not only "make it into the documentation" but even "make history." The historiography of apocalyptic movements necessarily must grapple not only with the cognitive dissonance of the believers, but also the unintended consequences of their deeds. No story, in such conditions, is "straight."

I start from the obvious and disconcerting observation that all oral discourse, which we historians cannot hear, went on constantly in the past and *necessarily* moved people and *motivated action more than "our" texts did.* This is true, if only because in order for a text to "act," it needed a living interpreter. What we do not know is far more important than what we do. Privileging the unknowable in this manner may strike the serious, empirical historian, trying to "get the story straight," as absurd. But I submit that it acknowledges more fully our situation as historians: the fact that we cannot hear this primary oral discourse does not lessen its importance for those who could.

In the case of recovering lost apocalyptic voices, this necessitates using working hypotheses as a flashlight with which to explore the bushes of people's thoughts and motivations... even of those who left us not a word in writing.[18] Among the crucial aspects of approaching what people thought and believed as they undertook

---

[17] Hans Kellner, *Language and Historical Representation: Getting the Story Crooked* (Madison: University of Wisconsin Press, 1989), 3–4.

[18] Interestingly enough, although Mario Vargas Llosa dedicated each chapter to speaking in the voice of different characters, he never has a chapter of his novel about the Canudos community giving the voice of the messiah, Antônio Conselheiro, see *The War of the End of the World* (New York: Farrar, Strauss, Giroux, 1984). On this extraordinary Brazilian movement, see Levine, *Vale of Tears* (above, chapter 2, n. 43). Messiahs are always the hardest to fathom.

their actions, we need to make a decisive shift in our temporal vectors. Most people think about the past, understandably, from the perspective of the present, with the knowledge of how things turned out. This has obvious advantages, and shapes how we ask our questions, about why things turned out the way they eventually did.

But the people we study looked into an unknowable future and acted without retrospective knowledge. If we would understand how they thought, rather than just what they did, we must go back and look with them at the unknowable future. And for them then, as for us today, the future is the great Rorschach screen onto which we project our hopes and fears. That is the screen upon which the millennial dreams are woven in apocalyptic time. Looking at apocalyptic history through the lens of the retrospective perfect is "like gazing at a Flemish tapestry with the wrong side out: even though the figures are visible, they are full of thread that obscure the view and are not bright and smooth as when seen from the other side."[19]

On some level, we historians are all bats in Plato's cave: we cannot see what happened or hear what people spoke in the past; we can only interpret the data that appears on the screens of our radar systems. We live in a world of shapes cast by those mysterious puppet makers who, standing behind us in time, fashion the texts that, passed in front of our philological light, throw flickering shadows on the walls of our historiographical present. And we give prizes to the best interpretations of those shadows.

There is a difference, however, between historians who seem unaware or unconcerned by their status as bats and do little to refine the sensitivity of their radar screens, and those who, conscious of their limitations, seek to compensate for their "oral" blindness. Historians who can dismiss an account of widespread apocalyptic activity throughout a large region as local nuisance, or who can write extensively about the period without even mentioning this activity,[20] are not bats *despite* themselves, they are *determined* ones. Rather than hone their radar with informed conjecture to pick up apocalyptic "oral discourse," they insist that the things that do not (sufficiently) register on their own highly literate screens do not matter, or that, rather, they are interested in recuperating other "lost voices."[21]

Charlemagne's Millennial Coronation in 6000 Anno Mundi

Take, for example, the case of the imperial coronation of Charlemagne in AD 801. According to a system of chronology that had dominated Western Christian

---

[19] Cited by Daniel Boorstin, *Hidden History: Exploring Our Secret Past* (New York: Vintage, 1987), epigraph.

[20] Goffart, *Narrators of Barbarian History*, above, n. 6; Peter Brown, *The Rise of Western Christendom: Triumph and Diversity, AD 200–1000* (Oxford: Blackwell, 1996).

[21] See, for example, Paul Freedman and Gabrielle Spiegel, "Medievalisms Old and New: The Rediscovery of Alterity in North American Medieval Studies," *American Historical Review* 103 (1998): 677–704, in which of all the alternative voices they chronicle none is identified as apocalyptic.

historiography from the fourth to the mid-eighth centuries, Charlemagne was crowned on the first day of the year 6000 since the creation of the world (Anno Mundi, or AM). According to the earliest sources in the tradition, the advent of the year 6000 promised the beginning of a "sabbatical millennium."[22] And yet, because the Carolingians had adopted Anno Domini in the 740s, and all the official documents dating the coronation used that new system, modern historians of the period have assumed—without discussion—that Charlemagne and his court neither knew nor cared about this calendar. For them, the coronation in the year 6000 was a coincidence without significance.

And yet, this notion of a sabbatical millennium had survived and shown remarkable vigor in Christendom for almost seven centuries. Even the formal opposition of the Augustinians who rejected any form of millennialism failed to dispense with it. Indeed, we can trace not only its presence, but also its unacknowledged power, over the course of at least seven centuries (from ca. 100–800 CE), during which two different dating systems for the age of the world were adopted in succession, AMI (Incarnation in 5500, 6000 in AD 500), and AM II (Incarnation in 5199, 6000 in AD 801). And each time, the chronology got discarded in its 5900s, at the approach of the fabled year 6000.

Vesperian historians, as we have seen, take the sources at face value: if it disappears, then, they reason, the chronographers of the day just adopted a more accurate one. But analyze these (extraordinary) chronological shifts in terms of the shifting value of such calculations for roosters and owls over time, and a different picture emerges. When attached to a chronology of the "Age of the World" (Anno Mundi), the sabbatical millennium permitted what was doubly forbidden: dating the End *and* promising the millennium. Such a clearly counter-indicated system could only work because it offered, at least at its introduction, a distant date, an owl's date. When Hippolytus first linked the sabbatical millennium to a calendar, he placed his present in the year AM 5700. He thus promised a non-apocalyptic earthly millennium: "From the birth of Christ one must count another 500 years, and only then will the end come."[23]

But over subsequent centuries at the approach of 6000, what had served the owl so well threatened to become the rooster's favorite weapon. Far-sighted theologians like Eusebius (ca. 5800), Jerome, and Augustine (ca. 5900) saw the problem coming and took action, forging and deploying a new calculation of Anno Mundi that reset the apocalyptic clock. Thus, at the turn of the century before the year AM I 6000, the dominant chronology dated Jesus' first *Parousia*, the Incarnation, in 5199, not 5500. And so, when the latter's apocalyptic date arrived, prominent figures like Cassiodorus dated it 5699, not 6000. The very need to change the calendar suggests not the insignificance of the issues involved, but quite the contrary, the

[22] See Landes, "Lest the Millennium."

[23] Hippolytus, *In Danielem* 4:26, Hippolyte, *Commentaire Sur Daniel*, trans. Maurice Lefèvre, Sources Chrétiennes 14 (Paris: Éditions du Cerf, 1947), 193; see Landes, "Lest the Millennium," 147.

imperative that at least Western ecclesiastics felt in denying the roosters such a weapon.

Like Hippolytus' AM I, the new AM II seems to have found favor as long as it served the owls' agenda, gaining the adherence of all the major Latin historians of subsequent centuries. Indeed, with Eusebius' and Augustine's systematic hostility to any millennial reading, the uninformed historian might imagine that the new system "had abandoned all implied eschatology, renouncing all speculation on the end of the world."[24] But if that were the case, then one might expect that chronologers would pay no attention to a "coming" year 6000 and continue to use the dominant system regardless of the advent of a now allegedly insignificant date of 6000.

And yet, no. Historians began counting down to this new year 6000 from the late 5800s onward, right up to 6000. And so, much in the same way that Jerome and Augustine had done at the dawn of the AM I 5900s (early 400s CE), Bede went to great pains to get his contemporaries to drop AM II for Anno Domini at the dawn of his 5900s (early 700s CE). For his pains, he got accused of heresy. Apparently for most owls, a hundred-year buffer still seemed big enough.[25]

The Carolingians, however, came to power in the two generations before the year 6000, and they found Bede's solution appealing. At their first major reforming council, in 5942 AM II (741 CE), under the aegis of the English Boniface, they dropped that dating system. And so, reading our Carolingian annalists, at the advent of AM II 6000, we find our sources dating (with exceptional precision) the coronation of Charlemagne to the first day of the year AD 801. Only marginal figures (at least to the historian's eye), in the most allusive of ways (hence escaping both contemporary censure and the inattentive glance of modern historians), continued the calculations of how many years remained in the millennium.[26]

Of course, alerted historians, like Wolfram Brandes and Johannes Heil, find a rich harvest of such "marginal" evidence if only they look.[27] But to integrate such evidence in a larger framework, one that involves reconsidering the key figures of the age, demands a paradigm shift: it requires that, at least provisionally, we imagine that these shards of a discourse that made it into the Augustinian medium of writing represented a much larger conversation in progress. That seems more than the profession at present seems capable of handling. Brandes' effort to publish on the topic met with the following rejection: "I cannot believe that Charlemagne had anything whatsoever to do with eschatological thinking."[28] An apocalyptic or millennial Charlemagne, is an anomaly too indigestible to even contemplate.

---

[24] Bernard Guenée, *Histoire et culture historique dans l'occident médiévale* (Paris: Aubier-Montaigne, 1981), 150; see analysis in Landes, "Lest the Millennium," 150.

[25] Landes, "Lest the Millennium," 174–78.

[26] Ibid., 178–91.

[27] Brandes, "'Temporapericulosasunt,'" Heil, "Approaches to Reconceptualizing Eschatology after AD 800 (AM 6000)," *Traditio*, 27 (2000): 77–103.

[28] "Ich kann nicht glauben dass Karl der Grosse irgend etwas mit eschatologische Dingen zu tun hatte." In rejection of the work of Wilhelm Brandes, text provided by Johannes Fried.

So conventional historians, in thrall to a level-headed Charlemagne who kept his wits about him, will not, cannot, imagine a role for the *outillage mental* of millennialism in his world. Perhaps, like Saladin, he laughed at stories of people panicking over apocalyptic rumors;[29] but neither he, not his court succumbed to such nonsense. However sophisticated these historians might be on other topics, when it comes to apocalyptic beliefs, they continue to look backward, *ex post defectu*. Thus, their backward gaze scans a near-solid wall of documented contempt and indifference for anything millennial, anything apocalyptic. It *seems* more than reasonable, then, to conclude that this documentary wall represents the overwhelming consensus of the culture, especially of the elite culture. It would be pointless to wonder about what kind of oral disputes stand behind these anti-millennial tropes that appear with such unwonted regularity in the texts.[30]

Given that the imperial coronation was, in the words of the great Carolingian historian Rosamond McKitterick, "an act that was to have far-reaching ideological repercussions in the succeeding centuries,"[31] this may be a good example of positivist historians "straightening the story." After all, could not one of the *major* impacts of Charlemagne on the imperial imagination in the West have been precisely this millennial dimension? Could that have been what motivated the young and infinitely ambitious Emperor Otto III to visit Charlemagne's tomb on Pentecost of 1000?[32] Could that not explain the extraordinary life of messianic imperialism in medieval Europe with its once and future emperors waiting in caves and volcanoes to reemerge at the apocalyptic time?[33]

The benefits of such an exegesis may seem considerable. But the hidden costs may be equally high. If we consider the possibility that those occasional flashes of apocalyptic fervor that appear in our documentation represent longer periods, both before and after the composition of our retrospective narrative, we get a radically different reading of events. Here we face the possibility that some important aspects of humankind's history may have been shaped by apocalyptic waves; and that these waves, which have, till now, been only partially identified, may have come far more often than we now imagine. At least one reading of the documentation about apocalyptic episodes in the early Middle Ages (500–1000) suggests that millennial dating may be among the *most* privileged terrains for understanding the discourse *between* elites and commoners in the early Middle

---

[29] See Schwartz, *Centuries' End* (New York: Doubleday, 1995), 49–52 and Dorothea Weltecke, "Die Konjunktion der Planetenim September 1186. Zum Ursprungeinerglobalen Katastrophenangst," *Saeculum* 54 (2003): 179–212.

[30] Janet Nelson, "Review of *Peace of God*," *Speculum* 69 (1994): 165.

[31] Rosamond McKitterick, *Atlas of the Medieval World* (New York: Oxford University Press, 2004), 33.

[32] Benjamin Arnold, "Eschatological Imagination and the Program of Roman Imperial and Ecclesiastical Renewal at the End of the Tenth Century," *Apocalyptic Year 1000*, chap. 13; and Johannes Fried, "Awaiting the End of Time around the Turn of the Year 1000," ibid., chap. 1.

[33] Cohn, *Pursuit of the Millennium*, 89–126.

Ages.[34] One might compare the various incarnations of the sabbatical millennium with the Burgess shale that Stephen Jay Gould studied in *Wonderful Life*: rare fossils of soft-shelled life forms that normally pass without any fossil record, in this case records of an oral discourse between elites and commoners.

Instead, most historians write histories that do not, cannot handle the phenomenon of millennialism. They are like scientists who refuse to do subatomic physics out of disdain for the weak "trace" evidence for subatomic particles.[35] It is as if they cared more for sparing the reputation of their culture heroes from the taint of apocalyptic irrationality (Jesus, Paul, Akiva, Constantine, Muhammad, Charlemagne, Francis of Assisi, Newton, the Vilna Gaon, Marx, Lenin, Mao) and proscribing their fools or villains for having succumbed (Emicho of Leiningen, John of Leiden, Sabbatai Zvi, Hong Xiuquan). Bad millennial historiography is *vesperian*: bat-historians take at face value the documents produced by owls narrating *ex post defectu*.

All this may seem understandable. But the resistance of historians to paying attention to millennialism sometimes reaches astonishing proportions. Indeed, when one looks closely at the argumentation, one finds an (unconscious) adoption of the owls' rhetorical project(ion) and sensibility. Such owl-historians, hostile to the very phenomenon they claim to analyze and explain, consistently speak of apocalyptic beliefs as irrational fears and imply that *if* there were roosters back then (whom they claim they cannot find), contemporaries would have ignored them for "crying wolf."[36] Even when they encounter the notion that most apocalyptic passions—especially those of the roosters—derive their most powerful fuel from hope, not fear, they seem unable to register the outrageous *hopes* of the millennium.[37]

This may relate to a secondary overlap between bats and owls, a psychological one. In addition to sharing the retrospective perfect, they often share a negative attitude toward apocalyptic irrationality. Indeed, in a number of cases, historians asserted a non-apocalyptic reading of the year 1000 specifically in the context of dismissing fears of 2000. At the end of the 1980s and beginning of the 1990s, two major French historians—Jacques Le Goff and Jean Delumeau—both held interviews aimed at "le grand public" in which they articulated the theme "no terrors in 1000, no terrors in 2000." And they did so despite the fact that neither had published anything scholarly on the year 1000, and offered only a loose collection of

---

[34] For a good beginning in this direction, see Aaron Gurevich, *Medieval Popular Culture*, chap. 1, "Peasants and Saints" (Cambridge: Cambridge University Press, 1990); for recent examples, see Abigail Firey, *A Contrite Heart: Prosecution and Redemption in the Carolingian Empire* (Leiden: Brill, 2005), 111–54; Rachel Fulton, *From Judgment to Passion: Devotion to Christ and the Virgin Mary, 800–1200* (New York: Columbia University Press, 2005), 60–89. This will be the focus of my *While God Tarried*.

[35] Subatomic particles cannot be seen; only their trail can be detected.

[36] G.L. Burr, "The Legend of the Year 1000," *American Historical Review* (1901): 435.

[37] See Pierre Riché, *Les Grandeurs de l'an mille* (Paris: Bartillat, 1999), 11–23.

the least rigorous arguments of the previous scholarship.[38] What audience did they conceive of when they spoke thusly? And why did other historians pay heed?

To do valuable historical analysis of apocalyptic moments and millennial movements, we must develop an ability to fly into that seemingly solid, textual, "wall" of indifference and hostility to millennialism that so marks our sources, to make the imaginative leap back in time to a moment when the future was unknown (as it is for us and every generation), a time when it was not at all clear that the world would *not* end. We must be able to imagine a culture and a discourse in which, at certain times of crisis, virtually no one, even the most rigid Augustinian, could still insist that nothing portentous was happening.

In order to fathom the phenomenon in question, we need to constantly peel away our layers of cognitive and psychological resistance to granting serious attention to such embarrassing, even humiliating, errors. In such matters of shame, above all, one slides easily from difficult attempts at empathy with rather bizarre roosters to the easy cognitive egocentrism of the owls: we have difficulty imagining people so crazy, a fortiori, on a grand scale. It seems somehow disrespectful.

One needs, therefore, to understand clearly just how powerful our resistance to the study of this bizarre and disturbing phenomenon. To clear away the rubbish that clutters the mouths of our caverns of perception, let us begin with a millennial reading of the great parable, *The Emperor's New Clothes*.

■ THE EMPEROR'S NEW CLOTHES AS APOCALYPTIC — REVELATORY — NARRATIVE

Andersen's tale has a long history within the larger tradition of trickster narratives.[39] But it also represents a tale of public revelation and judgment. As a result, the story maps onto the apocalyptic curve in interesting ways. Granted, it is not a perfect analogy: while most apocalyptic prophets attack figures of authority, and therefore seem determinedly subversive from the point of view of power holders, this one represents a "top-down" affair, like Akhenaten. And there are such occasions, where emperors and kings are swept up in the enthusiasm/terror of such prophecies, as, for example, the bishop and emperor in Constantinople in the final years of the fourth century,[40] and possibly Charlemagne. The Emperor's New

---

[38] Jean Delumeau, "La grandepeur de l'an 2000? L'angoisse du vide," *Le nouvel observateur*, no. 1282 (June 1–7, 1989): 38; Jacques Le Goff, "Faut-il avoir peur de l'an 2000?" *Télérama*, no. 2086 (January 3, 1990): 8–10. See also E. Randolph Daniel, "Medieval Apocalypticism, Millennialism and Violence," in *Millennial Violence: Past, Present, and Future*, ed. Jeffrey Kaplan (London: Taylor & Francis, 2002), 275–99.

[39] Archer Taylor, "The Emperor's New Clothes," *Modern Philology* 25, no. 1. (August 1927): 17–27. The tale is one of Aarne-Thompson types (number 1620); see several variants from around the world: D. L. Ashliman, "The Emperor's New Clothes and Other Tales of Aarne-Thompson type 1620," online: http://www.pitt.edu/~dash/type1620.html#silkrobe, February 15, 2010.

[40] See above, chapter 2.

Clothes represents just such an incident. Here the initiators of the Doomsday moment are charlatans (as the owls wish us to believe about all roosters)—not prophets but out for profit.

Stage 1: The Waxing Wave

In this tale, apocalyptic (revelatory) time begins when the tailors arrive in town with their announcement of a wondrous way to judge people's wisdom or folly—a this-worldly "Last Judgment." Those who can see the magical clothes are wise; those who cannot, are foolish. The implications here for "real power"—that is, who has the emperor's approval, and who does not—make this a *highly significant* revelation. Of course, the cutting edge of the story is that, just like apocalyptic prophecy doomed to failure, this Day of Judgment will backfire and reveal the opposite: those who "see" the clothes are the fools, just as those who count on the tribulation for the wicked will be confounded.

The Doomsday (*doom* is Old English for judgment) prophecy enters public discourse when the emperor accepts the tailors' claims and pays them to create his new wardrobe. From the time they set to work until the public procession marks the apocalyptic countdown. Anticipation grows as the date of the revelation nears. As the tailors' work drags on (and costs a fortune in gold cloth), the emperor wavers, not so much in his faith in the tailors, as in his faith in himself: will he "see" the invisible cloth, will he be saved? So he sends his trusted chamberlain to check out the tailors' progress.

With the conversion of the chamberlain to the tailors' claims, the apocalyptic discourse becomes official; the apocalyptic prophecy has not only entered into the public sphere, but seized the reins of power. Suitably empowered by the reassurance of his chamberlain, the emperor ups the ante: a great procession planned, a Day of Judgment for all. The court and the public are both primed and anxious at the prospect of judgment—who will see and who will not see the wondrous clothes?[41]

The first disappointment comes with the tailors' revelation of the clothes to the emperor and the court: no one sees any clothes; everyone is thrown into cognitive dissonance. At this moment, a collective admission that there are no clothes would rob the tailors of their charismatic claims, put an end to the "apocalyptic" prophecy, and spare the emperor public humiliation. Instead, everyone, afraid of admitting foolishness (and insulting the emperor by revealing *his* folly), praises the creation that only exists in their minds and their conversation. Rather than admit their error, they up the ante. Thus, the failure of every member of the court to admit not seeing the clothes leads the emperor to undertake his fateful public procession, amplifying both the intensity and reach of the apocalyptic moment.

---

[41] This represents a fairly rare kind of apocalyptic moment (how rare?) where the authorities themselves are not only drawn into the expectation, but lead it. Augustine describes a similar situation in Constantinople in 398 (see appendix at website).

Stage 2: The Wave Reaches Its Peak

The momentum endures as long as the crowd continues to praise the clothes at the sight of a naked emperor. Their cognitive dissonance is so great, the mimetic consensus so powerful, that no one dares utter his or her thoughts, a nice illustration of how people can deny the very evidence of their eyes.[42] The first part of the procession represents the height of public adherence to the prophecy. Like the emperor and pope outside the walls of Constantinople, offering prayers of penitence up to an absent God, the public offers up praise to a vain and foolish Emperor.

> Everyone said, loud enough for the others to hear: "Look at the Emperor's new clothes. They're beautiful!"
> "What a marvellous train!"
> "And the colors! The colors of that beautiful fabric! I have never seen anything like it in my life!" They all tried to conceal their disappointment at not being able to see the clothes, and since nobody was willing to admit his own stupidity and incompetence, they all behaved as the two scoundrels had predicted.

Stage 3: The Wave Breaks

The bubble bursts when the boy contradicts the crowd, and the father affirms his son's comment—"'Good heavens! listen to the voice of an innocent child,' said the father"—and the crowd follows their lead—"and one whispered to the other what the child had said. 'But he has nothing on at all,' cried at last the whole people." Here, in a reversal typical of apocalyptic moments, the tables turn: those who expected the tribulation for others undergo their own tribulation, their own humiliation. Immediately, the realization sets in: those most committed to the illusion are revealed to be fools, those least committed are released from their thrall.

And yet at this point in the story, one might suggest a different ending. Rather than public acknowledgment of the boy's comment, the father could have said, "Hush child, the emperor wears a full suit, and it's beautiful!" and the crowd could have glowered at the child for revealing their folly along with the emperor's. Historically speaking, this is probably the most common outcome—normally voices of dissent are repressed. Indeed, in the first version (which he sent to the editor), Andersen had the parade go off without contradiction.[43]

---

[42] As the saying goes, "Are you going to believe me or your lying eyes?" For an interesting case study, see Martha Beck on the Egyptian papyri interpreted by the Mormon's founder Joseph Smith even though he could not read hieroglyphics (*Leaving the Saints: How I Lost the Mormons and Found My Faith* [New York: Crown Publishers, 2005], 150–60); for a Mormon critique of the book, see Alan Wyatt, "Loss and Sadness," http://www.fairlds.org/Reviews/Rvw200502.html.

[43] When Andersen first wrote the tale, he had it end with a successful procession and the king noting that he had never had so successful an event. The ending with the boy—which is radically ambiguous on the nature of the crowd's reaction—came to him after the tale was already at the publishers and he made the changes at the last second. See Jackie Wullschlager, *Hans Christian Andersen: The Life of a Storyteller* (New York: Knopf, 2001), 176–78.

Stage 3: Varying Reactions of Disappointment

Let us follow Andersen's revised, authoritative account, in which the cat got out of the bag, and this choked, hidden perception swelled from whisper to shout. The child has released this crowd of individuals from the painful cognitive contradiction between what they saw and how they acted. This would qualify as one of those moments, analyzed by James Scott, when hidden transcripts can burst to the surface, when the emperor's own foolishness has endowed the populace with the power to mock him openly.[44] This could be a moment where, as Bakhtin said about Rabelais, explosive laughter had turned the world upside down.[45] But would the crowd respond with hilarity or horror? Andersen makes no mention of laughter.

Was the public delighted or terrified by the shattering of the icons of power, by the revelation that their emperor was a public fool?[46] If they had predatory neighbors—the norm for most cultures in most of history[47]—this omen bode much ill. For example, in France, in 1356–60, with King John, the hapless loser of the battle of Crécy, captive of the English, and the countryside at the mercy of unemployed mercenaries, the millennial rantings of an imprisoned Franciscan spiritual contributed to the most widespread and violent commoner's revolt in French history—the *Jacquerie* of 1358.[48] The public might well be terrified by having a fool for an emperor.

The end of Andersen's story offers us a particularly revealing insight into the problem of documentation. The remainder of the procession went on as scheduled, despite the crowd's response. Even though everyone knew that the emperor was naked, Andersen has the royal court persevere as if all were well. "'But he has nothing on at all,' cried at last the whole people. That made a deep impression upon the emperor, for it seemed to him that they were right; but he thought to himself, 'Now I must bear up to the end.' And the chamberlains walked with still greater dignity, as if they carried the train that did not exist." Thus, the emperor maintains the public transcript of his revelatory procession even as its meaning has reversed. To save face, he prolongs his humiliating procession, despite the calls from the now transformed audience. The turmoil of public cognitive dissonance, of two competing narratives—emperor as naked fool, emperor as august presence—continues until the last courtier in the procession disappears behind the palace gates.

[44] Scott, *Domination*, 226–28.

[45] Bakhtin, *Rabelais and His World* (Bloomington: Indiana University Press, 1984); on Bakhtin, see Scott, *Domination*, 122–23, 175–76.

[46] As we shall see in the course of the book, the answer to this has a great deal to do with the civic potential of the culture in question: terror characterizes cultures ill-suited for civic autonomy, and vice-versa.

[47] See below, chapter 6. For a good contemporary example of the problem, see the case of Saddam Hussein pretending to have nuclear weapons to discourage Iran from invading.*

[48] Although John of Rupescissa wrote apocalyptic prophecy precisely about the years (1356–60) Robert Lerner sees the revolt as a confirmation of the prophecies (*The Feast of Abraham* [Philadelphia: University Pennsylvania Press, 2000], 77–83), rather than the latter as a spark to the former, as suggested by the contemporary, Froissart (*Chronicles*, trans. Geoffrey Brereton [Baltimore: Penguin Books, 1978], 165–66).

In "buying into" the scam of the apocalyptic (revelatory) "new clothes," the court made the public moment one of utter humiliation, rendered all the more horrifying by the knowledge that any of them could have prevented the whole disaster if only he or she had spoken earlier. (The courtiers all, after all, saw the emperor before the procession.) But they were so committed to the "prophecy," so slavish in their mimesis of their "betters," that they now found themselves forced, by the rules of the very ritual they started, to suffer their drawn-out humiliation in impotent silence. Able neither to lash out at the crowd nor to break and run, they must do what no sane elite would think of doing under ordinary circumstances: they parade their naked emperor down the streets of his capital "holding the invisible train still higher."

Stage 4: The Receding Wave, the Return to "Normal"

The shared apocalyptic moment—anticipation, dread, celebration, humiliation, terror—was only over when the last courtier in the procession disappeared behind the gate of the palace and the emperor disappeared into his chambers. At that point, the collective experience, broken in the prism of the revelatory "failure," scatters over a large spectrum. What happened? What can this mean?

As historians, let us take the story past the point to which Andersen's fable brings us, to the social *memory* of this event. As soon as the "moment of reversal" has ended, "normal time" returned, and with it, the power of the court and emperor. And their primary effort would be to suppress any public memory of the event. The morning after, only a fool would remind the courtiers of what happened. Indeed they, with their ritual denial even in the face of public perception at the end of the procession, have already indicated the official court position. Their version, the official version, will contain no mention of the hoax, of the enormous humiliation they all endured.[49]

The *Volk*, the commoners who saw the parade and agreed with the lad's revelation, whose cries reached the emperor's ears, may well have told their tale of imperial humiliation repeatedly, to peals of laughter and running tears; and they may have been rebuked by others warning that such events can promise nothing but catastrophe. But they will have done so in the privacy of their homes and hearths and taverns. Theirs is the oral social memory, one more item in the lore whose recital keeps the winter months warm. Little wonder, then, that this narrative comes to us as a "folk" tale.

The court, on the other hand, prepares, shapes, defines the public transcript. Not only did the incident never happen, it is most decisively over, closed, terminated.

---

[49] This gives us the "newspeak" of Orwell's typical dystopia. The Russian joke tells of a communist historian noting that we can hope to know the present and the future, but the past is unpredictable. Some might accuse postmodern historiography of contributing to making that remark normative rather than a mordant comment on totalitarian propaganda.

What happened that day has *nothing* to do with anything subsequent. Apocalyptic moments have *no* carry-over in the public transcript. Even when major changes may have been instituted as a result—the firing of the chamberlain, the rapid rise of another, uncompromised court faction, the gradual replacement of many courtiers—the reasons given will identify *anything but* a response to that humiliating nonevent.

Thus, the journalist who comes to the imperial capital a week after the naked parade and interviews only courtiers, without visiting the taverns, will tell a bland tale: "Emperor Parades in New Clothes: Populace Enthused." Any modern paper would hopefully fire so inept a journalist. And so, we historians, therefore, should also remember that, in almost every case where we have access to the documents, the narrators of past apocalyptic movements energetically sought to produce these public, court transcripts. Their audience was not us, but a learned, Augustinian-trained peer group. If we forget, if we make no effort to imagine the tales of the taverns,[50] we risk being the only rubes who do not know that the emperor paraded naked. We become vesperian historians.

■ HISTORIANS OF MILLENNIAL PHENOMENA:
TURKEYS

This book argues that if we are to understand what motivates our actors, we must pay attention to the rhetorical stance of the texts we read, and hear not only the loud, insistent, and formal voices of the owls, but also the muffled ones of the roosters and their audiences.[51] We must understand that depending on whether one feels guilty or innocent, the apocalyptic news has opposite effects. For some— Aggy's Southern slave owner, for example—belief in the advent of *The Day* (should) provoke terror, while for others—Aggy herself—it unleashed great hope, joy, and, potentially, sacred violence.[52] And we must always keep in mind that the owls' fear and the roosters' hopes normally lie buried beneath the hostile silence of the keepers of the historical record.

Let us call millennial historians—among whom I wish to be identified—as turkeys. By empathizing with those who hope so outrageously, we can stand in the barnyard as roosters crow and observe their electrifying impact on the other animals. Turkey-historians do not assume that dramatic gestures need to be "de-dramatized," that roosters and their followers were either crazy, or that they should, in cases where they admire one of the roosters, neatly iron out his or her deeds and assign them "rational" (non-apocalyptic) notions. Nor do they need a "smoking gun"

---

[50] Taverns are an active site for hidden transcripts; Scott, *Domination*, 122–23; E.P. Thompson, *Making of the English Working Class* (New York: Vintage, 1966), 51–52.

[51] Kenneth Burke, *The Rhetoric of Religion* (Boston: Beacon Press, 1961).

[52] See above, chapter 2 n. 13.

before they will consider millennial dimensions of peoples' behavior. Familiar with the patterns of roosters, they look for their signatures.

Turkey-historians understand that apocalyptic faith can take many forms. They listen carefully for the sounds and look for the impact of this evanescent and protean set of beliefs. Some of these roosters may have crowed only to themselves, isolated in the cloister, like Ademar of Chabannes, 1029–33, pouring out his anguish and venom in folio after folio of forged accounts of a virtual reality that continues to fool historians.[53] Or they may have crowed to a huge and combustible audience, whether from the depths of a papal prison cell, like John of Rupescissa,[54] or in the light of day, like Savonarola, who took over the most dazzlingly enlightened and secular city of Renaissance Europe.[55]

And when these historians detect roosters gaining public purchase, they anticipate that owls change their behavior in characteristic ways. These latter, largely hostile responses, are invariably better documented than that of the roosters and their credulous followers... the *defecturi* those about to be disappointed. Jerome's and Luther's anti-millennial denunciations far outweigh, both in literary bulk and in the attention historians pay them, the writings of the "delirious Judaizers" and the *Schwärmerei*.

In the post-apocalyptic return of the owls' dominance in normal time, no successful rooster can survive without shedding his original plumage, and no apocalyptic community survives if it does not find a useful niche for itself in which it provides the *saeculum*—that world that should have passed away—with valued services.[56] No turkey-historian would thereby conclude that, *post defectum*, they no longer have anything to do with millennialism and therefore their (mistaken) past need not interest us.

Nietzsche warned of the dangers of a "functionalist" approach as anachronistic.

> There is for historiography of any kind no more important proposition than the one it took such effort to establish but which really *ought to be* established by now: the cause of the origin of a thing and its eventual utility, its actual employment and place in a system of purposes, lie worlds apart; whatever exists, having somehow come into being, is again and again reinterpreted to new ends, taken over, transformed and redirected by some

---

[53] On Ademar's final forgeries, see Landes, *Relics*, Part III; on their apocalyptic nature, Michael Frassetto, "Heretics, Antichrists, and the Year 1000: Apocalyptic Expectations in the Writings of Ademar of Chabannes," in *The Year 1000: Religious and Social Response to the Turning of the First Millennium*, ed. Frassetto (New York: Palgrave-MacMillan, 2002), 73–84. For a good example of using the forgeries uncritically, see Barthélemy, *L'an mil et la paix de Dieu*, 369–72.

[54] See above, n. 48.

[55] On Savonarola, see Donald Weinstein, "Savonarola, Florence, and the Millenarian Tradition," *Church History* 27, no. 4 (1958): 291–305; Christopher Rowland, "Imagining the Apocalypse," *New Testament Studies* 51 (2005): 303–27.

[56] In this sense, demotic millennialism makes the easiest return since, by valuing manual labor, it often reforms its community around a new and valuable technology (e.g., the Shakers).

power superior to it;[57] all events in the organic world... [involve] a fresh interpretation, an adaptation through which any previous "meaning" and "purpose" are necessarily obscured or even obliterated.[58]

And yet, that which really ought to have been established by the late nineteenth century remains the exception more than a century later. One can understand how, with the failure of apocalyptic expectations (e.g., in the case of early Islam, the non-arrival of *Al-Kiyama* [the day of Judgment]),[59] subsequent believers would want to clear their founder of having preached any such mistaken beliefs. Luke reassures us that when Jesus said, "The kingdom of heaven is at hand," he did not mean it literally; on the contrary, it refers allegorically to the kingdom "within" all of us; and subsequent ecclesiastics and modern church historians have insisted that "kingdom of heaven" has nothing to do with this earth, despite the observable fact that all Jewish popular messianism was "this worldly."[60]

But why would historians insist on taking these later revisions, these narratives *ex post defectu*, as valid reports on the situation before the disappointment? Why would we, who wish to identify the forces that move people to act the way they do, ignore such valuable insights into one of the most powerful forms of rhetoric known?[61] Why would we willingly choose to be as obtuse as the characters in a DC comic book who cannot tell Clark Kent from Superman, even though the only difference is a change in clothing and the addition of eyeglasses?

A Turkey's Reconsideration of the Tale of Thiota, the Pseudo-Prophetess

To have a sense of how this works, let us return one last time to the example with which we began chapter 2. Composed by a monk from an important monastery near Mainz with close connections to the imperial court, the account exudes the retrospective perfect. Thiota is a *pseudo-prophetess*, a monetary fraud with a ludicrous apocalyptic prediction, who was justly punished and humiliated. Open and shut case; the incident is over.

But looking closer, we find some valuable and revealing details of the woman's spectacular if temporary success at least among two constituencies. First, among commoners who, in large numbers, showered her with gifts—the ultimate sign of commitment for commoners. (Imagine the frustration of clerics whose efforts at collecting tithes rarely met with such generosity.) And second, among some clerics who, ignoring their Augustinian training, followed her—O how scandalous—as a

---

[57] Whatever Nietzsche had in mind here, for the case of apocalyptic beliefs, that power superior to it is the inexorable passage of time and the continuation of the *saeculum*.

[58] Nietzsche, *Genealogy of Morals*, Essay 2, section 12, 77.

[59] See below, chapter 14.

[60] Gershom Scholem, *The Messianic Idea in Judaism and Other Essays* (New York: Schocken, 1971), 1–36.

[61] O'Leary, *Arguing the Apocalypse*.

divine teacher who had superseded church doctrine! In 847–48, apocalyptic time had turned the world upside down in Mainz. This success even among clerics may indeed have had something to do with clerical apocalyptic calculations. In this case we may be dealing with the earliest evidence of a tradition that would become particularly strong at the advent of 1000—the belief that when the Annunciation coincided with the Passion (Friday, March 25), the end would come.[62]

For how long did Thiota maintain her status as *magistra*? Did the bishop intervene as soon as word came to him of the scandal? The chronicler understandably, like the courtiers in Andersen's fable, would like to tell us that those of sound mind quickly brought this nonsense to a close. But the historian should at least consider an alternative hypothesis, whereby the bishop waited *until prophecy failed*.

As we have seen, during the crescendo of an apocalyptic wave, roosters dominate public discourse and only the most severe measures—killing, execution, massacre—have any effect. And all too often, they backfire, creating martyrs. In Thiota's case, with some clerics fully in her camp, a mere whipping would only have inflamed hostility to the church among her numerous following. As we saw, moreover, in the case of the "False Christ of Bourges," even the execution of the pseudoprophet and the harsh disciplining of his followers could not bring such a story to an early end; indeed they led to a metastasis of the movement.[63]

We find just this dynamic in thirteenth-century England, where an "uneducated ascetic visionary" named Peter of Wakefield predicted the end of John's reign on Ascension Day 1212. The king initially ignored him, then imprisoned him, producing a notable spike in Peter's fame, and in the prophecies attributed to him. John *awaited the passage of the day* before executing him and his son. But even then, his believers redated the prophecy from May 23 (Ascension Day, 1212) to May 27 (the thirteenth anniversary of John's coronation on Ascension Day 1199). And even after the passage of both days, they continued to interpret the man's prophecies allegorically. All this follows classic patterns of prophecy failed.

In the case of Thiota, it may well have seemed more advisable to some key policy-makers to wait (with prudence worthy of an owl) until her prophecy failed, than to confront such a rooster at the height of popular influence. Indeed, some of their hesitation may have come at least as much out of a (secret) fear that Thiota was right—after all, even Augustine had to admit that it was a *duty* of Christians to prepare for the end which *could come at any time*—and given the political conditions, it was certainly possible. Some of their colleagues had already trod that slippery path to apocalyptic delirium and ended up in Thiota's court.

---

[62] David Van Meter, "Christian of Stavelot on Matthew 24:42, and the Tradition that the World Will End on a March 25th," *Recherches de Théologie ancienneet médiévale*, 63 (1996): 89–90.

[63] The assassination of "False" Christ of Bourges (591 CE) at the height of his mission by the men of the bishop of Clermont (whose disciples therefore viewed the Church as deicides), led to a multiplication of charismatics spreading his message throughout Gaul (above, n. 4).

Thus the most likely reconstruction of this incident has a female commoner come to the archepiscopal city of Mainz in 847 and, through apocalyptic rhetoric, dominate public discourse, even serve as a judge in the biblical sense, for many months even up to a full year. Such a reading implies a variety of not commonly accepted notions about the Early Middle Ages, from the pervasiveness of apocalyptic discourse among the populace and its potential impact on public life, to the insecurity of the ecclesiastical elite, and the fragility of what looks like—to judge from the surviving sources, lay and clerical—the supposedly dominant male (and Augustinian) discourse of authority. How long did such things last and how often did they occur? How deep into the culture did such attitudes reach and what were the consequences? One historian has recently offered a general answer these questions:

> Rather than imagining a Carolingian episcopacy that exercised considerable control over the Christian flock, one may discern an elite corps of bishops and scholars, educated in demanding but perhaps at times *recherché* hermeneutic, riding out swells of popular piety that they at times perceived as outright heresy, preached by "false priests," "false Jews," or "false prophets."[64]

■ MILLENNIALISM: THE TWICE-UNTOLD TALE

Given the preceding analysis, it should come as no surprise to the reader that the history of millennialism remains to be written. Indeed, it is a twice-untold tale. This is not to say that there is a lack of millennial scholarship, including excellent studies by first-rate and highly respected historians. The bibliography of millennial studies is enormous, indeed, a burgeoning field.[65] But it does mean that that work has, by and large, remained at the margins of any kind of grand narrative of the West since the advent of Christianity, even in the times when the very chronological shape of history was conceived in millennial terms.

The first time the "grand narrative" of Western history was told (fourth to fifteenth centuries), *religious* historians chose not to include millennialism in the story. Theological owls like Eusebius (ca. 300), Orosius (416), Gregory of Tours (ca. 570), Isidore (ca. 600), Bede (ca. 700), Otto of Freising (ca. 1150), and Baronius (ca. 1600), reconstructed a history of the Church, purged as much as possible of both apocalyptic and millennial elements.[66] The second time, in the massive revision of modern historiography from Gibbon to Charles Homer Haskins, *secular* historians, determined to push religion into the background of their story, were hardly interested in highlighting religious phenomena that even the ecclesiastical historians considered ridiculous. In both of the "grand

---

[64] Firey, *Contrite Heart*, 145.

[65] Daniels, *Millennialism: An International Bibliography*.

[66] Note the importance of "as much as possible." In cases like Orosius, Gregory of Tours and Otto of Freising, they let in a great deal that they should have kept out.

narratives" of European history to date, therefore, millennialism remains a marginal, insignificant phenomenon.

And despite the current "postmodern" challenge to modernism, and the attempt to reclaim the "religiosities" of a past age, many historians continue to ignore millennialism.[67] Perhaps it reflects too much of a "grand narrative." In any case, both religious and secular historiography seems to gravitate toward the vesperian. Too often, they obscure rather than clarify the history of perhaps the greatest and most tenacious grand narrative of all.

This issue goes deep. The very foundations of Western literate consciousness come in significant part from two of the most profoundly millennial religious cultures in world history—Judaism and Christianity. The faithful of both religions, even more than others, have been subjected to repeated and repeatedly inaccurate apocalyptic prophecies, and both produced profoundly vesperian literary and historiographical traditions. And both began major writing projects in the centuries after what was for both a profoundly apocalyptic century (the first century CE).[68] If, on one level, deconstruction views texts as built upon unavowed silences, then the Western tradition calls out for a millennial deconstruction.[69]

The paradox resides still more intensely in the Christian world, because unlike Judaism, the very religion comes into existence at the height of apocalyptic expectation, from John the Baptist and Jesus' millennial hopes for the imminent arrival of the "kingdom of heaven" on earth, to Paul's expectations of an instantaneous cosmic transformation in "the twinkling of an eye."[70] For Christianity to survive these disappointments without destroying the vital appeal of its foundational promise of imminent, collective redemption meant the development of a discourse of denial—Jesus never made so wrongheaded a claim—that permeates the very mindset of its intellectuals, especially the apologists. As Ernst Käseman put it: "Apocalyptic [disappointment] is the mother of theology."[71] The continued

---

[67] Speigel and Freedman, "Medievalisms Old and New"; Elizabeth A. Clark, *History, Theory, Text: Historians and the Linguistic Turn* (Cambridge, Mass.: Harvard University Press, 2004).

[68] Alan Segal, *Rebecca's Children: Judaism and Christianity in the Roman World* (Cambridge: Harvard University Press, 1984), 1; Yisrael Yuval, *Two Nations in Your Womb: Perceptions of Jews and Christians in Late Antiquity and the Middle Ages* (Berkeley and Los Angeles: University of California Press, 2006).

[69] See above, chapter 1, n. 12. The principle of *différance*, the permanent postponement of a definitive reading, suggests an almost Augustinian asceticism of exegetical restraint in refusing to "finalize the grand narrative." Instead, it seems to have produced scarcely disciplined semiotic arousal.

[70] One could read Moses and the Exodus as a millennial movement, with the narration and laws of the Pentateuch establishing a demotic millennial legislation for a nation of free peasants (see below, chapter 8). In such a reading, the forty years in the desert represent a response to an initial disappointment (God's/Moses') that the Israelites were not ready to go from slavery directly to the Promised Land.

[71] Ernst Käseman, "Die Anfange christlicher Theologie," *Zeitschrift für Kirchengeschichte* 57 (1960): 162–85; see also Florentino García Martínez and Eibert J. C. Tigchelaar, "Is Jewish Apocalyptic the Mother of Christian Theology?" in *Qumranica Minora: Qumran Origins and Apocalypticism* (Leiden: Brill, 2007), 129–52.

hostility to Schweitzer's observations about Jesus' apocalyptic expectations illustrates the taboo nature of the issue, and profound resistance remains characteristic of much even recent, indeed "cutting-edge," analysis of New Testament texts.[72]

It is, however, little wonder that religious historians, scholars committed to preserving the identity of their ecclesiastical communities, tell a story that follows this retrospective voice. They have other agendas, like the preservation of the faith, and the stability of the social order based on their teachings. Thus, those Catholics who would even admit that millennialism sometimes darkened their theological doorstep, treated such occasions as aberrant and minimal, as "Judaizing" infections that did not reflect the true nature of Christianity.[73] All of this shares the same retrospective imposition of meaning that characterizes Whiggish views of evolution[74] and produced a narrative about one "true orthodoxy" in early Christianity that produced many deviant "heresies" (including millennialism).[75]

In this sense, Augustine, as the most powerful anti-apocalyptic, anti-millennial thinker in the Latin Church, founded the dominant school of vesperian historiography for the "middle ages"—that lengthy middle period between the two *Parousiai*, during which the End has not yet come. His insistence that millennialism never had any part of true Christianity and that responsible leaders (clergy) should never espouse apocalyptic beliefs, should never "read" contemporary events by the light of the book of Revelation, dominated ecclesiastical circles. And, since time *always* gave victory to the adherents of this school, the documents composed and preserved for the eight centuries from Augustine to Joachim (ca. 400–1200) seem to confirm his assertion.

Now when Augustine first established the vesperian school of historiography, he did so for *theological* reasons. His reading of the past record reflected an urgent anti-apocalyptic agenda, a rhetorical stance aimed at his unstable contemporaries.[76] He had no interest in a balanced assessment of the past. He and the centuries of theologians, copyists, and archivists who followed in his lead worked diligently to muffle the voice of the roosters in their texts for the sake of the Church, the social order, and the salvation of souls.

---

[72] Paula Fredriksen, "What You See Is What You Get: Context and Content in Current Research on the Historical Jesus," *Theology Today* 52, no.1 (1995): 75–90.

[73] Léon Gry, *Le millénarisme dans ses origines et son développment* (Paris: Alphonse Picard, 1904).

[74] Stephen Jay Gould denounces the ways in which such Whig history informs so much evolutionary thinking (*Wonderful Life: The Brugess Shale and the Nature of History* [New York: W.W. Norton, 1989]), and Robert Wright illustrates just how tempting the trap can be by falling into it (*Nonzero: The Logic of Human Destiny* [New York: Vintage Books, 2001]).

[75] See Walter Bauer's deconstruction of this "orthodox" and retrospective narrative and his proposal that "orthodoxy" was the most successful version of the wide range of products that the early Christian movement generated: *Orthodoxy and Heresy in Earliest Christianity* (Mifflintown, Pa.: Sigler Press, 1996).

[76] On the importance of identifying the rhetorical stance of the writer, see Kenneth Burke, *Attitudes towards History* (London: Editorial Publications, 1937); also Stephen O'Leary, *Arguing the Apocalypse*, 3–20.

Thus Christian historians *by training* ridiculed and despised millennial believers whose work they disliked (and feared); and at the same time, they absolved anyone of stature—a prominent bishop, theologian, ruler, reformer—who might have entertained such forbidden and (eventually) mistaken beliefs, by passing over the details of their rooster phase in silence. The literate elite in Judaism and Islam similarly mistrusted and tried to marginalize the disruptive qualities of apocalyptic beliefs.[77] So anyone consulting an "in-house" history of any of the three most intensely eschatological religions the world has ever known—Judaism, Christianity, and Islam—would find little or no mention of millennialism.

The problem, however, lies less with these religious thinkers whose theological and social agenda is clear and compelling, than with modern "secular" historians, who have no good conceptual reason to affirm, continue, and, in some cases, actively participate in this collective effort by vesperian historians to muffle the sounds of apocalyptic discourse and minimize the role of millennial dreamers. And yet, at the end of the eighteenth century,[78] when a new secular, enlightened historical voice emerged, seeking to rewrite our history and liberate it from these blinkers of religious superstition and slavish adherence to dogmatic demands, the ideological hostility to millennialism and apocalypticism remained strong.

Ironically, however, millennialism became even less prominent in secular narratives.[79] Despite an emerging critical consciousness that submitted all documentation to grave doubts about its surface meaning (dating and identifying forgeries being among the first techniques of the new historiography, and casting off the superstitious dogmas of religion being an axiomatic approach), these new historians accepted the evidence on millennialism at face value. "Few texts, few beliefs," was Ferdinand Lot's formula for rejecting the notion that AD1000 was an apocalyptic date, as if the documentary record were transparent on reality.[80]

It was as if, in rejecting religious superstition, a fortiori they rejected that which even the religious considered foolishness. Certainly the earliest stages of enlightenment thought came within the context of a vigorous, one could even say intolerant

---

[77] For Judaism, see Scholem, *Sabbatai Sevi*, 1–15; for Islam, see David Cook, *Studies in Muslim Apocalyptic* (Princeton, N.J.: Darwin Press, 2002), and below, chapter 14.

[78] For drama's sake, let us take 1776, the year that Smith published his *Wealth of Nations*, and Gibbon his *Decline and Fall*, two works whose historical vision changed our perspective on the workings of time. A decade later, James Hutton's *The Theory of the Earth* (1785–88), which dated the life of planet earth in the millions of years, constitutes the turning point in a new and dramatic shift in historical awareness, of dramatically deepened historical perspective. This is about the time that biblical historiography first begins to explore the documentary hypotheses.

[79] For the phenomenon in general, see Gry, *Le millénarisme*, 118–29; Vincent Ermoni, "Les phases successives de l'erreur millénariste," *Revue des questions historiques* 70 (1901): 353–88. The "pay-off" is most visible in the attack on the romantic's notion of an apocalyptic "year 1000"; see R. Landes, "Historiographical Fear."

[80] Ferdinand Lot, "Le mythe des terreurs de l'an mille," *Mercure de France*, 300 (1947), 647.

pursuit of "reason" and a horror of religious "enthusiasm."[81] Thus millennialism plays virtually no role in the secular recasting of the tale—neither Gibbon's nor Voltaire's.[82] This tendency became even more pronounced in the "scientific" corpus of positivist historiography at the end of the nineteenth century, the matrix of the modern historical profession, and the moment when an apocalyptic year 1000 became a "fable," a "myth," an invention of the fevered brain of "romantic" historians. Vesperian historiography continued to thrive despite secularization, and modern historians are most often Augustinian without knowing it.[83] Indeed, many a modern historian, secular as well as religious, will still say "Amen" to that.[84]

And yet, secularism and the Enlightenment hardly brought on a decrease in apocalyptic activity.[85] On the contrary, apocalyptic conflicts are among the few religious phenomena to survive secularization,[86] indeed develop (mutate into) recognizable and powerful secular forms of millennialism that have dominated the history of the last century—Democracy, Communism, Nazism, Zionism.[87] Ironically, millennialism actually *intensified* with the advent of modernity, since the new *secular* forms took more consistently activist paths precisely because there was no "God" for whose omnipotent intervention one should wait. Hence, "rational" owls and "enthusiastic" roosters continued to fight their rhetorical battles for the heart and soul of the public throughout the eighteenth, nineteenth, and twentieth centuries, and, as the string of successful revolutions indicate, with increasing success for the new mutant form, secular millennialism.[88]

---

[81] On the character of thought in the seventeenth century, see Stephen Toulmin, *Cosmopolis: The Hidden Agenda of Modernity* (Chicago: University of Chicago Press, 1990); on the hostility of the emerging secular and scientific thinkers religious passions, see Ronald Knox, *Enthusiasm: A Chapter in the History of Religion, with Special Reference to the XVII and XVIII Centuries* (Oxford: Clarendon Press, 1962).

[82] Voltaire was especially hostile to millennialism, which he and his enlightenment colleagues labeled "enthusiasm" and "fanaticism" (see Diderot et al., *L'encyclopédie*, q.v.). Gibbon also gives millennial beliefs short shrift—a brief summary that acknowledges millennialism's early importance to Christianity, but then decisively dismisses it: "[Millennialism] appears to have been the reigning sentiment of the orthodox believers; and it seems so well adapted to the desires and apprehensions of mankind, that it must have contributed in a very considerable degree to the progress of the Christian faith. But when the edifice of the church was almost completed, the temporary support was laid aside." (*Decline and Fall*, chapter 15, p. 404).

[83] Landes, "Owls, Roosters, and Apocalyptic Time: A Historical Method for Reading a Refractory Documentation," *Union Seminary Quarterly Review* 49 (1996):165–85.

[84] "Many of us remain unconvinced of the need for such a [this-worldly] transitional episode," John Polkinghorne, *The God of Hope and the End of the World* (New Haven: Yale University Press, 2000), 86–87. See also E. Randolph Daniel, "Medieval Apocalypticism, Millennialism and Violence," *Terrorism and Political Violence* 14 (2002): 292.*

[85] See Weber, *Apocalypses*, 83–147; Katz and Popkin, *Messianic Revolution*; Peter Schäfer and Mark R. Cohen (eds.), *Toward the Millennium: Messianic Expectations from the Bible to Waco* (Boston: Brill, 1998). Below, chapter 8.

[86] Another, directly related religious belief to thrive in both religious and secular forms in the following two centuries is anti-Judaism, something to which both Voltaire and Gibbon contributed.

[87] See below, chapters 10–13. On Zionism, see below, chapter 14.

[88] Katz and Popper, *Messianic Revolution*.

From this perspective, then, the continuity of the vesperian school seems less the product of a genuine indifference to a marginal, even vanishing phenomenon, than the continuation of that the determined silence of owls to a threatening discourse from roosters. And like their religious predecessors, these modern historians sometimes engage more in wishful thinking than historical analysis, a trend particularly noticeable at the advent of 2000: "pas de terreurs en l'an mil; pas de terreurs en l'an 2000."[89] This studied dismissal, and the broad scholarly consensus it rallied behind it, may explain some of the difficulty French and other Western intellectuals have had in confronting the phenomenon of apocalyptic Islam in the decade after 2000.[90]

To some extent, the poverty of mainstream thought about millennialism may derive from a lack of familiarity with the phenomenon. In that case, I think this book can help. Perhaps, with a greater understanding of how rich the tale of the long and winding road from apocalyptic episode through disappointment to strategies for re-entry into normal time and the founding of more stable and enduring forms of social organization, we can better analyze those phenomena we all agree deserve our attention. But for those who will not entertain this approach, even as a working hypothesis, I can only hope that the range of incidents I present below over time and space, outside of Christian and Jewish orbits, can overcome some of the resistance.

---

[89] Landes, "Historiographical Fear."
[90] See below, chapter 14.

PART TWO

Tribal Millennialism

4 Suicidal Millennialism

Xhosa Cattle-Slaying (1856–1857 CE)

In the spring of 1856 in what is today South Africa, an orphan girl of about fifteen from the tribe of the amaXhosa named Nongqawuse went to the fields to work with her uncle's sister-in-law, Nombanda, a girl of eight. According to her own account, strangers approached her, claiming to be dead ancestors who came with a conditional promise: if the Xhosa would slay all their cattle, destroy their grain stores, cease planting crops, and purify themselves of all witchcraft, a great day would dawn when the British would vanish from the land and the ancestors would live again, bringing with them new and more plentiful cattle and grain. Then would the Xhosa live again in peace and prosperity.[1]

Those to whom she reported this prophecy of terrible hope at first responded with skepticism. But her uncle and guardian, himself a soothsayer in the tribal tradition and a man who had spent time with Christians, took up her claims and swiftly won over large numbers of believers from many of the Xhosa tribes. When the anticipated date of the alleged return passed without any sign of fulfillment, Nongqawuse and her uncle insisted that the failure stemmed from an imperfect fulfillment of the demands: the tribesmen had not slain *all* the cattle, and had even sold many for profit.

So believers undertook an even more bloody slaughter that not only wiped out their own stocks, but also put enormous pressure on those who did not believe Nongqawuse's millennial prophecy to kill their cattle as well. Each subsequent disappointment led to a greater slaughter of cattle until, when it was all over, according to some estimates, the Xhosa had killed some half a million cattle. By the end of 1857, some thirty thousand to fifty thousand Xhosa had starved; the British had herded many others into labor camps; white settlers took over and cleared more-land; and the colonial authorities had either sent Xhosa chiefs to prison on Robben Island or broken them to British rule.

How can we understand this self-inflicted catastrophe? Why did not or could not people stop the madness before it did so much damage? Why did Nongqawuse's many detractors fail to discredit her after the first or second failures of her ridiculous prophetic promises? Can we pronounce on such terrible developments without exploring what Freud called *thanatos*, or the "death

---

[1] The only extant scholarly monograph on the Xhosa Cattle-Slaying is J. B. Peires, *The Dead Will Arise: Nongqawuse and the Great Xhosa Cattle-Killing Movement of 1856–7* (Johannesburg: Ravan, 1989), recently critiqued by several contributors to Chris Andreas, Sheila Boniface Davies, and Andrew Offenburger, eds., "The Xhosa Cattle-Killing," *African Studies* 67, no.2 (2008).

instinct"?[2] And can this self-inflicted tragedy tell us anything about our own world and our way of dealing with its problems?

For the Xhosa unbelievers (the *amagogotya*), a British plot lay behind this madness and was designed to destroy the Xhosa. For the British, the Xhosa warrior chiefs plotted to make their people so utterly desperate with this prophecy that they would attack the British troops and drive them out. Both read it wrong, each according to the desires and fears of their hearts, each as conspiracies of malevolent men, much like themselves.[3] The prophecies, however, were not conspiratorial deceits, but sincere beliefs, and those who embraced them did so with full heart and great rejoicing. And it was the logic of their commitment that explains the dynamic of the movement. In order to understand how this could happen, we need to explore the mindset of apocalyptic millennialism. As the biographer of Lord Grey, the British governor of the province at the time, put it: "She uprose, a dark but comely Maid of Orleans, a Messiah to her people and her message swept Kaffraria like a wind."[4]

With the advent of Nongqawuse's prophecy, the dominant public voice embraced prophecies of an imminent and utter transformation of the workings of this world. In the "apocalyptic moment" created by such anticipation, the majority of people, including some of the most powerful and influential among the great clans, slaughtered all their cattle and ceased to plant their crops in order to bring on a new, transformed world—the *millennium*, or the messianic kingdom. This means that for some critical period of time—in this case over a year—the majority of people believed in and acted according to the conviction that they stood at the vortex of cosmic salvation. And in this case, these unhappy Xhosa undertook a terrifying act of cultural self-mutilation. Anyone reading the account of their hopes and deeds cannot escape a feeling of immense sadness.

In order to approach such a phenomenon—whose full depths I think scholars should have the modesty not to pretend to understand in any set manner—we need to understand why and how the prophecy might have made sense to Nongqawuse's listeners. What was it in her rhetoric that persuaded them to the radical, indeed shocking, promises of a clearly disturbed (disheveled, sick) young girl. From an understanding of that nexus, we can begin to trace the lineaments of

---

[2] The staggering slaughters of the European armies during World War I, the "Great War," forced Freud to identify this counterintuitive instinct. The participants of that war also responded to disappointment by increasing their self-destructive behavior, in this case for a four-year period at the loss of millions of lives. Freud first advanced it as a hypothesis in *Beyond the Pleasure Principle* (1920), and developed it further in *Civilization and Its Discontents* (1930). It was one of the least accepted of his ideas even among his disciples. See the discussion in Frank Sulloway, *Freud: Biologist of the Mind: Beyond the Psychoanalytic Legend* (Cambridge Ma.: Harvard University Press, 1992), chapter 11.

[3] J. P. Peires, "The Late Great Plot: The Official Delusion Concerning the Xhosa Cattle Killing, 1856–1857," *History in Africa* 12 (1953): 253–79.

[4] James Milne, *The Romance of a Pro-Consul: Being the Personal Life and Memoirs of the Right Hon. Sir George Grey, K.C.B.* (London: Thomas Nelson & Sons, 1911), chap. 13.

the apocalyptic moment that this prophecy created, and the dynamics of the inevitable disappointment that followed.

▪ CULTURAL ORIGINS OF THE CATTLE-SLAYING PROPHECY

The tale of the Cattle-Slaying becomes slightly less incomprehensible when we understand it as a particularly dramatic response to a larger situation. Like so many other millennial movements, the Xhosa here reflect a characteristic tribal response to the brutal incursions of European imperialism. For more than a century, the British had carried on a war against the Xhosa and adjoining tribes, seeking either to break them up or subject them. The Xhosa had put up vigorous military resistance, some of it led by prophets, including one great warrior messiah who like his Chinese contemporary, Hong Xiuquan of the Taiping (The Great Peace), thought he was Jesus' younger brother and promised his warriors magical protections from the weapons of the white man.[5]

In the previous decade, the struggle had become especially nasty, and the Xhosa had taken to the Amathole Mountains, carrying on a guerilla campaign that stymied the efforts of the British commander, Harry Smith who retired in disgrace. His replacement, Sir George Grey, had earned his stripes in some ruthless campaigns in South Australia and New Zealand and had no intention of allowing humane policies toward the enemies of the crown to tarnish his reputation for victory, even as he nominally espoused principles of freedom and dignity for the indigenous tribes.[6] Along with his commander, Lieutenant-Colonel William Eyre, he carried out a campaign that struck not just at the warriors who fought against British dominion, but at their homesteads, their women, and their goods. As one historian noted dryly, Grey "applied his 'civilization' policy with a rigour untempered by sympathetic restraint," determined to wrench the Xhosa from the "idle vagabond pastoral life" and teach them the "habits of industry."[7]

Grey's campaign, which by modern standards would readily earn the epithets of ethnic cleansing and racist genocide, proved far more effective than his predecessor's civility. An increasing number of Xhosa chiefs found themselves forced to submit to his exacting conditions in order to save their tribes from extinction. The resulting "settlement" involved the death of many and the domesticating of most tribal leaders, lost land, displaced populations, and the inability to resist. The "old ways" of military resistance no longer worked, however intolerable the new.

---

[5] On the previous Xhosa millennial movements, see J. B. Peires, "Nxele, Ntsikana and the Origins of the Xhosa Religious Reaction," *Journal of African History* 20, no. 1 (1979): 51–61; Brian Wilson, *Magic and the Millennium*, 236–38; on the Taiping, see below, chap. 7.

[6] See James Gump, "The Imperialism of Cultural Assimilation: Sir George Grey's Encounter with the Maori and the Xhosa, 1845–1868," *Journal of World History* 9, no.1 (1998): 89–108, esp. 97–101.

[7] Peires, *Dead Will Arise*, 55; Gump, "Imperialism," 98.

In addition to the political crisis, a series of natural disasters had struck at the material well-being of the Xhosa people: a severe drought began in 1850; a blight struck the roots of their cereal crop; and worst of all, a terrible plague, first brought from Holland in 1853, devastated their cattle. This last disaster had a particularly demoralizing effect. Cattle played an essential role in Xhosa culture, defining wealth, fixing dowry price—the very definition of power and prestige.[8] To the Xhosa, these misfortunes were the product of some invisible force wreaking havoc in the Xhosa's system of values. And traditional sacrifice stood helpless before this onslaught.

The Xhosa attitude toward their cattle went well beyond mere material interests. They knew their beasts personally and treated them with great care and respect. The plague, therefore, was particularly cruel, since it killed them with a slow, excruciating death that had them literally starving on their feet, unable to eat, scarcely able to breathe, living bags of skin and bones. Such death—also a "gift" from the English as far as the Xhosa knew—served as a terrifying symbol of the looming death of their culture. If, as Steven O'Leary put it, the first task of the apocalyptic prophets is to convince those to whom they preach that *now* evil rules the world as *never before*,[9] then Nongqawuse and any of the numerous other "prophets" of the time had little problem accomplishing the first step. All the signs of the times pointed in the same direction.

Nor did Nongqawuse appear out of nowhere. Xhosa culture had already experienced a number of prophetic figures and millennial movements, some of them classic uprisings whose leaders promised the natives that they would be immune to the white man's bullets.[10] And in addition to warrior prophets, Xhosa culture accepted the notion that young girls might indeed have a privileged relationship with the ancestors. Her prophetic message, although more extreme than earlier ones, took up well-established themes, including the sacrificial killing of cattle and the return of the ancestors.[11]

So when Nongqawuse first offered her prophetic solution, it struck at least some people as the key to an unanswerable and agonizing dilemma. Everywhere death loomed, every path to survival seemed blocked, and she opened a path to far more than mere survival. Her prophecy promised the elimination of the British oppressors and social redemption—a great age of messianic abundance, rejoicing, and fellowship. The dead would return in a great new age of restored bounty—the

---

[8] This was also true of the Germanic tribes of early medieval Europe, whence we get the term *capital* from the Latin *capita* or head (pl.) [of cattle].

[9] O'Leary, *Arguing the Apocalypse*, 34–44

[10] Peires, "Nxele, Ntsikana and the Origins." On the belief that millennial incantations would render warriors immune to the enemies weapons, which we find also among the New Zealand Maori, the Chinese Boxers, the Native American Ghost Dance, just to name a few; see Wilson, *Magic and the Millennium*, 221–71 passim, and Kenelm Burridge, *New Heaven, New Earth*, 15–22, and next chapter.

[11] J. B. Peires, "The Central Beliefs of the Xhosa Cattle-Killing," *Journal of African History* 28 (1987): 43–63.

millennial kingdom. And although the cost of the demanded purification was high, the reward was even greater. Believers dreamed of a world before the white invaders had come and destroyed the great age that was. They were millennial restorationists.[12]

The apocalyptic sacrifice also has its logic. Like most religions, Xhosa beliefs centered around the notion of giving in order to receive (what the Romans called *do ut des*), and in such a crisis, the more extravagant the gift, the greater the reward. Indeed, like so many millennial prophecies, this indigenous one combined aspects of local beliefs with the narrative of biblical apocalyptic theodicy in which justice prevails throughout the world. It projected that local narrative onto a cosmic stage. As one of the survivors of the Cattle-Slaying, William Philip, commented: "When, therefore, the girl spoke of the rising up, she was [merely] setting a spark to things that were already known concerning the ancestors."[13]

Nor did this moral vision about redemption engage in pure self-pity, with its corollary of blaming the other alone (here, the white man) for the punishing reality in which the Xhosa found themselves. Part of Nongqawuse's prophetic teachings demanded that the Xhosa purify themselves from their own evil inclinations, including eliminating witchcraft, a longstanding social problem that the believers acknowledged had defiled them, their culture, and the very crops they planted and cattle they bred. Nongqawuse was one of the *amathamba*, one of the "soft" ones—generous, open souls, who shared, who "allowed in." These were the people who received the visions, the people who retained their solidarity with their tribe and its ways.

Her most vocal opponents came from the ranks of the *amagogotya*, the "hard ones," the closed, individualistic, stingy, calculating souls, those who most frequented the white man and adopted his ways. It was the spread of such narrow and selfish calculation—that "greed" that Adam Smith had assured his readers three generations earlier actually served the collective good through the workings of an "invisible hand"—that had poisoned Xhosa culture from within. The cattle and grain are blighted, said the "soft ones," because we Xhosa are a defiled culture. In a sense, the sacrifice represented a collective atonement for the Xhosas' own sins, sins which currently prevented them from moving the forces of the cosmos (here, the ancestors) to act in their favor. And the two corrupting forces that Nongqawuse's teachings targeted for purging were the malevolent traditions from within, Xhosa witchcraft (envy), and from without, British-inspired selfishness.

Upon completing this great sacrifice and purge, the Xhosa's role in the apocalyptic drama would come to a close. From there on, Nongqawuse promised, the Xhosa would become the beneficiaries of everything to follow: the ancestors would return—the dead would rise—with abundant and healthy cattle and grain, the British would vanish into the sea whence they came, and everyone would celebrate

---

[12] See above, chapter 1; Wilson, *Magic and the Millennium*, 238–40.
[13] Peires, "Central Beliefs," 52.

the best of the old world of feasting and sharing, all at the prime of their vigor, all delighting together. Like the Ghost Dancers who believed that the earth would shed the white man like a snake sheds a skin and restore the lost perfect world, they believed they would achieve the great abundance of a peaceful and just society.[14] Their apocalyptic scenario moved from active cataclysmic—we destroy our goods—to passive transformative—the ancestors bring the millennium.

■ RECONSTRUCTING THE COURSE OF THE PROPHECY: APOCALYPTIC TIME AND DOCUMENTATION

But we must beware of leaning too heavily on a set depiction of Nongqawuse's teaching. Apocalyptic prophets notoriously shape their message to their audiences (and vice-versa), and not necessarily cynically. Their charisma resides not in them, but in their ability to arouse others, and almost invariably (at least in the cases where documentation preserves details) they follow the gravitational pull of the messianic wave, in which the enthusiasm they generate demonstrates the truth of the prophecy. From the beginning, then, apocalyptic discourse changes constantly, and in particular, after the inevitable disappointment, prophets improvise so much, so rapidly—apocalyptic jazz—that one should never take any recorded articulations as anything more than the record of a stage in a complex, ever-accelerating journey.

Since all our insider accounts of the event, including the oral accounts the British wrote down, came from after the failure—*ex post defectu*—they inevitably contain a retrospective quality that shapes all their information with the hindsight of skeptics back in the saddle. One historian criticized the bias of the texts as well as the historians working them:

> [S]tate records supply the backbone of most scholarly accounts. With monotonous regularity, footnotes cite Government House documents, Colonial Office documents, British Kaffrarian documents, Imperial Blue Books discussing "Kaffir Tribes." That is, historians of African peasants [sic] have relied heavily upon Englishmen paid to further the interests of the British empire, who wrote texts in an alien tongue, organised them under western categories, and denigrated a movement seeking to sweep them off the face of the earth. Not surprisingly, scholarly narratives and state archives often share concepts, content, conclusions.[15]

---

[14] On the Ghost Dance, see Wilson, *Magic and the Millennium*, 283–306; Shelley Anne Osterreich, *The American Indian Ghost Dance, 1870 and 1890* (New York: Greenwood Press, 1991). For an original meditation on millennialism starting from an examination of the Ghost Dance, see Weston La Barre, *The Ghost Dance: Origins of Religion* (Prospect Heights, Ill.: Waveland Press, 1990) and below, n. 17.

[15] Helen Bradford, "Akukho Ntaka Inokubhabha Ngephiko Elinye (No Bird Can Fly on One Wing): The 'Cattle-Killing Delusion' and Black Intellectuals, c. 1840–1910," *African Studies* 67, no. 2 (2008): 209–32. Bradford cites a whole school of "orientalist" critiques of both the imperialist nature of the primary sources and the gender bias of the secondary sources. See Jeff Guy, "A Landmark, Not a Breakthrough," *South African Historical Journal* 25 (1991): 227–31.

The later work of the Christian William W. Gqoba represents the only text from a Xhosa.[16] As historians, we must consider these hostile post-mortem accounts as minimally reliable in the basics, and doubtful in the specifics, especially the details of sequence. The British sources in this case do provide us with some accounts from before the collapse of the prophecy, including some relatively empathic accounts.[17] But most of these accounts come from uncomprehending outsiders, and while they may offer valuable access to voices, they tell us at least as much about the mental world of the observer as of the observed. The English, for example, were in the grip of a revealing (if characteristic) paranoia, with which they built their own narrative of the "chief's plot."[18] Vesperian and orientalist discourse compounded each others tendencies to produce narratives that have offended, indeed "aroused the ire" of native historians.[19]

Roosters and the Creation of a Xhosa Apocalyptic Moment

To get an idea of how the movement played itself out, then, we must plot its path through this terrifyingly exhilarating experience of repeated waves of soaring hope and crushing despair, as intense as they were brief…the briefer, the more intense. The real issue in such cases, however, concerns not the actual message (which will mutate significantly over the brief but powerful period of its public dominance), but what permits the prophecy to spread first from the solitary visionary to a group of believers, and from there to wider public discourse.

Most apocalyptic discourse dies out long before it reaches that stage. And skeptics are too determinedly hostile to allow any to last long if they can possibly repress them. But in some rare cases, the opposite occurs: an apocalyptic prophecy *gains support* by entering public space, and then a path from the margins to the center opens up. This is what happened with Nongqawuse and her uncle Mhlakaza, and in all the subsequent movements we will study in this book.

When Nongqawuse began to prophesy, she had help. Her friend and relative, the eight-year-old Nombanda, echoed and confirmed her claims, and both received powerful amplification from her enthusiastic uncle Mhlakaza, whose appetite for

---

[16] W.W. G[qoba], "Isizatu Sokuxelwa Kwe Nkomo Ngo Nongqause," *Isigidimi Samaxosa* no. 1, 2 (March, April, 1888), 22–23, 29–31; an abridged translation is available from A.C. Jordan, *Towards an African Literature: The Emergence of Literary Form in Xhosa* (Berkeley and Los Angeles: University of California Press, 1974), 70–75. On the value of this text, see Bradford, "Akukho."

[17] The empathy of modern anthropology first appears at the level of scholarship with James Mooney's reports on the millennial Ghost Dance: *The Ghost Dance Religion and Wounded Knee* (New York: Dover, 1896).

[18] On the "paranoid imperative," see below, chapter 8. On the "Chief's Plot," see Peires, "Late Great Plot" and Bradford, who blames belief in this *after* the event for most of the inadequate, British-inspired historiography on this episode ("Akukho").

[19] N. Mndende, "The Prophecy of Nongqawuse: A White Man's Lie About the Xhosa Cattle Killing—1856–57," Seminar Paper presented May 8, 1997, University of Cape Town, cited in Bradford, "Akhuko."

preaching had been much whetted by his time with the missionaries.[20] As a result, they rapidly gained entry into public space and, we know from subsequent evidence, won a significant following. Eventually chiefs, even the biggest, Sarhili, became active believers. Sarhili's adherence probably came after enthusiasm had already spread bottom-up. Political forces rarely side with subversive apocalyptic prophecies that have not first excited enthusiasm among the larger population, especially in the case of self-mutilating prophecies.

The Loosening of Normal Time's Grip and Semiotic Arousal

Apocalyptic time first begins when the shape of "normal time" falls apart. The relentless British oppression, generation after generation—sometimes with a relatively kind face, sometimes with unimaginable barbarity, always through the missionaries with their messianic discourse—guaranteed that at some point, the normal world of the Xhosa would crack irreparably and their cultural mazeway through reality collapse.[21] It is not by accident that the Christian elements in Nongqawuse's prophecy identified the British as the party of Satan. There is also another *inkosi*, riding a grey horse, his name is the Grey One, otherwise known as Satan. And everyone who did not slaughter his cattle would become Satan's own subject. . . .[22]

Anyone in Xhosaland after the last colonial war six years earlier had to ask himself what precarious future held for the Xhosa. Notes Bradford, "What was remarkable about these times was not the 'Cattle-Killing delusion,' but the unleashing of horsemen of the apocalypse."[23]

Such a situation created the necessary preconditions for an irruption into public space of a millennial dream, one that actually created apocalyptic time. In its earliest phase, when public discourse has no answer to the devastating problems that face everyone, when the owls have no solutions, the air is pregnant with speech, signs, wonders reported and believed. Rumors fly—the most exciting and unlikely things, enthusiastically repeated. This condition, which the prophetic message inflames still further, constitutes a kind of semiotic arousal, in which all things

---

[20] On Mhlakaza, see Peires, who tracks down his extensive relationships with Christian missionaries and his failed attempts to "make it" in the world of Christian preaching (*Dead Will Rise*, 33–6).

[21] For a novelesque rendition of the kinds of pressures under which African cultures operated with the advent of Western imperialism, see Achebe, *Things Fall Apart* (Nairobi: East African Publishing House, 1973). The expression "mazeway" comes from Anthony Wallace, and refers to the way a given culture navigates its relationship with the external world through culture. The breakdown of a mazeway often triggers what Wallace calls "revitalization movements" (which, in terms of this book, represent an active, largely transformational, millennialism): *Revitalizations and Mazeways: Essays on Culture Change* (Omaha: University of Nebraska Press, 2003).

[22] G[qoba], "Isizatu," 22.

[23] Bradford, "Akukho."

become signs, messages that we either fail to understand or, with salvation's message, that confirm the prophecy. Nothing in this state of arousal can be merely coincidental. The tiniest occurrence must be "read"; everything has meaning. For those who fail to understand, the times are confused. For those who understand, they are apocalyptic.

In the case of Nongqawuse, one of the key rumors tells us much about the feelings of the Xhosa after the previous, disastrous war. The news arrived (interesting to imagine the possible lines of transmission[24]) from the Crimean warfront that in November 1854, the Russians had killed General Cathcart, slayer of the last great Xhosa prophet, Mlanjeni. The news understandably rejoiced Xhosa hearts—someone had taken vengeance for them. But they took it much further.

The Xhosa version differed from the news that came from abroad. The Russians who had killed Cathcart were Europeans whom the British were defeating despite Cathcart's folly.[25] But in the fiercely proud and deeply humiliated soul of the Xhosa warrior, such an act was no mere coincidence. In the local rumor-mill, the Russians were not whites at all, but the spirits of resurrected Xhosa warriors; and they were not going down to defeat, but rather driving the British from Crimea and heading down to help their people in Xhosaland, land of prophecies and of redemption.

Such dreams of celestial role in worldwide battle appears in the visionary narratives of many cultures from which we have literature, including accounts of oral cultures. In this case, the Xhosa showed that they were ready to think on a global scale. And their misinterpretation tells us how eagerly this people consumed the rhetoric of tribal battle and honor revenged, even—especially!—in their millennial fantasies. Indeed, their apocalyptic fantasies invited them to project their hearts' desires on this emerging global community that, under British lead, Europeans were creating as they carved out their dominion over the rest of the globe. For them, wherever the British were defeated, the Xhosa were fighting against them.

Take-Off: A Rooster Crows and the People Awake

However semiotically aroused people may get, we still do not have enough for a millennial movement to take hold. For a full-fledged episode of apocalyptic time to occur a visionary must convincingly announce the apocalyptic path that will lead this generation to the millennial goal. This, of course, is no easy process, since the prophet must overcome the innate common sense of most people:[26] owls are a majority most of the time. And since the very threat of an apocalyptic voice in public space brings down heavy punishments, the hostility of owls intensifies

---

[24] One path may have been through orderlies in a hospital.

[25] Apparently, he wandered into the midst of the Russian army and found himself dead shortly after dryly remarking, "I fear we are in a mess."

[26] See Jeff Peires, "'Soft' Believers and 'Hard' Unbelievers in the Xhosa Cattle-Killing," *Journal of African History* 27 (1986): 443–61.

especially at times of semiotic arousal. Despite such immense odds, every once in a while, a rooster's prophecy "catches," and a mighty apocalyptic wind begins to blow scattering the owls' hoots of caution like chaff.

Here in Xhosaland, we find many of the classic features. We have ample prior evidence of a millennial dream (that would rid them of the British) in the range of the apocalyptic revolts it had produced in earlier wars. Probably each of the eight wars against the British started with an apocalyptic prophet-warrior.[27] The millennial dream itself had the widest appeal. It promised a world where all people rejoice. A world where the good would enjoy the delights of the messianic age, and the wicked would suffer the punishment they so richly deserve. A world of honor and integrity restored, of the victory of the just.

Above all, such a prophecy flies on the wings of a great hope: those who join will earn the great prize—all of them.

> Nongqawuse said that nobody would ever lead a troubled life. People would get whatever they wanted. Everything would be available in abundance.[28]
>
> All the people who have not arms and legs will have them restored, the blind people will also see, and the old people would become young.
>
> There would rise cattle, horses, sheep, goats, dogs, fowl and every other animal that was wanted and all clothes and everything they would wish for to eat the same as English people eat, and all kinds of things for their houses would all come out of the ground.

In these allusions to British well-being, one finds the same sentiments that produced the cargo cults of the Pacific southwest, where natives conceived of the millennium in terms of cargo, like the that coming to the whites, landing for the natives. Obviously there are significant differences between the Xhosa path and the cargo cults', between "we must undergo an immense self-sacrifice and then we will receive the restored agricultural plenty" and "we must carry out certain rituals and we will have the wealth and mastery of the white men." But they both share the same crisis (culture collision) and the same millennial framework of response (acquire the white man's abundance).[29]

But with every promise must come a path to its realization. In Nongqawuse's case, as we have seen, the price was steep. To join the movement, players must burn bridges, in this case the most precious good of the culture (and eventually every last bit of food). From the perspective of an owl, this was a mad fool's gamble. No matter how badly the disease had hit, there remained great herds of cattle (well over half a million), and no matter how bad the famine, there remained food and further planting seasons. Nongqawuse's call demanded a dramatic, public

---

[27] See Peires, "Origins of the Xhosa Religious Reaction"; Peires, *The House of Phalo: A History of the Xhosa People in the Days of Their Independence* (Johannesburg: Ravan Press, 1981).

[28] Peires, *Dead Will Arise*, 80 n. 6.

[29] For further discussion of the cargo cults and the ghost dances of the tribal world, see below, chapter 5.

act of self-mutilation as the price of entry. Radical sacrifice was the ticket to the new kingdom.

But there was more. Nongqawuse had something to say about a long-standing custom among the Xhosa, namely witchcraft. Witchcraft narratives readily transform into apocalyptic narratives. They inhabit the zero-sum landscape of the wars between good and evil. In many millennial scenarios (especially demotic ones), those who will inhabit the kingdom to come (the "saints" or elect) renounce the evil acts of witchcraft. This attack on witches, however, suggests that the prophecy is not "merely" based on an innocent Xhosa beset by evil British. There were problems within Xhosa society that those who wished to bring back the good old days must also address, internal rot manifested externally in the terrifying cattle and grain diseases that devastated their very lives. And among the culprits Nongqawuse fingered was the malevolent, envious, zero-sum world of magic. As with so many apocalyptic ironies, this concern with malevolent witchcraft ends up being one of the great moral failings of the movement: it would turn zero-sum malevolence into negative-sum rage.

The Movement in Its Public Success

Although the movement reached its greatest strength with the support of the Xhosa chiefs, it would be a mistake to take so important a victory for granted. Few such movements reach "court" unless they already have aroused notable public enthusiasm. And even fewer succeed with their messages in court unless they have that popular support.[30] The first successes for the prophecy came quickly for the young visionary who showed so much talent in a highly prized art of *amathamba*, of ridding oneself of personal concern and opening oneself to the spirits. Her prophecy was embraced by a wide range of people, some of whom flocked to her residence near the mouth of the Gxarha River to learn more of her teachings. There they not only met Nongqawuse and her uncle, but also Nombanda, Nongqawuse's younger relative, also a prophet of the movement.

Apparently, as the quotes above about the imminent "good news" indicate, people were eager for her promises, and once they had accepted them, they entered by anticipation into the community of the saved. Mda's novel catches this feeling beautifully:

> People were beginning to gather from all directions. Others had already camped at the banks of the Gxarha River. They had been there for many days, listening to Nongqawuse, who was still seeing the Strangers almost every day. Sometimes she would be overwhelmed by the spirit so much that she got sick. Then Mhlakaza would take over and make his pronouncements. But the favorite of the people, and even of the chiefs, was

[30] Most apocalyptic scenarios that circulate in courts tend to be paranoid, conspiracy-driven catastrophes.

young Nombanda, who talked so sweetly of the beautiful life that awaited those who carried out the instructions of the Strangers.[31]

Despite the popularity of Nombada's pleasing rhetoric, the key figure in this success was Nongqawuse's uncle, Mhlakaza, a known diviner within his own culture, and a frustrated but knowledgeable preacher within the Christian world as well.[32] He published the news, visited the chiefs and convinced Sarhili, the great king, to visit Nongqawuse. Mhlakaza preached the new way to the crowds and interpreted the visionary's mysterious sayings. In a sense, he created the movement from his niece Nongqawuse's visions. Visionary females who shape the inner community and males who mediate with the outside world is not uncommon.[33]

The movement flew on wings of rumor. As we have seen, the British had been defeated in the Crimea by the Xhosa ancestors who were on their way to Xhosaland to help defeat them there. Reflecting an observable pattern of apocalyptic waves coming in (at least two) successive generations, this excited reading of history reopened apocalyptic time from earlier failures decades earlier, and the prophetic voice of Nongqawuse resonated against the very contours of the cosmos.

Rumors sustained the movement at every step of its career. The *amathamba* had entered a stage of such semiotic arousal that people saw the cattle coming everywhere, heard them below ground, across the sea, in the reeds by the river bed. All nature vibrated with the sounds of revitalization and redemption.

> Tidings of the marvellous sights witnessed near Mhlakaza's village filled the country. The horns of oxen were said to be peeping from beneath the rushes that grew round a swampy pool near the village of the seer; and from a subterranean cave were heard the bellowing and knocking of the horns of cattle impatient to rise.... There were those who said they had actually seen the risen heroes emerge from the Indian Ocean, some on foot, some on horseback, passing in silent parade before them, then sinking again among the tossing of the restless waves. Sometimes they were seen rushing through the air in a wild chase as of old. Then again they were marshaled in battle array....[34]

And Nongqawuse made extensive use of this semiotic arousal in her dealings with believers. We have an account of a visit of a group of chiefs and advisors—the guardians of public space and discourse, in which she took them on what we today would call a guided meditation:

> They heard the crashing of great stones breaking off the cliffs overlooking the headwaters of the River Kamanga, whereupon the men gazed at one another wondering. They were seized with dread...While they stood wondering, the girl was heard saying, "Cast

[31] Zakes Mda, *The Heart of Redness* (Oxford: Oxford University Press, 2000), 78.

[32] Peires, *Dead Will Arise*, 33–36.

[33] I speak here of an active agent spreading the movement, no matter what the gender (see Moshe Idel, *Messianic Mystics* [New Haven, Conn.: Yale University Press, 1998]).

[34] Peires, *Dead Will Arise*, 94.

your eyes in the direction of the sea." And when they looked intently at the waters of the sea, it seemed as if there were in truth people there. There was the bellowing of bulls and oxen, and there was a black mass coming and going, coming and going until it disappeared over the horizon, there in the waters of the sea. Then the people began to believe.[35]

The apocalyptic vision can work as a drug, drawing people into the crucible of belief based on pure wish-fulfillment, hallucinated wish-fulfillment. The vision, even as it recedes from sight, by the mere (very) experience of it, the memory of intensity, affirms belief.

Burning Bridges and Speaking Hidden Transcripts Aloud

One of the key dynamics of the apocalyptic gamble involves the burning of bridges. Because the present world so teems with evil, because evil so dominates and corrupts people at all levels of society with its mimetic power, the true believer must demonstrate dramatically and publicly his or her breaking loose from the mind-forged manacles of "normal time" and its capitulation to evil. The more dramatic the gesture, the more thorough the transformation. The *amathambas*, perhaps because they were *collectively* sacrificing their cattle, made their native (organic) communities also apocalyptic (saved) communities. By breaking with the "public transcripts" of the dominant culture, they committed fully to the new community, where they found a new and far more intense intimacy and intensity.

Charles Brownlee, the commissioner of the Ngqika Xhosa, wrote, "The people are led by a strange infatuation. In the midst of their ruin they are happy and contented and in the confidence of the fulfillment of their expectations they now no longer make a secret of what was at first so carefully concealed."[36] On the wings of deep conviction, the apocalyptic belief has entered into public space and begun to affect the public transcript, that is, the relations of submission and obedience that keep public life relatively predictable.[37] Major Gawler, a particularly disliked magistrate in one region, found that the local chief, now a believer, had visibly changed: "His formerly dull and frequently sullen and uncivil demeanor towards me has lately changed. He is now very civil, high-spirited, and witty."[38]

In the Xhosa movement, apocalyptic time did not bring on violence because the aggression was entirely—to the British, unbelievably—directed against the believers themselves. Formerly angry and depressed Xhosa, especially the chiefs, could speak their minds with the British, not because they wanted to provoke

---

[35] Peires, *Dead Will Arise*, 88, n. 21.

[36] Peires, *Dead Will Arise*, 145. The Ngqika Xhosa were led by Sandile, a powerful chief who remained on the fence as long as he could, but whose people largely supported the movement.

[37] James C. Scott, *Domination and the Arts of Resistance* (New Haven, Conn.: Yale University Press, 1989), 206–12.

[38] Peires, *Dead Will Arise*, 145.

anger, but because they felt they now had a secret—the return of the ancestors—which made British dominion imminently a thing of the past. They could afford banter precisely because they savored the coming humiliation of their enemies. They felt no need for anger or violence because everything would happen while they watched. They could see the burning coals to be heaped on British heads (Romans. 20:12).

Social and Gender Composition of the Movement

It is always hard to assess the motivations for adherence to millennial prophecies. The general distribution tends to favor a rough split along hierarchical lines. Those with more power, more investment in "the world" and public space tend to dislike prophecies that claim that their world of dominion is "about to pass away," whereas those who bear the greater burden of the world's stigmatized tasks and duties—manual laborers—tend to favor them. Thus the poor, the dispossessed, women, and educated people who feel they should run the world but do not, form an important component of almost all these millennial movements. After all, adherence to the prophecy, observance of its moral injunctions, offered believers a tremendous promotion. At the very least, they acceded to a life of honest labor where neighbors could enjoy sharing the world's abundance in peace, and previously haughty aristocrats had to put their backs to the plough. In some more hierarchical versions, they would receive a special kingship over the world with slaves to command. Such generalizations, in the case of the Xhosa, seem to work, although, as with all millennial movements, exceptions abound.

Brownlee noted early on that the "the movement seems peculiarly to have been one of the common people," and a missionary named Bryce Ross reported that "when the people are reminded that their chiefs disapprove of this work, their answer is that they don't care for their chiefs."[39] One of the characteristic appeals of apocalyptic prophecies derives from the vast range it gives to insubordinate behavior. When one is convinced that the immediate future will bring a radical reversal of fortunes, then much of the inhibitions that normally restrain inferiors from defying their superiors—the threat of *eventual* punishment—vanishes.[40]

But these movements are not purely "materialistic," limited to the poor and the meek. They can also recruit members among those who should, by this principle, be most opposed—elders, the powerful, the rich, men, fathers, older brothers. Indeed, people from such authoritarian circles—alpha males—join, sometimes

---

[39] Ibid., 176, n. 101.

[40] The highway police in Montana stopped several of Clare Prophet's disciples going up there from Los Angeles at her apocalyptic call, and recall how when they were informed of their court date, laughed happily because it was after the world, according to their prophet, would no longer exist. Ron Harris, "Sect Members Flock to Bomb Shelters, Ready for a Holocaust," *Los Angeles Times*, March 15, 1990, 3.

showing remarkable docility in their relationship with women prophets. And, just as we find roosters among the dominant, so we find owls among the subordinate. Sometimes it was a son who tried to stop his father from killing the cattle, or a woman who urged her husband to join her in planting, although more often, it seems, the reverse held true. While apocalyptic prophecies may follow observable patterns of social behavior, at their core lie some attractions whose working on the human psyche takes place at a radically individual level. Too much of what leads the millennial believer to enter apocalyptic time relates to forces beyond our grasp, that any effort to "explain it" is tentative at best. The factors involved are perhaps best grasped with the use of chaos theory.[41]

Women played a prominent role in the Xhosa movement, especially in the early period, from its origins in a young girl prophet, through first expansion. This characterizes many millennial movements. In the upswing of apocalyptic enthusiasm and hope, women frequently have important public voices that inspire this kind of behavior. As Susan Juster wrote about the first "Great Awakening" in the colonies in the 1720s–40s, the spontaneous public behavior of women, including preaching to men, reflected their contribution to the holiness of the moment; but when the movement had peaked and started to wane (return to normal time), that behavior became disorderly and was once again repressed.[42]

Women generally find that apocalyptic time offers them an opportunity to make their voices heard, and some take vigorous advantage of it. Young women visionary prophets thrive in this unusual public discourse and become prominent (if later demoted) leaders of the movement, like the two prophetesses who fueled Montanus' outbreak of pneumatic millennialism in the second century after Jesus' death,[43] or the woman who led the early phases of what eventually became Bahai.[44] While some of the crusaders were following Charlemagne leading heavenly armies in 1096, others joined a young girl following her goose to Jerusalem.[45] And, as we saw in previous chapters, a particularly powerful and mature apocalyptic prophetess could become the acknowledged *magistra* of a major town.[46] A number of other female prophets complemented and amplified Nongqawuse's prophecies: her relative Nombanda, and independently, the eleven-year-old "prophet" Nonkosi of the Mpongo River.

[41] On chaos theory, see L. Douglas Kiel and Euel Elliott, eds. *Chaos Theory in the Social Sciences: Foundations and Applications* (Ann Arbor: University of Michigan Press, 1996).

[42] Susan Juster, *Disorderly Women: Sexual Politics and Evangelicalism in Revolutionary New England* (Ithaca, N.Y.: Cornell University Press, 1994).

[43] Trevett, *Montanism*, 151–96.

[44] On the early history of the Baha'i and the initiatory role of the poetess-seer Táhirih, see Abbas Amanat, *Resurrection and Renewal: The Making of the Babi Movement in Iran (1844–50)* (Ithaca, N.Y.: Cornell University Press, 1989), 299–330.

[45] Ekkehard of Aura, *Chronicon Universale*, ad. an. 1099, *Monumenta Germaniae Historica Scriptores* (Stuttgart: Anton Hiersemann Verlag, 1844), vol. 5, 215, lines 3–4.*

[46] See above, chapters 2 and 3.

As in the case of Nongqawuse and Mhlakaza, often in millennial movements, women play a critical role in the building of the communities of believers, while their men play the role of intermediaries, of interpreting the community to those on the outside.[47] Also, since most apocalyptic prophesies start out opposing their "power of the word" to that of this evil and ruined world of the sword, the moral discourse they engage in favors women's discourse, as does that of civil society.[48] Where discourse dominates violence, women find themselves at the very least on a significantly more level playing field than "normal time" and the gravitational pull of "might makes right" will tolerate. In order to imagine how a millennial movement can gain momentum, the observer should look for the myriad places where new behavior for women—in this case refusing to plant even if it means leaving their husbands—contributes.

Since we scholars are on the outside of most of these movements, however, we tend to exaggerate the role of men because of their prominence in bringing us evidence to interpret, including their *ex post defectu* demotion of women from apocalyptic holiness to a subordinate place in the "order" of normal times.[49] In this retrospective narrative, we hear mostly derogatory stories about silly girls from the now-triumphant owls; and from the now-chastened roosters, grateful tales of enduring faith in the face of devastating disappointment. Despite the skew of the sources, women's role in millennial movements constitutes a major component of the phenomenon. Indeed, one could even claim that apocalyptic time produces some of the earliest examples of prominent voices for women (especially commoner women) in recorded history. One could ask for no more dramatic example than the success of this young girl Nongqawuse, who could hardly lie closer to the bottom of the Xhosa hierarchy of prestige. Women and millennial movements constitute a major field of investigation for both millennial scholars and gender scholars.[50]

In the case of Nongqawuse, we see these women not only behind some of the more powerful figures who do end up as believers (Sarhili's mother, for example), but also at the core of the movement's commitments. Indeed, they prove the critical support for the prophecy's first test of public credibility (not its accuracy, its ability to induce belief). One observer, Tiya Soga, a Xhosa missionary, noted a

---

[47] See, for instance, the Marian Apparition Cults. Victor Balaban, "Self and Agency in Religious Discourse: Perceptional Metaphors for Knowledge at a Marian Apparition Site," in *Metaphor in Cognitive Linguistics: Selected Papers from the Fifth International Cognitive Linguistics Conference, Amsterdam, July 1997*, ed. Raymond W. Gibbs, Jr. and Gerard J. Steen (Philadelphia: J. Benjamin, 1999).

[48] Indeed, one might argue that millennial values are the most precocious source of "modern liberal values" like emancipation (see below, chapter 8).

[49] Susan Juster argues that this "reordering" of what had previously been considered holy behavior as "disorderly" happened in the later stages the "First Great Awakening" (*Disorderly Women*).

[50] See Brenda Brasher and Lee Quinby, eds., *Gender and Apocalyptic Desire* (London: Equinox Publishing, 2006); Helen Bradford argues strongly for the gender-biased failure of earlier historiography of the Nongqawuse drama ("Akukho").

connection that, with the necessary changes, applies to most millennial prophecies: they appeal with particular vigor to those who do the dirty work: "The women, the cultivators of the soil in Africa, were the warmest supporters of the prophet, as they rejoiced in the anticipation of getting crops without labor."[51] So gender (male-female) and class divisions (rulers–manual laborers) overlap significantly in the Xhosa case.

In particular, older women, well past their prime, seem to have had a particular enthusiasm for this movement, anticipating eagerly the return of their dead husbands and the return of the vigor and prestige that had marked their youth. Indeed, Sandile's mother admonished him for his wavering in the face of the prophecy: "It is all very well for you, Sandile. You have your wives and children but I am solitary."[52] A great deal of pressure to meet the prophecy's demands came from the women throughout the movement, although in some cases daughters criticized their fathers for killing their cattle.

Although an unusual number of cattle were killed in the wake of the first announcements, most cattle still lived at the end of 1856, the final weeks of planting season. People had to choose whether to plant crops or not: one cannot imagine a more public commitment to Nongqawuse's prophecy. According to our sources, the women, on whom the greater burden of agricultural labor fell, refused their men's commands to plant or even to join their men in planting: "The women are now the strongest supporters of the delusion, most of the men who have cultivated have had to break up their ground themselves, and when the husbands have insisted that their wives take a part, they have left and gone to their parents."[53] Historically, this particular act of burning bridges—not planting—constitutes one of the most enduring and spectacular of the public commitments to an apocalyptic prophecy designated to climax within the year—from the second-century Mediterranean to nineteenth-century northeastern America.[54] This report gives the scholar valuable insight into how, at least in one case, gender contributed to the decision.

The Politics of Successful Millennialism

We have a somewhat more detailed understanding of the critical moment when Nongqawuse got political support, especially from the greatest of the Xhosa chiefs

[51] Peires, *Dead Will Arise*, 173 n. 90 with further references.

[52] Ibid., 173. The comment recalls uncomfortably the joke about the man who has a 24-hour terminal illness and takes his partner on the town one last time. As he drags her from one bar to the next, she finally refuses, insisting he take her home: "But darling . . ." he protests, trying to guilt her with his condition. "Look," she snaps, "*you* don't have to wake up in the morning!" Only in the Xhosa case, the impatient wife actually induces the terminal condition.

[53] Ibid., 117 n. 37.

[54] See above on the second-century Christian community, chapter 1, n. 1; on the Millerites, see O'Leary, *Arguing the Apocalypse*, 93–133.

then alive, Sarhili. Until authorities pronounce themselves on new prophecies, most people stand back. And when they do pronounce, the mass of mimetic players will follow. Once "it pays" to believe in the prophecy, many will turn to it.

In the case of Nongqawuse, as in the case of the emperor's new clothes, most of her believers never spoke with her or made their own judgments. The vast majority of believers based their beliefs on the reports of others, who themselves were often influenced by previous reports.[55] At various times Nongqawuse seems to have used a variety of tricks including figures seen in the mist—the "new people"—who would not speak with anyone but her, and who complained about the behavior of the Xhosa *amagogotya*. But overall, the prophecy's appeal to the deep-seated desires of this unhappy people to live in freedom and abundance overrode all criticisms, however sharply some of the opponents of the prophecy articulated them.

At that point, mimetic desire—the need to want what others want—can act infectiously to bring large crowds into supporting roles. The expression "*Vox populi, vox Dei!*" derives its initial significance from the role of the people in precisely such apocalyptic moments, when a discourse of fairness makes radical claims in public. In such cases, a reversal occurs—the world turned upside down—in which the owls, who once dominated public space (even if incompetently), now find their rhetoric blown away by apocalyptic winds carrying radical new voices. The reassuring assertions owls made with such success in normal time, dismissing and ridiculing the roosters, no longer have the "power of words." That has passed into the hands of the prophetic radicals who lead the people to their ruin. Indeed—from the owl's point of view in apocalyptic time—the world does totter on the brink!

Why did Sarhili and so many chiefs side with the prophetess? Peires suggests one important element that we find in many cases of anti-imperial millennial forces. The British impact on Xhosa traditional culture had been devastating, and both the long-term impact of the market in "freeing" entrepreneurial Xhosa from the grip of their chiefs, and the last war, in which many chiefs had lost a great deal of land, justifiably alarmed those whose powers lay with the old system. In acceding to the enthusiasm of his commoners, a chief showed loyalty to his people in the face of the destructive forces that threatened him and his nation. Peires concludes: "It is thus no exaggeration to describe the Cattle-Killing as a popular mass movement of a truly national character, uniting both chiefs and commoners, the major social classes of the pre-colonial social order, in a communal defense of their way of life."[56]

In this sense, the chiefs follow a pattern often noted in demotic millennial movements. External imperial forces tear at the very fabric of the culture, specifically at the line the divides the elites from the commoners. Essentially, these conquerors offer the local leaders a chance to enter the larger imperial elite at the cost of abandoning their own people to the exploitation these new political powers reserved for

---

[55] Peires, *Dead Will Arise*, 165–66.
[56] Ibid., 176.

the great mass of commoners.[57] In the case of the leaders of the Zealot rebellions of ancient Judea, both warriors and rabbis preferred a national millennial response that preserved the people to one that joined them to the Greek or Roman political world.[58] Similarly, the chiefs of Xhosaland, in siding with the young prophetess, stood by their own people. These noble sentiments, however, were not enough to prevent a catastrophe to their people far greater than had they refrained from crowing in the first place. Just as the Zealots provoked the destruction of the Temple and the second exile of the Jews (70–1948), so we know only too well what fearful consequences rained down upon the Xhosa for following Nongqawuse.

When a major chief sides with the new revelation, one finds a characteristic split. Older and more prudent councilors resist and find themselves replaced by a younger group who, sincerely or not, ride the prophetic ardor around them to positions of great prominence. The British officer Gawler noted that one chief in his district, Mhala, himself an old man enthused by the prospect of being "made young again," had alienated his older councilors and "surrounded himself with a number of young second-rate councilors ambitious of distinction and ready to take their chances in forwarding any of the current nonsense."[59] Like the fabled emperor's court, when the official word from the chancellor, backed by the king, approves of the tailors' "new clothes," both mimetic and political power drives most people to side with the new teachings.

In a sense, Sarhili took the greatest wager. Nongqawuse and her uncle had gone from virtual social invisibility to become two of the most talked-about players in Xhosa public discourse, so their commitment makes sense in purely self-serving terms. Sarhili, on the other hand, and his fellow chiefs already dominated that public discourse, and to bind their fate so closely to such a dangerous prophecy and so quixotic a pair of prophets did not make any kind of "rational" sense.

Sarhili had the most to lose (but also, in his own mind almost certainly, the most to win). With both British and natural catastrophes inexorably strangling the culture he ruled over, he understandably might view a magical jump from this to the next world as being all the more attractive. In any case, the adherence of Sarhili to Nongqawuse's prophecy proved to be one of the most important aspects of its apocalyptic career. Eventually, the full weight of both the prestige of the chiefs, including threats of violence, came down upon the unbelievers.[60] Political power within Xhosa society resided with the believers.

---

[57] For a further discussion of this process and its role in generating apocalyptic movements, see below, chapter 9.

[58] Jonathan Price, *Jerusalem under Siege: The Collapse of the Jewish State, 66–70 C.E.* (Leiden: Brill, 1992); I will treat this at greater length in *While God Tarried*, chapter 3.

[59] Peires, *Dead Will Arise*, 172.

[60] We will discuss the pressure at the end of the apocalyptic wave below. At least one report mentions a Mfengu woman was murdered when she attempted to turn her Thembu husband against the killing of his cattle (Peires, *Dead Will Arise*, 173); and more than one unbelieving wife was forced by other wives to side with the believers.

Any historian not willing to play psychologist stops here. We have no real evidence of what motivated the man to behave as he did—virtually nothing "from his mouth," and the rest, unreliable reports in which both Sarhili and his recording interlocutors are playing a host of political games.[61] So who are we to hope to imagine the mind of a failed messianic believer?

Unfortunately, the historian of millennial movements cannot afford such admirable if prudent modesty. We need to understand certain aspects of Sarhili's motivation if we are to understand the believers' *behavior*, in particular the choices they make for handling their coming *post defectum* tribulation. And since the most dangerous turns that disappointed millennialism takes are political—totalitarianism and revolutionary terror[62]—the motivations of Sarhili and the other chiefs above all demand attention and analysis.

Resistance: The Owls

Despite signal victories, Nongqawuse's prophecy never won the open adherence of all, and the struggle between believers and unbelievers marks the sociability of the Xhosa to this day.[63] Whatever the eventual politics of position-making at the higher level, once the chiefs had committed, one can reasonably postulate that the nonbelievers had, and tried to appeal to, a native common sense. They denounced the prophecy as a ghastly gamble with a bad outcome. True owls—right in the long run.

One daughter, for example, laughed at her father for his credulous stance. When by moonlight they looked at a neighboring hillside as Nongqawuse had instructed them, he *saw* the cattle and the ancestors, but she insisted that she only saw thorn trees.[64] He, in turn, called her a "mad English girl" (which suggests that opposition to the prophecy was considered a form of British assimilation) and threatened to disown her.[65]

What makes for such a configuration, where the young girl is the unbeliever and the father a believer? Perhaps she had something of an English education or

---

[61] The urgency with which British officials "kept the record clean" in this period produced a virtually useless supply of official dispatches (see Peires, *Dead Will Arise*, 218–26), although their field correspondence offers some fairly candid insights.

[62] See below, chapters 9–12.

[63] The current tensions as a reflection of the fault lines of the cattle-slaying forms the basic structure behind Mda's novel, which flips back and forth between the movement and the present (*The Heart of Redness*).

[64] Peires, *Dead Will Arise*, 92–93, 172. The father and others who had come to visit Nongqawuse had been told to look over at another hill covered with thorn bushes and see the ancestors and cattle showing themselves in anticipation of their coming. This then offers evidence of a fight between believers and nonbelievers over the products of the believers' semiotic arousal. He saw an apocalyptic sign of imminent salvation; she saw something normal and refused to join in his suspension of disbelief. See also Peires, "'Soft' Believers and 'Hard' Unbelievers."

[65] Peires, *Dead Will Arise*, 173–74 and n. 91.

some form of contact with the English. One suspects that, in many more cases the relationship was reversed, parent-skeptics against children-believers (as much of the evidence suggests), but not being noteworthy, this did not get recorded. What accounts for the distribution of believers and unbelievers after accounting for the sociological *Wahlverwandtschaften*. Perhaps, we should side with Descartes when he commented, "common sense is the most evenly distributed trait in humanity...."[66]

In the case of Nongqawuse, the nonbelievers were a strong voice, but a minority. Some of them vigorously denounced Nongqawuse as a fake and refused to kill their cattle. Some came to hear her and walked away unconvinced, disparaging her as a sex-troubled teenager, in one case beating her thoroughly.[67] Sarhili had two brother nonbelievers who constantly urged him to abandon the mad prophecies. Families and couples split apart over this issue. And Nongqawuse and her followers showed in the ways they handled the evidence of disappointment soon to come, just how much the opposition's disbelief troubled them.

The terms that the Xhosa believers used to describe the believers and unbelievers tell us a great deal about one of the major faultlines of Xhosa culture under pressure from European colonial invaders. The believers called themselves the *amathamba*, or the soft ones. This does not mean "soft in the head" as most rational thinkers might be tempted to conclude, but yielding and receptive, open to influences, ready to set aside personal and selfish desires and act in ways that helped others (what the Chinese might call *yin*). Prophets and diviners must practice a radical self-abnegation and thereby open themselves to the messages from the spirits.[68] *Amathamba* were also open-handed people, practitioners of the kinds of cultivated generosity that had marked Xhosa tribal culture, where no one should eat without sharing.[69]

By contrast, however, the *amagogotya* were the hard ones—stingy, selfish, even disloyal, those who "eat alone." In the continuous struggle that the British presence provoked among the Xhosa, the *amagogotya* represented those who found themselves drawn to the British capitalist meritocracy. Often councilors and other wealthy men, these hard ones realized that, by selling their surplus rather than sharing it, they could accumulate wealth and influence and, above all, independence from their chiefs and the demands of the tribes. These were the heroes of the British administration, both religious and imperial. These people were prepared for the necessary transformation by which the British could transfer their White

---

[66] Descartes, *Discourses on Method* (Leyden: Ian Maire, 1637) 1:1. The statement continues with classic Gallic bite:...for each one thinks he has enough and none thinks he has too much. ("Le bon sensest la chose du monde la mieux partagée; car chacun pense en êtresi bien pourvu, que ceux même qui sont les plus difficiles à contenter en toute autre chose n'ont point coutume d'en désirer plus qu'ils en ont.")

[67] Peires, *Dead Will Arise*, 172, n. 87.

[68] Another translation of *amathamba* is "those who drill like soldiers," which Peires notes is far from contradicting the meaning of soft and underlines the discipline and sense of responsibilities to others such an attitude demands; *Dead Will Arise*, 175.

[69] Ibid., 175 and n. 98, n. 100.

Man's Burden.[70] Autonomous individuals, prepared to "play" the British game despite the social costs, formed the core of the opposition.[71]

In this sense, Nongqawuse's prophecy drove a sharp wedge right into the heart of this conflict. The soft ones, who embodied the most noble traits of the tribal world now under siege, would make the supreme sacrifice of killing their cattle and purging themselves of the malevolent impulses of witchcraft in order to bring in a new and vastly improved world. They would go out to greet the ancestors returning with superior cattle in abundance for all of them. The hard ones, who embodied the most cowardly and miserly traits of the imperial world, refused, condemning themselves—and (the *amathamba* argued) eventually their whole people—to death. But the *amagogotya* argued the opposite (and, like so many owls, they were right). The choices could not be starker, nor the stakes, higher.

The historian must never overlook the moral dimension of this and any other millennial movement. Millennialism is above all a moral critique of the world, and its spread to believers invariably includes a moral message that, on the one hand, demands a sacrifice, but on the other, assures believers that they are the truly righteous.[72] If they now suffer, it is precisely because for the evil "might makes right." But prophets promise that all this, the world of evil, will soon turn upside down. So when they are wrong, it is their world—and, if they seize power even momentarily, everyone's world—that is turned upside down.

Defectum and the Onset of Cognitive Dissonance

The bigger the bridges you burn on your way out, the harder to return to that normal time and to that society you thought was about to pass away. Here in Xhosaland, the apocalyptic waves threw believers onto a jagged rocky coast— devastating, self-inflicted famine. The ancestors did not come.

The real question in the case of all apocalyptic movements, most of them millennial, is how they handle this disappointment. This involves two distinct if overlapping stages: (a) when do they realize/admit that the prophecy has failed? and (b) what do they then do? The first stage is that of cognitive dissonance, the awareness that something that radically contradicts our understanding of the world is afoot, something unbearable to acknowledge. Hence most of the first phase of any cognitive dissonance is unconscious. But Nongqawuse had told her enthusiasts to expect the ancestors at the new moon, and the passage of several of those moons, when the sun failed to rise red and two moons to appear in the sky, marked moments of devastating disappointment, of *post defectum* tribulation for her followers.

---

[70] George Grey, in particular, earnestly wished this transformation of the Xhosa. For the larger pattern, see Adas, *Prophets of Rebellion* (above, chapter 2, n. 47).

[71] Peires, *Dead Will Arise*, 175–77.

[72] Among the best discussions of this dimension is Burridge, *New Heaven, New Earth*, 4–8.

For Nongqawuse and her uncle, the first such moment came with the August moon of 1856, widely understood—but not "officially sanctioned"—as the appointed time. It came and went without sign of change. Typically for cases where there is no set time in the original discourse but just a promise of *very* soon, these unofficial disappointments lead the roosters to fix a new date to come, in order to keep their followers' attention on the future. After August came the October moon, and this one received official sanction.

> In October, the prophets ordered the people to adorn themselves beautifully in celebration of the coming of the new day, "and withered old hags who had discontinued painting and ornaments for years, though tottering with age and want, are found covered with red clay and ornaments, hoping soon to have youth restored and an abundance of food."[73]

As with the Anabaptist leaders in Münster, public spectacle formed the natural stage for these fantasies of celebration designed to distract from cognitive dissonance.[74]

Failure takes believers from elation to the depths of depression and doubt, a bipolar roller-coaster ride that will endure until the grip of outrageous hope is broken. After the failure of October, believers fell into an earnest and increasing apathy as the consequences of their actions began to affect their diet. Leaders wavered, and some turned to drink. Now the cognitive dissonance surfaced at least to consciousness, and in some cases into conversations. Of these conversations, the most valuable to us are the private ones, whose content may reflect trust and intimacy, but we can still learn from the politically motivated reflections of the great chief Sarhili, who, when all was said and done, had risked the most on this prophetic gamble. In January, Brownlee wrote McLean that Sarhili had admitted that "he had had doubts but that having started with this thing, he was determined to see it through."[75]

This remark deserves note, because it suggests a common theme in the most destructive phases of *post defectum* apocalypticism. What the chief indicated here was the value he put on "face" and not losing it—precisely how Andersen has his naked emperor behave. To admit error would mean a permanent demotion, a fundamental loss of position in his culture. But the inexorable passage of time *without* the promised fulfillment forced him repeatedly into moments of self-awareness and the horror they brought. After the particularly public and humiliating Great Disappointment in October, with catastrophe looming, Sarhili acknowledged the magnitude of the disaster for him:

> I have been a great fool in listening to lies. I am no longer a chief. I was a great chief, being as I am the son of Hintza, who left me rich in cattle and people, but I have been deluded into the folly of destroying my cattle and ordering my people to do the same;

---

[73] Peires, *Dead Will Arise,* 145.
[74] Middlefort, "Madness and the Millennium at Münster."
[75] Peires, *Dead Will Arise,* 146 n. 4.

and now I shall be left alone, as my people must scatter in search of food; thus I am no longer a chief. It is all my own fault; I have no one to blame but myself.[76]

On the way home from this incident, Sarhili attempted suicide, and his councilors took away his weapons to prevent any further attempts. Once "recovered," however, Sarhili returned to the prophecy. Rather than contemplate such catastrophic blows to his personal face, Sarhili preferred to play out the hand, no matter what the consequences.

> I have undertaken a thing of which I now entertain certain doubts, but I am determined to carry it through…No one opposed me when I first undertook what I have undertaken, I consider therefore that they have approved of what I have done. I have sent to Sandille [sic], Macoma, Pato and Umhala, and our views are one. I have now no cattle left, but I cannot starve, there are still cattle in the land, and they are mine. I will take them when I require them.[77]

Thus, the suspicions of the *amagogotya* were not unfounded. They had claimed: "You were simply slaughtering yours, saying that you will send the White man across the sea today, were you all along surreptitiously hoping to come and pester us? Haven't yours arisen yet, you having said they would simply arise?"[78] In a sense this remark gives us an insight into a kind of cannibalistic Samson, someone who, recognizing his coming destruction, chooses to bring down with him standing around—and mocking. In Sarhili's case, alas, it was his own people, his own fellow believers, whom he mass-murdered with his suicidal pride. Such a response traces the lineaments of those dynamics which, in the hands of a modern messiah equipped with technology, bureaucracy, and political power, can wreak catastrophe and create totalitarianism.

These politics of shame deserve a much more prominent place in our social sciences than they now hold.[79] Although modern cultures demand that their political leaders *not* make decisions based on their own personal dramas of honor and shame,[80] this is emphatically not the norm in most political cultures, neither those in the rest of the non-Western world today nor even, too often, in our own. On the contrary, personal dramas of honor and shame, projected as the "face" of the nation itself, have dominated history for the millennia since the earliest civilizations deployed the great technologies of the Neolithic revolution—the sword, the plow, and the pen.[81] We cannot begin to count how many great decisions—for example the process

---

[76] Ibid., 158 n. 43.

[77] Ibid., 153 n. 27. This is precisely *not* true. He would not listen, and he now will not acknowledge.

[78] G[qoba], "Isizatu," 30, cited in Bradford, "Akukho."

[79] For some interesting reflections, see Harold Lasswell, *Psychopathology and Politics* (Chicago: University of Chicago Press, 1930); more recently, see Jon Elster, *Alchemies of the Mind: Rationality and the Emotions* (Cambridge: Cambridge University Press, 1999), 145–238.

[80] Hence it was widely understood in American public culture that to claim in the winter of 2003 that Bush was going into Iraq to "avenge his father," was a criticism, not a justified motive.

[81] See below, chapter 8.

leading to the "Great War" in 1914—have been made on the self-indulgence of rulers determined to subordinate all of the concerns of their people to their own psychic needs for honor.[82] And such motivations become all the more prominent as apocalyptic time intensifies the pressures under which millennialists labor.

All in all, Nongqawuse's prophecy went through at least a half-dozen distinct moments of disappointment: the full moons of June, August, October, and February were the high points, but one must imagine people who expected it any day, who every day worked through a small but painful disappointment. The most powerful of these disappointments came on February 16, 1857 and later became known by the same term used to describe William Miller's followers in 1844: the "Great Disappointment." A traveler's report from the Transvaal a week after gives a striking portrait of the believers in the morning after the dawn of the great day, the day of two moons, when the sun would turn red, the ancestors would return with cattle and grain in abundance, and the British would be swept from the land.

> The sun just like any other sun. The believers withdrew into their houses all the day, fastened tightly behind their many doors, peeping outside occasionally through the little holes in their dwellings until the sun disappeared. Meanwhile those who had never believed or done any of the things prescribed went about their usual work.[83]

The basic premise/promise of all the extraordinary sense of adventure and intimacy of purpose had collapsed. Our source, however, speaks of the *amagogotya* going about their tasks as quotidian both in the nature of the tasks and the manner of carrying them out. If the report comes from one of the central areas of the movement, then the behavior our observer noted that day was not quotidian, but one of the few days when *amagogotya* could carry on their chores publicly and in peace. It was a great day for the owls, a fearful day of shame for the roosters.

In some senses, one must wonder how this "Cattle-Slaying" could have survived so many disappointments, so many visible proofs that the prophecies had no substance, especially given the costs involved. Nor would this wonder merely reflect our modern skeptical mentality. Xhosa contemporaries held similar attitudes. With every failure, the unbelievers (and the British) raised their voices in protest. From the first big disappointment in August of 1856, it seemed, repeatedly, that the movement faltered and might die out. But it did not. On the contrary.

The Tragic Response to Apocalyptic Disappointment: Upping the Ante

The solution to which the *amathamba* came when their prophecy failed represents the most terrible path any apocalyptic movement can take. Faced with consistent

---

[82] See the analysis of Thomas Schiff, *Bloody Revenge: Emotions, Nationalism, and War* (Boulder: Westview Press, 1994), 75–100.

[83] Informant from the Transkei (independent Xhosa territory), 24–2–1857; quoted in Peires, *The Dead Will Arise*, 157.

evidence of the failure of the prophecies and the inevitable doubts that had begun to arise among believers, doubts intensified by the increasingly aggressive opposition of the owls, the roosters responded with apocalyptic scapegoating. If the prophecy had failed, then someone was to blame, and in this case, the full weight of responsibility fell not on those who had rashly issued the prophecies and the orders to slay the cattle, but on the *amagogotya*, the *unbelievers*. The ancestors had not come with the promised cattle and grain because the Xhosa had not slain *all* their cattle. Only when they had sacrificed all the old cattle, it emerged in the *post defectum* period, could the new come, and not until. Further, those cattle that believers had dispatched were often sold, or their hides sold. The sacrifice would only work when it was unclouded by profit. Only the most wanton destruction could work.

Thus, with each disappointment, believers, instead of questioning the prophecy, questioned the behavior of their own half-hearted supporters and their opponents within Xhosa society. After all, most had only reluctantly killed their cattle, always holding back from a total destruction. Not until the Great Disappointment of February 1857 did enthusiastic but wealthy chiefs, including Sarhili, kill all their cattle. "Many who have listened have only done so with one ear: the cattle are not all dead, and there is still a little corn left," commented one Thembu believer.[84]

Thus, from the earliest disappointments in August of 1856 through the madness that continued to drain Xhosa life to the last drop late in the summer of 1857, the believers always had an excuse. First their own shortcomings—after all, if they reproached the *amagogotya* of miserliness, how could they, the *amathamba*, in good conscience hold back their own goods from the demanded sacrifice? But then, progressively, as they killed more and more of their own and *still* nothing happened, they turned more ominously to the shortcomings of the *amagogotya*.

At the heart of this response lies a typical tendency of *post defectum* apocalyptic thinking. All apocalyptic scenarios are some mix of active and passive elements. In religious and magical ones, the passive scenario often looms large because God or the cosmic magical forces (here the ancestors) play such an extensive role in bringing on the millennial kingdom. In this case, the scenario called for a mutual exchange—in exchange for the sacrifice of the old, the ancestors would bring the new. Disappointment tends to act as a kind of trip switch, shifting passive movements into more active modes, and vice-versa. In this case disappointment produced a far more aggressive and demanding role from the Xhosa, *amathamba* and *amagogotya* alike.

This in turn raises a second key issue in apocalyptic millennial scenarios. What are the consequences of unbelief in the prophecy? In the case of Nongqawuse's prophecy, we have two versions, both prominent at the end, although it is probable that one emerges only *defectum*. In one version, those who sacrifice cattle, the

---

[84] Peires, *Dead Will Arise*, 315, no note.

amathamba, will receive their reward, while the unbelievers, the *amagogotya*, will suffer fates similar to the British. In the later versions, after prophecy has failed, the ancestors will *only return when all have become believers,* only once the whole tribe has become *amathamba*.

The former was probably the initially understood scenario. It so dominated most minds that even in the throes of multiple disappointments, after the December debacle, Mhlakaza claimed that the Napakade had been about to arrive with six hundred new cattle when the ancestors of the *unbelievers* interceded on their behalf and asked him to delay, lest their descendents be damned for not killing their cattle.[85] This explanation, probably improvised in the wake of this particularly humiliating failure, may nonetheless have made it possible to switch the blame onto the backs of the *amagogotya*. Their disbelief delayed the return of the ancestors.

One can readily imagine why this explanation would meet with approval among the *amathamba* as they struggled with their disappointment. The failure of our expectations, they could thus reason, is not our fault for believing so ridiculous a promise, but theirs for not believing it. Thus an apocalyptic scenario in which the ancestors separated the sheep (the saved believers) from the goats (the damned unbelievers), could shift imperceptibly but inexorably as the ancestors' unbearable delay continued, into a scapegoating scenario in which the resistance of the goats prevented the sheep from achieving their salvation. This, one of the favorite riffs of those playing apocalyptic jazz, helped to transform an active cataclysmic scenario, directed at the self, into an aggressive one directed at the "other." A similar logic has informed countless Christian apocalyptic movements which, in their disappointment, most commonly but not exclusively turn against Jews for not converting and thereby preventing the advent of the messiah.[86]

Such coercive apocalyptic scenarios generally appear in the post-apocalyptic wake of disappointment. They do not suit the earliest stages partly because they appeal to harsh feelings that rarely serve as the initial evangelizing emotions of a millennial movement, partly because the earliest prophecies ordinarily impress upon listeners the imminence of the event. Apocalyptic prophecies—especially ones that promise results within the year as Nongqawuse's listeners thought she said—tend to emphasize both the imminence and ineluctability of the event. Nothing can be done to change the prophetic decree, *but* believers can do something to position themselves so as to benefit from it.

Only after disappointment do the more active apocalyptic scenarios take on momentum. In the later stages of the Cattle-Killing, the ancestors—also known

[85] Ibid. 149 n. 14.

[86] R. Landes, "What Happens when Jesus Doesn't Come? Jewish and Christian Relations in Apocalyptic Time," in "Millennial Violence: Past, Present, and Future," ed. Jeffrey Kaplan, special edition of *Journal of Terrorism and Political Violence* 12 (2001).

as the "new people"—became increasingly capricious in their reasons for not appearing. At first, explained Mhlakaza, they did not come with the promised cattle because they responded to the prayers of the *amagogotyas'* ancestors trying to give the unbelievers another chance...later, they were so offended by the presence of *amagogotyas* that they refused to appear...still later, they were angered by the lack of enthusiasm with which the *amathamba* had sacrificed their cattle...eventually, all reasonable explanations exhausted, the ancestors were delayed because, apparently, they could not agree on what order of rank they should appear (!). None of these explanations would have drawn people into the movement. They were designed, on the contrary, to keep them in once disappointment hit.

Ridden like a Horse: Millennial Movements as Possession

As in so many other movements, what the prophet and her uncle, her public spokesman, set in motion eventually escaped their control. "The prophets of the Gxarha were totally unprepared to deal with the crisis which their prophecies initiated. They were obviously unable to produce the 'new people' on demand, or to cope with the consequences of the failure of their prophecies."[87] Over time, however, they could not continue, and Nongqawuse withdrew, becoming too "sick" to prophecy, and Mhlakaza began to distance himself from her prophecies. But the collapse of the core had little effect on the movement, now playing out a collective logic that no one except, *perhaps*, Sarhili could decisively influence. Just as William Miller, crushed by the failure of his date of 1843, had a minimal role in resetting the apocalyptic clock to the following year, so the two originators of the movement played ever smaller roles by the end.

The tragedy of the story, of course, is that having chosen the path of scapegoating to explain the failed prophecy, Nongqawuse and her uncle set in motion the fire that consumed the Xhosa. Such "explanations" for failed prophecy only work when people want to hear them, and as such they tell us much about the internal conflicts and deep hostilities that cut through Xhosa culture at this time. If the Cattle-Slaying drove Xhosa culture to commit suicide, then that reflected, in part, a readiness to tear itself apart.

Thus the initial, and all subsequent responses to disappointment, took the form of encouraging still-more-extensive and wanton destruction, first of the believers and then of those brought by pressure, often from their wives, from the ranks of unbelievers. Certain chiefs, like Sandile, hesitated constantly, alternating between wanting to appease the British commander, who lived uncomfortably close, and wanting to appease the believers who insisted he neither plow nor plant, but rather that he slay his cattle. Thus, paradoxically

---

[87] Peires, *Dead Will Arise*, 310.

from our "rational" point of view, with every disappointment, the pressure increased and the killings waxed in number and ferocity. By the "Great Disappointment" of February 1857, the movement should have reached its term. Absolute famine faced the people.

And yet it went on for more than half a year, and the devastation wreaked in that period—including open attacks by the now-destitute *amathamba* on the remaining cattle of the *amagogotya*—added terrible consequences to already catastrophic beliefs. If tribulation was coming, it was not coming to those whom the believers had at first expected to punish, but to themselves. The more they denied this classic twist of apocalyptic fate, the worse they made their tribulation; and the more they denied this ironic reversal, the more damage they did to their apocalyptic "enemies" in an effort to *make* the scenario come out *right*. If the ancestors (or God, or the forces of the universe) did not punish those who deserved it, the believers would.

Few millennial movements show the devastating logic of negative-sum responses to apocalyptic disappointment than the Xhosa Cattle-Slaying. The initial dream promises a land redolent with peace and joy, people reunited with their ancestors, rejuvenated and vigorous all, a land filled with the bounty of nature, healthy cattle and grain, and freed from the talons of that great bird of prey that held the Xhosa in its death grip—European imperialism. But between this world caught in British talons, and the future world of abundance, lay a great sacrifice that the Xhosa had to carry out. With the failure of the promises came a critical moment when believers, in order to cling to the dream, turned to the most ferociously aggressive and coercive measures directed against themselves. Everyone lost but the British.

This path, so often trod by millennial movements in their moment of crisis, represents the key issue for the policy implications of millennial studies. At some moment, some millennial groups that have achieved even a modicum of success in their first, voluntaristic and enthusiastic stage, turn from a discourse of egalitarianism, free choice, and fair play to one of coercive purity in which the previously *unthinkable*—hierarchy, aggression, violence, mass murder—becomes increasingly central. In post-apocalyptic disappointment, a transformative scenario based on the harmonious cooperation of the cosmic and human forces of good becomes a negative-sum rage to force the solution, to *carve the millennial kingdom* out of the very body social.

When all is said and done about the Xhosa Cattle-Slaying, one of its most outstanding lessons deals precisely with this violent, scapegoating response to prophetic failure. The empathic historian, who can readily imagine the appeal of millennial promises, has more difficulty understanding how often believers faced staggering evidence of their failure and continued on in their beliefs. And without that understanding, along with the matrix of violence and hatred it released *in order to survive*, we cannot understand why the prophecy had such a devastating effect on Xhosa culture.

The Return of Normal Time and the Re-Ascendance of the Owls and Foxes

The owls warn against waking the barnyard prematurely lest the foxes seize the occasion. This was the fate of that poster boy for apocalyptic stupidity, Chicken Little, who led his following into the lair of Foxy Loxy. In the case of the Xhosa, the British turned out to be both owl and fox. The British, although astonished at their staggeringly self-destructive behavior and occasionally ready to intervene in order to limit the damages, prepared to take full advantage of their folly. When Sarhili and the other believing chiefs at long last gave up and turned back to the British to see if they could get the deal they had been offered and refused at the end of the last war, they ran into a stony silence. Like so many inhabitants of apocalyptic time, the chiefs had spoken their mind, their normally hidden transcripts, with no fear of the consequences, and made abundantly clear to anyone listening, just how contemptuous they were of the British (and of their fellow *amagogotya*). Now the British were in no mood to compromise. On the contrary, the Xhosa had set themselves up to be dismantled, and that is precisely what the British proceeded to do.

Above all, they permitted and even encouraged the famine to take its toll. Not only did they not help, they discouraged any "benevolent" foundation from doing much either. In this, they followed the policies, already put in practice by a group of English evangelicals who had imbibed "free market" teachings with a thick patina of pre-Darwinian "survival of the fittest." This attitude was on particularly clear display in the case of the Irish famine. There, a school of intellectuals and officials including Trevelyan had greeted the potato famine that devastated Ireland as a "divine intervention" with which they must not interfere.[88] *Surtout pas.*

On the contrary, the death of about a third to half the population was precisely the blow necessary to crack the tribal society of the Xhosa that had proven so resistant to English efforts to "civilize" it. For Grey, the Irish and the Xhosa had the same problem: unable to understand the glories of individuality, discipline, and autonomy—the very things that had made Britain great—these primitive peoples had clung to tribal solidarities and all the stunting superstitions that accompanied them.

For Grey, it was a fight to the death between what German sociologists, a generation later, would call *Gemeinschaft* (community) and *Gesellschaft* (society), with a winner-take-all, survival-of-the-fittest outcome. In game-theory terms, he played a prominent role in the English imperial offer of a closed positive-sum game: "we both win, but we Brits win (much) more than you." As Grey put it in a letter,

---

[88] "God and nature had combined to force Ireland from diseased backwardness into healthy progressive modernity," Peter Gray, *Famine, Land and Politics: British Government and Irish Society, 1843–1850* (Dublin: Irish Academic Press, 1998), 331–32; Brendan Ó Cathaoir, *Famine Diary* (Dublin: Irish Academic Press, 1999), Introduction.

"we wish to make the Xhosa a part of ourselves, with a common faith and common interests…." He then specified his revealing expectations: they would become "useful servants, consumers of our goods, contributors to our revenue."[89] The famines, in other words, were, then, heaven-sent executioners of the old world. In the case of the Irish, the damage was largely inflicted; the Xhosa dispatched themselves.

In any case, the English, led by Grey's vision, did not hesitate to ruthlessly exploit the advantage so inexplicably, so irrationally opened up for them by Xhosa society itself, to do another version of what they had done in Ireland. They allowed large numbers on the verge of starvation to die. They rounded up the chiefs and sent them to Robben Island for decades. They pushed the destitute commoners off their land and opened whole new tracts to white settlement. They sent the sons and daughters of the chiefs to schools where they could learn to play the game by the English rules, and incorporated huge numbers of now indigent and homeless workers into labor camps and domestic service, including, possibly, Nongqawuse.

Even the *amagogotya* who had shown such loyalty to the English ethos found themselves on the short end of the stick. Only one officer, Major Gawler, showed any concern for them, and he ended up creating with them a renegade police force that clearly worked toward cleansing the land of Xhosa.[90] In later years, British administrators would refer to the events after the Cattle-Slaying as times when ethical standards were suspended, when deeds one would not want recorded occurred.

Now, the English had a reasonable excuse act this way, at least by their perception of things. They fully believed in what they called the "Chiefs' Plot." Unable to fathom the possibility that the warriors they had had so much difficulty mastering in the past would take seriously a mad prophecy pronounced by a deranged teenage girl, the British assumed it was a ruse. The chiefs, in their minds, must have supported the movement not because they believed it, but—much like the British— they planned to exploit its stupidity. Since one of the major holds that the British had on Xhosa behavior centered on the Xhosa's attachment to their goods and families—precisely what Cathcart and his commander Colonel Eyre had devastated in the previous war—the imperial officers assumed that the idea was to make the Xhosa so desperate that they would attack the British with the ultimate zeal of those on the brink of annihilation—the warrior with nothing to lose, not even his house and family.[91]

This conspiratorial reading of the phenomenon made a great deal of sense to the British. Given that the British represented the root cause of this millennial madness owing to their own remorseless *libido dominandi*, they assumed that

[89] Peires, *Dead Will Arise*, 318 and chap. 2/2.
[90] Ibid., chap. 6.
[91] Ibid., chap. 7.

nothing less drove their enemies whom they considered, in any case, far inferior to them morally. Hence it would be close to unthinkable to the British to imagine that this was *not* a plot against them. It would, therefore, have been sheer imprudence to take pity on these people and help them in their distress. Those who live by the sword, think by the sword, even when they try to do otherwise. And so, despite their fervent desires, the millennium-addled Xhosa fell to the British foe.

5 Commodity Millennialism

Papuan Cargo Cults (Twentieth Century)

■ VAILALA MADNESS AND MAMBU

In the waning months of 1919, alarmed reports came out of some southern Papuan coastal villages in the Gulf District. The natives had stopped working or going to the Christian mission services; they dressed in Western clothes and sat on chairs at tables set with flowers in empty beer bottles. And at night they drank the drug kava and carried on in wild dancing and visionary episodes, including women stripping off their clothes and falling to the ground. They abandoned much of traditional ritual practice, burning ceremonial wooden vessels in large bonfires. New moral codes demanded the renunciation of witchcraft, stealing, adultery, and rituals of public confession elicited admissions of guilt, repentance, and forgiveness in vast outpourings of emotion.[1]

The explanation that inquiring whites received recounted how an old man with much experience with Europeans had had a vision while hunting. He died shortly thereafter, but then visited his sons and told them that the ancestors were coming to them aboard a steamer full of cargo for *them*. In some versions, the cargo included European weapons. In order to prepare, they purified themselves by burning traditional ritual objects, and adopted new sacred objects—photographs from the West, including a picture of George V, an advertisement for Lifeboy soap, and the cover to a cheap novel depicting an airplane.[2] The movement spread like wildfire, carried by, among others, a native who worked for the European government, Kori, the "Paul of Papua," who had first come to investigate for his superiors and ended up joining, then leading the movement.[3]

The authorities responded with alarm—the missionaries at the loss of those souls they were shepherding to heaven, the administrators at the loss of labor and the potential for disruption. For the religious, the blow landed with particular force since many of the most active participants called themselves "Jesus Christ

---

[1] On the Vailala madness, see the account of the regional magistrate, Francis Edgar Williams, "The Vailala Madness," in *"The Vailala Madness" and Other Essays*, ed. Erik Schwimmer (Honolulu: University Press of Hawaii, 1977) and the assessment and retelling by Peter Worsley, *The Trumpet Shall Sound*, 2nd ed. (New York: Shocken Press, 1968), 75–104. On Mambu, see Kenelm Burridge, *Mambu: A Study of Melanesian Cargo Movements and Their Social and Ideological Background* (New York: Harper Torch Books, 1960); and Worsley, *Trumpet*, 104–08.

[2] Worsley, *Trumpet*, 75–83.

[3] Similarly, Hitler was initially sent by the government to observe the workings of the NAP, which he rapidly joined and then led.

men". They claimed to receive messages from Jesus, and, in at least one case, messages from *Ihova Yesu-nu-ovaki*—Jehovah the younger brother of Jesus. Elaborate descriptions of the God's European clothing circulated,[4] emphasizing the direct link between heaven and cargo. They viewed the coming of the cargo as the fulfillment of the millennial promise of the Christian missionaries. Indeed, the movement may have been triggered by an apocalyptic sermon on the Resurrection preached by a white missionary.

Like the Xhosa, they synthesized Christian mythology with their own. They innovated in ritual acts, marrying some of the Christian missionary practices— Sabbath observance, "reading" prayers (often by illiterates), classes, work groups— with some of the more ecstatic native ones—kava drinking, dancing, feasting, singing. And in their giddy enthusiasm, they talked back to the white man. Set free from the fear of the white man, like the Xhosa chief Sarhili, they could at last let him know what the black man really thought, speak the hidden transcript of resentment and envy. In recognition of its ecstatic elements—trances, glossolalia— Europeans called it Vailala Madness.[5]

The administrators also found this behavior infuriating. Wrote one:

> They sat quite motionless and never a word was spoken for the few minutes I stood looking at them. It was *sufficient to raise anybody's ire* to see them acting in such an idiotic manner; a number of strong, able-bodied natives, in mid-afternoon, dressed in clean, new toggery, *sitting as silently as if they were sticks and stones*, instead of being at work or doing something else *like rational beings*. They appeared fit subjects for a lunacy asylum.[6]

The administration sought, with relatively mild measures (fines, rounding up participants and giving them work and food, suppression of the practices), to stifle the movement, and succeeded after a manner, and largely *after* the cargo manifestly failed to appear. The wave peaked and receded, but continued to flare up for years, and even after its supposed demise in 1931, the movement carried with it an aura of magic. Natives remembered it as a "brief age of miracles."[7]

There were various outbreaks of cargoism over the years, including a major incident in the western areas of the Madang district on the northern shore. This time the movement was led by a baptized Roman Catholic and former migrant

---

[4] Note the analogy to the Taiping visions of God's clothing (chapter 7).

[5] E. F. Williams, an anthropologist published the first major study of the movement, *Vailala Madness and the Destruction of Native Ceremonies in the Gulf Division* (Papuan Anthropology Reports 4 (Port Moresby: E.G. Baker, Government Printer, 1923).

[6] *Papua, Annual Report*, 1919–20, Appendix V, cited in Worsley, *Trumpet*, 84 (italics mine).

[7] F.E. Williams, "The Vailala Madness in Retrospect" in *Essays Presented to C.G. Seligman*, ed. E.F. Evans-Pritchard et al. (London: Routledge & Kegan Paul, 1934), 373, cited in Worsley, *Trumpet*, 90. Cf. Radulfus Glaber's account of people looking back after the passage of the first Christian millennium, a time of "prodigies and wondrous events," and wondering why miracles did not happen anymore, *Five Books of Histories* 5.1.10, ed. John France, Niethard Bulst and Paul Reynolds (Oxford: Clarendon Press, 1993), 229.

laborer named Mambu who broke away from the mission, where the priests had considered making him a mission helper, and began to preach a new version of the millennial advent of cargo. His movement also spread rapidly, this time in the hinterland. Mambu called himself the "Black King" and the "King long ol kanaka" and claimed supernatural powers including invulnerability. His followers ritually discarded their tribal dress and, after having their genitals sprinkled in baptism, burned their former garb and donned that of the white man. In exchange for their new lives, Mambu told them the ancestors dwelt in the volcano of Manam Island where they prepared the cargo that their living descendents would receive *if* the living kept faith with them though Mambu's instruction. Alarmed by the spread of the movement, and the (to them) erratic behavior of the enthusiasts who no longer attended mission schools and churches, no longer planted crops or produced goods for market, government forces arrested Mambu and exiled him. With the Japanese invasion both the administrative records and any trace of him disappear.

■ YALI AND JOHN FRUM: POSTWAR CARGOISM

During the war, both Japanese and Americans tried to use the willingness of natives to see outsiders (themselves) as bringers of millennial salvation in order to gain cooperation with the native population in their war against each other. So after the war, cargoism revived rapidly, this time fully integrating the huge new array of cargo goods and delivery systems—especially airplanes—that had recently visited these normally isolated lands.

This time, the natives copied the magic of the Americans, imitating their army camps, using American flags, clearing runways for planes to land, carving sticks to look like guns, and making uniforms. They drilled as did the army, and stood in ranks, as did the American soldiers, at the landing of cargo. The enthusiasm of these cults survived disappointment in their expectations and the disapproval and mockery of the whites, who thought them mad, and referred derisively to their activities as "Cargo Cults."[8]

Into this volatile mixture stepped a man named Yali, a former migrant worker who had helped the Allies (Americans and Australians against the Japanese) and risen to the rank of sergeant major, been in Australia and returned to Papua New Guinea.[9] Both races respected him, the approval of the whites intensifying his charismatic appeal to his fellows. The whites expected him to work for them and keep the population docile—he even received a pension; the blacks looked to him for salvation. At the time of his return, administrative records speak of him as

---

[8] Lamont Lindstrom, *Cargo Cult: Strange Stories of Desire from Melanesia and Beyond* (Honolulu: South Sea Books, 1993). For further deconstruction of this term, see below.

[9] On Yali, see Peter Lawrence, *Road Belong Cargo: A Study of the Cargo Movement in the Southern Madang District, New Guinea* (Manchester, U.K.: Manchester University Press, 1964).

"sincere, energetic, and...a beneficial influence on the natives."[10] He urged the people to reorganize their villages and lives along the lines of European culture. His "rehabilitation scheme" aimed at bringing his people into the modern world.

But the Europeans treated him badly. He experienced deep and humiliating disappointments at the hands of the administrators even as his fellow blacks treated him with extraordinary honor. They insisted on granting him exceptional status, holding special ceremonies for him wherever he went, dancing and singing in his honor, holding great feasts. Yali was "idolized to the point that [he] generated 'millennial' or 'miraculously transformative' hopes beyond [his] control or wishes."[11] This determination on the part of the natives to see Yali as their savior had its effect. He finally began to approve and eventually lead an enthusiastic cargo movement that spread far and wide, one in which a nativized, apocalyptic Christianity spread its good tidings. Native "Lutheran" evangelists baptized in droves.

Yali developed a whole cadre of lieutenants to carry out his orders, spread the message of cargo, and baptize and organize communities. Hostility to Europeans, administrative and missionary, informed his teachings. He purged the movement of Christian elements and restored indigenous myths, retold in a millennial idiom. The native deity Kilibob became the god of cargo; the promised salvation lay around the corner. At its height, whole regions had been removed from colonial administrative control; Yali collected taxes and organized social life.[12] By 1950, the colonial administration arrested Yali and kept him in prison until 1955. During this period, the Yali movement appeared to have disappeared.

When Yali was released from prison in 1955, however, he returned to his followers and the Yali movement began anew. But the movement now took new forms. Yali, embittered still more by his experience with whites, looked to pay them back for their betrayal. He turned to nativistic magical and "cultic" practices, reintroducing, for example, the great Ngaing harvest festival, shifting from "progressive" to "restorative" themes, rejecting Western ways.[13]

Perhaps overwhelmed by the intensity of his followers' desire to believe in his powers, he assumed a royal persona and indulged his sexuality to its fullest. Like Hong Xiuquan of the Taiping, he kept multiple wives. His followers brought young

---

[10] *Pacific Islands Monthly,* April 1947, 69, cited in Worsley, *Trumpet,* 216.

[11] Garry Trompf, *Payback: The Logic of Retribution in Melanesian Religions* (Cambridge: Cambridge University Press, 1994), 215. (The original passage spoke of both Yali and his contemporary, Paliaup; I've modified it to the singular.) On the role of followers in producing messianic leaders, see Moshe Idel, *Messianic Mystics* (New Haven, Conn.: Yale University Press, 1998).

[12] Compare Yali with Thiota, who only lasted a year, but had a similar unofficial but political status (above, chapters 2–3).

[13] Elfriede Hermann, "The Yali Movement in Retrospect: Rewriting History, Redefining 'Cargo Cult,'" *Oceania* 63 (1992): 58. According to Garry Trompf, this represents a widespread shift in cargo cults after (and as a result of) the war, from "advent dancing" to military drills, from "so called 'classic' to 'modern' cargoism." *Payback,* 207–09.

maidens, or "flower girls," to him. Yali's followers collected his semen in bottles, believing that it could produce wealth or that it had curative powers.

Yali's personal predilection for indulging his charismatic powers coincided with a dramatic shift in his movement toward coercive purity, and its accompanying legal and political hierarchy. Followers began to refer to Yali as the King of New Guinea, and he simultaneously established a group or lieutenants, or *lo bos*, to enforce his laws. In 1964, and again in 1968, Yali ran for a seat in the New Guinean House of Assembly. Yali and his followers believed that the House of Assembly in Port Moresby was a secret source of wealth. If elected, Yali planned to go to there in order to distribute to all New Guineans the vast treasures that lay within.[14] But, perhaps as a reflection of how coercive religiosity and democracy do not mix well, Yali was never elected. He died in 1975, and his movement disappeared to the point where his own villagers from Sor-Yabilol deny that Yali was ever a cargo prophet.[15]

At least Yali was a real person and exerted his charisma directly. John Frum, if he ever existed, remains unknown, as does the origin of his name.[16] And yet expectation of John Frum's *return* with cargo has inspired a series of movements of apocalyptic expectation on the small island of Tanna in the New Hebrides chain (today part of Vanuatu). As early as 1940, islanders reported seeing John Frum at kava-drinking rituals around the campfire. The extravagant promises made in his name were unmistakably millennial. A cataclysm would at once drive the white man from the land, level the volcanic mountains and turn everything into fertile plain, and join Tanna to the nearby islands in one large landmass; the natives would get back their youth, no sickness would trouble them, the earth would bring forth its abundance without labor, and chiefs and teachers would receive salaries. A new heaven and a new earth.

His disciples, on his reported command, reinstituted kava-drinking, dancing, polygamy, and other customs forbidden by the missionaries. They ceased to work, began to either spend all their money or throw it into the sea,[17] and to eat up their food supplies in lavish feasts. All this they did on a premise similar to that of the Xhosa: they would drive the white man from the island and please the ancestors, who would return with cargo. But unlike the Xhosa, who felt guilty eating from their slain cattle, these movements embraced antinomian excess, not asceticism.

The initial outbreak in 1940 did not draw much attention, but the next one, in May 1941, drew the ire of administrators, who arrested leaders and alleged John Frums. December's news of Pearl Harbor triggered another wave, as did the arrival

[14] Louise Morauta, "The Politics of Cargo Cults in the Madang Area," *Man* 7, no. 3 (1972): 442.

[15] Hermann, "Yali Movement in Retrospect," 58–59.

[16] The name may refer to "John *from* [America], or John [the Baptist] *Broom* [who will sweep away the whites]." On John Frum, see Edward Rice, *John Frum He Come: A Polemical Work about a Black Tragedy* (Garden City, N.Y.: Doubleday, 1974), and Lindstrom, *Cargo Cults*, 73–146.

[17] In the May 1941 outbreak, natives brought hundreds of pounds of cash, including gold sovereigns not used since the early part of the century; Worsley, *Trumpet*, 155.

of American troops which—to the natives' astonishment and delight—included blacks like them. New variants on the prophecy appeared, this time holding out America as the great millennial hope, the land from which the cargo would come.

These apocalyptic communities have developed a wide range of rituals and techniques, including extraordinarily energetic dance techniques, the extensive use of American paraphernalia (including war medals and discarded metal objects), American flags, and crosses. Despite repeated failure to either bring back John Frum or bring on cargo, and the withering mockery of both whites and Westernized islanders, the island of Tanna continues to this day to have live cults centered around John Frum.

Explaining the Phenomenon

Cargo cults have precipitated an epistemological crisis for anthropology as a discipline. The sudden emergence of a variety of seemingly ridiculous cults in the period after the war, and their recurrence no matter how "wrong" the predictions, profoundly challenged the "functionalist" paradigm whereby anthropologists of the period tried to "understand" the things they observed in terms of the uses (including structural functions) that they served in the culture in question. The challenge prompted an interesting "Popperian" response from an epistemological philosopher.[18] Unfortunately, his reflections, despite their telling criticism, found little favor with the ascension of a postmodern paradigm that prized narrative above all.[19]

In one sense, the challenge to anthropologists came from the deeply irrational, almost "silly" nature of these cults. Certainly the conditions that produce millennial responses the world over—imperial Western cultures invade and subjugate indigenous tribes—applied here. Like the Xhosa, these islanders had to deal with rapacious Europeans who used their vast superiority of force to enforce their dominion, and whose racial aspects—these islanders are black, rather than brown skinned—were hard to miss. As one European put it: "I want the nigger to work for me so I can make my pile and leave the *#@*& country."[20] Or as one native upbraided a fellow Papuan for being lazy: "D'you think you're a white man, doing nothing?" As with all millennial movements, anger, resentment, and a desire for retribution runs through almost all the cargo cults.[21]

But unlike outright rebellions, which, no matter how hopeless, could still be explained as "rational" behavior designed to assert independence and reassert dignity, these cults seemed at once silly and doomed from the start. Their open admiration for aspects of Western culture—especially the wild pro-Americanism of the

---

[18] J.C. Jarvie, *The Revolution in Anthropology* (London: Routledge & Kegan Paul, 1967).
[19] See discussion below.
[20] Williams, *Vailala Madness*, xii, cited in Worsley, *Trumpet*, 82.
[21] For a thorough and thought-provoking analysis, see Trompf, *Payback*.

John Frum cult[22]—became almost embarrassing to any anthropologist, a fortiori any still secretly in search of noble savages, or at least locals who could "see through" Western materialism. The fascination of *kago* continued to seduce the natives despite its apparent folly. It illustrated the "irrepressible longings for a redemptive illusion" to which even the most sophisticated of Westerners might fall prey.[23]

The embarrassment was not merely among anthropologists who did not like the inherently invidious comparison implied in an indigenous movement that so radically misunderstood and slavishly imitated the West. Anthropologists wanted nothing to do with the contempt among administrators, missionaries, and white settlers for the stupidity of *kago* cults. Lindstrom calls the Western "take" on cargo cults "Birdism," named after Norris Mervyn Bird, who wrote one of the first published analyses of the phenomenon after World War II.[24] Here the cults illustrated native childishness and reinforced the claims to political dominance of white colonialists and settlers, "a discursive way of exercising power and control…an artifact of colonial interest."[25] Orientalism incarnate.

And this contempt found an echo among the native owls, the equivalent of what the Xhosa had called the *amagogotya* ("hard ones"): natives *not* (or formerly) drawn to the cargo cults. Lattas notes the anger of those who had been part of earlier cargo cults not only toward "the Europeans and Melanesian officials who had suppressed them, but also toward *relatives and neighbors who assumed the overbearing attitudes of government officials and missionaries…*"[26] For these folk, often those readiest to play by modern rules, the cargo cults became an embarrassment, much as the Xhosa "cattle-slaying" embarrassed modern Xhosa over a century later.[27]

Kago "Cults" as Millennial Movements

In the '50s and '60s, anthropologists found millennial dynamics a compelling way to analyze cargo cults. Peter Worsley drew extensively on the burgeoning scholarship on millennialism, including Norman Cohn's study of the Middle Ages, to

---

[22] The American presence, with the (comparatively) striking "egalitarianism" of black-white relations in the army, triggered a whole new postwar phase of cargo enthusiasm. See comments by Trompf, *Payback*, 207–12.

[23] The phrase comes from David Horowitz, "The Sick Mind of Noam Chomsky," *FrontPage Magazine*, September 26, 2001. Online: http://97.74.65.51/readArticle.aspx?ARTID=24447, February 23, 2010. (Such hostility is a common feature among owls; see below, chapter 12 on UFOs.)

[24] Norris Mervyn Bird, "Is There Danger of a Post-War Flare-Up Among New Guinea Natives?" *Pacific Island Monthly* (November 1945).The question was answered, correctly, in the affirmative.

[25] Lindstrom, *Cargo Cult*, 92; Ton Otto "Cargo Cults Everywhere?" *Anthropological Forum* 9, no. 1 (1999). See above, n. 7.

[26] Andrew Lattas, *Cultures of Secrecy: Reinventing Race in Bush Kaliai Cargo Cults* (Madison: University of Wisconsin Press, 1998), xii (italics mine).

[27] See Daniel and Magdalene Crowley's article on the groan of embarrassment they received from a Vanuatu official when they told him they were going to see the celebrations of John Frum: "Religion and Politics in the John Frum Festival, Tanna Island, Vanuatu," *Journal of Folklore Research* 33, no. 2 (1996): 161.

"explain" these movements as expressions of the discontent of the masses that specifically used Christian apocalyptic texts to create movements of liberation from oppression and advent to a Promised Land at the End of time.[28] Burridge's work explored more existential dimensions of this millennialism in *Mambu*, an approach that climaxed in one of the great conceptual works on the subject, *New Heaven, New Earth*.[29] From the perspective of postwar anthropologists, the behavior that so struck earlier Western observers as bizarre, turned out, on closer examination, to reflect profound and ubiquitous dramas of human destiny. If the local natives at times behaved strangely, so had—and did—Westerners.

The movements contained a wide range of both millennial myths and varied apocalyptic scenarios. In some, we find contours very similar to the Xhosa Cattle-Slaying: on the basis of a revelation from benevolent and powerful ancestors, some groups rejected both the white man's culture and the indigenous culture degraded by the white man. Somehow, slaying pigs and destroying money would sweep the whites from the islands. Others, the more notable and curious for Westerners, announced the arrival of cargo and imagined the millennial kingdom in terms of Western consumer culture. Endless cargo became the modern version of the "millennial banquet" at which the elect—the believers in the prophecy—will sit in glory.

And such movements "appear" in moments of widespread apocalyptic expectation of an imminent and cosmic transformation in which each player saw him- and herself acting. Indeed, the zenith of a prophet's influence correlates closely with the intensity of the apocalyptic fervor.[30] Those natives sitting in their white European clothes at tables with flowers on a work day were, at a simple level, just saying that in their world of fairness, they had earned what the European had—a (long) pleasant day of rest. But to get up the nerve to do so in defiance of the Europeans' will, they imagined themselves acting at the edge of the vortex. *Kago* was coming *soon*!

The cargo cults illustrated so many of the dynamics characteristic of millennial movements that they soon became for some scholars the epitome of millennial movements. However ludicrous the premises that motivated these movements, however wrong and irrational the expectations of these millennial groups in apocalyptic time, these movements galvanized participants. In the renewed enthusiasm created by the sense of imminence, the cults were able to introduce new forms of celebration, of organization, and of social relations. They could be understood as revitalization movements,[31] as a form of acculturation with modernity,[32] or as

---

[28] Worsley, *Trumpet*, credits long conversations with both Cohn and Eric Hobspawm in the first preface (1957), p. 9; see also pp. 221–56; and his second edition appendix.

[29] Burridge, *New Heaven, New Earth*.

[30] Lawrence, *Road Belong Cargo*, 195–99.

[31] Anthony Wallace, *Culture and Personality* (New York: Random House, 1961).

[32] This is my impression of the current scholarship. Christianity has made huge strides in these regions over the last generation; see discussions of the advent of the year 2000 in "Millennial Countdown in New Guinea," ed. Pamela Stewart and Andrew Strathern, special issue, *Ethnohistory* 47, no. 1 (Winter 2000).

crucibles in which societies discover and deploy their cultural creativity.[33] They actually made sense.

Indeed, one might argue that the works of these anthropologists on the cargo cults and that of Norman Cohn, Christopher Hill, and Eric Hobspawm on medieval and early modern millennial movements constitute the origins of millennial studies as a scholarly field.[34] Anthropological observations of millennial movements in the South Pacific supplied sound and fury to dry pages of medieval manuscript describing similar prophets bringing on similar episodes of apocalyptic millennialism.[35] In particular, the cargo movements illustrate the most remarkable and counterintuitive of apocalyptic dynamics, the power of apocalyptic jazz to sustain a moment/movement well past the failure of its (ludicrous) initial prophetic claims.

Moreover, the millennial approach permitted these anthropologists to address not only perceptions, but also experiences and passions. They could, by dealing with this data, see how people handled the staggering cognitive and emotional impact of dealing with the West, and the immense appeal of an apocalyptic millennial transformation in formulating a response. Any native could see how the dominant white culture used its technological superiority to subjugate the indigenous people, producing an insoluble dilemma. "'The white phenomenon' was itself an eschatological event, bringing to an end the age-old lithic order by revealing an astounding mode of existence, full of power and magic."[36]

The experience of contact with so vastly superior a culture provoked a mental and spiritual convulsion among people who found that Westerners broke so many rules of the universe that they imagined these strangers could do anything. Indeed, initial contact sometimes prompted the belief that the newcomers were gods. In slang terms, the arrival of the whites blew their minds. And one of the major forms of the "thinking" and "feeling" that natives did as a result of this contact was to think in millennial and apocalyptic terms.

Islanders both reasoned and dreamed their way through the new mazeway. They used their concepts of magic to understand the European invaders, in much the same way that we use our "rationality" to understand them. They reasoned: "If we had what they have [*kago*], life would be perfect." They engaged in cognitive egocentrism: "Westerners must operate as do we: taking care of matters of success

---

[33] Michele Stephen, "Cargo Cultism, Cultural Creativity, and Autonomous Imagination," *Ethos* 25, no. 3 (1997): 333–58.

[34] For an example of a later scholar's recognition of the earlier pioneers in this field, see Michael Barkun's Introduction to *Disaster and the Millennium* (Syracuse: Syracuse University Press, 1986), 1–10.

[35] The insights that Cohn gleaned from his conversations with Worsley (see above, n. 28) certainly gave a force to his argument that earlier work in medieval millennialism largely lacked. But the marriage of medievalists and anthropologists, so successful for Cohn, did not have a ripe future; the latest generation of medieval scholars' forays into anthropology have, most often, by-passed millennialism.

[36] Trompf, *Payback*, 172; see also Andrew Lattas, "Skin, Personhood and Redemption: The Double Self in West New Britain Cargo Cults," *Oceania* 63 (1992): 27–54; Steven C. Leavitt, "The Apotheosis of White Men? A Reexamination of Belief about Europeans as Ancestral Spirits," *Oceania* 70 (2000): 304–23.

and failure by working in the world of unseen forces with magic. We will follow their lead, do their rituals, and the cargo will land for us." It made perfect sense. At this level, the *kago* cults reflect the desperate effort of these people—still largely at a stone-age level of social and technological organization—to try and catch up on millennia of Western cumulative development. And since that process had accelerated with geometric intensity over the past two centuries, that effort would inevitably be faulty.

So, to sustain itself over time and inevitable failure, that layer of thought rode on a far more powerful surge of expectation—a collective dream of millennial redemption. Believers sought (and continue to seek) dramatic answers to drastic events. And they found theirs in dreams about the future, dreams in which they now stood at the edge of redemption, center stage in the human drama. Prophets discovered, willy-nilly, that the way to attention and power was to use millennial rhetoric, to promise the perfect world of collective salvation, and to lead the faithful on the necessary path to its gates.

Many of these movements took the form of break-away congregations, led by charismatic leaders who, having trained as missionaries, took the Christian playbook and ran the plays of a transformative apocalyptic scenario that promised a demotic millennium. They used the storehouse of Christian apocalyptic and messianic symbolism to its fullest, including anointing charismatic leaders like Jimmy Stevens as a Moses leading his people to the Promised Land.[37] They invoked the end times to spur repentance, offered a comprehensive ethical and legal discipline for those who wished to accede to the millennial kingdom, innovated in a wide range of traditional practices (baptism,[38] banana-slice Eucharist[39]), and added their own creations, many of which involved sexual freedom that defied not only (conventional) Christian precepts, but local customs as well.[40] At their height, in apocalyptic time, waves of conversion to these native churches made the long, patient, and grudging success of the foreign missionaries look paltry.

The truly strange in this tale, then, may have less to do with Melanesian culture, than with the differences between normal and apocalyptic time. One gets the same impression from the anthropological reports as one does from discussions of the

---

[37] Garry Trompf, "Independent Churches in Melanesia," *Oceania* 54, no. 1 (1983): 51–72; and ibid. 54, no.2 (1983): 122–32.

[38] Lattas, *Cultures of Secrecy*, 131–33.

[39] Francis Hagai, Marist trained teacher, high officer in the Hahali movement's Church, Trompf, "Independent Churches in Melanesia, Part 1," 54–55.

[40] See, for example, the "Baby Garden" of the Hahali movement, which William Blake might have called "The Garden of Love." The leader of the Hahali is a good representative of the native, educated and elevated within the Church by missionaries, who breaks away and founds his own movement. See Trompf, "Independent Churches in Melanesia"; Ryan, *The Hot Land: Focus on New Guinea* (Melbourne: Macmillan, 1969), 290–303; Griffin, "The Hahalis Welfare Society (Buka, North Solomons)," in *Melanesian and Judeo-Christian Religious Tradition*, ed. Garry Trompf (Port Moresby, 1975), Part C Pkg 4 Opt.3, 38–43; M. Rimoldi, "Love, Kinship and Marriage in Hahalis," PhD Dissertation, University of Auckland, 1984.

Xhosa: outsiders (both native and Westerner) amazed (and disturbed) by the folly they witness, dealing with people who, in eager response to the promises of apocalyptic time, have ceased to adhere to the public transcripts. They no longer accept what their fellow islanders and the Westerners do under the impression that normal time, with its normal rules, will go on indefinitely as it had since time immemorial. For them this is not, *cannot* be, "normal time"—too great a paroxysm, too much suffering unexplained.

And from there, only a small step leads to full-blown apocalyptic time where, freed from these constraints, denizens are free to mix and match the elements of native and Western culture that they wish. They are free to express moral contempt for both the white man *and* the traditions of the ancestors; to bring out the bones of their dead *and* don the white man's clothes. They are free to drink kava and feast continuously and free to adopt new codes, new languages, new mythologies, new dreams. And each different outbreak of apocalyptic time produced a different mixture of progressive and restorative millennial expectations.

It is precisely when we step into the world of dignity and self-worth that we begin to understand both the attraction and the creativity of these apocalyptic messages for people who feel crushed by material *and* psychic forces.[41] But in millennial moments, apocalyptic discourse takes over and sweeps aside the owls, emptying villages, missions, and whole regions while enthusiasts go to the sacred places, gateways to the new heaven on earth. When we look at the social energy such ideas unleash, we begin to understand the dynamics of apocalyptic time. The prophecies operate as massive shortcuts: by creating the apocalyptic vortex, everything is at stake all at once, and redemption, total redemption, brings vindication to the victims.

But at what a price! Short-term heaven—the proleptic community of the saved—in exchange for long-term devastation—ruin, disgrace, death. What Festinger found among the followers of Dorothy Martin in the 1950s, we find among the *kago* cultists: the community formed in apocalyptic time has a sense of urgency and intimacy that some, once they have tasted it, will renounce only with great reluctance.[42] These movements illustrate a wide range of behaviors, from ascetic (renunciation, destruction of wealth) to antinomian (sexual promiscuity, wild dancing, kava drinking), and can move from one end of the spectrum to the other in the course of apocalyptic rhythms.

Perhaps one can discern in the works of Burridge and Worsley a sympathetic resonance between this inebriating element of *kago* cults and the Dionysian

---

[41] On dignity in the cargo cults, see Burridge, *New Heaven New Earth*, 119–22; on dignity and the stakes in "public transcripts," see Scott, *Domination*, 113–15; also, Avishai Margalit, *The Decent Society* (Cambridge, MA: Harvard University Press, §996). See also below, chapter 8.

[42] Festinger, *When Prophecy Fails*. The study protected her by calling her "Marion Keech"; see also Michael Barkun, *A Culture of Conspiracy: Apocalyptic Visions in Contemporary America* (Berkeley and Los Angeles: University of California Press, 2003), 156–57.

fervor that swept through Western culture in the 1960s.[43] Lindstrom suggests that in the 1960s people began to read Burridge's *Mambu* "against the grain," not, as Burridge had intended, with the hero as the good, modernizing, Westerner, but Mambu, the rebel, "...the true future. Young Dionysus chases away boring Apollo. Trance, dance, free love, drugs, cult communitarianism, the New Man, the New Age, living the myth-dream—all this, through cargo culting, becomes the human solution and not the problem."[44]

And like the '60s and many other such movements, the wave of enthusiasm builds by addressing issues of morality from an egalitarian perspective. Thus among cargo-cult discussions, most of the more sympathetic ones, starting with Worsley's 1956 pioneering study *The Trumpet Shall Sound*, favor a neo-Marxist approach to capitalist imperialism and the resistance it provokes. Here the natives' hostile attitudes attract their special attention, and the world, free of white devils, holds pride of place.[45] Their millennialism, like that of peasant rebels in the Middle Ages studied by Norman Cohn, *makes sense*. These kago cults, however, show the same (if slightly milder) forms as the Xhosa's suicidal millennial vision—destroy your crops, throw away your money, and the ancestors will return with better (salvic) goods, and the white man will be swept away.[46] Indeed the administrators faced with the phenomenon of *kago* cults thought John Frum meant John Broom who would sweep the white men out of the land.[47]

Notions of brotherhood through morality offer important points of cargoist interaction with Westerners, to the point of investing disinterested and empathic anthropologists with millennial significance. Peter Lawrence's sympathetic account of Yali, the postwar cargo cult leader, became a sacred text for Yali's successors, a kind of "Yali Gospel according to Lawrence."[48] Burridge, sharply aware of the forces at work, noted the expectations heaped on Westerners who display even "disinterested generosity." This is hardly what one might consider an apocalyptic emotion, but perhaps a sign of how remorselessly zero-sum the islanders experienced other exchanges with whites. Natives eagerly sought "messages" from Burridge, ready to suspect reluctance as deceit rather than honest modesty in his protestations of

---

[43] See Norman O. Brown, *Life Against Death: The Psychoanalytical Meaning of History* (Middleton, Conn.: Wesleyan University Press, 1959) and *Love's Body* (New York: Random House, 1966).

[44] Lamont Lindstrom, "Cargo Cult Horror," *Oceania* 70 (2000): 301–02.

[45] Trompf, *Payback*.

[46] In some cases, this involved the command to kill one's pigs (the local equivalent of the Xhosa's cattle) as a necessary preliminary to the arrival of *kago*, for example, the Tombema Enga in the 1940s: see Daryl Feil, "A World without Exchange: Millennia and the Tee Ceremonial System in Tombema-Enga Society," *Anthropos* 78 (1983): 95–99; Trompf, *Payback*, 236.

[47] Alexander Rentoul, "John Frum: Origin of New Hebrides Movement," *Pacific Islands Monthly* 19 (1949): 31, cited in Lindstrom, *Cargo Cult*, 83. It is altogether possible that this information came from a native. Lindstrom thinks it is true.

[48] Gary Trompf, "What Has Happened to Melanesian 'Cargo Cults'?" in *Religious Movements in Melanesia Today*, ed. Wendy Flannery (Goroka: Melanesian Institute for Pastoral and Socio-Economic Service, 1984), 3:35; cited in Lindstrom, *Cargo Cult*, 6.

ignorance. "I felt in some small way, the pressures that Yali and Mambu must have felt."[49]

▪ EX POST DEFECTU: KAGO CULTS AFTER THE FAILURE

And just as we find with so many other examples of this kind of transformative apocalypticism which arouse strong collective enthusiasms, these movements proved astonishingly resilient in the face of failure. The tenacity the believers demonstrated, no matter how often their predictions failed, draws our attention to the reluctance with which denizens of apocalyptic time renounce their magical world. The medieval historian, looking back centuries *ex post defectu*, tends to assume that the passage of an apocalyptic date meant the end of the belief, a "boy who cried wolf" effect.[50] But to the anthropologist watching the extraordinary ability of leaders like Mambu and Yali, and even the nonexistent John Frum, to survive failed prophecy, the evidence before their eyes contradicted such "rational" assumptions. They could hear the compelling apocalyptic rhetoric that turned failure into occasions for new and reoriented frenzies of expectation—the scapegoating accusations of betrayal,[51] the upped ante and the accompanying coercive strategies to assure compliance,[52] the need for new dates[53] and new scenarios.[54]

The results of such a teeming culture of apocalyptic outbreaks, and the struggles to handle disappointment that they set in motion, offer a dazzling array of examples of millennial dynamics and the unintended consequences of these failed expectations. Among these, the most fruitful come from new religious movements (often native churches) which "land in normal time" with a new discipline, an acculturation to the modern world. They combine new codes of regulations and punishments to create enduring communities, efforts to introduce

a new order of *lo* (law)—of peace and cooperation...to create a cohesive, rigorously ordered and rule-bound situation full of miraculous potential, on the understanding

---

[49] Burridge, *Mambu*, 237–43, quotation from p. 239.

[50] See appendix to chapter 3 at website: Interpreting Abbo of Fleury's Letter.

[51] Cognitive dissonance and scapegoating (Yali and the churches; *Road Belong Cargo*, 176); child sacrifice in the Halhali movement (Trompf, *Payback*, 224).

[52] See the discussion in Trompf, *Payback*, 232–37.

[53] Take the interesting case of the *Peli* (Hawk) association, which organized a massive human chain gang around the summit of the (traditionally sacred) Mount Hurun of east Sepik. They gathered on the seventh day of the seventh month of 1971, according to the apocalyptic calculations of a Melanesian prophet (Patrick Gesch, "Cultivation of Surprise and Excess in the Sepik," in *Cargo Cults and Millenarian Movements: Transoceanic Comparisons of New Religious Movements*, ed. Garry Trompf [New York: Mouton de Gruyer, 1990], 213–38). Their task was to restore the mountain's sacral qualities by taking away American geodesic concrete marker from the summit.

[54] Many of the new scenarios are in fact appearing in the native churches. See Jan Bieniek and Garry Trompf, "The Millennium, Not the Cargo?" *Ethnohistory* 47, no. 1 (2000): 113–32.

that the greater-than-ordinary-human forces were about to intervene to tip the balance of power and remove both oppression and oppressor.

The *lo* of these cargo movements was never *only* a system of penalties, nor the social pressures within them mere repression. They were "totalistic" in their drive for support, fired by fervent desires for the coming of the new, group wealth (the achievement of which demanded unwavering faith and loyalty, frequently toward a 'charismatic leadership')....

Whatever their negative retributive stance toward external oppressors and surrounding critics, furthermore, cargoist visions of the world are only half comprehended if they are not also grasped as the welcoming of that other dimension so close to the heartbeat of Melanesian religions: the celebration of abundance, the excitement of exchange, the preparedness for generosity and sacrifice—in other words, positive reciprocity.[55]

The medievalist rarely has someone even remotely like a sympathetic anthropologist there to record this extraordinary, rapidly shifting yet compellingly powerful post-apocalyptic discourse and preserve it for the "record." And yet the parallels seem more than intriguing. Trompf, invoking H. I. Hogbin's phrase, calls these communities "experiments in civilization."[56] The term recalls Brian Stock's characterization of eleventh-century "textual communities," specifically cases of demotic "heresies," as "laboratories of social change."[57]

In the longer run, however, even apocalyptic jazz begins to wear thin, and leaders have to change their tune. People will make enormous sacrifices under the understanding there will be a payback. When the leaders fail to deliver and normal time reasserts its heavy gravitational pull, the tricks of the trade of prophet cease to work.[58] When the Hahalis movement ran aground in the 1970s, followers began accusing the prophet Teosin of ritually killing defectors and embezzling funds (cargo!). His disaffected followers returned to Western churches; and his "Baby Garden" become a brothel for factory workers.[59]

And with these troubles for the roosters, the owls reasserted their hegemony, and the roosters either repented of their folly ("Was *I* wrong!") or went into the closet ("We were only wrong about the timing, you'll see!"). Unless they witness an actual outbreak of these "madnesses," anthropologists deal with their wake, *ex post defectu*,

---

[55] Trompf, *Payback*, 236–37.

[56] Herbert Ian Hogbin, *Experiments in Civilization: The Effects of European Culture on a Native Community of the Solomon Islands* (Routledge & Keegan Paul, London, 1969); Trompf, *Payback*, 234.

[57] Brian Stock, *Implications of Literacy: Written Language and Models of Interpretation in the Eleventh and Twelfth Centuries* (Princeton, N.J.: Princeton University Press, 1983). On the apostolic movement of the early eleventh century as post-apocalyptic textual communities bound by an egalitarian code, see R. Landes, "The Birth of Popular Heresy: A Millennial Phenomenon," *Journal of Religious History* 24 (2000): 26–43.

[58] Jimmy Stevens (Moses) used to communicate with world leaders on a make-believe radio, to organize the evacuation of the English and French (Trompf, *Payback*, 220; Bernard Hours, "Leadership et Cargo Cult. L'irresistible ascension de J.T.P.S. Moïsé," *Journal de la Société des Océanistes* 32 [1976]: 207–31.

[59] Trompf, *Payback*, 225.

a world where cargo (apocalyptic) beliefs are taboo, and only spoken of with people one trusts.

In the following passage, already partially cited, from Andrew Lattas, we see the roosters, *ex post defectu*, back in the closet, the object of disapproval from owls of all kinds:

> Some cargo cult followers initially refused to tell me their secret cult stories…and even then, some people would tell me their stories only at night, when only trusted family and friends were around. When they disclosed their secrets, they often did so with a mixture of urgency and anger at their unfair treatment, not only at the hands of Europeans and Melanesian officials, but also *at the hands of relatives and neighbors who assumed the overbearing attitudes* of government officials and missionaries.…Those who reported neighbors and relatives to government officials and missionaries did so not because they did not have cargo cult beliefs of their own, but because *they often had a sense of rivalry and outrage at the deception of some of the cult leaders* [italics mine].[60]

These conversations take place in a post-apocalyptic world (the highpoint had passed by the mid-1970s),[61] where the roosters have been "deserted by virtually all [their] followers,"[62] where many retain their cargo (millennial) beliefs in private, and where rivalries pit owls and ex-roosters against closet roosters.

And the difficulty that we have eavesdropping on this most dangerous of moral discourses should alert us to a core dimension of anthropological epistemology. How do anthropologists gather evidence when intercultural trust plays so much of a role in the nature of information exchange? Lattas, working with adherents of a banned set of beliefs, mentions only the names of the dead, and of those who had already suffered the pains of failed expectation, or, as they call it, "eaten the cane" of "criticisms, humiliations, and imprisonments."[63] Like Burridge, like any anthropologist working with "live" millennial movements, Lattas operates in a world where information can have dire consequences. Here the observer can, as the historian cannot, view the playing out by living people in oral conversation, of a "post-apocalyptic" period when the owls, briefly silent at the momentary triumph of millennial roosters, re-impose their authority.

Cargo Discourse: At the Intersection of Apocalyptic and Postmodern

One of the major dilemmas for "postmodern" anthropologists is whether to even use the term cargo cult, an expression in which both components raise

---

[60] Lattas, *Cultures of Secrecy*, xii.

[61] See the articles cited in Holger Jebens, "Trickery or Secrecy? On Andrew Lattas' Intepretation of 'Bush Kaliai Cargo Cults,'" *Anthropos* 97 (2002): 181–99, online: http://anthropology.uwaterloo.ca/WNB/Trickery%20or%20Secrecy.html, February 23, 2010.

[62] Dorothy and David Counts, "Review of Lattas," *Paideuma* 56 (2000): 325.

[63] Lattas, *Cultures of Secrecy*, xiv; see Jebens' critique of Lattas' (lack of) awareness of the problem using Lattas' own characterization of the Kaliai as a culture that revels in deception ("Trickery," 186–87).

serious epistemological problems.[64] Every aspect of the expression is troubling:

- "Cargo" clearly carries far more weight for believers than it does for their Western observers. For them it carries salvific significance, what Burridge calls a "myth-dream." Modern scholars may then misinform Western readers for whom cargo primarily has quotidian associations.
- "Cults" is a word that much scholarship on new religious movements has eschewed because it has negative connotations—irrationality, brainwashing, danger—and partakes of a hegemonic discourse that robs these movements of their voice and permits the "authorities" to intervene and prevent these allegedly "pathological" movements from running their course.[65]
- "Cargo cults" together carries an indelibly derisive sense—the exotic, the ridiculously sublime curiosity of *Mondo Cane* (1962).[66] To use the term partakes of the contempt it embodies.[67]

What stood out about *kago* cults was their embrace of Western cargo as a salvific force. Unlike the Xhosa, they did not view the coming age as a great shudder (*intifada*) that would sweep away the white man or, as did the Sioux Ghost Dancers, that the earth would peel him away as a snake does a skin. When they mistrusted the white man and grew angry, they told stories of how the ancestors had sent them cargo and the white man had switched the shipping bills of lading.

We can understand the misunderstanding. These white brothers did not share what they knew, even as they pretended to do so. Native contacts with whites produced disorientation and millennial fervor even when the whites wanted to help and offered to teach. Even the nice ones—the best-intentioned missionaries, the American armed forces,[68] the anthropologists, the sympathetic travelers—just confused matters.

The native kagoists lived in and looked for a coherent culture with a coherent worldview. They assumed the same is true in the West. Instead they ran into a cacophony of Western discourses—the political (imperialist, and with Americans,

[64] See the most recent compendium of this critique in Holger Jebens, ed., *Cargo, Cult, and Culture Critique* (Honolulu: University of Hawaii Press, 2004).

[65] For a discussion of the problems of using the word "cult" and the apparent consensus among New Religious Movement scholars not to, see remarks by James Lewis and Gordon Melton in *Oxford Handbook of New Religious Movements* (Oxford: Oxford University Press, 2004), 5–7, 17–21.

[66] The movie, a documentary about the strange and bizarre, chose cargo-cult practices as its grand finale. See Michelle Stephen, "Cargo Cults, Cultural Creativity, and Autonomous Imagination," *Ethos* 25, no. 3 (1997): 334–37. See above, n. 24, on Lindstrom's critique of "Birdism."

[67] Hermann, "Yali Movement"; see relevant remarks in Crowley's brief travel narrative ("Religion and Politics").

[68] The American presence triggered a whole new round of cargo hopes, with the Americans offering an image of messianic redeemer in contrast to the thoroughly despised Europeans and Australians. See Trompf on this aspect of American presence during and after World War II (*Payback*, 212–14).

democratic), economic (capitalist, philanthropist, and tourist), religious (Christian missionary), and intellectual (journalist, anthropologist). Natives understandably concluded that these Westerners confused them on purpose, systematically trying to keep them ignorant. For example, a key moment in the launching of the Yali Movement in an anti-Western direction came when a prospective prophet told Yali that the white man had two myths of origin, one about Adam and Eve and one about monkeys.[69] Yali assumed intentional deception rather than self-censorship and confusion. Why should he not?

But even when one understood this much, the problem remained: in comparison with other millennial movements, even ones notable for their "irrationality" (i.e., self-destructiveness), *kago* cults have an indelible element of the silly. The Xhosa might have been mad, but tragically, even nobly suicidal; the Taiping mad, but catastrophically omnicidal. None of them had so obvious an aspect of unconscious self-parody. Here we have people doing an endless variety of ritual actions in order to produce cargo, talking into phones and taking pictures with cameras carved of wood, dancing at furious rates, singing, sacrificing, killing. And all of them, at best, do not fail too drastically. Most of them, to be honest, engage in foolish childish, mistaken, and ultimately self-indulgent fantasies.

But we may not say that—too judgmental, too much an inscription of our supposed rationality onto their narratives. Lindstrom chides Burridge at the re-edition of *Mambu* (in time for the millennium), for thinking too highly of his own culture, too little of the one he studies. In Burridge's work, "Papua New Guineans think and live in terms of their culture, but European culture disappears behind a gauze of commonsense, unanalyzed presumptions of normality and *rationality*. The anthropological message is that Tangu truths are true within the world of their myth-dreams, but European truths are just true."[70] Indeed, some anthropologists, like Patrick Gesh, remain unapologetic about referring to the Western hegemonic discourse as "objective" and "rational" as they point out the fundamentally "magical" (and hence ineffective) assumptions of cargo behavior.[71]

Many anthropologists, however, have rejected the Eurocentric grand narrative of Western rationality and its mission to subjugate irrationality.[72] Postmodernism offers a particularly satisfying way to tackle so exquisite a dilemma. By destabilizing terms like "cargo" and "cult," by freeing discourse from the need to stand by the values of its own culture, by rejecting psychological terms like "madness," "hysteria,"

[69] Lawrence, *Road Belong Cargo*, p. 174.

[70] Lindstrom, "Mambu Phone Home," *Anthropological Forum* 9, no. 1 (1999): 102.

[71] Patrick Gesch, "The Cultivation of Surprise and Excess: The Encounter of Cultures in the Sepik of Papua New Guinea" in *Cargo Cults and Millenarian Movements*, 213–36.

[72] Nancy McDowell, "A Brief Comment on Difference and Rationality," *Oceania* 70 (2000): 373–79. She argues that we need to embed our understanding of rationality in culture (our own), rather than imagine that our Western rational notions transcend culture. Note that all her "we too..." examples are also millennial (Christian fundamentalism), and therefore by "Western rational" (i.e., owl's) standards irrational.

and "irrationality" as "a process of scientising race and scientising colonial domination,"[73] by focusing on narratives rather than facts, one can not only describe—often quite powerfully—the workings of these movements, but even turn the analysis back on the West, destabilizing our own comfortable verities.

This generational effort produced what some refer to as the "self-reflexive turn in anthropology," a heightened, even radical, self-criticism. Here we encounter the cargo cults as a disturbing mirror of ourselves, a cartoon version of our own past, one that mocks *us*, not them.[74] These "crazy" natives have in fact perceived the salvific promises of material goods that lie behind so much of the dynamics of modern culture and played them back to us in a grotesque parody.

In so doing, *they* reveal to us one of the more disturbing aspects of our culture, our *own* salvific relationship to cargo. Madison Avenue has a whole dimension of hidden persuaders that offer to the purchaser little fragments of the redemptive results promised by cargo prophets.[75] Commodity fetishism drives the modern world—in Marxian terms, it drives the dialectic of history. The never-ending false promise of cargo as salvation plays the same role in modern Western economies that the natives' cargo has played in theirs. Indeed, one might call Black Friday (the big day of sales after Thanksgiving), with its lines at shopping malls that begin to form before midnight, as the High Mass of consumerism. We get material well-being without joy; and *they* get fleeting joy without material benefit.[76]

Lamont Lindstrom, one of the analysts of cargocult *discourse*, describes the dilemma of insatiable desires in the shaping of these movements. He uses the language of love and desire; I have inserted the millennial terminology in brackets.

> Cargo cults are a kind of late capitalist romance. Like love, cargo [millennial] desire metaphorically is a form of madness. And even apparent acquisition of the love object [millennial cargo] cannot end the story. [Millennial d]esire is never satisfied and lovers lust after the never-ending emotion of aching desire itself [apocalyptic expectation] as much as they covet some particular lover. A lover in the end, like the [millennial] marketplace where one may never stop shopping [hoping], never fully satisfies.[77]

---

[73] Andrew Lattas, "Hysteria, Anthropological Disclosure and the Concept of the Unconscious. Cargo Cults and the Scientisation of Race and Colonial Power," *Oceania* 63 (1992): 5, cited in Jebens, "Trickery," 185.

[74] For a summary with multiple references, see Jebens, "Trickery," 181–82.

[75] See Vance Packard, *The Hidden Persuaders* (New York: D. McKay Company, 1957); Garry Trompf, "The Cargo and the Millennium on Both Sides of the Pacific," in *Cargo Cults and Millenarian Movements*, 35–94; for an analysis of the Reagan years' "obsessive pursuit of material accumulation" as a "cargo cult unleashed by the bourgeoisie and its charismatic leaders," see Gerrit Huizer, "Cargo and Charisma: Millenarian Movements in Today's Global Context," *Canberra Anthropology* 15 (1992): 106–30.

[76] There is a similar dynamic at work the never-ending false promise of unenjoyed wealth accumulation offered to the Puritan drivers of industrialization. See Max Weber, *Protestant Ethic and the Spirit of Capitalism*, trans. Stephen Kalberg (Los Angeles: Roxbury Publishing Company, 2002); on the insatiability of narcissistic needs and their aggregate cultural impact, see Christopher Lasch, *The Culture of Narcissism: American Life in an Age of Diminishing Expectations* (New York: Warner Books, 1980).

[77] Lindstrom, "Cargo Cult Horror," 294.

Millennial desire is a form of hope addiction, and what cargoism teaches us, among other things, is that the more "realizable," the more "conceivable" the promise—for example, something concrete like cargo—the more easily can one hold out hope for its advent. In a profound sense, these natives echo in grand millennial terms the basic secret hope of so many members of consumer society—"if I could only have *that*, then I'd be happy." Some of the edgier recent anthropological literature emphasizes this ironic critique of the West embedded in the apparently foolish "reading" of cargoists.[78]

■ DECONSTRUCTION'S DOWNSIDE

The attempt at deconstruction, however, creates its own problems. A politically correct discourse aimed at preserving the dignity of the indigenes becomes a new coin of the realm, and Western hegemonic thought slips in the back door. For example, argue some, scholars should not be so racist as to imagine that other human beings would not be capable of basic rationality.[79] Gananath Obeyesekere makes an argument aimed specifically at modern liberal taste when he doubted that the Hawaiians saw Captain Cook as their god Lano because "depicting a rogue European traveler as a 'god' was inherently implausible, as a violation of a general human practical rationality."[80] Obviously the Hawaiians, on first contact, did not know what a rogue European traveler was, much less that Cook was one. But the offense to native pride and our sympathy for that badly abused pride favors such formulations, explicit or implicit.

But projecting rationality, no matter how well intentioned, has its pitfalls. The functionalist model, to which it ultimately resorts, holds that some cunning of human nature makes it inevitable that cultures adapt, and adapt successfully. Everything is "eventually" rational, even if that is not evident in the early phase. But at the very time as it posits an evolutionary force of considerable interpretive power, functionalism continues to project Western rationality (really *ex post defectu* learning) back onto people and movements who dance to a different drum.[81] The cognitive egocentrism of Western functionalism, historiographic or anthropological, is to project onto other cultures some (hidden) rational calculus that makes them "like us," and hence, understandable to us.

[78] Doug Dalton, "Cargo Cults and Discursive Madness," *Oceania* 70 (2000): 345–61.

[79] For an interesting and courageous discussion of this as far back as 1964, see Jarvie, *Revolution in Anthropology*. The flaws he addresses in this "methodological egalitarianism" have, if anything, become more severe with the advent of postcolonialism.

[80] Leavitt's paraphrase of Obeyesekere's argument in *The Apotheosis of Captain Cook* (Princeton: Princeton University Press, 1992), 8, 19–21; Leavitt, "The Apotheosis of White Men?" *Oceania*, 70 (2000): 304. See comments on Edward Said, below, n. 85.

[81] See discussion of these matters in chapter 3, above, and appendix on the apocalyptic genealogy of suicide terrorism at website.

Eager to avoid mocking cargo cults, some anthropologists so contextualized these movements in Melanesian religion and culture that the larger culture in which these movements arise becomes "cargoized."

> Melting down cargo and cult into ordinary Melanesian cultural practice establishes an awful equation between cargo cult and Melanesian culture. Cargo cult sinks down and disappears into the fundamental structures of Melanesian cognition and sociability; but in so doing it contaminates and consumes these. What used to be Melanesian culture becomes cargo cult writ large.[82]

And often enough, clarifying and acknowledging the constructed nature of Western cargo discourse has led to more self-reflection than to a better understanding of these movements. For some the phenomenon "cargo cults" cease to exist, or at least takes a back seat to discussions of Western "desires" that make cargo cult discourse so intriguing to us Western intellectuals.

We end up with a form of anti-Orientalist discourse that mostly attacks the West. In avoiding value judgments on the islanders, the Westerner self-abases before their (perceived) value judgments against us. Lattas, in the eyes of his critics, falls into a classic "postcolonial" morality play where the Westerners are the bad subjugators, and the Kaliai are the subjugated good guys.[83] By mapping a postcolonial discourse about inscribing hegemony on subalterns, the anthropologist can "identify himself with and speak for the [subjugated native] and speak for the latter from a position of assumed moral authority."[84]

We find a similar, disguised neo-positivism in the work of someone like Edward Said, who forbids "othering" with his invocation of a "common humanity" that assumes basic "rationalist" elements favored by the very Western culture he critiques.

> At all costs, the goal of Orientalizing the Orient again and again is to be avoided, with consequences that cannot help but refine knowledge and reduce the scholar's conceit. Without "the Orient" there would be scholars, critics, intellectuals, human beings, for whom the racial, ethnic, and national distinctions [note the lack of mention of *religion*] were less important that the common enterprise in promoting human community.[85]

To do otherwise would be racist.

---

[82] Lindstrom, *Cargo Cult*, 42.

[83] Jebens, "Trickery," 195–98. The most recent expression of this dilemma comes in the immensely popular movie *Avatar* (2010), in which the plot is a paper-thin tale of good, nature-enmeshed natives versus predatory, technology-addicted white folks, all delivered with the most magisterial application of the latest movie technology.

[84] Jebens, "Trickery," 197.

[85] Said, *Orientalism* (New York: Vintage, 1979), 328. For an analysis of the noxious effect of Said's impact on anthropology, see Herbert Lewis, "The Impact of Edward Said on Anthropology, or: Can the Anthropologist Speak?" *Post-Colonial Theory and the Arab-Israeli Conflict*, ed. Phillip Salzman and Donna Divine (London: Routledge, 2008), 96–108.

In so doing, however, we run the risk of replicating the very effects of "silencing the discourse of others in order to read [our] own discourse on top of them," that these same anthropologists decry.[86] "The Kaliai appear as equally voiceless, faceless, anonymous, and homogenous...By representing the Kaliai this way, Lattas ultimately widens the cultural distance between them and the Western reader, instead of bridging that distance, which could be seen as one of the most important objectives of anthropology."[87] Empathy becomes sympathy,[88] and yields to cultural self-effacement: Who are we to judge? We dare not, even if, as Kenelm Burridge repeatedly points out, *they* never cease to judge. And even if, in their own version of millennialism, postmodern anthropologists enlist themselves on the side of the oppressed, thus joining rather than studying millennial currents. Rather than reading a Western owl's discourse of reason, they read a Western rooster's discourse of (national) liberation.

The dilemma is deep. How can we heal the wounds that "we," by our very presence, have and continue to inflict on "them"? How can we teach them about the "real" cargo they seem to want so—how one makes and acquires it—without destroying their culture? How to share, without turning them into the "soulless" rational zombies that we fear we have become? How can we acknowledge the radical "otherness" of this culture's workings and still keep it within the realm of ("rational," i.e., not self-destructive) humanity?

■ POSTMODERN DISCOURSE AND MILLENNIALISM

The problem may not be that we are dealing with another, radically different culture—although we may—but also, and more certainly, with a radically different aspect of cultural existence which, despite its importance, lies beyond our cognitive reach, and seems desperately alien. In that sense, what we face with *kago movements* is, indeed, something radically other. Trying to understand the phenomenon genuinely challenges our cognitive egocentrism at the same time as it challenges our self-perceptions.

But why should we Westerners look on in such amazement, as if members of our culture and race had not done equally "stupid" things—like following a goose and a goat to the Holy Land (1096)?[89] Why should we act as if the postwar movements of John Frum and Yali were weird nativistic behavior, when they rode in the wake of the most terrifyingly destructive Western millennial movements—Nazism and

---

[86] Andrew Lattas, "Primitivism in Deluze and Guattari's *A Thousand Plateaus*," *Social Analysis* 30 (1991): 111.

[87] Jebens, "Trickery," 197.

[88] Lawrence's treatment of Yali is at once nuanced and sympathetic. One is therefore not prepared from his depiction to encounter the version of Yali proffered by a fellow islander as a sexual predator (on young women, some of whom mysteriously die after he leaves); see "A Short Note on the Mythology of Yali," *Journal of the Polynesian Society* 71, no. 3 (1982): 449–52.

[89] Above, chapter 4, n. 45.

Communism—the very causes of the World War?[90] Why should we even show surprise at *kago cults*, when we have our own, based not on analyzing the real presence of a technologically superior civilization, but on imagining the existence of a superior civilization in space that will come with their *kago*—vastly superior technology and wisdom—and save us from ourselves?[91] The answer to the question of "otherness," then, may not concern so much the "otherness" of the black-skinned islanders and the white-skinned invaders, but *the otherness of the rooster and the owl*.

After all, if the postmodernists are right, *kago* cults are a parodic critique of our own irrational desires. These Paleolithic tribal folk actually saw (without realizing it) what we could not: that our manufactured goods are also salvific cargo, that behind these technological wonders with which they were confronted as if from a ten-millennia-long sleep, lay a millennial genealogy.[92] When Lindstrom chides Burridge for not including the Western myth-dream in his analysis (he uses the word "dissecting"), he is thinking of modernity. If anything has emerged from the first two generations of millennial scholarship, it is that modernity itself is a European millennial dream with a long genealogy, especially in monotheism.[93] So now we have what Burridge did not: a discussion of how many pioneer scientists drank deeply from the well of millennial dreams, from the early "scientists" like Bacon, Priestly, and Newton, to the latest crop of geniuses pushing the limits of Artificial Intelligence and Artificial Life.[94]

And yet, ironically, even though anthropology provides one of the most fruitful and important sources of knowledge about millennialism—and Melanesia is a virtual petri dish of millennial experimentation—the self-reflexive turn in anthropology does not seem to have included much attention to the West's millennial myth-dreams. And this seems to be the case even though the anthropologists have one of the major conduits of Western millennialism in their very field of research—the missionaries and their Bible. Once local peoples get a hold of that Bible, they "inscribe" their indigenous narratives about the past and the future on its grand narrative of cosmic salvation in history. The missionaries, whose zeal always burns brighter in apocalyptic time, spread versions of apocalyptic dramas over which they rapidly lose control. If we were to identify and compare all the

[90] See below, chapters 10–11. Note that when McDowell calls Western rationality into question, she focuses on Christian fundamentalists and apocalyptic nuts ("Brief Comment"), not on the millennialism of Marxist and post-Marxist deconstruction. See below, chapters 10 (Marx) and 11 (Communism).

[91] See below, chapter 13.

[92] For the millennial dreams behind the peculiarly Western (Promethean) passion for science and technology, see David Noble, *Religion of Technology: The Divinity of Man and the Spirit of Invention* (New York: A.A. Knopf, 1997).

[93] Burridge himself was probably not familiar with the millennial genealogy about which most Westerners remain largely ignorant where it concerns the origins of science (below, chapter 8). Even had he had known that Newton was a millennialist when he went to do his fieldwork, he could hardly have argued that.

[94] Noble, *Religion of Technology*, 143–208.

Western narratives that local people have appropriated for their own use, often in defiance of the colonial authorities, millennial ones would stand in first place: their "madness" is ours, indeed, it is human.[95]

The pattern is familiar. The white man brings his Christianity (one largely purged of enthusiastic millennialism), and the native hears another (one largely based on millennial enthusiasm).[96] The outbreaks of apocalyptic time, when large numbers embrace a prophecy about the imminent advent of the *kago*, mark particularly creative moments of religious synthesis. In their aftermath of apocalyptic failure, some believers abandon the faith, some return to Western churches, and some "congeal" into a native, church movement, able to survive in "normal time."

Aside from Garry Trompf, however, most recent anthropologists working on cargo cults seem to know far less about non-Melanesian millennialism than did Peter Worsley.[97] Rather than try and supply the millennial myth-dream that Burridge lacked, Lindstrom prefers to de-center that of modernity. Neither he, nor Lattas, use millennialism as an analytic category;[98] neither pays much attention to the role of apocalyptic expectations in producing the narratives they study.

Indeed, if anyone has done their homework on this one, it is the missionaries who begin to acknowledge both the millennial origins of these *kago* hopes, and their own religion's contribution to that situation. They have begun to see their own work in terms of taking these local religious manifestations more seriously. Nor are they unmoved by the values that animated anthropology's reflexive turn. These missionaries are a far cry from their predecessors driven by the need to *impose* their grand narrative:

> We need to do everything possible to ensure the full measure of human dignity, equality of being and potential for self-determination among those with whom we serve and minister. This is going to mean learning to act as brothers, not as bosses; of giving suggestions, not orders; of setting standards and making decisions that are subject to consensus opinion which carries the weight of group support, rather than our own arbitrary personal demands; it is going to mean having to see some of our choice plans and ideas being "mangled" by co-workers who fail to share our perceptions.[99]

---

[95] Weston La Barre, *Ghost Dance*.

[96] For a parallel in American slavery, see Albert Raboteau, *Religion and the Slave Family in the Antebellum South*, Center for the Study of American Catholicism Working Paper Series 7 (South Bend: Notre Dame University Press, 1980).

[97] See Gary Trompf, *Early Christian Historiography: Narratives of Retributive Justice* (London: Continuum Press, 2000).

[98] And, at least in the case of Lindstrom and Lattas, in the process, millennialism disappears as an analytic category (see Ton Otto on Lindstrom, "Cargo Cults Everywhere?" *Anthropological Forum* 9, no.1 [1999]: 90–91; Lattas does not have an entry for either millenarianism or messianism in his index; alterity and hegemony have large entries.

[99] Douglas Hayward, "Melanesian Millenarian Movements: an Overview" in *Religious Movements in Melanesia Today*, vol.1 (Goroka, Papua New Guinea: Melanesian Institute for Pastoral and Socio-Economic Service, 1983), 20.

The missionaries may be still driven by a Western "grand narrative" of global conversion to Christianity, but it is no longer the top-down imposition of salvation, but a demotic one of equality and dignity. What may distinguish them from anthropologists, ironically, is that they are more aware of what they are doing than those postmodern radicals who think they have slipped the net.

PART THREE

Agrarian Millennialism

6 Imperial Millennialism

The Monotheist Pharaoh Akhenaten
(1360–1347 BCE)

How manifold it is, what thou hast made!
They are hidden from the face (of man).
O sole god, like whom there is no other!
Thou didst create the world according to thy desire,
Whilst thou wert alone: All men, cattle, and wild beasts,
Whatever is on earth, going upon (its) feet,
And what is on high, flying with its wings.
The countries of Syria and Nubia, the land of Egypt,
Thou settest every man in his place,
Thou suppliest their necessities:
Everyone has his food, and his time of life is reckoned.
Their tongues are separate in speech,
And their natures as well;
Their skins are distinguished,
As thou distinguishest the foreign peoples.
Thou makest a Nile in the underworld,
Thou bringest forth as thou desirest
To maintain the people (of Egypt)
According as thou madest them for thyself,
The lord of all of them, wearying (himself) with them,
The lord of every land, rising for them,
The Aten of the day, great of majesty.

—Great Hymn to Aten, ca. 1350 BCE*

Somewhere around 1400 BCE, the Eighteenth-Dynasty Egyptian pharaohs reached the height of an imperial conquest and consolidation quite uncharacteristic of earlier Egyptian dynasties. From Thutmose I to Amenhotep III (ca. 1500–1350 BCE[1]), Egyptian power, normally Nile-bound, had spread over an area from Sudan to Libya to the borders of Syria, bringing under pharaonic rule large numbers of foreign peoples.[2] The

---

* James B. Pritchard, ed., *The Ancient Near East*, vol. 1, *An Anthology of Texts and Pictures* (Princeton, N.J.: Princeton University Press, 1958), 227–30; Robert Hari, *New Kingdom, Amarna Period: The Great Hymn to Aten* (Leiden: Brill, 1985).

[1] In matters of chronology, Egyptologists working in this period have approximately a twenty-year wobble between their data (given in regnal years) and any overarching dating system like the Common Era one.

[2] William Hayes, *The Scepter of Egypt: A Background for the Study of Egyptian Antiquities in the Metropolitan Museum of Art*, Part 2, *The Hyksos Period and the New Kingdom (1675–1080 B.C.)* (New York: Metropolitan Museum of Art, 1959), chap. 2–7; Ian Shaw, ed., *The Oxford History of Ancient Egypt* (Oxford: Oxford University Press, 2000), chap. 9–10.

rulers and ideologues of this dynasty dealt with this unprecedented situation by articulating a language of divinity and kingship that was less parochial than previous Egyptian formulas and better suited to Egypt's prominence in the family of nations. Among the most popular elements of this discourse, we find the intensification of a sun-cult that associated the emperor with the sungod, and a corresponding imperial ideology that made the pharaoh the cosmic ruler not only of Egypt but of the world.[3]

The climax of this development came around 1370 BCE when, in his thirtieth year of reign, Amenhotep III celebrated his first Sed festival (Jubilee). He subsequently held two more in years thirty-four and thirty-seven before dying two years later. These celebrations were spectacular affairs, and the immense expenditures both for the enduring memorials in stone and the logistics of the celebration have left an extensive body of evidence in their wake.[4] They mark an apotheosis of this sun-king imagery, with its attendant deification of the living pharaoh, which had been building since early in the dynasty.[5] Nothing comparable to this magnificence existed anywhere else in the world at this time.

This precocious society also had a highly evolved elite culture. Its realistic, dynamic, and imaginative art predates that of Greece by almost a millennium.[6] And ruling over this empire we find an exceptionally effective administrative body of highly trained and cooperative officials, one that used multiple forms of literate communication and used them imaginatively.[7] They showed a correspondingly acute interest in the historical record, and used it to shape the present, as in the case of the Sed festival.[8]

---

[3] "The term 'ruler of that which the sun-disc encircles' has, by the Eighteenth Dynasty, become firmly established as indicating Pharaoh's worldwide dominion," Donald Redford, "The Sun-Disc in Akhenaten's Program: Its Worship and Antecedents, I," *Journal of the American Research Center in Egypt* 13 (1976): 47–61, at 49.

[4] On the Sed festivals, see below, 159–63.

[5] The deification of the living pharaoh that took place in the New Kingdom develops a tradition of Egyptian royal theology (pharaoh the "good," perfect, present god). For a sense of the predominance of Egypt internationally, see the Amarna letters (found at Amarna, but dating from the reign of Amenhotep III). They offer a striking dossier of international relations based on positive-sum principles. See Raymond Cohen and Raymond Westbrook, eds., *Amarna Diplomacy: The Beginnings of International Relations* (Baltimore: Johns Hopkins University Press, 2000).

[6] Arielle Kozloff et al., *Egypt's Dazzling Sun: Amenhotep III and His World* (Cleveland: Cleveland Museum of Art, 1992), 7.

[7] For instance, commemorative scarabs from the beginning of Amenhotep III's reign have been found throughout the Levant and even in Crete. These scarabs may have been sent to foreign rulers or Egyptian agents as gifts or announcements; see James M. Weinstein et al., "The World Abroad" in *Amenhotep III: Perspectives on His Reign*, ed. David O'Connor and Eric H. Cline (Ann Arbor: University of Michigan Press, 1998), 234, 245–46.

[8] Tiy, Amenhotep III's principle queen and the mother of both Thutmose (the eldest son who would have been Pharaoh had he lived) and of Akhenaten, had an archive/collection of historical documents. The Brooklyn Museum contains a First Dynasty tablet with a note on the back indicating that the piece belonged to the queen; Donald Redford, *Akhenaten: The Heretic King* (Princeton, N.J.: Princeton University Press, 1984), 52.

Indeed, so much information survives about this bureaucracy, that scholars can even attempt a prosopography of these administrative superstars whose elaborate and eloquent tombs inform us on both their accomplishments and the tone of court life.[9] Among its officials, we find someone whose cult lived on after him, and who, along with Imhotep (the "inventor" of the pyramids, 27th century BCE) became deified in later centuries.[10] Amenhotep sa-Hapu (son of Hapu), a commoner from the delta, rose to the top of the imperial hierarchy, regulated it felicitously for decades, and must rank among the most extraordinary viziers in the history of world culture.[11] Among his many accomplishments rank his engineering of the (misnamed) Colossi of Memnon,[12] and his crowning success, the staging the great Sed festival of regnal year 30, which will play a pivotal part in the tale we are about to examine.[13]

Amenhotep sa-Hapu and his pharaoh seem to have presided over one of the most extraordinary periods in Egyptian history. One rarely finds so much evidence for a truly "civic" culture in the long and largely belligerent history of humankind. It is not often that the emperor of Babylon wrote to the pharaoh complaining "when you celebrated a great festival (the Sed festival), you did not send your messenger to me saying, 'come to eat and drink.'"[14] Amenhotep III was the "sunking," and sa-Hapu was the impresario of his divine cult.[15]

And yet, at the very height of this imperial splendor, everything fell apart rapidly during the reign of Amenhotep III's successor, Akhenaten. Within two decades, the empire had imploded, Egyptian imperial hegemony shattered in the restless warfare of "plunder-or-be-plundered" kings of the Near East. And Egypt was laid waste. As a restoration stela from the next reign claims:

---

[9] W. Helck, *Zur Verwaltung des Mittleren und Neuen Reichs* (Leiden: Brill, 1958), 285–443. Much of the debate surrounding the transition from Amenhotep III to his son, the future Akhenaten, turns around the contents of these tombs of high officials; see F.J. Martin Valentin, "Indications et évidences d'un ecorégence entre Amenhotep III et IV" in *Proceedings of the Seventh International Congress of Egyptologists, Cambridge, 3–9 September 1995*, ed. C.J. Eyre (Leuven: Peeters, 1998), 741–57.

[10] Dietrich Wildung, *Imhotep und Amenhotep* (Munich: Deutscher Kunstverlag, 1977); Wildung, *Egyptian Saints: Deification in Pharaonic Egypt* (New York: New York University Press, 1977).

[11] I use the term vizier here anachronistically. It derives from Arabic in a later period and is often used by Egyptologists to designate the "*tjaty*," a figure similar to the prime minister, e.g., Andrew Gordon, "Who Was the Southern Vizier during the Last Part of the Reign of Amenhotep III?" *Journal of Near Eastern Studies* 48, no.1 (1989): 15–23. Cf. another extraordinary case: Gerbert of Aurillac, the commoner who became Pope Sylvester II.*

[12] See below, n. 50.

[13] On sa-Hapu, see Alexandre Varille, *Amenhotep fils de Hapou* (Cairo: Imprint de l'Institut français d'archéologie orientale, 1968) and William J. Murnane, "Servant, Seer, Saint, Son of Hapu: Amenhotep, Called Huy," *KMT* 2, no.2 (1991): 8–13, 56–58. He probably died one to three years after Amenhotep III's thirty-year Sed festival.

[14] Amarna Letter EA 3, *Amarna Letters*, trans. William J. Moran (Baltimore: Johns Hopkins University Press, 1992), 7; cited in O'Connor and Klein, *Amenhotep III*, 18.

[15] See W.R. Johnson on the role of the first Sed festival as the deification of Amenhotep III ("Monuments and Monumental Art under Amenhotep III: Evolution and Meaning," in O'Connor and Cline, *Amenhotep III*, 87–88); also Reeves, *Akhenaten: Egypt's False Prophet* (New York: Thames & Hudson, 2001), 71–73.

...the temples and the cities of the gods and goddesses, starting from Elephantine as far as the Delta marshes...were fallen into decay and their shrines were fallen into ruin, having become mere mounds of overgrown grass. Their sanctuaries were like something which had not yet come into being and their buildings were a footpath—for the land was in rack and ruin...When an army was sent to Djahy [Canaan], to broaden the boundaries of Egypt, it was unsuccessful....[16]

Ancient Egyptian historiography is not normally known for its honest admission of such catastrophic failure.

How did such a rapid collapse occur in what seemed like the most splendid and successful imperial adventure the world had ever seen? There is only one answer: the deeds of the most controversial and unusual pharaoh in Egyptian history, the legendary "heretic pharaoh," Akhenaten, the first documented monotheist in history.[17] And in the argument of this book, Akhenaten is also the first millennial monotheist in history.

Taking over the empire that his father had given him, Akhenaten proceeded to dissipate it all in a frenetic series of moves inspired by an overwhelming commitment to the Aten, the sun-disk, as the manifestation of the only God, the creator God, in whose image he, Akhenaten, ruled over the world. Beginning with an unprecedented Jubilee *early* in his reign (year 3), which he repeated at least once,[18] Amenhotep IV then changed his name to Akhenaten, *beneficial to Aten* (year 5/6); built and moved to a new capital halfway between the northern capital (Memphis) and the southern (Thebes); set off an Egypt-wide campaign of iconoclasm and mutilation of the public record in an effort to eliminate all cults other than that of the Aten and in particular obliterate the name of Amun (year 12). Within a few years, he was dead, leaving behind a churning wake of hostility that obliterated almost every trace of his existence. He remained unknown to history until nineteenth-century European archeological digs uncovered the evidence of his bizarre career. Few reigns in ancient history are more spectacular, better documented, and yet, leave so many unanswered questions.

We do not know, for example, how to interpret the sudden death of his eldest daughter Meritaten and the disappearance of his beloved wife Nefertiti in year 12. Did she die? Did he have her eliminated? Did she disappear (fall out of favor?) and reappear later, this time as Pharaoh Smenkhare?! We are not sure who were the parents of the next young pharaoh, Tutenkhaten, or under whose influence he changed his name to Tutenkhamen. We do not know whether Tutenkhamen acted alone, or others launched and sustained the counter-campaign, aimed at systematically destroying the memory of his predecessor (father?) and restoring, as much

---

[16] Restoration Stela of Karnak (ca. 1330), cited in Reeves (his translation), *Akhenaten*, 182.

[17] In principle, Abraham, the first monotheist in the biblical tradition, dates back to the eighteenth century BCE, but Akhenaten is the first verifiably historical figure to deploy some form of explicit monotheism in a systematic political program aimed at transforming society.

[18] On the "co-regency" hypotheses, see discussion below.

as possible, the status quo ante. So many wild and wildly opposing scenarios—and yet each in its own way plausible for such a unruly time, leaving us in the dark about how the Egyptian court navigated its way back from Akhenaten's world to the norms of Egyptian political behavior.

We do know Akhenaten was reviled in Egyptian memory, banished from the "public" (inscribed) record except as "the rebel" (*sebiu*) or "the criminal" (*kheru*) of Akhetaten, and recalled in oral discourse as a mad and heinous figure.[19]

> The simplest and commonest technique of forgetting is *the destruction of memory* in its cultural objectifications such as inscriptions and iconic representations. This is what happened to the monotheistic revolution of Akhenaten, and the destruction was thorough enough to keep this event completely irretrievable until its archaeological rediscovery in the course of the nineteenth century.[20]

First the 1840 discovery of the remains of his first Sed festival in Thebes and still later, that of the city of Akhetaten in Amarna, permitted modern Egyptologists to finally reconstruct this extraordinary episode in Egyptian history.[21]

All this constitutes a fascinating combination of high drama, paparazzi gossip, and exceptionally precocious expressions of monotheism, against the backdrop of the great Egyptian empire of the later fifteenth to early fourteenth century BCE. The discovery of Akhenaten's traces transformed religious history, prompting a wide range of studies that considered his possible influence on Moses (including Freud's), with a number of scholars (like the great Egyptologist Breasted), arguing that he prefigured Jesus:

> Love! One stands amazed at the reckless idealism, the beautiful folly, of this Pharaoh who, in an age of turbulence preached a religion of peace to seething Syria. Three thousand years later mankind is still blindly striving after these same ideals in vain. Nowadays one is familiar with the doctrine: a greater than Akhenaten has preached it, and has died for it.[22]

Akhenaten has served as the subject of plays, novels, operas, movies, psychoanalytic and medical studies, and a host of historical reconstructions that go from the most serious (and rather dry) analyses to the most imaginative speculation.[23] The stunning museum exhibit on just this historical period—*Pharaohs of the Sun* (1999)—was one of the best attended since that of Akhenaten's "son," Tutenkhamen.

---

[19] Manetho, an Egyptian priest under Ptolemy II (first half of the third century BCE) managed to fuse what the ancient Egyptians might have considered two black spots in the history of the Middle Kingdom (the reign of Akhenaten and the Exodus) into one narrative. See Jan Assmann, *Moses the Egyptian* (Cambridge, Mass.: Harvard University Press, 1997), 30–33.

[20] Assmann, *Moses the Egyptian*, 216.

[21] Amarna's remains were first noted by Napoleon's savant, Edmé Jomard, in 1798, but its significance only appeared after the deciphering of hieroglyphs and the first "reading" of the Amarna inscriptions by Karl Richard Lepsius in the 1840s.

[22] Arthur Weigall, *The Life and Times of Akhnaton Pharaoh of Egypt* (Edinburgh: William Blackwood & Sons, 1911), 227–28. For the best treatment of this trend, see Assmann, *Moses the Egyptian*, especially his discussion of Freud's *Moses and Monotheism* (1939), 144–67.

[23] See Dominic Montserrat, *Akhenaten, History and Fantasy* (London: Routledge, 2000), chap. 6–7.

For both the lowest motivations of popular culture, and the highest concerns of historical analysis, Akhenaten is a superstar. One historian called him, "history's first individual."[24]

■ ANOMALIES

Despite the relative richness of the historical record (documents, artwork, archeological remains) we understand very little of what we would like to know about so fascinating a historical moment. Among the puzzles, however, let us note some of the more striking anomalies of the Akhenaten episode.

The Speed of the Transformation and Its Disappearance

Jan Assmann noted that "two aspects of Ahkenaten's religious revolution are especially astounding: its incredible speed and radicalism, and the total obliteration of all traces of it in the aftermath."[25] Normally, given Egypt's political traditionalism, even if a pharaoh were to introduce major changes, he would disguise them in forms from the past. Here, on the contrary, not only does Amenhotep IV openly embrace the most radical change, but does so at near-lightning speed. And the rapidity with which his successors buried his efforts suggests just how unnatural Egyptian elites found this particular episode.

Origin and Nature of Monotheism

Above all, we do not know whence the monotheism and, still more, the iconoclasm came. Although some historians may try to dismiss some of the development of the Aten cult and its monotheistic language as a "mere" nuance of difference from earlier religious ideas,[26] the very transformations of imagery, particularly the sudden appearance of the sun-disk with emanating rays terminating in hands, hallmark of Akhenaten's "mature" style, underlines how radical the nature of the religious imagination at work.[27] The poetry this strange ruler composed

---

[24] James Breasted, *A History of the Ancient Egyptians* (New York: Scribner & Sons, 1908), 265. Having read Amenhotep sa-Hapu's details (see below, n. 52), I would propose him as both a predecessor in individuation and in visionary projects, and a direct influence on the pharaoh, since the future Akhenaten grew up in the court over which sa-Hapu presided.

[25] Jan Assmann, *The Mind of Egypt: History and Meaning in the Time of the Pharaohs*, trans. Andrew Jenkins (New York: Henry Holt, 1996), 214.

[26] "The sun-worship of Akhenaten, which most modern observers have accepted as a new and revolutionary religion, differed from these re-edited doctrines of the Re-cult by a mere nuance, by placing a little more emphasis upon the Aten, or visible manifestation of godhead, than upon Re, the hidden power that motivated it," Cyril Aldred, "Egypt: The Amarna Period and the End of the Eighteenth Dynasty," *Cambridge Ancient History*, vol. 2 (London: Cambridge University Press, 1975), chap. 19 and 87.

[27] Redford, "Sun-Disc," 53–56.

(or inspired)—most famously, the hymn to Aten quoted as epigraph to this chapter—replicates the intense religiosity and even the language of the Hebrew Psalm 104. Indeed, most Egyptologists argue that this hymn inspired the psalm that, according to Jewish tradition, would only be composed about four centuries later by David (ca. 1000 BCE).[28]

Origin and Nature of Iconoclasm

Less than a decade after assuming power, Akhenaten took this religious fervor into a ferocious iconoclastic campaign that violated every norm of Egyptian religious culture—a *damnatio memoriae* of all the (other) gods. Nor was this iconoclastic campaign merely a personal pique. He gave the orders from his solar capital at Akhetaten, and though he never left it, an army of zealots proceeded to hack out names all over Egypt. Even private possessions like scarabs bear the marks of this extraordinarily intrusive campaign that will often recur in the history of iconoclasm. Many Egyptians, however, reviled these innovations. And the mark their anger at this intrusion appears clearly in the energy with which the next generation wiped out every trace they could of the rebel.

Relationship of Akhenaten with His Father Amenhotep III

There is a very difficult dispute among Egyptologists on the transition from Amenhotep III to Amenhotep IV (later Akhenaten). Three scenarios have support:

1. the long co-regency, in which the son already shared the throne with his father as early as the twenty-eighth year of his reign, in which case Akhenaten's three Sed festivals are also his father's;[29]
2. a short co-regency of about two years in which case the first Sed festival of the son is the last of the father's;[30] and
3. a succession at death, in which case Akhenaten's three Sed festivals follow his father's.[31]

Each of these scenarios has important implications both for our understanding of family relations (father-son/son-mother/son-wife) and for our understanding of

[28] On the two texts, see K.H. Bernhardt, "Amenophis IV und Psalm 104" *Mitteilungen des Instituts für Orientforschung* 15 (1969): 193–206; Donald Redford, "The Monotheism of the Heretic Pharaoh: Precursor of Mosaic Monotheism or Egyptian Anomaly?" *Biblical Archeology Review* 13, no. 3 (1987): 27; Jan Assmann, "Die 'Häresie' des Echnaton," *Saeculum* 23 (1972): 121–22; V. A. Tobin, "Amarna and Biblical Religion," in *Pharaonic Egypt: The Bible and Christianity*, ed. S.I. Groll (Jerusalem: Magnes Press, 1985), 231–77.

[29] The strongest advocates are Cyril Aldred, "The Beginning of the el-Amarna Period," *Journal of Egyptian Archeology* 45 (1959): 19–33; W.R. Johnson, "Amenhotep III and Amarna," *Journal of Egyptian Archeology* 82 (1996): 65–82; Francisco Jose Martin Valentin, "Indications et évidences," 741–57.

[30] Reeves suggests the possibility in *Akhenaten*, 76–78.

[31] Donald Redford, "On the Chronology of the Egyptian Eighteenth Dynasty," *Journal of Near Eastern Studies* 25 (1966): 113–24; Reeves, *Akhenaten*, 75–78.

the theology whereby a pharaoh achieves divinity while still alive, thus leaving the historian some three and a half millennia later deeply confused. All these elements take on even more puzzling shades when we add to this mix the oddly Oedipal behavior of Akhenaten in his twelfth regnal year,[32] when he went on his campaign to hack out all mentions of Amun, including, therefore, all inscriptions with his father, Amenhotep's, name. According to the first scenario, this took place the year after his father's death; according to the other two, more than a decade after it.

Creation of Akhetaten (Amarna)

Moving the capital to Amarna defied all previous patterns. The pharaohs had often built new palaces and even new capitals, which they may have favored, but they did not, as did Akhenaten, "reduce their personal world to a matter of a few square miles."[33] His exclusive focus on Amarna as both his residence and cultic center, *to the detriment* of the rest of Egypt and the empire, constitutes the core of his "problem" as a ruler. Moreover, the extraordinary artistic depictions of life at Amarna, with their dynamism, spontaneity, and affection, defied all earlier norms of pharaonic representation. And although the city's vestiges clearly show how much (cosmic) thought went into the layout of Aten's capital and its pervasive temple cult to the Aten,[34] the actual construction occurred at breakneck speed, with a resulting shoddy product that one observer called "jerry-built."[35]

Role of Nefertiti and Family Relations

Among the more exceptional aspects of Akhenaten's reign was the role his wife Nefertiti played. Shown in many more scenes than any previous pharoah's wife (with the exception of the female pharaoh Thutmose III's stepmother, Hatshepsut, ca. 1502–1483? BCE), Nefertiti appears as virtually an "equal partner" with her husband Akhenaten, not only in some remarkably affectionate family scenes, but also in cultic settings.[36] This importance only intensifies the mystery of her disappearance and

---

[32] This was dealt with very early in the psychoanalytic movement by Karl Abraham and Freud. See Immanuel Velikovsky, *Oedipus and Akhenaten* (Garden City, N.Y.: Doubleday, 1960); Sigmund Freud, *Moses and Monotheism*, trans. Katherine Jones (New York: Vintage Books, 1967); for a recent psychoanalysis, see Gérard Huber, *Akhenaten sur le divan: L'origne égyptienne de la psychanalyse* (Paris: Jean-Cyrille Godefroy, 2001).

[33] Assmann, "Die 'Häresie' des Echnaton," 109.

[34] On the layout of the city, see Redford, *Akhenaten*, 142–49.

[35] On the shoddy construction work at Amarna, see ibid., 144–45.

[36] On the prominence of Nerfertiti, see John A. Wilson, "Akh-en-aton and Nefert-iti," *Journal of Near Eastern Studies* 32 (1973): 235–41. On the affectionate nature of the royal family, see Reeves, *Akhenaten*, 147–49, and Cyril Aldred on the only "kiss" in Egyptian art (now at the Brooklyn Museum): *Akhenaten, Pharaoh of Egypt: A New Study* (London: Thames & Hudson, 1968), 136–37. On the prominence of Tiye in the court of her husband Amenhotep III, see O'Connor and Cline, *Amenhotep III*, 7. Tiye may have set a precedent, but Nefertiti clearly took it to a new level.

makes it possible to imagine that she is the figure of a pharaonic ruler that appears late in Akhenaten's reign.[37] And behind Nefertiti lies a complex of confusing family scenes that have provoked conjectures on everything from incest to murder.

Artistic Styles and Ahkenaten's Psychosomatic Condition

The artwork of Amarna has long attracted the attention of historians and connoisseurs for its extraordinary talent, rapidly changing styles, dynamism, and new symbols. Indeed, the shifts in style are so sharp and rapid that art historians have difficulty establishing a chronology of the many distinctive styles within the short reign. Certainly in comparison with the formal and rather stiff style of earlier statues, Amarna art burgeons with examples of spontaneous behavior, especially expressions of affection (the pharaoh and wife, enthroned, with children climbing all over them; Nefertiti kissing a daughter on the lips, and grieving at the bed of a dead child).

Akhenaten himself seems to undergo a major transformation in stone: his initially colossal images have a grotesque anti-idealism to them that sometimes shocks with its depiction of peculiarities in shape and proportion not traditionally used in depicting pharaohs. In particular, his form becomes increasingly feminized (including one nude colossus without penis) until it almost seems as if he were a pregnant female. Similarly his facial features run from pronounced to caricatural.[38] There is an entire literature that, assuming these depictions are realistic, has searched for the disease it chronicles,[39] which the most recent DNA study contradicts.[40] Nor do these distortions apply only to Akhenaten, but also to members of his family whose distended skulls and strangely shaped bodies have elicited considerable surprise among analysts. When we add to this mix the extraordinary iconoclastic campaign that, itself, underlines the religious importance of this art, we have a unique episode in art history.

Foreign Policy

Perhaps the most confusing dimension of Akhenaten's behavior was his foreign policy. When he came to sit alone on the throne, he inherited an empire

---

[37] See below.

[38] It is quite difficult to look at these depictions without having one's canon of taste profoundly disoriented: that such pictures, which would be at home in a Disney cartoon, should be etched in massive stone sculptures some 3500 years ago, is hard to compute.

[39] See A.Burridge, "Did Akhenaten Suffer from Marfans Syndrome?" *Biblical Archeologist* 59, no.2 (1996): 127–28; J. B. Risse, "Pharaoh Akhenaten of Egypt: Controversies among Egyptologists and Physicians Regarding His Postulated Illness," *Journal of the History of Medicine and Allied Sciences* 26 (1971): 3–17.

[40] Zahi Hawass et al., "Ancestry and Pathology in King Tutankhamun's Family," *Journal of the American Medical Association* 303, no. 7 (2010): 638–47, online: http://jama.ama-assn.org/cgi/data/303/7/638/DC1/1, March 1, 2010.

unprecedented in Egyptian history both in its scope and in its hegemonic primacy. Egypt was, to use modern terms, at the head of the "First World." The cache of cuneiform tablets found at Amarna testifies to the wide reach and close relations that Egypt maintained with the outside world during the reign of Amenhotep III.[41] The first impression of historians looking at the letters was that Akhenaten had allowed this vast empire to collapse for lack of attention, that the later letters repeatedly express dismay at his lack of responses. As one Egyptologist concluded: "he handed over Palestine and Syria to chaos and misery and the rule of his intriguing Hittite enemy."[42] Some subsequent readings have softened the conclusions, insisting that much of the complaints are a form of ritualized rhetoric, and cautioning against interpreting the sequence of an undated correspondence for which we only have the incoming mailbox. Nonetheless, Akhenaten's rule seems to represent a marked, puzzling, and sudden lack of interest and involvement in foreign policy.

So how can we understand this bewildering, overwrought, and ultimately catastrophic episode in Egyptian history?[43] Some historians have sought to explain Akhenaten's extraordinary career as "mere," rational political activity.[44] "All of this was accomplished according to a well-conceived plan. Akhenaten was certainly not a "visionary" but a methodical rationalist. His reforms were implemented one by one, as soon as the necessary political conditions had been created."[45] And yet, the innovation, the intensity, and ultimately, the self-destructiveness that mark so many aspects of the historical record militate against such reductionism.

Despite the reluctance of historians to attribute agency to religious fervor, here it seems an inescapable conclusion. The composition of the "Great Hymn to Aten" alone (unless it was borrowed from the Hebrews), attests to an exceptional level of religious commitment and imagination. More significantly, however, when one examines specifically the most spectacular and self-destructive aspects of his career, in particular the founding of Akhetaten/Amarna and the iconoclastic campaign—one finds religious (ontological) issues predominate.

Indeed, the evidence suggests that what Akhenaten himself *felt* to be a cosmic truth overrode any earlier practices in maintaining social order. In terms of Paul

---

[41] See Cohen and Westbrook, *Amarna Diplomacy* for the latest discussion of this extraordinary cache of documents.

[42] H. R. H. Hall, "Egypt and the External World in the Time of Akhenaten," *Journal of Egyptian Archeology* 7 (1921): 53.

[43] For some historians, this marks the permanent decline of Egypt: "But all originality had abandoned Egypt with Akhenaten; and she became soon a mere museum of doddering priests and mummies and remained so under the rule of Libyans or Ethiopians, till the artificial renascence of the Saïtes (26th Dynasty, 664–525 BCE) endeavored to rejuvenate her, but without originality or inspiration." Hall, "Egypt and the External World," 52.

[44] Reeves (*Akhenaten*) tries most recently to give us a shrewd or at least largely rational Akhenaten; for objections to this form of cognitive egotism, see below.

[45] Erik Hornung, *Conceptions of God in Ancient Egypt: The One and the Many* (Ithaca, N.Y.: Cornell University Press, 1982), 244.

Zweig's felicitous expression, Akhenaten was the first "heretic of the self," the first man who, swayed by his own convictions, rejected the very fabric of the culture into which he had been born.[46] And, indeed, we can make much sense of this exceptional episode if we consider it in light of the dynamics of apocalyptic time in which Akhenaten thought he inaugurated the millennial kingdom.

■ AKHENATEN, AKHETATEN, AND THE APOCALYPTIC CURVE

What follows will necessarily be a brief sketch of what the millennial dynamic has to offer to the study not only of Akhenaten's reign, but also that of his father, Amenhotep III, the "sun-king." By plotting their careers on the apocalyptic curve, we find the earliest example of a hierarchical millennial movement that deploys specifically the iconic monotheistic formula, "One God, one King." Given the vast influence this iconic millennialism would have in subsequent history (especially Christian), such a case deserves all the attention its dazzling creators invite us to pay. The historical treasures here run very deep.

The Preconditions to Take-Off: Amenhotep III's Sed Festival

Akhenaten's millennial adventure began before he got directly involved. His father Amenhotep III had already taken the imperial millennial model to heights that would have been the envy of his (unconscious) emulators in subsequent millennia, rulers like Constantine, Charlemagne, Frederick II, and Louis XIV. As a court project, then, this millennial movement arises not, as so many better-known ones like the Xhosa and other tribal movements, from cultural catastrophe and the anxieties of when "things fall apart." Rather, such imperial millennial projects arise as the result of a great—unheard of!—worldly success. Inspired courtiers then translated that success into still-more-ambitious schemes of ruling the whole (known) world, with the monarch as the cosmic ruler.[47]

From the time of Thotmose III's great military successes in the middle of the fifteenth century, Egypt had been on an unprecedented trajectory toward empire. As it did so, it developed a new discourse of royal hegemony not only over Egyptians inhabiting what one scholar has called Egypt's "thousand mile trench through the desert," but also an imperial hegemony over their newly subject peoples. At the core of this discourse lay an ideology that has repeatedly produced imperial

---

[46] Paul Zweig, *The Heresy of Self-Love* (Princeton, N.J.: Princeton University Press, 1980). He begins with the gnostics of the early first millennium CE, who looked to Egypt as their source of truth. The author of the *Corpus Hermeticum* (composed in the first century CE), was allegedly Hermes Trismegistus, an older contemporary of Moses who corresponds quite closely to the figure of Amenhotep son of Hapu. The Egyptians of the second century worshipped him as a deity and also associated with the their garbled version of the Akhenaten tale (see below, n. 163).

[47] One might argue the same for the 1960s: see Mendel, *Vision*, 223–64.

millennial projects since then: the principle of the "sun-king" and the icon of the one God/man ruling the earth in perfect harmony. The pharaoh was always, throughout Egyptian history, regarded as a living god on earth and an image of the highest god (sun-and-creator), but Amenhotep's court played this theme insistently, creatively, aggressively. The emergence of the sun-king imagery around Amenhotep III had developed throughout the Eighteenth Dynasty, especially at the Heliopolitan School in the Delta.

Amenhotep III, however, took this solar theology one major step further, affecting all the cults somewhat, but especially transforming the cult of Amen, the titular god of Thebes and the pharoah's namesake. In contrast with Akhenaten, however, at this stage the symbolism of the sun still had multiple forms, from the disk in the wings of a falcon, to the falcon-headed god, to the sun bark that crossed the sky every day. It had visible forms (the disk or *Aten*) and invisible forms (*Amun*). The king was the visible manifestion of the sun god; he is the *Aten*. Only under Akhenaten did the sun-disk become part of a name of God—*pa-aten* (the sun-disk); *pa-aten-ankh* (the living aten).

This traditional sun imagery served the empire well by joining the pharaoh to this unifying and vivifying sun. The pharaoh became more explicitly the beneficent center from which the blessings of the universe flowed. And such a marriage became magnificently manifest in spectacular works of architecture, sculpture, and engraving. The symbolism of royal construction at Karnak under Amenhotep III, as it moved away from the military triumphalism of his immediate predecessors (Thutmose III and Amenhotep II), took on a program of piety that increasingly made the king both the servant of the sun god and his earthly incarnation.[48]

All the splendor of these building and sculpting campaigns were organized by a burgeoning and increasingly assertive class of courtly entrepreneurs led by Amenhotep sa-Hapu. A contemporary flourishing of urban life, increasingly planned in its layout, began to transform Egyptian settlements, from the royal palace of Amenhotep III at Malkata with its surrounding habitations to various sites along the Nile. The new style, which would become standard by the time of the Amarna constructions, appears also in the buildings around the temple associated with sa-Hapu.[49]

This generation's feats in paving the valleys of Karnak and Luxor with spectacular temples to Amun and tombs for the court and its courtiers attest to the stunning vigor and talent of these people. And among their many feats, perhaps the

---

[48] Betsy Bryan, "Antecedents to Amenhotep III," in O'Connor and Cline, *Amenhotep III*, 32; see also the more detailed discussion in Kozloff, *Egypt's Dazzling Sun*, 96–102. See also Jan Assmann, *Egyptian Solar Religion in the New Kingdom: Re, Amun and the Crisis of Polytheism* (New York: Kegan Paul International, 1995), especially the hymn of twin brothers/architects under Amenhotep III (Zuti and Hor).

[49] Peter Lacovara, *The New Kingdom Royal City* (London: Kegan Paul International, 1997), on the association of a new floor plan that would become standard at Amarna with sa-Hapu, see 56.

most outstanding, from the point of view of engineering, was the transport *upstream* of massive quartzite rocks from the quarries in the Western Delta to Karnak to make the famous and misnamed Colossi of Memnon (actually of Amenhotep III), in this case, specifically the work of sa-Hapu.[50]

The climax of this vast and powerful cultural, royal, and religious ascension came with the thirty-year Sed festival that Amenhotep sa-Hapu prepared in his final year for his king Nebmaatre Amenhotep III.[51] Here we find a combination of religious imagination, extraordinary wealth, bureaucratic and logistical capacity, rapid monumental construction, and even archival historical research,[52] on a scale rarely if ever achieved in pre-industrial times.

Sed festivals were an ancient custom and represented on a grandiose scale what all religious festivals in Egypt were supposed to do: to make whole the "riven world," to join heaven (the gods) and earth (man), to mark and rejuvenate the feeling of *communitas* that bound the society together.[53] At the Luxor Temple, a yearly festival reenacted the divine birth of the king, engendered by god and woman. At the heart of this particular Sed festival, one of the best-attested of its kind, however, we find a systematic articulation of the unity of the sun god and the

---

[50] The Colossi of Memnon represent an astounding engineering feat, taking two massive blocks of granite from quarries in the north, hundreds of miles upstream to Karnak near Thebes, and unloading them at a newly constructed port there; see Kozloff, *Egypt's Dazzling Sun*, 138–39; picture, 33. They are statues of Amenhotep III misidentified as statues of Memnon. For sa-Hapu's involvement, see Varille's inscriptions (*Amenhotep fils de Hapou*).

[51] For a description of the scenes of this Sed festival depicted at the temple of Amenhotep III, see Jocelyn Gohary, *Akhenaten's Sed-Festival at Karnak* (London: Kegan Paul International, 1992), 11–18; for a discussion and list of other sites that depict this occasion, see Lawrence Berman, "Overview," in O'Connor and Cline, *Amenhotep III*, 16 and n. 78; for sa-Hapu's role, see his statue at Karnak, "Scribe of the Recruits." "... on the occasion of his first Jubilee of thirty years of his majesty, the king ordered me to effect revisions (renovations?) of the domain of Amun ... The king named me the ceremoniary of Amun for all his festivals" (Varille, *Amenhotep fils de Hapou*, 20). For further details on his funerary chamber, see C. Robichon and A. Varille, *Le temple du scribe royal Amenhotep fils de Hapou* (Cairo: Imprimerie de l'Institut français d'archéologie orientale, 1936), pl. XXXV.

[52] On the search for precedents in the record, see comments in O'Connor and Cline, *Amenhotep III*, 17–18; Queen Tiye's "document" from the first dynasty is about a Sed festival (see above, n. 8); the allusions to sa-Hapu's role are both explicit (Alexandre Varille, *Inscriptions concernant l'architect Amenophis fils de Hapou* (Cairo: Imprimerie de l'Institut français d'archéologie orientale, 1968), 41–42) and implicit in an interesting remark in his biographical statue where the text states that "he is a man who wants to change nothing of the customs that have existed since the most distant times, ignoring [really or seeming to] that he is their raison-d'être ... " Varille, 40. This may mean that, wrapped in appeals to ancient custom, Amenhotep sa-Hapu was in fact innovating extensively ... something borne out by the evidence.

[53] "The 'riven [*gespalten*] world' was made whole for the duration of the festival. The Egyptian religious feast centered on the belief that ... the rift between heaven and earth might be suspended and the gods could walk the earth once again in person." Assmann, *Mind of Egypt*, 231. On the notion of *communitas*, see the work of Victor Turner which, for all the criticism it has received, remains a valuable approach to the workings of religion on a society-wide scale. Victor Turner, *Dramas, Fields, and Metaphors: Symbolic Action in Human Society* (Ithaca, N.Y.: Cornell University Press, 1975).

sun-king, one that literally and unprecedentedly deified the pharaoh *before* his death.[54]

This particular Sed festival, then, could mark a major point on the apocalyptic curve, the point when a millennial ideology successfully entered public discourse. Like most imperial millennial projects, it came top-down, and the fact that it had the weight of the court behind it obviously gave it an advantage that the visions of a fifteen-year-old girl from the bottom of the social hierarchy would not initially have had. But whether from above or below, the key to apocalyptic discourse concerns how it is received once it enters the public sphere. Not all enormities that come from courts elicit enthusiasm.

The intense foregrounding of solar imagery, the use of dazzling sun-disk (*itentjehen*) as title…placed the king at the center of the earthly universe, a world no longer conceived of as Egypt alone. Now the vision included foreign countries, suggesting the expansive apotheosis of the Egyptian state as not only the center of the cosmos, but as the ruler and beneficiary of the entire world.[55] Amenhotep III's favorite epithet was *Nebmaatreatentjehen* or "Nebmaatre, the Dazzling Sun Disk," and in honor of his Sed festival, he had a large statue of quartzite made for himself in which he appears deified, and characterized as the ruler of the world, the "Dazzling Sun Disk of All Lands."[56] This ideological expansionism also appears in Amenhotep III's diplomacy, which, in the Amarna cache, displays an extraordinary level of interest in and interaction with the rest of the world.[57]

The vision behind such grandiose symbolism, and the vast crews of artists and workers it set in motion, earned Amenhotep the title of the most extensive and intensive "builder" in the history of Egyptian pharaohs.[58] "The king's apparent campaign of splendor was not merely a real estate development. Rather…it was the concrete realization of his view of cosmos—with himself at the center representing the three major aspects of the sun-god Amon-Re."[59] It is as millennial

---

[54] The elements of this deification of the pharaoh go well beyond the level of detail possible here. See Assmann "Die 'Häresie' des Echnaton," 109–26, and Erik Hornung, *Akhenaten and the Religion of Light*, trans. David Lorton (Ithaca, N.Y.: Cornell University Press, 1999), 24–27; Raymond Johnson, "Monuments and Monumental Art," in *Amenhotep III*, 86–88; Tobin, "Amarna and Biblical Religion." Alexander the Great went through the same crisis of megalomanic deification *before* his death; see Peter Green, *Alexander of Macedon 356–323 B.C.: A Historical Biography* (Berkeley and Los Angeles: University of California Press, 1991), 451–64. The same situation was endemic among the Roman emperors after Augustus, particularly Caligula and Nero.

[55] On the novelty of this ecumenical vision, see Hornung, *Akhenaten and the Religion of Light*, 55–57.

[56] Berman, "Overview," 3. For a discussion of the statue discovered in 1989 at the Luxor cachette along with the innovative (shocking?) elements whereby Amenhotep III is presented as a living God, see Kozloff and Bryan, *Egypt's Dazzling Sun*, 132–35, color plate 5, figures V. 14–16. See also Georges Posener, *De la divinité du Pharaon* (Paris: Imp. Nationale, 1960).

[57] On the Amarna documents, see below, pp. 131–32.

[58] "No king of Egypt left more monuments, more tangible proofs of his greatness, than Amenhotep III…." Berman, "Overview," 1.

[59] Kozloff and Bryan, *Egypt's Dazzling Sun*, 5; cited and discussed by David O'Connor, "The City and the World," in *Amenhotep III*, 142–72.

sun-king—perhaps the first in recorded history—that Amenhotep III acted out his astounding reign.

Both Amenhotep III and his namesake vizier sa-Hapu were probably aware that this did not reflect reality, that there were inhabited regions where the sun shone and the pharaoh's writ did not run, that a good deal of wish-fulfillment lay behind such grandiose claims. But the discourse of a universal, pacific rule emanating from the place where the heavens and the earth meet—the pharaoh and his temples—had now become the official symbolism of the Egyptian monarchy. "It is not a distant march from the characterization of solar power here [Amenhotep III's Sed festival] to Akhenaten's exultation of the sun-disk's life-giving sunlight."[60]

Transition from Amenhotep III to Akhenaten: Divine Kingship in Mutation

One of the most contentious aspects of Akhenaten's reign concerns the transition from his father to him. Co-regencies were not uncommon in Egypt, more common still in the earlier Twelfth Dynasty, and for half a century now, some researchers have argued for either a short or a long co-regency.[61] The long co-regency places the accession of Amenhotep IV in the twenty-eighth year of his father's reign, two years before the first Sed festival; the short, sometime in the final two years of his reign. Many historians have no co-regency.[62] The arguments are compelling when reading both sides of the debate, and the split seems to some extent to follow the inclinations of art historians (co-regency) and historians (none or short). Although both scenarios can accommodate a reading of Akhenaten's career as a millennialist, the millennial account that makes the most sense follows either the no co-regency thesis, or at most, a short one.[63]

One large problem with a long co-regency is that it makes Akhenaten's behavior almost completely incomprehensible. According to the long co-regency, Akhenaten founded Akhetaten and shifted to his solar imagery all while his father still lived.

---

[60] Kozloff and Bryan, *Egypt's Dazzling Sun*, 135.

[61] See Valetin, "Indications et évidences"; Johnson, "Amenhotep III and Amarna," 65–82; Aldred, *Akhenaten*, 100–32.

[62] Donald Redford, *History and Chronology of the Eighteenth Dynasty of Egypt: Seven Studies* (Toronto: University of Toronto Press, 1967), 88–169; William Murnane, *Ancient Egyptian Coregencies* (Chicago: Oriental Institute, 1977); Hornung concludes: "A co-regency between the two kings is untenable" (*Akhenaten and the Religion of Light*, 30). Berman notes that the art historians tend toward co-regency, the historians against it ("Overview," 23).

[63] This is not the place to go into all the arguments, although I will cite some below when they arise. But generally the idea that Akhenaten would have been preparing "his" version of the Jubilee at Karnak coincidentally with his father's first one at his palace at Thebes seems highly unlikely. Also the lack of any mention of Amenhotep IV in the depictions of the first (thirty-year) Jubilee makes co-regency this early still more unlikely. Depictions of Amenhotep IV standing with his father, such as on the Third Pylon at Karnak (*Amenhotep III*, 79–80) may in fact have been added on later or may in fact be Tutankhamen (Murnane). See below, n. 67.

While that in itself may not be impossible, it seems highly unlikely. The building of Akhetaten would have been a colossal folly from Amenhotep III's point of view. Moreover, it suggests a harmonious relationship between the father and son, which makes his sudden virtually Oedipal turn to Amun-smashing iconoclasm immediately after his father's death difficult to understand.[64] Even in the chronology of successive reigns, the speed with which the Amarna revolution occurs is almost blinding; to posit only five years of independent reign for Akhenaten seems to defy even the warping influences of apocalyptic time.[65] In what follows, then, I follow the principle that all the major deviations from both longstanding Egyptian practices *and* from his father's own innovations come after the young king ruled on his own. Psychologically, it makes the most sense.

If there is something to be said for a co-regency, it concerns the significant overlap between Amenhotep III's notions of divine kingship and those of his son,[66] who, whether in public fact, or in his mind (and retrospectively inserted into the public record), considered himself deified along with his father.[67] This overlap, which concerns the transmission of public megalomania from one generation to the next, should certainly stand at the center of any discussion of Akhenaten and his father.

The most significant first development of the new king's reign was his decision to build a huge temple to Aten, the *Gem-pa-Aten*, or "Aten is found" at Karnak. This rapidly built structure was covered with (relatively small) carved blocks called *talatat* that presented a vast elaboration of solar imagery and Egypt.[68] Although the next dynasty, the Ramses, tore the structure down, they fortunately used the *talatat* as filler for their own construction. Thus, over forty thousand of these *talatat* survive. Each is a puzzle piece of a vast iconic program that may have covered two huge facing walls.[69]

The mobilization of resources necessary for this structure was immense. As a contemporary inscription noted: "First occurrence of his Majesty's giving command to muster all the workmen from Elephantine to Sama-behdet, and the leaders of

[64] Huber, *Akhenaten sur le divan*, 111–14. The hostility might eventually lead to an abreaction against his father, perhaps, but not immediately after a substantial and still critical joint project.

[65] Assmann remarks on the "incredible speed" of the revolution (above, n. 26), and accordingly rejects the co-regency hypothesis. On the intensity of apocalyptic time, see above, chapter 2; and below on Sartre's visit to Cuba, chapter 11, n. 102.

[66] See W. Raymond Johnson's discussion of the Hebti ritual and Amenhotep IV's role in the deification of his father ("Monuments and Monumental Art" in O'Connor and Cline, *Amenhotep III*, 90–93).

[67] Some of the discussions of co-regency emphasize the role that Akhenaten would have played in his father's deification (Johnson, "Amenhotep III and Amarna," 81–82). Some of the evidence for co-regency suggests later tampering with the record: (1) the addition of a small Amenhotep IV to the Sed festival procession (Johnson, "Monuments and Monumental Art," 90–91); and (2) the sculpture of the two Amenhoteps with the son in front of the father (see Redford's discussion, *History*, 141–43).

[68] For a discussion of this temple, see Redford, *Akhenaten*, 102–36.

[69] On the *talatat* see Gohary's 110 plates illustrating them and her reconstruction of part of one wall (*Akhenaten's Sed-Festival*, plate 1).

the army, in order to make a great breach for cutting out sandstone, in order to make the sanctuary of Re-Harakhti in his name, 'Sunlight which is in the Aten' in Karnak...."[70] In one sense, this signaled Amenhotep IV's intention to continue his father's massive building campaigns, specifically the one at Karnak.[71] But this temple, the first in honor specifically of Aten, sounded a new—and for the practitioners of traditional Egyptian piety, possibly ominous—note. Built to the east of Amun's Karnak Temple in Thebes, where a newly powerful priesthood served that god, Amenhotep IV's new temple pointedly slighted the great god of the place. No mention, no depiction of Amun appears in the program; indeed almost all the "old gods" have disappeared.[72]

Furthermore, the temple seems to have been built at tremendous speed in order to hold a Sed festival at Karnak in Amenhotep IV's second or third year.[73] Such a move was most daring, since kings normally waited at least until their thirtieth year to hold their first Sed festival.[74] In these depictions, moreover, we find the first appearance of the "new style" of the sun-disk with rays shining down on the pharaoh.[75] This new iconography took the divinization of the pharaoh still further than under Amenhotep III: with the god no longer anthro- or zoomorphic. The king no longer celebrates before, or offers to, a god. The disc is above him. "The effect is to make the celebrant, the king, the focal point of attention."[76] At the same time a new epithet appears between the cartouches (containing the god's name) and the disc designating the Aten as "[t]he great living Aten who is in Jubilee, lord of heaven and earth who resides in [the temple]."[77]

Evidence from the inscriptions suggests enormous expenditures, "staggering totals" of various provisions probably assembled for the Sed festival. These expenses

---

[70] Inscription at Silsileh, Urk. IV, 1962. There is also a correspondence between Ramose and Akhenaten about this building program; N. de Garis Davies, *Tomb of Vizier Ramose* (London: The Egypt Exploration Society, 1941), pl. 36; see also Redford, *Akhenaten*, 59–60.

[71] See above on Amenhotep III's development of a massive construction plan to link Karnak to Luxor first begun by Hatshepsut, see Betsy M. Bryan, "Antecedents to Amenhotep III," in O'Connor and Cline, *Amenhotep III*, 29–30.

[72] Redford, *Akhenaten*,130. On the previous rather limited role of the sun-disk in sun god worship in Egypt, see Redford, "Sun-Disc."

[73] Gohary, *Akhenaten's Sed-Festival*; for the date, see discussion, 29–33. The symbolism all predates the new Amarna style (disk and rays ending in hands) and the name Akhenaten (hence before year 5).

[74] This of course adopts the working hypothesis that there is no long co-regency, according to which the Karnak Sed festival is the "same" (or co-eval) with Amenhotep III's thirty-year Sed festival. Indeed, one might argue that one of the attractions of the co-regency is that it explains the rapid repetition of the Sed festival. The alternative explanation is Akhenaten's megalomania, which seems indubitable if, at this point, early for its full public expression. On the escalation of claims by a messianic figure, see above, chapter 2, n. 8; and below on Hitler, chapter 12, pp. 361–63.

[75] See the illustrations in Gohary, *Akhenaten's Sed-Festival*, 1; discussion in Redford, "Sun-Disc." It is interesting to consider the fact that the engraved illustrations revealed what the actual Sed festival that it depicted could not, but that Amenhotep IV already "saw," namely the Aten's rays with small hands at the end shining down *on him alone*.

[76] Redford, "Sun-Disc," 55.

[77] Ibid.

underline the celebratory and popular aspects of this cult of divine kingship. Redford reconstructs the impression the documentation suggests, of enthusiastic triumphalism.

> The sheer mass of foodstuffs brought together by the state to be bestowed upon the people at the jubilee as the king's largesse, helps us better to appreciate the atmosphere of hilarity and fervent loyalty with which the plebs anticipated the festival. No better means could be imagined to bring the nation together and to remind its citizens of the political system to which they owed their all. Such a festival was one of the few occasions in the course of their relatively short lives when peasant, laborer, and artisan would enjoy a square meal. No wonder hands are lifted in adoration to the "window of appearance," and the royal courts resound to the chorus of thousands of voices raised in a paeon of praise! To serve pharaoh meant that one would eat![78]

This unorthodox celebration, of course, inaugurated far more radical departures from custom, but it can tell us a good deal about the young king's frame of mind. Although he had yet to break fundamentally with earlier symbolism and ritual, he here made the Aten, the sun-disk, the focus of the ceremony to such an extent that he seems reluctant to even acknowledge other gods. Does this suggest that already he had a commitment to an exclusive monotheistic interpretation of the Aten? Certainly, he claims Aten has given him permission to have this Sed festival[79]: the first sign of things to come—the Aten, which shines on the pharaoh alone, directly communicated with the young king, directing him to break with past precedents.[80]

Amenhotep IV's first Sed festival at Karnak constitutes an unconventional continuation of a practice that his father legitimately inaugurated. It suggests not only his sense of his continuity with his father's reign, but more specifically his attachment to these celebrations. The first Sed festival contributed to divinizing the living pharaoh and inaugurated a public millennial discourse—festival celebrations, erection of monuments, issuing of scarabs. In the terminology of this book, Amenhotep III had launched "apocalyptic time," and his son took it even further.

Amenhotep IV's enthusiasm for subsequent festivals, particularly in the context of his peculiar interest in the Aten, both prolonged and intensified the experience of apocalyptic time and his own divination. The son's Sed festivals allowed him to renew this experience and intensify his sense of divinity though his association with the Aten who now took on the epithet "Aten who lives in Jubilees."[81] And the

[78] Redford, *Akhenaten*, 136.

[79] One of the Sed festival *talatat* bears the following inscription: "Admitting the magistrates, friends and standard-bearers of the army, to cause them to stand in the king's presence at the first Sed-Festival of his majesty which [his beloved father] the living Aten, granted to him." Gohary, *Akhenaten's Sed Festival*, 95; pl. XLVIII, scene 115.

[80] Note: no matter how innovative, Amenhotep III and sa-Hapu avoided any show of innovation (see above, n. 52).

[81] Battiscombe Gunn, "Notes on the Aten and His Names," *Journal of Egyptian Archaeology* 9, no. 3/4 (1923): 170–72.

worship of the "one God, the Aten," with its rays exclusively bathing him (and his wife Nefertiti), proved a particularly fruitful direction in which to develop the political theology of his father: *one God, one King.*

The Artistic "Realism" of the Karnak Period

Among the many puzzles posed by the Akhenaten episode concerns the timing of the almost grotesque distortions in the representation of Akhenaten and, eventually, the rest of the royal family. Still more puzzling, the *most* bizarre statues seem to date from the *earliest* period in the reign, while still at Karnak, where we get a decisive shift from the heroic style of pharaoh so favored by earlier members of the dynasty, to a startlingly peculiar depiction of the new pharaoh. Here we find, for example, a monumental sculpture of a nude feminine-looking pharaoh without a penis,[82] with a long face and huge lips that seem to border on caricature, and an elongated head that inspires UFO enthusiasts to speculate on his alien identity.[83]

Although historians do not quite know how to interpret these presentations, most agree that they represent a remarkably frank depiction of pharaonic deformity, a "grotesque realism" that violated every earlier norm of pharoanic representation. Certainly it deviated sharply from the narcissistic norms that characterized the reign of the just-dead, divine, "sun-king," his father Amenhotep III, whose sculptures got younger and more handsome the older he got.[84] Some suggest that he had Marfan's syndrome, a hereditary condition with physical consequences close to some of the stranger elements of Akhenaten's iconography. The latest research on Akhenaten's mummy (KV55), however, shows no evidence of Marfan's.[85]

And if one tried to imagine when this kind of macabre development might emerge, one would think sooner of the strange and overheated despair of late Amarna, when all canons of normalcy might be jettisoned in the search for answers to the painful cognitive dissonance of millennial failure. But instead it seems to be directly linked to the pre-Amarna period, to early Karnak and to the work of the king's chief sculptor, Bek. Indeed, at Bek's death, the new chief sculptor, Tuthmose "tamed Bek's exuberance and bravura into a style of greater elegance and sophistication."[86] The movement, therefore, starts with this startling artistic

---

[82] Perhaps to denote the a-sexuality of the one God.

[83] See, for example, the "New Age" historical novel by Daniel Blair Stewart, *Akhunatan: The Extraterrestrial King* (Berkeley, CA: Frog Limited, 1996).

[84] Amenhotep III's portrayal in his later years resembles that of Elizabeth I, in that, as they got older, the portraits produced of them got younger. On Elizabeth, see Roy Strong, *Gloriana: The Portraits of Queen Elizabeth I* (New York: Thames & Hudson, 1987), 146–51 and Susan Frye, *Elizabeth I: The Competition for Representation* (Oxford: Oxford University Press, 1993), 98–114.

[85] Hawass, "Ancestry and Pathology," Appendix.

[86] S. Hochfield, "The Revolutionary Art of the Sun King of Egypt," *Art News* 72, no. 8 (October 1973): 37. For more on Tuthmose, see below, pp. 175–76.

departure rather than terminates with it. As the most recent study of Akhnaten's mummy concludes: "Therefore, the particular artistic presentation of persons in the Amarna period is confirmed as a royally decreed style most probably related to the religious reforms of Akhenaten."[87]

One psychological dynamic characteristic of apocalyptic time might explain this very strange anomaly. Akhenaten knew he was not at all like his father, including sexually. Whereas his father had numerous consorts (much of the Amarna archive contains requests for beautiful foreign women), Akhenaten was different and, by alpha male standards, radically inferior. It could not have escaped the court's notice that the new pharaoh did not express his manhood in traditional ways, which may have included physical manifestations of effeminate and oddly-shaped features that he had since childhood. One might imagine that a "normal" young pharaoh would try denying this embarrassing reality for the sake of vanity, pursuing the same flattering and heroic self-representation his father favored in his late years (after the Sed festival).

Instead, by an alternative conjecture, he took the realist path and embraced his peculiarities. Fairly early on, perhaps in the immediate aftermath of his father's death, the son appears to have read his peculiarities not as signs of inferiority and failure, but as signs of mission and election; indeed, given the evidence of his mummy, he may well have accentuated the very physical features that most concerned him. He was *different* from his father because he was chosen for a different, *still higher task*: to fulfill—and surpass—his father's work. This interpretation permitted him to embrace his perceived deformities, to assert, to *reveal* his messianic identity through this startling iconography.

Nefertiti would have played a critical role in this turn of affairs, since, as his wife and (clearly from contemporary and subsequent depictions) intimate partner in this venture, she alone would have the emotional and psychological power to convince him that his deformities were beautiful and not ugly—an early version of beauty and the beast. She alone could arouse the king semiotically to the point where he could transform his fears of inferiority or inadequacy into proof of messianic status.

The royal couple then, saw the young king's peculiarities as chosenness. Precisely the elements that, in "normal" conditions, marked him off as a weird and flawed creature, now marked him as the specially selected vessel for the cosmic transformation of Egypt and the world. And all this happened at the same time as the Sed festival, followed closely by the change in name to Akhenaten or "Beneficent/Effective one of/for the Sun Disk,"[88] and plans to move to Akhetaten. So, this working hypothesis would argue, this public "solution" to his embarrassing physical

---

[87] Hawass, "Ancestry and Pathology."

[88] On the meaning of the name, see discussion in Montserrat, *Akhenaten, History and Fantasy*, 21–22. Redford suggests "sunlight which is in the disc" ("Sun-Disc," 54).

features released a burst of visionary activity. In a sense, in stripping himself naked and revealing his deformities, he became, in a strange version of Andersen's emperor, a test of whether his advisors saw him as savior or madman.

The widespread imitation of this style and the appearance of weird deformities in all the members of the royal family—in particular the alien-like elongated heads—would, in this scenario, have the whole family participate in this chosen status. It represents the victory of the feminine over the masculine, of the pregnant over the conqueror, the beneficent over the tyrant. "Whatever the reasons for this radical departure from the normal mode of depicting Pharaoh with muscular physique and heroic gaze, the new canon of proportions seems to have become a mark of the elect."[89] And once this corner turned, Akhenaten and his partner in millennial utopianism, Nefertiti, could embark on the great and mad adventure of building Akhetaten.

■ AKHETATEN, THE MILLENNIAL CITY

This city, built along the Nile about halfway between Thebes and Memphis, stood roughly at the center of the kingdom. It was carefully planned, with nine stelae containing lengthy inscriptions placed in a complex geometrical pattern that mapped out the space, using the royal tombs in the hills on the east side and the temple to Aten in the center.[90] Thereupon rose up out of wasteland in less than a decade a city that housed some twenty to fifty thousand people![91] Here the king moved the capital, royal residence, archives, officials, diplomats, temples, and the finest artisans of the realm.

Some historians have tried to minimize the significance of this move, arguing that it was entirely within the range of normal behavior for an Egyptian pharaoh—or any king—to change capitals.[92] But this move seems to involve far more than a "rational" choice. Even those who insist on seeing a relatively shrewd and realistic Akhenaten during the Karnak period admit that "the big political mistake that Akhnaten committed was his decision to leave the former capital of the empire (Thebes) and move permanently to Akhetaten."[93] Akhenaten's move involved a

---

[89] Hochfield, "Revolutionary Art," 36.

[90] William J. Murnane and Charles C. Van Siclen III, *The Boundary Stelae of Akhenaten* (London: Kegan Paul International, 1993).

[91] Montserrat notes that the area of habitation was so large that nineteenth-century observers assumed it must have been occupied for centuries to have grown so large (Montserrat, *Akhenaten: History and Fantasy*, 24). Hornung suggests as many as 100,000, but that seems excessive (*Akhenaten and the Religion of Light*, 67).

[92] Reeves compares the move to the one the Japanese emperor Kanmu effected in the eighth century CE from Nara to Kyoto (*Akhenaten*, 104). He emphasizes in both cases the rulers' desire to get away from powerful clans (in Akhenaten's case the Amun priesthood) who may have planned assassination.

[93] Z. Zahn, "Akhenaten and the Amarna Period," in *Exotic Art*, ed. W. Forman and B. Forman (London: Spring Books, 1956), 11.

radical constriction of activity and attention. As one historian noted: "the royal sphere of activity and influence which had previously filled the horizon of the Thutmosid realm from Nubia to Syria, now shrank to a couple of square miles."[94] Far from a shrewd move, this royal initiative proved catastrophic for the empire and the nation.[95]

Indeed, the Akhetaten endeavor seems to have drained the nation of capital, resources, and administrative talent. The expenses of this construction taxed even the limitless wealth of Amenhotep III's treasury, leading Akhenaten to divert funds from the Amun priesthood toward his inexhaustible projects. Moreover, the exclusive focus on the worship of the Aten—to the point of closing down other temples—affected Egypt not only financially but culturally. The average Egyptian experienced this religious revolution up close: even burial practices had to change and the beloved *shawabtis* (figurines buried with the dead) were banned.[96] And once relocated to Akhetaten, the king never left.[97] Akhenaten closed himself within the sacred precincts of his new capital.

There he seems to have combined two elements of pharaonic life that he emphasized more than any previous Egyptian ruler, a bizarre combination of solar rituals and lively family life. His daily displacements in the city combined worship of the Aten—in which he was both high priest and incarnate god—with ceremonial processions in a dazzling chariot that replicated the movements of the Aten.

In contrast to this elaborate ritual, the artistic depictions of his family life portray a spontaneity, family affection, and physical intimacy that startles in comparison with a millennia-long tradition of stiff hierocratic depictions of the pharaoh.[98] Here in this new world we find Nefertiti playing exceptional roles for a pharaoh's wife, appearing as his equal in political scenes,[99] and he as her equal in loving and intimate family scenes.[100]

> Entirely new is the overwhelming concentration on representing the domestic life of the royal family... reclining within a garden pavilion, the king tenderly embracing his eldest daughter and the next two perched on Nefertiti's lap, the tiny Ankhesenpaaten playing with an ornament dangling from her mother's crown. Over this relaxed evocation of domestic harmony hovers the great disk of the Aten, its rays ending in little hands that bless the monarchs and offer them signs of life and power... members of the family are

---

[94] Assmann, "Die 'Häresie' des Echnaton," 109.

[95] See below, pp. 176–78.

[96] Erik Hornung and Betsy Bryan, eds., *The Quest for Immortality* (New York: Prestal-Verlag, 2002), 141.

[97] There is some disagreement as to whether one of his engraved statements represents an oath not to leave. See William Murnane, *Texts from the Amarna Period in Egypt* (Atlanta: Scholars Press, 1995).

[98] Hochfield, "Revolutionary Art," 36.

[99] See her presence in depictions of the execution of captives; her equal size and place in ritual occasions; and her as recipient of the Aten's rays.

[100] For example, depictions of getting ready for bed on the *talatat* and numerous "family scenes."

frequently shown embracing and even kissing one another. Such frank expressions of emotion are almost unknown in Egyptian art of earlier ages.[101]

Historians who grapple with the bizarre nature of the move to Akhetaten tend to attribute it to religious fanaticism, an explanation that at least has the advantage over the "pragmatic" school of acknowledging how counterintuitive the king's behavior was. And yet, what kind of religious fanaticism? The easiest answer focuses on the "natural" intolerance of monotheism and the extraordinary grip it had on the young king's mind.[102] Mingled with the megalomanic tendencies of Akhenaten, this seems like a reasonable, if opaque, explanation that hovers close to the less sympathetic view of a kind of (ultimately incomprehensible) religious madness. I would like to suggest that we understand Akhenaten as gripped by a particular form of religious zeal, namely that apocalyptic millennialism which possesses its believers and "rides" them to their destruction.[103] Let us consider then the millennial significance of Akhetaten before returning to the intensity of family relations.

Akhetaten represents one of the earliest documented cases of a hierarchical millennial city based on monotheistic principles. Like many cult centers, it represents for its inhabitants the earthly center of the cosmos, where the benefits of the heavens descend to earth and where cultic activity assures the regularity of the universe. In this case, Akhenaten's worship of the Aten assured the daily circuit of the sun.[104] In radically replacing the earlier mythology of the sun's circuit, in which, after setting, it faced particularly grave dangers before reemerging, Akhenaten had relocated the cosmic process in his (and his wife's) person and his (their) city. Using the notion of a single creator god whose rays beneficently bathed his creation with light and life, Akhenaten conceived of himself (and his wife) in precisely the same terms. As the Aten shone upon him (them), so he (they), beneficently, shone upon the world, the entire world.

---

[101] Hochfield, "Revolutionary Art," 37.

[102] There is a growing school of "essentialist" criticism that seems to see in monotheism (rather than a particular form of monotheism) the seeds of violent intolerance. For the most recent expressions of this, see Garth Fowden, *From Empire to Commonwealth* (Princeton, N.J.: Princeton University Press, 1993), chap. 4. Fowden seems unaware that he is studying specifically iconic monotheism. See above, chapter 1, n. 68); Jonathan Kirsch, who has a chapter on Akhenaten in *God against the Gods: The History of the War between Monotheism and Polytheism* (New York: Viking, 2004), chap. 1.

[103] The relationship of millennialism to monotheism specifically deserves close attention. Certainly non-monotheistic millennialism is possible, (Matreya Buddhism, Xhosa, cargo cults, Ghost Dance, etc.), but the elective affinity of monotheism for millennialism remains indisputable. Indeed, the question is better formulated, what forms of monotheism are not millennial?

[104] The new style abolishes earlier mythology of the navigation of the sun boat beneath the horizon, in conflict with chaos. The sun no longer experiences conflict (i.e., it has entered the millennial realm); the rituals of Akhenaten are "thanksgiving" offerings for the new dispensation. Contrast this to the earlier mythology of the battle and Atem as the invisible (i.e., set beneath the horizon, and threatened) sun who must win his nightly victory "assuring the daily circuit of the sun."

Thus Akhenaten at Akhetaten makes most sense as someone who believes that he, as the incarnation of the divinity, by living his life as he does, "magically" assures the welfare of the entire world. Akhenaten posed as the personal god on earth vis-à-vis Aten as the cosmic god in heaven. Indeed, one scholar argues that he chose the spot because a total solar eclipse passed directly over the site on the Nile, according to the boundary stela that read: "Now, it is the Orb, my father, who advised me concerning it, namely the Horizon of the Orb."[105] He and Nefertiti represent a cosmic couple of love and fertility.[106] As they rejoice in the wonders of nature and the joys of life, so do they assure the same for all.[107] As one of the founding stelae engravings reads, Akhetaten was Akhenaten's "great monument which he founded for himself; his horizon [in which his] circuit comes into being, where he is beheld with joy where the land rejoices and all hearts exult when they see him."[108] The prominence of Nefertiti and their rejoicing in his daughters (even though they had no male heir) reflects the characteristic prominence of women in the upswing of millennial movements.

One might call what happened a narcissistic implosion. If Nero fiddled while Rome burnt, Akhenaten and Nefertiti seem to have fondled their children and each other while the Egyptian empire fell around them. Indeed, one might even consider them some of history's earliest documented "flower-children" when one looks at the extraordinary display of spontaneity and simple delights with which the art of the time depicts them.[109] *Nothing* in earlier Egyptian art leads us to expect *anything* like this; and nothing in subsequent art comes anywhere near this.

Of course, all pretenses to perfection, no matter how attractive the imagery, fail to accord with messy reality. At the same time as the reliefs depict a blissful family, the documentary record suggests exceptional upheavals within the family, which historians still cannot sort out. They do, however, suggest the untimely death of daughters, the disappearance (and reappearance as a pharaoh!?) of Nefertiti, and possibly incest between Akhenaten and one or more of his daughters.[110] Meanwhile,

---

[105] William McMurray, "Dating the Amarna Period in Egypt: Did a Solar Eclipse Inspire Akhenaten?" (2003), online: http://www.egiptomania.com/EEF/DAPE.pdf, March 1, 2010.

[106] The presence of Nefertiti at the heart of the millennial vision suggests the possibility that Akhenaten was working within a framework of a "myth of origin" that, like the Hebraic one, involved the creation of man "male and female."

[107] If they had heard the Hebrew account of the creation, they could well have seen themselves as "restoring" the pre-lapsarian relationship between Adam and Eve.

[108] Nick Wyatt, *Space and Time in the Religious Life of the Near East* (Sheffield: Sheffield Academic Press, 2001), 191–92; translation adapted from Murnane, *Texts*, 74.

[109] In particular, see the tableau of a pharaoh (variously idenitifed as Akhenaten or Smenkare, his successor) leaning on his staff smelling the flowers that Nefertiti or Merytaten offers to him as the breeze blows their hair and clothes (from Staatliche Museen zu Berlin, illustrated in Reeves, *Akhenaten*, 148).

[110] The most recent DNA studies reveal that Tutenkhamen was the child of an incestuous union of Akhenaten and a close relative; Hawass, "Ancestry and Pathology."

even the people who moved to Akhetaten kept their distance from the new "way of being."[111]

Like so many millennial thinkers, the magical beliefs that they held about how their actions would bring on the era of messianic perfection led them to behave in ways that failed to take account of the realities they firmly believed they had permanently escaped. It was one thing for Amenhotep III to play with notions of divinity and celebrate Sed festivals at the end of his reign: he added these flourishes to a brilliantly working system. But Akhenaten turned the flourishes into a new, and dysfunctional system.

In the case of this royal couple, we have an unusual case of top-down millennialism. Unlike the tribal movements like the Xhosa and the Melanesian Cargoists, where dispossessed people responded to the cruel blows administered by enemies more powerful than they, here we have rulers at the very height of worldly success. This was, thus, a top-down movement that, like the sun's rays, emanated from Akhenaten throughout the world. As such it represents perhaps the earliest example of iconic monotheism that combined a wide range of both demotic elements (spontaneity, pacific relations) with hierarchical ones (authoritarianism, royal/ imperial center).

In terms of apocalyptic time, we can identify the move to Akhetaten as the equivalent of the moment when Sarhili slaughtered his most precious heifer. Not only had apocalyptic discourse entered public space, it had taken over political decision-making. And as we saw with the case of the Xhosa, the move often means the replacement—if not a purge—of the older ministers and advisors with new ones who, either from sycophancy and ambition or religious zeal, offer the king their unquestioned obedience.[112] A number of historians note, with evident distaste, the kind of obsequious style these men used—many claiming to have been "made" or raised from obscurity by the divine majesty.[113]

In one sense, Akhenaten built on the work of his predecessors; indeed one might even argue that he could not have *imagined* this project without the work of the previous reign. Similarly, Akhetaten constitutes, despite a long history of town planning in Egypt during the Middle Kingdom, an extraordinary development of urban planning, a powerful extension of efforts that had already appeared in the previous reign.[114] It mobilized the huge and talented workforce of Amenhotep III's

[111] Albrecht Endruweit, *Städtischer Wohnbau in Agypten: Klimagerechte Lehmarchitektur in Amarna* (Berlin: Gebr. Mann Verlag, 1994), Appendix 3: "Die Comfort Zone."

[112] On the lack of continuity between the administrators from Thebes and the new group at Akhetaten, see Redford, *Akhenaten*, 164–66. Note the parallel phenomenon with the "conversion" of various chiefs to Nongqawuse's prophecy, above, chapter 4.

[113] See Jan Assmann, "Die loyalistische Lehre Echnatens," *Studien zur Altägyptischen Kultur* 8 (1980): 1–30.

[114] On the Middle Kingdom, see Barry Kemp, *Ancient Egypt: Anatomy of a Civilization* (London and New York: Routledge, 1989); on the immediate precedents, see Peter Lacovara, *The New Kingdom Royal City* (New York: Kegan Paul International, 1997).

day and pushed them to work at a feverish rate that itself reflected the impact of apocalyptic time. No site, even in modern times, has gone from desert to fully operative city of tens of thousands in so short a time.[115]

One can even suggest a direct link between the theology of the sun-god-king and the working of this extraordinarily adept and pervasive administration built up during the previous decades under the stewardship of sa-Hapu. Just as the rays of the Aten shine down on Akhenaten, so, through his ministers, that is, his administrative rays, the instruction emanates from Akhetaten and shines down upon the entire kingdom. In the tomb of Ramose, one of the few viziers in which we find evidence of the actual switch to the "new teaching," we have one panel in which Ramose receives instruction from the king, while in the next he imparts it to the rejoicing population.[116] We find a similar dynamic, at just the same time, in Akhenaten's relationship with Bek his sculptor over the decision to depict Akhenaten "realistically."[117]

The sycophantic attitude of the new generation of officials at Akhetaten may not represent so much (or just) a base groveling of favor-seekers as it does a self-image appropriate to those who at once served a—*the*—god, and represented him to the rest of the (benighted) population. Rather than take this as "mere" self-serving propaganda, it may represent the way that those who embarked on this new venture viewed themselves: their teaching should, would result in the harmony of the universe and the joy of its inhabitants. That it had to fail represents the wisdom of our *ex post defectu* hindsight.[118] Everything we know about Akhenaten suggests that he believed fully in his cosmic mission and destiny.

What else can explain the staggering pretension of his adventure, although as psychoanalysts might say, that may have been "overdetermined"? In particular, his dismissive attitude toward the mythological explanation of the cosmos that had, in varying ways, informed the Egyptian *Weltanschauung* for millennia implies that *time itself* had come to a completion with his reign at Akhetaten.

The Impact of Akhenaten's Revolution on the Egyptians

With Akhetaten and its rituals now replacing an earlier cosmology, the sun no longer rose, and set, and rose again because of an elaborate struggle that daily took place between the sun god Ra and the forces of chaos that attacked the bark of the

---

[115] The urban planning behind Akhetaten, the "green and pleasant land" watered by a host of carefully planned wells, represents a tour de force of extraordinary proportions; see Reeves, *Akhenaten*, 113–37. On the haste with which it was built, see above, n. 35.

[116] Most of the iconography in this Theban period is part of the "old" style of Amenhotep III (including a festive meal with sa-Hapu), but the last two tableaux show the new iconography of the sun-disk and rays. See Davies, *The Tomb of the Vizier Ramose*, pl. XXXII–XXXV, 30–35; Tobin, "Amarna and Biblical Relgion," 249.

[117] Bek speaks in his tomb inscriptions (at Amarna) of receiving the king's instructions in all that he did.

[118] This is not to say that there were no "owls" who predicted the failure of this venture (and were purged for their opinion), but that those who "believed" in it, no matter how wrong, were not therefore either cynical or stupid.

sun every night and every day. On the contrary, Akhenaten abolished these rituals, replacing them with his own.[119] Similarly—at least in (new) principle—no longer did people die and go to an afterlife with the assistance of Osiris and a wide range of funerary rituals, but all were to rejoice in the present and lived anew (dead or alive) with the sun's daily rebirth.[120]

> When you dawn, they live.
> When you set, they die.
> You yourself are the time in which and thought which one lives.[121]

Even festivals were outlawed since Akhetaten had transcended the "riven world." Akhetaten was a permanent Sed festival, one that put an end to all others.[122] Those who articulated this new vision may have rejoiced; but the rest of the population almost surely suffered severely from this enlightened reductionism.

Such extraordinary discarding of rituals that had governed a people's public and private piety since time out of mind cannot come from a "hard-headed realist."[123] It is the work of someone who, in true apocalyptic millennial fashion, believes that time has come to its climax and its end with its millennial fulfillment in the now, a now into which public and private, past and future, local and universal have all collapsed. "The concept of eternity is abandoned in favour of an obsessive attention to a detailing of the here and now; previously differentiated, heaven and earth were now one and the same."[124] "Time, in a sense, was redundant."[125]

In this sense, the "break" or decisive change in direction under the new chief sculptor of Akhetaten at the death of Bek, Tuthmose, may actually represent an extension of the ideology of the pharaoh's beneficences to the kingdom. We know

---

[119] On the previous notion of the sun's progress and the participation of the entire Egyptian pantheon in assuring its regular progress against the forces of chaos embodied in the god Apopis, and the radically anti-mythical approach of Akhenaten, see Assmann, *Mind of Egypt*, 207–18.

[120] See Aldred, *Akhenaten*, 165–67.

[121] M. Sandman, "Texts from the Time of Akhenaten," *Bibliotheca Aegyptica* 8 (1939): 95:18; cited in Assmann, *Mind of Egypt*, 220.

[122] "For [Akhenaten] god is nothing but light and time. He overcomes neither evil nor death, as neither has any place in this new vision of the world. Akhenaten's vision was the most consistent Egyptian attempt to transcend the idea of a 'riven world.' But Akhenaten's emphatically *undivided* world has no place for the moral aspect of the divine and the claims that attend it" (Assmann, *Mind of Egypt*, 221).

[123] See Reeves in particular (*Akhenaten*, 145–47), who, interestingly enough, compares Akhenaten to other millennial rulers—Stalin and Mao (see chapter 12).

[124] Ibid., 147.

[125] Ibid., 101. The fullness of time no longer refers to eternity of time after death but here and now, Akhenaten *as* eternity. Eternity now! The concept of eternity is not abandoned (on the contrary, the word "nhh" abounds in the text) but perhaps redefined in terms of "here and now" (personal communication from Jan Assmann).

that Bek's studio represents a factory for mass-producing images of the pharaoh, many meant to be "used" in ceremonial processions.[126] This image factory may have produced images of Akhenaten to be sent out throughout Egypt for cultic purposes: just as Akhenaten's courtiers worshiped the divinely royal family at their Amarna tombs, so all of Egypt may have been expected to perform the ceremonies that assured the regular beneficence of the Aten through his earthly incarnation. That these statues—far more traditional in their depictions of the pharaoh—might compromise with "reality" in order to appeal to the aesthetic of the broader population makes sense: this is "popular" millennial art. Only the initiates (*et encore!*) at Akhetaten could truly appreciate the real truth.

■ Things Go Awry: Defectus

When a millennial movement reaches such a point of public and political commitment, there is no return. To go back would constitute an impossible admission of error. From this point onward, the more magical the notion, the more terrible the damage at its inevitable failure. We know more *that* Akhenaten failed than precisely how. Strange disturbances in the record offer fleeting glimpses that we can only speculate about, many of which happen in regnal year 12. The year started out well: foreign dignitaries bearing gifts from many lands came to pay homage to the great pharaoh in his new residence, and, at least in the Egyptian renditions of the event, showed the proper abjection before the god.[127] But shortly thereafter, Akhenaten's mother Tiye died, his eldest daughter Merytaten died, a second consort, Kiya, died in childbirth, and Nefertiti suddenly disappeared from the record. The serpent of mortality had struck in immortal Eden. The divine family no longer lived in the blissful "now."

This same year, or shortly thereafter, Akhenaten ordered the most astounding deeds of his revolutionary rule: an iconoclastic campaign that scarred Egyptian art permanently. He ordered the hacking out of the name Amun from any inscription (including many with his father's name[128]), the destruction of statues of the gods, in some cases, the word gods in the plural, even symbolic representations of them, like geese or cabbages. Nor was this merely in public sculpture. We find examples of this erasure even in private and small objects like engraved scarabs. Moreover, this campaign had to have the approval of zealots given how far and wide its impact was felt, from the Fourth Cataract in the south to places outside of Egypt. Indeed, many historians posit an army of enforcers who went throughout the countryside

---

[126] Hochfield, "Revolutionary Art," 37.

[127] "…the king appeared in a kiosk, while all around flocked emissaries from Nubia, Libya, Syria, and the Hittites. Gold, silver, precious jewels, costly garments and manufactures were placed on the ground in the royal presence, while livestock milled about lowing—all constituting the expected 'benevolences' due from the grandees of the empire" (Redford, *Akhenaten*, 186). See also N.D. Davies, *The Rock Tombs of El Amarna* (London: Egypt Exploration Fund, 1903), v. 2, pl. 29; v. 3, pl. 13.

[128] With the notable exception of Amenhotep III's personal tomb.

imposing the orders on one and all. The rays of the sun suddenly turned cold and their extending hands, harsh.

Historians have justifiably found such unprecedented behavior difficult to understand, and I do not pretend to explain why the violence took the specific form of iconoclasm. But the dynamic of apocalyptic time can explain why it happened when it did, and why it took such a far-reaching and coercive form, supported by so many "agents." Disappointment inevitably disorients millennial believers, and when they have burned as many bridges and made as many enemies as had Akhenaten, the failure of the millennial project to work out as imagined threatens them with annihilation: the incomprehensible failure produces unbearable dissonance.[129]

People who hold political power, often respond by upping the ante, by denying the evidence of failure, and by carving out of the real world the millennial reality they cling to so mightily: coercive purity. Like the Xhosa chief Sarhili, rather than admit error to the "unbelievers," roosters with power prefer to terrorize them. What combination of monotheistic exclusivity and Oedipal behavior, unleashed by the death of his mother,[130] actually drove Akhenaten to this particular form of coercive purity remains unclear. But *that* an episode of massive coercive purity should come precisely as the movement began to implode makes perfect sense within the framework of the apocalyptic wave.

This internal campaign coincides with a collapse of the empire in western Asia, where letters from several allies begging Egypt to intervene failed to arouse Akhenaten's interest.[131] Some earlier historians have presented his quiescence as an exalted form of pacifism that was, like Jesus', beyond the comprehension of his generation.[132] Later ones have sought to "play down" the range of the damage, although the only real disagreement is over how great a decline this represents.[133]

Whatever the causes of the neglect, the negative consequences became quickly apparent. "By the end of the reign of Akhenaten, Egypt had proved a broken reed in its failure to support the independent states of South Syria with effective military aid."[134] Apparently, to those allies outside the utopian preserve of Akhetaten,

---

[129] For a diametrically opposing view, see Hornung, *Conceptions of God in Ancient Egypt*, 244–50.

[130] She apparently came to Akhetaten with statues of her husband, and one can well imagine that until her death (and with the manifest failure of his mad gamble), Akhenaten would not allow the full range of his hostility to his father to become manifest.

[131] Commenting on the Amarna letters, Reeves wrote: "Pharaoh's determined, almost pathological lack of interest in the world outside inevitably took its toll on Egypt's prestige abroad" (*Akhenaten*, 153). For a parallel case of domestic iconoclasm while the borders collapsed, see the discussion of the Roman Empire circa 400 CE in Markus, chap. 6.

[132] See Weigall, *Life and Times* (above, n. 22).

[133] That assessment depends largely on how seriously one takes the entreaties for help or dismisses them as so much diplomatic "rhetoric of crisis." Michael Several, "Reconsidering the Egyptian Empire in Palestine during the Amarna Period," *Palestine Exploration Quarterly* 104 (1972): 123–33; most recently, Cohen and Westbrook, *Amarna Diplomacy*, 101–38.

[134] Aldred, "Egypt: The Amarna Period," 84.

the sun-king-god's millennial self-absorption had disastrous results. It should even be possible, upon close examination, to detect the earliest hints that rulers outside of Egypt had found out that Akhenaten was mad, and that the political reach of his father had vanished.

Monotheism and the Akhenaten Revolution

Monotheism plays a critical role in Akhenaten's thought, and historians have often commented and speculated on its relationship to Hebraic monotheism. Indeed, Hebraic claims to Abrahamic monotheism aside, Akhenaten constitutes the earliest documented case of monotheism in the historical record.[135] For some, the relationship to Hebraic monotheism seems extremely close, including the nearly verbatim passages in Psalm 104 and the "Hymn to Aten" found in one of the tombs at Akhetaten.[136] In particular, the earliest Egyptologists, often Protestants eager to see in Akhenaten a precursor of Jesus, extolled his lucidity and principled pacifism.[137] Even Freud, who had his own reasons not to notice the difference, assumed that Akhenaten's monotheism and Moses' were essentially identical.[138]

For others, especially more recently, the relationship is at best tenuous. Redford has underlined what many have noted, that Akhenaten's "cold" monotheism has little in common with the emotional and ethically demanding Hebrew God, and Tobin notes that it is hard to imagine how Moses could have known much about Akhenaten's banned heresy.[139] In fact, Akhenaten's monotheism actually diminished some of the shared elements of Hebrew and Egyptian religiosity, turning the Ma'at, which in so many ways resembled the principles of Hebraic moral concerns

---

[135] Most historians believe that "real" monotheism (one God for the universe), as opposed to "henotheism" (one God for the people) did not appear until late in the Jewish religion; see Mark Smith, *The Early History of God* (San Francisco: Harper & Row, 1990) and Diana V. Edelman, ed., *The Triumph of Elohim* (Grand Rapids, Mich.: Eerdmans, 1995).

[136] James Breasted, "Ikhnaton, The Religious Revolutionary," in *Cambridge Ancient History*, 1st ed., vol.2 (Cambridge: Cambridge University Press, 1924), chap. 6; Aldred, *Akhenaten*, 187–89; Hari, *The Great Hymn to Aten*, 15–18.

[137] Weigall, *Life and Times*, 226–30.

[138] For Freud, the assertion that the Mosaic religion is "nothing else but that of Aton" (*Moses and Monotheism*, 27) takes on the force of an axiom, and upon which his analysis rests. This leads him to make such statements as "he [Moses] was an adherent of the new religion, whose basic principles he fully understood and had made his own" (*Moses and Monotheism*, 31). On Freud's reasons for wanting to see them as the same, see Yosef Yerushalmi, *Freud's Moses: Judaism Terminable and Interminable* (New Haven, Conn.: Yale University Press, 1991). Apparently, Freud (like so many other modern scholars) had such contempt for religion that he did not notice the differences. He assumed ethical similarities precisely where there are vast differences between the egalitarian law code of Moses and the authoritarian kingship of Akhenaten. Freud actually does note one difference between Akhenaten's monotheism and that of the Jews, which "entirely relinquishes the worship of the sun," and he seems to link it to a "purposive contradiction" between Akhenaten's "deliberate antagonism" to popular religion and presumably (Freud does not even finish this thought), Moses' intense commitment to transforming popular religion. But he considers that these "easily discerned" differences "do not enlighten us much" (28–29).

[139] Redford "Monotheism of the Heretic Pharaoh," 32; Tobin, "Amarna and Biblical Religion," 233.

for the weak, the orphan, the poor and dispossessed, demanding honesty and truth from all men, into an assertion of Akhenaten himself as the embodiment of truth, a synonym for the pharaoh and *his* commands.[140]

Curiously, anyone who has considered the relationship between the Hebraic and Egyptian monotheism, however close or distant they consider them, has made the same assumption cherished by the hermetic school of the Renaissance.[141] Moses took his monotheism from Akhenaten.[142] Generally those who so view Akhenaten's relationship to Moses tend to represent a "philosophical" school of monotheism in which Akhenaten's accomplishment comes not from revelation but from mental speculation, and therefore represents a higher plane than that of the messy, emotional, often irritable nature of Moses' "one God."[143]

Before deciding on such matters, however, it seems important to specify the fundamental difference between Israelite and Egyptian monotheism: the relationship of the one God to kingship.[144] Curiously, historians either fail to note this striking difference, or, even noting, play it down.[145] Akhenaten's brand of monotheism may share its theological presumptions with the "Mosaic" version—its rejoicing in the abundance of God's creation, and its iconoclastic tendencies. But in terms of political thinking, it represents a thoroughgoing version of *iconic monotheism*: Akhenaten forbade statues of all *other* gods, but produced images of himself (and ceremonies) that emphasized precisely his role as the image of, indeed incarnation of, the one true God. His zealous destruction is not iconoclasm, but the authoritarian imposition of new icons mass produced at Akhetaten, ones glorifying his own personal divinity. His was top-down millennialism.

All of the other authoritarian characteristics of the hierarchical formula emerge as well. In particular, we find the substitution of the king's orders for ethical teachings. The "magic" of Akhenaten's millennium predicated an absolute role for his decisions that literally dispossessed, even as it claimed to fulfill, the needs of all the Aten's creatures. No festivals, no funeral rites, no decisions. The people received their plenitude, their salvation from the beneficent rays of the sun and the equally beneficent royal family and the king's ministers: they prayed before an altar with a

---

[140] R. Anthes, *Die Maat des Echnaton von Amarna*, Journal of the American Oriental Society Supplement 14 (Baltimore: American Oriental Society, 1952).

[141] On the hermetic tradition, see below, n. 163.

[142] This is Breasted's argument at the turn of the century ("Ikhnaton, The Religious Revolutionary"), picked up by Freud (*Moses and Monotheism*, 1934–38), and commonly addressed even by those who do not consider the connection particularly close (Redford, *Akhenaten*, 232–35).

[143] "We stand here at the threshold less of the monotheistic universal religions than of natural philosophy, and had this religion won out, we might have expected a Thales rather than a Moses," Jan Assmann, *The Search for God in Ancient Egypt* (Ithaca, N.Y.: Cornell University Press, 2001), 213; see also James P. Allen, "The Natural Philosophy of Akhenaten," in *Religion and Philosophy in Ancient Egypt* (New Haven, Conn.: Yale University Press, 1985), 97.

[144] Most historians who do distinguish have a tendency to make the case in terms of what one or the other was "lacking," rather than differing fundamentally.

[145] See above, chapter 2. For an example of someone who, despite noting the difference quite clearly, does not appreciate how significant they are, see Tobin, "Amarna and Biblical Religion" (and notes below).

picture of the king and his family.[146] No need for further Sed festivals: the world was no longer riven.

Viewed in these terms, Akhenaten's monotheism shows every sign of being not a purer and more abstract form of monotheism, but a megalomanic distortion of ethical monotheism's intense focus on demotic ethics. It is as if, having grasped some of the basic (and radical) principles of ethical monotheism—including the celebration of human life in all its particularities and activities and the beneficent desire of the one God that *all* his creatures rejoice in creation—Akhenaten believed that the only way for this brilliant insight to reach the rest of the population was through him. *He* guaranteed social order; *he* embodied Ma'at; *he* was a jealous god who suffered no other gods to stand before him in the eyes of his people.[147]

Thus, according to this reading, Akhenaten's monotheism does not represent the height of rational theology but of religious megalomania, even by Egyptian standards. His obsession with "monotheism" was actually an obsession with himself, and represents the exact opposite from Moses' demotic, anti-monarchical monotheism of "No king but God."[148] Indeed, for a king who considered all Egypt (and probably the entire world) to be his own possession, who commanded and spent the wealth of his nation as he willed and in particular in his enormously expensive fantasy at Akhetaten, it would have been incomprehensible to respond to a challenge to his authority as did Moses with the return challenge, "Whose donkey have I taken?"[149] Akhenaten's obvious answer would be: "Everybody's."[150]

Every contrast between the two men's vision of monotheism revolves around this fundamental contrast between the two principle monotheistic political formulas: "One God, one King" and "no king but God." This contrast constitutes the very fault line that separates the two: the iconic sun-god-king versus radical iconoclasm, the authoritarian and expensive monarchical apparatus versus the demotic leadership of charismatic judges, the ethics of hierarchy versus the ethics of *isonomia*.[151] They are both monotheistic; they are profoundly different.

---

[146] In Hornung's formula, playing on the Islamic one: "There is no god but Aten and Akhenaten is his prophet" (*Concepts of God*, 248). This is actually too modest for Akhenaten. His formula is "there is no God but Aten and Akhenaten is his earthly incarnation."

[147] Hornung, *Conceptions of God in Ancient Egypt*, 248–49.

[148] See Martin Buber, *Kingship of God* (New York: Humanity Books, 1967); and *Moses: The Revelation and the Covenant* (New York: Humanity Books, 1988).

[149] One of the characteristics of anti-monarchical monotheism was the reluctance of the "leader" of the people to expropriate their private property. Moses and Samuel both respond the challenge to their authority with the rhetorical question: "Whose donkey have I taken?" (Numbers 16:15; 1 Samuel 12:3). Weigall, perhaps disturbed by the huge expenses that Akhenaten incurred, gives a spirited defense of his right to do so on the basis that, as with all monarchies of the time, a fortiori the Egyptian one, the entire land was the king's personal possession to dispose of as he wished.

[150] Note the biblical narrative's apparent approval of Pharaoh's taking everybody's donkey in the Joseph story, Genesis 47:14–27.

[151] Tobin points out that at no point, even in the literature most favorable to kingship in ancient Israel, was the sun imagery ever used to refer to the king: "The Hebrew texts in general avoid the usage of sun symbolism, probably on purpose in order to escape any possible dangers of equating YHWH with the sun itself" ("Amarna and Biblical Religion," 255–58). Freud noted both the absence of solar worship and the demotic thrust without appreciating their significance (above, n. 139).

And like so many examples of this top-down, imperial form of overzealous monotheism, Akhenaten's revolution from above proved remarkably fragile and unpopular.[152] Within years it had shattered, provoking a backlash that would literally wipe away any trace of it for more than three millennia. This hardly meant the end for iconic monotheism. Indeed, in the hands of Christian imperial theologians it would become so common a theme—despite its fragility—that modern scholars seem to assume that this is monotheism's *only* political formula.[153]

■ THE OWLS STRIKE BACK: *DAMNATIO MEMORIAE EX POST DEFECTU*

Although, as we shall see in the next chapter with the Taiping, movements that begin "bottom-up" often turn authoritarian once they reach power, in this early Egyptian case we have an almost purely top-down phenomenon inspired by a megalomanic king and his ambitious cadre of administrators. That the project never had the support of the populace seems highly probable, especially given the ways in which Akhetaten drained both their economic and religious resources, leaving them to bathe in the wan sunlight of their mad king's fantasies. But we can make even more certain statements about the reaction of Akhenaten's successors, who reviled him and sought to destroy him in ways that mirrored his own campaign aimed at destroying any traces of Amun and the other gods of Egypt.

It is difficult to date the beginning of the "return to normal time," partly because the final years of Akhenaten's reign are shrouded in mystery.[154] We can, however, mark two key moments in the process. The first came several years after Akhenaten's death, in the third or fourth year of the reign of Akhenaten's second successor,[155] when the young boy-pharaoh changed his name from Tutenkhaten to Tutenkhamen (i.e., from *living image of Aten* to *living image of Amun*). In so doing, he reversed the name change that had first set off the millennial venture of Akhnaten and adopted

---

[152] For an interesting parallel, see the abreaction to the first great emperor of China, Qin, shortly after his death: Mark Edward Lewis, *The Early Chinese Empires: Qin and Han* (Cambridge, Mass.: Harvard University Press, 2007), 70–74. On the fragility of the imperial formula "one God, one king," see the reflections of Garth Fowden, *From Empire to Commonwealth*, 90–93, 169–75. See also Assmann, *Moses the Egyptian*, 22–29.

[153] Francis Dvornik, *Early Christian and Byzantine Political Theory*, 2 vols. (Washington, D.C.: Dumberton Oaks Center for Byzantine Studies, 1966); Peterson, *Monotheismus als politisches Problem* (Leipzig: Hegner, 1935).

[154] The most systematic study is that of Rolf Krauss, *Das Ende der Amarnazeit* (Hildesheim: Gerstenberg Verlag, 1978). The tale of the final years and succession of Akhenaten offers rich terrain for historical speculation of the most bizarre kind—Nefertiti as Pharaoh! (Reeves, *Akhenaten*, 172–73), incestual marriages, assassination, usurpation.

[155] The first is the mysterious Smenkare, whom some think was Neferiti; see Julia Samson, "Nefertiti's Regality," *Journal of Egyptian Archeology* 63 (1977): 88–97; for arguments against this theory, see Redford, *Akhenaten*, 191–92.

the name his father had so zealously gouged out of every Egyptian inscription he could.[156] That such a move came at the bidding of his handlers (the pharaoh was a boy at the time and died young) seems certain, and reflects a decided shift away from the millennial policies of Akhenaten, including a move out of Akhetaten. The Resoration Stela of Tutenkhamen eloquently describes the devastated condition of Egypt, and explicitly repudiated Akhenaten's adventure.[157]

But if Tutankhamen, through his advisors, turned away from Akhenaten's millennial fantasies, he retained a certain syncretism that sought to embrace both Amon and Aten.[158] The lad died tragically young and was buried in a tomb that marks a return to pre-Atenist practices despite retaining some aspects of the "Amarna style."[159] The full repudiation, the violent one, came still later, under Tutankhamen's third successor, Horemheb, the general (risen from the ranks of commoners via the bureaucracy) who, upon becoming pharaoh, wiped out all traces of Akhenaten's revolution. Horemheb struck Akhenaten's name from the records and pharaoh lists; he hacked out his name and any symbols of Atenism throughout Egypt; he usurped most of his monuments for himself; he systematically knocked down the walls of Akhetaten.

For this part of his campaign we have explicit evidence. At the same time we can surmise—if the initial conjecture is accurate—that Horemheb ordered the systematic destruction of the Akhenaten-as-only-god sculptures that Tuthmose's factory had produced and sent throughout Egypt. Indeed, their imposition in place of traditional religious objects might explain the ferocious revulsion over Akhenaten that surpasses anything previously know in the annals of Egyptian history, despite the frequent use of *damnatio memoriae* (the obliteration of memory).[160]

These activities suggest not merely disapproval of Akhenaten and his adventure, but violent repulsion. And without the work of modern archeologists, the only remaining traces of Akhenaten would be the occasional (and incomprehensible) negative reference to Akhenaten's evil, and a strange oral narrative, recorded some eleven centuries later in which Amenhotep sa-Hapu, Akhenaten, and Moses all mingle confusingly in a feverish nightmare.[161] As is so characteristic of millennial movements *ex post defectu*, the owls have the decisive word, and where they

---

[156] This is engraved in the restoration stelae at Karnak, on which see Reeves, *Akhenaten*, 182.

[157] Ibid.

[158] A wide range of material, including a throne originally prepared for Akhenaten, includes the names and the worship of both gods.

[159] Though evidence of the Amarna style in the tomb's imagery shows signs of continuity with the previous reign. Rita E. Freed, "Akhenaten's Artistic Legacy," in *Pharaohs of the Sun: Ahkenaten, Nefertiti, Tutankhamen*, ed. Rita E. Freed, Yvonne J. Markowitz and Sue H. D'Auria (Boston: Little, Brown and Co., 1999), 187–90.

[160] For earlier examples, see the work done on Senenmut, Hatshepsut's vizier; Peter Dorman, *The Monuments of Senenmut: Problems in Historical Methodology* (New York: Kegan Paul International, 1988).

[161] W.G. Waddell, trans., *Manetho* (Cambridge, Mass.: Harvard University Press, 1980); for an analysis, see Assmann, *Moses the Egyptian*, 29–44.

do not tell a distorted tale, they wipe out the memory entirely. And yet, as often happens, with enough attention, historians can reconstruct the story from the traces of their efforts to erase: not *e silentio*, but *e vestigiis*.

■ POSTSCRIPT: MILLENNIAL FASCINATION WITH EGYPT AND AKHENATEN

Although Akhenaten's mad episode vanished from the written record, myths of an older contemporary of Moses who had esoteric knowledge about creation, *prisca theologica*, circulated widely in the ancient world. Around the turn of the Common Era, a body of (Greek) texts attributed to this shadowy wise man known as Hermes Trismegistus, or Hermes the Thrice Great appeared. Although scholars in the Latin West knew about the existence of these texts, not until the fall of Constantinople to the Muslim Turks in 1453 did a copy reach the West, where Cosimo de Medici immediately ordered its translation into Latin. The extraordinary career of the Latin translation, and its impact on Western scientific thinking, has been chronicled by Frances Yates.[162] The ironic element in this particular story comes from the lack of any clear millennialism in the original corpus, which nonetheless, in the hands of Western thinkers, triggered a particularly potent millennial movement in the West—modern science.[163]

Two minor footnotes in the story however, bring the tale full cycle to our discussion. In 1599, a hermetic enthusiast from southern Italy, Tomasso Campanella, was arrested by the authorities for trying to create a (demotic) utopian community, the *City of the Sun* in the mountains of Calabria. While he rotted in prison, certain intellectuals in the court of Louis XIII read his work and were particularly drawn to his use of sun imagery. Richelieu, the king's great minister, had Campanella freed from prison and brought to court in Paris. The hierarchical principles of rulership that the grateful escapee fashioned for his new-found patrons provided the royal jelly to turn the king's young son, Louis XIV into the "sun king."[164]

And last, but hardly least, the Nazis had a particular fascination for Akhenaten. Hitler prized the bust of Nefertiti above all other art treasures as an image of

---

[162] See Francis Yates, *Giordanno Bruno and the Hermetic Tradition in the Renaissance* (London: Routledge, 1964); see also below on Tomasso Campanella and the sun-king Louis XIV). The discovery of Akhenaten at the end of the nineteenth century permitted modern historians to substitute him and monotheism for Hermes Trismegistus and "true gnosis."

[163] On the relationship of the "Magus" tradition to the emergence of modern science see Francis Yates, "The Hermetic Tradition in Renaissance Science," in Charles Singleton, ed., Art, Science and History in the Renaissance (Baltimore: Johns Hopkins, 1968), 255–74; on science as a millennial project, Noble, *Religion of Technology*; on more recent work on the millennial dimension of hermetic thinking, see Geoffrey McVey, "Giordano Bruno and the Rewriting of the Heavens," in Gutierrez and Schwartz, *The End that Does*, 85–96.

[164] Yates, "Giordano Bruno and Tommaso Campanella," in *Giordano Bruno*, 360–98.

Aryan [sic] perfection. The mysteries of Akhenaten provided those Nazi ideologues who had a particular fascination for the mystical, in particular Theosophy, with a great source of racial speculation[165] and novelistic fantasy.[166] The heady mixture of nudism, Theosophy, Egyptian mysticism, and anti-Semitism created a Nazi Akhenaten who could "justify the *furor Tuetonicus* that would soon engulf Europe."[167] As the French writer Savitri Devi wrote in dedication to the 1958 book on Akhenaten entitled *The Lightning and the Sun*:

> To the god-like Individual of our times;
> The man against Time;
> The greatest European of all times;
> Both Sun and Lightning:
> ADOLF HITLER
> As a tribute of unfailing love and loyalty, forever and ever.[168]

The attractions of iconic monotheism with its sun worship and imperial messianism cut across cultures and times.

---

[165] A number of German and English historians tried to argue that Akhenaten's mother Tiye was of Aryan descent (Weigall's argument, translated into German, picked up by Savitri Devi); in Montserrat, *Akhenaten, History and Fantasy*, 109). On the Nazis and the occult, especially Theosophy, see Nicholas Goodrick-Clarke, *The Occult Roots of Nazism: Secret Aryan Cults and their Influence on Nazi Ideology* (London: Tauris Parke, 2004), 192–204, and below, chapter 12.

[166] For a brief discussion of two prominent cases, the German historical novelist Josef Magnus Wehner (1891–1973) and the French-born Devi (Maximian Portaz, 1905–82), see Montserrat, *Akhenaten, History and Fantasy*, 111–14.

[167] Ibid.,108.

[168] Ibid., 113. The book, as Montserrat points out, was more than a dusty secondhand bookshop curiosity. Parts of it are on the World Wide Web, for example, at a Green Nazi site: http://www.natvan. com/cgi-bin/webc.cgi/st_prod.html?p_prodid=658. For Savitri Devi (née Maximine Portaz), see a website dedicated to her work, http://www.savitridevi.org/article-bolton.html.

7 Bipolar Millennialism

Taiping (The Great Peace, 1850–1864)

At the height of the open-air revivals in the United States, known as the "Great Awakening" (1820s–40s), a charged encounter occurred between two men in the city of Canton in southern China. In 1836, a Chinese Christian, touched by missionaries carrying this wave of enthusiasm to China, met, spoke with, and gave a missionary pamphlet to a young man who had just failed the exams to enter the Mandarinate. Although it took several years of incubation, that encounter set Hong Xiuquan on a path to claiming the messianic titles "God's Chinese Son" and "Jesus' Younger Brother." Over the course of a decade of work (1840s), he gathered around him a small, loyal band of followers who pursued a highly disciplined, demotic religiosity, inspired by the biblical Ten Commandments. They called themselves the *Bai shangdi hui* (Society of God Worshippers) and denounced both Confucianism and local religious cults as idol worship.[1]

By 1850, conflict broke out between them and the administrative agents of the Manchu dynasty, the Qing. Setting off to war, they adopted the Daoist messianic title *Taiping* ("Great Peace"). Although the tide of battle shifted back and forth initially, the swelling number of recruits to the Taiping permitted them, by 1853, to march north from the southern reaches of Canton to Nanjing, the former imperial capital of the Ming Dynasty, and take the city. Once in possession of the city, Hong Xiuquan proclaimed himself messianic emperor and inaugurated the "Great Peace." The land reform he enacted, which gave to every man and woman identical plots, may be the most egalitarian experiment on record up to that time.

The movement's spectacular success derived from its deep egalitarian appeal. Whenever they took a city or region, they carefully distinguished between the rich whom they plundered (and in some cases of especially hated men, executed) and the poor to whom they distributed some of the plunder and offered a three-year amnesty on taxes. As a contemporary British observer noted during the movement's most powerful moment (1856), their promise of "equality of

---

[1] The bibliography on the Taiping is immense. The works I will most frequently cite are: Robert Weller, *Resistance, Chaos and Control in China: Taiping Rebels, Taiwanese Ghosts, and Tiananmen* (Seattle: University of Washington Press, 1994); Jonathan Spence, *God's Chinese Son: The Taiping Heavenly Kingdom of Hong Xiuquan* (New York: W.W. Norton, 1996); Vincent Y. C. Shih, *The Taiping Ideology: Its Sources, Interpretations, and Influences* (Seattle: University of Washington Press, 1967); Jen Yu-Wen, *The Taiping Revolutionary Movement* (New Haven, Conn.: Yale University Press, 1973); Stephen Hunt, "The Revolutionary Dimension of Millenarianism: The Case of the T'aiping Rebellion," in *Christian Millennialism: From the Early Church to Waco*, ed. Stephen Hunt (Bloomington: Indiana University Press, 2001) and Thomas H. Reilly, *The Taiping Heavenly Kingdom: Rebellion and the Blasphemy of Empire* (Seattle: University of Washington Press, 2004).

property or at least of a sufficiency for every man...won to their cause the best sinew and muscle of the country."[2] If the early demotic religiosity of the Taiping had won tens of thousands by 1850, the egalitarian social program that accompanied open rebellion swelled their ranks to possibly over a million by the time they took Nanjing.[3]

But in Nanjing heaven turned to hell. Hong, the messiah, withdrew to an imperial heaven of elaborate rituals, magnificence, and sexual excess. He failed to press on to Beijing and, instead, let the Qing bring the battle to him. War continued to eat away at the borders of the half-born empire for over a decade; megalomania and court intrigue plagued the inner circles to whom Hong had left the details of the revolutionary struggle; and expressions of disappointment brought on paranoid attacks of revolutionary terror. A dynamic familiar to all historians of revolutionary movements set in with vigor.

And yet, despite such exceptionally dysfunctional behavior, the millennial forest fire continued to rage. The Taiping held out against the Qing for another ten years of merciless war. Two years before the Xhosa began to kill their cattle, the Qing extinguished the last flames of this millennial revolt in a massive slaughter. Before the final resolution, however, some 20–35 million (!) Chinese lost their lives. This constitutes the most massive bloodletting in recorded history at the time, one that stands alongside the death tolls of Hitler, Stalin, or Mao a century later.

■ COMPARISON WITH AKHENATEN

The differences between Hong Xiuquan and Akhenaten abound. Obviously, Xiuquan's death toll seems at opposite poles from the inwardly directed "pacifism" of Akhenaten, as do their sexual proclivities. The Taiping represent an egalitarian movement that arose from the margins and depths of the social hierarchy, while Akhenaten was born to the purple. Xiuquan hated the established authorities, especially the Mandarins who had turned him away, and his group represented a radical alternative to the accepted norms of social order. Akhenaten, on the other hand, carried his revolution out from above, using the very bureaucratic elite that Hong so radically rejected. The pharaoh had no need for violence precisely because he controlled the political structures of the time.

---

[2] Thomas Taylor Meadows, *The Chinese and Their Rebellions: Viewed in Connection with Their National Philosophy, Ethics, Legislation and Administration* (London: Smith, Elder & Co., 1856). He appropriately compared the early Taiping with the English revolutionaries of the 1640s, also millennialists, and he could just as well, and perhaps with more accuracy, given the violence that both of these movements engendered, have compared them with the Jacquerie and the other such, considerably bloodier rebellions of the Middle Ages.

[3] John Newsinger, "Taiping Revolutionary: Augustus Lindley in China," *Race and Class* 42, no. 4 (2001): 59. The Qing sources of the time estimate two million members of the Taiping. It is hard to rely on such sources: alarmist figures might arouse an effective response, but such an enormous figure could also be discouraging. The population of China at the time was about 300 million.

Even the documentary record differs dramatically. Unlike Akhenaten, whose deeds took place almost three and a half millennia ago, and whose limited documentary record lay buried in the sands and under the subsequent building projects of hostile successors, the Taiping produced a profusion of documents that survive. Some of these came from their own side—decrees, legislation, religious texts, poetry, theology, even a highly edited translation of the Bible, all churned out at the printing presses of Nanjing. Some came from outsiders, whether the Qing police officials who worked to defeat and suppress them, or the Europeans (political and religious figures) who collected their documentation to figure out how to deal with them.[4] We even have several eyewitness accounts including one voluminous memoir by a European disciple of the Taiping.[5]

Rare are the scholars of China who do not consider the Taiping a millennial movement. Egyptologists, on the other hand, have never thought of Akhetaten as a millennial experiment. The differences seem so obvious that no historian to my knowledge has ever thought to connect them.

Under these obvious differences, however, we find a host of similarities in these two movements that, despite occurring almost four millennia apart, both take place in agrarian empires. In particular, both messiahs, once they acquired power, followed a similar pattern. They shared the same conviction that the current generation stands in a unique and privileged position vis-à-vis a world at the brink of transformation. They both isolated themselves in a millennial capital whose sacred activity would somehow transform the entire world; and their same inward focus became so obsessive that the outside world collapsed. And last but certainly not least, they shared the same megalomanic tendencies, rendered all the more eccentric and self-destructive by the failure of apocalyptic expectations, and eventually alienated even their own following.

■ ORIGINS IN THE EXPERIENCE AND BELIEFS OF HONG XIUQUAN

Hong Xiuquan poses a paradox for us. On the one hand, he seems the least likely candidate for the role he played. A brilliant young man with a promising career in the Mandarin elite of China, he mastered the Confucian teachings, and even without success in the exams, he had a career as a teacher that he pursued from his earliest years (ca. 1830 when he was only sixteen) until the "conversion" experience of 1843. Why he would leave such a lifestyle for the extraordinary rigors of an apostolic mission leading to a total war with the Qing dynasty, raises important questions, and draws our attention to the frequent presence of aspiring and

---

[4] A brief collection of translated sources is available in J.C. Cheng, *Chinese Sources for the Taiping Rebellion, 1850–1864* (Oxford: Oxford University Press, 1963).

[5] A.F. Lindley (Lin-li), *Ti-Ping Tien-Kwoh: The History of the Ti-Ping Revolution* (London: Day & Son, 1866; reprint, New York: Prager Publishers, 1970).

failed "intellectuals" in the ideological ranks of millennial and revolutionary movements.[6]

The key to understanding his transformation seems to lie in the devastating humiliation he experienced when he failed multiple times to pass the exams and enter the Mandarinate. Hong was a Hakka peasant, an ethnic minority, living among the Han Chinese majority. Born to a family that, despite its peasant status, had a long history of scholars, Hong Xiuquan was a boy prodigy—the greatest of his line. Stories of his youth emphasize both how much his family sacrificed so that he might study and how proudly his father bragged about his son's accomplishments. Having mastered the recital of the *Five Classics* and the *Four Books* within a matter of years, he had first presented at these exams at the astonishing age of thirteen. Failure at that point, however disappointing and humiliating, was nonetheless understandable. But nine years later in 1836, at the age of the other candidates, the failure and the deep disappointment that it would inspire in his family and clan made the humiliation all the more intense. And each of the next two failures made it unbearable.

The Visit to Heaven: Compensatory Visions (1837)

We have an early account of the experiences that compelled Hong Xiuquan into his messianic career, a series of visions that came to him at the nadir of his humiliation. A close study of them offers valuable insights into the process whereby someone becomes a messiah. In particular, it sheds important light on the dichotomy between the psychocultural dynamics of honor-shame versus integrity-guilt; and these, in turn, relate directly to the difference between hierarchical and demotic religiosity. Since Hong's millennialism registers exceptionally high in both forms of religiosity—egalitarian fairness and imperial privilege—an understanding of these emotional issues should be particularly valuable.

The missionary Theodore Hamberg, the greatest Western expert on Hakka culture and language, composed a document of exceptional interest for our purposes with lengthy descriptions of Hong's early visions. In 1852, he met Hong's cousin Hong Ren'gan, an active participant in the early part of Hong's messianic career as well as a witness to the events in question. Ren'gan had become separated from the movement and spent much of the 1850s in Hong Kong, where he recounted a great deal of the information Hamberg wrote down.[7] This account of Hong's life-changing encounter with a Christian on the occasion of his taking his second examination in 1836 is remarkably free of either the piety or bitterness that characterizes later accounts of his early career.[8]

---

[6] See discussion of Arab nationalism and al-Qaeda in chapter 14; Hitler, chapter 12; and Mendel, *Vision and Violence*, chap. 5.

[7] The year of his death, Theodore Hamberg published *The Visions of Hung-Siu-tshuen, and Origin of the Kwang-si Insurrection* (Hong Kong: China Mail Office, 1854). On these visions, see Weller, *Resistance, Chaos and Control*, 36–38; Spence, *God's Chinese Son*, chap. 4.

[8] P. M. Yap, "The Mental Illness of Hung Hsiu-Ch'uan, Leader of the Taiping Rebellion," *Far Eastern Quarterly* 13, no. 3 (May 1954): 288–89.

Of course, that still does not mean that the account is accurate. Visions/dreams are notoriously difficult to remember and record, especially when one does not understand them. And according to Hong himself, this vision did not make any sense at the time, and neither he nor any in his circle initially paid it any mind.[9] Indeed, it would not take on its meaning for another seven years, when Xiuquan failed the exam for a fourth and last time. So on one level, it is hard to know what stage of the process of retrospectively creating a coherent narrative of Hong's "calling" this account represents. Furthermore, since this vision constituted the charter of the Taiping movement, it was too important to survive unadulterated by retrospective narrations, even the ones that Ren'gan retained. But even taken as a self-conscious statement by Hong Xiuquan, it reveals a great deal.

Let us take the biographical text piece by piece (italics mine).[10]

> Near the examination hall he saw *a man dressed in the custom of the Ming dynasty without a pigtail, but tied his hair in a knot upon his head.* It seemed that the man could not understand or speak Cantonese because he employed a Chinese as his interpreter. *The stranger was surrounded by group of people.* Hong Xiuquan heard him *telling the people through the interpreter about the fulfillment of their wishes.* Hong Xiuquan *approached the stranger and asked him through the interpreter if he could attain a literary degree.* The stranger told him that "You will attain the highest rank, but do not be grieved, for grief will make you sick. I congratulate your virtuous father." Hong Xiuquan thought it was strange to hear that.
>
> The next day Hong Xiuquan again met these two men in the street. One of them had in his possession a parcel of books consisting of nine small volumes, which were a complete set of work entitled, *Good words for exhorting the age.* When Hong Xiuquan came out from the examination hall, the man gave him the whole set. Hong Xiuquan took them home and after glancing through their contents he placed them in his bookcase thinking that they were unimportant.

The author of the texts Hong received was the Christian Liang A-Fa, and according to some accounts, the figure in the story is Liang.[11] Whoever he was, this Chinese convert had clearly had done several things that Hong Xiuquan had not:

- he had broken with the mimetic and legal demands of the Confucian culture of the day in both hairstyle and clothing;

---

[9] "...beyond interpretation, by common consent it can have no meaning." Spence, *God's Chinese Son*, 50.

[10] This analysis, done from a translation, by someone with limited knowledge of Chinese culture, can only touch on specific aspects of the document, but it can, I hope, identify some of the apocalyptic dynamics. I am working with the translation provided by Theodore de Bary and Richard Lufrano, *Sources of Chinese Tradition* (New York: Columbia University Press, 2000), 213–15.

[11] Liang A-Fa was in Malaysia from 1834–39 (Spence, *God's Chinese Son*, 31–32). So if this encounter occurred during Xiuquan' second exam (1836), then the person in question could not have been Liang (who was born in Guandong province and therefore spoke Cantonese). On the other hand, the man is probably not a Westerner.

- he had separated himself from the exam system: so while others, filled with anxiety, entered the halls to undergo the exacting exams and almost surely fail, he sat calm and untroubled;
- he had a following, companions who cared about what he said;
- he dispensed opaque (and to judge by his comments to Xiuquan, largely optimistic) prophetic advice about the fulfillment of people's wishes.

According to later (retrospective, although not *ex post defectu*) accounts, this conversation was short and Xiuquan put the pamphlet away without reading it.[12] But the following year, he failed the exam again, and this time the burden of failure became unbearable. He became so ill on the way home that he could not even travel, racked with a fever, passing into delirium for forty days and almost dying.

> The following year in 1837 Hong Xiuquan again attended the public examination at the provincial city Guangzhou. When the results were out Hong Xiuquan saw *his name placed high upon the board, but afterwards it was lowered to the bottom. Deeply grieved, disappointed and discontented, Hong Xiuquan had to go home with his ambition dashed.* Shortly afterwards he felt very ill, he engaged a sedan chair with two stout men, who carried him back to his village. That day was the first day of the third moon in the 17th year of Emperor Daoguang. He confined himself to bed. During this period he had a succession of dreams or visions.

The detail about his name on the board being high and then lowered is of utmost importance, whether or not it happened. Public results of the examinations are, of course, major occasions of both honor and humiliation.[13] For Xiuquan to fail this third time was personally catastrophic. But if he had passed and then had his results changed, that would contribute to a rage that could easily spill over into hostility to the entire system of Confucian exams. Certainly, he believed he had been cheated.[14] In any case, with no chance to appeal, this third failure left Xiuquan a broken man, sick, incapable of making it home where his family awaited eagerly the news of his success. He was literally dying of shame. And in his fevered collapse, the vision came.

> He first saw *a great number of people welcoming him to an unknown place.* When he woke up he thought it was a strange dream. He presumed that the place arrived at was the

---

[12] This account may be true, although it may represent a retrospective narrative that makes the tale more stark. What we can probably deduce from it is that Xiuquan did not "understand" what he read in any substantive way, although he may well have found both the conversation and the initial reading of the text intriguing. The elements of his subsequent vision suggest that he had been more deeply touched by this encounter both emotionally and substantively than his later account suggests.

[13] Only a tiny fraction of candidates passed. Public posting of exam results has long dominated most universities in Europe, although the "invasion of privacy" inherent in the practice has raised objections (see "Is There a Better Way to Get Exam Results?" *BBC News*, July 2, 2004, online: http://news.bbc.co.uk/2/hi/uk_news/magazine/3860119.stm, April 13, 2010).

[14] See the remarks of Augustus Lindley (*Ti-Ping Tien Kwoh* [1866]), who received the biographical narrative while with the Taiping in Nanjing. According to Lionel Jensen, Hong's writings do not suggest he had the kind of command of the classics to ensure success on the exams. As for the claim of precocity is a topos and does not necessarily mean that he was so brilliant he should have passed (personal communication).

palace of *Yan Luo Wang* [the king of the underworld] and he was going to die soon. So he called his parents and other relatives to assemble at his bedside. He told them in the following terms:

My days are counted, and my life will soon be closed. O my parents! *How badly have I returned the favor of your love to me! I shall never attain a name that may reflect its luster upon you.*

After saying this Hong Xiuquan closed his eyes and was in coma.

So far, both the vision and the interpretation show no sign of Christianity. His resignation at his coming death prompts his "final words"—shame for having let his parents down. "I shall never attain a name that may reflect its luster..." As the Chinese expression goes, "a man needs face like a tree needs bark."[15]

Those, standing next to his bed, thought he was going to die, but as soon as Hong Xiuquan closed his eyes he saw a dragon, a tiger, and a cock entering his room. Soon after he observed *a great number of people playing musical instruments. They approached with a beautiful sedan chair inviting him to be seated.* Once he was seated on the sedan chair they carried him away. *He was astonished at the honor and distinction bestowed upon him. He did not know what to do.* They soon arrived at a beautiful and luminous place, where on both sides were assembled *a multitude of fine men and women who saluted him with expressions of great joy.* As he left the sedan chair, an old woman took him down to the river and said, "Thou dirty man, why hast kept company with yonder people, and defiled thyself? I must now wash thee clean."

The dragon, tiger, and cock are all Chinese symbols of power and dominion. The enormous—bewildering—honors shown to him replace in this alternative reality the shame and humiliation he felt in the real world.[16] The beautiful sedan chair replaces and transforms the sedan chair he took home, paralyzed by the examination failure. The cleansing specifically removes him from the world of corruption and defilement—the shame—of the "real" world.

After the washing ceremony, Hong Xiuquan, in company with a great number of old virtuous and venerable men, among whom he remarked many of the ancient sages, entered a large building where they opened his body with a knife, took out his heart and other parts, and put in their place others new and of a red color. Instantly when this was done, the wound closed, and he could see no trace of the incision which had been made. Upon the walls surrounding this place, Hong Xiuquan remarked a number of tablets with inscriptions exhorting to virtue, which he one by one examined. Afterwards they entered another large hall the beauty and splendor of which were beyond description.

---

[15] 人要臉，樹要皮 (ren yaolian, shu yao pi). See below, n. 55.

[16] For an interesting case of such a situation, in which the subject, a Christian monk who had been humiliated unbearably, created an alternative reality on parchment in which he triumphed gloriously, see R. Landes, *Relics, Apocalypse, and the Deceits of History* (Cambridge, Mass.: Harvard University Press, 1995), part III.

A man, venerable in age, with golden beard and dressed in a black robe, was sitting in an imposing attitude upon the highest place. *As soon as he saw Hong Xiuquan, the old man began to shed tears, and said,*

"All human beings in the whole world are produced and sustained by me; they eat my food and wear my clothing, but not a single one among them has a heart to remember and venerate me; the worse is that they take my gifts and they worship demons; they purposely rebel against me, and arouse my anger. Do thou not imitate them."

This surgery, conducted by "ancient sages," makes him a new man, inside as well as out. It has parallels in shamanistic cultures the world over.[17] Hong is prepared for his meeting with the chief figure who appears to have the features—like everyone in this vision—of Chinese court figures. On one level, a father figure, on another, the all-powerful emperor, this bearded man's emotive response to the visionary again restores the "order" that the "real world" had so grievously violated: Xiuquan was specially chosen. The words of this figure represent the first, possibly retrospective, hint of monotheistic beliefs: this imperial figure produced and sustains "all human beings in the whole world." Here Hong's anger with the world appears in the mouth of a cosmic father figure, who at once condemns them for rebelling against him and warns Hong not to follow them—that is, not to pursue his efforts to join the Mandarinate.

After saying this the old man gave Hong Xiuquan a sword, *commanding him to exterminate the demons, but to spare his brothers and sisters.* He also gave Hong Xiuquan a seal and said it was for him to overcome the evil spirits. After that he gave Hong a yellow fruit to eat and Hong said it was very sweet. After having received the sword and the seal from the old man Hong Xiuquan began to exhort to those people waiting in the hall and to perform the duties for old man. Some replied to his exhortations,

"We have indeed forgotten our duties towards the venerable."

Others said,

"Why should we venerate him? Let us only be merry, and drink together with our friends."

Hong Xiuquan continued his admonitions with tears. The old man said to him,

"Take courage and do the work; I will assist you in every difficulty."

Shortly after this the old man told the people in the hall that,

"Hong Xiuquan is competent to this charge."

The imagery remains profoundly Chinese. The sword to exterminate demons and the seal to overcome evil spirits are both classic Taoist images.[18] Hong Xiuquan

---

[17] For example, Philippine shamans, debunked by Philip Singer, "'Psychic Surgery': Close Observation of a Popular Healing Practice," *Medical Anthropology Quarterly*, n.s., 4 (1990): 443–51, online: http://www.jstor.org/pss/649226, April 13, 2010.

[18] "The seal and the sword are important exorcist objects of the Taoist priest. Exorcism normally plays no role in underworld iconography, except when Taoist priests visit the underworld 'to destroy the fortress of hell' and enable deceased souls to gain safe passage through the underworld toward a better incarna-

leaps into his newly assigned role—in *this* world he *is* worthy—only to meet with the resistance of the self-indulgent courtiers. He alone, on heaven and earth, has the courage and drive to purify the world.

He then led Hong Xiuquan out and told him to look down and said,

> Behold the people upon this earth!
> *Hundredfold is the perverseness of their hearts.*

Hong Xiuquan looked down and saw such a degree of depravity and vice that he was flabbergasted.

This view of the mass of humankind will be a key element in all of Hong's career (indeed of any messiah's or eschatological thinker's). The degree to which the apocalyptic enthusiast believes his or her fellow humans to be corrupt—still worse, irredeemably corrupt[19]—correlates directly to the intensity of the cataclysm that must precede the earthly redemption. The angrier and more unforgiving the messiah, the more destruction necessary to purify the world of sin; and the more divine assistance fails, the more he will feel fully justified in raining down vengeance on the world. In subsequent visions, this issue will become still more pronounced.

> He then woke up in trance and he felt the very hairs of his head raise themselves. Suddenly, *seized by a violent anger* and forgetting his feeble state he put on his clothes and left his bedroom. When he saw his father he bowed to him and said,
>
> "The venerable old man above has commanded *that all men shall turn to me and all treasures shall flow to me.*"
>
> When his father saw him speaking in this manner, he did not know what to think, but [was filled] with joy and fear.

Reentry to the world of failure after such compensatory visionary experiences is always difficult. Hong's report to his father expresses none of the salvific dimension of his experience, only the personal vindication. He was now a full-fledged megalomaniac, as suits any angry messianic pretender. The father's mixed response (as reported years later after Xiuquan had come out of the experience successfully), suggests that he was more terrified than overjoyed, a painful reminder to his son

---

tion. In Hakka culture in Guangdong province (Hong's culture of origin), it was the custom for adults to be initiated in a Taoist exorcist tradition. This custom lasted into the twentieth century," Barend J. terHaar, "God's Chinese Son: The Taiping Heavenly Kingdom of Hong Xiuquan [Book Review]," *Journal of Social History* 30, no. 4 (Summer 1997): 1007–08; see terHaar, "China's Inner Demons: The Political Impact of the Demonological Paradigm," *China Information* 11, no. 2/3 (1996–97): 54–88; Rudolf Wagner, *Reenacting the Heavenly Vision: The Role of Religion in the Taiping Rebellion* (Berkeley: Institute of East Asian Studies and Center for Chinese Studies, University of California–Berkeley, 1982).

[19] Augustine had a similar view of what he called the *massa damnata*, that vast majority of humankind condemned justly by original sin to eternal damnation, see Gerald Bonner, *Freedom and Necessity: St. Augustine's Teaching on Divine Power and Human Freedom* (Washington, D.C.: Catholic University of America Press, 2007).

that whatever the joys of his visions, in the real world he has no "face"; he is still a failure even to his father. He returns to the world where he can breathe.

> The sickness and visions of Hong Xiuquan continued about forty days. In these visions he often met a middle-age man whom he called elder brother who instructed him how to act. This elder brother of his went with him wandering to the uttermost regions in search of evil spirits. *Together they slew and exterminated the evil spirits.* Hong Xiuquan also heard the venerable old man with the black robe *reprove Confucius* for having omitted in his books to expound clearly the true doctrine. *Confucius seemed much ashamed, and confessed his guilt.*

Later, Xiuquan will identify this elder brother as Jesus. For the time being, there is no hint of that. This incident, which recurs several times and eventually leads to Confucius' beating, represents the ideal reversal: he who failed to pass the Confucian exams receives favor from the cosmic figure who orders Confucius' punishment. He gets to see the man who inspired those who failed him, repeatedly admonished, ashamed, beaten. Not Hong, but Confucius "eats the cane."

> Hong Xiuquan, during his sickness, often, as his mind was wandering, used to run about his room, leaping and fighting like a soldier engaged in battle. His constant cry was,
>
> > Tianzhu, tianzhu, tianzhu, tianzhu; [Jesuit term for "master of heaven" (God)]
> > Slay the demons! Slay the demons! Slay, slay:
> > There is one and there is another;
> > Many, many cannot withstand one single blow of my sword.
>
> His father felt very anxious about the state of his mind and attributed the calamity of his family to the fault of the geomancer who selected an unlucky spot of ground for the burial of their forefathers. He engaged conjurers to drive away evil spirits; but Hong Xiuquan said,
>
> > How could these imps dare to oppose me?
> > I must slay them, I must slay them!
> > Many, many cannot resist me.
>
> In his imagination he pursued the demons who seemed to undergo many changes and transformations: one time flying as birds, and another time appearing as lions. In case he was not able to overcome them he held out his seal against them... at the sight of which they immediately fled away. *He imagined himself pursuing them to the most remote places under heaven. Wherever he made war with them he destroyed them. Whenever he succeeded he laughed joyfully and said, "They can't withstand me."* He was constantly singing one passage of an old song, "The virtuous swain he travels over rivers and seas; he saves many friends and he kills enemies. During his exhortations he often *burst into tears*, saying, "You have no hearts to venerate the old father, but you are on good terms with the impish fiends; indeed, indeed, *you have no hearts, no conscience more.*"

The split here between his psychological elation and reality are nearly complete: he has retreated into a state of fantasy omnipotence. His father, understandably concerned, assumes that the invisible forces of the world have been violated and seeks to repair the breach, redoubling his son's fury. Here we find the visionary, totally identified with his salvific "father," reproaching those in the "real world" for their lack of heart, of conscience. Good and Evil have now been realigned in dangerous ways, and his apologetic shame before his family—O my parents! How badly have I returned the favor of your love to me!—has become reproach.

> Hong Xiuquan's two brothers constantly kept his bedroom door shut and watched him because they did not want him to run out of the house. After Hong Xiuquan had tired himself by fighting, jumping about, singing, and exhorting, he lay down upon his bed and went to sleep. While he was asleep people would come and look at him. The news about his condition was spread far and wide. *Soon the whole district knew that he was a madman.*

Even as his fantasy world advances, his position in the "real world" retreats. He has now passed from "failure" to "madman" in the eyes of his community. He is "beyond shame."

> Hong Xiuquan often said that *he was an appointed emperor of China.* He was *highly gratified when someone called him the emperor of China.* However, if any one called him mad, Hong Xiuquan would laugh at him and said, *"You are indeed mad yourself, and do you call me mad?"*

He has, by now, passed from utter humiliation, to megalomania, to some kind of genuine grounding in his new experience. He wants to be called—he believes he is—the emperor of China, but he is sufficiently aware of "the real world" to expect others not to accept his claims. His laughter—someone purely in the world of honor and shame would grow angry—suggests so great a level of confidence in his visions as revelations of his destiny that he can afford to ignore the "slings and arrows." Indeed, he seems to have been filled with a sense of cosmic omnipotence, all expressed within a Chinese idiom.

> When undesirable persons came to see him, he rebuked them and called them demons. All day long he sang, wept and exhorted. During his sickness he composed the following piece of poetry:
>
> > *My hand now holds both in heaven and earth,*
> > *the power to punish and kill.*
> > *To slay the depraved, and spare the upright;*
> > *to relieve the people's distress.*
> > My eyes survey from the North to the South
> > beyond the rivers and mountains;
> > My voice is heard from the East to the West
> > to the tracts of the sun and the moon.
> > The Dragon expands his claws,
> > as if the road in the clouds were too narrow;
> > And when he ascends,

> why should he fear the bent of the milky way?
> Then tempest and thunder as music attend,
> and the foaming waves are excited.
> The flying Dragon the Yik-king describes,
> dwells surely in Heaven above.

One early morning when Hong Xiuquan was about to leave his bed, he heard the birds of the spring singing in the trees which surrounded the village. Instantly he recited the following ode:

> The Birds in their flight all turn to the light,
> In this *resembling me*;
> For *I'm now a King, and every thing*
> *At will to do I'm free.*
> As the sun to the sight, *my body shines bright*
> Calamities are gone;
> *The high Dragon and the Tiger rampant*
> *Are helping me each one.*

This poem suggests that as he returns to his embodied persona, he returns with an inner sense of certainty and even serenity. Without this, he never could have succeeded in gathering a following.

Hong Xiuquan's relatives engaged several physicians to cure his disease. They gave him medicines to take, but [this] was of no avail. One day his father noticed a slip of paper put into a crack of the doorpost, upon which were written the following characters in red:

> The noble principles of the Heavenly King,
> The Sovereign King Quan.

His father took the paper and showed it to the other members of the family, but they could not understand the meaning of these seven characters.

If the meaning is as clear in translation as in the original, than the family's incomprehension comes from the fact that the meaning so violates the possibilities of the "real world" that they could not allow themselves to acknowledge their son's claims. But, as the dynamics of millennialism will illustrate, apocalyptic time makes all things possible.

From that time onwards Hong Xiuquan gradually regained his health. Many of his friends and relatives came and visited him. They wanted to know and to hear from his own mouth what he had experienced during his disease. Hong Xiuquan related to them, without reservation, all that he could remember of his extraordinary visions. All his friends and relatives could say was that it was very strange indeed.

He reenters the social world as something of a new kind of prodigy, his tales at least worth the hearing. Like all messiahs, his needs for attention and admiration are strong, and apparently, if only in this opening period of his new career, he manages to satisfy them, if only minimally.

At this point, according to sources, including above all his cousin Ren'gan, Hong's personality changed: from a fairly spontaneous and lively youth, he now became far more sober, poised and stately in his bearing, impressing some with the inner conviction with which he comported himself. And yet, he did not pursue the destiny offered him in his visions. For the next six years, he continued to teach, and some might have even thought that he had come to terms with his diminished, but still prestigious, social standing as a Confucian tutor. And at this point, the imagery in these retrospective accounts of his visions is still almost entirely Chinese: "It has, above all, nothing to do with Christianity or any knowledge of Christian teachings."[20]

Fourth Examination Failure: Exegetical Arousal (1843)

Six years later, Hong Xiuquan attempted a final time to take the exam, and failed again. Such a move was exceptionally dangerous, particularly in that it risked the (inevitably) fragile persona he had reconstructed in the aftermath of his visions—his dignified self-possession. Why he chose to do so, we cannot know—Was he challenged? Did he grow weary of his low station? Did he have a sense that this time he could not fail? Certainly the willingness to do this suggests that he had yet to break with the Mandarinate no matter how much he had delighted to see how "the father" rebuked Confucius.

And again he failed. And again he returned home in disgrace.

It was only then that his cousin Li Jingfang borrowed the religious tract by Liang A-Fa from him and told him how important it was that he reread it in 1843. This time, not only did the text have meaning, but it also unlocked the key to his wondrous vision of seven years earlier. The "old father" of his vision was, in fact, the God of the Bible, and his "elder brother" was Jesus.[21]

At that point, the tract, and particularly the extensive passages from the prophet Isaiah, seemed to describe the agony of China in this period of unprecedented crisis, with European imperialists imposing their will on a weak government, winning the Opium Wars, and flooding China with narcotics. The tract was truly a warning to "this age."[22] In it, Hong found out that long ago Jesus—his older brother—had come to earth to bring the "Great Peace."

---

[20] "Offensichtlich erwuchsen die Gesichte Hungs auf konfuzianischen, taoistichen und buddhistischen Vorstellungen; se hatten mit dem Christentum und einer Kenntnis der christlichen Lehre überhaupt nichts zu tun." Georg Franz-Willing, "Die Ideologie der Taiping," *Zeitschrift für Religions- und Geistesgeschichte* 24, no.4 (1972): 321. He cites Shih, *Taiping Ideology*, 277; see also Eugene Boardman, "Christian Influence upon the Ideology of the Taiping Rebellion," *Far Eastern Quarterly* 10, no. 2 (1951): 115–24. online: http://www.jstor.org/stable/2049091, April 13, 2010.

[21] The source for this is a Taiping publication, the *Taiping Heavenly Sun*, in Cheng, *Chinese Sources*, 7–12.

[22] For a discussion of the way in which the tract and Isaiah's words seemed uncannily to describe the current situation, see Spence, *God's Chinese Son*, 51–65. The situation here is less dire than that of the Xhosa and the Native Americans who were faced with cultural extinction, but in the case of imperial China, we are dealing with a long cultural tradition that assumed dominion of surrounding cultures. The perception of decline, therefore, may have been significantly greater and more painful than the "objective" situation.

The importance of this pamphlet, addressed to his entire generation, could not be understated. It confirmed Hong Xiuquan's sense of importance by linking him with people on the other side of the world. Nor was he alone in finding this missionary material inspiring. Hong's mission only had power because large numbers—millions—of this generation of Chinese were prepared to believe that they constituted "the chosen generation"—subject to unbearable suffering, destined to redemption.

From another angle, one can also argue that millennialism here serves as the means whereby Christianity finds a Chinese idiom. In concrete terms, the vision is so fundamentally Chinese in content, with its emphasis on family, its imperial tone, its imagery, that historians of the Taiping ideology identify all its sources in Confucian, Daoist, and Buddhist conceptions. And yet this moment marks the beginning of a vast shift in Hong and in southern China's thinking about Christianity. The fusion of Hong's Chinese vision and millennial Christianity proved far more powerful than either force on its own. In particular, Hong's Christian millennialism would gain far more converts to the Christian "word," Christian texts, and Christian demotic principles, than any other missionary effort before or after. Notes Rob Weller, "In a country where intensive missionary activity throughout the nineteenth century had only a tiny effect, and in a region of Guangxi so cut off it would not see its first missionaries for several decades, Taiping Christianity was new and radically different."[23] Like the charismatic (false) prophets of early medieval Europe ("False" Christ of Bourges, "Pseudoprophetess" Thiota, Adalbert the "eccentric"), the indigenous population showed far more enthusiasm for the millennial variant of Christianity than the ecclesiastical one.[24]

But, just as Peter Brown pointed out that the conversion of Rome to Christianity was also a conversion of Christianity to imperialism,[25] so, via Hong, the spread of Christianity to large numbers of Chinese involved a transformation of European Christian monotheism into a Chinese idiom, with a heavenly family. The very term "Taiping" was part of a Chinese "millennial" tradition.[26]

Hong's movement gained from this syncretism one of its great strengths, but also an enduring and ultimately fatal conflict with Western Christians.[27] On the one hand, this revolutionary movement made the first concerted effort to transform China according to Western principles—open to Western technology and to its demotic deployment (e.g., printing). On the other, Hong's commitment to

[23] Weller, *Resistance, Chaos and Control*, 34.

[24] See the examples of the "False Christ of Bourges," Thiota and Aldabert, discussed above, Part I, chapters 1–3.

[25] Peter Brown, *The World of Late Antiquity* (New York: Harcourt Brace Jovanovich, 1971), 82–94.

[26] See Hunt, "Revolutionary Dimension of Millenarianism," 123–27.

[27] See also the exchanges between Yang Xiuquan, The East King, and Captain Mellersh on what God wears, what his appearance is, and who his children are, Spence, *God's Chinese Son*, 230–31.

Christianity—he, like all true believers, thought his brand was the "true one"—left him open to accusations of heresy from more traditional Christians. And his megalomania encouraged just such a judgment. Indeed, the missionary Issachar Roberts refused to baptize him in 1845, precisely because he felt that the young man had not grasped some of the key elements of the religion he wished to join.[28] Nonetheless, despite what we might call Confucian elements, Confucius himself and all his teachings received radical censure: the dream liberated Hong from the thrall of a tradition that had rejected him.

Incubation (later 1840s)

All things great start small. Initially, the movement consisted of Xiuquan and his cousin "Yunshan": Feng Yunshan. They baptized each other. Eventually it involved the rest of the Hongs—immediate family and some clan. Over the years, the movement made headway, mostly in the Thistle Mountains, the back hills of the Penghua Mountains, the region around Sigu village, and the area to the south of the Xiang township.[29] Its relatively modest success derived from its demotic emphasis: dignity of manual labor, brotherhood of all discipline, equality.[30] The movement rejected the vices plaguing Chinese society at the time—gambling, opium, magic, banditry.[31] Despite his megalomanic tendencies, Hong Xiuquan was a forthright man who spoke with all regardless of their outward importance and readily accepted criticism from his fellow believers.[32]

At the core lay Hong's understanding of the Ten Commandments whose text, by 1847 at the latest, he possessed. Its prominence in the religion of the Taiping became so distinctive that Western observers commented that it "was known among the common people as the 'Ten Commandments religion.'"[33] Most notably,

---

[28] See the deliberations of Issachar Roberts, the only Western Christian to give Hong Xiuquan instruction: Yuan Chung Teng, "Reverend Issachar Jacob Roberts and the Taiping Rebellion," *Journal of Asian Studies* 23, no. 1 (1963): 55–67, online: http://www.jstor.org/pss/2050633, April 13, 2010. See also J.S. Gregory, "British Missionary Reaction to the Taiping Movement in China," *Journal of Religious History* 2, no. 3 (2007): 204–18. For a full discussion, see S.Y. Teng, *The Taiping Rebellion and the Western Powers* (Oxford: Clarendon Press, 1971), part III.

[29] Spence, *God's Chinese Son*, 110–11.

[30] See the parallels with early Protestantism discussed in Reilly, *Taiping Heavenly Kingdom*, 130–35.

[31] Weller, *Resistance, Chaos, and Control*, 60–64.

[32] Spence, *God's Chinese Son*, 118.

[33] Reilly, *Taiping Heavenly Kingdom*, 97. Reilly argues that Hong did not get this emphasis from Liang A-Fa's tract, which rarely cites the "Old Testament," but from his brief study with Issachar Roberts, and that (like many non-Western cultures) the Taiping's Christianity was "more of an Old Testament religion than a New Testament one" (98). Note that, according to Lindley, the Taiping celebrated the Sabbath on Saturday (*Ti Ping Tien Kwoh*, 315). For a contemporary example of this tribal attraction to the Ten Commandments, see the Movement for the Restoration of the Ten Commandments of God in Uganda (above, chapter 2, nn. 24 and 65).

Hong's comments on the sixth commandment—"thou shalt not kill"—express a remarkable benevolence and nonviolence, so apparently odds with subsequent developments.

> The Sixth Heavenly Commandment: *Thou shalt not kill or injure.* He who kills another kills himself, and he who injures another injures himself. Whosoever kills and injures another breaks the Heavenly Command. A poem reads: 'The world is one family and all men are brothers....Let us all be at peace, enjoy the *Taiping*.'[34]

The strong inner discipline of the group—we might compare them with some of the lay apostolic movements of the Middle Ages, or the *Salaf as-Saaleh* (early companions) of Islam—provided solidarity, identity, purpose. It also permitted them to appear to the outside world as upstanding citizens,and to escape the hostility of the police force, which had its hands full of robber gangs, including the Triads, who dominated much of the rural terrain in the south (and created problems for Xiuquan's followers as well).

This period of the movement deserves close attention since it represents the earliest core from which the larger movement arose, and to some extent, its profile at this moment shows little of the future explosiveness which would mark the first case of total war and mega-death in modern times. Among the most important aspects of this period, we need to understand how a group that seemed to have so low and industrious a profile, with such strong egalitarian and peaceful commitments, could turn into one of the most murderous, imperialistic ventures in human history.

Rob Weller offers a particularly interesting analysis of this process by focusing on the role of spirit possession in the nascent movement. Spirit-possession cults were a distinctly Chinese form of religiosity, a kind of semiotic arousal that often spilled over into enthusiastic incoherence.[35] Drawing on anthropological studies (including his own extensive work) on the role of spirit possession in China, he notes a proliferation of possessions within the movement in the late 1840s, which permitted a significant number of independent and new voices to emerge within the movement. This demotic surge of divine inspiration—"Would that all God's children were prophets!" (Numbers 11:29)—gave an enormous boost to bottom-up elements within the movement. Hong's benign neglect, a combination of tolerance and absence, allowed the phenomenon to gain great traction within the group. In addition to "speaking in tongues," some of the charismatics proved capable of curing illness; in the case of someone like Yang Xiuqing, a farm laborer and charcoal

---

[34] "The Book of Heavenly Commandments," issued in Year 2 (1852); see Franz Michael, *The Taiping Rebellion: History and Documents,* 3 vols. (Seattle: University of Washington Press, 1966–71), 2:121. Note that Hong is working with a Christian translation. The Hebrew reads "Thou shalt not murder"— with no mention of "or injure".

[35] Weller, *Resistance, Chaos and Control,* 69–85; on the role of the "spirit" in charismatic movements, see the case of Montanus, who "talked in tongues" and added a third "testament" to the biblical corpus, as did the Taiping: see Trevett, *Montanism.*

burner become incarnation of the Holy Spirit, his healing talents surpassed even those of Hong.[36]

This "surprising" reorientation toward traditional (even local) Chinese spirit-possession cults, which had no part in Hong's initial ideology, redefined the movement. The principal "possessed" were local (non-Hakka) commoners with little education, "men very different from the hopeful scholars like Hong, Feng and the other original converts."[37] Their rise within the movement intensified group dynamics, drawing much larger numbers and more agitated followers.

"Possession cults that do develop into social movements usually collapse in fairly short order; long-lived movements like the Taiping rebellion arise only rarely."[38] Most movements with such anarchic tendencies tend to either remain at fairly low levels of activity, to self-destruct, or to arouse the hostility of the authorities and get suppressed.[39] By 1849, as Weller puts it, the movement was "saturated" with voices and interpretations.[40] And it had, with its iconoclastic campaigns, aroused considerable hostility from both Qing officials and local magistrates.

Over the course 1849, the movement once again shifted focus. Hong Xiuquan retook the reins and redirected the energies of the faithful into a full-fledged—and successful—military revolt. He began by restricting legitimate prophetic speech to two leaders who spoke respectively for the Holy Spirit (Yang Xiuqing) and Jesus (Xiao Chaogui). And at the same time, Hong began to retaliate more boldly against the harassment of Qing and local authorities. It is at this point that the language of the demonization, "imps" or "demon officials," becomes the common designation for the enemy, and they deserve nothing short of extermination. They fell outside the embrace of those human brethren whom it would be a sin to kill.

Not coincidentally, the two major "possessed" voices that he still permitted had the singular virtue of supporting the idea of launching a military movement, the *Taiping-Tien*: the Heavenly Kingdom of Peace and Prosperity.[41] As Hong put it in

---

[36] Weller, *Resistance, Chaos and Control*, 64–68.

[37] Ibid., 94–95.

[38] Ibid., 88.

[39] Weller cites the Watchtower movement in Rhodesia/Zimbabwe and the Shakers in North America, ibid., 88–93.

[40] There is obviously a problem here in causal argumentation. We know the situation had reached saturation point because it precipitated a drastic shift away from this semiotic anarchy toward a hierarchy. But we know that other movements (Weller discusses a number of such millennial movements that do not become violent) do not make the shift, or made it "prematurely" as it were. So we should consider timing in these matters. It is possible that by tolerating the cacophony of visionary voices as long as they did, Hong and his inner core of disciples made the eventual shift to unifying violence all the sharper and more powerful. Weller remarks that the numbers increased from a few thousand to over ten thousand in the visionary period (1847–50); Weller, *Resistance, Chaos and Control*, 50.

[41] Perhaps the most militant figure was Yang Xiuqing, the future "East King," and de facto ruler of Nanjing. Shih considers Yang's "most prominent contribution to the Taiping ideology ... the subordination of everything else to the military, and eventually to the political success of the Taiping army" (*Taiping Ideology*, 109).

1850: "Too much patience and humility do not suit our present times, for therewith it would be impossible to manage this perverted generation."[42] When he first viewed humankind through the lens of a bountiful single God-creator back in 1837, he had felt rage at people's ingratitude and urged God to wipe them all out. Now, he had the means to slay the "demon officials." He had an insurrectionary, anti-Manchu army.

This millennial notion of establishing God's kingdom on earth through the agency of his younger son, of conquering the land and ruling it for God in the place of the blasphemous Qing (Mongols, not Chinese!), now became the central focus of the movement. In quick order, visionary revelations led to solemn declarations and proclamations, military and civil legislation, a new calendar which began with year 1 in 1851...all under the new banners reading *Taiping* that rallied the troops.[43] This millennial vision that borrowed from both Buddhist White Lotus and Christian millennialism galvanized the movement and solved all its problems: in mobilizing against the authorities and channeling the energies released by the possession cults, Hong could turn his faithful into fanatic soldiers prepared for the battle to come, willing to suffer the worst discomforts in order to bring on the millennial *Taiping*.

The turn to violence here seems over-determined by a combination of social dislocation and apocalyptic ideology. Certainly, the "times" confirmed the imminence of collapse of Chinese culture under the assault of the modern West, both commercial (Opium Wars), and religious (Protestant preaching).[44] Ancient Taoist and Mohist doctrines explained this as one of many great cyclical catastrophes as part of the cosmic order that had regularly, in past centuries, produced messianic figures who, at such times, called for rebellion.[45] Hong certainly had a receptive audience, in particular among some of the most marginal members of society, starting with his own ethnic group the Hakka, and including miners, charcoal-makers, peasants dislocated by sudden impoverishment, unemployed dockworkers and transporters. And Hong's peculiar brand of messianic Christianity had little difficulty accommodating native scenarios, which mapped nicely onto his revolutionary millennialism.[46] In such conditions, Hong's original vision seems to have inspired (or justified) among believers a profound contempt for the lives of anyone deemed the apocalyptic "other"—all demon enemies of the "Great Peace."

The language of demonization—present from the first (memories of the) 1836 vision—strengthened such attitudes. God had told Hong back in 1836 that he must

[42] Hamberg, *Visions*, 43, cited by Spence, *God's Chinese Son*, 115.

[43] For the documents produced as a result of the change, see Michael, *History and Documents*, vol. 2, part 2; on this period, Spence, *God's Chinese Son*, 110–25; Jen Yu-Wen, *Taiping Revolutionary Movement*, 52–70; Weller, *Resistance, Chaos and Control*, 86–110.

[44] Hunt, "Revolutionary Millenarianism," 118–23.

[45] Both Hunt (ibid., 120), and C. K. Yang (*Religion in Chinese Society* [Cambridge: Cambridge University Press, 1961], 227) place Hong's wide appeal in this context.

[46] In his commentary on the book of Revelation 21, Hong identified the "New Jerusalem" as the Taiping "Heavenly Capital" (Cheng, *Chinese Sources*, 91). For an extensive analysis of the various strains of millennialism in Hong's Taiping ideology, see Reilly, *Taiping Heavenly Kingdom*, 104–16.

wait a while longer, thus putting a brief brake on a war that would, the apocalyptic moment arrived, explode onto the scene. Hong's sense of mission involved not a passive apocalyptic scenario, not the quiet transformation of some few (thousands of) lives in anticipation of God's intervention in history (e.g., the Shakers). On the contrary, it was an active cataclysmic scenario, the violent destruction of the unjust government that ruled this world, the Qing dynasty, and then the inauguration of the millennial peace, the *Taiping*. The iconoclasm of the early movement, along with their discourse on demons, suggest that they were, from the earliest times, ready for a war with the enemies of the true religion, and only awaited the right moment to show their hand. In our terms, from an early point onward, this movement's apocalyptic scenario was active cataclysmic aiming at a demotic (egalitarian) millennium; and Hong Xiuquan was God's instrument, messiah, chosen to bring about the necessary cataclysm. Now, in 1850, the time had come.

Does this mean that the movement was inherently violent? Or could it have been what Catherine Wessinger calls a fragile or aggressed millennial group, whose violence and paranoia arise as a result of some combination of inner flaw—a failed prophecy, an anarchic visionary leadership—and an attack from outside authorities.[47] Certainly, local authorities began to attack and arrest the followers of Hong Xiuquan, although it seems clear they were responding to an increasingly aggressive iconoclasm and anti-Confucianism that Hong began to preach. That led to open clashes with local authorities, both religious and civic.[48] But for the authorities (local and imperial) not to oppose them might well have encouraged further defiance. Every time Hong and his disciples smashed idols without suffering retaliation, they struck one more blow at the strength of the existing order. Often enough, in the history of such movements, a distinct dance of defiance and response between the believers and the authorities spirals out of control. Apocalyptic time demands constant change; the belief rides the believer like a rider his horse.

■ THE ADVENT OF APOCALYPTIC TIME AND POWER

This is not the place to go over the extraordinary career of the *Taiping* armies, starting with the first battles in Jintian 1850 and culminating with the seizure of Nanjing in 1853.[49] Some of the elements of their success, however, come clearly from the demotic elements of their religiosity, which prepared them to make the transition from a relatively stable agrarian lifestyle to that of an army. Their discipline, the initiative and creativity of their generals, the rapid deployment of earth-

---

[47] Catherine Wessinger, *Millennialism, Persecution, and Violence: Historical Cases* (Syracuse: Syracuse University Press, 2000), 3–39. See also, Daniel L. Overmyer, *Folk Buddhist Religion: Dissenting Sects in Late Traditional China* (Cambridge, Mass.: Harvard University Press, 1976).

[48] On the period from 1847–49, see Spence, *God's Chinese Son*, 96–109. On rewriting the visions to increase the anti-Confucian passages, see 98. On the first public act of iconoclastic vandalism, see 100.

[49] For a description, see Spence, *God's Chinese Son*, chap. 12.

works that call for sustained manual labor, and their fanatic dedication suggest the kind of highly motivated behavior that, from the time of the ancient Israelites and Greeks, has allowed the few to defeat the (initially incompetent) many.

In particular the strict separation of men and women reflected the nature of apocalyptic time—until the millennial *Taiping*, for virtue's sake, they had to remain apart. This policy led to remarkable efforts to break up couples and families, and immensely increased the "inorganic" nature of this voluntary community. The result, not surprisingly, intensified the single-minded zeal of the warriors for God's millennium. As they swept through rural regions, giving the local peasantry the choice of death or membership in the salvific army, they managed to incorporate huge numbers of recruits—according to some counts, as many as two million by the time they reached Nanjing.

But what was sauce for the geese—the masses—at Nanjing, was not at all sauce for the gander—the leadership. If Lord Acton's dictum about power and corruption has validity, then the remarkable absolutism of millennial beliefs make millennial power the pinnacle of absolute corruption. What more unquestionable authority than that of the younger brother of Jesus, the son of the unique God? The period of power at Nanjing provides us with one of the most startling examples of the paradoxes of demotic millennialism come to power on the wings of revolutionary violence. Although its millennial ideal continues to promise a world of peace, equality, and plenty, the behavior of the leadership grows increasingly authoritarian.

Shortly after his arrival at Nanjing, Hong Xiuquan enacted two radically incompatible sets of policies. On the one hand, he pursued a land-reform program that represents the most radically egalitarian in recorded history—all property evenly distributed among all followers, men and women alike. On the other hand, he declared himself the emperor of the Taiping, and far from behaving in the "progressive" (anti-imperial, anti-Confucian) fashion with which he announced his millennial orientation, Hong began to behave like a restorationist Chinese emperor ruling from the last Chinese imperial capital, that of the Ming dynasty at Nanjing.

The shift to apocalyptic emperor, which represents the culmination of imperial millennialism, occurred rapidly and apparently without much opposition.[50] The first use of such language came with the preparations for war, and the only opposition—at least in its surviving form—concerned when imperial titles were appropriate (not yet), rather than whether the Taiping would be an imperial or demotic regime. Hong had a court that became increasingly isolated from the world outside itself (much like Akhenaten's), with a harem, a vast proliferation of rules and regulations surrounding court etiquette, and a very strong hierarchical

---

[50] Of course, the opposition to such a move is generally among the most rapidly suppressed narratives, appearing only in the tales, largely demonizing, of internal groups of dissidents who betray the revolution (mostly to outside forces). For an example of such a narrative, see Gregory of Tours' account of the "Vase of Soissons," *History of the Franks*, 2.27, 139–40. Mao underwent the same transformation, on which see Jonathan Spence, *Mao Zedong* (New York: Penguin, 2006), 100–01.

emphasis of lines of authority and deference.[51] The closer one got to the leader of this movement, the farther one retreated from demotic values. As Rob Weller notes, this represents a classic Chinese religious and political trope of the "receding center."[52]

In addition to his own court, he permitted three other ones, each with their own kings. In this world of domineering alpha males we find all the themes of hierarchical culture proliferating. The ego-conflicts between them were driven by the classic concerns of honor and shame in the establishment of who was superior to whom.[53] And these pervasive conflicts led to the deep and ultimately murderous hostilities that tore the movement apart. When the West King Xiao Chaogui (Jesus' incarnation) cited the proverb about man's face and a tree's bark to describe the attitude of his rival, the East King Yang Xiuqing (the Holy Spirit's incarnation), he acknowledged indirectly that any demotic expectation that people in power can put aside their own cravings for honor long enough to assure the well-being of the people they serve goes against human nature.[54]

And yet, to whatever extent the court life in Nanjing had hierarchized (Sinified, Confucianized), the Taiping's social legislation suggests that they wanted to have the best of both worlds. Produced by the city's printing presses and made available publicly, this legislation represents the most egalitarian land distribution on record in world history to that time, and the first time that any Chinese ruler had ever taken so public and authoritative commitment to the egalitarian and free nature of his "subjects."[55] And so it seemed to sympathetic outsiders. Indeed, the disappointed but still-hopeful Karl Marx wrote enthusiastically about the movement for the *International Herald Tribune* in 1853, hailing the Taiping as the spark that would set off the international workers' revolution.[56]

■ THE TENSION BETWEEN IMPERIAL AND DEMOTIC IN A PERIOD OF APOCALYPTIC POWER

The Taiping offers a wide range of examples of the immense tension that builds up within a movement between its demotic roots and its imperial tendencies once it has power in its hands and, inevitably, its expectations are disappointed.

---

[51] The model for this imperial administration was the Zhou-li," the blueprint for the Zhou dynasty some three millennia earlier.

[52] Rob Weller, "Mountains and Valleys: Multiple Natures and Their Consequences in China," Paper delivered at Boston University, November 9, 2008.

[53] Michael, *History and Documents*, 2: 125–31.

[54] On the proverb, see above, n. 15.

[55] "The Land System of the Heavenly Dynasty" in Michael, *History and Documents*, 2:309–20. See also Spence, *God's Chinese Son*, 173–74; for a discussion of the failure of the Taiping's idealistic system, see Kathryn Bernhardt, "Elite and Peasant during the Taiping Occupation of the Jiangnan, 1860–1864," *Modern China* 13, no. 4 (October 1987): 379–410.

[56] See below, chapter 10, n. 79.

- *Sex and the Millennium:* Among the premillennial, apocalyptic demands that Hong made of his believers was the radical separation of the sexes and the renunciation of sexuality. He did this because under battle conditions, to mix the sexes was to invite the kind of immoral behavior that, by his understanding of the Ten Commandments, must not occur. The costs of such a process strike some of us as unbearable, but in the framework of an apocalyptic war, such sacrifices actually can galvanize rather than depress.[57] Once arrived in Nanjing, however, the "theological" question with immense practical implications arose: has the millennium of *Taiping* begun? If yes, then the separation of men and women should end; if not, then it must continue until complete victory. Hong's choice was classic elitism: for the commoners, the disciplines of apocalyptic imminence; for the elite, especially for him, the delights of millennial immanence. Again, one could make a strong case that the failure of the Taiping to press on to Beijing and finish the job resulted from Hong's falling down the imperial and sexual rabbit hole, rendering him incapable of effective behavior in the world of real politics, whether it be fighting the Qing or keeping his own lieutenants in line.
- *Women and the Taiping Millennium:* In the same way that we find women play a prominent role in the popular millennialism of the Cattle-Slaying, we find them again here. The Taiping banned foot-binding, concubinage, bride-price, the seclusion of women, and their separation from men. Women served in the army, even as commanders, had access to education, sat at the civil service examinations and could hold high office. Outside observers expressed astonishment at seeing women walking the streets of Nanjing, mingling freely with men. It was the "rural 'female barbarians with unbound feet' of the Taiping movement who pulled back the curtains of modern history for Chinese women and allowed them on to the public stage."[58] As with Thiota in 847 and the Great Awakening of the early eighteenth century, apocalyptic time and demotic millennialism allow commoner women to mount the stage of history.
- *Politics and Religion of Honor:* Honor mattered immensely for Taiping elites. One finds this not only in the murderous plottings that resulted in the slaughter of thousands of Taiping by their own fellow believers, but even in the religious thought of Hong Xiuquan. One notes, for example, in his new

---

[57] Joan of Arc demanded that the Dauphin's soldiers renounce the three key elements of a soldier's life—wenches, swearing, and gambling. Rather than create problems, it created a powerful sense of solidarity among them and devotion to her; Régine Pernoud, *The Retrial of Joan of Arc: The Evidence at the Trial for Her Rehabilitation, 1450–1456*, trans. J. M. Cohen (New York: Harcourt, Brace, 1955), 107, 132, 142, 158–59, 163–64.

[58] Fan Hong, *Footbinding, Feminism and Freedom: The Liberation of Women's Bodies in Modern China* (London: F. Cass, 1997), 30, cited by Newsinger, "Taiping Revolutionary," 60; see also Kwame Anthony Appiah, *The Honor Code: How Moral Revolutions Happen* (New York: W.W. Norton, 2010), chap. 2.

translation of the Bible into Chinese, that he eliminates all those passages which might set a bad example, might bring "shame" to the proffered role models: Abraham lying about Sarah, Lot and his daughters, Judah and Tamar.[59] Instead of making available a self-critical demotic text as a challenge to readers expected to be autonomous moral *agents*, Hong wanted a clean version that would serve as a model to impose on moral *subjects*. This attitude may be closely tied up with his lack of confidence in his "rank and file" (and therefore his separation of men and women).

• *Iconic and hierarchical religiosity:* The relationship between images and imperial (iconic) religiosity comes across with particular poignancy in the exchange between the Taiping and some Englishmen to whom they pose some urgent theological questions, many of which betray the importance for Hong's theology that God have a body and be visible. Indeed, some of the questions specifically betray a concern for God's sumptuary habits—what kind of beard and clothing does he wear, a matter of great concern for the honor codes at courts as well.[60] The religion that had banished Confucian icons invented "monotheist" icons, and in the process of Sinifying the God of the Bible, turned him into a patriarchal family man.[61]

• *Executions:* The readiness with which the Taiping executed their own reflects the move away from demotic religiosity and the ensuing ravages of paranoia. The harshness with which discipline generally was enforced, the number of executions for violations of the rules, and the overriding concern with preventing sexual transgressions, all testify to the waxing power of coercive purity and its accompanying paranoia. Hong's cousin and early follower, Hong Ren'gan, rejoined the group in Nanjing and expressed horror at the ease with which Hong ordered executions. Reflecting demotic style that surely dated from the early years of the movement, he suggested that executions "should be left to God's divine judgment, according to the commandment that stipulates *Thou shalt not kill.*" Hong responded: "Our holy Father's sacred edict instructs us to behead the evildoers and sustain those who are upright. Thus killing demons and those who have committed crimes is something that cannot be avoided."[62] As with most coercive purity, the practitioners tended

---

[59] Spence, *God's Chinese Son*, 254–61; for a collection of Hong's annotations to the Bible see Cheng, *Chinese Sources*, 81–91.

[60] Note that Yang's rise to highest power came from a demotic critique of Hong's sumptuous attire (Spence, *God's Chinese Son*, 223–24), testimony to Xiuquan's commitment to honest criticism; but Yang's own subsequent behavior suggests that, as Nietzsche would have us expect, when it came to his own imperial behavior, no forms of abasement for others was too much.

[61] For the extremely revealing and agitated corrections that Hong added to the theological response from Joseph Edkins, see Spence, *God's Chinese Son*, 288–89, and the illustration between 274–75.

[62] Ibid., 274. See also the proliferation of executions among the radical pacifist Anabaptists at Münster, in their brief moment of apocalyptic power, 1533–35, discussed in Middlefort, "Madness and the Millennium at Münster," 115–34.

toward paranoia, best illustrated by the successful deceit of Zhang, a captured Qing spy, who denounced the Taiping's most loyal and competent commanders as secret agents for the Qing. When Yang had them all executed (apparently without a very thorough investigation), he in fact decimated his own best people.[63] As with the French Revolutionary Terror and the totalitarian developments in Soviet Russia and Mao's China, the victory of radical egalitarianism gave birth to the most horrific excesses of the paranoid imperative.[64]

One of the more revealing aspects of this incompatibility between demotic and imperialist tendencies within the movement comes from the comments of an outsider, a Confucian member of the gentry who raised and led the decisive forces against the Taiping. Observing their threatening posture and their demotic values, Zeng Guofan made a macro-historical argument that echoes eerily the *Protocols of the Elders of Zion* in its contrast between the good, hierarchical world of order and the subversive anarchy of egalitarianism.

> Since the days of the T'ang, Yu, and the Three Dynasties, the sages of all ages have been sustaining the traditional culture and emphasizing the order of human relationships. Hence, ruler and officials, father and children, high and low, honored and humble, were as orderly in their respective positions as hat and shoes, which can never be placed upside down. Now, the Yueh [Taiping] bandits steal some dregs of foreign barbarians [the Bible] and adhere to the religion of god; from their fake king and fake ministers, down to the soldiers and menial servants, they address one another as brothers, alleging that only Heaven can be called father. [No king but God.] Aside from this, all the fathers of people are brothers and all the mothers are sisters.... In short, the moral system, ethical relationships, cultural inheritance, and social institutions and statutes of the past several thousand years in China are at once all swept away. This is not only a calamity in our great Qing dynasty but is, in fact, the most extraordinary calamity since the creation of the universe, and that is what Confucius and Mencius are crying bitterly about in the nether world.[65]

Here we see the horror that a demotic movement arouses in the eyes of someone raised within a profoundly hierarchical society.[66] Demotic millennialism strikes this imperial owl as a catastrophe on a cosmic scale. Given how many people died

---

[63] Spence, *God's Chinese Son*, 228.

[64] Here I use the paranoid imperative both as Eli Sagan does, especially in *Citizens and Cannibals: The French Revolution, the Struggle for Modernity and the Origins of Ideological Terror* (Lanham, Md.: Rowman & Littlefield, 2001), where he investigates the French revolutionary dynamic, and as I distinguish it—exterminate or be exterminated—from its "normal time" formulation, the dominating imperative—"rule or be ruled" (see below, chapter 8).

[65] Spence, *God's Chinese Son*, 227–28.

[66] See Louis Dumont, *Homo Hierarchicus: The Caste System and Its Implications* (Oxford: Oxford University Press, 1988).

from this madness, it is hard not to empathize. But at the same time, two points seem noteworthy: (1) that this demotic zeal made it so attractive to the traditionally "inert" peasantry that they joined by the millions, and (2) that the movement became so violently destructive precisely as a result of the swiftness and zeal with which it abandoned its demotic principles and moved toward coercive hierarchy. We will find the same phenomenon with Communist millennialism, once come to power.[67] Demotic religiosity may be attractive, but it is extremely hard to sustain.

Hong's turn to an Akhenaten-like isolation in his millennial city and palace doomed his movement, despite the pervasive incompetence of the Qing troops opposing him and the considerable talent of some of his generals. His followers, torn by often-murderous rivalries and largely abandoned by their leader, failed to coordinate strategies and either consolidate their hold on the areas they had conquered, or to push on to other major cities. In addition, their religious orientation, which might have, had it been capable of some compromise, won the support of the Western powers, actually repelled them. Hong's only Western missionary teacher, Issachar Roberts, visited the Nanjing capital in 1860 to assess the movement, and concluded that Hong had lost his mind.[68] In the final years of the war, Western troops and generals fought for the Qing.[69] In 1860, the Taiping's effort to take the key port city of Shanghai failed, and from that point on, in a horrific war of attrition, they steadily lost ground.

When the final siege of Nanjing starved the city in 1864, Hong died of food poisoning from eating rotten food. When the Qing troops took the city, they disinterred his body, cremated it, and shot the ashes from a canon lest anyone try and create a relic cult. Some 20–35 million (!) Chinese lay dead as a result of this millennial war. It had literally decimated the population of around three hundred million.

▪ SUBSEQUENT ROLE IN CHINESE HISTORY

In the West, the Boxer Rebellion of 1896–1901 is far better known than the Taiping, despite the fact that the Boxer Rebellion only produced casualties in the thousands, perhaps tens of thousands, a mere fraction of the fatalities caused a generation earlier by the Taiping.[70] As a sad illustration of whose ox is gored, the West remembers the Boxer Rebellion—indeed the expression "Yellow Peril"

---

[67] For the most recent analysis of Mao's tendency toward imperialism, see Spence, *Mao Zedong* and Jung Chang and Jon Halliday, *Mao: The Unknown Story* (New York: Knopf, 2005).

[68] On Roberts' visit to Nanjing, see Spence, *God's Chinese Son*, chap. 20.

[69] In particular, the "Ever Victorious Army" of Frederick Townsend Ward, who had set out for China with dreams of joining the Taiping and becoming one of their kings, but, upon realizing the opposition of the Western powers in Shanghai, offered his services to the Qing (see discussion in Jen Yu-wen, *Taiping Revolutionary Movement*, 89–93.)

[70] On the differences in memory, see Paul A. Cohen, *History in Three Keys: The Boxers as Event, Experience and Myth* (New York: Columbia University Press, 1997), 14–15.

entered our vocabulary as a result—because among those casualties some hundred or so were Westerners, and the Boxers targeted both Manchus and Westerners. But in Chinese history, especially in the narratives of modern Chinese revolutionary movements, from Chiang Kai-shek to Mao Zedong, memory of the Taiping dominates, in particular among the Communists who saw themselves and presented themselves to the Chinese as the continuators of the egalitarian revolutionary struggle of the Taiping.[71]

The irony here lies in the double mistake committed by the Chinese Communists in making this connection. They were convinced that they had improved in a critical way over the Taiping by eliminating the religious fanaticism that drove them, thus purifying the revolutionary ideology and permitting them a success that had eluded Hong Xiuquan. And yet, they were victims of the same millennial zealotry that drove the Taiping to sacrifice tens of millions of lives for the sake of "Heaven on Earth." The staggering contempt for human life,[72] the compulsion to impose purity from above, the radical land-reform principles that destroyed the economic life of the country,[73] all replicate the errors of the Taiping. Still more striking, we find in Mao's behavior as he came closer to taking power the same shift to imperialism that marked Hong Xiuquan's ascension. In part, this was a response to the [perceived] "needs" of the masses, but in part it was a response to the megalomanic dynamic of the messianic leader, including the imperial harem.[74]

So, having convinced themselves that they represented the best of the Taiping and had, with their renunciation of the obscurantist and superstitious religious element, learned their historical lesson, the Maoists used Taiping history to promote their cause and made the same mistakes that their earlier "criticized" heroes had made. This error, based on a perception that the critical difference

[71] James P. Harrison, "Chinese Communist Interpretations of the Chinese Peasant Wars," in *History in Communist China*, ed. Albert Feuerwerker (Boston: MIT Press, 1968), 189–215; Harrison, *The Communists and Chinese Peasant Rebellions: A Study in the Rewriting of Chinese History* (New York: Atheneum Press, 1971); Alex Volkoff and Edgar Wickberg, "New Directions in Chinese Historiography: Reappraising the Taiping: Notes and Comment," *Pacific Affairs* 52, no. 3 (Autumn 1979): 479–90; Robert Weller, "Historians and Consciousness: The Modern Politics of the Taiping Heavenly Kingdom," *Social Research* 54, no. 4 (Winter 1987): 731–55.

[72] The Maoists did not discuss the death toll of the Taiping, whose memory they invoked so approvingly. They were equally averse to discussing the death toll of the "Great Leap Forward."

[73] Zhang, quoted above, notes that "[t]he farmers cannot cultivate their own fields to pay taxes because it is said that all the land belongs to the Heavenly King. The merchants cannot do their own business to make profits, because it is said that all the commodities belong to the Heavenly King" (Spence, *God's Chinese Son*, 327).

[74] Mao, apparently, spent many long hours and days fornicating as often as he could; see the accounts of his doctor, Li Zhisui, *The Private Life of Chairman Mao* (New York: Random House, 1994).

between modern revolutionary movements and millennialism lies in seculari-zation, and that consequently secular revolutionary movements are not millen-nial and need not understand themselves in that framework, continues to dominate both scholarship and political rhetoric. The consequences of such superficial assumptions in the twentieth century, to which we shall turn in the next part of the book, have been nothing short of catastrophic, for China, for Russia, and for Europe.

PART FOUR

Modern (Secular) Millennialism

8 Demotic Millennialism

Civil Polities and the Dismantling of the Prime Divider

A peasant plowing his field uncovered a lamp.
When he rubbed off the mud, a genie appeared and offered him
any wish, only whatever he asked for, his neighbor would get double.
"Poke out one of my eyes," he responded.

And it shall come to pass at the end of days
That the mountain of the Lord's house
Shall be established as the top of the mountains, And it shall
be exalted above the hills; And peoples shall flow onto it.
And many nations shall go and say:
Come ye and let us go up to the mountain of the Lord,
And to the house of the God of Jacob;
And he will teach us His ways,
And we will walk in His paths;
For out of Zion shall go forth the law,
And the word of the Lord from Jerusalem.
And he shall judge between many peoples,
And shall arbitrate between many nations;
And they shall beat their swords into plowshares
And the spears into pruning hooks.
Nation shall not lift up sword against nation,
Neither shall they study war any more.
But they shall sit, every man
Under his vine and under his fig tree;
And none shall make them afraid… Micah 4:1–4; cf. Isaiah 2:1–3.

To understand the dynamics of millennialism in modern industrial societies, one has to understand the cultural and psychological framework of "agro-literate" societies from which they arise.[1] This contrast maps well onto the two major varieties of millennial dream: hierarchical and demotic. Premodern societies have a variety

[1] There are a number of terms used by various social scientists to characterize such cultures. John Kautsky calls them *aristocratic empires* (*The Politics of Aristocratic Empires* [Chapel Hill: University of North Carolina Press, 1982]). Ernst Gellner calls them *agro-literate*, since literacy and agriculture are the two key technologies that permit the emergence of prime dividers from the more egalitarian tribal cultures (*Nations and Nationalism* [Oxford: Blackwell, 1983]), a term taken up by John Hall (*Powers and Liberties: The Causes and Consequences of the Rise of the West* [Berkeley and Los Angeles: University of California Press, 1986]). The anthropologist George Foster calls them *deprivation societies*, reflecting their low levels of production and the subsistence levels at which the peasantry lives ("Peasant Society and the Image of Limited Good," *American Anthropologist* 67 [1965]: 293–315). I suggest the term *prime-divider societies*.

of key features in common, all of which center around the creation of a vast and profound division between elites and commoners. In such societies, the elites monopolize weapons, communications technology, and wealth, while commoners, primarily peasants working the land, live at subsistence level. This primal structure is characteristic of most, if not all, "premodern" agrarian "civilizations" from the empires of the ancient world, East and West, to most of the countries of the "Third World" today. In such cultures, elites, especially the armed warriors, had a great deal of discretionary power in their dealings with commoners.

The broad cultural generalizations I am about to set forth are meant to orient rather than to assert dogmatic positions. Research supports the idea that prime dividers dominate the structures of agrarian societies the world over. This does not mean that all prime dividers are identical or that all regulate relationships between above and below the same way. But in each of these societies there is a *prime* divider that—by Western democratic and by demotic millennial standards—is oppressive.[2] In this sense, the history of "higher civilizations" around the world is a catalogue of the varieties of prime-divider politics.

■ THE PRIME DIVIDER AND THE PARANOID IMPERATIVE

Elites construct prime dividers along four major lines: legal privilege, stigmatization of manual labor, restricted access to the technologies of knowledge, and weaponry—all imposed by *potentes* who possess "honor" and status. Although each society works these various elements differently, the overall effect is remarkably similar. The gravitational field of stratified society forms around a prime divider and its maintenance.

- *Privilege Legalized*: Aristocrats have special status before the law: they legislate, they judge, they execute. They pay fewer (if any) taxes. Laws favor their persons and their property over the person of the commoner. According to such systems, stacked in favor of the incumbents, commoners "steal" (often a capital crime) while elites "expropriate."[3]
- *Manual Labor Stigmatized*: Labor defines commoners. In the eyes of the elites, it represents a disgrace that disqualifies laborers from public life, public discourse, and elite education. Elites are defined by their freedom from manual labor: the *liberal* arts are precisely for those "liberated" (by slaves)

---

[2] James C. Scott's study suggests without actually stating it that the more oppressive a society, the more repressed and violent the "hidden transcripts" (*Domination*).

[3] Kautsky, *Politics of Aristocratic Empires*, 197–205; Arthur S. Diamond, *Primitive Law: Past and Present* (London: Methuen, 1971).

from banausic concerns.[4] Indeed, one might even argue that the prime divider is drawn precisely at the divide between the vast majority who labor and the few who do not.

- *Technologies of Knowledge and Weaponry Monopolized*: Elites try to maintain as much control over information as possible, traditionally monopolizing writing and its power to transform both religion and record keeping. Similarly, they try and keep weapons, especially the best weapons, out of the hands of commoners. The clerical elite in the Middle Ages, for example, maintained control of the Bible by severely restricting translations;[5] while the warrior aristocracy jealously guarded its violent privileges. "Violence was built into the very texture of aristocratic life."[6]

- *Honor and the Elite:* The basic elements of honor-shame cultures, which in tribal cultures tend to involve all male members of the tribe in the same honor class, become, under conditions of conquest and state-building, a particular privilege of the elites, whose recourse to force allows them to establish their dominion in a quotidian sense by their possession of honor. "Honor is inherently possessed by the aristocrat, not as an individual, but as a member of the aristocracy."[7] In an honor-shame culture, one may, even must, shed blood for the sake of honor. It is a notoriously zero-sum mentality in which one takes one's honor at another's expense: I can only win if you lose; I make myself look bigger by making you look smaller.[8] And, of course, the most exalted form of violence is war, the sport of kings, the passion of the warrior aristocracy.

The prime divider between elites and commoners acts as a kind of social membrane that maintains two different cultural spheres, each supporting subgroups which, no matter how internally diverse, nonetheless group into two radically different *cultures*, with different family relations, different educational systems and religious practices, and above all, dramatically different expectations and senses of entitlement. Indeed, the differences created by variable access to resources actually

---

[4] *Banausic* comes from the Greek meaning "artisan" or "manual labor." Oligarchs used it as a derogatory term meaning "smacking of the workbench, cramped in body" to refer to manual labor and laborers. Kautsky has an overall discussion, *Politics of Aristocratic Empires*, 177–87.

[5] R. Landes, "Literacy and the Origins of Inquisitorial Christianity: The Exegetical Battle between Hierarchy and Community in the Christian Empire (300–500)," in *Social History and Issues in Human Consciousness: Some Interdisciplinary Connections*, ed. A.E. Barnes & P.N. Stearns (New York: New York University Press, 1989), 137–70. See below, Walter Map's reflections on Waldo's French Bible (n. 18).

[6] Reinhardt Bendix, *Kings and People: Power and the Mandate to Rule* (Berkeley and Los Angeles: University of California Press, 1980), 228.

[7] Kautsky, *Politics of Aristocratic Empires*, 170, discussion, 169–77.

[8] See the discussions in Christopher Boehm, *Blood Revenge: The Enactment and Management of Conflict in Montenegro and Other Tribal Societies* (Lawrence: University Press of Kansas, 1984); Foster on the notion of limited good, "Peasant Society"; and Philip Salzman, *Culture and Conflict in the Middle East* (New York: Prometheus, 2008).

create marked physical differences between tall and muscular aristocrats and small, gaunt commoners.[9] Elites protect prime dividers by making the passage from below into their advantageous situation difficult, most often a process of osmosis that takes families generations to accomplish. In the case of individuals, every caution is taken that the newcomers (*arrivistes*) adheres strictly to the rules of the elite to which they have acceded. They are the last in, and the first out.[10]

Prime dividers rise out of political cultures that take the "dominating imperative" as axiomatic: *rule or be ruled, dominate or be dominated, enslave or be enslaved.* This "golden rule"—do unto others before they do onto you—takes its imperative nature from its assumption about the other's response. If "we" do not subject "them," then "they" will subject us. One *must* dominate as a *defensive* measure. When the Melians complained that the Athenians were unfair in killing the men and enslaving the women and children were they not to submit, the Athenians responded:

> Our opinion of the gods and our knowledge of men lead us to conclude that it is a general and necessary law of nature to rule whatever one can. This is not a law that we made ourselves, nor were we the first to act upon it when it was made. We found it already in existence, and we shall leave it to exist forever among those who come after us. We are merely acting in accordance with it, and we know that you or anybody else with the same power as ours would be acting in precisely the same way.[11]

Obviously in a world where others palpably intend to do precisely the same, it not only makes sense to play by those rules, but it becomes dangerous to abstain.[12]

And so, those above had to police the prime divider in every possible way: monopoly of weapons, debasement of manual labor, crushing and humiliating exactions from the commoners. For example, a hostile ecclesiastical chronicler expressed a harsh (Augustinian) attitude toward the behavior of peasants who, in the early 1180s, formed a *conspiratio* (sworn association) in France led by a carpenter named Durandus. Called the *Capucciati* (because of the white hoods they wore as a sign of their *conspiratio*), they challenged seigneurial dominance.[13]

> The league of the sworn of Le Puy was only a diabolic and pernicious invention. There was *no longer fear or respect for superiors.* All strove to acquire liberty, saying that *it*

[9] Charles Tilly, *Durable Inequality* (Berkeley and Los Angeles, University of California Press, 1998), 1–8.

[10] For two good contemporaneous examples, see the fates of Joan of Arc (1412–31) and Jacques Coeur (1395–1456), both commoners who took prominent places above the prime divider, both jettisoned when it no longer suited their aristocratic patrons.

[11] Thucydides, *The Peloponnesian War* 5: 105, Penguin edition, 405.

[12] Eli Sagan, *The Honey and the Hemlock: Democracy and Paranoia in Ancient Athens and Modern America* (Princeton, N.J.: Princeton University Press, 1991).

[13] Still the best historical account of this unfortunately neglected episode in the religious and social history of medieval France is that of Achille Luchaire, *Social France at the Time of Philip Augustus*, trans. E.B. Krehbiel (New York: F. Ungar Publishing Co., 1957), 12–19. See also, John France, "People against Mercenaries—The Capuchins in Southern Gaul," *Journal of Medieval Military History* 8 (2010): 1–22.

belonged to them from the time of Adam and Eve, from the very day of creation. They did not understand that *serfdom is the punishment of sin!* The result was that there was *no longer any distinction between the great and the small, but a fatal confusion* tending to ruin the institutions which rule us all, through the will of God and the agency of the powerful of this earth.[14]

Medieval elites held *in*equality as self-evident, and hierarchy as endowed by the Creator. The aristocracy controlled productive surpluses: they had leisure time, ate meat to their fill, and lived by the sweat of other men's brows.[15] The very definition of the powerful man, the dominator, was how much he ate—a man without an appetite could not be king over the Franks.[16]

> By God! Fair sire, he's of your line indeed,
> Who thus devours a mighty haunch of boar,
> And drinks of wine a gallon at two gulps.
> Pity the man on whom he wages war![17]

The social order depended upon their superiority, their honor.

Similarly, when the other major players above the prime divider, the clergy, met with a threat to their monopoly on writing and scripture, they found commoner pretensions inacceptable. Faced with the Waldensians, whose vernacular Bible and public demotic preaching had deeply disturbed the clergy of Lyon, Walter Map, after humiliating Waldo with a trick question, went on to note:

> Shall then the pearl be cast before the swine, the word be given to the ignorant, whom we know to be unfit to take it in, much less to give out what they have received? Away with such a thought! Uproot it! From the head let the ointment go down to the beard and thence to the clothing; from the spring let the water be led, not the puddles of the street....They are beginning in a very humble guise because they cannot get their foot in; but if we let them in, we shall surely be turned out.[18]

---

[14] *Gesta Pontificum Autissiodorensium,* ed. and trans. Michel Sot, *Les Gestes des évêques d'Auxerre.* Les classiques de l'histoire de France au Moyen Âge 43 (Paris: Les Belles Lettres, 2002), 180–81; discussed in Luchaire, *Social France,* 17. Note the similarities with the complaint of the Mandarin scholar about the Taiping, above, chap. 7, n. 66.

[15] Cf. Abraham Lincoln's Second Inaugural Address: "It may seem strange that any men should dare to ask a just God's assistance in wringing their bread from the sweat of other men's faces, but let us judge not, that we be not judged." Online: http://www.bartleby.com/124/pres32.html, April 13, 2010.

[16] Massimo Montanari, "Peasants, Warriors, Priests: Images of Society and Styles of Diet," in *Food: A Culinary History from Antiquity to the Present,* ed. Jean-Louis Flandrin and Massimo Montanari (New York: Columbia University Press, 1999), 180.

[17] *Chanson de Guillaume,* lines 1428–31, trans. *La chançun de Willame,* ed. Elizabeth Stearns Tyler (New York: Oxford University Press, 1919), 62, cited and translated in Marc Bloch, *Feudal Society* (London: Routledge & KeganPaul, 1965), 1:13.

[18] Walter Map, *De nugiis curialium,* trans. Montague Rhodes James (Oxford: Oxford University Press, 1983), 124–27. An early argument for "trickle-down."

Or, as one British aristocrat who lived at a time of rapidly increasing literacy and print production for commoners exclaimed: "Should a horse know as much as a man, I should not like to be his rider."[19]

The gravitational force field of political activity naturally produces prime dividers not because everyone is driven by the urge to dominate. Rather, as Augustine pointed out, those driven by *libido dominandi* rise to the top of political organizations.[20] But the dominance of these "alpha males" imposes on the entire range of relations and reflects evolutionary forces immensely difficult to control or even sublimate.[21] Thus, those who achieve power within any given polity show the most aptitude for the negative projections involved in the dominating imperative, and justify their efforts to assure their dominance by assuming that, were someone else in their position, they would do the same. Thus, no matter how well a young "aristocracy" (rule of the *best*) deserves to rule, the tendencies of incumbency come to dominate polities. Most of the cyclical visions of civilizations, from Plato and Aristotle to Ibn Khaldoun to Spengler, assume this tendency as a law of political life.

Prime dividers are, therefore, ubiquitous in stratified societies themselves based on the technologies of weaponry (metals), communications (writing), and agriculture (plow).[22] Prime-divider societies, therefore, show remarkable stability not so much in their particulars—empires and kingdoms come and go—but in the durability of the form.[23] The conquerors of prime-divider societies (as well as the revolutionaries who overthrow them) have an uncanny tendency to reproduce the prime divider in some form or variant.[24] These kinds of societies characterize almost all forms of "higher civilization" over the last three millennia. Indeed, Eli Sagan, who approaches the political problem from a (social-) psychological point of view, considers it a near-miracle that any civilization has escaped the predatory talons of the dominating imperative: "Paranoia is the problem. The paranoid position ["rule or be ruled," which produces prime dividers] is the defense. Democracy is a miracle, considering human psychological disabilities."[25]

---

[19] Bernard Mandeville, "An Essay on Charity and Charity Schools" (1719) in *The Fable of the Bees: Or Private Vices, Public Benefits* (London: C. Bathurst, 1795), 181; quoted in Paul Starr, *The Creation of the Media: Political Origins of Modern Communications* (New York: Basic Books, 2005), 61.

[20] Peter Burnell, "The Problem of Service to Unjust Regimes in Augustine's City of God," *Journal of the History of Ideas* 54, no. 2 (1993): 177–88.

[21] See Richard Wrangham and Dale Peterson, *Demonic Males: Apes and the Origins of Human Violence* (New York: Houghton Mifflin, 1996); Michael Ghiglieri, *The Dark Side of Man: Tracing the Origins of Male Violence* (Cambridge, Mass.: Perseus Books, 2000).

[22] Ernst Gellner, *Plough, Sword and Book: The Structure of Human History* (Chicago: University of Chicago Press, 1992).

[23] Kautsky, *Politics of Aristocratic Empires*, 3–10.

[24] For early examples, see Garth Fowden, *Empire to Commonwealth*; Ephraim Karsh, *Islamic Imperialism*. For more "modern" revolutionary examples, see above, chapter 7 (Taiping), and below, chapter 9 (French Revolution) and 11 (Communism).

[25] Sagan, *Honey and the Hemlock*, 22. For a historical-sociological analysis of some of these issues, see Tilly, *Durable Inequality*, esp. chap. 7: "The Politics of Inequality."

From the perspective of someone living in a relatively advanced civil polity, it may seem "reasonable" to consider the inability to rise above the "paranoid" position as a psychological disability. From the perspective of prime-divider societies, however, the willingness to trust others not to try and dominate is the psychological inability.[26] The logic of the peasant in the epigraph of this chapter, is not merely envy: granted, to have a neighbor become twice as wealthy as oneself is psychologically painful and destroys the pleasure in what one has gained, no matter how large a sum; but it also *endangers* him. The neighbor could use his position to gain dominion over him. His move, were this a chess game, would get a "!!": in the kingdom of the blind, the one-eyed is king. Perhaps that explains why escaping the gravitational pull of the prime divider is a miracle.

■ CIVIL SOCIETY AND THE DISMANTLING
OF THE PRIME DIVIDER

Civil polities attack the ideological and institutional foundations of prime-divider societies, that is, their cultural and legal supports. Instead of privilege before the law, they insist on equality before the law, what the Greeks called *isonomia*. Instead of the disgrace of manual labor, they emphasize its dignity and the rights of those who engage in it. Instead of restricted access to information, they encourage widespread knowledge (even literacy), and publish the laws and religious texts (sometimes the same) for all to see. Instead of an old-boy network that guarantees that most, if not all, positions of authority in the culture are manned by aristocrats, they reward merit regardless of birth. And instead of legally privileging one religion, they guarantee that religious choice is voluntary and not coerced.

Such societies, rather than yielding to the demands of a warrior aristocracy, reject the use of "private" violence as a legitimate means to get what one wants. They insist on the accountability of the ruling authorities, on transparency in government, on the ability of a population to rid themselves of rulers that they feel do not live up to such standards. Such societies systematically *substitute a discourse of fairness for violence in dispute settlement*, and therefore protect citizens from the assaults of armed elites or legally privileged castes. I refer to such cases, where unarmed people can count on the security of person and property, where discourse rather than violence governs decision-making and dispute settlement, as "civil polities."[27]

One might describe civil polities, to borrow the metaphor of the German medieval aristocracy, as cases where, in principle, by constitution, the "pruning shears" are taken out of the hands of a predatory elite and placed in the hands of the

---

[26] Indeed, Hong Xiuquan's trust of Yang Xiuqing proved fatal (above, chapter 7).

[27] There is an enormous literature on "civil society," most of which defines civil society in terms of nongovernmental organizations. See Adam Seligman's critique of this terminology in *The Idea of Civil Society* (Princeton, N.J.: Princeton University Press, 1992). To avoid the problems involved in using the heavily overused term, I prefer "civil polities" to refer to the former. Democracies then, are the major but not unique subset of civil polities.*

populace as a whole: a government "of the people, by the people, and for the people."[28] They trim back the excesses of the aristocracy, limiting their ability to use force, subjecting them to the same laws, and hopefully preventing the emergence of the kinds of huge disparities of wealth and power between elites and commoners that favor the consolidation of prime dividers.

But in order to overcome the dominating imperative, such civil polities have to come up with an alternative to the coercive, fear-induced obedience that characterizes "top-down" polities. They must foster a counter-ethic to the "paranoid position." Civil polities seek social cohesion and order from consensus rather than coercion, from a social contract or covenant, from bottom-up rather than top-down. The golden rule—"do unto others as you would have them do onto you"—demands a degree of empathy and mutual respect that aristocrats (or ruling elites) categorically reject in their dealings with the peasantry (subjects). Only when such principles of empathy and equality become widely accepted can a society attempt to dismantle the prime divider: to replace legal privilege with *isonomia*, contempt for manual laborers with their dignity and equality, pre-ordained commoner illiteracy with autonomous participation in an educated, public sphere. These, I submit, are important cultural preconditions to democratic forms of government, preparing the terrain, as it were, for so radical a political experiment.[29]

In the succeeding sections, I try to (a) define the four components of a civil polity that contrast directly with those of a prime divider in purely secular terms; (b) explore the religious dimension of these components in a particular, demotic, reading of the Bible; (c) link this biblical religiosity to the emergence and dynamics of demotic millennialism in the West; and (d) in a final section, explore how that demotic millennialism became secularized in the ideology of the Enlightenment. The following chapter explores one of the first apocalyptic movements of this new secular millennialism and its efforts to dismantle the prime divider—the French Revolution.

The Proto-Democratic Quaternity: Civil Polity Inverts Prime-Divider Structures

(1) Isonomia

The Greek term *isonomia* has a variety of possible meanings over which philologists and historians have argued for decades, it can mean either equality *before* the law or *through* the law. Most famously, Solon and Kleisthenes introduced *isonomia*

---

[28] Gadi Algazi, "Pruning Peasants: Private War and Maintaining the Lords' Peace in Late Medieval Germany," in *Medieval Transformations: Texts, Power and Gifts in Context*, ed. Esther Cohen and Mayke de Jong (Leiden: Brill, 2000), 245–74.

[29] In addition to Sagan (above, n. 11), see also the discussion in Adam Seligman, *Modernity's Wager* (Princeton, N.J.: Princeton University Press, 2000). Lincoln's opening lines of the Gettysburg Address alludes specifically to this experimental issue: "a new nation conceived and dedicated to the proposition that all men are created equal...testing whether that nation, or any nation so conceived and so dedicated can long endure."

(with the latter meaning) as the legal foundation of Athenian democracy.[30] Historians of ancient Greece present this as a victory for the common people greater "than anywhere else since the dawn of history."[31]

Herodotus has a Persian character, Otanes, praise this egalitarianism—*isonomia*—as the fairest of all notions.

> Contrast this [the tyrannical excesses of monarchy] with the rule of the people [*demokratia*]: first it has the finest of all names to describe it—equality under law [*isonomia*]; and secondly, the people in power do none of the things that monarchs do. Under a government of the people a magistrate is appointed by lot and is held responsible for his conduct in office, and all questions are put up for open debate...."[32]

One might even call this a "public secret." *Everyone* knows that *isonomia* is the best, most just system—the "finest of all names." But given the impossibility of getting the powerful to play the game by rules that make them equal to commoners, it is as unrealistic as it is obviously preferable.

Accordingly, some historians consider equality before the law as a notion whose "boldness and rarity cannot be overstressed."[33] From the perspective of modern democracies, the basic elements of judicial *isonomia*, or "procedural justice" as Rawls calls it,[34] may be taken for granted, but from the perspective of aristocratic polities (i.e., the vast majority of former and present-day, literate, sociopolitical structures), *isonomia* challenges the core of hierarchy. Popper argued that *isonomia* was the one definition of justice that Plato could not refute, but also could not tolerate, and therefore he passed over it in silence when discussing "justice" in his *Republic*.[35] And one need only look at the resistance of the fifth-century BCE Roman patriciate to the prospect of "permanent laws, permanently exhibited where all can see them," even though the laws privileged them, to realize how threatening aristocratic groups find such measures.[36]

---

[30] See the discussions in Gregory Vlastos, "*Isonomia*," *The American Journal of Philology* 74 (1953): 337–66; Martin Ostwald, *Nomos and the Beginnings of Athenian Democracy* (Oxford: Clarendon Press, 1969); H.W. Pleket, "*Isonomia* and Kleisthenes," *Talanta* 4 (1972): 63–81; Michael Taylor, *The Tyrant Slayers: The Heroic Image in 5th Century B.C. Athenian Art and Politics* (New York: Arno Press, 1981); for an unconventional meditation, see J. R. Lucas, *Isonomia* (1990), online: http://users.ox.ac.uk/~jrlucas/libeqsor/isonomia.pdf, April 13, 2010.

[31] Vlastos, "*Isonomia*," 355.

[32] Herodotus,*The Histories* 3.80, 6, trans. Aubrey de Sélincourt (London: Penguin, 1972), 239.

[33] Moses I. Finley, *Economy and Society in Ancient Greece* (New York: Penguin, 1953, 1981), 84–87; see also B. Borecky, "Die politische Isonomie," *Eirene* 9 (1971): 5–24, on the dual meaning of the term.

[34] John Rawls, *A Theory of Justice* (Cambridge, Mass.: Harvard University Press, 1971), 83–89.

[35] Karl Popper, *The Open Society and Its Enemies* (London: Routledge, 2002), 1:93–119. For another sharp critique of Plato from a millennial analysis, see La Barre, "The Greek Ghost Dance," in *The Ghost Dance*, 517–47.

[36] For a translation of the (eventually) Twelve Tables of the Law engraved in bronze, see *Roman Civilization: Sourcebook*, vol. 1, *The Republic*, ed. Naphali Lewis and M. Reinhold (New York: Harper & Row, 1966), 101–09, with bibliography. For Livy's lurid account of the difficulties in establishing and publishing these tables, see *Early History of Rome*, 3.32–60, trans. Aubrey de Sélincourt (London: Penguin, 1971), 216–50, quotation from 3.58, p. 247–48. For commentary, see Alan Watson, *Rome of the XII Tables: Persons and Property* (Princeton, N.J.: Princeton University Press, 1975), who does not feel that the class distinctions were effectively so great (177–86).

We should not underestimate the anger and resistance that this loss of arbitrary power provokes in the ruling classes. To the "noble one," the idea of equality before the law constitutes what Nietzsche called "slave morality," which, upon infecting the strong with "bad conscience," sickens them. And so, the argument in defense of aristocratic privilege goes, all society falls ill.[37]

(2) Literacy

Isonomia entails literacy—some might even argue that alphabetic literacy was a prerequisite to *isonomia*. In ancient Greece, literacy spread (relatively) rapidly with the dissemination of the alphabet from the late eighth century BCE onward.[38] Solon (sixth century BCE) and Kleisthenes (fifth century BCE) come two centuries later, inaugurating reforms based on isonomic laws. Publication of the laws played a crucial role in the institution of many polities in the ancient world and in any constitutional system of the modern world.[39] But in every case of *isonomia*, the founders published the laws since only an informed citizenry could hope to protect its legal rights against the constant encroachments of those in power.[40] The fate of the laws in Orwell's parable *Animal Farm* illustrates the troubled relationship between egalitarian laws and egalitarian community, on the one hand, and the incapacity of authoritarian elites to tolerate such limiting public law codes, on the other.[41]

In his book, *The Implications of Literacy in the 11th and 12th centuries*, Brian Stock has argued that "textual communities" constitute a crucial social unit formed around a text—possibly very brief—whose moral and spiritual demands constitute the goal of those members who join.[42] These voluntary societies, "laboratories of social organization," underline the fact that strict literacy (i.e., people who can read) is perhaps less vital than *access* to texts. Many of the members of the early eleventh-century textual communities that Stock highlights could not read. But their access to the text through oral, communitarian

---

[37] Nietzsche, *Genealogy of Morals*, 1:10–11, trans. Kaufmann, 36–43. On the contribution of this resistance to modern conspiracy theories, see below, chapter 11.

[38] E.A. Havelock, *The Literate Revolution in Greece and Its Cultural Consequences* (Princeton, N.J.: Princeton University Press, 1982).

[39] To which numerous cases of law codes engraved in stone attest: Hammurabi's Code (ca.1790 BCE); Mosaic Commandments (ca. 1200 BCE); the Gortyn Code in Crete (ca. 450 BCE), the Twelve Tables of the Law in Rome (ca. 450 BCE), etc..

[40] Here we see one of the peculiar capacities of script at play: by objectifying the law, by setting it in stone, writing permitted a whole new level of public scrutiny and the accountability of judges and rulers. Vlastos actually reintroduces the significance of "mere" equality before the law, in discussing the role of political equality in supporting the "rule of law" ("*Isonomia*," 356–66).

[41] George Orwell, *Animal Farm* (New York: Harcourt Brace, 1945).

[42] Brian Stock, *The Implications of Literacy: Written Language and Models of Interpretation in the Eleventh and Twelfth Centuries* (Princeton, N.J.: Princeton University Press, 1983), 88–240.

media (readings by people they trusted) nevertheless transformed their lives. In more than one of Stock's cases, the texts serve as laws that apply equally to all members.[43]

Historians identify such communities appearing within the Church (and therefore gender separated) as a critical part of the great developments in legal and intellectual culture in the High Middle Ages (twelfth-century Renaissance and beyond).[44] When such communities and movements (like the Waldensians) appeared among the laity (and therefore were gender-mixed), ecclesiastics viewed them with deep suspicion, and when mockery failed, pursued them as "heretics." In conjunction with the "rule of the law," widespread access to the text of the law means widespread awareness of rights and protection.[45]

(3) Manual Labor

Manual labor serves prime-divider cultures as a kind of mark of disgrace, a stigma that excludes the laborer from participating in political and cultural life, and the positive valuation of manual labor represents perhaps the most radical of the egalitarian principles discussed here.[46] Even Aristotle clearly parts paths with any more radical democratic notions of considering the opinions of manual laborers of any value in public life.[47]

Not everyone, of course, shares the attitudes of the elites. Obviously peasants, who labor all their lives and must convey a work ethic to their children, have a different view of the dignity of their task and the value of their opinions.[48] The real significance would then seem to lie in the conditions under which the affirmation of this commoner's self-respect manages to penetrate into the elite. Athens honored manual laborers to an unusual degree, granting commoners the right to speak in the agora and to vote. And at least some part of Athenian attitudes came close to

---

[43] This is not a point brought out by Stock in his theoretical discussion, but every example he then gives, in particular of what we might call "apostolic communities," indicates that whether explicitly as a law, or implicitly as a moral imperative, the texts serve this function. The Church's objections emphasize the scandal of not distinguishing between clerics and layfolk; ibid., 88–151.

[44] Richard Southern, *The Making of the Middle Ages* (New Haven, Conn.: Yale University Press, 1963); Caroline Bynum, "Did the Twelfth Century Discover the Individual?" in *Jesus as Mother: Studies in the Spirituality of the High Middle Ages* (Berkeley and Los Angeles: University of California Press, 1982).

[45] R. Landes, "Between Aristocracy and Heresy: Popular Participation in the Limousin Peace of God (994–1032)" in Thomas Head and Richard Landes, *The Peace of God* (Ithaca, N.Y.: Cornell University Press, 1992), 184–219.

[46] For a general statement see Kautsky, *Politics of Aristocratic Empires*, 177–87.

[47] See Aristotle's remarks in the *Politics*: "for a man who lives the life of a mechanic or laborer may not aspire to the things which belong to excellence" (3.5.20).

[48] Robert Redfield, *Peasant Soceity and Culture: An Anthropological Approach to Civilization* (Chicago: University of Chicago Press, 1956).

what one historian has compared to the Protestant Ethic.[49] For them, any kind of idleness was unacceptable, and they inverted the law to insist that *only* men who *worked for a living*, and taught their sons a profession, could enjoy the full range of citizens' rights.[50]

(4) Shift from Zero-Sum Honor to Positive-Sum Integrity

The least visible, least documentable, but perhaps most fundamental element in the creation of a civil polity comes from the notable increase in the tolerance of adult males for public contradiction. This results to some extent from an internal shift in ability to contain anger, and to some extent from a change in the peer group, which ceases to honor violence as an appropriate response to insult.[51] In the United States and Britain, for example, the duel only faded when the public opinion changed.[52] This shift occurred in Western civilization in the context of a contrast between rational and irrational behavior. "Rational" described the positive-sum interactions that, in benefiting all, made sense; "irrational" described the hot-headed often self-destructive demands of overwhelming emotions like rage at humiliation, destructive envy, or the drive to dominate.[53]

The logic of positive-sum interactions seems clear to people brought up in civil polities. Compromise is the essence of democracy; going for hard zero-sum outcomes blights growth and mutual prosperity. But despite its obvious advantages, the *emotions* of positive-sum interactions can be quite arduous. They demand that we renounce (or at least sublimate) such pervasive and nearly irresistible emotions as envy and *Schadenfreude*. In any open-ended positive-sum exchange, neither side can predict who will gain more, and to sustain such exchanges, one has to learn to tolerate, even take pleasure, in other people's success. The "rational" response to the genie's dilemma of one wish that gives twice as much to one's neighbor is to say, "give me ten million bucks and good for my neighbor who gets twenty." But generosity can render one vulnerable just as can much as laying down one's weapons. If the neighbor uses his wealth to attack and impoverish me, my

---

[49] M. Balme presents a rather homiletic picture: "Attitudes to Work and Leisure in Ancient Greece," *Greece and Rome* 31 (1984): 140–45; for a more balanced view, see Sinclair, *Democracy and Participation*, 112–13, 226–27; R. Hopper, *Trade and Industry in Classical Greece* (London: Thames & Hudson, 1979), 61–70.

[50] Balme, "Attitudes," 143.

[51] On dueling and the psychological issues at stake, see Jon Elster, *Alchemies of the Mind: Rationality and the Emotions* (Cambridge: Cambridge University Press, 1999), 216–28.

[52] In the north, see the response to Aaron Burr after he killed Hamilton in a duel; see Joseph Ellis, *Founding Brothers: The Revolutionary Generation* (New York: Vintage, 2002), 20–47; for Britain, see Kwame Anthony Appiah, *The Honor Code: On the Origins of Moral Revolutions* (New York: W.W. Norton, 2010), chapter 1.

[53] The rational dimension of economic choices (that makes the "invisible hand" possible) pervades the writing and thinking of Adam Smith, a Lowland Scot who knew well the economically regressive character of the proud Highlanders.

rational decision will be my ruin. Both sides of a positive-sum encounter need to maintain the high emotional ground: that path involves significant vulnerability and demands not only trust but also trustworthiness. Sustaining rationality takes emotions that are not, themselves, rational.[54]

Perhaps the most critical dimension of this problem of honor concerns the ability of commoners to criticize elites publicly without incurring a violent reaction. This, in turn, depends on the capacity of those criticized elites to tolerate such public "affronts," rather than treat them as assaults on their manhood. While "honor" demands violence in response to "insult," a civic polity substitutes a discourse of fairness for that violence in dispute settlement, and insists that one respond to criticism on its substance, not as an *ad hominem*. In order for an elite to tolerate things like a "free press" and "freedom of petition," it must have a high tolerance for the kind backtalk that no "man of honor" would tolerate. *Away with such thoughts! Uproot them!* It is difficult to exaggerate the importance of this particular cluster of concerns—honor, integrity, self-criticism, tolerance—for civil polities which cannot thrive (and therefore not, in the long run, survive) without a highly developed culture of self-criticism. Both morality and science depend upon it.

These four elements—*isonomia*, widespread literacy, dignity of manual labor, and positive-sum attitudes that transcend honor-shame dynamics—show an extremely high correlation with democratic tendencies. If one examines any of the places in which democratic sentiments, and, on occasion, institutions, manage to emerge, despite the vigorous objections of the aristocratic classes, one finds these four elements have already established firm bases in the culture of the society. The communes of eleventh-century Europe, the peasant rebellions of the late Middle Ages (e.g., England, 1381) and early modern period (e.g., Germany, 1525), the Puritan Revolution of the seventeenth, the American and French of the eighteenth, and the Socialist and Zionist movements of modern times—all made appeals to equality before the law, all spoke of manual labor as a unique source of dignity, all leaned heavily for their support on the existence of a class of commoners who could read or cared about the contents of texts, and all, at least in their nascent stages, emphasized the importance of overcoming the obsession with externally defined "honor." From a purely sociohistorical perspective, then, the rise to prominence of these four factors in any given culture seems like an excellent indicator of future democratic and economically productive developments.[55]

Because they reverse the zero-sum thinking of the dominating imperative, such societies, when they successfully stabilize, have remarkably strong economies.[56] Markets, after all, operate most efficiently when accurate information circulates, property is secure, and, in a voluntary exchange, both sides stand to

---

[54] For an excellent analysis of these issues, see Elster, *Alchemies of the Mind.*

[55] R. Landes, "Economic Development and Demotic Religiosity."

[56] D. Landes, *Wealth and Poverty of Nations*; and Lawrence Harrison and Samuel Huntington, eds., *Culture Matters: How Values Shape Human Progress* (New York: Basic Books, 2001).

win.[57] Again Pericles underlines the implications: "The greatness of our city brings it about that all the good things from all over the world flow in to us, so that to us it seems just as natural to enjoy foreign goods as our own local products." Karl Popper called this an "open society"[58]: a thriving, culturally creative city in which, as Pericles put it: "each single one of our citizens, in all the manifold aspects of life, is able to show himself the rightful lord and owner of his own person."[59] As opposed to the hierarchical world of the prime divider, where every man has a "master," this culture lays claim to be one where freedom empowers all its citizens to act autonomously. The "atmospheric pressure" of such a polity differs markedly from that of prime-divider ones.

Civil Polity as a Historical and Theoretical Concept

Obviously the reality, even at the height of Athenian democracy, fell far short of these fine-sounding ideals. At any given time, the citizens of which Pericles speaks so favorably represented a minority of the inhabitants—foreigners had limited rights, women fewer, and slaves, none. And they were less known by their stability and magnanimity, than by their devouring envy and ferocious rivalries.[60] But merely the embrace of *isonomia* for so limited a number of people, and the shift of significant amounts of envy and rivalry to constructive modes of competition, stands out as a rare exception in the historical record. Nor did it happen easily.[61] It was, whatever the contrast with reality, a huge anomaly in a world dominated by prime dividers and intellectuals ever ready to defend and justify them.

So between the antinomies *prime-divider societies* and *civil polities*, we find a continuum. Few actual societies embody an absolute example of either case, especially of the latter. All societies have elites; all societies recognize, at least minimally, their debt to their commoners. What distinguishes different sociopolitical systems, then, concerns above all the approach of the elite toward dominion. Prime-divider societies, with their hierarchies of power, work *with* the natural gravitational pull of *libido dominandi*. People, primarily alpha males, need to dominate. So the political system gives that urge ways to play itself out in battle for the dominance of the fittest. If war is the sport of kings, it has much to do with how war "created such joy in the hearts of men, for whom daring and contempt for death were, in a sense, professional assets."[62]

---

[57] This is the central theme of Nathan Rosenberg and L.E. Birdzell Jr., *How The West Grew Rich: The Economic Transformation of the Industrial World* (New York: Basic Books, 1987).

[58] Popper, *Open Society and Its Enemies.*

[59] Thucydides, "Pericles' Funeral Oration," in *Peloponnesian War*, 2: 35–42, 145–46.

[60] For a devastating critique of Greek society from this point of view, see both Phillip Slater, *The Glory of Hera* (Princeton, N.J.: Princeton University Press, 1992); and Peter Walcott, *Envy and the Greeks* (New York: Aris & Phillips, 1978).

[61] Josiah Ober, *Mass and Elite in Democratic Athens: Rhetoric, Ideology, and the Power of the People* (Princeton, N.J.: Princeton University Press, 1989).

[62] Bloch, *Feudal Society*, 1: 13.

Civil polities, on the other hand, represent experiments against the grain, struggling against the dominating imperative, always resisting its gravitational pull, with its "rational" paranoia and its incumbent hierarchical elites. Rather than think of them as two opposing models, one should rather conceive of prime dividers as the norm of a longue durée from the ancient empires to the present, and civil society as deviation from that norm, *experiments* in freedom, never perfect (i.e., millennial), but necessarily limited by the gravitational pull that shapes prime dividers—or, as Augustine would say, a *corpus permixtum*.

All civil polities have, therefore, so far achieved only limited degrees of success in dismantling the prime divider. All cultures and groups will have elites and commoners, and all elites confront Acton's law: *power corrupts; absolute power corrupts absolutely*. Indeed, some critics dismiss all the alleged "advances" of civil society as disguised forms of *libido dominandi*. Commerce, money, and knowledge substitute for weapons of violence in the battle for domination; lawyers and judges, whatever the principles of the legal system, still stack the cards in favor of the powerful, producing a de facto privilege; people who can, avoid manual labor and look down on those who cannot. As far as the more radical critics of modernity are concerned, modern democracies are only thinly disguised prime-divider societies.[63]

But that inability to distinguish between prime-divider and (necessarily flawed) civil polities is, in itself, a form of millennial thinking in which anything short of perfection gets dismissed as just "more of the same." And at the same time, it obscures any understanding of the relationship between different types of millennial thinking on the one hand, and these, in fact, significantly different social structures, on the other. The question is not whether elites exist, but how they interact with commoners, not whether elites grow corrupt, but what mechanisms a polity builds in for correction—venues for rebuke, for the expression of informed public opinion, for holding powerholders accountable (venues which such critics like exploit to the fullest extent) without suffering the consequences that a real prime-divider elite would administer.

■ DEMOTIC RELIGIOSITY AND THE DEMOCRATIC QUATERNITY

Most modern thought about civil society, democracy, and modernity emphasizes the importance of "secular" values in their emergence. Religion, as Marx so famously informed us, "is the opiate of the masses"—a superstructure of superstitious opacity manipulated by priests and designed to justify the prime divider as

---

[63] See, for example, Herbert Marcuse, "Repressive Tolerance," in Robert Paul Wolff, Barrington Moore, Jr., and Herbert Marcuse, *A Critique of Pure Tolerance* (Boston: Beacon Press, 1969), 95–137. This critique was carried on by figures like Noam Chomsky and Edward S. Herman, *Manufacturing Consent: The Political Economy of Mass Media* (New York: Pantheon, 1988); Howard Zinn, *A People's History of the United States: 1492–Present* (New York: Harper Collins, 1999); and, through Edward Said's *Orientalism* (New York: Vintage, 1979), into a whole school of postcolonialism.

either inevitable or necessary.[64] But such an approach obscures important elements of the story. First, it assumes that all religion—and certainly all monotheism— represents an authoritarian, imperialist impulse: "one God, one emperor, one religion."[65] But this approach ignores a whole range of religiosity—especially strong in monotheistic traditions—that I would like to call "demotic"[66] and which inform, if not create, the demotic millennial tradition.

Once we shift our attention from institutions and political thought to the social and cultural values outlined above, democratic Athens finds a serious and older "demotic" rival in the ancient world—the Hebrews.[67] Indeed, this culture emphasized the importance of *isonomia*, mass education, manual labor, and the substitution of integrity for honor, long before, and with much greater consistency and depth, than Greek or even Athenian society. And perhaps because of this consistency—unlike Athens, there were few voices of dissent on any of these matters—the culture and its traditions survived in an unbroken chain from the ancient world to the present.[68] Moreover, since the principal (but not sole) source of these values, the Hebrew Bible, became the canon of the dominant religion of European society, these attitudes found much more accessible expression—and to a much wider audience—through religious than through classical studies.[69]

Although both forms address the commoners and their religious needs, *demotic religiosity* differs from *popular religiosity* in intent, style, and content.[70] Popular religiosity condescends, offering a wide variety of attractive elements that at once appeal to and reinforce commoner tastes—icons, relics, magical ceremonies,

---

[64] Marx's remark on the opiate of the masses appears in his introduction to *A Contribution to the Critique of Hegel's Philosophy of Right* CW, v. 3, 3. On the distinctions between thick and thin hegemony, see Scott, *Domination*, 66–89.

[65] On the indictment of monotheism for intolerance and imperialism, see (in addition to works cited above, chapter 2, n. 68), Jonathan Kirsch, *God against the Gods: The History of War Between Monotheism and Polytheism* (New York: Viking Compass, 2004); Regina Schwartz, *The Curse of Cain: The Violent Legacy of Monotheism* (Chicago: University of Chicago Press, 1997).

[66] For a more elaborate discussion of demotic religiosity and the economic "take-off" of the eleventh century in Western Europe, see R. Landes, "Economic Development and Demotic Religiosity."

[67] For the most recent articulation of this idea, see Moshe Weinfeld, *Social Justice in Ancient Israel* (Jerusalem: Hebrew University Magnes Press, 2000); and Joshua Berman, *Created Equal: How the Bible Broke with Ancient Political Thought* (New York: Oxford University Press, 2008).

[68] On the role of community solidarity across "class" lines in the survival of Jewish communities, see the magnum opus of Simon Dubnov, *History of the Jews in Russia and Poland from the Earliest Times until the Present Day*, trans. I. Friedlaender (New York: Ktav Publishing House, 1975).

[69] In the past decades a new field, "Political Hebraism" has emerged, which traces the surprisingly powerful role that a "demotic" reading of the Bible played in the emergence of modern political thought. See the work of Yoram Hazony and the journal *Hebraic Political Studies* (Jerusalem: Shalem Press, 2005–present); and Eric Nelson, *The Hebrew Commonwealth: Jewish Sources and the Transformation of European Political Thought* (Cambridge Ma.: Harvard University Press, 2010).

[70] Both English words come from foreign words meaning "of the people" (Latin: *populus*; Greek: *demos*).

miracle stories, scapegoating narratives, even, in some cases, human sacrifice.[71] By and large, these appealing forms of religious practice tend to reinforce the status quo, to support the prime divider. Demotic religiosity, on the other hand, elevates, educates, demands discipline, renunciation, education, self-criticism. Like prime dividers and civil polities, these two forms of religiosity always manifest in real societies as some kind of mix. Too much demotic religiosity, however, can undermine the social order that popular forms are designed to support.[72]

For example, in the Middle Ages, the Catholic Church encouraged *popular* religiosity by presenting commoners with sculptured and painted illustrations of biblical narratives, the "Bible for the illiterate." The prime-divider assumption here is that commoners could not learn to read, that they were, culturally, a different species. As a result the Bible's contents were mediated by a professional, Latin-speaking, clerical elite, who, like Walter Map, did not view with favor any effort on the part of commoners to gain independent access to the text. Demotic religiosity, on the other hand, encouraged translation into the vernacular for a public capable of learning to read. Similarly, unlike Hong Xiuquan's attitude toward the Bible, in which honor and emulation of models of perfection predominated, demotic religiosity encourages the autonomy of a critical (and self-critical) reader.[73]

Demotic religiosity offers a key to understanding the emergence of democratic culture in two senses. On the one hand, in its stable, quotidian form, it produces the kind of reliable morally autonomous agents that must make up a critical mass of any society experimenting with civil polities. On the other, under conditions of apocalyptic enthusiasm, demotic millennialism can generate that critical mass, can inspire citizens to make a covenant, to enter into a contract, with each other, collectively, that they all commit to exercising their freedoms in such a way as not to impinge on the freedoms of others. The *Encyclopédie* defined the natural law as the product of "in each man an act of pure understanding that reasons in the silence of passions about what man may demand of his neighbor (*semblable*) and what his neighbor has a right to demand of him."[74]

Let us begin with the four proto-democratic cultural principles of civic polities as they appeared in ancient Hebrew and rabbinic traditions in their quotidian form, as exercised in "normal time."

---

[71] On human sacrifice and its relationship to priesthood and hierarchy, see the reflections of Rene Girard, *Things Hidden Since the Foundation of the World*, trans. Stephen Bann and Michael Metteer (Stanford: Stanford University Press, 1987); and Eli Sagan, *At the Dawn of Tyranny: The Origins of Individualism, Political Oppression, and the State* (New York: Knopf, 1985).

[72] Some historians have organized the history of Western Christendom around this antinomy: Jeffrey Burton Russell and Douglas W. Lumsden, *A History of Medieval Christianity: Prophecy and Order* (New York: Thomas Crowell, 1968). They were equally averse to discussing the death toll of the "Great Leap Forward," Frank Dikötter, *Mao's Great Famine: The History of China's Most Devastating Catastrophe (1958-1962)* (New York: Walker and Co., 2010).

[73] See above, p. 207.

[74] Diderot, "Droit naturelle," *Encyclopédie*, vol. 11, 116:9, online: http://artfl.uchicago.edu/images/encyclopedie/V5/ENC_5-116.jpeg, March 8 2010.

Isonomia

Despite a lack of democratic (elective) institutions, no polity in the ancient world so systematically pursued the principles of judicial equality as ancient Hebrew society.[75] Whether one takes the Decalogue as the founding document of the late second-millennium BCE Hebrew religious community, or a later (post-exilic) reformulation of a founding event (in which case it would be roughly contemporary to Solon and Kleisthenes),[76] these commandments, allegedly published on stone tablets, and applicable to all the members of the community regardless of status or wealth, constitute the earliest extant case of an isonomic code. And most remarkably, this particular code produced the most enduring case of an isonomic textual community—a civil polity—in history.[77]

The Bible, as a collection of texts composed over the course of more than a millennium, is the product of this isonomic community, and the subsequent texts bear every mark of adhering to these principles regardless of the form of government practiced in Israel.[78] The admonitions to judges insist on impartial justice, regardless of the status of the defendants: one should favor neither the rich (and take bribes) nor the poor (out of pity).[79] The privilege of Sabbath rest applies to all, including non-Jews, servants, slaves, even animals.[80] The principle of equal treatment on these matters of social privilege is explicitly enunciated at a number of points, in particular with reference to the poor, the defenseless, "the stranger in your midst"[81]: "You shall have one ordinance, both for the stranger, and for him that was born in the land."[82]

The rabbinical tradition elaborated on all of the passages in question and insisted that the pursuit of justice "without respect of person" (i.e., status) constituted a central task of Judaism. "To every judge who judges truly…the Scripture reckons it as if he had been a partner with God in the work of creation."[83] Moreover, clearly any decision Jewish judges handed down applied to themselves as well as to others, Gentiles as well as poor Jews.[84]

---

[75] Berman, *Created Equal*, 61–80, esp. 68–70.

[76] See John Bright, *The History of Israel* (London: S.C.M. Press, 1972), 141–45, esp. 142 n. 5.

[77] The issue of equal status before the law constitutes the single most fundamental difference between the Mosaic code and the Hammurabi code with which it has often been compared. Hammurabi's Code clearly gives legal privilege (greater compensation for damage) to a descending hierarchy of the king's subjects—the *amelu* (chieftans, men of substance), the *muskinu* (free men without substance), and the *ardu* (a large chattel population); it punishes theft with execution, as well as the failure to return slaves to their masters. Martha Roth, *Law Collections from Mesopotamia and Asia Minor* (Atlanta, Ga.: Scholars Press, 1995).

[78] Berman notes that although Hammurabi's Code was copied for almost a millennium, no extant decisions cite it; the opposite is true of biblical code, which pervades all subsequent legal reasoning and judgments (*Created Equal*, 84).

[79] Exodus 23:1–9; Deuteronomy 16:18–20; Berman, *Created Equal*, 68–70.

[80] Exodus 20:8–11; Deuteronomy 5:12–15.

[81] E.g., Leviticus 19:33–4.

[82] Exodus 12:49, Numbers 9:14.

[83] See the collection of exegetical sayings in C.G. Montefiore and H. Loewe, eds., *A Rabbinic Anthology* (New York: Schocken Books, 1974), 382–411.

[84] Ibid., no. 1055, 1056, p. 390–91.

Although not elaborated into an explicit doctrine, certain political implications of this notion of justice are clear from the biblical texts. For example, just rulers had no right to dispossess or confiscate property from individuals: both Moses and Samuel, when faced with objections to their rule, invoke as their primary defense the claim never to have taken another's ox or donkey;[85] and conversely, royal injustice is when the king takes from his subjects without their consent.[86] Such actions would scarcely be viewed by most rulers of the day as transgressions; and still fewer of their subjects would dare criticize them for it. As one commentator has pointed out, amid all the voices of the ancient world, the prophets stand as some of the few who denounced the "idolatry of power" with such fervor and impartial consistency.[87]

Literacy and Education

Although actual literacy did not reach high proportions in Israelite society until relatively late (in their history, but not in comparison with other cultures),[88] *access* to the text of the law, and encouragement of public knowledge of the law, constituted one of the highest priorities of the earliest communities.[89] By the time of the return from the first exile in the late sixth century BCE, public readings of the Torah (i.e., the Law) took place not only on the Sabbath, but also on the two main market days, Monday and Thursday, accompanied by translations into the vernacular of the day (*targumim*).[90] Such customs attest to the community's commitment to carry out the isonomic aims of the texts that they thus further shaped and transmitted.[91] Long before "literacy rates" had reached the unwonted proportions of a majority of men, oral transmission of the law and its commentary had involved the whole of Jewish society. The "people of the book" thus constitute the largest

---

[85] Numbers 16:15; 1 Samuel 12:3. See above, chapter 6, nn. 150–51.

[86] Nathan upbraids David for his adultery with the imagery of taking a poor man's lamb (2 Samuel 12); and Ahab and Jezebel, the archetypical tyrants, seize a commoner's vineyard and kill him when he refuses to sell to the king (1 Kings 21).

[87] Joshua Heschel, *The Prophets* (New York: Harper & Row, 1962), 1:159–86. Note the contrast between Akhenaten and Moses' monotheism on precisely the issue of expropriating property, above, chap. 6, n. 150.

[88] On literacy in ancient Israel, see the recent review of several books on the subject by William Schneidewind, "Orality and Literacy in Ancient Israel," *Religious Studies Review* 26 (2000): 327–32; on the larger context, see William V. Harris, *Ancient Literacy* (Cambridge Ma: Harvard University Press, 1991).

[89] For an excellent discussion of these issues, see Berman, "Egalitarian Technology: Alphabet, Text and Class," in *Created Equal*, 109–34.

[90] Josephus insists on the importance of these public readings, *Against Apion*, trans. Henry St. John Thackeray (New York: Putnam, 1926), 2.175–78, pp. 362–65.

[91] For a particularly good example of the demotic tendencies of rabbinic culture, see the account of the conflict between the aristocratic Rabban Gamliel and the more egalitarian rabbis, Joshua ben Hananiah and Akivah, recounted in the Babylonian Talmud (*Berachot*, 28a); discussion in Menachem Fisch, *Rational Rabbis: Science and Talmudic Culture* (Bloomington: Indiana University Press, 1997), 63–78.

enduring isonomic "textual community" in recorded history. Correspondingly, one might even argue that, the medieval elite's resistance to biblical translations represents a resistance to allowing commoners access to the isonomic law code embedded in the Hebrew Bible.

Manual Labor

The value of labor as a fundamental part of humanity's destiny appears throughout the Bible: indeed, God's first actions are deemed labor, from which he rests on the seventh day, and establishes thereby a model of how society should work in this regard. Of all the versions of that universal myth of a past Golden Age, Judaism's alone includes work;[92] similarly, the future age of perfection envisages a world where justice means each man enjoys the fruits of the labor of his own hands.[93] All the great leaders of the people worked: Abraham, Isaac, Jacob, Judah, Joseph, Moses, Saul, David, Amos, Elijah, and so on; and the ordinances established by Moses clearly place the tiller of the soil at the center of the new society. The first two kings went from the stable to the throne. The Wisdom literature repeatedly contrasts the well-being of the worker who eats from the labor of his own hands and the rich man who lives off the labor of others.[94]

The commandment of the Sabbath embodies the peculiar combination of manual labor and isonomia so characteristic of biblical legislation: "Six days shall you labor and do all your work; but the seventh day is the sabbath of the Lord your God. In it you shall not do any work, you, your son, your daughter, your manservant, your maid servant, your cattle, nor the stranger within your gates" (Exodus, 20:9–10). First it commands work to the owner of slaves (presumably a reminder necessary for the rich and powerful, and in distinct contrast to the behavior of the ruling class in Egyptian society); second, it explicitly commands rest to all including servants, Gentiles, even animals.

The contrast between this attitude and those found commonly in Greece and Rome, where foreign and slave labor provided the occasion to avoid manual labor, deserves attention beyond the obvious difference in the respect paid to commoners so strongly attested to in the Hebraic tradition.[95] For Hebrews and their later descendents, the Jews, whose emphasis lay not on logic and philosophy but on morality and ethics, manual labor did not exclude one from participating in the

[92] "And the Lord God took the man, and put him into the Garden of Eden *to work it* and to keep it" (Genesis 2:15).

[93] At that time—the end of days—the instruments of war (hence violent domination and dispossession of the working classes) are turned into agricultural instruments (tools of manual labor): Isaiah 2, Micah 4 (epigraph to chapter); S. Kalischer, "Die Wertschätzung der Arbeit in Bibel und Talmud," *Judaica: Festschrift zu Hermann Cohens siebzigstem Geburtstage* (Berlin: B. Cassirer, 1912), 589.

[94] Ecclesiastes 2:10, 15:12; Wisdom of Solomon 22:29; Psalms 104, 128:2.

[95] See Kalischer, "Wertschätzung," 583–84; also Moses I. Finley, "Technical Innovation and Economic Progress in the Ancient World," *Economic History Review*, ser. 2, 18 (1965): 29–45.

intellectual life of the culture; to the contrary, it was necessary. Hence, alone of cultures of the ancient Mediterranean, Hebrew society considered labor appropriate for all its members, including the intellectual class. "Rabbi" was not a legitimate profession but an avocation; these learned men were expected to have a trade.[96] Again, this hardly means that there were no class divisions in rabbinic communities, but as the tale of the rebellion against the aristocratically minded Raban Gamliel illustrates, there were mechanisms for rebuke on both the public and private scale.[97]

The perceived value of manual labor provides a key to a larger attitude in the biblical and rabbinical texts: the importance of the "commoners."[98] Whether protecting the rights of the powerless, providing a safety net for the poor, enjoining compassion and charity toward the disadvantaged, forbidding the exploitation of hired hands, or providing a periodic enfranchisement and a roughly egalitarian redistribution of property and status through the Sabbatical and Jubilee years, the social world envisaged by the biblical text is one in which the central figures are the simple, honest, working individual.[99] Of all the "high culture" texts from Antiquity, none gives so much information about working the land, trade, and crafts as the Bible and the Talmud.[100]

Transcending Honor-Shame Culture and Positive-Sum

The Hebrew Bible contains an extended discourse on the difference between integrity and honor, from the quintessential dilemma of Judah when faced with either admitting fault or killing his daughter-in-law Tamar for blackening his family's honor (Genesis 38), to the classic redefinition of the mighty man in Proverbs (16:32): "One who is slow to anger is better than the mighty, and one whose temper is controlled than one who captures a city."[101] Indeed, a number of

---

[96] See *Rabbinic Anthology*, 440–50.

[97] Note that Rabbi Joshua, one of the successful opponents of the aristocratic Gamliel in the Sanhedrin, was a poor blacksmith (above, n. 92).

[98] For a discussion of this term, see Peter Blickle, *The Revolution of 1525: The German Peasants' War from a New Perspective* (Baltimore: Johns Hopkins University Press), 123–24, 220 n. 43.

[99] See the injunctions against oppressing the disadvantaged (the common trio: widows, orphans, strangers) in such key texts as the "holiness code" (Leviticus 19–21); the two covenant commentaries (Exodus 22:21–28; and Deuteronomy 15:7–11, 24:17–22); payment of workers daily, no pledges overnight, general injunctions (Exodus 21, Leviticus 25, Deuteronomy 15); compare this with Solon's poem "On the Constitution of Athens," trans. David Shavin, *FIDELIO Magazine* 2: 2 (1993), online: http://www.schillerinstitute.org/fid_91-96/fid_932_solon.html, April 13, 2010. Aristotle, "The Constitution of Athens," 12.4 in *Ancient Greece: Documentary Perspectives* (Dubuque: Kendall Hunt Publishing, 1985), 6–7. For an extended survey of the Israelite material, see Weinfeld, *Social Justice in Ancient Israel*.

[100] See Jacob Neusner, *The Economics of the Mishna* (Chicago: University of Chicago Press, 1990).

[101] Note that Hong Xiuquan found the story of Tamar unacceptably shameful (Spence, *God's Chinese Son*, pp. 257–60). Proverbs 16:32, which is taken up as proof of the rabbinical formulation, "Who is mighty? He who conquers his own passions," *Pirkei Avot [Ethics of the Fathers]*, 4:1; *The Koren Siddur*, ed. trans. Rabbi Jonathan Sacks (Jerusalem: Koren Publishing, 2009), 660.

"psychological" commandments specifically target the zero-sum emotions, pro-hibiting envy,[102] vengeance,[103] even *Schadenfreude*.[104]

At the same time, the biblical text emphasizes positive-sum relations, and the generosity toward others that sustaining those relations demands. Abraham's voca-tion is to found a chosen people through whom "all the families of the world will be blessed"—in other words, the chosen people fulfill their destiny not when they are "on top," but when others are blessed. The commandment to "love your neighbor as yourself," exacts an empathy that makes mutual freedom possible. As a result, biblical legislation can prescribe a rigorously fair system of courts and judges, which rapidly (in the course of half a millennium) replaced the self-help justice system.[105]

Jesus' teachings as recorded in the New Testament take many of these demotic elements to even greater levels of intensity: rather than love your neighbor and help your enemy, he demands that people love their enemy;[106] rather than not bear a grudge and not take vengeance, he demands that one forgive seven times seventy and turn the other cheek. As a result, the ethical demands of the New Testament represent a massive attack on—indeed a superhuman negation of—the most elementary aspects of honor-shame culture. The contribution of such tendencies both to apostolic movements in the Middle Ages and to the most demotic Protestant movements contributed significantly to the emergence of both civil polities and their productive economies.[107]

Mosaic Utopian Legislation: Free Peasants without a Prime Divider

Indeed, one could take Mosaic legislation as a prescription for a (utopian) society of free and autonomous peasants who, rather than bowing before their lords, living

---

[102] "You shalt not covet your neighbour's house, you shalt not covet your neighbour's wife, nor his man-servant, nor his maidservant, nor his ox, nor his ass, nor any thing that is your neighbour's" (Exodus 20:17).

[103] "You shalt not bear a grudge or take vengeance" (Leviticus 19:18).

[104] "If you meet your enemy's ox or his ass going astray, you shalt surely bring it back to him again" (Exodus 23:4). For a discussion of rabbinic attitude toward the matter of shame (i.e., the importance of *not* embarrassing/humiliating others), see Jeffrey L. Rubenstein, *The Culture of the Babylonian Talmud* (Baltimore: Johns Hopkins University Press, 2003), 54–79.

[105] On the "cities of refuge," see Alexander Rofé, "The History of the Cities of Refuge in Biblical Law," *Deuteronomy: Issues and Interpretation* (Edinburgh: T. and T. Clark, 2002), 121–48; by the second com-monwealth (sixth century BCE), there were no more cities of refuge and the "redeemer of blood" had become a court appointee. While a half a millennium may seem like a long time, some Mediterranean cul-tures have yet to replace "self-help" justice (see Boehm, *Blood Revenge*) and Arab societies, below, p. 427.

[106] The Gospel of Matthew quotes Jesus saying, "You have heard that it was said, 'Love your neighbor, and hate your enemy.'" Nowhere does the Hebrew Bible enjoin hating one's enemies (at most, hating God's enemies, Ps 139:21), but specifically *not* hating your personal enemies.*

[107] On medieval demotic religiosity and its relationship with economic growth, see Landes, "Economic Development and Demotic Religiosity"; on the modern cases, see Max Weber, *Protestant Ethic and the Spirit of Capitalism*, ed. and trans. Stephen Kalberg (New York: Oxford University Press, 2008). All four of Weber's principle case studies—Calvinism, Methodism, Quietism, and Baptism—are profoundly "demotic" by my definition.

at the margins of subsistence, and farting their displeasure silently, "walk upright," and eat (meat) to satiety.[108] In that sense, the period of the judges, for all its recorded turbulence and moral failures, seems guided by the principles of a civil polity as defined above: self-regulating communities, united by religious commitments (including demotic pilgrimage rituals and egalitarian laws of work and rest) and a pervasive system of *isonomic* justice with charismatic (i.e., meritocratic) judges as the highest court of appeals. And underlying those social structures lies a profoundly anti-monarchical monotheistic principle of Hebraic origin: "No king but God."[109]

Of course, the reality is far from the ideal, especially when one considers the sordid details of both periods of judges and kings. But even that information, so embarrassing in the face of the ideal, reflects a biblical commitment to self-critical honesty, no matter how shameful. What great "people" tells the story of its own origins in slavery, taken out by a mighty God, whining and accusing its benefactor every step of the way? If self-criticism is a mark of overcoming the demands of public honor, then no ancient civilization can offer anything to compare with the corpus of self-accusing texts from the biblical account of the patriarchs through the prophetic denunciation of kings, to the immensely revealing narratives of the Talmud.

▪ DEMOTIC MILLENNIALISM AND THE PRIME DIVIDER

This, then, provides the context for the discussion of demotic millennialism, first broached among the varieties of millennialism in the opening chapter of this book. The high overlap between demotic religious values and the development of civil polities in the West suggests a link which demotic millennialism readily illuminates. Indeed, the very origins of "revolutionary" (i.e., cataclysmic apocalyptic), demotic millennialism arise in the contest between imperial hierarchies and the surviving Israelites after the Babylonian captivity, those from the tribe of Judah (i.e., the Jews).

---

[108] See the rabbinic blessing at the end of the meal: "and you have eaten to satiety…and the merciful one will bring us, upright, into our land…" *Koren Siddur*, pp. 980, 986.

[109] See discussion above, p. 27. For the two clear articulations of this principle, see Gideon's response to the offer of kingship (Judges 8:23) and Samuel's response to a request for a king (1 Samuel 8–11). Joshua Berman's formula for the freedom involved is "The Commoner's Upgrade from King's Servant to Servant King," *Created Equal*, 15–50. The ambiguity of the biblical and rabbinical corpus on kingship has produced a large and difficult literature. For the rabbinic debate over monarchy, see Gerald Blidstein, "The Monarchic Imperative in Rabbinic Perspective," *AJS Review* 7–8 (1982–83): 15–39. For a recent article on the role of anti-monarchical Talmudic thought on the emergence of the anti-monarchical strain of republicanism in seventeenth-century Latin Christendom, see Eric Nelson, "'Talmudical Commonwealthsmen' and the Rise of Republican Exclusivism," *Historical Journal* 50 (2007): 809–35.

These imperial conquering armies—Babylon, Persia, Greece, Rome—spread not only through their military might, but through their increasingly sophisticated ability to peel off the elites from the conquered cultures. And they found a readily serviceable seam along the prime divider. They could thus absorb the surviving and cowed conquered elites into the lower levels of their ruling class and together exploit conquered peoples.

Alone of these societies—and not without great difficulty—the Jews managed to withstand this process. Partly this came from their almost pathological tendency to self-criticism. While most of the "leaders" of ancient peoples interpreted their loss at the hands of their enemies as a sign that the conqueror's gods were stronger than theirs, the Jews preferred to believe that they had done something wrong, and their God was punishing them.[110] But their ability to resist came also, according to this analysis, from both their elite's commitment to solidarity *across* the prime divider and their demotic texts that demanded that commitment. Thus, while some of the Jewish elite did "Hellenize" and "Romanize," a critical mass remained committed to the common people more than to their personal careers.[111]

Of course, such an exegesis of history, in addition to the painful and often masochistic self-criticism involved in blaming your own people's immorality for losing at the hands of ruthless imperialists, also left the "true believer" with the desperately painful question of theodicy: how could God allow the evil to flourish and the good to suffer? Granted, God might use imperial oppressors as a scourge of his people, but how could he continue to punish them even after they had repented and returned? We are at the opposite end of the spectrum here from the Athenians' articulation of the principle: "Those who can do what they will; and those who cannot, suffer what they must." Jewish apocalyptic thinking reveals how at least some of those who "suffer what they must" interpreted their suffering as contingent. The "evil" present is a test, a prelude to the mighty victory of the Lord; and those who remain faithful to him regardless of how much they must suffer, will eventually get their reward.

So the more powerful the talons of empire dug into Israelite society, the more fantastic the millennial imagination became—about both the apocalyptic violence that would clear the way, and the magical abundance that would mark the messianic age. In this sense, the messianic imagination, with its rich complement of

---

[110] See, for example, the book of Lamentations attributed to Jeremiah, in which, for the first time, we find the expression "turn the other cheek" (3:3). Max Weber argued this position in 1917–19: *Ancient Judaism* (New York: Free Press, 1951), chap. 12; for a more recent analysis, see James Luther Adams, *An Examined Faith: Social Context and Religious Tradition* (Boston: Beacon Press, 1991), 234–43. For the rabbinical response to the apocalyptic catastrophe of the Temple's destruction in 70 CE as the product of "*sinat hinam*" or "gratuitous hatred," see the story of Kamtza and Bar-Kamtza recounted in the Babylonian Talmud, *Tractate Gittin*, f. 56a, and in the Midrash, *Lamentations Rabbah* 4:3.

[111] For a good analysis of the relationship between the Jewish elite and the Romans, see Martin Goodman, *The Ruling Class of Judaea: The Origins of the Jewish Revolt against Rome*, A.D. 66–70 (Cambridge: Cambridge University Press, 1987).

apocalyptic violence, represented the cry of anguish that arose from a culture torn at the seam, where there was no seam. The millennial vision imagined a time when honor was restored and the shame of subjection, the cognitive dissonance of having God's chosen people subjected, would be set aright.

Most Jewish apocalyptic of the time was resolutely passive: *God* would take vengeance for his oppressed people; heavenly forces would do the often cosmic damage, and reward the crushed but faithful believers. Jesus, as described in the Gospels, called to radical forms of repentance (Matthew 5), in the shadow of a violent apocalypse (Matthew 24). On the other side of that imminent Apocalypse, he and John the Baptist promised a "kingdom of heaven" in which the last (those who repented) would be first and the meek (the crushed) would inherit the land.[112]

Other Jews at the time took a more active stance. Adopting the demotic slogan, "No king but God," they dreamed of throwing off the Roman yoke and restoring Israel through their own violence. By the mid-60s CE, according to Josephus, these Zealots managed to arouse the entire Jewish people in Palestine into a disastrous revolt against Rome which ended in the destruction of the Temple in Jerusalem, the death and enslavement of about a million Jews, and the second exile.[113] The result: the victory of Roman imperialism and its prime-divider as the public transcript, and the spread, via both Christians and Jews, of some of the most demotic and anti-imperial religious traditions the world has ever seen, carrying a wide range of apocalyptic hopes for a future millennial kingdom.

▪ DEMOTIC MILLENNIALISM AND CIVIL POLITY

In the language of social science, the goal of demotic millennialism (as imagined in the millennial song of Isaiah/Micah) is to dismantle traditional, belligerent authoritarian and socially stratified (prime-divider) societies, and replace them with a universal network of free, productive civil polities, living in mutual and voluntary peace and exchange, enforced by a discourse of judicial fairness. It is at once a modern ideal and an ancient prophetic dream. And while at the approach of the year 2000, it seemed within reach, in the twenty-first century, the modern version seems no less outrageously hopeful than the prophetic one some 2700 years ago.[114]

One could attribute the astonishing success of civil polities over the last two centuries to sober reformist policies: wise men (and women) who instituted limited but significant changes that led, bit by bit, to better forms of government. This kind of Whig history, however, looks backward and evens out the bumps along

---

[112] See a good summary of the scholarship in Bart Ehrman, *Jesus: Apocalyptic Prophet of the New Millennium* (New York: Oxford University Press, 1999).

[113] Josephus, *Antiquities*, 18:23; *Jewish War*, 7:323; Goodman, *Ruling Class of Judaea*, 93–94; Jonathan Price, *Jerusalem Under Siege: The Collapse of the Jewish State, 66–70 C.E.* (Leiden, Brill, 1997).

[114] Compare Michael Walzer (ed.), *Toward a Global Civil Society* (Oxford: Berghan Books, 1997) with Lee Harris, *The Suicide of Reason* (New York: Basic Books, 2007).

the way. It is essentially vesperian and therefore constructs, *ex post defectu*, a linear narrative. It gets the story "straight."

From the millennial perspective, however, the key to "launching" an experiment in civil polity begins with apocalyptic enthusiasm, navigates disappointment, and stabilizes upon reentry to normal time. Initially fueled by the belief in an imminent radical transformation of the world, riding on the surge of enthusiasm such beliefs inspire, movements attempt to inaugurate a millennium of equality, and dignity of manual labor, made up of autonomous individuals inspired by mutual love for each other, voluntarily renouncing violence, envy, and greed. They fail of course, but to the degree that they pursued their goals "tautologically"—that is, remained faithful to their demotic values during the period of post-apocalyptic transition—to that degree their "reentry" into normal time can preserve significant features of their millennial ideal.[115]

So rather than return to prime-divider status, as most movements that either aim at a hierarchical millennium from the beginning (e.g., Akhenaten) or shift to that mode in the course of apocalyptic time (e.g., Taiping, Communism), some demotic movements can stabilize without necessarily returning to the status quo ante. Even the French Revolution, after its detour via terror and imperialism, returned to a monarchy significantly more meritocratic and socially mobile than the one it overthrew, and set in motion a dynamic (dialectic?) that by the end of the century produced a relatively stable republic. One might argue that sustaining civil polities is like bicycle riding: in order to get the experiment to work, you need to get an initial push of enthusiasm just to get the population to embrace the "social contract," discarding the prime divider political culture where such an embrace is virtually irrational. Viewed in this manner, one might argue a modified Weberian position: modern democracies are the unintended consequences of inevitably failed demotic millennial experiments.

The Ironies of Demotic Millennialism

The path to a (relatively) successful reentry is, however, perilous. Demotic millennial experiments are highly vulnerable in a world where *homo homini lupus*, man is a wolf to his fellow man. Ironically, the greatest danger that all these egalitarian millennialists run is success. At that point, the millennial presuppositions upon which the movement predicated its apocalyptic strategy—take power and get rid of the forces of evil (money, property, privilege, selfishness) and the "new human" (fellow, citizen, comrade) will spontaneously emerge—are *always* disappointed.

---

[115] The fate of the radical egalitarianism of some of the English millennial movements that participated in the "Civil War" of the mid-seventeenth century offer a good example of this process of constructive failure; see David Zaret, *Origins of Democratic Culture: Printing, Petitions and the Public Sphere in Early Modern England* (Princeton, N.J.: Princeton University, 2000). On tautological millennialism, see below, n. 122.

And as a result, the leaders of the movement often set in motion the transition from demotic freedoms to authoritarian control.

Whatever its millennial hopes and its apocalyptic urgencies, over time, demotic religiosity must make its peace with hierarchy. No matter how egalitarian the culture, strong elements of authoritarianism necessarily emerge. The fate of the Maccabean revolt, perhaps the first successful millennial movement whose fate the historian can follow closely, illustrates the process. Initially inspired by anti-imperial apocalyptic visions, and radically demotic in its goal—"each sat under his own fig and vine, and none made them afraid" (1 Maccabees 14:12)—the new regime, the Hasmoneans, turned into a troubling mimesis of Greek imperialism.[116]

A similar, if more lengthy, dynamic played out in the Christian journey to imperial glory. Demotic millennialism—sometimes pragmatic, sometimes magical, almost certainly shared by John the Baptist and Jesus—constitutes precisely what the Church fathers rejected as they formulated a salvific Christology that found favor above the prime divider and permitted the Christianization of the Roman Empire. The imperial fathers of the Catholic "Golden Age," for whom the promises of perfection lay in heaven not on earth, virulently denounced millennialism as carnal, as *Judaizing*:[117] carnal, because it takes the textual promises of a millennium of peace and abundance *literally*; Judaizing, because it expects the millennium to transform the *saeculum*.

Not surprisingly, this violent turn against the demotic millennialism of its origins drove Christian theologians ever more into the embrace of iconic, imperial millennialism: from "No king but God," to Eusebius' pregnant formula—"One God, one emperor."[118] Ironically, Eusebius, raged against "millennialism" as an insane and rabid belief completely at odds with Christian "truth," even as he articulated the principles of hierarchical millennialism. For those familiar with the twice-untold tales of vesperian historians, it is perhaps not so surprising that most Church historians have taken Eusebius at his word, considering him one of the great foes of millennialism, when he was one of the Church's most consequential hierarchical millennialists and only attacked the demotic brand.

Nietzsche "predicted" much of this behavior in his analysis of the envious *ressentiment* that undergirded the millennial "slave morality."[119] While they are powerless, the weak complain about the unfairness of aristocratic oppression and their

---

[116] Gerbern S. Oegema, *The Anointed and His People: Messianic Expectations from the Maccabees to Bar Kochba* (Sheffield: Sheffield Academic Press, 1998), 39–72.

[117] One might almost define the period as one in which millennialism became an increasingly and finally, with Augustine, overwhelmingly shunned belief.

[118] See above, pp. 24–25.

[119] The Nazi use of Nietzsche represents one of the great ironies of history since they arise in a cesspool of self-pitying *ressentiment* at loss of power—"stab in the back"—that Nietzsche so tirelessly denounced. See below, p. 356.

goal of an egalitarian society sounds noble. But when such arguments stem not from a desire to put an end to dominion, but to substitute your own dominion for that of those who now oppress you, the results of "attaining power" can veer rapidly from demotic to hierarchical.

The question that faces millennial historians at this point is not whether Nietzsche was right about Tertullian and the Athenians about the Melians.[120] Undoubtedly, there are people who only whine about fairness while they are weak, but as soon as they are strong, they will turn on others. There are unquestionably many *hommes (et femmes) de ressentiment* in the annals of millennial behavior— perhaps most of them. And one important branch of millennial rhetoric appeals to precisely such desires, among other things, for retribution.[121] Whole movements can be the product of envy and *ressentiment* and their impact, if they gain power, can be devastating.

But do all who speak prophetically speak in bad faith? And do all who listen and become aroused at this discourse listen in bad faith? The fate of millennial movements turns not on whether their presuppositions and predictions are wrong—they will always prove to be so—but on how believers handle the disappointment and what changes they go through when reentering normal time. The most self-destructive tend to be those that most readily abandon earlier, irenic positions and turn to a demonizing narrative that generates violence. The most constructive tend to cleave to the values of justice on whose wings they first rose from popularity to power—the dignity of manual labor and equality—what Mendel calls "tautological millennialism."[122]

The dilemma, of course, comes from the entirely predictable and entirely denied fact that taking power virtually guarantees that the movement faces disappointments, including the reappearance within the ranks of the new and redeemed people of all those corrupt and selfish attitudes that Augustine had insisted would exist till the very end of the *saeculum*. The new millennial body rapidly becomes a *corpus permixtum*, in which good and evil continue to struggle for control of human souls.

When demotic millennial movements face the failure—the *defectus*—in a position of power (e.g., successful revolutionary groups), they are faced with a particularly acute choice. Either they stick with their ethical ideology that force, even if necessary at the start, should rapidly shift to education and voluntarism, or they abandon it for a more cataclysmic, apocalyptic scenario in which they take an increasingly coercive role.[123] Most often, adherents, once engaged in apocalyptic time, resist giving up its promises. Instead, they "up the ante" and follow ever-more-radical paths. Like the Xhosa, they greet every disappointment by raising the stakes.

---

[120] On the Melians, see above, n. 11.

[121] O'Leary, *Arguing the Apocalypse*, 63–73, 83–84; Trompf, *Payback*; see below, chapter 10, on Marx's analysis of "crude communism" and the role of envy, see below, p. 315.

[122] Mendel, *Vision and Violence*, 83–84.

[123] See below, chapter 11.

The key to the inevitable apocalyptic reentry into normal time revolves around the way in which the leaders and power holders handle the imperfections that all millennial experiments must confront. Those that view even insider opposition as betrayal, who seize upon demonizing narratives about the sins of "others" (as was the case with the Xhosa and the Taiping), are capable of killing vast numbers of people. The Chinese *Great Peace* ceased only after some 20–35 *million* Chinese had lost their lives in a "total" millennial war, and their successors under Mao may have killed as many as 70 million of their own people, most of them in peacetime! The ideologies of revolutionary terror, *shahada*, and apocalyptic devastation come out of frustrated totalitarians, who, unable to coerce reality to fit their desires, conclude that only by destroying the world can they save it.[124]

Whatever the outcome, however, the early passions of apocalyptic movements make little sense without understanding the widespread appeal of demotic millennialism and its vision of a world at once free and just. This may or may not be the tone of the movement once both success and later failure take their toll. But *at origin*, religious movements, in particular monotheistic ones, draw deeply from this demotic well. People hold back from such visions out of a combination of fear of offending the powers that be and conviction that the world is a cruel place where such dreams designate one as a victim not a victor. But if the meme spreads fast enough in apocalyptic time and this "full-throated" hidden transcript comes roaring into public discourse, if it looks like the new world has become an irresistible force...then many will gladly join.

How these movements of demotic enthusiasm "turn out"—how they manage both the temptations of success (power) and the tribulations of failure (humiliation)—mark the character of a movement. The temptation of violence, especially in disappointment, makes Mendel's "tautological" millennialism—peaceful means lead to peaceful ends—difficult to achieve. Does repeated failure have any impact on such outrageous apocalyptic hopes? Does a learning curve exist over the long run of episodes repeating within a given culture for generations, centuries, millennia?

Yes and no. If we conceive of apocalyptic beliefs as memes, they have a tendency to mutate constantly in order to survive and to spread. Thus failure drives people to reshape their apocalyptic scenarios and their millennial visions of a "just" society, and in the West, in the period after printing, it tended to tether the messianic dream to more realistic and exacting standards, even to "dress it up" in more rational, scientific, even Greek and Roman *secular* clothing. In response to a God who perpetually tarried, the apocalyptic meme, rather than fading, moved further along the activist scale, and substituted faith in deliberate human actions for hopes of a divine intervention. But even as that may have weaned millennial hopefuls away from a deus ex machina, it has not rid us of the passion for a just—a perfect—society. Constant, repeated failures have not led to fewer but more apocalyptic

---

[124] Lifton, *Destroying the World to Save It.*

scenarios and millennial destinations, some long-term (Bacon's "project" for science),[125] some more immediate (secular revolutions).

■ THE ENLIGHTENMENT AND REVOLUTIONARY IDEOLOGY: SECULAR DEMOTIC MILLENNIALISM

For quite some time now, some scholars have argued that the Enlightenment secularized millennial dreams and formulated them in nonreligious terms.[126] As Kant put it: "Everyone can see that philosophy can have her belief in a millennium (Chiliasmus)... but her millenarianism is not wildly exuberant(*schwärnerisch*)."[127] John Mee notes: "The possibility of a Millennium wherein the world would be reformed into the perfect society had permeated deep within the thought patterns of Christian Europe over many centuries; its presence persists even in the most secular of the utopian projections that were essential to the eighteenth century's interest in progress."[128]

Most historians of the Enlightenment have, however, found these arguments either unconvincing or too banal for comment. To the extent that millennial discourse appears in the scholarly discussion, it revolves around the enthusiasm of identifiable millennialists for the Enlightenment project rather than the millennialism of the Enlightenment.[129] Any effort to move in the latter direction inevitably runs afoul of specialists in the field, "splitters" who object to lumping something so variegated, but primarily rational and secular, as the Enlightenment, with something so irrationally religious as millennial enthusiasm.[130]

---

[125] Steven Matthews, "Francis Bacon's Scientific Apocalypse," *End that Does*, 97–114 and, more broadly on science as a millennial project, see Noble, *The Religion of Technology*, chap. 6; and several other articles in *The End that Does.*

[126] Lee Tuveson, *Millennium and Utopia: A Study in the Background of the Idea of Progress* (Berkeley and Los Angeles: University of California Press, 1949); more recently, David Nash, "The Failed and Postponed Millennium: Secular Millennialism Since the Enlightenment," *Journal of Religious History* 24, no. 1 (2000): 70–86.*

[127] *Idea for a Universal History from a Cosmopolitan Point of View* (1784); from Immanuel Kant, *On History*, trans. Lewis White Beck (New York: Bobbs-Merrill Co., 1963), thesis 8, online: German, http://www.korpora.org/Kant/aa08/027.html, April 13, 2010. On the derogatory cluster of terms *schwärmerisch, Schwärmerei, Schwärmgeister*, which Luther introduced in the sixteenth century, see below n. 130. chapter 10, n. 66.

[128] John Mee, "Millenarian Visions and Utopian Speculations," in *The Enlightenment World*, ed. Martin Fitzpatrick (New York: Routledge, 2004), 536–50, citation, p. 536.

[129] Recently a series of studies edited by Richard Popkin and others have taken up the former issue with regard to early modern period: *Millenarianism and Messianism in Early Modern European Culture*, 4 vols., International Archives of the History of Ideas (Dordrecht: Kluwer Academic Publishers, 2001). See especially the final two volumes: James E. Force and Richard H. Popkin, eds., *The Millenarian Turn: Millenarian Contexts of Science, Politics and Everyday Anglo-American Life in the Seventeenth and Eighteenth Centuries* and John Christian Laursen and Richard H. Popkin, eds., *Continental Millenarians: Protestants, Catholics, Heretics.*

[130] It is in vain that one looks for discussions among historians of the Enlightenment on the role of millennialism, even those where one might expect it, like Franco Venturi, *Utopia and Reform in the Enlightenment* (Cambridge: Cambridge University Press, 1971). On "lumpers versus splitters," see above, Introduction, n. 3. On the differing attitudes toward "enthusiasm" (*Schwärmerei*) in precisely these several decades of the mid-late eighteenth century, see Knox, *Enthusiasm.*

In the terms of this book, the Enlightenment "project" can be expressed as follows: (1) the secularization of demotic millennialism's goal: a society without a prime divider, (2) a progressive process of transformation toward that end, and (3) by the end of the eighteenth century, a rapidly quickening set of expectations that produced an active apocalyptic episode known to us as the French Revolution.[131]

Improving the World and the Notion of Historical Progress

Enlightened thinkers developed an increasingly strong sense of progress through history over the course of the eighteenth century, which they understood as the increasingly rational, egalitarian, and humane organization and regulation of society.[132] For Kant, this was nothing less than "the realization of Nature's secret plan to bring forth a perfectly constituted state as the only condition in which the capacities of mankind can be fully developed, and also bring forth that external relation among states which is perfectly adequate to this end."[133] He anticipated a still-distant world in which war will seem senseless, and an "international government for which there is no precedent in world history" that will arbitrate between nations, the secular (and equally ethereal) replacement for a God who "will judge and rebuke nations…" (Isaiah 2:4).

Many figures in the Enlightenment felt that they participated in a great historical process that began with the "revolution" of the printing press, "and whose progress nothing can stop; the force, wealth, and happiness of nations have become the prize of the enlightenment."[134] Notes Baker: "It was a fundamental claim of the Enlightenment that it represented a process of universal transformation, a world-historical revolution in human affairs."[135]

> In this sense, the Enlightenment itself was a profound revolution, already under way: Lived as a process of cultural transformation, it was already separating past from present and reorienting expectation toward the future. "I see with pleasure that an immense republic of cultivated minds is forming in Europe," wrote Voltaire to Prince Golitsyn in

---

[131] For a more detailed analysis, see website: appendices.

[132] J. Bury, *The Idea of Progress* (London: MacMillan, 1920), chap. 8; Robert Nesbitt, "History of the Idea of Progress," in *Literature of Liberty*, ed. Leonard P. Liggio, 2:1 (1979): 7–37; more recently, G. M. Ditchfield, "Religion, 'Enlightenment' and Progress in Eighteenth-Century England," *Historical Journal* 35, no. 3 (1992): 681–87; James H. Moorhead, "Between Progress and Apocalypse: A Reassessment of Millennialism in American Religious Thought, 1800–1880," *Journal of American History* 71, no. 3 (1984): 524–42. For the relationship to (and derivation from) millennialism, see Tuveson, *Millennium and Utopia*.

[133] Immanuel Kant, *Idea for a Universal History from a Cosmopolitan Point of View*, para. 8; in Kant, *On History*, trans. L. W. Beck (New York: Bobbs-Merrill Co., 1963), online: http://www.marxists.org/reference/subject/ethics/kant/universal-history.htm, April 3, 2010.

[134] Nicolas de Condorcet, *The Progress of the Human Mind*; cited in Baker, *Inventing the French Revolution* (New York: Cambridge University Press, 1990), 213.

[135] Ibid., 214.

1767. "Enlightenment is spreading on all sides...In the past fifteen years or so a revolution has occurred in people's minds that will mark a great epoch."[136]

Condorcet's essay, published after his death in 1796, but composed while on the run from his Jacobin enemies in 1794, offers one of the most eloquent expressions of this historico-philosophical faith.[137] And his "reactionary" foes immediately perceived the millennial heresy embedded therein, and denounced the "apocalypse of this new gospel."[138] Carl Becker formulated the orientation: "To the future the Philosophers therefore look, as to a promised land, a new millennium."[139] Or, as Richard Rorty recently described the "political project" of the Enlightenment, "to create heaven on earth: a world without caste, class, or cruelty":[140] in my terms, a world without a prime divider.

One might posit as a critical dimension of all millennialism that the more secular the outlook, the more active its apocalyptic scenarios. Without an omnipotent God to intervene, you must do it yourself. Of course, the passive apocalyptic eschatological scenario favored by the ecclesiastical authorities in Europe—pie in the sky by and by—did not exhaust the religious options. On the contrary, demotic millennialism with an active transformative apocalyptic scenario represented the best of both secular and religious ideologies for transforming *this world*.

Enlightenment and Revolution

The arguments over the relationship between the Enlightenment and the French Revolution have raged from the time of the events themselves to the present, often at the mercy of complex and convoluted ideological agendas.[141] I neither want to "accuse" or "credit" the Enlightenment with, or "hold it responsible for" the Revolution and its excesses. My argument is that the Enlightenment both accommodated and reinforced certain demotic millennial tropes that, in turn, produced a particularly powerful apocalyptic movement—the French Revolution—in which people who believed they were carrying out the "true goal" of the Enlightenment, were the central actors. Not for them the long-term patience of Kant's faith in a providential progress. *Now* was the time.

[136] Ibid.

[137] Keith Michael Baker, "On Condorcet's 'Sketch,'" *Daedalus* 133, no. 3, *On Progress* (2004): 56–64.

[138] Ibid. on Louis de Bonald.

[139] Carl Becker, *The Heavenly City of the Eighteenth-Century Philosophers* (New Haven, Conn.: Yale University Press, 1932), 118. See further elaboration of precisely this theme, which Becker did not pursue in detail, in Darrin McMahon, "Happiness and the Heavenly City of the Eighteenth-Century Philosophers: Carl Becker Revisited," *American Behavioral Scientist* 49 (2006): 681–86.

[140] Richard Rorty, "The Continuity between Enlightenment and 'Post-Modernism,'" in *What's Left of Enlightenment? A Postmodern Question*, ed. Keith Michael Baker and Peter Hanns Reill (Stanford: Stanford University Press, 2001), 19. Rorty continues: "Despite the need for patience, this goal is as desireable as ever." Of course, patience is precisely what the rooster abhors.

[141] Dorinda Outram, *The Enlightenment* (Cambridge: Cambridge University Press, 1995), 126–40.

Perhaps because of the Enlightenment's own explicitly anti-religious discourse, however, political and social historians (themselves largely "secular") tend to ignore the parallels between religious millennialism and the ideology of the Enlightenment.[142] For many modern historians, who see in the Enlightenment their own genealogy, the key players—and the most striking new ones on the scene, the most modern—were those figures who played by the new rules of the "Republic of Letters," the public sphere, where reason and transparency ruled.[143] Here free-thinkers stripped away the mystifications and superstitions of religion—what Blake called "the mind-forged manacles"—and replaced them with a moral reason built on the axiomatic "equality of man."

And yet, just as the demotic millennialism of an earlier (medieval and early-modern) era had violently opposed the Church as an agent of Antichrist, and sought to bring about a just egalitarian society on earth, so did the gospel of reason that the revolutionaries invoked.[144] In this sense, the Enlightenment's dream of a society based on reason, equality, brotherhood, transparency/honesty, and justice represents a secular version of the millennial dream, all the more potent *because* secular. If the medieval chiliast awaited God's intervention (even after over-throwing the "powers that be"), the modern, enlightened one considered humanity the millennial agent.

The very slogan *liberté, égalité, fraternité* constitutes a lapidary reformulation of the demotic millennial ideal expressed in the prophetic expectation of a time when honest laborers would live free from a rapacious aristocracy and share the fruits of their labors in fellowship.

- *Liberty*: "You will proclaim freedom throughout the land..." (Leviticus 25:10, Isaiah 61:1).
- *Equality* (before the law): "They will beat their swords into plowshares..." (Isaiah 2:4); "When Adam delved and Eve span, who was then the gentleman?"
- *Fraternity*: "On that day, says the Lord of Hosts, everyone of you shall invite his neighbor to come under his vine and under his fig (Zechariah 3:10)."[145]

---

[142] Ironically, in defending the Enlightenment from Becker's criticisms, Peter Gay makes precisely Becker's point about the millennial tradition: "The philosophes were, above all, radical social reformers...impatien[t] to get to work...[they] knew exactly what they were doing; they were building a new earthly city": "Carl Becker's *Heavenly City*," in *The Party of Humanity: Essays in the French Enlightenment* (New York: Knopf, 1964), 192–93. Note the sly anti-Augustinianism of the formula "new earthly city."

[143] Jürgen Habermas, *The Structural Transformation of the Public Sphere: An Inquiry into a Category of Bourgeois Society*, trans. Thomas Burger (Cambridge, Mass.: MIT Press, 1991). For a critique of Habermas that focuses specifically on his secular prejudices and places a key moment in the emergence of the public sphere a century earlier, see Zaret, *Origins of Democratic Culture*.

[144] Mendel, *Vision and Violence*, 108–15; Mee, "Millenarian Visions."

[145] On the origins of the slogan in early modern France, see George Huppert, *The Style of Paris: Renaissance Origins of the French Enlightenment* (Bloomington: Indiana University Press, 1999), chap. 4.

Because the philosophers of the previous centuries had systematically reformulated the demotic principles of monotheistic theology into the reasoning of natural law, they presented such matters not as products of the religious mind, but as axiomatic, as obvious to "reason." "We hold these truths to be self-evident..." wrote the Francophile Thomas Jefferson in 1776, and then went on to articulate an idea whose intellectual inspiration may have been Stoic notions of natural law, but whose emotional commitments and implementation on a society-wide scale came from apocalyptic and millennial readings of a demotic Bible.[146] Millennialism is, above all, a form of applied social mysticism.

Such values derived from more than mere "logic," as the appeal to our rights-granting "Creator" and Kant's elision between "nature" and "providence" suggest.[147] The revolutions inspired by this radically demotic creed animated both the classical and nascent romantic strains of European culture.[148] Conceptually, ideologically speaking, the millennial dimension of Enlightenment moral and political ideology is a matter of how full or empty any historian sees the glass. Certainly there are plenty of issues in which the new, secular ideology self-consciously distanced itself from the unsavory enthusiasms of millennialism.[149] And, as Karl Mannheim points out, the ideology of systematic reason in establishing political organizations attempted to reorient hopes from a boundless and time-based expectation (with the emphasis on the destruction of the old system), to a bounded, spatially oriented project (with emphasis on the construction of a new one).[150]

These distinctions between revolution and millennialism, however, may be more conceptual than actual. When the adepts of the new, secular approach, entered into the apocalyptic time warp of revolution, they ended up behaving much more like millennialists of the older variety. As we shall see, when the French Revolution failed in its efforts to engineer the new nation with its new citizens, it turned increasingly to the more classic apocalyptic jazz, turning "Reason" into a religious cult, and reevaluating upward just how much destruction was necessary to succeed.

What makes them part of the same general category is the shared qualities of outrageous hope and the necessary disappointment to which any dramatic effort to effectuate that hope doomed its disciples, no matter what their worldly success.

---

[146] On the millennialism of the American Revolution, see Bloch, *Visionary Republic*; J. F. C Harrison, *The Second Coming: Popular Millenarianism, 1780-1850* (New York: Routledge & Kegan Paul, 1979). For an example of the millennial demotic reading of the demotic Bible, see Malcolm Chase, "From Millennium to Anniversary: The Concept of Jubilee in Late Eighteenth- and Nineteenth-Century England," *Past and Present* 129 (1990): 132-47.

[147] Kant, *Idea for a Universal History*, para. 9.

[148] Blake (above, chapter 1) provides the best example of the enthusiasm for revolution on the part of a proto-romantic poet. See below, chapter 9, pp. 250-53.

[149] The distaste, even revulsion, against enthusiasm comes from both the secular and the religious perspective. Knox's *Enthusiasm* is largely a compendium of millennial movements in Christianity from its earliest centuries.

[150] Mannheim, *Ideology and Utopia*, 196.

As a result, we find that just as religious millennial movements have a wide range of variant responses to the failure of their expectations, so do modern secular ones. Indeed, one might argue, these latter are like the little girl with the curl: when they are good, they're very, very good, and when they're bad, they are terrifyingly horrid. The connections become particularly clear when one maps the French Revolution on the apocalyptic curve.

9 Democratic Millennialism

French Revolution (1789–1815 CE)

> …crying *Empire is no more! and now the lion and the wolf shall cease.*
> Let the Priests of the Raven of dawn no longer, in deadly black, with
> hoarse note curse the sons of joy!
> Nor his accepted brethren—whom, tyrant, he calls free—lay the bound
> or build the roof!
> Nor pale Religion's lechery call that Virginity that wishes but acts not!
> For everything that lives is Holy! (William Blake)[1]

■ MILLENNIAL DIMENSIONS OF THE FRENCH REVOLUTION

The tale of the French Revolution is familiar to Western ears. It constitutes a key story in the *grand narrative* of Western freedom and stands alongside the American Revolution as one of the two inaugurating events of the modern world.[2] In terms of the definitions used in this book, the French Revolution as a whole constitutes a *progressive demotic millennial* movement—one inspired by a desire to *perfect the world* through *egalitarian* ideals. It entered apocalyptic time with an *active, transformative* scenario—*legislate* the just society in the context of widespread popular enthusiasm. But gradually, as the "voluntaristic" effort failed, the leaders of the movement increasingly shifted to more violent tactics, and with the inauguration of what they called the "Terror," adopted an *active cataclysmic scenario* (only through merciless violence could the transformation come). Eventually, the movement ended up in *hierarchical millennialism*—the Napoleonic empire. The return to monarchy in 1815 marks the *return to normal time*.

We have already discussed the way in which the Enlightenment secularized certain key demotic millennial themes, shifting the apocalyptic transition decisively toward an active transformative scenario. Matters ran in both directions. "Serious and respectable" millennialists like Richard Price and Joseph Priestly,

---

[1] Blake, conclusion to *Marriage of Heaven and Hell*.

[2] Ferenc Feher, ed., *The French Revolution and the Birth of Modernity* (Berkeley and Los Angeles: University of California Press, 1990).

despite their transformative (gradualist) beliefs, nonetheless viewed the French Revolution with great enthusiasm as the fulfillment of prophecy.[3]

The extraordinary career of Moses Dobruška, a Moravian disciple (and nephew) of the Jewish messianic antinomian, Jacob Frank, illustrates the close connection between the secular and religious manifestations of demotic millennialism—with Masonry as an intermediary.[4] After the collapse of Frankism, Dobruška handled his cognitive dissonance by moving westward, taking on a German identity (and a title of nobility) as a Freemason named Franz Thomas von Schönfeld. There he circulated easily among an aristocracy fascinated by his ability to incorporate Kabbalistic symbols into Masonic discourse. But by 1791, the call of revolution drew him and his brother to Paris where they joined in Jacobin circles. Here he found a new, secular, actively universalist outlet for his frustrated millennial yearnings.

Under his new name, Junius Frey, Moses fought for the Revolution; indeed, he became one of the Jacobin's most prolific ideologues, openly rejecting the obscurantism of the b iblical Moses for the radical passions of (his reading) of the Enlightenment philosophers (Locke, Rousseau, Kant) and the promise of "liberty for all."[5] Writing to his son just before his execution along with Danton and others, he urged him: "…despite all I have suffered for Liberty, you must come [with your mother and two sisters] live in Republican France and leave the impure soil of the Austrian tyrants. I have only one regret, to not have had the joy of seeing the consolidation of the Liberty of this immortal people in my lifetime…Paris, 29 Ventôse, year 2 of the Republic."[6]

In apocalyptic times, passionate people—roosters—transgress normally insurmountable boundaries, including the one that separates religious and secular. William Blake's utterly original visionary work illustrates how easily such boundaries could be crossed. His enthusiasm for both the American and French Revolutions—despite the fact that the American one challenged his own nation, Albion—reflects his uncompromising commitment to the demotic war on empire.[7]

---

[3] Jack Fruchtman, *The Apocalyptic Politics of Richard Price and Joseph Priestley: A Study in Late Eighteenth-Century English Republican Millennialism*, Transactions of the American Philosophical Society 73, no. 4 (Philadelphia: Diane Publishing, 1983) on their gradualism, 81–93; on their response to the Revolution in France, see Clarke Garrett, "Joseph Priestley, the Millennium, and the French Revolution," *Journal of the History of Ideas* 34, no. 1 (1973): 51–66.

[4] Gershom Scholem, *De frankisme au jacobinisme: La vie de Moses Dobruška, alias Franz Thomas von Schöfeld alias Junius Frey* (Paris: Gallimard, 1981).

[5] He and his brother received a certificate attesting to their bravery in the assault on the Tuileries, June 10, 1792, on which see Albert Mathiez, *The French Revolution*, trans. Catherine Phillips (New York: Grosset & Dunlap, 1964), 115; Scholem, *De frankisme au jacobinisme*, 69. Note that although Mathiez and other French historians were aware of the role of these Eastern Jews in the revolution, they were unaware of their millennial origins, something that Scholem pointed out (pp. 10–22). On his ideological writings, see Junius Frey, *Philosophie sociale dédiée au people français par un citoyen de la Section de la République française*, June 26, 1793; discussion in Scholem, *De frankisme au jacobinisme*, 72–76.

[6] Scholem, *De frankisme au jacobinisme*, 89.

[7] On Blake's radicalism, see David Erdman, *Blake, Prophet against Empire: A Poet's Interpretation of the History of his own Times* (Princeton, N.J.: Princeton University Press, 1954); and E.P. Thompson, *Witness Against the Beast: William Blake and the Moral Law* (New York: New Press, 1995); Robert Rix, *William Blake and the Cultures of Radical Christianity* (Burlington VT: Ashgate Publishing, 2007), 121–35.

At the height of the enthusiastic phase of the French Revolution, he wrote "A Song of Liberty," which concluded his *Marriage of Heaven and Hell* (epigraph to this chapter).[8]

Demotic strains of Christian religiosity, from the Huguenots and their Catholic cousins, the Jansenists, informed such work as the "Declaration of the Rights of Man," and the anti-monarchical reasoning that justified regicide.[9] The Universal Declaration of the Rights of Man adhered closely to the principles of demotic millennial legislation: equality before the law, dignity of manual labor, and freedom (of speech) for the individual. One of the earliest paintings publishing the rights has them surrounded by Masonic symbolism and inscribed on two tablets of stone: the new universal legislation.[10]

The first phase of the French Revolution, then, takes the form of a systematic dismantling of a prime-divider society and systematic constructing of a "civil polity" in which egalitarian rules, enforced by a discourse of fairness replaced a society of legal privilege and aristocratic dominion. It is precisely the systematic and relatively pragmatic effort to dismantle the old and construct an alternative political system that political scientists consider the key element that "medieval": distinguishes medieval millennial uprisings from modern revolutions. In terms of following the course of both the ideologies and the enthusiasms these ideas have had, however, this distinction does not so much separate the two phenomena as it does distinguish them as variants within the millennial worldview. More empirically (and technologically) based, more dedicated to systematic reasoning than to inspirations and revelations, modern revolutionary thought is, essentially, a more effective form of millennialism. But, like all perfectionist impulses, such effectiveness did not create a millennium; it merely meant that the failure of the attempt proved far more consequential than earlier forms.

How then did such non-, even anti-religious beliefs have anything to do with millennialism? According to Michelet, the secular turn of millennialism came—at last—from a shift from passive to active apocalyptic scenarios, which involved a mutation in the response to the failure of apocalyptic prophecies. Countless times,

---

[8] See Robert Rix, "William Blake's 'A Song of Liberty,'" *Explicator* 60:3 (2002): 131–34, who sees in the "accepted brethren" a reference to the battles within the Masonic movement over these issues.

[9] On the well-known links between Calvinist thought and egalitarian revolution (which among other things gave the English the Commonwealth), see Dale Van Kley, *The Religious Origins of the French Revolution: From Calvin to the Civil Constitution, 1560–1791* (New Haven, Conn.: Yale University Press, 1996), On Jansenists, see below, n. 75; Roger Chartier's *The Cultural Origins of the French Revolution* (Durham, N.C.: Duke University Press, 1991), chap. 5–6; and Dale Van Kley, "The Jansenist Constitutional Legacy in the French Prerevolution, 1750–1789," *Historical Reflections* 13 (1986): 393–454. On the Protestant genealogy of anti-monarchical republicanism and its debt to an anti-monarchical rabbinic reading of Deuteronomy 17, see Nelson, "Talmudical Commonwealthsmen" (above, chapter 8, n. 110).

[10] Musée Carnavalet, Paris; 1789 oil on wood painting of a stone monument. See Jonathan P. Ribner, *Broken Tablets: The Cult of the Law in French Art from David Delacroix* (Berkeley and Los Angeles: University of California Press, 1993).

an omnipotent and allegedly loving God had failed to appear and save the masses crushed by a cruel aristocracy. The wretched of the earth decided that they could wait for divine intervention no longer; that their freedom was *their* task. With his characteristic passion and empathy, Michelet meditated on the long and cruel history of the French commoner: "...and my very heart bled in contemplating the long resignation, the meekness, the patience, and the efforts of humanity to love that world of hate and malediction under which it was crushed...Right [just law], though postponed, shall have its advent; it will come to sit in judgment, on the dogma and on the world. And *that day* of Judgment will be called the Revolution."[11]

Popular Excitation: The Onset of Apocalyptic Time

In one sense, one can mark the first stirrings of apocalyptic time in France with the American Revolution. Circles of intellectuals all over Europe, but especially in France, showed immense enthusiasm for events triggered by "the shot heard round the world." One French observer noted: "The independence of the Anglo-Americans is the event most likely to accelerate the revolution that will bring happiness to earth. It is in the breast of this nascent Republic that lie the true treasures that will enrich the world."[12]

Plays, essays, poetry, and public displays of enthusiasm rippled across Europe from Paris to Moscow as an informed public followed the news from the new continent. "There is a hundred times more enthusiasm for this revolution in any café in Paris than there is in all the United States together," commented Louis de Portail on his return to Paris in 1777. Adam Zamoyski noted:

> Many believed that something in the nature of a miracle was taking place, that a whole society was throwing off not only the shackles of monarchical denomination but also the cultural and spiritual taints of the old world, that it was reinventing itself as an entirely new kind of human polity. It seemed to be on the point of bringing about the chiliastic dream of a utopian state on earth, to make up for the paradise which the children of the Enlightenment no longer believed in.[13]

As with the Xhosa, international news excited the apocalyptic fervor of a semiotically aroused people. But here, rather than wild rumors transformed to suit wild imaginations, it was real news, enflaming the most sophisticated elements of European society.

The enthusiasm reached new heights in August 1788, when King Louis XVI's call for an Estates General had an electrifying effect on the larger population,

---

[11] Jules Michelet, *History of the French Revolution*, ed. Gordon Wright (Chicago: University of Chicago, 1967), 28, 30.

[12] Quoted in Bernard Fay, *L'espritré volutionnaire en France et aux Etats Unis à la fin du XVIIIe siècle* (Paris: Edouard Champion, 1925), 133; cited by Adam Zamoyski, *Holy Madness: Romantics, Patriots and Revolutionaries, 1776–1871* (New York: Viking Press, 2000), 19.

[13] Zamoyski, *Holy Madness*, 20.

including the peasantry. Some took the call for electing representatives as a signal that the time had come to abolish the legal privileges of the Church and aristocracy. In January 1789, Abbé Sieyès published his groundbreaking essay on "What is the Third Estate?" which eloquently rejected any role for the first two, privileged, estates. Many peasants, for their part, assumed that the king sided with them; that evil came from his administrators and the aristocracy, and that he would soon show his true love for his people openly.[14] As one delegate from Aix noted at the time:

> The lower classes of the people are convinced that when the Estates General sat to bring about the regeneration of the kingdom we would see a *total and absolute change*, not only in present procedures, but also in conditions and income… The people have been told [sic] that the king wishes *every man to be equal*, that he wants neither bishops nor lords; *no more rank, no more tithes nor seigniorial rights*. And so these poor misguided people believe they are exercising their rights and obeying their king.[15] (Italics mine).

Lefebvre comments that both peasants and bourgeois viewed the calling of the estates as presaging a miraculous change in men's fates.

> It awoke hopes both dazzling and vague of a future when all would enjoy a better life… This vision of the future united the heterogeneous elements of the Third Estate and became a dynamic source of revolutionary idealism. Among the common people it gave to the Revolution a character that can be called mythical, if myth is taken to mean a complex of ideas concerning the future which generate energy and initiative. In this sense the Revolution in its early stages can be compared to certain religious movements in nascent form, when the poor gladly discern a return to paradise on earth… At the same time this great hope inflamed fearful passions, from which the bourgeoisie was not exempt. The revolutionary mentality was imbued with them; the history of the period bears their deep imprint.[16]

Albert Mathiez also remarked on the "messianic hope of regeneration" surrounding 1789, an observation confirmed by the medievalist Gabriel Monod, who wrote an introduction to his work.[17] While some of Mathiez's historiographical "enthusiasm"

---

[14] James Scott invokes this response as a classic example of how what officials proclaim (public transcript) and what people hear (private transcripts) can differ quite dramatically. And in this case, the call for electing representatives invited a public expression of these private transcripts that marks precisely what Scott considers the most dangerous moments in social dynamics: the potential breach into the public sphere of private transcripts. In particular, peasants project their own desires on rulers (*Domination*, 147–48).

[15] M. de Caraman, representative of Aix, cited by Georges Lefèbvre, *The Great Fear of 1789: Rural Panic in Revolutionary France* (Princeton, N.J.: Princeton University Press, 1973), 39–40, italics mine; cited in Scott, *Domination*, 146.

[16] Georges Lefebvre, *The French Revolution from Its Origins to 1793*, trans. Elizabeth Moss Evanson (New York: Columbia University Press, 1962), 116.

[17] Albert Mathiez, *Contribution sà l'histoire religieuse de la révolution Française* (Paris: F. Alcan, 1907), 32; Gabriel Monod, "Introduction," p. i–iv.

may reflect a (Marxist) retrospective perspective, as a description of the Revolution (for which "1789" becomes a symbol), it also accurately reflects contemporary feelings.

Nor were these expressions of a secular millennialism alone in responding to the French Revolution. Many religious millennialists, both in favor of and opposed to the French Revolution, interpreted it as a fulfillment of the prophecies of yore, not only biblical, but also the prophetic works of earlier figures like Nostradamus.[18] Millennial enthusiasm, as it so often does, transgressed the most "sacred" of boundaries.

As we have seen, the first critical moment in the career of a millennial movement comes when its apocalyptic discourse—now is the time to fundamentally change the social order—enters the public sphere. Normally such boldness results in immediate repression. Here, these voices not only did not get repressed, they became empowered.

And typically, women, even commoner women, played a powerful role. Vociferous crowds of men and *women*, inspired by radical egalitarianism, attended the discussions of the Estates General from its inception on May 5, and, if only by their vociferous presence, contributed to decision-making.[19] Rabble rousers, the wives of Jacobins and Sans Culottes who filled the galleries of the revolutionary tribunals with their noisy opinions, "played the role of firebrands."[20] A police chief wrote in a report echoed by countless others: "It is mainly the women who are stirred up, women who in their turn communicate all their frenzy to men, heating them up with their seditious propositions and stimulating the most violent effervescence."[21] This extraordinary popular voice, so important in early stages of a successful millennial movement, played a key role in the radicalization of the French revolutionary movement both in terms of its demands and in terms of its resort to violence, as in the case of the Bastille.[22]

Of course, as any student of millennial revolts knows, these passions can easily swing from wild enthusiasms to paranoid panic: once the challenge to the "old

---

[18] See discussions in Weber, *Apocalypse*, 106–17; Georges Minois, *Histoire de l'avenir* (Paris: Fayard, 1996), 444–48. Ironically, no one made use of the most extraordinarily accurate prophecy, that of Pierre d'Ailley who, in the 14th century predicted the Apocalypse in 1789; see Laura A. Smoller, *History Prophecy, and the Stars: The Christian Astrology of Pierre D'Ailly, 1350–1420* (Princeton, N. J.: Princeton University Press, 1994).

[19] Necker's agent notes the role of these crowds in his *Journal des Etats-Généraux*, May 26 1789; cited in Patrick Kessel, *La nuit du 4 août 1789* (Paris: B. Arthaud, 1969), 99; see also the classic studies by Gustave Le Bon, *The Crowd: A Study of the Popular Mind* (New York: Viking Press, 1960); and Georges Rudé, *The Crowd in History, 1730–1848* (New York: John Wiley & Sons, 1964). On women, see Joan Landes, "Women of the Revolutionary Crowd," with extensive bibliography (2005), online: http://chnm.gmu.edu/revolution/imaging/essays/landes.pdf, March 11, 2010.

[20] *Comité civil* of the *section du Nord*, Archives nationales, F(7) 4584, d. Baillet; cited in Dominque Godineau, "Masculine and Feminine Political Practice during the French Revolution, 1793–Year III," in *Women and Politics in the Age of Democratic Revolution*, ed. Harriet B. Applewhite and Darline G. Levy (Ann Arbor: University of Michigan Press, 1990), 74 n. 31. See also Carla Hesse, *The Other Enlightenment: How French Women Became Modern* (Princeton, N.J.: Princeton University Press, 2001), chap. 4.

[21] Godineau, "Masculine and Feminine," 76.

[22] See Kessel, *La nuit du 4 août*, chap. 6: "The Weight of the People: June–July 1789," 99–115.

world" goes public, once hidden transcripts openly defy public ones, retaliation is not far behind. The "Great Fear," which swept France from shortly after the fall of the Bastille to shortly after the night of August 4, illustrates how profoundly the events of the day shook people with cosmic anxieties, reawakening atavistic memories of wars with the English that dated back centuries, and ignited furious rages against the aristocracy characteristic of earlier millennial revolts.[23]

And yet, the initial response to these atavistic fears came in the form of a wave of demotic enthusiasm. Like all transformative apocalyptic believers, the revolutionaries emphasized free will. Isaiah and Micah foresaw a day when the nations of the world would *voluntarily* accept God's judgment and rebuke, and their weaponsbearers would beat their own swords into plowshares and spears into pruning hooks.[24] Here in France, on the night of August 4 1789, the most enlightened of the aristocrats—lay and clerical—voluntarily renounced their "feudal" rights, the very stuff of legal privilege and of one person's subjection to another.

Moreover, this famous "all-nighter" inspired vast enthusiasm precisely because of the voluntaristic element.[25] When the viscount of Noailles, the most determined of those aristocrats ready to renounce their unjust privileges, made his famous speech calling for the sale and/or abolition of all feudal rights, the effect was electric: "This devotion to the public matter (*chose publique*) aroused a universal enthusiasm in both the Assembly and in the galleries," wrote an observer in his journal.[26] This emotion carried the day. Other, more reluctant aristocrats (those who had the most to lose in this affair) found themselves inspired: "Immediately, a general feeling seized the souls of all the privileged ones, filling them with enthusiasm."[27] Eventually, "no one dared to contradict the intoxication which swept up everyone's spirits."[28] In apocalyptic time, even Kant's sober, philosophical millennialism became *schwärmerisch*.

Michael Fitzsimmons argues that this night marks the key moment in the French Revolution, when a stalemated tug-of-war between reformers and defenders of the status quo gave way to a paradigmatic reorientation.[29] After that night, legislators found a common purpose and "saw their task as the realization of the ideals that had emerged during that evening and believed that it would be done

---

[23] On the "grande peur," see Lefèbvre, *Great Fear of 1789*; more recently, see John Markoff, *The Abolition of Feudalism: Peasants, Lords and Legislators in the French Revolution* (University Park: Penn State University Press, 1996), chap. 7. On the medieval peasant revolts, their millennial drives, and the ferocious revenge exacted by nobles, see Cohn, *Pursuit*; and Rodney Hilton, *Bond Men Made Free: Medieval Peasant Movements and the English Rising of 1381* (New York: Viking Press, 1973).

[24] On this demotic millennialism and its relationship to demotic religiosity, see above, chapters 1 and 8.

[25] Kessel calls his chapter, "En une seule nuit…," *La nuit du 4 Août*, pp. 133–79.

[26] Gorsas, cited in ibid., 139.

[27] Brissot, cited in ibid.

[28] Anonymous composer of a letter later published in the *Bulletin*, cited in ibid.

[29] Michael P. Fitzsimmons, *The Night the Old Regime Ended: August 4, 1789, and the French Revolution* (University Park: Penn State University Press, 2003).

through the medium of the new constitution."[30] August 4 gave the French Revolution its "liberal" character. "Overnight, France went from a nation marked by feudalism and corporate privileges to one characterized by equal rights under the law, abolition of nobility, separation of church and state, and freedom of worship."[31] Moments in history when the aristocracy *voluntarily* renounces power (the core of a transformative demotic millennial scenario), are quite rare, and often attended by large and enthusiastic crowds.[32]

The historian underestimates at his or her own peril the power of enthusiasm at such moments, both at the time, and subsequently as spurs to both memory and the desire to recreate such feelings. I think it fair to say that such collective enthusiasm at the transformation of how a culture exercises power shares much in common with millennial sentiments. At the height of this wave of voluntaristic transformation, one painter produced perhaps the most optimistic vision of this scenario in which, in a sacred grove, the king and his family amicably hand over the reins of power to the Republic.[33]

And just as the excitement caused by the American Revolution had inspired the Europeans, so the French inspired both the Americans and other Europeans. To the west, Wordsworth, in a poem to the revolution describes the thrill of the rooster at dawn:

> Oh! pleasant exercise of hope and joy!
> For mighty were the auxiliars which then stood
> Upon our side, we who were strong in love!
> *Bliss was it in that dawn to be alive,*
> *But to be young was very heaven!*[34]

To the east, Hegel wrote,

> But now for the first time man gets to the point of recognizing that thought should rule spiritual actuality. So this was a glorious dawn. *All thinking beings* joined in the

---

[30] Ibid., 22.

[31] Stephen Auerbach, "Review of *The Night the Old Regime Ended*," *Canadian Journal of History* (2004), online: http://findarticles.com/p/articles/mi_qa3686/is_200408/ai_n9443931, April 13, 2010.

[32] On the Peace of God, see Thomas Head and Richard Landes, eds., *The Peace of God: Social Violence and Religious Response in France around the Year 1000* (Ithaca, N.Y.: Cornell University Press, 1992); on the Great Allelulia of 1233, see Augustine Thompson, *Revival Preachers and Politics in 13th Century Italy: The Great Devotion of 1233* (Oxford: Clarendon Press, 1991); on the events of 1989 and the fall of the iron curtain, see Aleksander Smolar, "History and Memory: The Revolutions of 1989–91," *Journal of Democracy* 12, no. 3 (July 2001), 5–19. On Michelet's excitement at the experience of July 1830, see his *Histoire de la Révolution Française*, ed. Ernest Flammarion (Paris: Près L'Odéon, 1898), "Introduction de 1868," 1.

[33] René Dubois, "Serment du roi, de la rein eet de la Garde Nationalesur l'autel de la Patrie," 1791, Musée Carnavalet, Paris.

[34] William Wordsworth, "The French Revolution as It Appeared to Enthusiasts," published by Samuel Taylor Coleridge in *The Friend, A Literary, Moral, and Political Weekly Paper* (October 26, 1809), lines 1–5. The poem is also included as part of Wordsworth's *Prelude* (Book 10 in the 1805 version and Book 11 in the 1850 version); see *The Thirteen Book Prelude*, ed. Mark L. Reed (Ithaca, N.Y.: Cornell University Press, 1991), vol. 1, 10:689–93/11:105–09, 285. Italics mine.

celebration of this epoch. A sense of *exaltation* reigned at this time, an *enthusiasm of the spirit thrilled though the world*, as if the actual *reconciliation of the divine with the world* had now *for the first time* come to pass.[35]

To the north, one enthusiastic Englishman described the "Fête de la Révolution" of July 14, 1790 as first "Grand Spectacle of Freedom": "Such a magnificent association of FREE MEN, emancipated from the shackles of despotism within so short a space of time, is hitherto unparalleled in the annals of History. It is a phenomenon on which surrounding empires look with Admiration—it is a subject that deserves the most minute attention..."[36]

Repeatedly, one finds in the rhetoric of the French revolutionaries an acute awareness of their position on the world stage. They stood at the center: indeed, in transforming themselves, they prepared a world transformation. The ideology of this period remains a central element of our ideology of civil society to this day, including much of the declarative rhetoric of the United Nations.[37]

The Demotic Millennial Moment: Revolutionary Festivals (Fall 1789–Summer 1790)

For Michelet, the first year was the true revolution. It was then that French people everywhere—men and women, young and old—stepped into the breach of collapsing royal administrative authority and built from below new organizations that restored order—not another top-down hierarchical order, but the bottom-up order of freedom and mutual respect. Michelet considered the *festivals of the revolution*, however ephemeral, as part of the core, the "real" revolution, the "*spontaneous organization of France*."[38] Under the aura of this magical moment of mutual forgiveness and reconciliation, vast assemblies met throughout the land, holding festivals and enacting a kind of social contract. From November 1789 until the climax with the great commemorative festival of July 14, 1790, these assemblies stepped into the breach brought about by the collapse of the *ancien régime's* administrative functions, bringing into the new civic accord the soldiers, who had previously played the role of enforcers of aristocratic dominance. These sites of

---

[35] Friedrich Hegel, *Vorlesungen über die Philosphie der Weltgeschichte*, ed. G. Lasson (Leipzig: F. Meiner, 1944), 4:926; cited in H.S. Harris, "Hegel and the French Revolution," 6 n. 2 (p. 17). See also Lewis Beck, "The Reformation, the Revolution and the Restoration in Hegel's Political Philosophy," *Journal of the History of Philosophy* 14, no. 1 (1976): 51–62. Italics mine.

[36] London Times, July 20, 1790, cited in Helen Maria Williams, *Letters Written from France* (Oxford: Woodstock, 1988), 253.

[37] "The Universal Declaration of Human Rights," online: http://www.un.org/en/documents/udhr/, April 13, 2010.

[38] Michelet, *History of the French Revolution*, chap. 10, p. 432 (italics his). Of course, the important festivals, were increasingly organized from the top down, but the early ones elicited a good deal of local spontaneity and improvisation. See Mona Ozouf, *Festivals and the French Revolution*, trans. Alan Sheridan (Cambridge, Mass.: Harvard University Press, 1988), 33–40.

open celebration became mythical events where past, present, and future collapsed into one vast destiny fulfilled: collective redemption.

In one case, the men in one of the provinces had met separately to listen to a reading of the proceedings of the National Assembly:

> The women draw near, listen, enter, and, with tears in their eyes, entreat to be allowed to join them. Then, the address is read to them, and they agree to it heartily. This affecting union of the family and the country filled every heart with an unknown sentiment. The *fête*, though quite accidental, was but the more touching on that account. It was short, like all human happiness, and lasted but one day. The account of the proceedings ends with a natural expression of melancholy and musing: "Thus passed away the happiest moment of our lives."[39]

Michelet reads and weeps over the expressions of messianic joy that swept though France, flying on the wings of a suddenly potent ideology of human dignity and freedom, equality and fellowship.

Many places that held these festivals sent to their parent, the National Assembly, letters describing the proceedings. Reading them as director of the Royal Archives during the 1840s, Michelet described them as "love letters":

> The only art, rhetoric, or declamation that appears therein is precisely the absence of art, the embarrassment of a youth who knows not how to express the most sincere sentiments, who employs the language of romance, for want of better, to confess his true passion. Such is the power of love. To attain unity, nothing was able to prove an impediment, no sacrifice was considered too dear. All at once, and without even perceiving it, they have forgotten the things for which they would have sacrificed their lives the day before, their provincial sentiment, local tradition and legends. Time and space, those material conditions to which life is subject, are no more. A strange *vita nuova*, one eminently spiritual, and making her whole Revolution a sort of dream at one time delightful, at another terrible, is now beginning for France. It knew neither time nor space.[40]

While the skeptical historians can dismiss Michelet as an enthusiast (*schwärmer*) who underestimates how much both the festivals and the letters were stage-managed, they also risk underestimating how much spontaneous emotions drove the early ethos of the Revolution. Michelet's description, itself partly a projection of his own experience in July 1830, captures well the transformative excitement of apocalyptic time.[41]

---

[39] Michelet, *History of the French Revolution*, 447.

[40] Michelet, *History of the French Revolution*, 444.

[41] Note the similarities between Michelet's depiction of deserted villages while *everyone* is at the festivals, and Augustine's depiction of Constantinople emptied when all are outside the city with the emperor in a vast assembly of public penitence (see appendix at website). Michelet well understood the relationship of this kind of collective freedom grounded in good will with apocalyptic expectations: his description of the apocalyptic "Year 1000" and the role of the Peace Assemblies follows close on his experience of the July nights of 1831 (above, n. 32).

Revolution: Anti-Religious or Anti-Clerical?

At a popular level, all these ideas of equality and freedom resonated with an ancient and still-vital Christian demotic millennialism, expressed, for example, in the multiple patois that marked the regions and (largely) oral cultures of France. In 1790, Hyacinthe Sermet published a sermon in Occitan that assured his brothers that now had come the time for that liberty Jesus had promised so long ago.[42] Later that year, a wool merchant in Albi named Salivas delivered a speech to the "good people of the countryside," which the Society of the Friends of the Constitution published in the original Occitan. The congruence of Christian (demotic) millennial imagery with the Revolution is complete:

> It is *now* that *the reign of God will flourish* in *this Kingdom*. It is *now*, in this *age of miracles*, that what he said in the prayer which He himself taught us, and which a good Christian says every day, will be fulfilled: *sanctificetur nomen tuum,* hallowed be thy name, which means let thy name spread and be worshipped thoughout the earth... France will be the first which in setting itself free will spread and propagate the *law of our Lord, and the Nations of Europe*, who already wish to imitate our Constitution, will also espouse all the purity of the Gospel, and thus the desire for our [collective] Redemption [i.e., in the terminology of this book, our millennial hopes] will be fulfilled. The name of the Lord, of God Almighty, will spread and be hallowed first throughout Europe, and from here will *reach to all parts of the universe*... God as heard our oath, it is written in the book of life, it is pleasing to Heaven and has brought joy to all the martyrs crushed by the former despotisms, the former tyranny... France will have no better comparison than Zion triumphant, that heavenly Zion which the Scripture speaks of.[43]

The enthusiastic acceptance of the revolutionary ideology by many members of the clergy tells us that for people raised within the Catholic Church, as much for the honest merchant Salivas as for the well-educated Abbé Grégoire, the demotic millennialism of the revolution was, precisely, the fulfillment of their own religious hopes and passions.[44] A host of visionaries, both in France and as expatriots in England, announced the advent of the millennium as a result of the Revolution, including a

---

[42] "So then, brethren, we are not children of the bondwoman but of the free. Stand fast therefore in the liberty wherewith Christ hath made us free, and be not entangled again with the yoke of bondage..." Antoine-Pascal-Hyacinthe Sermet, *Discours proinounçat dabant la legiou de Sant-Ginest, Pel R. P. Sermet, Exproubinical des Carmés Descaussés, Predicairé ourdinari del Rey, & c.* (Toulouse, 1790), 1, Bibliothèque Municipal de Toulouse, Réserve Dxix. 134, no. 4; cited by David Bell, "Lingua Populi, Lingua Dei: Language, Religion and the Origins of French Revolutionary Nationalism," *American Historical Review* 100, no. 5 (December 1995): 1403.

[43] Salivas, *Abissalutary de M. Salivas lou Xoubé al brabé moundé de las campagnos* (Albi, [1790 or 1791]), B.M.T. Réserve Cxviii .151, 7; cited in Bell, "Lingua Populi," 1419.

[44] On Grégoire's (Jansenist) millennialism, see below, nn. 74–79.

whole society of mystics at Avignon, featuring women visionaries like Suzanne Labrousse and Catherine Théot.[45]

More important, and less likely to register on the historians' "millennial radar," were the myriad local curés, men of the lower clergy who apparently, despite their training and service in the extremely hierarchical and aristocratic church of the *ancien régime*, were ready to shift gears quite rapidly. In the upper Saône, the curates not only participated, they led the movement of local organizations that spontaneously arose to implement the new dispensation in practice. One priest in particular, in Issy-l'Évêque, established himself as the ruling magistrate, retrying cases that had already been decided, promulgating laws which he gave to the country through the mayors, and even set out, sword in hand, to redistribute property equally to all.[46]

It is as if Rudolf of Fulda had written in 847 not about Thiota the false prophetess, but the National Assembly: "And what is still worse, men from the holy orders, *setting aside ecclesiastical doctrine*, followed [the Revolution] as if it were a [sacred cause] *sent from heaven*."[47] Indeed, something similar to this had happened more than seven centuries earlier, when a "peace league" led by millennial priests had gone to war against the aristocracy that refused to abide by the oaths of peace.[48] They too saw themselves as Zion triumphant—the new Children of Israel, fighting their Canaanites, aristocratic enemies. Like Hong Xiuquan, this curé understood that the time had come for an egalitarian land reform like the one Moses established for the children of Israel before when they entered and conquered the Promised Land.[49]

Thus, one might argue, the anti-religious nature of the French revolution revolves not around religion per se, or even *Christianity* or *Catholicism*, but around demotic versus hierarchical social attitudes. Demotic and visionary Christians and Jews, embraced the French Revolution, from the Christian mystic William Blake in London to the Jewish millennial sectarian, Moshe Dubroška to the priest of Issy-l'Évêque.[50] The Revolution, then, may be seen, not as *against* religion, but, as de

---

[45] Clark Garrett, *Respectable Folly: Millenarians and the French Revolution* (Baltimore: Johns Hopkins University Press, 1975); Hillel Schwartz, *The French Prophets: The History of a Millenarian Group in Eighteenth-Century England* (Berkeley and Los Angeles: University of California Press, 1980).

[46] Michelet, *History of the French Revolution*, 437; see also Nancy Fitch, "Whose Violence? Insurrection and the Negotiation of Democratic Politics in Central France, 1789–1851," paper presented at the conference on Violence and the Democratic Tradition in France, University of California, Irvine, 1994.

[47] See above, chapter 2, n. 1.

[48] On the peace league, see Thomas Head, "The Judgement of God: Andrew of Fleury's Account of the Peace League of Bourges" in *Peace of God*, 219–38.

[49] On Hong, see above, chapter 7. On the biblical land distribution, see Numbers 26: 52–56; Joshua Berman, *Created Equal*, 86–92; on Jubilee, see Moshe Weinfeld, *Social Justice in Ancient Israel*, 152–78 (both cited above, chapter 8, n. 67); on Jubilee land reform and the French Revolution, see R.B. Rose, "The 'Red Scare' of the 1790s: The French Revolution and the 'Agrarian Law,'" *Past and Present* 103 (1984): 113–30.

[50] On Blake's response to the French Revolution, see below, n. 59; on Dubroška, see Scholem, *De frankisme au jacobinisme*.

Tocqueville and Michelet described it, as *une religion nouvelle*,[51] and like most radical new religious movements, at once egalitarian and (therefore) *anti-clerical*.[52] Or, to paraphrase Marx, a move from the anti-millennial religion that served as an opiate for the masses to a millennial revolutionary religion that served as a psycho-stimulant that roused them from their torpor.

From this newly triumphant demotic enthusiasm, all the former divisions vanished: rivers became connectors of humanity rather than sites of aristocratic toll collection and oppression. Catholic priests, whose predecessors had only recently burned them as heretics, now embraced and honored Protestant ministers in the shade of this capacious joy. Describing the miracle, Michelet, always attentive to how people blame God for their own inadequacies noted: "God, so long accused, was at length justified."[53]

■ THE MILLENNIAL PREMISE OF THE FRENCH REVOLUTION: IF WE FREE MAN FROM UNJUST OPPRESSION, HE WILL BE FREE

The millennial premise of the French revolutionaries, the ideology that nourished the most enthusiastic players in the first, transformative part of the revolution, held out the notion that the aristocratic politics of the *ancien régime* had perverted, indeed crushed the people—the Third Estate, the nation—and made them bad. This was true not only of peasants, crushed by the burdens and humiliations of seigniorial obligations, but also the bourgeois with their obsession with money and their grotesque aping of the aristocratic styles, the Jews, sunk in their inveterate and superstitious practices, and the theater folk, corrupting a licentious public. All would be transformed by the miracle underway.

For once the Revolution had removed injustices, the new man and woman would spontaneously appear—autonomous moral agents, virtuous citizens, for whom "the law is engraved not in marble or stone, but in the hearts of men."[54] Kant expressed the same kind of thinking in his 1784 essay on the Enlightenment:

---

[51] Claude Lefort, "La revolution comme religion nouvelle," in *The French Revolution and the Creation of the Modern Political State*, vol. 3, *The Transformation of Political Culture, 1789–1848*, ed. François Furet and Mona Ozouf (New York: Pergamon Press, 1989), 391–99. Carl Schmitt also viewed the French Revolution in this light; see the discussion in S. D. Chrostowska, "Notes for a History of the Political: Capital Events and Bodies Politic in the French Revolution," *Telos* 147 (2009): 99–119.

[52] This is not to say that there were not revolutionaries who despised all religion, including the millennial brand I here invoke. On the other hand, just as with the American Revolution, these thinkers-may have played a more prominent role in both the documentary production and our retrospective appreciation, than they did at the time.

[53] Michelet, *History of the French Revolution*, 449. On the issue of the Church's notion of God's punishing human evil, see his reflections in *La Sorciere* (Paris: Collection Hetzel, 1862), 65.

[54] Robespierre, 17 Pluviôse, Year II, February 5, 1794; cited in Marie-Hélène Huet, *Mourning Glory: The Will of the French Revolution* (Philadelphia: University of Pennsylvania Press, 1997), 75.

"indeed, if it is only allowed freedom, enlightenment is almost inevitable."[55] We hear precisely this enthusiastic hope in Robespierre's speech in favor of giving full-citizen status to the Jews and the actors, yet another long-oppressed class. "Actors will deserve public esteem when an absurd prejudice no longer opposes them from enjoying such esteem. Then the virtues of the individuals will contribute to purifying the spectacles, and the theatres will become public schools of principles, of good behavior (*bonnes moeurs*) and of patriotism."

This speech illustrates nicely both the millennial premise and the legislative agenda that such rhetoric supports. Notes Patrice Higonnet, "[The revolutionaries] thought that society would bloom harmoniously of its own accord if the institutions of public life were made more rational and natural."[56] No wonder that William Blake, whose "Glad Day" represents an extraordinary pictorial representation of the transformed and energetic *new man*, showed as much enthusiasm for the early Revolution in France, as he had for the American.[57] If, as the antinomian Proverb of Hell states, "Prisons are built with stones of law and brothels with bricks of religion,"[58] then by a genuine liberation, society will need neither prisons nor brothels.

This approach resembles closely the kind of thinking that had moved earlier religious millennialists. As he prepared for war against "the powers that be," Thomas Müntzer had articulated the same transformational hopes. For him, the removal of human slavery to unjust rulers (and ruling classes) was a prerequisite to the natural spread of the Gospel. "Creation must become free before the pure Word of God can grow upon the earth." If commoners behaved badly and showed a limited appreciation for the call of the Gospel, it was because of their economic hardships.[59] Indeed, Müntzer's approach to the revolt of the commoners—known as the Peasants' War or the Peasants' Revolution—was a rearticulation of Luther's belief that, were the commoners given access to a Bible in a language they could understand, they would embrace *his* salvific reading—and this, despite Luther's profoundly pessimistic view of mankind's depraved human nature. Millennialism doth make many hopeful fools.

For the French Revolution, the millennial hope lay not in scripture, but in Rousseau's theories of freedom and the general will. The popular voice, once freed, would express the "general will," the desire of all. Of course, as aristocrats had always argued, in reality freeing the popular voice could lead to mob violence and

---

[55] Immanuel Kant, *Was ist Aufklärung?* para.4, online: http://www.korpora.org/Kant/aa08/036.html, April 13, 2010.

[56] Patrice Higonnet, *Goodness beyond Virtue: Jacobins during the French Revolution* (Cambridge, Mass.: Harvard University Press, 1998), 101.

[57] Blake, *The French Revolution* (unfinished? 1791), in *Poetry and Prose of William Blake*, 282–95. Blake got into political trouble for wearing the tricolor in public, but he removed it in response to the Terror rather than to reactionary opinion in England. On Blake's "America: A Prophecy," see above, chapter 2.

[58] One of the *Proverbs of Hell*, Blake, Marriage of Heaven and Hell, Plate 5f, *Poetry and Prose*, 34.

[59] Abraham Friesen, *Thomas Muentzer, a Destroyer of the Godless: The Making of a Sixteenth-Century Religious Revolutionary* (Berkeley and Los Angeles: University of California Press, 1990), 259.

vigilantism. But, at least at the outset, the most idealistic of the revolutionaries believed that liberty went hand in hand with virtue, and that the free and virtuous individual would wish the same for his neighbor as he wished for himself. As Robespierre put it, "Ambition, force and perfidy have been the legislators of earlier societies... now [they] are subjected to reason."[60] Now was the time for the general will to legislate, "that is to say, to make men happy and free by your laws... It is in the virtue and sovereignty of the people that one finds protection against the vices and despotism of government."[61] This optimism was a necessary component of revolutionary enthusiasm.

And just as Robespierre favored the freedom and dignity of actors, so he supported the freedom of the people. It was literally a religious belief that the people, once freed, were incorruptible:

> But the people! But corruption! Ah, cease to profane this moving and sacred name of the people, in linking it to the idea of corruption. Who among men equal in rights, dares to declare his neighbors unworthy to exercise those, to strip them of those rights for his own advantage![62] And surely if you permit people to found a similar condemnation on presumptions of corruptibility, what terrible power do you arrogate for yourselves. Where will your proscriptions end?[63]

In this early, optimistic stage of the Revolution, Robespierre opposed the death penalty as fervently as he endorsed the freedom of the press.[64] These journalists "were not only [in] a struggle for values good in themselves, but a fight against the instruments of traditional governmental tyranny, and for means of popular self-expression."[65] And given the glorious response of the French people throughout the realm, the great explosion of generosity, fellowship, and industry that they showed in the first year of the Revolution, the leaders had every reason to believe that their premises were gloriously correct.

[60] Charles Vellay, ed., *Discours etrapports de Robespierre* (Paris: Charpertier et Fasquelle, 1908), 257; cited in Jacob Talmon, *Rise of Totalitarian Democracy*, 91.

[61] "C'est dans la vertu et dans la souveraineté du peuple qu'il faut chercher un preservatif contre les vices et le despotisme du gouvernement" (Vellay, *Discours et rapports de Robespierre*, 12; cited in Talmon, *Rise*, 92). See above on the "silent reasonings about one's *semblable*," chap. 8, n. 74.

[62] As Sagan argues, the previous 2500 years of political thought at least held that anyone, or most everyone, given the opportunity to claim more rights than his neighbor, will do precisely that. The very nature of Robespierre's rhetoric—damn the empirical evidence, it is *unthinkable* to disagree—suggests the heady expectations of apocalyptic time (*Honey and the Hemlock*). The disconnect with reality suggests that Robespierre has been listening to the sirens' millennial song and is headed for an unhappy meeting with a rocky reality.

[63] Robespierre's speech on universal suffrage, National Assembly, August 11, 1791; online: http://www.assemblee-nationale.fr/histoire/Robespierre1791.asp, April 13, 2010.

[64] Robespierre on the freedom of the press, speech before the Société des Amis de la Constitution, May 11, 1791; online: http://membres.multimania.fr/discours/presse.htm, March 8, 2010. On the death sentence, speech before the National Assembly, May 30, 1791; online: http://membres.multimania.fr/discours/peine_mort.htm, March 8, 2010; and below.

[65] Talmon, *Rise*, 92. We find the same ideology early in the Russian Revolution, on which see below, chapter 11.

Jews and the Rational Millennium: Emancipation and the Redemption of Mankind

Based on the same millennial presupposition that oppression makes people evil rather than vice-versa, we even find some revolutionaries arguing for the emancipation of the Jews.[66] The logic seemed impeccable, especially to the young moral zealot Robespierre who argued that not emancipating them defied all notions of justice: "How can the social welfare be founded on the violation of eternal principles of justice and of reason which are the basis of all human society?"[67] Of course, such noble sentiments may seem "reasonable" (really according to demotic, millennial reasoning), but to act on them made high emotional demands: (1) an ability to transcend the invidious feeling of Christians that the very existence of Jews was a slap in the face and that their degradation was proof of Christian theology;[68] and (2) the self-critical admission that the French (as Christians) were responsible for the current base conditions in which the Jews found themselves.[69]

The fight was sharp, the process lengthy and subject to recurring crises and regressions. But, as often with demotic millennial movements, at least in the early stages of optimism, a philo-Judaic tendency carried unwonted emotional and rhetorical weight. Nor was this philo-Judaism a one-way street. As we saw, there were Jews from far-away Eastern Europe like Moses Dobruška and his brother who, upon hearing of the Revolution, hastened to join, ready to caste of the obscurantism of Moses the Lawgiver for the clear, open, universal thinking of this demotic revolution.[70] As Maurice Bloch, an assimilated French historian of the Jewish persuasion, put it over a hundred years later and in the midst of the Dreyfus Affair: "The New Jerusalem will be everywhere when the idea of the French Revolution triumphs...and before this New Jerusalem, people will be able to say once again, 'God acts through the French!'"[71]

---

[66] The subject receives scant attention in the general histories of the Revolution. See Arthur Hertzberg, *The French Enlightenment and the Jews* (New York: Columbia University Press, 1968), 314–68; and more recently, Shmuel Trigano, "The French Revolution and the Jews," *Modern Judaism* 10 (1990): 171–90.

[67] Robespierre, *Pour le bonheur et pour la liberté*, ed. Y Bosc, F. Gauthier and S. Wahnich (Paris: La fabrique-éditions, 2000), 32.

[68] On the widespread perception, even in revolutionary circles, that the Jews *qua* Jews observing their Torah represent "more a hostility to Christians than a desire to please God," a sentiment drawn from Spinoza's works (and replicated in Sartre's), see Trigano, "French Revolution and the Jews," 176. On the role of Jewish subjection in Christian theology, see Jules Isaac, *The Teaching of Contempt: Christian Roots of Anti-Semitism* (New York: Holt, Reinhart and Winston, 1964); for a more recent analysis with an intentionally provocative subtitle, see Paula Fredriksen, *Augustine and the Jews: A Christian Defense of Jews and Judaism* (New York: Doubleday, 2008).

[69] On the willingness to accept blame, see Robespierre, "It is on the contrary national crimes that we must expiate in rendering them their imprescriptible rights of man which no one can take from them...To whom can we impute these vices [sectarianism and usury] if not to our own injustices?" (Robespierre, *Pour le bonheur*, 31). On the reversal in attitudes toward the Jews that accompanied a shift in the definition of honor during the Enlightenment, see appendix on Napoleon and the Jews at website.

[70] See above, n. 5.

[71] Maurice Bloch, "La société juive en France depuis la Révolution," *Revue des etudes juives* 48 (1904); the allusion is to Guibert of Nogent's account of the first crusade, which, among its many deeds, slaughtered Jews by the thousands: *Gesta dei per francos* [The Deeds of God through the Franks].

Among the proponents of Jewish emancipation we find the Abbé Henri Grégoire (1750–1831), one of the most openly religious, active members of the Revolutionary elite.[72] Grégoire, working with Jansenist piety and theology,[73] married Enlightenment idealism with a version of the relatively new (Protestant) chiliasm that viewed Jewish conversion at the end of time as essential, but to be preceded by a period of voluntary assimilation though improved conditions and internal Christian reform.[74] The key to their conversion lay in convincing them that Christianity—Catholicism—professed "the true religion, that of justice and toleration."[75]

Grégoire thus pressed hard for the emancipation of the Jews (and slaves) as citizens and viewed this as a key step toward hastening the advent of the millennium. He formulated a political program based on an active transformational apocalyptic scenario, which he successfully hitched to the star of the egalitarian Revolution. Thus one of the driving forces behind the emancipation of the Jews was a religious chiliasm that could effortlessly disguise itself in the secular language of reason and natural rights. Where Jews were concerned, the atheist Robespierre and the Catholic Grégoire were on the same ideological and legislative page. The consequences of this demotic millennial philo-Judaism in the following centuries would prove significant.[76] We will pick up this strain of revolutionary ideology subsequently in dealing with Napoleon, Marx, and Hitler.

On the other hand, Grégoire's desires carried forward into the secular idiom all the supersessionist tendencies of Christianity.[77] Grégoire's policy called for

---

[72] On Grégoire, see Ruth Necheles, *The Abbé Grégoire, 1787–1831: The Odyssey of an Egalitarian* (Westport, Conn.: Greenwood Publishing, 1971). He was among the representatives of the first order (clergy) to defect to the National Assembly, and became an active member of the most radical (Jacobin) Breton Club.

[73] On Grégoire's Jansenism, an issue of some controversy, see Rita Hermon-Belot, *L'abbé Grégoire: La politique de la vérité* (Paris: Seuil, 2000); and Dale Van Kley, "The Abbé Grégoire and the Quest for a Catholic Republic," in *The Abbé Grégoire and His World*, ed. Jeremy D. Popkin and Richard Henry Popkin (Dordrecht: Kluwer Academic Publications, 2000), 71–108. Compare Alyssa Sepinwall, who is unconvinced of the importance of Jansenism: *The Abbé Grégoire and the French Revolution: The Making of Modern Universalism* (Berkeley and Los Angeles: University of California Press, 2005), esp. 52–55.

[74] The origin of the new apocalyptic scenario that joined long, pragmatic premillennial projects to a cataclysmic finale go back to the contact of Menasseh ben Israel, the Marrano rabbi from Amsterdam, who found more approval among Dutch Calvinists than he did among his fellow rabbis (Katz and Popkin, *Messianic Revolution*, 80–88). More generally, see David Katz, *Philosemitism and the Readmission of the Jews to England, 1603–1655* (Oxford, Clarendon, 1982). On this "philo-" Judaic Protestant millennialism, which eventually produced such avid Zionists as Balfour, see Eitan Bar-Yosef, "Christian Zionism and Victorian Culture," *Israel Studies* 8, no. 2 (2003): 18–44. The first glimmerings of Grégoire's "philo"-Judaic millennial thinking arise in the high Middle Ages; see Robert Lerner, *The Feast of Abraham: Medieval Millenarians and the Jews* (Philadelphia: University of Pennsylvania Press, 2001).

[75] Cited by Edmond Morse-Levy, *Droit et liberté*, December 7, 1950, 1; in Necheles, *The Abbé Grégoire*, 16 n. 29. This led him to urge the clergy to reverse the teaching of deicide that lay so close to the heart of an invidious Christian anti-Judaism.

[76] See Rita Hermon Belot, "The Abbé Grégoire's Program for the Jews: Social Reform and Spiritual Project," in *Abbé Grégoire and His World*, 13–27; Sepinwall, "A Physical, Moral, and Political Regeneration of the Jews," in *Abbé Grégoire and the French Revolution*, 56–80.

[77] Although Grégoire did argue against coercion in converting the Jews, he started from the Catholic premise that only Catholics can be saved (creedal eschatology, on which see above, chapter1).

destroying the Jewish community and the nefarious hold that rabbis exercised on Jews; the now "liberated" Jews would be dispersed throughout the country, taught in public schools and integrated into an honest (i.e., not money-lending) economy. This combination of good conscience and social engineering that tears families apart, so much a part of Hong's millennial army, foreshadowed the even more violent strains of Jacobinism to come. One modern student of religious history has commented on how the revolutionaries "haughtily rectify this moment of contrite weakness [Robespierre's self criticism], by turning it into a moment of domination over the Jews and the Jew's being...."[78]

The Jacobin version of this homogenizing egalitarian individualism was stated in the still-operative principle of Jewish emancipation: to the Jew as citizen, everything; to the Jew as nation, nothing.[79] Grégoire had plenty of trouble just getting his revolutionary colleagues to focus on the issue. (He only made real headway with Emperor Napoleon.) At no time did it occur to anyone that Jews might have an independent culture that was valuable in its own right, and valuable for the French. Thus, when Frenchmen attended their festivals and gazed upon the "tablets of the law"—that is the representation of the Declaration of the Rights of Man on Mosaic tablets—they saw this new declaration as *replacing* and superseding the Decalogue, not as *an additional* attempt to legislate a civil polity that borrowed the imagery of the former in order to graft itself onto that tradition. In a move that would characterize much of the revolutionary spiral into terror, they saw themselves in a zero-sum relationship to a past that they sought to eliminate, rather than a positive-sum relationship with a past they needed to reinterpret, to sublimate.

Thus, just as Voltaire did, the Revolution, even as it rejected Christianity, accepted many of the prejudices of Christianity about the Jews and reproduced accordingly the same supersessionist relationship to Judaism. In taking the tablets for their frame, they invoked the "universalist" elements of monotheism even as the rejected not only their own iconic and hierarchical ecclesiastical traditions (which the Reforming Protestants also hated), but they also threw out demotic Jewish and Christian traditions as well.

As with most such legislation of the modern period, the emancipators had a sense of radical moral superiority to both their predecessors, whose superstitions had so long oppressed the Jews, and this curious, fossilized people, whom they condescended to free.[80] And yet, over the succeeding decades and centuries, the surprising success of Jews under the new, modern dispensation—constitutional governments that allowed Jews to play by the same rules as others—disconcerted

---

[78] Trigano, "French Revolution and the Jews," 175. This is an aggressive variant of the normally self-flagellating messianic complex known as "masochistic omnipotence syndrome"—everything is our fault, and if we were only perfect, we could fix everything.

[79] See Trigano's close analysis of the denial of the Jew as Jew in this legislation (ibid.).

[80] Hertzberg, *French Enlightenment and the Jews*, 268–314.

many observers. As we shall see, the conspiracy theories about democracy as a cover for world domination that targeted the Masons in 1800, shifted to the Jews as the arch-plotters by 1900.

■ COGNITIVE DISSONANCE AND THE TERROR: MILLENNIAL PARANOIA'S TWIN SOURCES

The "descent" of the Revolution into terror constitutes the most troubling issue for historians, particularly ones who thrill to the messianic slogan, *liberté, égalité, fraternité*.[81] The more traditional approach insists that the revolutionaries were engaged in improvisational behavior from the very start, and that the Terror represents an aberration that the Revolution might have avoided. A school of revisionists, however, have detected the seeds of the Terror from the earliest stages—indeed, in the very thinking of Jean-Jacques Rousseau, the revolutionaries' favorite political theorist, insisting, in the sharpest version of this argument, that the Terror was predetermined by the ideology.

Rather than view 1789 and 1793 as two radically different phenomena because they are so different, or assimilate 1789 to 1793 in order to view them as the same phenomenon, it may be more profitable to see them as two different stages of the apocalyptic curve. Looking at the advent of the Terror as a result of millennial disappointment can help us understand the paradoxical dynamics of this deliberately terrifying turn of events.

Trouble Within: Disappointment in the Millennial Premise

The problem for the revolutionaries, as for all active apocalyptic believers, arose when, inevitably, their millennial premises proved false. Apocalyptic time does not last long; millennial moments rapidly lose their ardor. And when they do, they come crashing down to earth. Soon enough people realize how they can take advantage of those naive souls who engage in trust and generosity.[82] For the French Revolution, perhaps the first sign of trouble came in the form of hoarding supplies. Food shortages, a constant presence from the very beginning of the Revolution, became still more severe with each succeeding year.

But the problem went far beyond merely selfish behavior. While legally emancipating actors and Jews and "rationalizing" the institutions of public life did change society, it hardly operated the way the revolutionaries hoped. Just as Luther discovered, much to his dismay, that many people did *not* read his biblical translation the way *he* did, Robespierre and his fellow enthusiasts discovered that freeing the French did not produce a mass of people who agreed with them, much less *reveal* a "general will." On the contrary, the brief period of collective unity did not last. Religious folk showed too much attachment to their old ways, cultic practices,

---

[81] For a detailed discussion of the debate, see below, pp. 279–85.
[82] Hypocrisy is the compliment that vice pays to virtue.

and even traditional rivalries;[83] and as time passed, secular revolutionaries thought that the solution to this divide was to press ever harder for the elimination of Christianity entirely (after 1792). All those quaint patois and dialects that had spoken enthusiastically for the new *religious* world began to grate on the ears of the educated French-speaking revolutionary elite.

Alas, the theater, now liberated from old lies, merely produced new ones. The revolutionaries came, unhappily, to realize that while they might destroy lies, they could not, however, uncover truth. As Marie-Hélène Huet notes,

> What is disclosed when masks are removed and veils are torn, is acting, duplicity, lies, untruth. Revolutionary rhetoric does not speak of unveiling truth, but of unveiling treason, bringing to light treachery and falsehood. Saint-Just again made explicit the function of the mask in his definition of the ideal revolutionary: "he thinks that [the peasant's] coarseness is a mask of duplicity and remorse, and that it covers deceitfulness with enthusiasm."[84]

From an explosion of mutual trust never before seen, the revolution began to tread the path of suspicion and distrust—from betrothal to betrayal. Suspicion had become systematic: enthusiasm deceives the unwary, and commoners, coarse fellows all, resist their own liberation.

Most outside observers, familiar with the workings of the real world and human nature, do not necessarily appreciate how surprising this turn of events might have seemed to the revolutionaries. What may seem obvious to us can strike the millennial enthusiast as incomprehensibly, indeed impossibly, wrong. They believe that their trajectory goes straight up into the orbit of millennial salvation, and the cognitive dissonance of finding themselves still stuck in the banal reality of human failure and corruption (the very reality owls like Augustine take for granted) fills them with fear and loathing.

The millennial premise made high-level assumptions about the "natural propensity" of humanity once freed from oppression, toward rational, positive-sum behavior. In a sense, it built on a widespread belief of Enlightenment thought laid out in detail by John Locke—people were "blank slates" and education could, therefore, thoroughly transform them.[85] As a result, it depended on an almost magical hope in the goodness of human nature and the reliability of reason. No

---

[83] See the example of the tensions in Nîmes analyzed by Arno Mayer, *The Furies: Violence and Terror in the French and Russian Revolutions* (Princeton, N.J.: Princeton University Press, 2000), 492–501.

[84] Marie-Helene Huet, "The Revolutionary Sublime," *Eighteenth-Century Studies* 28, no. 1 (1994): 53. In a terms of Scott's analysis of "hidden" and "public transcripts," one might describe this as the revolutionary belief that now that oppression had ended, so would "hidden" transcripts; it did not. As a result, the revolutionaries tried to *impose* a "thick hegemony" in the form of total transparency.

[85] John Locke, *Essay Concerning Human Understanding*, book 2, chap. 1:2. For a lively discussion of the notion and its impact on political thought and action, see Steven Pinker, *The Blank Slate: The Modern Denial of Human Nature* (New York: Viking, 2002), below, chapter 10, n. 29.

room here in this Rousseauesque romanticism for Augustinian pessimism about the *corpus permixtum,* no tolerance for the messy world of the Federalist papers. Indeed, Rousseau and his readers did contemplate the possibility that individuals, once free, might respond inappropriately and thus corrupt the general will. But the general will could deal with that corruption.

While most historians have focused on the anxiety of the revolutionaries as their expectations fail, Mendel has emphasized their impatience, a rooster's impatience:

> Once in power, the rationalist revolutionaries would see to it that all of society corresponded to their model of purity and perfection as precisely as did the planets to their objective laws. With little or no experience in compromising pragmatically with reality or with opposing points of view and accustomed to shaping theories at will to suit their private needs (unresisting paper taking anything), they would have little patience with anything or anyone inconsistent with their theories. If character and biography predisposed the revolutionary rationalist to totalitarian domination, the ideological heritage guided him to it and justified the way he used it.[86]

Their response, the ominous formula: "they must be *forced to be free.*"[87]

Attack from Without: Paranoia and the War against Democracy

As we have seen, millennial movements provoke apocalyptic responses: *one person's messiah is another's antichrist.* The French Revolution had universal ambitions. France merely marked the starting point of a movement of freedom that would, eventually—soon—transform the world. Robespierre exclaimed:

> Eternal Providence has called you forth, *only you since the beginning of the world* to re-establish on earth the empire of justice and freedom, in the midst of the liveliest lights which have ever shone upon public reason, in the midst of almost miraculous circumstances which it has pleased it to bring about in order to give you the power of securing man his happiness, his virtues and his dignity.[88]

This and similar sentiments permeate the expressions of self-perception among the revolutionaries. "Here is the state of the great trial that we plead before the universe...Let it judge between us and our enemies, between humanity and its oppressors."[89]

---

[86] Mendel, *Vision and Violence,* 119.

[87] This is, of course, the burden of Talmon's argument about Rousseau, for which, see discussion below on historiography. The important point to underline here is that this almost mystical notion of the general will comes from an attempt to reconcile freedom and discipline/virtue, and focuses on precisely the kinds of issues that had Kant's and Diderot's attention. See discussion of natural law in the *Encyclopédie,* above, chapter 8, n. 74, cited in Talmon, *Rise,* 41. See also the discussion in Isaiah Berlin, *Freedom and Its Betrayal Six Enemies of Human Liberty* (London: Random House, 2002), 27–49.

[88] Vellay, *Discours et rapports de Robespierre,* 92.

[89] Robespierre, "Defenseur de Constitution, IV"; Vellay, *Discours et rapports de Robespierre,* 174–75; cited in Talmon, *Rise,* 80.

This grandiose scale is a classic expression of the megalomania of roosters: we are the center of cosmic history; all of human history culminates in our efforts.[90] Nor did they delude themselves entirely. The whole (Western) world—at least the intelligentsia in the coffee houses—was watching; the revolutionaries did perform on a global stage. And, as in so many egalitarian millennial movements, people who act on such grandiose notions provoke the determined hostility of those surrounding political units who saw in its success a threat to their own existence.

The crowned heads of Europe trembled and gathered their armies for war, determined to throttle this infant horror in its crib.[91] In February of 1792, Prussia and Austria joined in a coalition (at least in principle) against revolutionary France. The revolutionary government responded in April by declaring war on Austria. All this occurred against a backdrop of growing domestic crisis—bad crops, hoarding, inflation, resistance in some of the provinces. Whether the revolutionary war caused the dynamics of terror, or those dynamics brought about the war, there is little doubt that they crystallized together.[92]

For the radical revolutionaries, such domestic woes and foreign threats were not coincidental, and certainly could not have been caused by their own errors of judgment, or even the honest disagreements of a loyal opposition. On the contrary, to the mind of an increasingly paranoid revolutionary like Robespierre, they arose from the malevolent will to undermine the new and glorious experiment— the work of traitors to the Revolution. In a move that describes in terrifying detail the workings of the paranoid imperative, the newly empowered revolutionary forces—Montagnard Jacobins—came to view any dissent as a conspiracy to betray the Revolution to the forces of reaction. Their opponents were not brothers exercising their newly granted freedom; they were diabolic traitors.[93]

Having just overthrown the monarchic principles of the dominating imperative— "rule or be ruled"—the revolutionary vanguard now passed into the most extreme

---

[90] On the inherent megalomania of apocalyptic believers and its relationship to paranoia, see above, chapter 1.

[91] Blake's poetic version runs:

And then their end should come, when France received the Demon's light [revolution].
Stiff shudderings shook the Heav'nly thrones! France, Spain and Italy in terror viewed the bands of Albion....
—William Blake, *America*, in *Poetry and Prose*, plate 16, lines 15–17; see Erdmann's commentary, 816.

[92] On the complex issues surrounding the onset of the revolutionary wars, see Timothy Blanning, *Origins of the French Revolutionary Wars* (London: Addison Wesley, 1986), 83–113, who concludes that "the Terror was latent in revolutionary ideology but needed the strains of war to be activated" (p. 139); and Gunther E. Rothenberg, "The Origins, Causes, and Extension of the Wars of the French Revolution and Napoleon," *Journal of Interdisciplinary History* 18, no. 4, *The Origin and Prevention of Major Wars* (1988): 771–93. See also, below, n. 99.

[93] For an extensive discussion of the paranoia attendant on this move to terror, see Eli Sagan, *Citizens and Cannibals: The French Revolution, the Struggle for Modernity and the Origins of Ideological Terror* (Lanham, Md.: Rowman & Littlefield, 2001): "Modernity Psychosis," 327–510.

form of the paranoid imperative—"exterminate or be exterminated." Robespierre explained:

> The two opposite genii…contesting the empire of nature, are in this great period of human history interlocked in a mortal combat to determine irretrievably the destinies of the world and France is the stage of this redoubtable struggle. Without, all tyrants are bent upon encircling you; within, all the friends of tyranny are banded in conspiracy: they will go on plotting until all hope will have been wrested from crime. We have to strangle the internal as well as the external enemies of the Republic, or perish with her; and, in a situation like this, your first maxim of policy must be the guiding principle that the people shall be led by reason, but the enemies of the people by terror.[94]

Barras commented: "Il faut guillotiner, ou s'attendre à l'être [one must guillotine or expect to beguillotined]."[95] For Robespierre and Saint-Just, it turned out to be both.

Of course, not all the public voices favored the paranoid descent into terror. In May of 1793, a delegate to the Convention denounced the greatest danger to the Revolution: "The spirit of denunciation that now prevails…[that] calumny is a species of treachery that ought to be punished as well as any other kind of treachery. It is a private vice productive of public evils; because it is possible to initiate men into disaffection by continual calumny."[96] Thus spoke Thomas Paine, who barely escaped the guillotine that cut down both Danton and Junius Frey. The point here is not whether a culture has people to articulate saner postures, but to whom do the key players (including the crowds) listen? Everyone agrees, in revolutionary France paranoia carried the day. "The rhetorical marking of hoarders as blood-thirsty and inhuman beasts was a sign of the terrorists' own impatience to shed the blood of their real and imagined enemies."[97] That any culture might produce such demonizers goes without saying; that the "public" and the decision-makers listen to them is another matter.

In any case, the logic of the Terror followed a classic (if not inevitable) psychological and apocalyptic dynamic. Once successful, the best of intentions and finest expressions of demotic values launch an egalitarian experiment at once immensely powerful and enthusing, and also extremely vulnerable. Having shed blood, the fear of vengeance from the (now overthrown) powers becomes a

---

[94] Vellay, *Discours et rapports de Robespierre*, 332; Talmon, *Rise*, 119.

[95] Louis Villat, *La Révolution et l'Empire, 1789–1815* (Paris: Presses Universitaires de France, 1936), 255; cited in Talmon, Rise,121.

[96] Paine, letter to Danton, May 6, 1793, *The Writings of Thomas Paine*, vol. 3, *1791–1804*, ed. M.D. Conway (New York: G.P. Putnam's Sons, 1895), 138; cited in J.M. Thompson, *The French Revolution* (Oxford: Blackwell, 1985), 350; Sagan, *Citizens and Cannibals*, 371 n. 37. Charles Walton, "Policing Public Opinion in the French Revolution: The Culture of Calumny and the Problem of Free Speech," *French History* 24 (2010): 113–14.

[97] William Sewell "Sans-Culotte Rhetoric of Subsistence," in *The French Revolution and the Creation of Modern Political Culture*, vol. 4, *The Terror*, 259; cited in Sagan, *Citizens and Cannibals*, 334 n. 18.

major concern. And not without reason: the promises of vengeance, the threats of "terror" by triumphant foreign troops and aristocratic émigrés, did not escape the attention of those who had rebelled. The Brunswick Manifesto of July 1792 threatened those who resisted the king's justice with "an ever memorable vengeance by delivering over the city of Paris to military execution and complete destruction, and the rebels guilty of the said outrages to the punishment that they merit...."[98] News of the fall of Verdun to Brunswick's invading forces in early September panicked Parisians. Fears were not unrealistic; and the violence of the response—the massacres of September 1792—hardly inexplicable.[99]

And yet, all too often, in these experiments that come to life in bursts of megalomaniacal enthusiasm, fears of vulnerability give way to a ruthless paranoia.[100] The early period of the Revolution—1789–91—has men like Robespierre convinced that the transformation will occur with a minimum of violence (as in America), that the natural conditions of nations is peace and justice. As late as 1791, Saint-Just, the most merciless member of the future Committee of Public Safety, reproached Rousseau for justifying the death penalty.[101] Robespierre in this early period was a determined opponent of the death penalty and of any restrictions on the press.[102] Even after the king's execution, Robespierre still hoped the violence would stop there.[103]

Historians have puzzled over the seeming incongruity of the pacifist sentiments of precisely the most bloodthirsty drivers of the Reign of Terror. They note the startling contrast between the Festival of the Supreme Being, with all its imagery of peace and concord on the 20 Prairial year II (June 8, 1794) and the decree only days later that removed the last legal constraints of the judicial terror, permitting summary executions and inaugurating the "Great Terror."[104] Such sentiments are more familiar to millennial scholars.[105]

---

[98] Brunswick Manifesto, July 25, 1792, issued by Charles William Ferdinand, Duke of Brunswick-Luneburg, para. 8; online: http://personal.ashland.edu/~jmoser1/brunswick.htm, March 8, 2010. For a discussion of this issue, see Mayer, *Furies*, 171–226.

[99] See Ronald Schechter's discussion of the internal contradictions of Blanning's (largely revisionist) arguments that it was the revolution's paranoia that drove the war, "Yet when [Blanning] writes, 'Never has there been a revolution so paranoid,' and then lists the reasons why it had cause to be fearful (p. 72), he simultaneously denounces the revolutionaries and offers an opportunity for their defenders," online: H-Net review, http://www.h-net.org/reviews/showrev.php?id=1877, March 8, 2010.

[100] See above, chapter 2, for a discussion of paranoia as a negative form of megalomania in which everyone else has nothing better to do than plot against oneself.

[101] Saint-Just, *Oeuvres complètes de Saint-Just, avec une introduction et des notes,* ed. Charles Vellay (Paris: Charpentier et Fasquelle,1908), 1:344; cited in Talmon, *Rise,* 90. See above on Robespierre, n. 66.

[102] Talmon, Rise, 92.

[103] See discussion in Marisa Linton, "Robespierre's Political Principles," in *Robespierre,* ed. Colin Hayden and William Doyle (Cambridge: Cambridge University Press, 1999), 42–53.

[104] Huet, *Mourning Glory,* 49 n. 43.

[105] Although the differences are significant, it seems worth noting that two days before the beginning of the Nuremberg Party Days of September 1939 whose theme was "Friede" [Peace], Hitler went to war against Poland and canceled the ceremonies. See below, pp. 380–82. See also Hong Ren'gan's rebuke of how bloody his cousin Hong Xiuquan had become during his Nanjing period, above, chapter 7, n. 63.

Indeed, the revolutionaries themselves had recourse to apocalyptic rhetoric to make their points. Speaking of a locksmith named Geoffroy, who had been wounded defending Collot d'Herbois (an ex-actor and member of the Committee of Public Safety), one enthusiast wrote to the Convention in the immediate aftermath of both the Festival of the Supreme Being and the onset of the "Great Terror":

> What a day of dread for the depraved is that on which, Legislators, you have recalled man to his original dignity, to another life, that day on which you have engaged the very Divinity in the cause of liberty. What a day of terror for the corrupt is that on which the martyrs raise themselves by the thousand to make a rampart of their bodies facing the blows of assassins. They are unaware that the reign of virtue has created millions of Geffroys in the Republic! It will be sublime, our regeneration, it will consume the old man to form the new man; it will annihilate the kings and the priests. Instead it will offer a God, virtue, the law; it will present a great fatherland of thinking, free, happy beings. Yes! A people which recognizes the Supreme Being, which is ready to sacrifice absolutely everything for the law, is a virtuous people, and a virtuous people never perishes: it has a right to the immortality of the soul.[106]

The passage contains precisely the relationship between regeneration in peace and happiness on the one hand, and terror on the other.

Terror, here, serves as the destructive force that clears away the rot of the old world, and provides the trial by combat for the new man. Michelet's depiction of the terror that struck the French aristocracy at the approach of the year 1000 and their participation in the "Peace of God" movement follows the same pattern, although in that case, God inflicted the terror in the forms of plagues and famines: "These excessive miseries shattered the hearts [of the aristocracy] and brought a small measure of gentleness and pity. They put their swords in their sheathes, themselves under the sword of God. It was what one called the *Peace*, later the *Truce of God*."[107] And when God fails to inflict the terror, the task falls to those who would carry out God's millennial promises.

Anxiety, Paranoia and Apocalyptic Bloodlust

To *active transformational* apocalyptic believers, ones whose loosened tongues have encouraged them to *speak* their hidden transcripts, to engage in prophetic denunciation, to "speak truth to power," but whose only sins are verbal, disappointment brings primarily humiliation. But to *active cataclysmic* ones, who have struck blows, drawn blood, and shown their fangs, disappointment brings panic at the retaliation

---

[106] Geoffroy the Locksmith, *Archives parlementaires de 1787 à 1860, première série (1787–1797)*, ed. M.J. Mavidal, M.E. Laurent et al. (Paris, 1867–?), 91:663 (27 prairial II); cited in Antoine de Baecque, "The Trajectory of a Wound: From Corruption to Regeneration. The Brave Locksmith Geoffroy, Herald of the Great Terror," in *The French Revolution and the Creation of Modern Political Culture*, vol. 4, *The Terror*, ed. Keith Michael Baker (London: Pergamon Press, 1989), 167 n. 30.

[107] Jules Michelet, *Le moyen age*, ed. Claude Mettra (Paris: Laffont, 1981), 231.

that will surely result from failure. Roosters typically behave aggressively, reveal to those in power their hidden feelings, all under the impression that those in power will shortly, imminently pass away. When that expectation fails, the "revelation" becomes a nightmare of anticipated retribution.[108] When this realistic fear joins with the cosmic humiliation of prophecy failed, such post-apocalyptic activists can plunge headlong into the paranoia of "exterminate or be exterminated."

The first clear manifestation of this anxiety and panic came almost immediately with the calling of the Estates General in the winter and fall of 1789, with rumors of attacks by brigands. By the summer, and especially after the destruction of the Bastille, the panic becomes the "Great Fear" of brigands, hoards of genocidal Huns, and a ruthless aristocracy led by the Comte d'Artois. Paranoia produces aggression, and the French peasantry behaved as did their medieval counterparts, although with considerably less bloodshed and gratuitous violence.[109]

The response to foreign attack follows a similar pattern: first fear, then aggression. Historians have long debated the nature of this external threat, and to what extent the revolutionary government merely responded, and to what extent, like the Taiping, they exacerbated it with both provocative rhetoric and behavior. Of course, asking roosters to tone down their universal claims lest the offend neighbors is to ask for acts of pragmatic calculation that defy the very logic of millennial ambitions.

However one might characterize the provocative behavior of the revolutionary government, there can be no doubt that the war fueled many of the instincts that led to the terror. The rhetoric of the *Marseillaise* echoed the bloodiest apocalyptic imagery: "*Qu'un sang impura breuve nos sillons.* [Let an impure blood (of our enemies) water our furrows]."[110] The passage was added as a caption to the engraving of Louis XVI's severed head held up to the roaring crowd, and finds its echo in Barère's famous remark: "the tree of liberty grows only when watered with the blood of tyrants."[111]

Robespierre and Saint-Just attributed to the "general will" of the people much of the sacrality that had previously qualified both "the Church" and the absolutist monarchy and made them omnipotent.[112] As a result, when "the citizenry" failed

---

[108] See, for example, the first proto-totalitarian episode of the (initially) pacifist Anabaptists at Münster (Middlefort, "Madness and the Millennium at Munster").

[109] On the Jacquerie's excesses (1356), see Hilton, *Bond Men Made Free*, 96–134.

[110] "Sillon" suggests a characteristic millennial symbolism in which it could mean the wake/tracks of the revolutionary armies, but since "abreuver" is a term for watering plants, the army is seen as a plow, turning over the soil of unredeemed societies and watering it with the blood of tyrants. The bloody imagery is biblical: "and the mountains shall flow with blood...and the land shall be soaked with blood" (Isaiah 34:4, 70); "Blood flowed from the wine press as high as a horse's bridle, for 1600 stadia" (Revelation 14:20). See also the American Civil War song, "The Battle Hymn of the Republic": "Oh mine eyes have seen the glory of the coming of the Lord, He has trampled out the vineyards where the grapes of wrath are stored."

[111] "L'arbre de la liberté...croît lorsqu'il est arrosé du sang de toute espèce de tyrans," *Archives Parliamentaires de 1787 à 1860*, vol. 57 (1900): 368.*

[112] This is one of the major arguments of Talmon's book, perhaps the one that has attracted the most hostility. See below.

to manifest it, the revolutionaries found themselves at once immensely vulnerable within, even as they provoked the hostility of their monarchical neighbors. Their combined impatience *and* paranoia—both of them millennial, that is, megalomaniac—drove the logic of the Terror. Here, what might have been a rhetorical excess—Rousseau's dictum that, in some cases, the general will could "force a man to be free"—became the driving ideological force of the Terror, or, in religious terms, "coercive purity."

Terror's Offspring: The Apocalyptic Genealogy of Totalitarianism

The path that leads from limited violence in order to free people's "nature" so they exercise peaceful freedom, to a ruthless coercive purity that forces them to be "free" in a state that uses terror to exact conformity, is a very short one in apocalyptic time. These positions are only contradictory if one tries to impose an intellectual and moral consistency upon them. But apocalyptic thinking rapidly becomes improvisational as time passes—rationality, consistency with the initial scenario, or morality, quickly cede to the imperative of sustaining the heat of apocalyptic time.

Once set in motion, the logic that the true revolutionary had to carve the perfect state out of the body social seems to have advanced pitilessly and inexorably partly because the most dynamic actors espoused this attitude and found a ready ear among the "Sans Culottes," the rowdy mobs drawn from the urban labor force.[113] It was in these contexts that the paranoid litanies of "enemies of the Revolution" and xenophobic denunciations of the "strangers" who invaded the land, and "speculators" who starved the people, made their greatest impact.[114]

In their disorientation, anxiety, and fear of vulnerability, the people demanded blood. It reassured them. It allowed them to project the evil and feel aggrieved; it slackened their thirst for vengeance.[115] As one police agent noted at the guillotining of twelve Breton traitors in June of 1793:

> These executions produce the greatest effects politically, the most important of which is that they calm the resentment of the people at the ills that it endures. In them is vengeance satisfied... [those who see themselves as victims] perhaps consent to reconcile themselves

---

[113] See Sewell, "Sans-Culotte Rhetoric of Subsistence," 249–70; R. P. Levy, "Babouvism and the Parisian Sans-Culottes," *Journal of European Studies* 11 (1981): 169–83.

[114] See Francois Furet, *Interpreting the French Revolution*, trans. Elborg Forster (Cambridge: Cambridge University Press, 1981), 53–58; Lynn Hunt, *Politics, Culture and Class in the French Revolution* (Berkeley and Los Angeles: University of California Press, 1984), 38–44; Mona Ozouf, "War and Terror in the French Revolutionary Discourse (1792–1794), *Journal of Modern History* 56, no. 4 (December 1984): 579–97. How much the fears were justifiable or blown out of control is a matter of historiographical judgment; but I suspect there is plenty of room here for apocalyptic time as a factor in intensifying paranoia.

[115] For a discussion of the psychology here, which Sagan considers a form of cannibalism, see Sagan, *Citizens and Cannibals*, chap. 15.

to the ills which they endure only when they see men whom they believe to be their enemies, more unfortunate than themselves.[116]

For Marat, who as early as May 1791 already envisioned the execution of *half a million* enemies of the Revolution by year's end, considered the massacres of prisoners in September 1792, which so horrified public opinion around the world, "*des vengeances nationales.*"[117] In September 1793, at the very beginning of the Terror, a Parisian Sans Culotte, leaving one of the meetings of the new assemblies, remarked, "The guillotine is hungry, it has been ages since she had something to eat." In so doing, he projected his own desires onto the machine of execution. He and his comrade Sans Culottes earned their sobriquet, "*buveurs de sang*," drinkers of blood. Soon thereafter, and not long before he and his wife went to the guillotine, Camille Desmoulins remarked "*les dieux ont soif.*" *Vox populi, vox deorum.*

Were this fear rational, it might have spent its furor with the passing of the main danger, that is, with the victories of the revolutionary government over both its external and internal foes in the early autumn of 1793, the beginning of the year II of the revolutionary calendar. But this terror had an ideological and psychological component that would not let go now that it had seized hold of the imaginations of people in the grip of grandiose visions. On the contrary, the Terror *worsened* after the situation has settled down: the devastation of both the rebellious Vendée and Lyons come in a situation where "realistic" threats had become far less pressing.[118] Millennial passions ride believers, digging their spurs deep into their mount's flanks.

But anxiety and fear did not alone drive on the terror. "Reason" did so as well. Reason provided the revolutionaries with a paradigmatic guide to actions. Reason dictated the path to those sufficiently free of emotions to pursue it. Reason argued that everything should, in order to be equal, be uniform and regular. And in order to impose such reasoned order, directions must emanate from the center: Paris. "Reason" became the focus whereby the revolutionaries shifted in midstream from their initial capacious politics of enthusiasm and bottom-up diversity, to the exclusive politics of top-down uniformity. The apocalyptic turn from transformative to violent, even cataclysmic scenarios, from persuasion to coercive purity, had begun in earnest and brought with it a shift from demotic to imperial millennialism.

From Happy Babble of Many Tongues to Francophone Imperialism

Among the many examples of the kind of Jacobin, centralized, top-down thinking, which included the successful introduction of the metric system and the unsuccessful

---

[116] Duttard, cited in Mathiez, *French Revolution*, 396–97; Sagan, *Citizens and Cannibals*, 343.

[117] Marat, *The Principal Speeches of the Statesmen and Orators of the French Revolution, 1789–1795*, ed. Henry M. Stephens (Oxford: Oxford University Press, 1982), 1:369; Sagan, *Citizens and Cannibals*, 344–48.

[118] On understanding this aspect of the terror, see Donald Greer, *The Incidence of the Terror during the French Revolution: A Statistical Interpretation* (Cambridge, Mass.: Harvard University Press, 1935).

attempt to introduce a ten-day week, perhaps one of the most interesting cases involves linguistic purity. The way in which the language question played out in the French Revolution follows closely the pattern of capacious diversity turning into dogmatic uniformity that so consistently marks the shift from demotic, voluntaristic to hierarchical, coercive apocalyptic styles.

Initially, patois and foreign languages participated in the French Revolution.[119] Indeed, increased literary activity operated as a "translator" of the revolutionary impulse into the language of the provinces: texts from Paris were translated, revolutionary sermons and exhortations in the local tongue, printed. And one of the tropes with which this translation took place was the invocation of the biblical millennial vision, the demotic one whose presence one can trace back to the earliest traces of Christianity in Western Europe. The happy babble of tongues all, individually, speaking a single and capacious message, naturally recalled the founding scene of the Church: the tongues of Pentecost.[120]

But the enthusiasm that this initial wave of apocalyptic fervor inspired, mixed as it became with immense fears and anxieties, did not last. The countryside's enthusiasm for an increasingly radical anti-monarchical and anti-Catholic government in Paris rapidly waned, even reversed, bursting out in violence that culminated in the catastrophic Revolt of the Vendée in 1793. Both sides slaughtered each other with the pitiless violence so characteristic of the earlier Christian religious wars. And as the revolutionaries considered this retrograde behavior and the coarse and foreign dialects that inspired it, they became far more receptive to the argument that *French* itself constituted one of the revolutionary virtues, its acquisition a revolutionary discipline, and the elimination of these other tongues—languages of the traitorous "other"—a revolutionary necessity.[121]

Already by 1792, a more compulsive attitude took hold. The revolutionary government established French as the unitary language over all the patois and regional languages still actively used in France. The "homogenization of mankind" commenced in earnest.[122] One of the keys proponents of *sola franca*, the Abbé Grégoire, mirrors in his attitude toward the provincial's relationship to French, what he thinks of the Jew in relationship to the new civic culture: both the Jews and the provincials should shed their own culture of origin to become unified with the rest, the higher, superior culture. Not that Grégoire's God was as bloodthirsty as

---

[119] This paragraph owes a great deal to David Bell's fascinating article, "Lingua Populi."

[120] Bell, "Lingua Populi," 1426. See Michelet's depiction of the letters that came to the National Assembly from the departmental administrators about the festivals: "The language is still dissimilar, but their words agree so well that they all seem to spring from the same place—from the same bosom. Everything has gravitated towards one point, and that point now speaks forth; it is a unanimous prayer from the heart of France" Michelet, *History*, 444 (book 3, chap. 11).

[121] Bell, "Lingua Populi," 1415–17.

[122] Ozouf, *Festivals*, 279; see also Lynn Hunt, *Politics, Culture and Class in the French Revolution* (Berkeley and Los Angeles: University of California Press, 1984), 52–86; Bell, "Lingua Populi." Note that we regress here from Pentecost, the myth that resolved the dispersion of Babel, back to Babel's hubristic project: the single tower to the sky, the unifying project, the use of a single language.

other revolutionaries. But once the logic of this uniformity became widely accepted, it best suited the camp of coercive purity. By the height of the Terror, one official suggested that German—the language of the Austrian and Prussian enemies—might be eradicated from Alsace by "guillotining a quarter of the population and expelling all others who had not actively participated in the revolution."[123]

The mindset of the revolutionaries once they had shifted toward coercive purity has all the earmarks of a self-justifying paranoia. As they threaten and victimize their opponents, they bathe in a sea of self-pity and sense of their own victimization. Talmon notes: "Here we are faced with a paranoiac streak, a strange combination of the most intense and mystical sense of mission with a self-pity that expressed itself in an obsessive preoccupation with martyrdom, death and even suicide."[124] In its worst forms, this paranoid omnipotence complex produces the apocalyptic principle of the most nihilistic of cataclysmic scenarios: "destroying the world to save it."[125]

And yet all the time, these agents of apocalyptic destruction insist they have nothing but the best intentions. Saint-Just protested that on the day he would become convinced that it was impossible to give the French people *"moeurs douces"* (sweet, gentle customs) he would commit suicide.[126] In his indictment of Danton, Saint-Just wrote: "there is something terrible in the sacred love of the fatherland, it is so exclusive that it immolates all for the public interest, without pity, without hesitation, without any human respect."[127] When these men and their Sans Culottes allies had finished, some four hundred thousand French, men, women, and children, monarchists, revolutionaries, and bystanders, lay dead. Terrible hopes produce terrible loves. Indeed, the bloodiest crusading can present itself as an "act of love."[128]

■ HISTORIOGRAPHY OF THE REVOLUTION: MILLENNIALISM AND THE *THÈSE DE CIRCONSTANCES*

Historians of revolutionary France have shown little interest in understanding their Revolution in light of the dynamics of other millennial movements.[129] The

---

[123] Bell, "Lingua Populi," 1416; citedfrom Paul Lévy, *Histoire linguistique d' Alsace et de Lorraine* (Paris: Les Belles lettres, 1929), 2, 64–65.

[124] Talmon, *Rise*, 81.

[125] R.J. Lifton, *Destroying the World to Save It*.

[126] Vellay, *Oeuvres complètes de Saint-Just*, 2:504.

[127] Ibid., 2:305; cited in Talmon, 82–83.

[128] Jonathan Riley-Smith, "Crusading as an Act of Love," *History* 65 (1980): 177–92.

[129] When Crane Brinton published a revised version of his widely read analysis of the dynamics of revolutionary movements, *Anatomy of Revolution* (New York: Random House, 1938, 1965). He mentions some millenarians at three points (pp. 153, 168, 194), but neither uses millennialism as an analytic category, nor cites Talmon, published more than a decade before the second edition. He did have Karl Mannheim's *Ideology and Utopia* (1929) available even at the time of his first edition, especially Mannheim's discussion of the "chiliastic" mentality (pp. 211–19) discussed above, chapter 8.

general case I have argued above—that the French Revolution was such a movement, that its shift to terror was characteristic of millennial movements that take power—were already laid out in detail by Jacob Talmon in his study, *The Origins of Totalitarian Democracy*, published in the early years of the Cold War, in 1951.[130] Talmon unerringly honed in on the psychology of messianism with its zeal, contradictions, and megalomaniac paranoia, and tracked the slide of well-intentioned believers from an imminently perfect world into a nightmare of self-destructive terror.[131] And like so many millennial historians, he ran into the vesperian historians' resistance, the determination to tell again the "twice-told tale" of Western history in which millennialism remains marginal.[132]

While Talmon's work was reasonably well received in some circles, historians gave it the cold shoulder.[133] When major volumes on the French Revolution appeared around the bicentennial of its onset in 1989, none of the ample bibliographies even mentioned the work,[134] despite (or perhaps because) of a widespread belief that "Neo-Conservative Revisionism had clearly become the ascendant interpretation of the historical establishment in England, France and the United States by the 1989 bicentennial."[135] This absence is especially notable in 1989, when historians of the Revolution framed the debate in terms of "was the Terror a response to circumstances?"[136]—the *thèse de circonstances*—"or a response to ideology?"[137] with a corollary dichotomy between "inevitable or avoidable?"[138]

---

[130] Alfred Cobban, Talmon's thesis supervisor at University College London, criticized the argument on several occasions: *Rousseau and the Modern State* (London: Allen and Unwin, 1964), 29–31; *In Search of Humanity: The Role of the Enlightenment in Modern History* (New York: George Brazillier, 1960), 182–85.

[131] Cobban's criticism (see previous note) ignores (or dismisses) precisely this key link that Talmon (and the phenomenon of millennialism) establish between (exalted) ideology, (less exalted) emotions like revenge, paranoia, and rage, and (murderous) action. Perhaps one of the major blocks to recognizing the link derives from the profound attachment of progressives to those who claim to work for "the underdog," sympathy for whom is "a psychological feature common to all humanitarian movements," (Howard Schuman and John Harding, "Sympathetic Identification with the Underdog," *The Public Opinion Quarterly* 27, no. 2 [1963]: 230; with note to Cobban, *In Search*). Note that Mannheim considers the excessive valuation of ideas in analyzing movements as an anachronistic "distortion produced by the liberal-humanitarian stage of the utopian mentality" (*Ideology and Utopia*, 213).

[132] See above, pp. 83–88. Talmon's fate (not accepted in his own field, but popular in others), is similar to the fate of Norman Cohn's work, *Pursuit of the Millennium*, and James Rhodes, *The Hitler Movement* (below, chapter 12).

[133] Gary Kates, "Introduction," in *The French Revolution: Recent Debates and New Controversies*, ed. Gary Kates (London: Routledge, 1998), 10. For a "systematic" analysis that is more assertive than analytical, see José Brunner, "From Rousseau to Totalitarian Democracy: The French Revolution in J. L. Talmon's Historiography," *History and Memory* 3 (1991): 60–85.

[134] *The French Revolution and the Creation of Modern Political Culture*, vol. 4, *The Terror*, ed. Keith Michael Baker (Oxford: Pergamon, 1994).*

[135] Kates, "Introduction," 10. Note that Talmon's work precedes the phenomenon by two decades.

[136] E.g., Higonnet, *Goodness beyond Virtue* and Mayer, *Furies*, 171–226.

[137] E.g., Francois Furet and Ran Halévi, "L'annee 1789," *Annales* 44, no. 1 (1989): 3–24; David D. Bien, "Francois Furet, the Terror, and 1789," *French Historical Studies* 16, no. 4 (1990): 777–83.

[138] "There is no denying, however, that historically terror has been an essential property of revolution and inherent in its dynamics" (Mayer, *Furies*, 93). See below, chapter 15 for a discussion of the Zionist revolution.

One school attributes the Terror to circumstances that drove the Revolution toward excess. Writes Patrice Higonnet: "Jacobins stumbled into the Terror. They did not plan for it to happen. They were dismayed when it unfolded and relieved when it stopped... The search for *absolute freedom* [?!] does not automatically lead to tyranny and bloodshed."[139] The "revisionist" school, led currently by François Furet and his disciples, argues that the Reign of Terror was ideologically driven and "inherent in the French Revolution from the beginning."[140]

[T]he dialectic between people and plot [i.e., the paranoid reading of domestic conflict] had existed as early as the summer of 1789, when the counter-revolution was still in limbo, and at any rate without serious support from outside. The dialectic grew until it came to dominate the entire political history of France in the spring of 1794... Robespierre's egalitarian and moralizing metaphysics then held sway over a Revolution that was finally living up to its principle.[141]

According to opponents of the revisionist position, there lies behind it a neo-conservative agenda, "palpably hostile... toward the French Revolution and toward the idea of revolutionary change in general,"[142] that goes back to Edmund Burke, Alexis de Tocqueville in the nineteenth century, and Jacob Talmon in the twentieth.[143] According to the revisionists, on the other hand, the "circumstantial" school identifies so much with the revolutionaries in search of "absolute freedom" that they apologize for these revolutionaries who failed in the past, and cheer on revolutionaries today who show no sign of having learned from those past failures. Sagan's book might best be summarized as asking the question: How could a moral genius like Robespierre in 1789 turn into the moral monster of 1794? And given that the history of leftist revolutions has, with terrifying regularity, gone from espousing the highest progressive values in the early stages, to mega-slaughters of *their own* people in subsequent stages, all to a chorus of approval and excuses from fellow travelers, such a question seems more than relevant.[144]

---

[139] Higonnet, *Goodness beyond Virtue*, 326 (italics mine). Hignonnet has since revised his views somewhat, "Terror, Trauma and the 'Young Marx': Explanation of Jacobin Politics," *Past & Present* 191, no. 1 (2006): 121–64.*

[140] For a lively discussion of this debate, see Stephen Kaplan, *Farewell, Revolution: The Historians' Feud, France, 1789/1989* (Ithaca, N.Y.: Cornell University Press, 1995); most recently, Paul Hanson, *Contesting the French Revolution* (Oxford: Wiley-Blackwell, 2009), 1–34.

[141] FranoisFuret, *Interpreting the French Revolution*, 69.

[142] Barry Shapiro, "Review of Gueniffey, *La politique de la Terreur*" *Journal of Interdisciplinary History* 31, no. 4 (2001): 635.

[143] Kates identifies the political agenda: "Both [Talmon and Furet], in short, view the Terror as the essence of the Revolution and view it as a harbinger of Bolshevism and Fascism" ("Introduction," p. 10).*

[144] See Ladan Boroumand, *La Guerre des Principes: Les assemblées révolutionnaires face aux droits de l'homme et à la souveraineté de la nation, mai 1789—juillet 1794* (Paris: Editions EHESS, 1999), whose analysis is informed by her experience with another millennial revolution that began as one of liberation and human rights—Iran 1979 CE/1400 AH. On both this revolution and Boroumond's scholarship on Muslim millennialism, see chapter 14. On Marx and Marxist denial of the millennial dimension to their own thought, see below, next chapter. On the fellow travelers of the Russian Revolution, see chapter 11.

Such dichotomies as inevitable/accidental, although useful in culture wars, seem poorly conceived for getting at historical understanding.[145] And certainly in the case of Talmon (and Eli Sagan), such dichotomies demand (perhaps are designed to insist on) a misreading of their arguments. Neither of these men argue that the terror was inevitable, and certainly not intentional from the start.[146] On the contrary, because they look at the psychological dynamics, they have particularly interesting things to say about what *circumstances*—external and internal—led the revolutionaries to tread so extraordinary path of betraying the very values with which they started. Nor are such matters "mere" academic discussion: current dramas play out similar dynamics.

Indeed, the most recent revival of the millennial thesis by Philippe Nemo inscribes itself at the heart of this political debate about the excesses of well-intentioned leftist revolutionaries. For Nemo, the Terror constitutes a regression to millennial passions.

> Although the ideas of *1793* can be designated by this date, since a number of them crystallized in the pivotal year of the Terror, it is appropriate to understand that they are much older, and owe virtually nothing to the Enlightenment and the great movement of science and of the trenchant criticism of prejudice and superstition that animated the 18th century. *They are the inheritors of the millenarian and apocalyptic collectivisms of Antiquity and of the Middle Ages.*[147]

Nemo notes that the denial that they are millennialists among both the eighteenth-century secular actors and their twentieth-century admirers at once disguises these origins and fuels the worst kind of repetition:

> *1793*...is millennialism. It is a shameful religion, unconscious of itself because it presents itself as atheism, secularism, and materialism, but actually functions psychologically and sociologically as millennialism. I call this ersatz religion the "Left" with a capital L, taking the word not in its parliamentary or partisan sense, but in its spiritual sense, a mysticism that will not brook discussion, resists all rational objection based on facts, and, on occasion, lifting whole mountains.[148]

---

[145] Steve Kaplan remarks on the elements that lead French historians to take the positions they do: "Outsiders may be surprised by the insularity of this sociology of the production and transmission of knowledge, by the practices of cultural patronage and brokerage, by the systems of clientage, promotion and punishment, by the clotted salience of ideology, and by the depths and range of institutional cleavages" (Kaplan, *Farewell*, 16).

[146] It is common to accuse Talmon of arguing inevitability (Brunner, "From Rousseau to Totalitarian Democracy," 65–66), although the only "inevitable" component of Talmon's argument, I think, is that attempts to perfect society (apocalyptic millennialism) will fail, not necessarily lead to totalitarianism.

[147] Philippe Nemo, *Les deux républiques françaises* (Paris: Presses Universitaires de France, 2008), 248; translation mine, italics his. See Thibaut Gress, "Philippe Nemo: Les deux Républiques françaises," *Actu Philosophia* (October 2008); online: http://www.actu-philosophia.com/spip.php?article54, April 13, 2010.

[148] Nemo, *Les deux républiques*, 248.

The rapidity with which a politically engaged scholar like Nemo can turn the identification of the secular passions of the Revolution with millennialism into an accusation of false consciousness or bad faith on the part of those progressives who still consider themselves "men of reason," but who savor this particular fragrance of millennial fervor, may explain why there is so much resistance to such a view.

I would like to propose a different kind of "millennial" reading of the Revolution. Rather than consider the Terror a regression to medieval chiliasm,[149] let us consider the entire episode millennial, one in which we find, over the course of an apocalyptic curve, a characteristic shift from transformational demotic to cataclysmic hierarchical millennialism. This has the disadvantage (at least for the "rationalist" school) of "tarring" the early Revolution with the millennial brush, but the great advantage of understanding the dynamics. For among the "models" for revolutionary change, the apocalyptic-millennial one focuses specifically on a central paradox: the clash between perfectionist ideals and bitter disappointment.

If one wants to argue that a sincere liberal impulse produced the "neo-liberal's" August 4, then one might argue that demotic apocalyptic enthusiasm for transformative millennialism—voluntarily aligning one's own desires with that of the "general will"—inspired the renunciation necessary to allow so paradigmatic a political reorientation. This was, quintessentially, the dismantling of the prime divider, the repudiation of that legal privilege that separated the elite from the commoners. Without the millennial passion, such fundamental—revolutionary— changes might never have occurred. After all, voluntary renunciations of power are extremely rare in human history.[150] The revolutionaries had incarnated Rousseau's general will in the most beneficent form: from Ideology to Utopia.[151]

And yet these same perfectionist drives, under different circumstances, driven by a coercive and increasingly paranoid apocalyptic scenario, can "read" the meaning of "general will" quite differently. Here, one might argue, the more perfectionist the search for the millennium—"absolute freedom"—the more devastating the failure and the more violent the response to it. Nor need that failure derive from "pure" motives: the base fears and desires that inform everyday decisions can mask themselves in "idealistic motives" both as public and private justification.[152] In apocalyptic time, the fly does not merely spoil the ointment, it renders it toxic.

---

[149] Note that Brinton's three mentions of "millenarianism" all come in the discussion of extremist tendencies that led to terror (above, n. 131). Mayer acknowledges the "secular millenarianism" of the entire venture: "Indeed Marxism, not unlike the Enlightenment, had its millenarian, Promethean, and redemptive cogency" (*Furies*, 145–46, 340); and he invokes it at a number of points in his narrative, primarily to explain the fanaticism of the true believer, religious or secular (e.g., the ferocious violence in the Vendée, 340).

[150] See above, n. 34.

[151] Mannheim, *Ideology and Utopia.*

[152] Gueniffey, *La politique de la Terreur.*

The paradox lies in the possibility that *only* with the absolutist tendencies of millennial passions could August 4 and the *fêtes de fédération* have "made" the liberal revolution cherished by the circumstantial school, while that very passion also drove the totalitarian directions so feared by the revisionists.[153] It is precisely the "good conscience" of the totalitarian, the conviction that he does this for his *victims*, that he is "saving" both them and others, that marks the true believer, whether it be Torquemada, Saint-Just, or Lenin.[154] The numerous differences between Bolsheviks and Jacobins should hardly blind us to the critical and disturbing similarities: for they both represent demotic secular millennial movements which, at the highest pitch of apocalyptic time, turned to state terror as a solution to the disappointments they faced.[155]

In other words, *neither* external circumstances *nor* ideology alone make for the potent brew that leads to terror and its institutional offspring, totalitarianism. Rather, it is what happens to demotic millennialism (Talmon calls it "democratic political messianism") when its millennial premises have failed, and cognitive dissonance sets in precisely as the revolution feels threatened from without and within. At once fear and impatience seize hold of at least some of the actors, who believe that they alone can save the perilous situation. At that point of crisis, the most messianic of revolutionaries engage in the apocalyptic improvisation whereby they turn a transformative scenario into a cataclysmic one, where they "up the ante" and move from persuasion to coercive purity.

These patterns may be powerfully compelling. What occurred in the French Revolution had already happened in the explicitly millennial cases of the Anabaptists at Münster,[156] and in a milder form in England in the mid-seventeenth century.[157] And it would happen again—often in even more violent forms—in Russia, China, Syria, Iraq, Cambodia, Iran.[158] But such developments are not inevitable: it had not happened in the United States in 1781, nor would it happen in Israel in 1948, and in the latter case, both the millennial currents and the "*circumstances*" of external

---

[153] Kates argues that the "neo-liberal school" does not—unlike the "neo-conservative" one—minimize the "oppressive character" of the *ancien regime*, or the "constructive, moderate and important accomplishments of the Constituent Assembly," or the "purposive, necessary violence" of the early period (in which he includes "even 10 August 1792"), "Introduction," 11–12. None of these positions undermines a millennial analysis of the revolution.

[154] Mayer, *Furies*, 340. See the ever-relevant meditations of Eric Hoffer, *The True Believer* (New York: Harper & Row, 1951), which came out the same year as Talmon's study.

[155] Higonnet categorically dissociates the two: "[Bolshevism's] relationship to Jacobinism is a social-scientific fiction" (*Goodness beyond Virtue*, 330–31); Mayer sees them as intimately related, as "secular millenarianism" (*Furies*, 145). Higonnet's latest article, in which he returns to Marx's early analysis, seems to move in Mayer's (and my) direction: the Revolution pursued an impossible task that it could not sustain ("Terror, Trauma," 142–45).

[156] Middlefort, "Madness and the Millennium at Münster"; see above, chapter 1.

[157] Christopher Hill, *The World Turned Upside-Down: Radical Ideas during the English Revolution* (London: Penguin, 1991).

[158] Below, chapters 11 (Russian Communism) and 14 (Iran).

threat and internal dissension, militated heavily for totalitarianism rather than a democracy tolerant of dissent.[159]

The year 1793 was not *in* 1789 in any linear sense, as Furet seems to argue, whereby he tries too hard to straighten the crooked tale. On the contrary, they represent two different locations on an apocalyptic curve that is not preordained: 1789 was the voluntaristic transformative, and 1793, the coercive cataclysmic apocalyptic drive for the demotic millennium. It was precisely because 1789 was so radically demotic and capacious—August 4—that 1793 came as an unanticipated response to its failure whereby the same revolutionaries transgressed so many of the very values they initially upheld. And until we begin to sort out what makes some revolutions, like the French and the Communist ones, turn in their disappointment to coercive purity and others to retreat from that headlong dive into apocalyptic mega-violence, we cannot hope to learn how to deal with future manifestations of revolutionary millennialism, homegrown or foreign.

Not all of the revolutionaries of 1789 rode the apocalyptic wave to 1793. Indeed, many crashed along the way, some out of conviction, some out of hesitation. Condorcet's "Sketch for the Historical Picture of the Progress of the Human Mind," which Keith Baker calls "perhaps the most influential formulation of the idea of progress ever written," was written in the most turbulent period of the apocalyptic curve.[160] Condorcet added his "tenth epoch," whose lineaments so resemble the French Revolution's highest ideals, while hiding from his Jacobin enemies during the Terror; in it he describes an era of moral and political progress that he put far off into a distant future. In the heart of the failure of his Revolution, *ex post defectu*, he preserved his millennial dream, and rewrote the apocalyptic timetable. In so doing, he articulated one of the major "grand narratives" that postmodernism rejects.

■ EPILOGUE: NAPOLEON AND THE VICTORY OF HIERARCHICAL MILLENNIALISM

It would take far too long to go into the next stage of the revolution, the Napoleonic episode in anywhere near the detail we have above for the earlier stages.[161] Sketching out a millennial reading of Napoleon, however, suggests that, as opposed to those who argue that his astonishing success came primarily because he was a good pragmatic thinker (which he was), his appeal went beyond mere military charisma. He appealed to a French public—and army—still hungry for someone who could revive their sense of destiny. They wanted someone who could resist the return of "normal time," could bring them back into apocalyptic time with its inebriating sense of empowerment, of standing at the center of world history.[162] As one historian noted:

[159] See discussion below, chapter 14.
[160] Baker, "On Condorcet's 'Sketch.'"
[161] See website appendix: Napoleon, the Muslims, and the Jews.
[162] Katia Sainson, "Le Régénérateur de la France": Literary Accounts of Napoleonic Regeneration, 1799–1805," *Nineteenth-Century French Studies* 30 (2002): 7–25.

Thus, in these texts Napoleon is represented as the God of the Last Judgment whose arrival on the French political stage would bring about the resurrection of French society and retribution for the Just, who had until then suffered. He is represented as the agent of the Second Coming—la Régénération—a cataclysmic event "in which the old world is replaced by a new and better world."[163]

And *that*, he both could and did do: with his rise to power the Revolution entered a second apocalyptic period, this time with a much stronger component of hierarchical millennialism.

As opposed to the first phase of the Revolution, in which a demotic, bottom-up impulse dominated, Napoleon represented an imperial messianic variant. As world conqueror, in the tradition of Alexander, he offered the most pragmatic way at once to protect and to spread the revolutionary gospel to the other nations. He retained, therefore, important elements of the demotic progressive millennium that marked the earlier stage of the revolutionary millennial moment—above all, with his egalitarian law codes.[164] He promised these modern benefits through a decisive use of violence in which he and his revolutionary troops would destroy the grip of the aristocracy so that freedom might flourish—a pattern quite similar to the one that permitted the spread of Islam.[165] In that sense, he worked with the formula proposed for the revolutionary army of 1792 in Belgium: "War on the castles, peace to the cottages!"[166]

And like all messianic promises, it failed. Promises of freedom clashed with the authoritarian behavior of conquering troops toward "liberated" populations, further reinforced by the increasingly imperial style Napoleon adopted in France. Beethoven's initial enthusiasm for Napoleon in dedicating the *Eroica* Symphony to him illustrates the kind of messianic appeal that the little general was able to inspire in the cultural elite of Europe. And when, upon hearing of Napoleon's imperial coronation, Beethoven tore up the title page, he, like William Blake, illustrated a rare quality in intellectuals who embrace messianic saviors—the honesty to admit error.[167]

By 1804, with his megalomanic coronation in Paris—he brought the pope from Rome only to have him stand by while he crowned himself and his bride

---

[163] Ibid.,17.

[164] David Wisner, "The Napoleonic Lawgiver," *Proceedings of the Annual Meeting of the Western Society for French History* 21 (1994): 1072–21.

[165] David Cook, "The Beginnings of Islam as an Apocalyptic Movement," in *War in Heaven/Heaven on Earth*, ed. Glen McGhee and Stephen O'Leary (London: Equinox Publishing, 2005), 79–94. There is some evidence that Napoleon understood this dimension of Islam in his appeals to Muslims when in the Middle East, on which see Christian Cherfils, *Bonaparte et Islam* (Paris:Pedon, 1914; Studly, GB, Alcazar Publishing, 2005), 105, 125.

[166] John Morris Roberts, *Revolution and Improvement: The Western World, 1775–1847* (Berkeley and Los Angeles: University of California Press), 107; Rothenberg, "Origins," 788–93.

[167] Despite widespread acceptance of this version of Beethoven's tumultuous relationship with Napoleon, the evidence appears more ambiguous: see Christopher T. George, "The Eroica Riddle: Did Napoleon Remain Beethoven's 'Hero'?" *Napoleonic Scholarship* 1, no.2 (1998); online: http://www.napoleon-series.org/ins/scholarship98/c_eroica.html, April 13, 2010. Kant, on the other hand, steadfastly defended the Revolution; Manfred Kuehn, *Kant: A Biography* (Cambridge: Cambridge University Press, 2001), 340–43.

Josephine—France reached the high point of the Revolution's second (hierarchical) wave of millennial enthusiasm. Having restored the Church to a position of official prominence and embraced the trappings of the former monarchy, including the accession of his entire family to royal status,[168] having reestablished the workings of a formal aristocracy, however modified with meritocratic appointments, Napoleon had begun the work of hierarchical restoration. Ambitious and talented young bourgeois could still ascend much higher on the social scale than before the Revolution, but the gears driving toward a demotic transformation of government had begun to grind in reverse. Had he won at Waterloo, Napoleon planned to move to Versailles.[169]

Unlike George Washington, who refused the monarchy when offered it, Napoleon seized upon it eagerly, indeed, offered it to himself.[170] Unlike the American republic that began more modestly in its pretensions to "absolute freedom" and equality, but which stabilized as a republic, France went through three iterations of "revolution" and monarchical restoration before stabilizing as a constitutional republic. Nor does this contrast necessarily suggest that Napoleon and his Frenchmen were any less dedicated to political freedom than the Americans. The combination of the radical nature of their moral pretensions and their geopolitical position—at once a military danger and opportunity—had the French enter a peculiarly erratic pattern of excess.[171]

In part, at least, it derived from the difference in location and trajectory. Had Washington enjoyed the spectacular military successes of Napoleon, he and his people might have found imperial models more difficult to resist. And had the new republic found itself threatened by armies after defeating the British, either Washington, or another military leader would have found much greater support among the population for monarchy. After all, historically speaking, the imperial messianism of the world-conquering hero is the most common formula for millennial success, and among the hardest to resist. But whether or not Washington's temptation was less than Napoleon's, the fact remains that Washington withstood the appeal of the dominating imperative, and the American Revolution constitutes one of that rare category that deserves a great deal of attention—demotic revolutions that do not turn totalitarian.

---

[168] Note that in David's painting of the coronation, all of Napoleon's family wears red soles on their shoes, a sign of royalty.

[169] For an interesting exercise in counter-history, see G. Macaulay Trevelyan, "If Napoleon Had Won the Battle of Waterloo," *The Westminster Gazette*, July 1907, reprinted in *Recent Essays*, ed. W.A.J. Archbold (London: Longmans, Green & Co., 1926).

[170] For an interesting movie that explores precisely the theme of Napoleon renouncing his imperial pretensions and finding the bourgeois joys of earned financial success, unpretentious love, and family intimacy, see *The Emperor's New Clothes* (2001).

[171] In this context, the criticism of the American Revolution as not *really* a revolution by historians like Howard Zinn, *A People's History of the United States: 1492–Present* (New York: Harper Perennial, 1995), 76–101, display the same millennial perfectionism as the French radicals, and straightens a crooked tale.

10 Egalitarian Millennialism

Marx the Rooster and Marxism (Nineteenth Century CE)

The French Revolution set off two great millennial shock waves that barreled down the nineteenth century, repeatedly churning up renewals of apocalyptic time in France, and throughout Europe. The first shock wave illustrates the law of apocalyptic dynamics, *when in doubt, up the ante.* It was the radical demotic paradigm, which saw in the French Revolution's failure, not the flaw of "going too far," but that of "not having gone far enough." It led to the articulation of both socialist and Communist ideologies, and produced a series of revolutions that spread through Europe throughout the succeeding century. The second shock wave illustrates the first law of apocalyptic dynamics: *one person's messiah is another's antichrist.* Following close behind, building up strength everywhere that the demotic paradigm went with its transformative impact on authoritarian societies, was the toxic wake of a profoundly paranoid discourse of the losing aristocracy: the conspiracy of modernity.

On the one hand, we find the frustrated communists: Babeuf was the first to take the step that Marx would later embed in his secular salvation history of an inverted Hegelian dialectic. The French Revolution had not failed because it had become a victim of excess and self-destructive paranoia; *it failed because it did not abolish property.* The millennial premise had shifted. No longer did the key to bliss lie in the breaking of aristocratic bondage and inaugurating an egalitarian law code, but in ridding everyone of the wretched behavior that comes with property ownership.[1]

This ideological development fueled a much broader movement of working people—what the Middle Ages called "the commoners"—manual laborers, working classes, the non-elites. They demanded levels of empowerment that no authoritarian society had ever permitted.[2] And one of long-term motivations for this permanent radicalism was the memory of—and the search for—the glory days of the French Revolution. During the Second Empire (1851–70), a

[1] On Babeuf, see Talmon, *Rise*, 167–247; Edmund Wilson, *To the Finland Station: A Study in the Writing and Acting of History* (New York: Farrar, Straus & Giroux, 1972), 83–93; Gerhart Niemeyer, "Babeuf and the Total Critique of Society," in *Politische Ordnung und Menschliche Existenz: Festgabe für Eric Voegelin zum 60. Geburtstag*, ed. A. Dempf, H. Arendt, and F. Engel-Janosh (Munich: C.H. Beck Verlag, 1962), 430–61. As Marx himself noted in his denunciation of "crude communism," one might see in all this a kind of politics of resentment: Equality cannot bear the feedback of meritocracy, and so reads all excellence as bad faith. See below, n. 102.

[2] August Nimtz, "Marx and Engels: The Unsung Heroes of the Democratic Breakthrough," *Science and Society* 63, no. 2 (1999): 203–31.

ninety-year-old manual laborer from Nantes, on his deathbed, "raised his eyes to the sky with a look of ecstasy and murmured 'O sun of [17]93, I will then die without seeing your rays again!'"[3] Apparently, for him, neither 1830 nor 1848— nor for that matter, 1789—came close.

On the other hand, we find the frustrated aristocrats. For them, the Revolution had stolen their right to dominate, and such theft could only bode an unprecedented evil: a conspiracy to enslave humankind far worse than anything *they* had ever done. Here Nietzsche, even as he deplored the demotic paradigm (especially because of its bad faith), read the soul of the conspiracist antimodern loser with merciless clarity: the politics of *ressentiment*, the fevered hatreds of people who want to rule and cannot. They accuse their (demotic) enemies of planning to rule the world even as they dream furiously about the day when they will rule again and inflict revenge on their enemies.[4] Once the revolutionaries had set "liberal" society in motion, and begun the process of dismantling the prime divider that had so favored them, the old aristocracy lost its open power to dominate. Now, anyone who could, learned to play by the new rules, and, like the common-born Michelet or the Jewish immigrant Meyerbeer, could rise to the very top of the system without betraying their origins to the elite's values. Those aristocrats who could not succeed by them, interpreted the victory of these new "democratic rules"—tolerance, freedom (of the press!), equality, meritocracy—as a vast conspiracy of people who, while pretending to play by the new rules, actually planned to enslave and rule the world.

This kind of thinking produces an antimodern apocalyptic scenario, whereby the forces of evil, disguised as angels of democracy, dupe the masses into overthrowing their elites only to then fall prey to a subversive plot to enslave them. For these antimoderns, the Masons were not involved in the benign conspiracy described by Mozart in *The Magic Flute* (1791), but a deeply malignant one, not magnanimous but malevolent.[5] For these conspiracists, the victory of democracies set off alarms. The revolutionaries may have thought they were spreading life-giving societies committed to justice and fairness *in this world*, and colored the map of the world with the spread of their constitutional states. But others viewed this cartographic transformation as tracking the spread of a cancer. They believed that they witnessed the final stages of a conspiracy of the weak to use democracy as a ploy to bind humankind.

These two strands of apocalyptic belief, both activated by the French Revolution, played significant roles in the two most powerful millennial movements of the twentieth century—Communism and Nazism. In this chapter we will deal with

---

[3] Story recounted by Gabriel Monod in his introduction to Albert Mathiez, *Contributions à l'histoire de la révolution française* (Paris: F. Alcon, 1957), i.

[4] Friedrich Nietzsche, *Genealogy of Morals*, 1:10–17, trans. Kaufmann, 36–54 (see above, chapters 1 and 8).

[5] On Mozart and the *Magic Flute*, see Appendix online.

Marxism as a millennial ideology, the next, with Communism as an apocalyptic movement dedicated to effecting that ideology, and the following one, with Nazism.

■ PRELUDE TO MARXISM: THE "RAW" COMMUNISM OF BABEUF

While historians tend to follow the story of the French Revolution by telling the big story that goes from the Directory to Napoleon, it is worthwhile pausing to consider a man whose solution to the crisis of a waning French Revolution was no less millennial than the future emperor's, but far less successful, in the short run at least. Noel (Gracchus) Babeuf was a Jacobin of no great importance.[6] After the Terror, however, he rose to prominence in a small group of radicals who articulated a theory of history as a class struggle between those with and those without property and predicted the imminent conclusion of this battle with the elimination of all private property. In grafting this "terrible simplification" onto Rousseau's *Discourse on Inequality*, he produced "a crude prototype of Marxist analysis."[7]

Babeuf did not think of himself as bloodthirsty: he distanced himself from the intention he attributed to Robespierre to slaughter millions of French in order to carry out the necessary redistribution of land for a just and equal society. Although he himself apparently preferred "persuading" people to lower their standards of living, one has to wonder what the taste of state power might have done to his reliance on rhetoric alone. Certainly his confidence in the power of a well-intentioned state to micromanage the economy seems boundless.[8]

Like religious millennialists, Babeuf was entirely convinced that his vision offered irresistible grace to everyone of honest and sound mind: "Where is the man who could be so mad as to reject this guarantee of never being in want, this promise of communal prosperity, this inexhaustible mine of perpetual individual well-being." Once the state had committed itself to this vision, the millennial kingdom was assured:

> Let that government make disappear all frontiers, fences, walls, locks on doors, all disputes, trials, all theft, murder, all crime, all Tribunals, prisons, gallows, torture, jealousy, insatiability, pride, deceit, duplicity, finally all vices. No more (and this is, no doubt, the most essential) of the ever gnawing tooth of general restlessness, of the personal, perpetual anxiety of every one of us, about our lot of tomorrow, next month, next year, in our old age, the fate of children and their children....Guarantee to every one of its

---

[6] Babeuf's baptismal name was Noel. He changed it to Gracchus (invoking the two great Tribunes of the Plebs from Republican Rome, Tiberius and Gaius Gracchus) in 1795.

[7] Talmon, *Rise*, 181. Talmon here echoed the language of Karl Marx, "*roher Communismus*," on which see below, n. 101.

[8] See his letter to Germain from the Arras Prison, July 28, 1795 (10 Thermidor, an. III) in Maurice Dommanget, *Pages Choisies de Babeuf* (Paris: A. Colin, 1935); cited in *Rise*, 193.

members a state of stable felicity, the satisfaction of the needs of all, a sufficiency inalterable, independent of the ineptitude, immorality or ill will of those in power.[9]

A classic millennial vision—boundless felicity, banishment of suffering—based on a new, but in fact medieval millennial premise: abolish private property and evil will vanish from the earth.

Such a vision obviously called for an enlightened vanguard, a revolutionary elite who, knowing what needed doing, could cut the Gordian knot of normal (i.e., corrupt) politics, and dissipate the fog of selfishness that confuses people into following the wrong leaders. The masses need to give their leaders full loyalty and full obedience. In turn, this revolutionary vanguard, which must not allow the people to act as they wish, but as they should act, also has the sacred, if painful, duty to use force.[10]

True to his vision, Babeuf and a small coterie of friends planned to take over the reins of government and inaugurate a totalistic regime based on the principles of absolute equality, universal obligation to work, and the unrestricted right of the "nation" to dispose of all property on French soil.[11] Betrayed by one of his conspirators, Babeuf and his revolutionary vanguard were arrested and imprisoned and executed by the Directory in 1796, the very year of Napoleon's ascendancy in the Italian campaign.

Babeuf's tale illustrates some of the dynamics of post-apocalyptic time. Like those members of the Committee of Public Safety who wanted to eliminate Robespierre and Saint-Just without ending the terror, Babeuf tried to fight against the return of "normal time." But in 1795, the radical demotic sentiments that had, in 1789, found such a powerful echo in a large and energized public sphere, now fell on deaf ears. That apocalyptic moment had passed, and only a military genius with a talent for imposing empire while convincing people that he came to liberate them could revive it. Conquest was a faster way back to the apocalyptic high than abolition of private property.

But Babeuf's post-apocalyptic analysis, his conclusions about why the Revolution had failed, had a long, fruitful, and destructive future. His insight that the revolution failed because it was not radical, like the Xhosa explanation that the ancestors had not come because some had yet to slay all their cattle, followed cognitive dissonance into still-more-coercive apocalyptic scenarios. It never put in question the behavior of these "rational" revolutionary agents in apocalyptic time, never questioned the revolutionary (millennial) premise that, once evil destroyed, earthly bliss would ensue.[12]

---

[9] Babeuf, *Le Tribun du people ou le Défenseur des droits de l'homme par Gracchus Babeuf*, 35:105–06; cited in Talmon, *Rise*, 195.

[10] Talmon, *Rise*, 219; K.G. Riegel, "Marxism-Leninism as a Political Religion," *Totalitarian Movements and Political Religions* 6 (2005): 97–126.

[11] Talmon, *Rise*, 229.

[12] For a good analysis of ideologies as responses to the disappointments of modernity, see the discussion of Friedrich Hölderlin in Lorelea Michaelis, "The Wisdom of Prometheus: Kant, Marx, and Hölderlin on Politics, Disappointment, and the Limits of Modernity," *Polity* 31, no. 4 (1999): 537–59.

■ MARX, THE SECULAR JOACHITE

Although there are many thinkers who developed aspects of this thought, none had so great an impact as Karl Marx (1818–83), the son of a lawyer from Trier. Marx's impact on the ideologies of the subsequent century and a half are nothing short of spectacular, a nice irony for someone who was at great pains to deny any real significance to ideologies. Marx's most important contributions to the millennial thought of his age concern his development of a "scientific" reading of history—the historical dialectic—that resembles in some important ways the historical exegesis of the Bible carried out by the medieval monk, Joachim of Fiore (d. 1202). Joachim had elaborated a system of exegesis that "read" history as an ineluctable process, a "history of mankind" that promised collective salvation.[13] Marx offered a secular variant, a historical dialectic that inexorably drove toward collective salvation in Communism.

With this historical feat, Marx accomplished a double victory. He formulated a "scientific" historiography that made his theories sound like the products of the cutting edge of modern culture.[14] And he gave all those who accepted his insights a sense of empowerment because, like Joachim's thirteenth-century readers, they believed they lived at the turning point of history. Like Auerliano Buendia, the character in Gabriel Marquez's novel, *Hundred Years of Solitude*, who labored ceaselessly to decipher a coded book and did so only to discover that he was reading an apocalyptic prophecy as it came true, Marx unraveled the hidden meaning of history just as, in his reading, it was reaching its climax. Unlike Auerliano, however, Marx was a step *ahead* of the process, and therefore had a chance to reveal it to a large audience.

In so doing, he inherited a secular tradition of apocalyptic teleology from two initial German enthusiasts of the French Revolution, Kant and Hegel, whose histories "took over the task of defining the modern age."[15] They sought to reveal the processes set in motion by human action, to articulate a Promethean history in which humankind was agent, not passive victim. The Promethean hubris behind this effort to replace a God who tarries with a technologically empowered and liberated humanity has drawn the attention of observers from its earliest moments to the present, from Hölderlin's *Hyperion*, via the Shelleys' *Frankenstein: Or, The Modern Prometheus* (1818) and *Prometheus Unbound* (1820), to David Landes'

---

[13] See Marjorie Reeves, *The Influence of Prophecy in the Later Middle Ages: A Study in Joachimism* (Oxford: Clarendon Press, 1969); Bernard McGinn, *The Calabrian Abbot: Joachim of Fiore in the History of Western Thought* (New York: Macmillan, 1985).

[14] "The dialectic, therefore, not merely associates Marxism and science, it makes Marxism appear as a kind of super-science," Donald MacRae, "The Bolshevik Ideology: The Intellectual and Emotional Factors in Communist Affiliation," *Cambridge Journal* 5 (1951): 165.

[15] The following paragraph owes much to Michaelis' article, "Wisdom of Prometheus." In the terminology of this book, the title would read "Apocalyptic Disappointment and the Limits of Secular Millennialism."

The Unbound Prometheus (1964) and Arthur Mitzman's *Prometheus Revisited: The Quest for Global Justice in the Twenty-First Century* (2003).[16] But if Hölderlin faced the bitter lessons of cognitive dissonance directly, others, better known to us, refused to accept the partial and painful successes of the Promethean millennial vision. For Kant, Hegel, and Marx, individual efforts may have failed, even single group efforts, but nonetheless a remorseless logic drove history forward. And there was a destination.

As a result, they all develop some version of gradual (in Hegel and Marx's case, punctuated) progress whereby the historical process continues to work toward the *telos* of history—collective salvation defined in secular terms. These men define the "modern age," as an age "that lives for the future," an age that "revels in novelty," a qualitatively new epoch, "in which the new and the unexpected constantly occur."[17] "All shared the basic experience of movement, of change in the perspective of an open future; disagreement prevailed only on the question of the tempo and direction which had to be taken. This dispute…challenged everyone to make a choice. From that time on, historical time exercised a compulsion that no one could escape."[18]

And among the things moderns could not escape was disappointment. Through the notions of time with a vector and humanity with agency, modern thinking assured a permanent recurrence of disappointment—this time, not with God but with ourselves. The disappointment that followed the spectacular failure of the French Revolution to accomplish its millennial goals operated for some, like Hölderlin, as a disillusionment with human hubris. But for others, in classic millennial style, it was only a disappointing delay, as if an appointment we had made with the future had been postponed. And it was the job of historical thinkers like Hegel and Marx "to bridge the gap between our plans and their realization."[19]

And of course, for such millennial stalwarts, the future holds out the promise of a radically better world. For Kant, this future derived from an ever-increasing role of reason and self-mastery, and he may even have coined the German word for

---

[16] Hölderlin's *Hyperion*, written in the immediate aftermath of the revolutionary Terror, "conceived in the love of freedom excited by the French Revolution and written in fluctuations of anxiety doubt and hope that came afterward," condemned the notion of unbounded human agency as hubris, Friedrich Hölderlin, *Hyperion, or the Hermit in Greece*, trans. Willard R. Trask, in *Hyperion and Selected Poems*, ed. Eric L. Santer (New York: Continuum, 1990), 539–40. David Landes, on the other hand, argues that "hubris is a start" for making the technological leap required by the industrial revolution in *The Unbound Prometheus: Technological Change and Industrial Development in Western Europe from 1750 to the Present* (Cambridge: Cambridge University Press, 2003), 555.

[17] Reinhart Kosellek, "'Neuzeit': Remarks on the Semantics of the Modern Concept of Movement," in *Futures Past*, trans. Keith Tribe (Cambridge, Mass.: MIT Press, 1985), 238–39; cited in Michaelis, "Wisdom of Prometheus," 541.

[18] Kosellek, "Neuzeit," 258; cited in Michaelis, "Wisdom of Prometheus," 542. See Sheldon Wolin, *Politics and Vision: Continuity and Innovation in Western Political Thought* (Boston: Light, Brown & Co., 1960), 195–238.

[19] Michaelis, "Wisdom of Prometheus," 542.

"progress"—*Fortschritt*.[20] Hegel took it to a new and more complex level with his notion of the dialectic, the complex interactions of forces in conflict and the non-linear passage from one stage to another. For him, the "cunning of reason" worked itself out in history *despite* what individual men willed; they were "the unconscious tools and organs" of the world spirit.[21] The present was always the *unintended consequences* of human agency.

Thus, despite the nonlinear movement of the "history of freedom" and of self-fashioning whose ups and downs those observers of the failures of the French Revolution knew only too well, the dialectic permitted one to maintain a sense of the overall trend regardless of what particular people or groups of people might (mistakenly) try to accomplish. "History," Marx later wrote, "is but a continuous transformation of human nature."[22] Such an approach enabled people, uninspired by Kant's gradualism, to welcome the upheavals they saw around them in good apocalyptic style as part of the process of redemption. For Hegel, reason points history ineluctably, if indirectly, toward the victory of freedom.

Marx took the elitist Hegel's dialectic and turned it on its head to create a demotic millennial historiography. The key to the millennial aspects of Marx's thought lay in three assumptions characteristic of apocalyptic thinkers.

- First, that he and his generation stood at the turning point from the penultimate to the final stage of world history. The dialectic patterns of thesis and antithesis and synthesis that mark human history were, in his own day, on the verge of a new and radically different synthesis. Capitalism had spawned its antithesis, and the shift to the new synthesis, Communism, was imminent. Like Joachim of Fiore, Marx focused on three great ages, and like his predecessor, he situated himself at the dawn of the new age.

- Second, that that new and coming stage represented a qualitative shift in the nature of the dialectic, its fulfillment: the next was the *last* stage. The driving motor of the dialectic throughout human history—class warfare—would, as Babeuf predicted, come to an end. Like the millennial week, which posited six thousand years of travail followed by a sabbatical millennium, Marx viewed the long past as a history of travail—the dialectic of class conflict—and the future age as fundamentally different.

- Third, that the motivating passion behind all this *Sturm und Drang* was a prophetic morality. It may be buried under mountains of abstruse

[20] For Kant, the conviction that humanity is gradually improving is a "philosophical prediction" ("Is the Human Race Continually Improving?" in *Kant's Political Writings*, ed. Hans Reiss, trans. H.B. Nisbet (Cambridge: Cambridge University Press, 1985), 185; Kosellek, "Neuzeit," 280; Michaelis, "Wisdom of Prometheus," 544.

[21] *Die Vernunft in der Geschichte*, 105; cited in G. H. R. Parkinson, "Hegel, Marx and the Cunning of Reason," *Philosophy* 64, no. 249 (1989): 291.

[22] Karl Marx, *Poverty of Philosphy* (New York: International Publishers, 1951), 124. According to Raymond Aron, "all Marxist philosophy loses its meaning if one forgets the philosophical inspiration according to which it is through history that human nature transforms itself or, even that man makes himself (*se façonne*)," *Le Marxisme de Marx* (Paris: Editions de Fallois, 2002), 291.

discussion in *Kapital*, or given an opaque rhetorical patina in *The Manifesto*, but beneath all Marx's writings lies a radical—indeed prophetic—moral outrage at how man exploits his fellow man and a passionate desire to see an end to this evil. Far from transcending morality, Marx's rage was above all moral, at its most profound, a cry for human freedom.

Arthur Mendel noted: [Marxism's] vision is that of the Biblical Prophets—social justice, the good society without (to quote the *Communist Manifesto*) "conquest, enslavement, robbery, murder," without "the poverty of the great majority that, despite all its labor, has up to now nothing to sell but itself; and the wealth of the few that increases constantly although they have long since ceased to work."[23]

As a form of secularized millennial historiography, Marx's work has a remarkable relationship to that of Joachim. Joachim built his exegesis on a study of history though the guidance of the Bible, especially the book of Revelation, and he developed a complex system to explain the hidden mechanisms of history. Marx built his on the study of history by working with the secular record and revealing the hidden mechanisms with the dialectic. Whereas Joachim's analytic technique was exegesis and his authority, scripture, Marx's was scientific analysis and the authority, the historical record.

The importance of this scientific claim as the authority cannot be underestimated. It offered a substitute for religious certainty and led both Marx, and still more, many Marxists, to make absolutist claims to "scientific" or "objective truth." No matter how accurate one might consider Marx's historiography, such posturing seems in retrospect like a form of *scientism*. But for contemporaries, the value of an absolutist claim to scientific truth represented above all a claim to reliably predict the future. Scientism replaced religion as the authority, and scientific prognostication operated as a form of secular prophecy.

■ CATACLYSMIC APOCALYPTIC: *LA POLITIQUE DU PIRE*

Marx's millennial historiography contributed yet another variant to the secular millennialism of the French Revolution. He developed a pronounced cataclysmic dimension to his apocalyptic scenario. Unlike many early enthusiasts of the revolution, for whom the role of violence was limited if not unnecessary, Marx shifted dramatically toward a scenario in which human suffering and alienation must reach absolute levels in order for the millennium to come. Like the scenario of Revelation, Marx foresees things getting much worse before they will get better, and that vision helps him articulate a revolutionary *politique du pire* which enabled Marxists to resist all calls to moderation and reform. Things had to get worse, much worse, *in order for* salvation to come.[24]

---

[23] Mendel, *Vision and Violence*, 150.
[24] Michaelis, "Wisdom of Prometheus," 547. See below, chapter 11, n. 13.

This cataclysmic scenario comes from Marx's work using Hegel's scheme from the perspective of the laboring masses. By focusing on the class wars *seen from below*, the desperation of the masses becomes the cry that sets in motion the final convulsion, and in order for that cry to occur, things had to get still worse.[25] This catastrophic direction of present trends also permits him to argue that *this time* the transformation, which must emerge from a *revolution*, will be total. It offers a decisive and absolutist (millennial) answer to the half-measures and bitter disappointments of the French Revolution.

The outlines appear in the *German Ideology* (1844?), where one finds a stark historicizing of philosophical discourse centered on the key apocalyptic turning point, the total alienation of the proletariat.

> *Only* the proletarians of the present day, who are *completely* shut off from *all* self-activity, are in a position to achieve a *complete* and *no longer self-restricted* activity, which consists in the appropriation of a *totality* of productive forces in the thus postulated development of a *totality* of capacities. All earlier revolutionary appropriations were restricted; individuals, whose self-activity was restricted by a crude instrument of production and a limited intercourse, appropriated this crude instrument of production, and hence *merely* achieved a new state of limitation... In all expropriations until now, a mass of individuals remained subservient to a single instrument of production; in the appropriation by the proletarians, a *mass* of instruments of production must be made subject to *each* individual, and property to *all*. Modern *universal* intercourse can be controlled by individuals therefore, only when controlled by *all*.[26]

Here we have a peculiar combination of, on the one hand, abstract philosophical notions—complete self-activity, modern universal intercourse—with, on the other, extremely concrete issues of forces of production and the lives of ordinary manual laborers, all wrapped up in a totalistic language that brooks no compromise.

The totalizing discourse operates as a kind of scientistic magic, making millennial promises about total liberation—"complete" control over the instruments of production and universal intercourse. But Marx offered this promise not to the intellectuals of his age, but specifically to those then suffering the most from the throes of industrialization.

> ...Marxist revolutionaries adopt Hegel's dialectic to prove that each step downward into deeper misery simultaneously and inevitably hastened the coming of paradise. "Imperialist" wars and "capitalist" depressions became, for the apocalyptic Marxists, what the "fortunate fall" and the "signs of the End" are for Christians, the same gratifying dialectic that Bakùnin had in mind when he announced that "the passion for destruction is a creative passion."[27]

---

[25] Note the parallel with the cry of the Israelites in bondage which triggers God's intervention, Exodus 2:23–25.

[26] Karl Marx, *German Ideology* in *The Marx-Engels Reader*, ed. Robert C. Tucker (New York: W.W. Norton, 1978), 191. Italics mine.

[27] Mendel, *Vision and Violence*, 153.

With such a promise comes a fury to console and soothe the agony of one's current condition—the very crushing pains the laborer now experiences will be transformed into the opposite, the very *totality* of their alienation will make it possible for *all* to achieve *complete* self-activity.

And behind the apocalyptic historical analysis lay an enticing millennial premise and promise: a "new man" would emerge on the other side of this wrenching process of alienation. Just as the French Revolution had promised a new citizen, so the Marxists promised a "new comrade"—an interesting shift, given the sad fact that "fraternity" was the first of the promises to vanish from the millennial formula of *liberté, égalité, fraternité*.[28] Here, over the course of the nineteenth century, revolutionaries availed themselves of John Locke's theories about humans as blank slates who had no "innate ideas," that is, no innate character, that rather sensory perceptions and experiences mold humans. Whatever Locke believed he meant, both Enlightenment thinkers and subsequent radicals seized eagerly on this nurture versus nature perspective to believe anything possible.[29]

As in the case of many millennial texts, this one seems far less compelling with hindsight; indeed, these expectations were and still are completely unrealistic.[30] But, "[o]ne may poke holes in the theories...mock any number of embarrassing contradictions. None of that matters. It is the myth, as Sorel saw, and its inspirational powers that count. And apocalyptic Marxism is the perfect myth."[31] One might argue that one of the reasons that Marx succeeded in winning so many fervent disciples was not *despite* the bizarre reasoning here displayed, but *because* of it.[32]

---

[28] By the time of the Directory (1794–99), it appears in the variant: "*Liberté, égalité, propriété.*" See, for example, a print of the three directors (Barras, La Révellière, and Reubell), after the coup-d'état of the 18 of Fructidor (September 4, 1797) entitled *La trinité républicaine*, BNP, Estampes, reproduced in François Furet and Denis Richet, *La Révolution du 9-Thermidor au 18-Brumaire* (Paris: Hachette, 1966), 123. See also Mona Ozouf, "Liberté, égalité, fraternité," in *Lieux de Mémoire*, ed. Pierre Nora, 3 vol. (Paris: Gallimard, 1997), 3:4353–89.

[29] Richard Pipes discusses the link between Locke and the Communists in *Russian Revolution, 1899–1919* (London: Harvill Press, 1997), 125–36; see above on the French revolutionaries' use of this notion, chapter 9 n. 85.

[30] For an attempt at a sympathetic but realistic review of the completely impracticable assumptions that underlie so much of Marx's thought about the Communist state to come, see Jon Elster, *Making Sense of Marx* (Cambridge: Cambridge University Press, 1985), 521–27. He repeatedly refers to the elements of Marx's assumptions and allusions that are "extremely" (522) and "irredeemably Utopian" (526), of coming from "Cloud-cuckoo-land" (524). See also Axel Van den Berg's characterization of Marx's salvific vision as an "absurdly bucolic...utterly cloudy millennium." *The Immanent Utopia: From Marxism on the State to the State of Marxism* (Princeton, N.J.: Princeton University Press, 1988), 56–7.

[31] Mendel, *Vision and Violence*, 152.

[32] "Such utopian images of the future command society, however scattered and fragmentary in the writings of Marx and Engels, form an essential component of Marxist theory—and one that is essential for understanding the appeals of Marxism in the modern world." Maurice Meisner, "Marxism and Utopianisn" in *Marxism, Maosim and Utopianism, Eight Essays* (Madison: University of Wisconsin Press, 1982); see also Frank E. Manuel and Fritzie P. Manuel, "Marx and Engels in the Landscape of Utopia," in *Utopian Thought in the Western World* (Cambridge, Mass.: Belknap Press, 1979), 697–716.

▪ APOCALYPTIC TIMING OF MILLENNIAL NARRATIVES: THE *COMMUNIST MANIFESTO*

In 1847, the newly forming "Communist Party" asked Marx and Engels, who had just joined, to write the manifesto of the movement. The opportunity enabled Marx to enshrine the millennial historical vision, which he had glimpsed in working through the *German Ideology*, into a brilliantly argued and coherent historical narrative, ending with a stirring call of the rooster: "Let the ruling classes tremble at a communist revolution. The proletarians have nothing to lose but their chains. They have a world to win. WORKERS OF THE WORLD UNITE!"[33]

The *Communist Manifesto*'s millennial grand narrative runs so: History is the tale of class conflict and the categorical victory of the ruling classes (prime-divider societies). From the dawn of polities, ruling classes have exploited working classes (dominating imperative). Earlier societies, however, despite being riven by class conflict, had multiple layers in their hierarchies, which, by mediating the conflict and rendering its workings opaque and inefficient, provided some stability even as they perpetuated their injustices. The modern bourgeoisie, however, has simplified this conflict in unprecedented ways. It has stripped away everything but the fundamental conflict between two classes: bourgeoisie and proletariat. Over time, history had worked to produce the apocalyptic prophets' favorite rhetorical trope—the simplifying dualism of good and evil.

The bourgeoisie is the most extraordinarily powerful of all ruling classes. Unlike earlier rulers who dominated others, bourgeois have used technology—new means and modes of production—to dominate both others *and* nature, and thereby they transformed the world in ways never before achieved. Although he claims that the bourgeoisie acts with a ruthlessness to match their power, one detects in Marx a certain admiration.

> The bourgeoisie has disclosed how it came to pass that the brutal display of vigor in the Middle Ages, which reactionaries so much admire, found its fitting complement in the most slothful indolence.[34] It has been the first to show what man's activity can bring about.[35] It has accomplished wonders far surpassing Egyptian pyramids, Roman aqueducts, and Gothic cathedrals; it has conducted expeditions that put in the shade all former Exoduses of nations and crusades.[36]

And this same colossus of modernity has an equally epic impact on the means and modes of production. By their very nature they are unstable:

---

[33] Karl Marx and Friedrich Engels, *Manifesto of the Communist Party* in *Marx-Engels Reader*, 500.

[34] This is another way to characterize the cultures of poverty that characterize prime-divider societies.

[35] In terms of this book: they have introduced the secular millennial imagination of modernity: humans can act and create at will; society is radically malleable.

[36] Marx and Engels, *Communist Manifesto* in *Marx-Engels Reader*, 476.

The bourgeoisie cannot exist without constantly revolutionizing the instruments of production, and thereby the relations of production, and with them the whole relations of society... *Constant* revolutionizing of production, *uninterrupted* disturbance of all social conditions, *everlasting* uncertainty and agitation distinguish the bourgeois epoch from all earlier ones. All fixed, fast-frozen relations, with their train of ancient and venerable prejudices and opinions, are swept away, all new-formed ones become antiquated before they can ossify. *All that is solid melts into air, all that is holy is profaned,* and man is at last compelled to face with sober senses, his real conditions of life, and his relations with his kind.[37]

Note the use of rhetoric that apocalyptic audiences want to hear—these are *unprecedented* times, and unprecedented things *will* occur. And at the very heart of this analysis lies a millennial promise: Marx believed that this immensely protean force of the bourgeoisie, which thinks itself in command, has played the sorcerer's apprentice and unleashed forces far greater than itself. The cunning of history has these new and technologically unfettered masters behaving atrociously in order to destroy them: those whom the gods would destroy, they first drive mad with greed and power. In their greed, they have driven workers to paroxysms of enslavement and alienation from the means and modes of production. With these productive forces now in the hands of the bourgeoisie, they performed on a scale that no other cultural elite, no matter how cruel, had—could have—ever done.

And in so behaving, they established the means of their own undoing, the creation of a laboring class–consciousness. They have created the people who will, suffering from the worst of their system, turn the tables on them and enjoy the best. The bourgeois do not realize it, but they are the messiah's donkey, the vehicle of the messianic age, not the inheritors of it. And like so many messianic vehicles, their fate upon arrival will be sacrificial slaughter.[38]

Most important, the dialectic, like Joachim's exegesis of scripture, provided the believer with an orientation in time.[39] Indeed, one might say, ironically, that this historical-dialectical orientation is *the good news*: "Have courage O you who hear this message, for *now* is the time of the final revelation/revolution." What the internal logic of the *Manifesto* suggests—that Marx believed he lived at the very edge of the apocalyptic transformation, on the brink of the revolutionary vortex— the final rhetoric makes clear. This is a work of exhortation, a rooster's crow. The

---

[37] Marshall Berman, *All That Is Solid Melts into Air: The Experience of Modernity* (New York: Simon & Schuster, 1982).

[38] See the disturbing analysis in Seffi Rachlevsky, *Hamoro shel meshiach* (Messiah's donkey) (Tel Aviv: Yedi'ot aharonot, 1998).

[39] Engels has some interesting remarks on Joachim of Fiore in his *The Peasant War of 1525*. Erich Voegelin traces the links between Joachim and both strands of modern "secular" apocalyptic readings of history, *The New Science of Politics: An Introduction* (Chicago: University of Chicago Press, 1952), 112–24. See also Eugene Webb, "Voegelin's Gnosticism Reconsidered," *Political Science Review* 34 (2005): 48–76, online: http://faculty.washington.edu/ewebb/EVgnost.pdf, March 23, 2010.

dawn has come. As Wordsworth put it at the time of the French Revolution: "Bliss would it be in that dawn to be alive, but to be young would be very heaven!"

And that moment was, in the mid-nineteenth century, very close. It was only a matter of the revolutionary vanguard, the radical demotic intellectuals who sided with the truely just—the oppressed—awakening them to their oppression, and convincing them that *now* was the time to arise and overthrow their enemies. In other words, in the terminology of this book, Marx's message constituted an active cataclysmic apocalyptic scenario leading to a demotic progressive millennium.

■ 1848: APOCALYPTIC MOMENT, MILLENNIAL WAVE

The question is, as with all millennial movements that want to spread: when and how will the apocalyptic transition shift gears from hell to heaven? For Marx, and most millennial modernists, that meant revolution, hopefully now. And the evidence suggests that, whatever earlier false alarms he might have experienced, the first major moment that Marx believed marked that great and final revolution was 1848, a moment that coincided with his own rise to prominence in the revolutionary ranks and his publication of the *Communist Manifesto*.

In 1848, starting in Italy in January and moving to Paris in February, a wave of revolutionary movements burst on the European continent like a roll of thunder.[40] The "people" in one capital after another, hearing the news from their neighbors, rose up to demand their rights—constitutional government, equality before the law, freedom. Roosters crowing awakened roosters all over Europe. The new day finally dawned.

The intoxication of this revolutionary enthusiasm, amplified by song and poetry, convinced people that this was the true international revolution, the one about which the French had only dreamed. A performance of Meyerbeer's opera, *Robert le Diable* (1831), in Paris after Louis-Philippe's abdication (February 1848), ended not only with the audience singing the "Marseilleise," but a new patriotic song: "Even to the depths of its roots/The old throne was corrupt…Long live Republican France! Liberty is on the wing!"[41] The descriptions of elation and fraternity, of joy and deeply felt drama, express the intensity of this apocalyptic time. But this time it was fueled not by celestial signs and wonders and human repentance—the standard Christian passive cataclysmic apocalyptic scenario—but by peoples rising up and taking their destiny into their hands. These active apocalyptic revolutions, part violent, part transformative, mark the use of the public sphere for a self-assertive discourse by people whom most cultures repress—commoners.

---

[40] Priscilla Robertson, *The Revolutions of 1848: A Social History* (New York: Harper & Row, 1960).

[41] See Hanna Lewis, ed., *A Year of Revolutions: Fanny Lewald's Recollections of 1848* (Providence, R.I.: Berghahn Books, 1997), 70.

Historians tend not to believe that the *Communist Manifesto* played much of a role in the wave of revolutions that swept through Europe in 1848, even though the violent uprising in Paris in June of that year occurred shortly after the *Manifesto* had first appeared in French there.[42] It was written rapidly in December of 1847 and first published in England at the end of February 1848.[43] On the basis of the documentary evidence one can argue either way—it came out after the outbreak of events, or it spurred on events already in motion.

One should not, however, view the spread of ideas in apocalyptic time according to the general rules of dissemination of texts in (relatively) normal time. Oral transmission goes faster and farther than written, and the *Manifesto*, like any good apocalyptic scenario, lends itself to oral recounting. Certainly, like the *Grande Peur* of 1789, whose rapid spread so surprises modern historians, apocalyptic news spreads orally, over unidentified paths, very rapidly. Given the extremely strong café and club culture that had arisen in Louis-Philippe's indulgent monarchy, where participants read and debated newspapers and other contemporary texts, a couple of months is ample time for the right publication to make its mark even indirectly, through word of mouth.[44]

Nor was Marx the only rooster crowing at the time. The same conversations through which the ideas of the *Manifesto* rippled found exaltation in Michelet's extraordinary *History of the French Revolution*, the first two volumes of which first appeared in 1847.[45] They described "the tale of the most beautiful days of the Revolution, still credulous, fraternal, clement...."[46] His colleagues at the Collège de France found his lectures on the French Revolution so incendiary—and wildly popular—that they prevented him from delivering them.[47] So the *Manifesto* fully reflected the feverish, radical expectation of the day, the same spirit that inspired the leaders of these revolutions to shape them along lines of class warfare and the destruction of all that stood in the way of a just society.[48]

---

[42] "The *Communist Manifesto*...exercised no influence on the February Revolution." Georges Duveau, *1848: The Making of a Revolution* (New York: Vintage, 1967), 206.

[43] Hal Draper, *Marx Engels Chronicle: A Day-by-Day Chronology of Marx and Engels' Life and Activity* (New York: Schocken Books, 1985), 30.

[44] On the growth and politicization of café culture, see W. Scott Haine, *The World of the Paris Café: Socialbility among the French Working Class, 1789–1914* (Baltimore: Johns Hopkins University Press, 1996), 140–42.

[45] "...my teaching, my history, and its all powerful interpreter—the spirit of the Revolution," Michelet, *Histoire de la Révolution Française*, ed. Ernest Flammarion, 5 vol. (Paris: Près L' Odéon, 1898); trans. Gordon Wright (Chicago: University of Chicago Press, 1967), 1:1.

[46] Ibid., "Introduction de 1868," 1.

[47] Arthur Mitzman, *Michelet, Historian: Rebirth and Romanticism in Nineteenth-Century France* (New Haven, Conn.: Yale University Press, 1990), 154–55; Oscar Haac, *Jules Michelet* (Boston: Twayne Publishers, 1982), 83–86; Wilson, *Finland Station*, 20. With Michelet's enthusiasm for the early years of the Revolution as a spur to further revolution, and his opposition among his colleagues, one might find the first iteration of the "revisionist debate" of the French Revolution (see above, chapter 9, for its current reiteration).

[48] The Communist Party was started by a group of German radicals in Paris who formed a club they modestly called the *Bund der Gerechten* or "Society/Covenant of the Just."

These revolutions differed from earlier ones (1789, 1830). They attempted to transform not just the structure of government, but also the social structure.[49] They began in the same demotic enthusiasm of the French Revolution, then, partly because of the massive task of restructuring society they tried to effect, rapidly devolved into violence and self-destructive failure.

Marx, thirty years old at the time, surfed the revolutionary wave with growing confidence in his conviction that *Now!* had at last come. "To Marx the outbreak and rapid spread of Revolution represented the fulfillment of a personal prophecy, and a chance to immerse himself in a struggle in which the whole destiny of humanity was at stake. Now his faith in the power of revolution both to reveal and to realize the meaning of history would find its rest."[50] He visited Paris briefly after the February overthrow of the monarchy, where he set up a Communist League club. Then after the March revolution in Berlin, he went to Cologne.

There he manned the *Neue Rheinische Zeitung* for three months, his "most formidable period as a publicist," during which every article, as Friedrich Engels later recalled, "struck like a shell and burst."[51] "Marx's goad dug the shanks of the Assembly, inciting it to bolder action, the breath of his freezing criticism blasted the backs of their necks."[52] He was his own "sans-culottes gallery" driving the revolution forward. Lenin later held up Marx's editorial work in this period as the "unsurpassed" model of an "organ of the revolutionary proletariat."[53] Marx, along with a host of others like Nicolas Restif de la Bretonne and Armand Marrast, had founded a major school of apocalyptic journalism.[54]

■ MEYERBEER AND MARX: DEALING WITH THE COGNITIVE DISSONANCE OF APOCALYPTIC FAILURE

But by late 1849, all the revolutions had failed, leaving a bitter legacy of half-baked democratic reforms. One of the more acute observers/participants of 1848, Massimo d'Azeglio used the metaphor of the stallion of liberty: "The gift of liberty is like a horse, handsome, strong, and high-spirited. In some it arouses a wish to ride; in many others, on the contrary, it increases the desire to walk."[55] If anything, these revolutions frightened people, who preferred to walk rather than mount that spirited stallion. Marx, along with many other millennial enthusiasts of 1848, found himself in the aftermath, bitterly disappointed, deeply embarrassed, and isolated. Ruefully, Marx

---

[49] Robertson, *Revolutions of 1848*, 4–7, 412–19.

[50] Jerrold Siegel, *Marx's Fate: The Shape of a Life* (Princeton, N.J.: Princeton University Press, 1978), 193.

[51] Wilson, *Finland Station*, 200.

[52] Ibid., 201.

[53] Ibid.

[54] James Billington, "The Magic Medium: Journalism," *Fire in the Minds of Men: Origins of the Revolutionary Faith* (New York: Basic Books, 1980), 306–24.

[55] *Recollections*, trans. Count Maffei (London: Chapman & Hall, 1868), 2:8; cited in Robertson, *Revolutions of 1848*, 415.

would later comment to Engels, "The pleasant delusions and the almost childish enthusiasm with which we greeted the revolution before February, 1848, are for the devil."[56] Another slip into *Schwärmerei* for those who had allegedly slipped that net.

The revolutionaries were in the depths of cognitive dissonance, and no matter what story they told themselves to keep going, things only got worse. Richard Wagner described with considerable honesty the intensity of his disappointment in 1852 when Louis Napoleon should have, in principle, stepped down from office.

> I always pointed…to this hopeful year [1852]…I cannot measure how deeply this hope had taken root in me; I soon, however, was forced to recognize that the confident pride of my assumptions and affirmations was largely due to the greatly increased excitement of my nerves. The news of the *coup d'état* of the 2nd December in Paris seemed to me absolutely incredible: I was certain the world was coming to an end. When the news was confirmed, and it became clear that events *no one had thought possible* had happened and seemed likely to endure, I turned away from the investigation of this enigmatic world, as one turns from a mystery the fathoming of which no longer seems worth while.[57]

If 1848 had disappointed bitterly, some, like Wagner, worked with a four-year buffer offered by the man who destroyed the initial dream, Napoleon III. The very intensity of the German Wagner's attachment to a French event in 1852—"the greatly increased excitement of my nerves"—testifies to the even greater passion surrounding the initiating moment of such delayed hopes, 1848.

Among those to reflect on the tragedy of 1848, rather than turn away from it, however, were two German Jews, one a reform Jew in the tradition of Moses Mendelssohn—the opera impresario Giacomo Meyerbeer—and one the son of a Jewish Kantian enthusiast who had converted to Lutheranism for the sake of his legal career—the Communist ideologue Karl Marx.

Meyerbeer's Penetrating Eye: Sympathetic Criticism for the Roosters

Meyerbeer's opera, *Le Prophète*, makes its reflections on 1848 via the tale of John of Leyden, the messiah-king of the Anabaptists at Münster in 1534.[58] This choice reflected a widespread sympathy among European radicals for the millennial

---

[56] Marx to Engels, February 13, 1863, *Marx-Engels Werke*, ed. Institut für Marxismus-Leninismus, 43 vol. (Berlin: Dietz Verlag, 1956–90) [*MEW*], 30:324; cited in Siegel, *Marx's Fate*, 233.

[57] Richard Wagner, *Mein Leben*, quoted in Siegel, *Marx's Fate*, 217. Note the inversion of norms here: "events no one thought could happen" refers here to the failure of the Revolution and the fairly predictable return to autocracy in the form of Napoleon III's empire. Thus in referring to "no one," Wagner speaks entirely from the perspective of the revolutionaries: the rooster's cognitive egocentrism. Compare Wagner's comments with those of Adam of Salimbene after the failure of the apocalyptic year 1260, the Joachite *annus mirabilis*: "I entirely laid aside this [apocalyptic] doctrine [of setting dates], and I am disposed henceforth to believe nothing save what I see," *Chronicle of Salimbene De Adam*, trans. Joseph L. Baird et al. (Binghamton: Medieval and Renaissance Texts and Studies, 1986), 440–41.

[58] I thank Stephen Agus, President of the Meyerbeer Fan Club for introducing me to this extraordinary figure and helping me with the material below. See the resource he has created online: http://www.meyerbeer.com, 23 March 2010.

Anabaptists as forerunners of modern egalitarian movements.[59] Heinrich Heine
went to Münster on pilgrimage in 1843, where he "kissed with burning lips the
relics of the tailor John of Leyden—the chains he had worn, the pincers with
which he had been tortured..."[60] Meyerbeer had made the choice of subject
already in 1838,[61] but the project lay dormant until 1848, when Meyerbeer witnessed the revolution in Paris.[62] He took it up again with great urgency, signing
a contract with the Paris Opera on March 11.[63] By early October of that year, we
find a frenzy of activity even as the revolution around him began to adopt repressive measures. In late November, Berlioz remarked on the courage this course of
action took: "Meyerbeer has begun rehearsing his *Prophète*. He is a courageous
man to risk launching a work of such dimensions at a time when riots or a change
of government can cut him short, however great his eloquence."[64]

The tale is full of the demotic revolutionary discourse that had, only the previous
year, echoed though the capitals of Europe. In the opening scene, three Anabaptists
make millennial promises to the peasants returning from their day's labor:

3 Anabaptists:	To us, the living spring,
	To us, come ye O people.
	Let us for freedom rise.
1st Peasant:	Those castles that rear—
2 Anabaptists:	Shall *all be yours.*
2nd Peasant:	The heavy burdens lain –
2 Anabaptists:	Shall *shortly be removed.*
Peasants:	And we, now vassals, slaves?
2 Anabaptists:	Shall all *at length be free.*
3rd Peasant:	And our proud ancient lords?
2 Anabaptists:	Shall *soon to us submit*
Peasants	They truly speak; it is the inspired will
	We all must follow them without delay.
	We have the power, we can defy the oppressor;
	No more shall tyrants reign, they all shall perish
	Let us now *rise to vengeance and to freedom*;
	And may destruction on our oppressors alight.

[59] See the parallel role that the Taiping played for the Communists, in which the "religious"
dimension counted for less than the demotic millennialism. On the Münster debacle, see Middlefort,
"Madness and the Millennium at Münster."

[60] François Fejto, *Heinrich Heine, A Bibliography* (Denver: University of Denver Press, 1946), 227;
see also Wilson, *Finland Station*, 194. One understands why the Qing fired Hong Xiuquan's ashes out
of a canon.

[61] The first contract was August 3, 1838 between Meyerbeer and his librettist Eugène Scribe, *The
Diaries of Giacomo Meyerbeer*, ed. Robert I. Letellier, 3 vol. (Madison, N.J.: Fairleigh Dickinson
University Press, 1999), vol. 1, entry for date, and n. 26. From the beginning, Meyerbeer played an
active role in shaping the text.

[62] See, e.g., his entry for February 24, 1848: *Diaries*, vol. 2.

[63] Heinz and Gugrun Becker, *Meyerbeer: A Life in Letters*, trans. Marc Violette (London: Helm,
1989), 118.

[64] Berlioz, Letter to Count Wielhorsky on November 28, 1848; see *Diaries*, vol. 2, n. 168.

The work weaves into this revolutionary plot a classic opera scenario worthy of a Hugo novel about love frustrated, vengeance sworn, identity mistaken, and trust betrayed. The opera ends with a grand finale where John of Leyden blows everyone up in a great banquet hall including himself, his mother, and (unbeknownst to him) his true love.

But beyond the plot-line pyrotechnics, the story explores the motives of revolutionaries—the Anabaptists, the reluctant messiah John, the eager masses. And even as it views their cause with sympathy, it emphasizes their base motives, including their desire for power and revenge. In comparison with Mozart's *The Magic Flute*, where the benign conspiracy of the Masons insists that revenge must not be taken, *Le Prophète* sees revenge as a—*the*—revolutionary motive.[65] In characteristic Meyerbeer style, the drama is at once spectacular and psychologically sophisticated, a sympathetic if remorseless meditation on the failure of revolutionary movements.

Marx's Fevered Search: The Failed Rooster's Compulsion

If Meyerbeer represents an owl meditating sympathetically but critically on roosters, Marx is a rooster trying desperately to explain why, despite being wrong about an apocalyptic 1848 (the unacknowledged motive), his millennial historiography still holds the key to the future. In particular, *Class Struggles in France* and *The Eighteenth Brumaire* represent elaborate efforts to say at once, "I knew that," and orient apocalyptic hopefuls toward a future still more cataclysmic and more brilliant.[66] Like so many roosters in post-apocalyptic disappointment, he tinkers with the basic apocalyptic scenario and *redates* it to the not-too-distant future.[67]

In March of 1850, Marx and Engels published an address to the Central Committee of the Communist League in London. It began:

> Brothers! In the two revolutionary years 1848–9 the League proved itself in double fashion: first in that its members energetically took part in the movement in all places,

---

[65] The reluctance of John of Leyden to accept the Anabaptists' invitation to be crowned king in Münster is overcome by his desire to hold power so that he might take vengeance on the lord who stole his bride (Act I, Scene 1).

[66] Already, during the revolution, Marx greeted the failure of the transformative phase of February ("the beautiful revolution") as a welcome tearing-away of the false masks of enthusiasm, and a revelation of what real revolution is about—the June days when workers got massacred on the barricades ("the ugly revolution"). See his remarks in the June 28, 1848 edition of the *Neue Rheinische Zeitung* (MEW 5:134), cited in Siegel, *Marx's Fate*, 198. Note that the disillusion of which Marx speaks in 1848 is not with "Revolution Now," but with the "confused enthusiasms of good will and flowers of rhetoric..." (*NRZ*, February 28, 1849, *MEW* 6:308; cited in Siegel, ibid.). Marx uses the term *Schwärmerei* for "confused enthusiasms"—See above, chap. 8, n. 132.

[67] "The historical failure of 1848 does not mean that the thinkers of the period were merely dreamers, fantasists, and abstract theorists. They made mistakes but their greatest error, to my way of thinking, was that they mistook the *pace of history*," Duveau, *1848*, 208 (his italics). In other words, they jumped the gun.

that in the press, on the barricades and on the battlefields, they stood in the front ranks of the only decidedly revolutionary class, the proletariat. The League further proved itself in that its conception of the movement as laid down in the circulars of the congresses and of the Central Committee of 1847, as well as in the *Communist Manifesto*, turned out to be the only correct one, that the expectations expressed in those documents were completely fulfilled and the conception of the present day social conditions, previously propagated only in secret by the League, is now on everyone's lips and is openly preached in the market places.[68]

This extraordinary text offers a striking insight into the mind of the rooster. Seen from the white-hot expectations at the height of the apocalyptic moment in1848, the current "achievements of the movement" they so proudly vaunt are a sad booby prize. But seen both *ex post ante* and *ex post defectu*—that is, from the perspective of normal time both before and after 1848—they are indeed significant accomplishments. The apocalyptic wave may have peaked and broken, but we have not returned to the status quo. Marx here claims that "Communism" has now successfully entered the public sphere, what, in this book's terminology should signal the onset of an apocalyptic movement.

But the passage is bravado. Marx and Engels and their comrades faced a far less rosy future than this passage might allow us to believe. They had participated actively, even at the forefront of the revolutions, and while it may be true that their ideas reached a much wider circle of people than before 1848, that only made their situation *post defectum* all the more dangerous. Even among the faithful, the "word on the street" held that Marx was utterly discredited: "However the revolution comes out, everybody agrees that Marx is done for."[69]

Indeed, this was surely Marx's darkest moment—exiled from France and Belgium, his young family terrorized, his wife subject to the indignities of a hostile police which even held her overnight "locked up in a dark room with prostitutes." Then, when he finally settled in London, he ended up in such indigent conditions that his wife's fourth child, Guido, died at her dried-up breast.[70] As Wilson comments, 1850 was an *annus terribilis* for the Marxes. And things did not get better for a long time.

But Marx in this period seems overwhelmingly committed to his intellectual challenge: "What went wrong? Can *I* have been wrong? *No!* I must prove I was

---

[68] Karl Marx and Friedrich Engels, "Address to the Central Committee of the Communist League," in *Karl Marx and Frederick Engels Selected Works*, 2 vol. (Moscow: Foreign Languages Publishing House, 1951), 1:98.

[69] Barrister Schramm, street gossip, Marx letter to Weydemeyer, August 2, 1851; cited in Wilson, *Finland Station*, 261.

[70] *The Letters of Karl Marx*, trans. Saul K. Padover (Englewood Cliffs, N.J.: Prentice-Hall, 1979), 56; account in Wilson, *Finland Station*, 255–59; Siegel, *Marx's Fate*, 253–56, 279–87: "The poor little angel drank in so much worry and hushed-up anxiety that he was always poorly and suffered horribly day and night," Jenny Marx to Joseph Weydemeyer, May 20, 1850 in *Marx and Engels through the Eyes of their Contemporaries* (Moscow: Progress Publishers, 1978), 144; cited in Siegel, *Marx's Fate*, 280.

right." And so he spent his time as a workaholic at the library of the British Museum, feverishly trying to discover the laws of the dialectic in the data of economic history. He even analyzed in depth the data from some factory reports that others used in bulk for ballistic tests.[71] Asked repeatedly to join revolutionary movements, Marx made it clear how bitter he had been disappointed as a result of the events of 1848–52, and how he had now committed himself to his "criticism" as his way of contributing to the revolution. Explaining to the poet Ferdinand Feiligrath why he had refused to help reorganize the Communist League in 1857, he wrote: "I have had no ties with *any* organization since 1852, that I stand by my firm conviction that my theoretical works help the working class more than joining associations, whose time is past on the continent…If you are a *poet*, I am a *critic*, and I truly had my fill of the 1849–52 kind of experiences."[72]

Engels admitted how much they had continued to misread the situation for another two years *after* the failure of the revolution in his 1895 introduction to Marx's *Class Struggles in France, 1848–50*: "Whereas in [early 1850] there was still the expectation of an early new upsurge of revolutionary energy, our publication [in the autumn of 1850] breaks once and for all with these illusions." But, this aside, Engels assures his readers, the text needed little to be changed in retrospect.[73] In other words, Marx very quickly forged his response to the apocalyptic disappointment of 1848 and convinced himself he had always known it. Henceforward, *ex post defectu* 1848, he had his dialectic narrative of the present.

One might even argue that what made Marx so imposing a figure in the second half of the nineteenth century—and beyond—was his ability to reformulate, and therefore sustain, the millennial dreams and hopes of his generation of demotic radicals. He offered them a "scientific" method whereby they could continue their revolutionary work in the certain knowledge that history was on their side, *despite* the revolutionary failures of the first half of the nineteenth century. Koselleck comments:

> In the place where he appeared as a historian of the present, *after his failure of 1848*, Marx outlined in an unsurpassed fashion the boundaries to the making [i.e., the millennial refashioning] of history: "Men make their history, but they do not do so freely…"[74] Marx made use of his clear insight to derive practical directives for action. It was, rather, the "makeability" of politics and not its socioeconomic conditions that he had under theoretical consideration here. It could be supposed that the practical-political influence that Marx has rests upon such formulations—on historical insights that are capable of

[71] The material was considered so useless that people fired bullets into them (Wilson, *Finland Station*, 241–42; Siegel, *Marx's Fate*, 226). Marx, apparently, thought he could find the traces of an invisible hand.

[72] Marx to Freiligrath, February 29, 1860, *MEW* 30:489–90; cited in Siegel, *Marx's Fate*, 231.

[73] Engels, "Introduction" from *The Class Struggles in France, 1848 to 1850*, in *Selected Works*, 1:111. See also his subsequent remarks about their feelings at the outbreak of revolution in February of 1848 (ibid., 112–13).

[74] Marx, *The Eighteenth Brumaire of Louis Bonaparte*, in *Selected Works*, 1:247; translation revised by Koselleck.

shifting the utopian horizon of expectation ever further into the distance. This can be proved by the route which is traversed from Bebel, Lenin, Stalin, to Tito or Mao.[75]

But rather than reading this work in light of its eventual success, let us consider it in the framework of Marx's experience at this time. From this perspective, in reading *Class Struggles* and *The Eighteenth Brumaire*, one gets the impression that Marx was working feverishly to reinterpret these events in order to salvage his historical (millennial) vision while jettisoning his mistaken (apocalyptic) sense of timing. He openly admits "...every important part of the annals of the revolution from 1848 to 1849 carries the heading: *Defeat of the Revolution!*"[76] He then proceeds to argue that what succumbed to defeat was not the revolution, but the "pre-revolutionary traditional appendages, results of social relationships which had not yet come to the point of sharp class antagonisms...etc." In other words, the scenario remained—class antagonism to the breaking point—now accompanied by a historical method for "reading" the "times"—shifting the horizon of expectation. Marx, forever semiotically aroused, after founding a school of apocalyptic journalism (first, mistaken draft), then founded a school of apocalyptic history (second, corrected draft), one in which he eagerly read the signs of the approaching Armageddon.

Nor, despite Engel's assurance that by late 1850 they had faced the truth that 1848 was dead, did Marx so readily abandon his belief in the imminence of the final revolutionary convulsion. Like many apocalyptic enthusiasts, Marx continued to believe the present so volatile that any spark could set off the great cataclysm. "During the summer of 1850 Marx acknowledged that the revolution's progress had been stalled...however, he still expected forward movement to renew itself within a few months."[77] Only Louis Napoleon's coup d'état of December 1851 convinced him—as it did Wagner—otherwise.[78]

And even then, his hopes remained high. When news of the Taiping rebellion reached him in London a year and a half later, he could scarcely contain his enthusiasm. Writing in the New York *Daily Tribune* in June 1853, Marx eagerly viewed events in "the Celestial Empire" as a prelude to the revolution he still awaited: "[I]t may safely be augured that the Chinese revolution will throw the spark into the overloaded mine of the present industrial system and cause the explosion of the long-prepared general crisis...It would be a curious spectacle, that of China sending disorder into the Western world."[79]

---

[75] Koselleck, "On the Disposability of History," in *Futures Past*, 208. Italics mine.

[76] Marx, *The Class Struggle in France, 1848 to 1850*, in *Selected Works* 1:128.

[77] Siegel, *Marx's Fate*, 201.

[78] See Siegel's discussion of the difference in perspective from this point of view between *Class Struggles* and *Eighteenth Brumaire*, in particular the shift from "metaphors of revelation so triumphantly employed" in the former to "veils and masks," *Marx's Fate*, 201–03. Note that this disappointment is also the one that drove Richard Wagner to abandon his revolutionary hopes as well, on which see above, n. 57.

[79] Marx and Engels, *MEW* 12:98; cited in John Newsinger, "The Taiping Peasant Revolt," *Monthly Review* 52, no. 5 (October 2000): 29. Compare Foucault's response to the Khoumeini Revolution in Iran (below, pp. 446–47).

What a curious spectacle, this dialectical historian, grasping at ominously murderous straws, just to keep his hopes alive. Mao, a century later, would bring both Hong Xiuquan and Marx's enthusiasms to life, with momentous, devastating consequences.[80]

But in the middle run, the failure of 1848 was a lesson in bridling enthusiasm and buckling down to a long, hard road, aimed at preparing the conditions for the revolution to return, and this time to succeed. Now, as Engels put it so delicately, Marx, bankrupt and exiled in London, had the "leisure" to review the historical documentation and show how his material dialectic remained the best guide to understanding the past and predicting the future.[81] But if the writing of Marx in this period shows immense depth, and repeatedly invokes a longer range of historical ups and downs, he and Engels use a discourse that betrays their expectation—"any day now"—of the revolution.[82] Intellectually, they resemble the rabbi who has his bags packed, expecting to have the messiah arrive at any moment. Only their messiah was the revolution.

▪ THE MILLENNIAL FANTASY: MAGIC AND THE "FADING AWAY OF THE STATE"

To approach Marx in light of a "post-apocalyptic" cognitive dissonance in the wake of 1848, also offers an explanation for Marx's lack of elaboration about the later stages of the apocalyptic process. Many have noted Marx's laconic and sparse words on the (millennial) look of the Communist paradise.[83] But he also says very little on the later stages of the apocalyptic process that take us from the *longue durée* of class conflict to the world of sharing without greed. Far easier for Marxists to imagine the collapse of Capitalism, and transition to "dictatorship of the proletariat" than that of the "withering away of the state" with its "freedom" and "self-

---

[80] Estimates of the "peacetime" casualties of Mao's millennial totalitarianism go as high as 70 million, Jung Chang and Jon Halliday, *Mao: The Unknown Story* (New York: Knopf, 2005); Frank Dikötter, *Mao's Great Famine* (New York: Walker and Co., 2010).

[81] Marx puts a brave face on their isolation in a letter to Engels of February 11, 1851, claiming that he was "much pleased with our public and authentic isolation in which we find ourselves now, you and I. It perfectly corresponds with our principles and our position…[freed from] the obligation to share in public with all these asses in the general absurdity of the party—all that is done with now," *Letters of Karl Marx*, 66; cited in Wilson, *Finland Station*, Appendix C. Engels' response (February 13, 1851) picks up where Marx left off, heaping abuse on these "incorrigible beasts" whom they had been forced to admit were in the party, but looking forward to the day when they could speak and write "without even mentioning any of these spiders" and when, "coolly," they could "dictate [their] own terms."

[82] Siegel discusses the constant renewals of hope in the revolution that characterized their thought (*Marx's Fate*, 218–52, passim). For example, Engels in a letter to Marx dated May 1, 1866, speculating on the possibility of Bismarck invading Italy: "the Berliners will blow off the lid. If they would only proclaim the Republic, then Europe would be upside down in a few days," in *Karl Marx, Frederick Engels: Collected Works*, trans. Richard Dixon et al., 50 vols. (New York: International Publishers, 1987), 42:270; cited in Wilson, *Finland Station*, 271.

[83] "…[T]he relevant texts [concerning the shape and tenor of the Communist world to come] are both few and extraordinarily ambiguous and elusive" (Elster, *Making Sense of Marx*, 527).

realization" that all will share in the new world. Marx's focus on the early stages of the process correspond precisely with the most "Promethean" elements of this millennial process, the revolution that destroys the corrupt world.

Thus his passion, and those of his disciples, focused primarily if not exclusively on bringing about the revolution, on the immense and immensely gratifying prospect of bringing down the system that they so hated. Therefore, the core of Marx's millennial appeal lay in the combination of a "secular" millennial historiography that gave people the sense of the sweep of salvation history on the one hand, and an active cataclysmic scenario that gave them a roadmap of the future. With it they could "read the signs of the times"—in newspapers! in our day!—and thereby navigate the coming whitewater and contribute to the imminent, inevitable, apocalyptic victory.

Marx and Engels: Not Millenarians, but Scientists

Thus Marx and Engels (and those who *read* them) could appear to themselves and others as hard-headed, no-nonsense thinkers. They heaped contempt on the fuzzy-brained utopians, with their silly communities and Christianity-tinged pacifism, and on the socialists who drained the revolution of its troops. Already in the *Communist Manifesto* Marx and Engels had heaped contempt on the utopians: "They still dream of the experimental realization of their social Utopias, of founding isolated *"palanstères"* [Fourier], of establishing "Home Colonies" [Owen], of setting up a "Little Icaria" [Cabet]—*duodecimo editions of the New Jerusalem*—and to realize all these castles in the air, they are compelled to appeal to the feelings and purses of the bourgeois."[84] Indeed, in comparison with the revolution that Thomas Müntzer had dreamed of, they were pocket-book versions of the millennium—modern, activist, secular, but also transformational, or, as Mendel would say, "tautological" millennialists.

The effort to distance themselves from millennialism occupied an important part of Marxists' self-identification, precisely because their opponents could see right through their transparent distinction. For his critics, Marx was a millenarian, a dangerous fool. As Bukharin later wrote defensively: "One of the most widespread forms of ideological class struggle against Marxism is its treatment as an eschatological doctrine, with all its accompaniments of chiliasm, of soteriology, of myth…All these analogies are playing with words."[85] Bukharin, the

---

[84] *Communist Manifesto*, in the *Marx-Engels Reader*, 499. Apparently no brown-nosing for Marx, although, like everyone who wanted to publish, he had to "raise money" for his endeavors (e.g., to keep the *Neue Rheinische Zeitung* afloat), which meant going to those with money, on which see Wilson, *Finland Station*, 202.

[85] [In other words: "one of the things our critics accuse us of, is being millennialists. Nonsense."] N. I. Bukharin, *Marxism and Modern Thought* (London: G. Routledge & Sons, 1935), 3.

rooster, quotes and rejects the owls' critique—that Marx *is* a apocalyptic millennial thinker—in order to legitimate the revolution.

Ironically, it was Marx and Engels who played with these words most persistently. "From their pre-communist days to their very last works" they went to great length to insist they were not millennialists.[86] In their eyes, their brand of outrageous hope was *completely different* from the millennial "dreamers"—the *Schwärmerei* that Luther so despised. *They* had "scientific" rigor.[87] Having "seen" the fundamental driver of human behavior—the means and modes of production—*in motion*, they could observe with Olympian perspective the choppy waves and white foam of culture and beliefs, of revolutions that come and go.

> The changes in the economic foundation lead sooner or later to the transformation of the whole immense superstructure. In studying such transformations it is always necessary to distinguish between the material transformation of the economic conditions of production, which can be determined *with the precision of natural science*, and the legal political, religious, artistic or philosophic—in short, ideological forms in which men become conscious of this conflict and fight it out.[88]

In Marx's "scientific" view, these latter superstructures depended on these deeper economic realities. Thus, Marx and Engels alone had banished the fantasies of silly utopianism with their transformative (i.e., impotent) emphases on moral suasion, their hopes of dramatically bridging the gap between the Kantian dualism of "is" and "ought." Marx and his colleagues alone focused, clear eyed, on the powerful forces of history, grinding and digesting the pitiful efforts of mere individuals trying to shape the world as they wish.

The Great Anarchist Promise: All the Springs of Cooperative Wealth

Behind their sarcasm about flakey chiliasts and their bitter scientific realism of the present lay a millennial promise as ludicrous as it turned out to be irresponsible. Marx fashioned an apocalyptic scenario out of the dialectic that actually contradicted the dialectic. Instead of having thesis, antithesis, and synthesis continue indefinitely, turning corners in centuries and millennia so distant that only a science-fiction writer on the order of an Asimov might think to predict them, Marx chose to bring closure to the very forces he argued ruled the life of humankind on earth with remorseless, scientific regularity since the dawn of man—from millennia of class struggle to millennial peace, all quite quickly.

[86] Axel Van den Berg, *The Immanent Utopia: from Marxism on the State to the State of Marxism* (Princeton NJ: Princeton, 2003), 44.

[87] See, e.g., Friedrich Engels, *Socialism, Utopian and Scientific*, ed. Edward Aveling (New York: International Publishers, 1935), 43–44, 52–53.

[88] Karl Marx, *A Contribution to the Critique of Political Economy* (Moscow: Progress Publishers, 1977), 21.

Instead of making the leap to the millennial kingdom via great acts of collective moral will like the socialists, Marx and Engels emphasized the ineluctable forces of nature in history. Nicholai Berdiaev understood well the millennialism behind Marx's vision: "A materialist who denied any higher principles, Marx transformed the idea of a messiah leading the Israelite people to an ultimate paradise on earth, into a theory envisioning the eventual redemption of the world from oppression and injustice by the new chosen people—the proletariat."[89] One can understand how so many Russian Jews of the turn of the century found this secular, universalist vision so attractive.[90]

According to Marx and Engels, all past utopian dreams were mistaken fantasies because they overreached—the time was not ripe—and they under-reached—they only worked for a small community. Now, because the work of the historical dialectic had reached the point when *everyone* would be transformed, *everything* was possible. It was not human *will* that brought the millennium, but the "will of history." And despite the ponderousness of its articulation, the historical dialectic had an important element of Paul's "twinkling of an eye."[91] Far from distancing himself from millennialism, Marx was *modern* millennialism writ large.

In this shift from the voluntarism and transformative nature of nineteenth-century millennialism, to a predestined and cataclysmic scenario, Marx was able to argue that the dialectic process, now in its last [*sic*] cycle (after which class conflict would vanish), had overcome the dualism of means and ends, of will and necessity.

> In a higher phase of communist society, after the enslaving subordination of the individual to the division of labor, and therewith also the antithesis between mental and physical labor, has vanished; after labor has become not only a means of life but life's prime want; after the productive forces have also increased with the all-around development of the individual, and all the springs of co-operative wealth flow more abundantly—only then then can the narrow horizon of bourgeois right be crossed in its entirety and society inscribe on its banners: From each according to his ability, to each according to his needs![92]

[89] Anna Geifman's paraphrase of Berdiaev's argument in *Smylistorii* (Paris: Aubier, 1948), 109–19; in *Thou Shalt Kill: Revolutionary Terrorism in Russia, 1894–1917* (Princeton, N.J.: Princeton University Press, 1993), 33.

[90] Robert J. Brym, *The Jewish Intelligentsia and Russian Marxism: A Sociological Study of Intellectual Radicalism and Ideological Divergence* (New York: Schocken Books, 1978); see also Anna Geifman, *Death Cults: The Vanguard of Modern Terrorism in Revolutionary Russia* (Santa Barbara CA: Praeger, 2010, chap. 4.

[91] "In a moment, in the twinkling of an eye, at the last trump: for the trumpet shall sound, and the dead shall be raised incorruptible, and we shall be changed" (1Corinthians 15:52). See the next chapter on Lenin's belief in the rapidity of the revolution's transformation of Russian society.

[92] Marx, *Critique of the Gotha Programme* chap. 1, *Marx and Engels Collected Works*, 24:87. On the final slogan, compare Acts, 2:45.

In this sense, the failure of 1848 had led Marx to emphasize the dialectic over the turning point. *Kapital* and his historical work managed to shift the emphasis from *immediately* to *certainly*. "Marx had participated in a series of mid-century failed revolutions, and the central purpose of his Herculean economic, social and historical research thereafter, was to prove that History would do for the revolutionaries what they had been unable to do for themselves."[93]

If the image of the cosmos for the Renaissance "new-ager" was the clock,[94] the most astonishing piece of technology developed in the fourteenth–fifteenth centuries,[95] for the Marxist it was the train. "We indeed know our way and are seated in that historical train which at full speed takes us to our goal...[The historical process is] going to its logical conclusion with the unswerving character of astronomical phenomena."[96] But whither the train? What was the goal of this movement? In a move that deployed the most radical biblical image of demotic transformative millennialism, Marx invoked the anarchist notion of the "fading away of the state."[97]

This idea comes directly from the most fantastic aspects of Marxian thought, the ones that most defy the lessons of the historical dialectic. Here and now, the current *saeculum* operates according to that dialectic—steeped in class conflict and the existence of a state that, by definition, reifies the exploitation and dominion of one class over another. But after the convulsions of the revolution—once property has vanished, and hence the source of exploitation—the state will fade away just like any organic substance denied the source of its nourishment. In a modern version of the Ghost Dance's belief in the passing of the whites, Marx imagined that a redeemed—egalitarian—society that had rid itself of the capitalist would shed its government like a snake sheds a skin. In the now-open space of human existence, at last breathing the fresh air of freedom, people would turn their utter alienation into utter self-realization.

Thus, in submitting to the exigencies of the dialectical process, humanity fulfilled its destiny—self-realization.

> They [the worker revolutionaries] know that in order to work out their own emancipation, and along with it, that higher form to which present society is irresistibly tending by its own economical agencies, they will have to pass through long struggles, through a series of historic processes, transforming circumstances and men. They have no ideals

---

[93] Mendel, *Vision and Violence*, 153.

[94] Erwin Panofsky, "Artist, Scientist, Genius: Notes on The *Renaissance-Dämmerung*," in *The Renaissance: Six Essays*, ed. Wallace K. Ferguson (New York: Holt & Co., 1962), 121–82.

[95] David Landes, *Revolution in Time* (Cambridge, Mass.: Harvard University Press, 1983), Part II.

[96] Plekhanov, cited in Mendel, *Vision and Violence*, 152; from Mendel, *Dilemmas of Progress in Tsarist Russia* (Cambridge, Mass.: Harvard University Press, 1961), 112. See the use of this train imagery by Trotsky in reference to Lenin's apocalyptic expectations, below, pp. 332–33.

[97] Andrzej Walicke, *Marxism and the Leap to the Kingdom of Freedom: The Rise and Fall of Communist Utopia* (Stanford, Calif.: Stanford University Press, 1995), 89–99.

to realize, but to set free the elements of the new society with which old collapsing bourgeois society itself is pregnant. In the full consciousness of their historic mission [thanks to Marx and Engels], and with the heroic resolve to act up to it.[98]

This attempt to present themselves as "scientists," and thus distinguish themselves in the prophetic market from harebrained utopians and chiliasts, apparently worked well, then *and* now. Few historians consider Marx and Engels as participating in the same (millennial) passions as either the medieval Christian chiliasts or the secular "utopians." But the distinction itself conceals far more than it reveals.[99] Marx may have freed himself of the sappy morality of the millennialists who looked to brotherhood and persuasion to transform the world, but his thought was millennial through and through. And in substituting for the too-tender transformationalism of the *duo decimo* chiliasts, a historical dialectic that could look impassibly on massive "human-made" catastrophes, he weaponized millennialism in ways that few previous such movements had ever achieved.[100]

In a sense, this invisible/disguised millennial dimension to Marx may partake of the same paradox as the role of ideology in his work. Even as he demoted ideology to serving as the handmaid of the means and modes of production (the "real" forces of history), his ideological formulations, played a central role in his thinking and the revolutionary action it eventually inspired. The magical quality of his "grand finale of the dialectic," which he wisely avoided elaborating on, illustrates the apocalyptic force field operating beneath the surface structures of "scientific" reasoning.

So Marx and Engel's claim that they had broken free of millennialism was "objectively" an effort to introduce a variant of millennialism, freed of the baggage of failure that the earlier, *religion*-based apocalyptic scenarios had acquired over the decades and centuries and millennia. Thus they could recruit for a bolder, Promethean millennial project that called on the workers of the world to unite.

■ ENLIGHTENED HATRED AND "SCIENTIFIC" MILLENNIALISM

In an early meditation on "raw" or "crude" Communism (*der rohe Communismus*), by which he meant the Communism of Babeuf and Buonnaroti, Marx explained

---

[98] David Fernbach, ed., *The First International and After* (New York: Random House, 1974), 213; cited in Van den Berg, *Immanent Utopia*, 50–51.

[99] "Yet, however meaningless and grotesque such claims, they are what distinguish Marxism from 'utopian' socialism as well as from various forms of positivism and Kantianism. Failure to see this has caused a great deal of confusion both among Marxists themselves and among a host of commentators," Van den Berg, *Immanent Utopia*, 51. See his references and long note 26.

[100] Both Hegelianism and Buddhism take a view that permits a claim to transcend the dichotomy of good and evil. On the attraction of antinomianism for millennialists, see chapter1.

its appeal as a universalization of envy. By implication, he distanced himself from it:

> Universal *envy* establishing itself as a power is only the disguised form in which *greed* re-establishes and satisfies itself in another way. The thought of every piece of private property as such is *at the very least* turned against *richer* private property as envy, and the desire to level, so that envy and the desire to level in fact constitute the essence [of the hatred of the results] of competition. Crude communism is only the fulfillment of this envy and leveling on the basis of a *preconceived* minimum.[101]

This is a highly sophisticated moral discourse that cuts to the quick of the mechanisms of *ressentiment* parading as idealism. But for all such insight, Marx ended up stoking the very fires he here critiqued. Helmut Schoeck notes: "It is only in Marxism, the abstract and glorified concept of the proletariat, the disinherited and exploited, that a position of implacable envy is fully legitimized."[102] Marx's aggressive brilliance took hold of history so powerfully that he could shake off the "utopian" fantasies that "all men are brothers" (here, *transformative* apocalyptic) and drive those who would participate in salvation history into a cataclysmic battle at the side of the true brotherhood, the proletarians.[103] And he accomplished this call to battle with the promise of a hopelessly impossible millennium that could only be "achieved" when alienation had produced so much rootlessness and anger that only a purging violence would clear the decks.

Such tendencies strengthened among those who inherited and implemented Marx's millennialism in the following generation, whose envy and *ressentiment* Max Scheler chronicled.[104] With an irony that became increasingly bitter with every passing generation, Marx may have written his own self-description in his vicious denunciation of the tailor-agitator Weitling for abusing prophecy. Annenkov, a witness to Marx's tirade, summarized Marx's assault then quoted him directly:

> It was simple fraud to arouse the people without any sound and considered basis for their activity. The awakening of fantastic hopes…would never lead to the salvation of those who suffered, but on the contrary to their undoing. "To go to the workers in Germany without strictly scientific ideas and concrete doctrine would mean an empty

---

[101] Karl Marx, "Economic and Philosophic Manuscripts of 1844," in *Writings of the Young Marx on Philosophy and Society*, ed. Loyd D. Easton and Kurt H. Guddat (Garden City, N.Y.: Anchor Books, 1967), 302. Italics and brackets mine.

[102] Schoeck, *Envy*, 418; see also remarks on 392.

[103] See Wilson, *Finland Station*, 188–99.

[104] Max Scheler (1874–1928), *Ressentiment im Aufbau der Moralen*, English: *Ressentiment*, trans. Lewis B. Coser and William W. Holdheim (Milwaukee: Marquette University Press, 1994). See remarks of Nietzsche on the *ressentiment* of millennialists like Tertullian in *Genealogy of Morals*, 2:17. See also the remarks of Wilson on the way in which the inheritors of Marx found themselves most comfortable imitating his dismissive, ridiculing, contemptuous style (*Finland Station*, 251).

and unscrupulous playing with propaganda, which would inevitably involve, on the one hand, the setting up of an inspired apostle and, on the other hand, simply asses who would listen to him with open mouth."[105]

It apparently never occurred to Marx that pseudo-science also constituted "empty and unscrupulous playing with propaganda."

Marx's unfortunate propensity to heap contempt on the self-educated commoner who dared disagree with him (e.g., Proudhon, Weitling, and Gottschalk) rested on deeply felt intellectual superiority and lack of respect for manual laborers.[106] It also reflected his conviction that he alone had done the *real* work, the *scientific* analysis that *guaranteed* the *right* approach.[107] As Techow, an embittered admirer put it, as he aged, Marx became possessed by the ambition for personal domination: he could now tolerate only inferiors, and despised his working-class supporters.

If Adam Smith justified greed by arguing for enlightened self-interest, then Marx justified revolution by invoking enlightened hatred. As another of Marx's disappointed disciples wrote: "If Marx had only as much heart as intellect, if he had only as much love as hate, I would go through fire for him, even though he has not only on several occasions indicated his utter contempt for me, but has finally expressed it quite frankly."[108] Decades later, Bakùnin, recalling long conversations with Marx in the late 1840s in Paris, commented:"I sought eagerly his conversation, which was always instructive and clever, when it was not inspired by a paltry hate, which, alas! happened only too often."[109]

In this sense, Marx represented a sharp turn away from the beneficent millennialism of the social engineers whom he so despised, to the kind of religious hatreds that marked so many medieval millennial movements, including the coercive purity of the Crusaders, the Flagellants, the Inquisition. He tore aside the mask of benign composure that had characterized the transformative demotic utopians—from Thomas More through (some of) the Masonic lodges to Owen

---

[105] Annenkov's eyewitness description of the scene "Eine russische Stimme über Karl Marx," *Die Neue Zeit*1 (1883), cited in Wilson, *Finland Station*, 197.

[106] This may explain Marx's disturbing behavior during the London exile, working feverishly in semiotic arousal, but never doing any remunerative work, manual or otherwise, to help his wretched family including his infant son who starved at his wife's shriveled breast. Marx himself saw this in terms of his own integrity and freedom, as a guarantee of his sincerity, not as the false consciousness of a bourgeois intellectual. See Wilson's discussion, *Finland Station*, 255–59; Siegel, *Marx's Fate*, 253–87. Compare Paul's genuinely demotic insistence on manual labor: 1 Corinthians 9.

[107] See discussion in Siegel, *Marx's Fate*, 143 (on Proudhon); Wilson, *Finland Station*, 197–98 (on Weitling) and 200–01 (on Gottschalk).

[108] Techow, letter included in attack on Marx by Vogt, cited in Wilson *Finland Station*, 265.

[109] Bakùnin in an 1871 manuscript, cited in *Bakùnin on Anarchy: Selected Works by the Activist-Founder of World Anarchism*, ed. Sam Dolgoff (New York: A.A. Knopf, 1972), 25–26.

and Fourrier. And then he plunged into the violent and beckoning future, armed only with his sword of dialectic and his fierce prophetic hatreds.

Perhaps, in this sense, Marx was the best prophet for the millennialism of the last generation of the nineteenth century. Too socially awkward, too lacking in charisma to play the role of messiah, he withdrew after 1848. And from the depths of his own intellect, in the silent corridors of his monumental meditation in the bowls of the British Museum, he wrote. His most appreciative audience was a generation of individuals, all of them too infused with the "heresy of self-love" to follow a messiah, and yet, all smart and semiotically aroused enough to read onto the Rorschach of Marx's convoluted yet brilliant historical prophecy, the revolutionary scenario that best suited his or her anguished soul on fire.

As for the promised millennium with which he roused his followers, it was as much mistaken as any earlier one, just this time magical millennialism presented as scientific analysis. Although we early twenty-first-century historians clearly speak *ex post defectu* some century and a half later, we do so, a great deal sadder and hopefully a little wiser. And if the history of the past century and a half have taught us anything, it is that Marxism/Communism not only never had a chance, but its promises and premises were absurd. "No such [Communist] society could exist," wrote a sympathetic critic recently, "to believe it will, is to court disaster."[110]

Come, come, comrade,[111] in light of the last century of history, yours seems too mild a formulation. Believing it *would* exist, *has* brought on staggering disasters, *repeatedly.*[112]

---

[110] Elster, *Making Sense of Marx*, 527; see equally mordant remarks from Van den Berg, *Immanent Utopia*, 43–77, esp. 49–51.

[111] The joke runs that the commissar asks the head of the collective farm about the potato crop. "If you were to pile the potatoes up it would reach as high as god's knee!" "Come, come, comrade, we both know there is no god." "Come, come, commissar, we both know there is no potato crop."

[112] Martin Amis, *Koba the Dread: Laughter and the Twenty Million* (New York: Talk Miramax Books, 2002); Stéphane Courtois et al., *The Black of Communism: Crimes, Terror, Repression*, trans. Jonathan Murphy and Mark Kramer (Cambridge, Mass.: Harvard University Press, 1999).

11   Totalitarian Millennialism

The Bolshevik Apocalypse (1917–1935 CE)

Looking at the trajectory of revolutionary movements in Europe over the long nineteenth century, from 1789–1914, they paint a depressing tableau of stuttering starts that rapidly collapse in mutual recrimination among the revolutionaries and successful counterattack by the forces of reaction.[1] It was as if the dialectic Marx had put in the service of revolutionary communism had managed only a series of false starts—a circular pattern rather than a spiral. While in the long run, these abortive convulsions may have served to "liberalize" some (Western) European cultures,[2] they were also the prelude to still-more-catastrophic experiments in "social utopianism" in (Eastern) Europe and beyond.

In the terms of this book, Marx's millennial ideology operated as he hoped: it triggered repeated attempts at violent, active cataclysmic apocalyptic movements (revolutions). In the West, this contributed to the dismantling of prime dividers (*ancien régime*) and the spread of constitutional democracies. But in Eastern Europe, the effort to destroy the tsarist regime by Marxist-inspired revolutionaries led to an enduring totalitarian society, and a reverse Napoleonic wave, a hierarchical millennium that stretched its top-down order from Moscow westward over Eastern Europe in the wake of World War II.

As with the case of the French revolution, little of the main argument here—that Marx and his disciples were millennial thinkers—has not already been argued by historians far more familiar with the material than I.[3] But, again, following the vesperian tendencies of the profession, few other modern historians have chosen to pursue this lead and therefore to identify the millennial dynamics at work here

---

[1] See Priscilla S. Robertson, *The Revolutions of 1848: A Social History* (New York: Harper & Row, 1960); Charles Tilly et al., *The Rebellious Century, 1830–1930* (Cambridge, Mass.: Harvard University Press, 1975); Roger L. Williams, ed., *The Commune of Paris, 1871* (New York: John Wiley & Sons, 1969).

[2] A. Nimtz, "Marx and Engels—The Unsung Heroes of the Democratic Breakthrough," *Science & Society* 63, no. 2 (1999): 203–31.

[3] For the analysis of an early observer of the Soviet Revolution, see F. Gehrlich, *Der Kommunismus als Lehre vom tausend jährigen Reich* (Munich: Bruckmann, 1920) and Karl Mannheim, *Ideology and Utopia*. More recent analyses: Jacob Talmon, *Myth of the Nation and Vision of Revolution: Ideological Polarization in the Twentieth Century* (New Brunswick: Transaction Publishers, 1991); Andrzei Walicki, *Marxism and the Leap to the Kingdom of Freedom: The Rise and Fall of the Communist Utopia* (Stanford, Calif.: Stanford University Press, 1995); Joshua Muravchik, *Heaven on Earth: The Rise and Fall of Socialism* (San Francisco: Encounter Books, 2002); K.G. Riegel, "Marxism-Leninism as a Political Religion," *Totalitarian Movements and Political Religions* 6 (2005): 97–126. Online: http://www.scribd.com/doc/39855870/Klaus-Georg-Riegel-Marxism-Leninism-as-a-Political-Religion, January 25, 2011.

over time.[4] Below, I sketch a trajectory of consistent responses to post-apocalyptic dissonance that might prove worthwhile pursuing in an effort to understand not only why the revolution happened in the least capitalist state, Russia, but also why it became totalitarian. Like the Xhosa, like so many apocalyptic hopefuls, European radicals faced terrible disappointments throughout the nineteenth century, and had to deal with all the cognitive dissonance such experiences inflicted.

■ COERCIVE PURITY AND THE *POLITIQUE DU PIRE*

How did the most determined of the modern roosters handle that dissonance? By clinging to the millennial promise; by redating the apocalyptic moment into the near future (postponing the event horizon); and by reframing the apocalyptic scenario and insisting that, to bring redemption closer, one needed to force things by a *politique du pire*. If the millennium had not yet arrived, it was because things were not yet bad enough. Not enough cattle had been killed.

Like so many disappointed apocalyptic hopefuls, the revolutionaries opted for coercive purity. And among the apocalyptic scapegoats they targeted, we find not only the evil bourgeoisie, the feudal aristocracy, and the numerous royal families, but also deviationists of all sorts from within their own camp. The narcissism of small differences that drove so many leftist groups to splinter in vitriolic animosity reveals, perhaps more than anything, the zero-sum mentality that, upon achieving power, would drive their coercive social engineering.[5]

Such a process explains the increasing prominence of the "dictatorship of the proletariat" in the Marxian paradigm, a notion that, in their latter years, even Marx and Engels came to accept would last quite a while.[6] This authoritarian transitional phase within the apocalyptic scenario, the narrow path whereby society would pass from the nadir of human exploitation to the pinnacle of fraternity, would inevitably, according to Marx, be "stamped with the birthmarks of the old society from whose womb it has emerged."[7] Although it still clung to a progressive demotic millennial goal, Marxism increasingly, indeed with every disappointment, grew more violent and authoritarian.

Speaking specifically of war, but more broadly of critical moments, Lenin describes the response of some to (apocalyptic) disappointment: "The experience of war, like the experience of every crisis in history, of every great disaster and every sudden turn in human life, stuns and shatters some, *but* it enlightens and

---

[4] Talmon's *Myth of the Nation* is a major exception, but as with his work on the French Revolution, the historical profession has not done much with his work. For a review of the material on Leninism/Stalinism as a "political religion," see Riegel, "Marxism-Leninism."

[5] See Riegel, "Marxism-Leninism," 101–10.

[6] See discussion in Axel Van den Berg, *The Immanent Utopia: From Marxism on the State to the State of Marxism* (Princeton, N.J.: Princeton University Press, 1988), 56–57.

[7] Ibid., 55.

hardens others."[8] Hardened enlightenment, the revolutionary style of the early twentieth century, emerges as the adamantine product of the tremendous pressures of disappointment. Van den Berg explains the "logic" needed to maintain faith in an impossible hope: "Marxism seems to have nothing to offer but an utterly cloudy millennium [withering away of the state] whose credibility can only be sustained, if at all, by postponing its eventual arrival indefinitely for all practical purposes, and an immediate program [dictatorship of the proletariat] that hardly appears attractive at all."[9] Or, to specify, "hardly attractive"—except to authoritarian personalities and desperate millennial hopefuls.

■ FROM WEST TO EAST: IN PURSUIT OF THE APOCALYPSE

At the same time as the Marxists'"method" for handling the cognitive dissonance of disappointment explains their growing authoritarianism, it also explains the passage of revolutionary Marxism from the West to the East, precisely where the dialectic predicted it would not go.[10] The *objective* historical logic of the *millennial* vision articulated in the *Communist Manifesto*, that is, Marx's dialectical path through the alienation of advanced capitalism to the world of self-actualizing individuals, should mean that the dialectic would reach its ultimate resolution, the "end of [the] history [of class struggle]," precisely where this process was most advanced...England, America.

But already in 1848, it was clear that advanced industrialization lessened the likelihood of revolution. Germany—a primitive economy by Marx's dialectical standards—had a much stronger revolutionary potential than England—the most advanced economic state. Rather than reconsider the [sacred] historical dialectic, Marxists—Marx included—came up with reasons why this "made sense." They would not question the axiomatic truth that lay at the heart of the apocalyptic scenario: that the bourgeoisie would exploit the workers so crushingly that they reached their state of evanescent alienation.[11]

This fudging of the "scientific" indicators of the historical dialectic followed an *emotional* logic, one that served to mobilize an *active cataclysmic apocalypticism*. Revolution at any cost.

> The question [Marx and Blanqui] put to themselves was how to prevent the come-back of the defeated class foe, how to stop the decline of the revolutionary momentum and

[8] *The Collapse of the Second International* (1915), cited in Edmund Wilson, *To the Finland Station: A Study in the Writing and Acting of History* (New York: Farrar, Straus & Giroux, 1972), 522.

[9] Van den Berg, *Immanent Utopia*, 56–57.

[10] After Marx and Engels,"the whole geographical axis of Marxist culture [shifted] towards Eastern and Central Europe," Perry Anderson, *Considerations of Western Marxism* (London: Verso, 1976), 7; for an extended discussion of the process, see Walicki, *Marxism and the Leap*, 208–68.

[11] This assumption is really a projection of the same prime-divider mentality that produced the *Protocols of the Elders of Zion*.

the ebbing away of idealistic exaltation in the face of the growing readiness to come to an accommodation with things as they were before? Through a revolutionary people's war on the model of 1793—was their answer. There was a common revolutionary cause which could be turned into a national cause of every one of the insurgent peoples—a war against Tsarist Russia, the only country on the European continent to have been left untouched by the revolutionary wave.[12]

Marx, and those who refashioned Marx's argument over decades, eventually centuries, of disappointment, trimmed their sails hard to the wind of this violent apocalyptic scenario. They had a greater passion by far for fomenting resentment and violence (consciousness raising) than for working to reform. The worse things got, the angrier the workers grew. The "slight" adjustment made to the apocalyptic scenario—from expecting Communism to emerge from the "advanced industrial capitalist" phase, to looking to the primitive agrarian state of Russia as the cutting edge—shows how little the specifics of the *intellectual* argument mattered to the revolutionaries. In that sense, Marxist ideology was indeed a mere superstructure driven not by the means and modes of production, but by the apocalyptic dialectic of "upping the ante."

From Marx to Lenin

The *masses*—the focus of the historical dialectic—did not respond nearly so well to the Marxist message of history and revolution in Western Europe as Marx and Engels hoped. Some Western *intellectuals*, on the other hand, responded enthusiastically. Again we find a similar logic born of cognitive dissonance. To many who still burned for that "sun of '48," Marx's violent apocalyptic scenario had much greater emotional appeal than the resigned maturity of a Hölderlin. The magical millennium, *via* the historical dialectic, exercised a continuous, motivating fascination. Marx soon found himself competing for control of the Communist movement with men even more dramatic and violent than he.

In the same way that the Xhosa chose, with every disappointment, to pursue coercive and scapegoating responses to failure—to seek still *more self-mutilation* in order to *earn the millennium*, so did some Marxists in pursuit of theirs. The worse it got, the better it would get, or, as the Russian revolutionaries put it: *chem-khuzhe, tem luchshe* [the worse, the better].[13] In the meantime, blame those who have not shown sufficient dedication to the revolution—including the cloddish peasants and workers who have not loved "their" (promised) freedom enough. The internecine conflicts within the left—classic expressions of the narcissism of small

---

[12] Talmon, *Myth of the Nation*, 33.
[13] Anna Geifman, *Death Orders* (New York: Praeger, 2010), 54.

differences already so visible in Marx's career[14]—reflect this sharp, zero-sum edge, with its predilection for coercive purity in the face of failure.[15] The climax of this tendency would come with the Russian Revolution, when the Bolsheviks followed the logic of coercive purity to totalitarianism, and their sympathizers in the West, including great thinkers like Shaw and Sartre—despite the massive betrayal of all the millennial values espoused—supported, justified, and concealed the madness of that coercive apocalyptic strategy.

■ PRELUDE TO CATASTROPHE: BAKÙNIN'S MESSIANIC PROMISES OF "FREEDOM" AND PREREVOLUTIONARY TERROR

Mikhael Bakùnin's life (1814–76) eloquently tells the tale of Communist millennialism and its active cataclysmic apocalyptic scenario.[16] The details, including the psychological issues involved, are far too complex to treat here, but the major outline of Bakùnin's life, thought, and influence are well worth a brief discussion. Few other thinkers reveal so clearly the deep connection between religious and secular apocalyptic thought, in particular the adoption of an active cataclysmic scenario in response to disappointment.

Born into an aristocratic family, Bakùnin began his career as a military officer and a staunch conservative, a great admirer of the tsar and of the Russian empire. A tempestuous youth with a difficult relationship to his authoritarian father, Bakùnin gave himself over to religious passions that slid easily into messianic grandeur, in which he saw himself as another Jesus.[17]

> How great I feel myself at this moment! I feel myself a man! My purpose is God. Vast storms and thunder shake the earth; but I do not fear you, I despise you, because I am a man! My proud and inflexible will tranquilly passes through your shocks in order to achieve my high destiny. I am a man. I will be God...I suffer because I am a man and want to be God. I am tranquil because I know my powers, because I see myself standing on the road that will continually bring me nearer to God...The animal will be destroyed, and the man will become God...Love is God. Passion is Man. Changing Passion to Love—this is man's task.[18]

---

[14] See above, p. 316.

[15] Raymond Aron, *Le Marxisme de Marx* (Paris: Editions de Fallois, 2002), 591–614; Riegel, "Marxism-Leninism," 99–110.

[16] Wilson has a characteristically vivid chapter on Bakùnin (*Finland Station*, chap. 14); he is a major figure in E. H. Carr's 1933 study, *The Romantic Exiles* (London: Serif, 1998), 192–204; Carr also dedicated a full study to him, *Michael Bakunin* (London: Macmillan, 1937); and there is a full-length study by one of the greatest millennial scholars, Arthur P. Mendel: *Michael Bakunin: Roots of Apocalypse* (New York: Praeger Publishers, 1981). I draw on both Wilson and Mendel in the following discussion.

[17] See Mendel's chapter, "The Fichtean Missionary: The First Crusade," in *Michael Bakunin*, 56–83.

[18] Cited in Mendel, *Roots of Apocalypse*, 60.

This is the same register of megalomania as Hong Xiuquan. And like Xiuquan, he early surrounded himself with a small circle of true believers who shared his opinion of himself.

But for all the thrill of these religious passions and the position of savior that he took toward others—his siblings, his acquaintances, the women he loved but, impotent, could not make love to—this path could not quench his thirst for grandeur. On the contrary, Bakùnin behaved badly—out of jealousy for his sister whom he loved too passionately—and the circle of the "saved" fell apart.[19] Like so many roosters, his need for adulation knew no limits, and the loss of his adoring following devastated him. The manic cycle brought him to the depths of depression—"hell, hell with all its terror."

Fascinated by Hegel, he went to Berlin in 1840 where, under the influence of the Young Hegelians, he became a radical and an atheist. There he studied the dialectic, the "algebra of revolution," and transmuted his religious passion to save those he knew and "loved" into a secular one to save the oppressed of the world. There he learned not to *leave* the world of suffering and evil, but to *destroy* it. In this abandonment of (formal, charismatic) religion and the zealous adoption of a (new religious) revolutionary creed, we find the roots of secular apocalypse.[20] Notes Mendel: "As with so many messiahs, before and after, Bakùnin will have then completed his voyage from personal anguish, though the fantasy of an infantile Eden, to the dream of a vengeful apocalypse."[21]

When the revolution came in 1848, he surfed the wave more eagerly than Marx, crisscrossing Europe to fan the flames. In Dresden, along with Richard Wagner, he took the initiative and ended up in a Prussian prison for his pains. Over the next fifteen years, he spent time in German and Russian prisons and in Siberian exile. Finally an epic escape to the east landed him in California, whence he made his way to England and finally Switzerland.

Upon return, he was like someone frozen in time, still passionately committed to the revolutionary spirit of 1848 when others had made their unhappy peace with its failure.[22] He clashed with Marx for the leadership of the Communist Party. In 1869, he met a young revolutionary in Geneva named Nechàev. The two composed a pamphlet entitled *The Catechism of a Revolutionary*, a militant "monastic" handbook that demanded utter and selfless dedication to the revolutionary cause.[23]

---

[19] On his relationship with VissarionBelinsky, see ibid., 77–83.

[20] Ibid., 84–112.

[21] Ibid., 86.

[22] See the description in Carr, *Romantic Exiles*, chap. 10.

[23] A translation is available in *Voices of Terror*, ed. Walter Laquer (New York: Reed Press, 2004), 71–75. On the debate over authorship, see Mendel, *Michael Bakunin*, 319–20. On Nechàev, see Philip Pomper, *Sergei Nechaev* (New Brunswick, N.J.: Rutgers University Press, 1979); Carr, *Romantic Exiles*, 255–73. On the relationship of monasticism to communist "political religion," see Riegel, "Marxism-Leninism," 101–04.

That cause took Marx's *politique du pire* to the extreme: the goal of the revolution was the happiness of the workers, but since the revolution could only come about through the eradication of the state, "the revolutionary must further with all his power the evils that will exhaust the people's patience."[24] "He is not a revolutionary if he feels pity for anything in this world," and the worst enemies must be eliminated immediately, while moderates "must be exploited in every possible way...we must make them our slaves" (¶13). The text argues that only secret societies of enlightened revolutionaries will be able to steer the world toward the desired end. We are far from the benevolent humanism of demotic transformational millennialism: on the contrary, the benevolence has transmuted into a revolutionary promise that only pure ruthlessness and power can implement. They had the best excuse for the worst deeds.

The role of these secret societies was to strive constantly for a volcanic eruption of destructive fury on the part of the people, the annihilation of the ruling elites, and, in the aftermath, to shape the new world. Wrote Bakùnin: "The aroused masses of people are like molten metal, which fuses into one continuous mass, and which lends itself to shaping much more easily than non-molten metal—that is, *if there are good craftsmen who know how to mold it* in accordance with the properties and intrinsic laws of a given metal, in accordance with the people's needs and instincts...."[25] Note the use of Promethean image married to a supreme confidence that he (and presumably his fellow revolutionaries) knew well "the intrinsic laws of *the metal*," that is, the people as molten metal. Such hubris confirms Augustine's warnings against millennialism[26] and at the same time, recalls the golden (really molten) calf.

In Bakùnin and his associates, we encounter a peculiar combination of glorious dreams of a happy and free humanity mingled inextricably with a *libido delendi*, a lust to destroy that reaches ecstatic paroxysm. Bakùnin's messiah complex combined hatred of this world with a megalomanic belief in his own power, and a passionate love of "freedom"—at least in theory.[27] Behind the radical call for freedom, however, lay a personality as conflicted as it was authoritarian, one which embraced an active cataclysmic apocalyptic narrative to answer the most profound insecurities.

Total detachment from and uncompromising denunciation of society, incessant prophecies of its imminent and complete annihilation, denunciation of all compromising Pharisees [like the revolutionaries of 1848 who had gone soft], self-justification for the

---

[24] Wilson, *Finland Station*, 324.

[25] Bakùnin, *Oeuvres*, ed. James Guillaume, 6 vols. (Paris: Stock, 1907),1:274; cited in Mendel, *Michael Bakunin*, 428.

[26] See above, chapter 1.

[27] Mendel reports how he began his study of Bakùnin because he felt that earlier ones, "did not take seriously enough Bakùnin's contribution to freedom. I finished the book convinced that neither the Carr biography nor other works on Bakùnin take seriously enough his *threat* to freedom" (*Michael Bakunin*, 1). Italics his.

cruelty by visions of a fine new and pure world to rise from the ruins, formation of successive circles of disciples who provided him with a monastic pseudo-family that he could "father," assurance that his own purity and that of his "intimates," his apostles, his cadre were in no way stained by the brutal violence that must inevitably pave the way to the kingdom of love and brotherhood.[28]

By the end of the nineteenth century, Bakùnin represented the anarchist wing of radical egalitarian thought, while Marx seemed comparatively mild. In the terms of this book, Marx had adjusted to an extended delay in the advent of the revolution by emphasizing the necessity of waiting for the moment when the dialectical forces had reached their fruition—a form of passive cataclysmic apocalyptic that counseled patience. Bakùnin, infuriated by the delay, argued for a still-more-active, still-more-destructive apocalyptic climax. In that sense, Lenin represented more of a Bakùninist than a Marxist.

■ THEORIZING THE MILLENNIUM: LENIN'S "WITHERING AWAY OF THE STATE"

Anyone reading Marx in the middle decades of the nineteenth century would never have imagined that the leading communist state of the twentieth century would be Russia. It defied all the logic of Marx's dialectical history.[29] And yet, it corresponded perfectly with the logic of apocalyptic disappointment. Disappointment acts as a trip switch, driving some from active to passive, and others from either passive to active, or active to hyperactive. For a realistic and honest revisionist like Eduard Bernstein, Engel's handpicked successor, this meant a shift to transformational *Evolutionary Socialism* (1899).[30] For those wedded to apocalyptic time, such revisionism was a betrayal of the faith. Muravchik explains the violent reaction Bernstein's shift elicited:

> The real fault with his argument was that by rejecting teleology, Bernstein's approach would rob socialism of the religious mystique in which Marxism had clothed it. No longer would it offer the promise of a "*new age...which established the 'kingdom of God' on earth and which will make all people into humans!*" as young, enthusiastic Kaustky had put it.[31]

In this case, the revolutionaries who could not bear the delay of the revolution shifted to still more active scenarios; they gravitated to violence—*active cataclysmic*.

---

[28] Mendel, *Michael Bakunin*, 422.

[29] For an excellent study of the kind of cognitive dissonance the economic and political developments of the later nineteenth century created for Marxists, in particular for Eduard Bernstein, see Muravchik, *Heaven on Earth*, 95–120.

[30] This becomes known as "social democracy." James T. Kloppenberg, *Uncertain Victory: Social Democracy and Progressivism in European and American Thought, 1870–1920* (New York: Oxford University Press, 1988).

[31] Muravchik, *Heaven on Earth*, 102. Italics mine.

As Lewis Coser put it, as far as Lenin was concerned, the evolutionary socialists were too patient; one had to "rape history."[32]

Built into such a move we find two elements that emerge sharply in Bakùnin: on the one hand, the active encouragement of the *politique du pire*, and the formation of revolutionary elites on the other. This current eventually produced the dictatorship of the proletariat, those enlightened revolutionary leaders who, considering themselves above all "human" (a fortiori phony "divine") laws, therefore felt empowered to act as they saw fit. "God is dead, everything is permitted." Since apocalyptic millennialism tends to produce an antinomian sense of superiority to the law, there was, for these men *and women*, no limit to what they might do. Indeed to act *above the law* was proof of revolutionary zeal and courage.[33]

Such a dynamic meant that Russia—the most retarded nation from the point of view of the historical dialectic—became the site of revolution rather than England, France, or the United States—the most advanced. As Muravchik notes:

> But a half century after the publication of the *Communist Manifesto*, the socialist idea hit another crisis as Marx and Engels' leading heir, Eduard Bernstein, observed that economic development was contradicting the prophecy. The theory was rescued by Lenin, who kept it alive by performing heart transplant surgery, replacing the proletariat by the vanguard.[34]

Lenin's *What Is to Be Done?* (1902), written in exile in Siberia, represented the most decisive response to Bernstein's "cowardly...unbounded opportunism."[35] It responded to revisionism the only way possible: "Smash its face in."[36]

An examination of Lenin's famous treatise, *State and Revolution*, which he wrote while in exile in Finland between the February revolution of 1917 and the Bolshevik takeover in October of that year, reveals all the characteristic millennial traits evident in Marxism combined with the impatient activism of Bakùninism. Riegel notes: "The carrier of the salvation work is not the proletariat [as Marxism anticipated] but its avant-garde, the intelligentsia motivated by its ethic of conviction. As disciplined virtuosos, this intelligentsia had activistically [sic] transcribed the Marxist economy of salvation to fit the special conditions of Russia."[37] Lenin

---

[32] Lewis Coser, *Greedy Institutions: Patterns of Undivided Commitment* (New York: Free Press, 1974), 130.

[33] See discussion in Laurent Murawiec, *The Mind of Jihad* (New York: Cambridge University Press, 2008), 59–90.

[34] Muravchik, *Heaven on Earth*, 8.

[35] Lenin, letter to his mother, *Collected Works*, 45 vols. (Moscow: Progress Publishers, 1977), 37:281; Muravchik, *Heaven on Earth*, 107. Note how, for Lenin, this cannot be an honest difference of opinion.

[36] Nikolay Valentinov, *Ecounters with Lenin*, trans. Paul Rosta and Brian Pierce (London: Oxford University Press, 1968), 184; Muravchik, *Heaven on Earth*, 106.

[37] Riegel, "Marxism-Leninism," 79. Already in 1920, Fritz Gehrlich detected the specific millennial signature of this text and of the larger phenomenon of Communism: *Der Kommunismus als Lehre vom tausendjährigen Reich*, 17–52.

provided his apocalyptic jazz in order to keep the hopes alive. As Riegel's translator's neologism suggests, this is still a further stage in a process of raising the ante. From Marxist activism that, in principle, rode the crest of the modern, industrial wave in the West, Lenin created a hyperactivism that pushed the redemptive process in an East where no wave of industrialism had occurred.

Given both the climate of terrorism that prevailed in Russia (and Eastern Europe) at the time, as well as the long history of uninterrupted authoritarian rule in Russia, one might expect the "withering away of the state" to take a long and painful time to work out; indeed, one might imagine that any realistic observer of the situation would want to avoid placing too much hope in the beneficent effects of the "dictatorship of the proletariat." And yet, Lenin's *State and Revolution* makes these ideas the center of his argument, and anticipates a relatively brief period of violence in the apocalyptic transition, moving rapidly to a transformative model. As opposed to the "utmost ferocity and savagery" necessary to depose the (fallen) state (by definition exploitative) and to the "seas of blood [that] it calls for," Lenin anticipated that the shift from *capitalist state*, via the *dictatorship of the proletariat* to the state's *withering away* "will entail far less bloodshed…and will cost mankind far less."[38]

The key element in this astounding fantasy, which proved so tragically wrong, is the notion that as opposed to the exploiters (state agents) who need "a highly complex machine for performing this task [oppression of the majority],…*the people* can suppress the exploiters even with a very simple 'machine,' almost without a 'machine,' without a special apparatus, by the simple organization of the armed people (such as the Workers' Soviets and Soldiers' Deputies…)."[39] Given how catastrophically wrong Lenin was, both in his estimate of the commoners' capacity to carry out the task he assigned them and in his estimate of how little violence the proletarian dictators would need (or want?) to use, one has to wonder what he was thinking as he wrote this. Was he fooling himself along with everyone else?

On one level, one could argue that no one had ever tried to do this before, so how could he know? But such an argument would ignore the painful (and apparently unlearned) lessons of the long nineteenth century (1789–1914), the consistent failure of the "people" to mount that stallion of liberty, their preference to be ruled, rather than, as required for the state to wither away, that they rule themselves. Perhaps as a believer in the simple truth of reason, Lenin assumed that it would be easy to mobilize a people to do what is right and reasonable. Or perhaps he gravitated toward whatever made the revolution enticing.

Only in communist society, when the resistance of the capitalists has been completely crushed [which alone can be crushed by the proletariat[40]], when the capitalists have

[38] V. I. Lenin, *State and Revolution*, in *Lenin on Politics and Revolution: Selected Writings*, ed. James E. Connor (New York: Pegasus, 1968), 220–21.

[39] Ibid.

[40] Ibid., 219.

disappeared, when there are no classes…*only* then "the state…ceases to exist" [Marx, Gotha] and "*it becomes possible to speak of freedom.*"…only then will the state *wither away*, owing to the simple fact that, freed from capitalist slavery, from the untold horrors, savagery, absurdities, and infamies of capitalist exploitation, people will gradually *become accustomed* to observing the elementary rules of social intercourse…they will become accustomed to observing them without force, without coercion, without subordination, *without the special apparatus* for coercion called the state.

Thus we have, after the initial violence, a radically transformative process whereby people "will voluntarily work *according to their ability*…[and] the 'narrow horizon of bourgeois right,' [i.e., envy and possessiveness], will then be crossed. There will then be no need for society, in distributing products, to regulate the quantity to be received by each; each will take freely 'according to his needs.'"[41] The confidence in humans as blank slates, or even more, as basically "good" beings only waiting to be free in order to behave responsibly, is astounding—and typical of demotic millennialism. "No king but the collective!"

How will all the organization of society work in such a world?

Accounting and control—that is *mainly* what is needed for the "smooth working," for the proper functioning, of the *first phase* of communist society. *All* citizens are transformed into hired employees of the state, which consists of the armed workers…All that is required is that they should work equally, do their proper share of work, and get equal pay. The accounting and control necessary for this have been simplified by capitalism to the utmost and reduced to the extraordinarily simple operations—which any literate person can perform—of supervising and recording, knowledge of the four rules of arithmetic, and issuing appropriate receipts.[42]

The naïveté of this formulation is astonishing. Given the data from past experience (which Lenin claims to have learned from),[43] to imagine mobilizing and arming the commoners as a relatively simple and peaceful way to move toward a stateless society seems like breathtakingly bad judgment.[44]

One would not know from such remarks that the Russia for which Lenin has such naïve hopes is the scene of widespread terrorism and that the terrorists were working with him.

---

[41] Ibid., 225.

[42] Lenin adds a footnote emphasizing this point, anticipating how this process of empowering the workers will lead to the ceasing of the "political state" and "public functions," which will thereby become "mere administrative functions." Ibid., 228.

[43] He follows this discussion with one that he never got around to finishing, on the "Experience of the Revolutions of 1905 and 1917" (ibid., 229).

[44] This is particularly relevant for someone who prides himself for appreciating their lives, having lived with them. Earlier in the same text he showed his contempt for the reformists, the "liberal professors and petty-bourgeois opportunists…the bourgeois publicists and politicians…who have never known want…and have never been in close contact with the oppressed classes and in their mass life…" (ibid., 219).

By their sheer quantity and devastating impact on the life of an entire society, these [acts of terrorism] and other forms of violence…represent not only a powerful, but also a unique social phenomenon. On the basis of new research it seems justifiable to argue that…premeditated acts against set targets—the most extreme form of radicalism…—played a primary role in the crisis of 1905–7 and in early 20th-century Russian revolutionary history.[45]

Bakùnin and Nechàev's *Catechism of a Revolutionary* had already proposed an alliance with "the intrepid world of brigands [who are] the only true revolutionaries in Russia."[46] Indeed, it was the thirst for authenticity, for passionate energy, as opposed to the paralysis of intellectual cogitation, that had driven the revolutionaries to admire "the brigands, thieves, tramps, outlaws, outcasts of Russian society. Distasteful as such an idea might be to beautiful souls, those forces had to be mobilized and utilized. It was a terrifying idea…but the Russian revolution was bound to be a terrible event."[47]

With all the confidence of a true believer, Lenin assures his audience of the soundness of his millennial premise: "With the removal of this chief cause [exploitation of the people, their want, and their poverty] excesses will inevitably begin to "*wither away*."

The expression "the state *withers away*" is very well chosen, for it indicates both the gradual and the spontaneous nature of the process. Only habit can, and undoubtedly will, have such an effect; for we see around us on millions of occasions [sic] how readily people become accustomed to observing the necessary rules of social intercourse when there is no exploitation, when there is nothing that arouses indignation, evokes protest and revolts, and creates the need for *suppression*.[48]

Here Lenin offers us a perfect illustration of the millennial premise: remove [what we believe is] the source of suffering and evil, and people will naturally become good and happy. Thenceforth,there will be no indignation, no envy, no protests, no need for "top-down" order—Holy anarchy. The idea that *envy* is not an "objective" (i.e., independent) emotion or that not all envy is justified (i.e., will not disappear once matters are "just") does not seem to have figured in this calculation.[49]

[45] Anna Geifman, *Thou Shalt Kill: Revolutionary Terror in Russia, 1894–1917* (Princeton NJ: Princeton University Press, 1993), 4–5. For a discussion of the ways in which this principled revolutionary terror often devolved into pure criminality that "terrorized the peaceful population," see 75–81, 154–80.

[46] Bakùnin and Nechàev, *Catechism*, 25; in Talmon, *Myth of the Nation*, 321–22. See above, chapter 7 for a similar development with the coordination between the Taiping armies and Triads.

[47] Talmon, *Myth of the Nation*, 295, summarizing Bakùnin, *Selected Writings*, ed. Arthur Lehning (New York: Grove Press, 1970), 186–87.

[48] Lenin, *Selected Writings*, 220.

[49] On envy, see Schoeck, *Envy*, esp. 421–24 on the phylogenesis of envy.

Everything millennial about Marx's logic, including the scientistic jargon about the nature of his analysis,[50] had been taken over by Lenin, if anything more confidently[51] and more aggressively naïve.[52] It is as if someone who was already hypnotized by Marx's magical millennium were to speculate further on the issue without questioning the millennial premises at all. Looking back on a half-century of Communist rule in the world, Donald MacRae noted the combination: "What has led Bolshevism in our time to dominate some eight hundred million human beings is the subtle alliance of what can be recognized as a modicum of scientific truth with a salvationist religion."[53]

And Lenin seems sober in comparison with the boundless utopianism of Trotsky, who concludes his *Literature and Revolution* (1924!) with a rhapsodic vision of the new man, born of communist revolution: "Man will become immeasurably stronger, wiser and subtler; his body will become more harmonized, his movements more rhythmic, his voice more musical. The forms of life will become dynamically dramatic. The average human type will rise to the heights on an Aristotle, a Goethe, or a Marx. And above this ridge new peaks will rise."[54] Despite the dire conditions of the revolution at the time, Trotsky's outrageous optimism resonated within a larger community of avant-garde artists,[55] and medieval millennialists.[56] "Harebrain plans," the party called such dreams when they began the painful return to "normal" time after Stalin's death.[57]

---

[50] "This question [what transformation will the state undergo in communist society?] can only be answered scientifically..." [thus far quoting Marx]"...[and] those seeking a scientific answer to it should use only firmly established scientific data" (Lenin, *Selected Writings*, 217).

[51] "[W]e are entitled to say with the fullest confidence that the expropriation of capitalists will inevitably result in an enormous development of the productive forces of human society" (ibid., 225).

[52] "[T]he escape from this popular accounting [by the parasites, sons of wealthy, the swindlers, and other "guardians of the capitalist traditions"], will inevitably become so incredibly difficult, such a rare exception, and will probably be accompanied by such swift and severe punishment (for the armed workers are practical men and not sentimental intellectuals, and they will scarcely allow anyone to trifle with them) that the *necessity* of observing the simple, fundamental rules of the community will soon become a habit" (ibid., 229). See discussion below, pp. 402–03, on the movie *The Day the Earth Stood Still* and Klaatu's equally bizarre if opposite "solution" to aggression.

[53] Donald D. MacRae, "Bolshevik Ideology: The Intellectual and Emotional Factors in Communist Affiliation," *Cambridge Journal* 5 (1951): 167.

[54] Leon Trotsky, *Literature and Revolution* (New York: Russell & Russell, 1957), 256; cited by Eric Goldhagen, "The Glorious Future—Realities and Chimeras," in *Problems of Communism* 9, no. 6 (1960): 10. Goldhagen cites the comment of Trotsky's biographer, Isaac Deutscher, who notes that "no Marxist writer before or after Trotsky has viewed the great prospect with so realistic [*sic*] an eye and so flaming an imagination," *The Prophet Unarmed* (Oxford: Oxford University Press, 1959), 197. Had Goldhagen not inserted the [*sic*], I would have.

[55] Rene Fülöp-Miller, *Geist und Gesicht des Bolschewismus: Darstellung und Kritik des kulturellen Lebens in Sowjet-Russland* (Zurich: Amalthea-Verlag, 1926); and Boris Groys, *Gesamtkunstwerk Stalin: Die gespaltene Kultur in der Sowjetunion* (Munich: C. Hasner, 1988).

[56] Emanuel Sarkisyanz, *Russland und der Messianismus des Orients* (Tübingen: J.C.B. Mohr, 1955).

[57] "The day of utopia, of arbitrary flights of fancy have passed, giving way to higher responsibility in analyzing reality and in foresight," *Kommunist* 12 (August 1960): 114; in Goldhagen, "Glorious Future," 14.

Goldhagen notes that this utopianism—denied by Bolsheviks as much as by Marx and Engels—served as a drug, not so much an opiate of the masses as an amphetamine for the (Communist) ruling class. "It would be difficult to exaggerate the élan derived by Bolsheviks from the utopian vision. It has endowed them with an unwavering singleness of purpose, with a missionary zeal which retains, undaunted, the fullness of its fervor even in adversity, and it has imparted to them an immunity to scruples in the pursuit of power."[58] Stalin turned these virtuosi into prelates of a new and institutional church.[59]

■ APOCALYPTIC TIME: A BOND BETWEEN LENIN AND TROTSKY

With a program like the one outlined in *State and Revolution*, Lenin's course once in power would surely fail. The only questions were: how seriously did he believe his own millennial rhetoric? And how would he deal with the (virtually immediate) negative feedback that would result from the effort to implement this utopian fantasy with such brutal methods? Or, put in terms of millennial studies, how, once in power, would he and his colleague handle the inevitable cognitive dissonance?

Forced to compromise and make a peace treaty with the Germans in the first months of 1918, Lenin defended his handling of such unrevolutionary behavior by invoking apocalyptic goals. The "breathing space" it provided would permit the radical transformation of Russia into the most powerful nation in the world.

> The reorganization of Russia on the basis of the dictatorship of the proletariat, and the nationalization of the banks and large-scale industry, coupled with *exchange of products* in kind between the towns and the small-peasant consumers' societies, is quite feasible economically, provided we are assured *a few months* in which to work in peace. And such a reorganization will render socialism *invincible both in Russia and all over the world*, and at the same time will create a solid economic basis for a mighty workers' and peasants' Red Army.[60]

Here was Lenin's technological version of Paul the Apostle's "in the twinkling of an eye."[61]

Was Lenin fast-talking in order to explain his unrevolutionary behavior? Or did he believe his own narrative? If he believed it, this passage would offer the millennial historian unusual evidence—a written testimony to Lenin's white-hot millennial hopes. Normally, such ludicrously wrong promises get dismissed as temporizing

---

[58] Goldhagen, "Glorious Future," 12; Riegel, "Marxism-Leninism," 66–83.

[59] Riegel, "Marxism-Leninism," 83–90; Riegel, "Rituals of Confession within Communities of *virtuosi*: An Interpretation of the Stalinist Criticism and Self-criticism in the Perspective of Max Weber's *Sociology of Religion*," *Totalitarian Movements and Political Religions* 1, no. 3 (2000): 16–42.

[60] Thesis 20, written January 7, 1918; published in *Pravda* 34 (February 24, 1918); in Lenin, *Collected Works*, 26:442–50; trans. Yuri Sdobnikov and George Hanna, online: http://www.marxists.org/archive/lenin/works/1918/jan/07.htm, April 13, 2010. First italics his, second two, mine.

[61] 1 Corinthians 15:51–52.

rhetoric ("he had to say that..."), or they get edited out of the record by either the rooster turned owl *ex post defectu*, or by the owl-editors of the rooster's work. And, normally, if the odd trace of such clearly mistaken beliefs or claims survives in the written record, bat historians can safely dismiss them as "slips of the pen."

Not so with Trotsky. In his biography of Lenin, the great revolutionary leader, Trotsky later reflected *ex post defectu* on Lenin's extraordinary optimism expressed in precisely this passage. Trotsky toys with the option of an owl's reinterpretation:

> *At present* [1924] such words seem *completely incomprehensible*: was this not a *slip of the pen*, did he not mean to speak of *a few years or decades*? But no, this was not a slip of the pen...I recall very clearly that in the first period, at Smolnyi, at meetings of the Council of People's Commissars, Lenin invariably repeated that we shall have socialism in half a year and become the mightiest state.[62]

Here we have an extraordinary insight into the role of apocalyptic, transformative rhetoric. Most ideologues, those for example who began to think in five-year plans, would have indeed corrected the "slip of the pen" and emended the document to read, "in a few decades." Trotsky does nothing of the sort. On the contrary, he tells us that this written remark (like so many other apocalyptic expressions to make it into print), represents merely the tip of the iceberg. Apparently, Lenin repeated this remark everywhere. He promised everyone who would listen, a lightning-fast *transformation* of the Russian nation. He apparently *believed* what he wrote in *State and Revolution*.

Certainly others did, especially those in his audience. And that, itself, accounts for his messianic charisma: he articulated a vision that people not only believed (*wanted* to believe) about an imminent millennium, but they also believed he could guide them there, speedily, in their day. He addressed a *chosen generation* and placed them, with him at their head, at the center of world history. *He* drove the train of history and *they* supplied the fuel.

Indeed, that is precisely how Trotsky used this story in his *Vita Lenini*. Lenin, he tells us, single-mindedly pursued certain issues to the exclusion of others. He would later decry this neglect and then gesture dismissively with his hand when reminded that he had himself forgotten. But, he tells us, "this 'defect' was only the reverse side of his faculty of the greatest inward mobilization of all his forces, and exactly this faculty made him the greatest revolutionary of history." He then tells the story in question in order to illustrate the messianic stance that, he says, Lenin "invariably" took. It is worth following Trotsky at length here, because he tells us how important this trait was in Lenin's overall personality.

First, he tells us, other leaders of the revolution were surprised and skeptical when Lenin made such claims. "The Left Social Revolutionaries, and not alone they, raised their heads in question and surprise, regarded each other, but were

---

[62] L. Trotski, *O Lenine* (Moscow, 1924), 112; cited in Richard Pipes, *The Russian Revolution* (New York: Alfred A. Knopf, 1990), 675; "Lenin: Forming the Government," online: http://www.marxists.org/archive/trotsky/works/1925/lenin/06.htm, April 13, 2010.

silent." Those on the inside (who were not listening fully to the speech, but rather looking down) "raised their heads in surprise" because, as Trotsky tells us next, this was a "sharp change" in tone (taking apocalyptic rhetoric from hot to boiling), and because to anyone with a remote grip on reality—of human nature and of the actual situation—such claims were ludicrous. But "they remained silent," because such rhetoric had a positive effect on the public—it made them compliant. A classic response of owls in an apocalyptic time that favors roosters: those who "know" this cannot be true remain silent before the aroused public.[63]

Trotsky goes on to place this in a larger context.

> This was his system of inculcation. Lenin wanted to train everybody, from now on, to consider all questions in the setting of their socialistic structure, not in the perspective of the "goal," but of today and tomorrow. In this sharp change of position he seized the method so peculiar to him, of emphasizing the extreme: Yesterday we said socialism is the goal; but today it is a question of so thinking, speaking, and acting that the rule of socialism will be guaranteed in a few months.

In other words, Lenin was engaged in apocalyptic jazz, speeding up the process, turning from soon to imminent, placing the promised land literally within reach. In so doing, he endowed every Russian who believed him with Promethean strength. He gave him (and her) the will to change, not in terms of a long-term goal of years or decades, "but of today and tomorrow." He made them existentially "free."

It seems like Lenin here was speaking from the pages of *State and Revolution*, as if he were addressing those crowds from whom he expected protean deeds. "How readily [they would] become accustomed to observing the necessary rules of social intercourse when there is no exploitation, when there is nothing that arouses indignation, evokes protest and revolts, and creates the need for *suppression*." In other words, how naturally and swiftly the millennium would take shape once the forces of evil had been removed!

Did he really believe it? Or was it just rhetoric—a way of keeping the natives docile, as the raised eyebrows and silence of his colleagues suggest? Trotsky addresses the question directly:

> Does that mean too that it should be only a pedagogical method [i.e., mere propaganda]? No, not that alone. To the pedagogic energy something must be added: Lenin's strong idealism, his intense will-power, that, in the sudden changes of two epochs, shortened the stopping places, and drew nearer to the definite ends. *He believed in what he said.* And this imaginative half-year respite for the development of socialism just as much

---

[63] This scenario offers a case contrary to E. Goldhagen's thesis that Communist millennialism was the drug of the revolutionary elite ("Glorious Future"). Here it seems to play the role of an drug of the public listening to the speech. This does not contradict Goldhagen's thesis that millennialism is the drug of the leadership—in this case Lenin and Trotsky—it just enlarges the group for whom millennialism serves that function. Note that the Left Social Revolutionaries opposed the treaty with Germany, and would have had good reason to object. For a similar dynamic, see Radulfus Glaber's account of a relic which the insiders knew was a fake, but remained silent while their leaders dedicated a church to that saint before throngs of enthusiastic faithful (*Five Books of Histories*, 4.3.6–8, 181–85).

represents a function of Lenin's spirit as his realistic taking hold of every task of today. The deep and firm conviction of the strong possibilities of human development, for which one can and must pay any price whatsoever in sacrifices and suffering, was always the mainspring of Lenin's mental structure.

Note the combination of idealism and willpower. We have will in order to will the ideal. And in the intense sense of apocalyptic time, in which the "stopping places" between two epochs—like those centuries between agrarian feudalism and advanced capitalism—are dramatically shortened, our will is exalted. Here we see that, as late as 1924, Trotsky, far from trying to rewrite Lenin, wants to recharge him. When the others lifted their heads in surprise, he, the author of the rhapsodic conclusion of *Literature and Revolution* in that same year, probably already had his head lifted, and thrilled to these daring words. This may have joined Lenin and Trotsky more closely than any ideological difference. They were both full-fledged roosters.

Alas, like so many bold roosters who reach positions of power, they had antinomian tendencies. Trotsky concludes with a restatement of the revolutionary's catechism. For so beautiful a goal, everything is permitted, including any price of sacrifice and suffering for those we are saving.

> There can be no middle course…Ruthless war must be waged on the kulaks! Death to them! Hatred and contempt for the parties which support them—the Right-Socialist Revolutionaries, the Mensheviks, and now the Left-Socialist Revolutionaries…To lament under these conditions…the civil war against the exploiters and to condemn it, or to fear it, means in reality to become a reactionary. It means that one fears the victory of the workers, which may cost tens of thousands of victims, and that one renders possible a new massacre by the imperialists, a massacre which cost millions of victims yesterday and will cost similar numbers tomorrow.[64]

Despite its intentions to cost tens of thousands rather than millions of lives, this calculus backfired. With Stalin's help, Lenin's Communism cost well over *twenty million* lives.[65] Far more than the Jacobins, the Bolsheviks cannibalized their own people.

■ THE JUGGERNAUT OF TERROR

Most Westerners know the tale of Lenin's "War Communism," with its purposive, ruthless, and radical uprooting of Russian society,[66] and the "Red Terror,"

---

[64] Cited in Mendel, *Michael Bakunin*, 177.

[65] See Stéphane Courtois et al., *The Black Book of Communism: Crimes, Terror, Repression,* trans. Jonathan Murphy and Mark Kramer (Cambridge, Mass.: Harvard University Press, 1999).

[66] Note that, as Richard Pipes points out, the expression "war communism" was first used in 1921, after that phase was over (i.e., had failed) as a way to explain the harshness of the governmental decrees (i.e., the state), as a response to war, when in fact its principle logic of implementation was that of Lenin's notions of eliminating the bourgeoisie and the aristocracy as the "solution," that is, improvisation on his millennial premise (*Russian Revolution*, 670–73). This offers a nice example of the way in which, *ex post defectu*, matters get reinterpreted "rationally" and apologetically.

with its staggering mortality rate. The unprecedented escalation of the contempt for human lives demonstrated by those revolutionaries of iron will rapidly surpassed anything that had come before with the exception of the Taiping.[67] Indeed the spectacle of revolutionary executioners, unable to "fortify" themselves with images of their own manhood, resorting to alcohol and drugs to dull the ghastly pain of slaughtering so many defenseless people, resembles the German police battalions carrying out the slaughter of Jews in Eastern Europe.[68] In both cases, the role of an apocalyptic sadism may be underestimated.[69]

But while the Germans proclaimed Jews and other "enemies of the Reich" guilty before executing them, the Bolsheviks pursued a policy of terror against the innocent. As Bolshevik Commissar of Justice Nikolai Krylenko put it: "We must execute not only the guilty. Execution of the innocent will impress the masses even more."[70] One aspect of this carnage deserves particular attention from the point of view of millennial studies. Among the early victims of the purges, we find party members who knew they were not guilty of the crimes for which they died, but who accepted their own deaths as completely justified.

In order to execute policies that not only hurt the innocent, but targeted them, the driving forces within the party had to override all of the demotic principles of justice that had first drawn revolutionaries into the Communist Party. This process follows closely the pattern of response to cognitive dissonance known as "coercive purity." In modern political terms, this meant "the party right or wrong." The case of Yuri (Gregory) Pyatakov, a party member who was eventually shot during the show-trials of the late 1930s, illustrates the process whereby a strongly independent thinker works his way to submission:

> None of us desires or is able to dispute the will of the Party. Clearly the Party is always right...We can only be right with and by the Party, for history has provided no other way of being in the right. The English have a saying, "My country, right or wrong..." We have much better historical justification in saying, whether it is right or wrong in certain individual cases, it is my party...[A]nd if the Party adopts a decision which one or other of us thinks unjust, he will say, just or unjust, it is my party and I shall support the consequences of the decision to the end...For such a Party a true Bolshevik will readily cast out from his mind ideas in which he had believed for years. A true Bolshevik has submerged his personality in the collectivity, "the Party," to such

---

[67] For a particularly disturbing collection of quotations about this process, highlighting the apocalyptic logic of the dynamic, see Mendel, *Vision and Violence*, 171–80.

[68] Cf. Mendel *Vision and Violence*, 178–81; on the Browning-Goldhagen debate, see below, chapter 12, n. 153.

[69] On Germany, see Daniel Goldhagen (discussed below, chapter 12); on Russia, see Anna Geifman, *Death Orders*.

[70] Adam Hochschild, *The Unquiet Ghost: Russians Remember Stalin* (New York: Mariner Books, 1995), 138.

an extent that he can make the necessary effort to break away from his own opinions and convictions, and can honestly agree with the Party—that is the test of a true Bolshevik.[71]

One ideology, one party, one communist heaven on earth.

Thus, for those who came out on the wrong side of a party struggle, submitting to death made a peculiar kind of sense:

> Could they now deny the judgment of History simply because their turn had come? To do so would have meant not only to deny the meaning of their lives as revolutionaries, but to reduce a sublimely pure revolutionary war for peace, justice, love and freedom into just another case of mass murder and to identify themselves as the murderers. It was better to surrender submissively, first to political defeat, and, later, to prison and death.[72]

In other words, at this point, after so much blood spilled, to deny their guilt would betray the apocalyptic narrative. Telling the truth would not avoid cognitive dissonance; it would intensify it. Suicidal self-sacrifice seemed a small price to pay to keep the millennial hope alive.

Thus, the logic of some apocalyptic revolution—Jacobin, Bolshevik—demanded that the dictatorship of the proletariat have no divided opinions, no "loyal opposition."[73] As Trotsky explained, shortly before he got purged, "Harsh as the demands on us by the Congress…we are obligated to bow our will and our views to the will and views of the party."[74] And the logic of cognitive dissonance argued that, when in doubt, rather than admit error, one should redouble the effort and the sacrifices. It was not only the Xhosa who killed their most precious capital.

■ MEGALOMANIA, PARANOIA, AND THE MILLENNIAL GENEALOGY OF TOTALITARIANISM

We have looked at the millennial aspects of three revolutionary movements that punctuate the period we might designate as "industrial society" (1750–1950)—the French Revolution, Marxism, and Communism—and made two major arguments, not particularly new, but still marginal to mainstream historiography.[75] First, "revolutions" represent the peculiarly modern contribution to the larger phenomenon

---

[71] Trotsky, in a speech from the Thirteenth Party Congress in 1924; cited in Boris Souvarine, *Stalin* (New York: Longmans, Green, 1939), 362–63; Mendel, *Vision and Violence*, 181. "That road [a second party], under the conditions of the dictatorship of the proletariat would be fatal for the revolution…."

[72] Mendel, *Vision and Violence*, 181.

[73] On the role of this attitude in generating the French revolutionary Terror, see above, chapter 10.

[74] Lev Kamenev at the Fifteenth Party Congress in 1928, cited in Mendel, *Vision and Violence*, 182.

[75] For earlier articulations of some or all the points I am making here, see Talmon, *Origins of Totalitarian Democracy*; Mendel, *Vision and Violence*; Eugene Weber, *Apocalypses*; Desroche, *The Sociology of Hope*. None of these arguments have yet made it into the historiographical mainstream.

of "active apocalyptic millennialism."[76] Here, self-consciously secular movements achieve power (with at least some recourse to violence) and then try with demotic millennial legislation to "free" the "people" from oppression and create a "just" (or "righteous") society.[77]

Second, totalitarianism is a technologically enhanced, coercive response to an apocalyptic disappointment that comes after—and as a result of—taking power. *Secular* millennial dreams, concocted, propagated, and "built" by "rational," technologically empowered humans, disappointed those who placed their faith in modernity's capacities for effecting collective salvation. When one has banished the source of evil in this world—aristocratic privilege, private property—and the "new human" that should emerge from the revolution—the new citizen, the new comrade—fails to measure up to the messianic expectations of the revolutionary vanguard, what should one do with one's power?

Often enough, those newly empowered zealots who see their earnest effort to generate the millennium turn rancid before them, take to imposing their will—no, not theirs, the "general will"—unto the body social. Indeed, the more fervently apocalyptic the believer, the more disappointed he or she is by the inevitable failure. In some cases, these disappointed *secular* zealots surpassed even the most terrible forms of *religious* millennialism in the violence and destruction they brought to those they sought to "save." Righteous, technologically endowed terror in the hands of apocalyptic paranoids is far worse than the worst of the Spanish Inquisition, which only killed thousands. Totalitarianism, then, represents the modern secular form of the coercive purity so characteristic of hierarchical (authoritarian) millennialists in the later stages of cognitive dissonance.

Put metaphorically, most demotic revolutions begin with a transformative apocalyptic premise that resembles gardening: if you remove the obstacles to healthy growth (turn over the ground, uproot the weeds, prune the plants), the millennial kingdom will naturally grow up in its wake. Here the violence is temporary and hopefully brief, a prelude to a time of peace and abundance. As the "Proverb of Hell" explains: "The cut worm forgives the plow."[78]

---

[76] I mean here specifically the major four studied by Crane Brinton (English, American, French, Russian) in his classic *Anatomy of Revolution* (discussed above, chap. 9, nn. 129 and 149). One of the standard points made in the "modern" narrative is that while medieval "revolts" were chiliastic, irrational, and incapable of implementing more than a burst of rage, modern "revolutions" applied reason and had a practical program to replace the regimes they overthrew. Note how the modern narrative writes the earlier millennial one out of the picture, when one could also tell the tale as one of "thinking through" the problem of demotic millennialism rather than abandoning it. Perhaps early revolutionary governments swung out of control of the reasoners because they had not yet sufficiently "thought through" the problem of millennialism.

[77] The next tale in Trotsky's *Vita Leninni* was his intense commitment to drafting a constitution. On the role of the law in Hitler's *tausendjähriger Reich*, see Carl Schmitt's contribution to totalitarianism in his work on political theology, most recently addressed by Gabriella Slomp, *Carl Schmitt and the Politics of Hostility, Violence and Terror* (New York: Palgrave Macmillan, 2009).

[78] Blake, "Marriage of Heaven and Hell", plate 7, line 6, in *Poetry and Prose*, 35.

But when, in apocalyptic time, believers seize power and enact their redemptive measures, eliminate the source of evil in this world, and yet, still the garden fails to respond and the millennium does not materialize, those now-powerful believers face a terrible dilemma. How do revolutionary elites, "the party," respond to this inexplicable delay, to the disproof of their millennial premise, to a generation of those they strive to redeem, but who could not throw off the bonds of slavery even when they had the chance?[79]

These leaders responded by shifting from gardening to sculpting. Henceforth these Promethean messiahs would *carve* out the lineaments of millennial perfection on the very body social. And with that move, we have the apocalyptic genealogy of totalitarianism: force the unwilling to be "free" by enslaving them to a perfectionist image of freedom. *Make* the millennium, whatever the cost to the recalcitrant who stand in the way of true good; they are demons, they are evil. So great can such impulses become that, even in the case of Marxists, that is, ideologues who dismissed ideologies as mere superstructures, people so moved forced millions to live and die by the demands of their scarcely-thought-out millennial ideology.[80]

Stephen Gould pointed out that if you ran the evolutionary clock backward and then ran it forward, you would get a radically different result because an intricate web of contingent events—the myriad choices, successful and not, that countless creatures make—governs the process.[81] Totalitarians want to run history forward at top speed to achieve their millennial goals. The infinite personal decisions that people make appear to them as resistance that must be crushed.

The justification comes, as Donald MacRae points out, by combining the "fear of freedom" with apocalyptic delay.

> In a world in which responsibility seems to grow as power lessens [i.e., the dynamic of civil polities], freedom is a burden; and Bolshevism is a system which excludes much of the weight of personal choice. I say "excludes", but to the communist a better word might be "postpones." After the revolution, after the dictatorship of the proletariat, comes freedom, but a freedom that does not burden, for human nature will have been remade to innocence and human life remoulded to simplicity.[82]

With such a typology, the French revolutionaries and Marxists represent two linked manifestations of demotic progressive millennialism: (1) they believed

---

[79] Note the similarity to the situation of God/Moses after the crossing of the Red Sea. Their patience—let the generation die out rather than smite them—is considerably greater than the revolutionaries who replaced the terrible "Old Testament" God. See above, chapter 3, n. 70.

[80] Klaus-Georg Riegel, "Inqisitionssysteme von Glaubensgemeinschaften: Die Rolle von Shuldgeständnissen in der spanischen und der stalinistischen Inquisitionspraxis," *Zeitschrift für Sociologie* 16, no. 3 (1987): 175–89.

[81] Gould, *Wonderful Life: The Burgess Shale and the Nature of History* (New York: W.W. Norton, 1990), 48–53.

[82] MacRae, "Bolshevik Ideology," 173.

axiomatically in equality and presented themselves as the best hope for true (radical) democracy. And (2) they both embraced characteristically active apocalyptic scenarios: the true believers must bring about the transformation. Although the French revolution, on the one hand, may have begun with a much more transformative scenario, it rapidly (over four years) passed to increasingly violent scenarios. On the other hand, the French revolutionaries drew back from bloodletting relatively quickly, especially when compared with what happened subsequently in Russia and China.

Marxism, however, partly as a child of the (disappointment in the) French revolutionary wave (*Babouvisme*), articulated from the beginning a sharply cataclysmic scenario in which things had to get worse before they could get better; indeed, in order for them to get "millennially" better, they had to reach apocalyptically catastrophic proportions. So once Marxists who took power began to use violence against those they claimed to have saved, they indulged an almost limitless appetite for death.

That both the French Revolution and the Russian traveled rapidly from a minimally violent, primarily transformative apocalyptic scenario (1789, February Revolution) to one that called for the systematic elimination of hundreds of thousands if not millions of people (1793, October Revolution), comes as something of a surprise, since both these movements explicitly promised that the new world would bring freedom and happiness to humankind. Invoking their commitment to the vision of a total salvation *in this world, now*, both revolutions steered—as if by the cunning of history—to the most appalling and contradictory style of apocalyptic millennialism. Their terrifying willingness to engage in coercive purification as a means to accomplish their visionary goals cost a staggering number of lives.

▪ THE PROBLEM OF "SECULAR" MILLENNIALISM

Dealing with millennialism in industrial societies presents particular challenges. In its more successful variants, industrial society embraces secular ideologies that explicitly reject the kind of religious language so characteristic of all previous forms of millennialism. Thus the self-image of modern secular societies insists that they have achieved their unique and uniquely powerful configurations precisely by rejecting all forms of religious superstition, especially the raving fantasies, the *Schwärmerei*, of millennial prophets. Nothing, it would seem, could be further from modernity than millennialism.

And yet, if one sticks to the definition of millennialism—perfect and just society *on earth* (however defined), and thereby, collective salvation for its inhabitants—and if one looks at the dynamics of apocalyptic time—from enthusiastic take-off to cognitively dissonant disappointment, to reentry into normal time—it seems justified to argue that, rather than having abandoned millennial beliefs, "modern" industrial society invented a new, secular variant.

Secular millennialism, like its religious progenitors, covers the full range of variants, from demotic to hierarchical, from progressive to restorative. But most often it falls in the demotic progressive quadrant of the millennial four-square. Industrial technology empowers us to generate wealth and free us from backbreaking labor in ways before unimagined. For the adherents of the most popular millennialism of the modern period (beginning, say, with the eighteenth century), bringing about equality among people seemed like it would solve the problems of injustice and human misery. The hierarchical variants, like Nazism (discussed in the next chapter), tend to emerge as secondary, antidemotic responses. Although, they may include restorative themes, like their admiration for Teutonic warriors, crusaders, and ancient symbols of power, modern millennialism is resolutely "progressive." Technology will assure that the new world will not resemble the old.

Technological prowess, with its offer of superhuman powers, has actually stimulated both the millennial and apocalyptic imagination among denizens of the modern world. We sinners can destroy the world with everything from nuclear weapons to ecological devastation. We true believers can build utopia with modern technology. And sometimes, we true believers must use the technology to destroy the world, precisely to save it.

Secular apocalyptic variants cover both squares of the cataclysmic-transformative axis; and fall primarily on the active side of the active-passive one. Indeed, technology-empowered, secular apocalyptic has produced the most radically active scenarios in the history of millennialism. When the believer awaits no God or supernatural force to intervene, apocalyptic transformations must take place as a result of human action, and both the destruction of the old world and the building of the new become key events. Even using the term secular in a religious sense,[83] "secular" apocalyptic is virtually *synonymous* with active, indeed hyperactive, apocalyptic: humans replaces God as the active agent in the creation of the millennium.

This peculiar (if not exclusive) aspect of secular millennialism—the complete shift of responsibility, of agency, from divine to human forces—sets many of these movements on the road to totalitarianism. This shift involved a level of megalomania that one normally associates with millennialists imbued with an enthusiasm that made them God's agents, even God incarnate. But here, with no God in play, the megalomanic dimension becomes almost a default mode: once the revolution in motion, anything that undermined its momentum—skepticism, dissent, doubt, scruples—became forces of evil. The empowerment of the moment became the raison d'être of the party.

> According to Lenin, the Communist Party is based on the principle of coercion that recognizes no limitations or inhibitions. And the central idea of this principle of boundless coercion is not coercion by itself, but the absence of any limitation whatsoever—moral, political and even physical, as far as that goes. Such a Party is capable of achieving mir-

---

[83] On Augustine's use of the word *saeculum* to refer to the time-space continuum, see chapter 1.

acles and doing things which no other collective of men could achieve...A real Communist...that is, a man who was raised in the Party and has absorbed its spirit deeply enough to become himself, is, in a way, a miracle man.[84]

Shades of Lenin and Trotsky's grandiose dreams of overtaking the West's industrial production in weeks! These revolutionary millennialists had erected their own icons of power—the scientific reading of apocalyptic history, the Party as infallible agent of apocalypse, the egalitarian messianic world to come—and were ready, in the face of time's insults, to sacrifice rivers of blood in order to keep their worship alive.

■ HANNAH ARENDT AND THE ORIGINS OF TOTALITARIANISM

This argument for the apocalyptic millennial genealogy of totalitarianism relates directly to the language used by Hannah Arendt in her *Origins of Totalitarianism*. For her, the outstanding quality of totalitarianism derives from the peculiar combination of "ideology and terror."[85] Totalitarian ideologies aim a perfect, "final" solution, where "all men have become One with Man, where all action aims at the *acceleration of the movement of nature or history*...[and] terror can be *completely relied on to keep the movement in constant motion.*"[86] Keeping the movement in constant motion is another way to identify the workings of apocalyptic jazz: systematic, increasingly desperate efforts to sustain apocalyptic time after the millennial promise has failed.

Arendt mistakenly thinks that ideologies of the kind that lead to totalitarianism are new.

> Ideologies—*isms* which to the satisfaction of their adherents can explain everything and every occurrence by deducing it from a single premise—are a very recent phenomenon and, for many decades, played a negligible role in political life. Only with the wisdom of hindsight [*ex post defectu*] can we discover in them certain elements which have made them so disturbingly useful for totalitarian rule. Not before Hitler and Stalin were the great political potentialities of the ideologies discovered.[87]

The ideologies she describes are forms of millennialism: they focus "not on what is, but what becomes...they predict the future."[88] And when they take power, they

---

[84] Yuri Pyatakov to N. V. Volsky in 1927 (defending himself from accusations of cowardice in abandoning his own convictions for the sake of the party), cited in Robert Conquest, *Reflections on a Ravaged Century* (New York: Norton, 2001), 77.

[85] Hannah Arendt, *The Origins of Totalitarianism* (New York: Meridian Books, 1958), 460–79.

[86] Ibid., 467. Italics mine.

[87] Ibid., 468.

[88] Ibid., 470. "Ideologies are never interested in the miracle of being. They are historical, concerned with becoming and perishing, with the rise and fall of cultures" (469). And yet, most millennialism begins with the miracle of being, for example, Akhenaten's "Great Hymn" and Psalm 104 (see above, chapter 6, n. 29). Early stages of demotic millennialism are grounded in human delight: "everyone of you shall invite his neighbor to come under his vine and under his fig" (Zechariah 3:10). Thus, (totalitarian) ideology as Arendt describes it here, would appear to be a late and particularly weaponized form of millennial thought.

consistently seek to change reality in accordance with their ideological claims, and interpret enmity as malevolent conspiracy.

Arendt has, here, described the dynamics of a later segment of the apocalyptic wave, which explain Hitler's and Stalin's original contribution. They did not articulate the millennial ideology (Hitler's came from the Ariosophists; Stalin's, from the Bolsheviks), but they did attempt what she calls "the process of realization." In that process, they fell in thrall to the (apocalyptic) logic of these ideas which "like a mighty tentacle seizes you on all sides as in a vise and from whose grip you are powerless to tear yourself away; you must either surrender or make up your mind to utter defeat."[89]

Cohn's controversial remarks about this dimension of Communist (and Nazi) behavior in the twentieth century make precisely this point: a small group of true believers, with a megalomanic sense of cosmic purpose, driven to seize power with the intention of decisively reshaping history and humankind, responds to frustration with paranoid violence. Cohn describes certain medieval chiliasts as the "true prototype of a modern totalitarian party…a restlessly dynamic and utterly ruthless group which, obsessed by the apocalyptic phantasy and filled with the conviction of its own infallibility, set itself infinitely above the rest of humanity and recognized no claims save those of its own supposed mission."[90]

> The megalomaniac view of oneself as the Elect, wholly good, abominably persecuted yet assured of ultimate triumph; the attribution of gigantic and demonic powers to the adversary; the refusal to accept the ineluctable limitations and imperfections of human existence, such as transience, dissension, conflict, fallibility whether intellectual or moral; the obsession with inerrable prophecies—these attitudes are symptoms which together constitute the unmistakable syndrome of paranoia. But a paranoiac delusion does not cease to be so because it is shared by many individuals, nor yet because those individuals have real and ample grounds for regarding themselves as victims of oppression.[91]

And it is in the inevitable frustration of these efforts that the totalitarian impulse emerges with remorseless logic. Thus, when Arendt writes her description of the process, she essentially *describes* one particular response to apocalyptic disappointment at the failure of the millennium. (I supply the millennial gloss in brackets.)

> It is in the nature [*sic*] of ideological politics—and is not simply a betrayal committed for the sake of self-interest or lust for power—that the real content of ideology (the working

[89] Stalin's speech of January 28, 1924; quoted in Lenin, *The Essentials of Lenin*, 2 vols. (London: Lawrence & Wishart, 1947) 1:33; Arendt, *Origins*, 472. See chapter 2 on the manner in which apocalyptic ideas "ride" the believer the way a horseman rides a horse.

[90] Cohn, *Pursuit of the Millennium*, 285; cited in Conquest, *Reflections*, 75.

[91] Cohn, *Pursuit of the Millennium*, 309. Citation from the first edition. Bertram D. Wolfe, the founder of the American Communist Party, whose copy I own (a birthday gift from my sister), marked this passage with a double underline and wrote PARANOIA in the margin.

class or the Germanic peoples [i.e., the "people" "chosen" for salvation]), which originally had brought about the "idea" (the struggle of the classes as the law of history or the struggle of the races as the law of nature [i.e., the key to seeing the timing and nature of the apocalyptic transformation]), is devoured by the logic with which the [millennial] "idea" is [apocalyptically] carried out.[92]

Totalitarianism, in other words, is not so much inherent in *ideology*, as it is in certain *millennial* ideologies that, following the "logic" of an active and violent apocalyptic scenario (buttressed by science and technology with particular force in the twentieth century), attempt to perfect the world. The "logic" of coercive purity, ultimately "attempt[s] to destroy every last crevice of human freedom."[93] Dictatorships want power and demand the people's corporeal obedience; totalitarian societies want "salvation" and demand the people's "soul." In Scott's terms, the millennial movement seeks to eliminate private transcripts by removing the public oppression that occasioned them; when private transcripts remain, it seeks to eliminate private transcripts as proof that they have succeeded. Thick hegemony demands not merely the accession of the body to the demands others place upon it, but the mind too. Winston must *believe* in Big Brother.[94]

Whereas the totalitarianism of Nazism came as less of a surprise, given the openly authoritarian ideology of the movement, that of both the French Revolution and the Russian surprised many, including the revolutionaries themselves, since both these movements explicitly promised that the new world would bring freedom and happiness to humankind. Thus, although Marxism and Nazism come from almost diametrically opposed ideological positions, by their commitment to a vision of a *total salvation in this world*, and in their violent engagement in apocalyptic time, they came to resemble each other in two of the most appalling aspects of millennialism—(1) their obsession with "redeeming" their chosen "people" at any cost to "private" life;[95] and (2) their terrifying willingness to engage in coercive purification as a means to accomplish their visionary goals with the stunning numbers of lives lost as a result.

▪ FELLOW TRAVELERS AND THE COGNITIVE DISSONANCE OF FAILED REVOLUTIONS

The reaction of Western Marxists to the Soviet debacle, namely, the length and depth of their denial that the dream had turned into a nightmare, has astounded

---

[92] Arendt, *Origins*, 472. Italics and parentheses hers, brackets mine.

[93] It seems appropriate that, in her concluding sentences, Arendt cites Augustine, the great anti-millennialist ideologue of the Christian Church (and the subject of her doctoral thesis), "Man was created so that a beginning might be made..." (*De Civ. Dei*, 12:20; Arendt, *Origins*, 479).

[94] George Orwell, *1984* (London: Secker & Warburg, 1948).

[95] Courtois et al., *The Black Book of Communism*; John Weiss, *Ideology of Death: Why the Holocaust Happened in Germany* (Chicago: I.R. Dee, 1996).

and puzzled most intellectuals not in thrall to Communist ideology. This is particularly true since some of these people, like George Bernard Shaw and Jean-Paul
Sartre, were both brilliant and otherwise known for their mordant observations on
people's "bad faith." And yet, just like believers incapable of allowing the evidence
of apocalyptic prophecy's failure to enter their consciousness, these people could
not admit to themselves or anyone else that the millennial experiment in which
they had invested so much (intellectual) energy could have failed.[96]

The best insights into the phenomenon come from examining the writings of
"political pilgrims," men and women who, out of deep sympathy for revolutionary
regimes in exotic lands, visited them and failed to remark upon any of the signs of
the holocausts that the revolutionaries carried out against their own people.[97] Paul
Hollander remarks on several traits that distinguish most "political pilgrims" in
the twentieth century, most of which involve commitment to apocalyptic millennial beliefs:[98]

- The fascination of the "distant or poorly known"[99]—that is, a valuable
  projection screen for the "not-self" of this fallen world.
- Revolutionary or post-revolutionary—that is apocalyptic or post-
  apocalyptic.
- Given to some variety of Marxist ideology—that is demotic millennialism.
- Hostile to the West—a rejection of self (world now) as the apocalyptic
  enemy.
- Image of the victimized underdog—preferably the victim of the West.

In other words, in the twentieth century, apocalyptic millennial dreamers were not
limited to the premodern condition, in which they could dream only of messianic
eras that existed in the future. These modern dreamers had a variety of choices of
"real world" utopias, namely demotic millennial experiments, to visit. Rather than
project all their hopes into an apocalyptic future, they could project them onto
these exotic, mysterious places that had only recently experienced apocalyptic
time. Such fantasies "only" required a denial that the apocalyptic wave had (already)
broken and that the millennial experiment had failed.

As a result, these pilgrims proved capable of the most extraordinary ability to
ignore whatever anomalies they observed in their terrestrial paradise. George

[96] One of the significant exceptions was Bertrand Russell, who, among other things coined the
expression the "fallacy of the superior virtue of the oppressed," in his 1937 essay "The Superior Virtue
of the Oppressed," *Unpopular Essays* (London: George Allen & Unwin, 1950).

[97] David Caute, *The Fellow Travelers: A Postscript to the Enlightenment* (New York: Macmillan,
1973); Paul Hollander, *Political Pilgrims: Western Intellectuals in Search of the Good Society* (New
Brunswick, N.J.: Transaction Publishers, 1998).

[98] Hollander, *Political Pilgrims*, 22.

[99] Hollander discusses a survey in Sweden after the fall of the Soviet Union in 1989, which considered *Albania* the most admired country (*Political Pilgrims*, 275–76). On the role of the South Seas as a
similar "fantasy utopia," see Richard Wrangham and Dale Peterson, *Demonic Males: Apes and the
Origins of Human Violence* (New York: Houghton Mifflin, 1996), 83–108.

Bernard Shaw's visit to Moscow in 1931 illustrates some of the psychology involved. A devastating critic of Western capitalism, he checked his skepticism at the border, along with the numerous tins of canned meat that his comrades had given him to bring to their starving Russian friends, since he "knew" there was no famine in the socialist paradise. He arrived in Moscow oblivious to all that surrounded him, including the dismay of the Russians when he told them about the jettisoned cans of meat.[100] Russia served not as a case of the "real world," subject to his penetrating criticism, but the foil for his own dislike of the world he inhabited, no matter how it welcomed the products of his socialist genius. Despite the horror that surrounded him in Russia, he came back with glowing reports. As Russell noted, Shaw "fell victim to adulation of the Soviet government and suddenly lost the power of criticism and of seeing though humbug if it came from Moscow."[101]

The combination of a profound dislike of one's own country—and in this case, of himself—and the fascination with the "supermen" of apocalyptic time comes across in Sartre's account of his visit to Cuba. Here Sartre met men who were dramatically unlike the nauseating men of *mauvaise foi* that populated his existential plays and philosophy (and his life), supermen living in apocalyptic time, men of purpose and meaning, authentic men.

> I heard the door close behind my back and I lost both the memory of my old fatigue and any notion of the hour. Among these fully awake men, at the height of their powers, sleeping doesn't seem like a natural need, just a routine of which they had more or less freed themselves…they have all excluded the routine alternation of lunch and dinner from their daily program. Of all these night watchmen, Castro is the most wide awake. Of all these fasting people, Castro can eat the most and fast the longest. [They]…exercise a veritable dictatorship over their own needs…they roll back the limits of the possible.[102]

All of a sudden, his own fatigue vanishes when he observes their intensity, their ability to override "normal" time with its routines and needs.

Behind this attraction for intensity-as-authenticity lies something still more disturbing, something already visible in the anti-intellectual rants of the nineteenth-century anarchists like Bakùnin and Nechàev—an admiration for the ability to commit violence in the name of the ideal and an ability to transcend the paralysis of the intellectual. Here we find the psychological dynamics that permit the alchemical transmutation of love into hatred, of the desire for peace and harmony into the embrace of war and (mega-) death. Behind the intellectual, paralyzed by a combination of ideological commitments to peace and nonviolence on the one hand, and the existential awareness of how meaningless the universe and

---

[100] Eugene Lyons, *Assignment in Utopia* (New York: Harcourt, Brace, 1937), 428–35.

[101] Bertrand Russell, *Portraits from Memory* (New York: Simon & Schuster, 1956), 59; cited in Hollander, *Political Pilgrims*, 139.

[102] Sartre, *Sartre on Cuba* (New York: Ballantine Books, 1961), 44, 99, 102–03; cited by Hollander, *Political Pilgrims*, 237.

how selfish and cowardly the bad faith of every individual, on the other, lies a longing to identify with the aggressor.

> But the primary attraction of Marxism cannot be to the sophisticated, though there can be no doubt that Marxism exercises a peculiar fascination over those who are susceptible to the worst intellectual heresy of our age: the romanticism of violence. (This is especially true because the individual who might well be afraid of his own inclinations in this direction can excuse himself to himself by the generosity of his goal and the "scientifically" established fact that history and society are intrinsically brutal and predetermined.) The main appeal is not here, however; it is the simple one of the Messiah and the Apocalypse."[103]

Such reflections may hold for some of the fellow travelers who inhabited the twentieth century, and continue to inhabit the twenty-first, but others show yet another mechanism, perhaps the most important, namely the hold of the community of believers. Festinger already pointed out the role of the community in producing certain forms of the cognitive dissonance of apocalyptic disappointment—the prophecy may have failed, but the intimate and purposeful community of believers *created* by that prophecy must not.[104] All of the adjustments demanded in order to lessen the pain of cognitive dissonance—the redating, the reformulation of what must be done in the meantime, the reshaping of relations within the group and to outsiders—reflect the need to keep the group alive in post-apocalyptic time. And the closer one was to the core of the group and the more one had burned bridges to "normal time," the more the commitment to maintaining group identity.

Eugene Lyons, one of the more thoughtful of the Communists to travel to Russia as a news correspondent in 1922, took over a *decade* to finally realize just what a nightmare the revolution had become.[105] Upon his return to the United States in 1934, it took him still another *three years* to decide to publish the truth. The hesitation came almost entirely from the sense of loss that such honesty would bring him—the exile from the community of true believers that had given his life so much purpose.[106] And not only did such shunning serve the purpose of preventing people on the inside from acknowledging reality—especially in public—but it shielded those still in denial from dealing with that reality. No one would trust someone who betrayed the revolution.

The power of this phenomenon of denial among leftist intellectuals in the West in the early twentieth century, has damaged our ability to think clearly about matters revolutionary, or, in the terms of this study, to think about active, violent, apocalyptic millennialism. Such matters go well beyond the issues of actual "fellow travelers" and the revolutions themselves, and include a wide range of issues that may seem, at first glance, to relate only marginally. Among the most difficult issues for academics to think about is the entire range of "Right-Left" political tendencies and all the

---

[103] MacRae, "Bolshevik Ideology," 168.
[104] Festinger, *When Prophecy Fails.*
[105] Lyons, *Assignment in Utopia.*
[106] Ibid., book 5, chap. 4.

submerged value judgments that scholars like to pretend they have put behind them.[107] In response to a question about resistance among his colleagues to a millennial genealogy to Marxism, Klaus-Georg Riegel responded:

> It is a widespread resistance among German historians and social scientists dealing with Marxism-Leninism to describe and analyze this movement in terms of a religious *fait social* in Emile Durkheim's sense. Most of the critics still are convinced that Marxism-Leninism is a historical fellow of the French Revolution, which brought humanity, the sun of reason, progress and a new brotherhood. Thus they believe that even Stalinism has some connections with this project of historical progress and any attempt to put this totalitarian system in the category of a closed and barbarian theocracy is very often vehemently refused. In this case, very emotionally seated aspirations and hopes of young or older intellectuals are at stake...Everybody who dares to take the Bolshevik world as a religious community is considered as a traitor betraying the humanitarian ideals of the modernity of the French Revolution...If you see it in this sense, say the proponents of the project of modernity, the distance between the old and the new modern world would shrink too much and the debts to the Christian tradition would become too heavy. Thus, when you treat the Bolsheviks as a millennial sect you are going to betray the project of modernity and treat the Bolsheviks despite their very modern efforts to industrialize backward Russia as a medieval sect of obscure believers.[108]

And among the historical issues of the twentieth century, nothing poses greater problems to scholars than the similarities and differences between the Soviet and Nazi totalitarian systems, both of which (by the definitions of this study) were active cataclysmic, apocalyptic millennial movements.

■ APOCALYPTIC PARANOIA AND THE *PROTOCOLS OF THE ELDERS OF ZION*

Before turning to Nazism, however, let us consider one of the more bizarre and millennial links between Communism and Nazism—the unusual career of one of the canonical documents of modern "political religions" from Nazism to Islamism, the *Protocols of the Elders of Zion*. Ironically, it was precisely the turn toward totalitarianism among the Communists that provided the most powerful empirical confirmation of the claims of the *Protocols*, that turn-of-the-century "warrant for genocide." In order to grasp both the power of the text and its millennial dimensions, we must begin with an understanding of Jews in modernity.

Paranoia, the Jews, and Modernity

One of the great surprises for almost everyone involved in the "modern project" was the phenomenal success of the Jews in the new world of constitutional governments,

---

[107] Martin Amis, *Koba the Dread: Laughter and the Twenty Million* (New York: Talk Miramax Books, 2002), 255–57.
[108] Email communications from Klaus-Georg Riegel, November 18 and 20, 2008.

meritocracies based on equality before the law. Demotic religiosity may explain this success retrospectively: having played by the rules of a civil society—equality before the law, self-criticism, meritocracy—for millennia, the Jews had little difficulty adjusting to the new conditions of civil polities of the nineteenth and twentieth centuries. Differently put, despite their humble/humiliated appearance, Jews eagerly rode the stallion of liberty, willing to take responsibility for the choices now offered them by civic polities.[109]

For antimodern foes of civil polities, however, this uncanny success became the focus of authoritarian fear and loathing. For centuries, the Jews were a pariah caste, legitimately looked down upon by even the lowliest of the low among the Christians. Now an alarming number of these pariahs moved into positions of social influence and prestige. "The unanticipated success of the Jews epitomized the awesome scope of social upheaval and served as a vivid, obtrusive reminder of the erosion of old certainties, of melting and evaporating of everything that was once deemed solid and lasting."[110] Indeed, the Jew became "the prime target of anti-modernist resistance," and the more apocalyptic [cosmic] the fears of modernity, the more virulent the Jew hatred. The Jews were behind it all.

Nor was this pure fantasy. Among the positions of prominence in modern society, assimilated Jews gravitated with a particular passion to the secular millennial vocation of radical revolutionary. From Junius Frey to Marx to Trotsky to Bertram Wolfe, messianics of Jewish origin pursuing progressive projects populated leftist revolutionary ranks in impressive numbers.[111] Their unusually high numbers in the highest levels of the Russian revolutionary ranks (Mensheviks as well as Bolsheviks) led to one of the more enduring myths of the contemporary world, that of Judeo-Bolshevism.[112] Brought over to Germany by White Russian refugees, this myth played a key role in the *Protocols*-permeated *Weltanschauung* the Nazis forged in the years immediately after the traumatic events of 1917–18.[113] In order to understand this world, and thus, how easily paranoia can take hold of a modern apocalyptic movement, it helps to understand the conspiracist world of the *Protocols of the Elders of Zion*.

This forgery, solicited by the Russian secret police at the turn of the century, and published by the paranoid mystic Sergei Nilus in 1905, combined two main strands of conspiracy thinking that had arisen in antimodern circles over the course of the

---

[109] On the "stallion of liberty," see chapter 10, n. 55. In his brilliant discussion of the "fear of freedom" (1941), Erich Fromm emphasizes the difficulty for those exercising freedom to take responsibility for making the wrong choice, something that the highly self-critical traditions of Judaism made possible, *Escape from Freedom* (New York: Macmillan, 1994), 23–38.

[110] Zygmunt Bauman, *Modernity and the Holocaust* (Ithaca, N.Y.: Cornell University Press, 2000), 45. Note the allusion to the *Communist Manifesto* (above, chapter 10, n. 37).

[111] See above, chapter 10, n. 90. Without understanding this profound demotic link between Judaism and modernity, one cannot grasp the daunting specter that emancipated Jews constituted for gentiles, especially conservative ones.

[112] On Judeo-Bolshevism, see Wistrich, *Revolutionary Jews*.

[113] See Michael Kellogg, *The Russian Roots of Nazism: White Émigrés and the Making of National Socialism, 1917–1945*, New Studies in European History (Cambridge: Cambridge University Press, 2006).

nineteenth century.[114] On the one hand, ever since the French Revolution, counter-revolutionary forces had attributed to the *Illuminati*, a Masonic order founded in 1776, a systematic and pervasive conspiracy to take over the world, an intention that Mozart inadvertently admitted in his *Magic Flute* of 1791.[115] For many conservatives in Europe, democracy was a cover for a plot to take over the world and enslave it, a conspiracy that was succeeding at an alarming rate all over Europe, indeed the world.

On the other hand, from before the origins of Christianity, writers had denounced the Jews as enemies of humanity to which medieval Latin Christians had added a worldwide rabbinical scheme to destroy the true religion.[116] As the impact of the civic revolutions of the late eighteenth and nineteenth centuries played out in the West, Jews enjoyed a success that astonished everyone, including themselves.[117] The great "discovery" that dawned on these antimoderns in the course of the nineteenth century was that the Masons were mere pawns in this conspiracy (as were Darwin and Nietzsche[118]). The real conspirators, who had been at work for millennia, were the Jews. As the century turned, the apocalyptic mood permeated ever-widening levels of discourse.[119] One person's messiah is another's antichrist.

The result of these two strands of conspiratorial thought coming together at the end of the nineteenth century resulted in the fabrication of the most powerful apocalyptic text in modern times, the *Protocols of the Elders of Zion*.[120] The *Protocols* forgery takes as axiomatic Sagan's *dominating imperative*—rule or be ruled. If all men—more specifically all political men—are ruled by *libido dominandi*, then any notion of a democracy/constitutional government/liberal experiment in self rule/

---

[114] *The Paranoid Apocalypse*, chap. 1.

[115] On Mozart's *Magic Flute*, see website appendix. The key articulation of this conspiracy, from which the forgers of the *Protocols* plagiarized, was already in Maurice Joly's *Le Dialogue en enfer entre Montesquieu et Machiavelli* (written in 1864); online: http://www.gutenberg.org/etext/13187, April 13, 2010. See the appendix of Cohn's *Warrant for Genocide*, for a list of the passages used.

[116] On pre-Christian anti-Judaism, see Peter Schäfer, *Judeophobia: Attitudes toward the Jews in the Ancient World* (Cambridge, MA: Harvard University Press, 1997); on the medieval Christian mania for demonizing the Jews, see Joshua Trachtenberg, *The Devil and the Jews* (New York: Harper & Row, 1966). On the medieval anti-Semitic contribution to the *Protocols*, see Jeffrey Woolf, "The Devil's Hoofs: The Medieval Roots of *The Protocols of the Elders of Zion*" and Johannes Heil, "Thomas of Monmouth and the 'Protocols of the Sages of Narbonne,'" both in *Paranoid Apocalypse*, chaps. 4, 5.

[117] Meyerbeer, who ran the Paris opera in the mid-nineteenth century, represents a good example of Jewish prominence, the Steven Spielberg of his day. For a larger discussion, see Yuri Slezkine, *The Jewish Century* (Princeton, N.J.: Princeton University Press, 2004), chap. 2. Although Slezkine considers the twentieth century to be the "Jewish Century," that merely attests to the continuing conditions from the late eighteenth to the late twentieth centuries, during which both civil polities and Jews thrived.

[118] *Protocols of the Elders of Zion*, trans. Victor Marsden (Costa Mesa, Calif.: Noontide Press, 1934).

[119] On the millennial stirrings around 1900, about which several books need to be written, see Hillel Schwartz, *Century's End: A Cultural History of the Fin de Siècle from the 990s through the 1990s* (New York: Doubleday, 1990), 156–98; *Jahrhundertwenden*, ed. Manfred Jakubowski-Tiessen et al. (Göttingen, Vandenhoeck & Ruprecht, 1999), 305–47.

[120] Michael Hagemeister, "'The Antichrist as an Imminent Political Possibility': Sergei Nilus and the Apocalyptical Reading of the *Protocols of the Elders of Zion*," in *Paranoid Apocalypse*, chap. 6.

civil polity that hopes to create order by freeing commoners and counting on them to act rationally/morally (to prefer self-control over dominion over another, positive-sum over zero-sum relations) is doomed to failure.[121] The *Protocols* espouses the fundamental aristocratic argument: the people cannot be trusted with power, and only when imposed from above with force—as the *Protocols* have the Jews say, "with violence and terror"—can there be any hope for order.

If democracy is a recipe for anarchy, then people who support, encourage, and benefit from democracy—like the Jews—cannot possibly do it for democracy's sake. They must have an ulterior motive. What motive? Obviously, the conquest of everyone else—the gentiles—and their subjection to slavery. The *dominating imperative*, here, constitutes not only the default mode, but the inescapable mode. *All* interactions are a struggle for power. This fundamental projection—everyone wants to dominate, even (especially!) the Jews—lies at the core of both the composition and the appeal of the *Protocols*.

Nor were these paranoids entirely wrong. On the contrary, all too often, when they took power, the behavior of the revolutionary democrats touting the messianic era of equality and peace fulfilled precisely the prediction of the *Protocols*. No sooner did these "democratic" revolutionaries take power and eliminate the aristocracy, than they introduced a much more pervasive form of dominion and human enslavement. Totalitarian tendencies on the radical demotic Left, then, confirmed the warnings of the paranoid, fascist, authoritarian Right.

And if the momentary madness of the French revolutionary terror was not enough to alarm some dupes, surely the sustained madness of Bolshevik Russia should suffice. To those living in the decade after the "Great War," and its 1917 revolution, the bad faith of the radical-Left-in-power was self-evident, certainly to all hostile observers. Only a fellow traveler could not see the problem. Nor did voices lack that blamed the Jews for the Soviets, whose seemingly "revolutionary" ideologues like Trotsky were actually rabbinical agents. No wonder, then, that even the *London Times* briefly entertained the possibility that the *Protocols* might be genuine.[122] It not only accurately warned of the Bolshevik revolution, but predicted its course—the unprecedented, totalitarian tyranny of the revolutionaries once in power. Hitler, aware that some considered the *Protocols* a forgery, argued in *Mein Kampf* that authenticity could be judged by how accurate their depiction of current events:

> They are based on a forgery, the *Frankfurter Zeitung* moans and screams once every week: the best proof they are authentic...The best criticism applied to them, however, is reality. Anyone who examines the historical development of the last hundred years from the standpoint of this book will at once understand the screaming of the Jewish press.

---

[121] Richard Landes, "The Paranoid Imperative and the Political Logic of the *Protocols*" in *Paranoid Apocalypse*, chap. 2.

[122] "'The Jewish Peril': A Disturbing Pamphlet," *London Times*, May 8, 1920, 15. The *Times* did publish a series of articles debunking the *Protocols* the following August, on which see Philip Graves, "The Protocols of Zion: An Exposure," *London Times*, August 16–18, 1921, online: http://emperors-clothes. com/antisem/graves-tran.htm, April 13, 2010.

For once this book has become the common property of a people, the Jewish menace may be considered as broken.[123]

As a result of these new historical developments, the text had an unmistakable prophetic and apocalyptic appeal. The "plot" it revealed may have been going on for millennia, but it was now coming to its terrifying climax in the present. Indeed modernity—the spread of egalitarian principles and all the attendant consequences—represented the victory of the conspiracy. This apocalyptic anxiety explicitly informs the preface that the Christian mystic Sergei Nilus wrote for the first edition of the text. And the 1905 Revolution right after publication, and the later victory of the Bolsheviks, spread that sense of apocalyptic foreboding far and wide.[124]

Many found its prophetic accuracy uncanny. Paul Zawadski argues that, in the increasingly disenchanted world brought on by secular modernity, the *Protocols* constitutes one of the first "sacred" documents of what Erich Voegelin called "political religions."[125] The fact that the *London Times* published an extensive analysis of the text as a forgery in 1921, and a Swiss court found two Nazis guilty of publishing the forgery in Berne in 1935, did little to prevent people's *faith* in its revelations.[126] On the contrary, the Bolshevik Terror starting in 1918 and the global Depression starting in 1929 made it a prophetic text revealing history as it happened.

Hitler and the Paranoid Response to the Challenge of Demotic Modernity

Perhaps the most consequential reader of the *Protocols* in the early twentieth century was Adolf Hitler. His profile suggests the kind of person who would find the forgery at once attractive and believable, precisely because it incarnated his own mentality. Indeed, Hitler constituted the most extreme example of the mentality the *Protocols* projects onto the Jews. In his own words he articulated the basic assumptions of the text:

- "The first fundamental of any rational *Weltanschauung* is the fact that on earth and in the universe, force alone is decisive. Whatever goal a man has reached is due to his originality plus his brutality."[127]

---

[123] Adolf Hitler, *Mein Kampf*, trans. Ralph Manheim (Boston: Houghton Mifflin, 1999), 307–08; David Redles, *Hitler's Millennial Reich: Apocalyptic Belief and the Search for Salvation* (New York: New York University Press, 2005), chap. 3.

[124] See the preface by Nilus; see also Hagemeister, "Antichrist as an Imminent Political Possibility."

[125] Paul Zawadski, "Jewish World Conspiracy" and the Question of Secular Religions: An Interpretative Perspective," in *Paranoid Apocalypse*, chap. 8.

[126] On Graves, see above, n. 122; on the Swiss court's saga, see Urs Lüthi, *Der Mythos von der Weltverschwörung: Die Hetze der Schweizer Frontisten gegen Juden und Freimaurer, am Beispiel des Berner Prozesses um die "Protokolle der Weisen von Zion"* (Basel: Helbing & Lichtenhahn, 1992); and more recently, the imaginative reconstruction of Hadassah Ben-Itto, *The Lie That Wouldn't Die: The Protocols of the Elders of Zion* (Edgeware: Vallentine-Mitchell, 2005).

[127] Robert G.L. Waite, *The Psychopathic God: Adolf Hitler* (New York: De Capo Press, 1993), 76–77.

- "He who wants to live should fight, therefore, and he who does not want to battle…does not deserve to be alive."[128]
- "Force is the first law…only through fighting have states and the world become great. If one should ask whether this struggle is gruesome, then the only answer could be: for the weak, yes, for humanity as a whole, no…"[129]
- "Politics is nothing else than the struggle of a people for its existence in this world…Man [is] the most brutal, the most resolute creature on earth. He knows nothing but the extermination of his enemies in the world."[130]
- "One creature drinks the blood of another. The death of one nourishes the other. One should not dribble about humane feelings…the struggle goes on."[131]

Not surprisingly, the man who so vigorously denounced the ruthlessness of the "Elders of Zion" (which the forgers had projected onto the Jews) took the *Protocols* as his strategic guide. Hermann Rauschning quotes Hitler's reflections: "We must beat the Jew with his own weapon. I saw that the moment I read the book…down to the veriest detail I found the *Protocols* immensely instructive [on such topics as] political intrigue, the technique of conspiracy, revolutionary subversion, prevarication, deception, organization."[132]

Having lost the zero-sum game of the dominating imperative (the dream on all sides of the "Great War") to the comparatively more positive-sum, liberal, allies, German authoritarian "losers" chose negative sum. In their minds, there was no "positive sum," and anyone who pretended to pursue such a system worked to destroy everyone else. So they took the fateful step from the (now-frustrated) dominating imperative to the paranoid imperative: from "rule or be ruled" to "exterminate or be exterminated." Hitler's genius was to articulate this paranoia in racial terms, terms that had a particular appeal to the German people who found, in their identification with the Aryan race, a message of empowerment worthy of heroic, indeed millennial proportions.[133]

---

[128] Ibid., 77.

[129] Ibid.

[130] Ibid.

[131] Ibid. Compare the *Iliad*: "And they, as wolves who tear flesh raw, in whose hearts the battle fury is tireless, who have brought down a great horned stag in the mountains and then feed on him till the jaws of every wolf run blood…" (16:156–59); discussed by Eli Sagan, *Lust to Annihilate: A Psychoanalytic Study of Violence in Ancient Greek Culture* (New York: Psychohistory Press, 1979), 53–65.

[132] Hermann Rauschning, *The Voice of Destruction* (New York: Putnam Books, 1940), 238–41. Notes Waite: "In reading…the *Protocols*, one has the feeling that one is reading descriptions of Hitler's own…plans. Page after page, all one needs to do is substitute the words 'Hitler will…' whenever the *Protocols* say 'the Jews will…'" (*Psychopathic God*, 119). Redles addresses the issue of Rauschning's reliability in "The Turning Point: *The Protocols of the Elders of Zion* and the Eschatological War Between Aryans and Jews," in *Paranoid Apocalypse*, chap. 9.

[133] Redles, "Turning Point."

12 Genocidal Millennialism

Nazi Paranoia

No historical incident has more marked the imagination of the West than Nazism. None is more central to whatever sense of moral compass exists in the postmodern age of moral relativity—Nazis are the gold standard of evil. Indeed, they are *so* evil that many refuse to allow anyone to be compared with them: they are unique, incomparable in their evil. Perhaps this explains some of the resistance to seeing the Nazis as a millennial movement: that very act of categorization makes them comparable, not just to other millennial death cults like the Taiping, and the Russian, Chinese, and Cambodian Communists, but even to such demotic movements as the American, early French, and Zionist revolutions. The mere acknowledgment of any connection is profoundly disorienting.

■ MILLENNIAL HOPES, APOCALYPTIC TIME, AND HITLER'S SUCCESS

Millennial studies focus on how beliefs travel from the disreputable margins of a culture to the center. In the case of Hitler, this question takes on particular importance since he and his Nazi Party seemed so ridiculous at the outset (the early '20s) and the results of his success were so catastrophic for everyone involved.[1] From a millennial perspective, the key to such sudden movement from the margins to the center generally lies in the advent of apocalyptic time. In order to succeed as he did, Hitler had to convince the German people of four things:

1. that *the apocalyptic battle had begun*;
2. that *the Germans needed a ruthless Führer to lead them into battle*;
3. that *Hitler was the man to do the deed*.
4. that *victory would bring a millennial kingdom*.

He was able to do precisely that in the course of a decade and a half (ca. 1919–1934).

The Final Battle Had Begun

Hitler did not have to invent the argument that the German people—and the world—were now in apocalyptic time. Behind the *Protocols* lay a host of

---

[1] Robert G. L. Waite, *The Psychopathic God: Adolf Hitler* (New York: De Capo Press, 1993), 211; for more on Hitler's image, see *Psychopathic God*, chap 1; on Hitler and the Nazi Party in the early '20s, see Ian Kershaw, *Hitler, 1889–1936: Hubris* (New York: W.W. Norton, 1999), chap. 5–6.*

apocalyptic reactions to modernity, both pro (communist) and anti (fascist). The "Great War" had had a distinctly apocalyptic flavor both in its enthusiastic inception and in its terrifying scale.[2] But even before that, one could argue for apocalyptic times from the turn of the twentieth century onward. Wilhelmine Germany engaged in extensive use of apocalyptic and millennial imagery, largely around the nascent *Reich* (the second, according to Hitler), much of it linked to various occult beliefs that associated the worship of power and hierarchy to the wisdom of the ancients.[3] Hitler emerged in the midst of a millennial stew.

More painfully, Germany came out of World War I with terrible psychic wounds. Millions of Germans, indeed millions of Europeans, had gone off to war in 1914 with zeal.[4] Hitler's own description of the enthusiasm with which he went to war as a young man of twenty-five echoes that of many Germans—and other Europeans.

> Thus my heart, like a million others, overflowed with proud joy that at last I would be able to redeem myself from this paralyzing feeling. I had so often sung *Deutschland überAlles* and shouted "*Heil*" at the top of my lungs, that it seemed to be almost a belated act of grace to be allowed to stand as a witness in the divine court of the Eternal Judge and proclaim the sincerity of this conviction. From this hour I was convinced that in case of a war—which seemed to me inevitable—in one way or another I would at once leave my books. Likewise I knew that my place would then be where my inner voice directed me.[5]

Of course, such hopes were destined to be shattered. And the war's failure brought on deep depression and despair in Germany. In the unbearable disappointment, one solution found particularly strong purchase among Germans: They had been betrayed, stabbed in the back, robbed of rightful victory by evil forces.[6]

In this context, the Weimar Republic represented a powerful incitement to apocalyptic feelings. The loss of the "Great War" had left Germans at the bottom of the European heap, deprived of key provinces and under a heavy burden for war repayment. Still worse, the victorious allies from the West had imposed on them the curse of democracy—the rule of market forces in an ever-industrializing world,

---

[2] Eugene Weber, *Apocalypses*, 140–41. Klaus Vondung, "Deutsche Apokalypse 1914," in *Das wilhelminische Bildungsbürgertum*, ed. Klaus Vondung (Göttingen: Vandenhoek & Ruprecht, 1976), 153–71.

[3] On Hitler and the occult, see Nicholas Goodrick-Clarke, *The Occult Roots of Nazism: Secret Aryan Cults and Their Influence on Nazi Ideology* (New York: New York University Press, 1992); Raymond L. Sickinger, "Hitler and the Occult: The Magical Thinking of Adolf Hitler," *Journal of Popular Culture* 34, no. 2 (Fall 2000): 107–25. Further discussion below, pp. 367–69.

[4] Weber, *Apocalypses*, 141. John A. Moses, "Justifying War as the Will of God: German Theology on the Eve of the First World War," *Colloquium*, 31 (1999): 2–20.

[5] Hitler, *Mein Kampf*, trans. Ralph Manheim (Boston: Houghton Mifflin, 1999), 163.

[6] For a study of the "stab in the back" theory (*Dolchstoßlegende*), see Lindley Fraser, *Germany between Two Wars: A Study of Propaganda and War-Guilt* (London: Oxford University Press, 1945), chap.1–2. Moeller van den Bruck, invoker of the *tausendjähriger Reich* (see below, n. 50), was a major advocate of this theory. See Fritz Stern, *Politics of Cultural Despair: A Study in the Rise of the Germanic Ideology* (Berkeley and Los Angeles: University of California Press, 1961), 214–21.

the impotence of parliamentary systems of rule that empowered leftist revolutionary forces, the prominence of Jews in politics and culture, the chaos and moral corruption of avant-guard art, the destruction of the simple life of the German commoner, *das Volk*.

As Germans saw the modern juggernaut of wealth and technology crush them and the malfunctions of Weimar constitutionalism paralyze them, as things spiraled out of control with the staggering inflation of the early 1920s and returned with a worldwide depression in the early 1930s, the argument that this was all part of a worldwide plan to destroy Germany became increasingly credible. Rudolf Hess, an instant convert to the Hitler cult, described the situation in the 1920s.

> Since then [the war] Germany writhes as in a fever. It can barely hold itself erect. Blood drained for years from its aorta as a consequence of the Versailles Treaty; wasteful state administration—empty coffers...grotesque inflation. In the *Volk* gleaming feasts next to glaring misery...The mightiest strain discharged at a moment's notice in plundering, murder and rioting.[7]

For many Germans, the "war to end all wars" was not over.[8] On the contrary, the 1920s were only an intermission. Indeed, one can detect in many of the returning soldiers—Hitler not the least among them—what one historian has called a "messianic-revolutionary outlook of the returning warriors," a synthesis of "nationalist ideology and an apocalyptic Christian mythology. The warrior-dictator can lead Germany to the Promised Land only once he has destroyed evil, sin, and death in their earthly embodiment as the potent, satanic Jew."[9] As EugenWeber and others have argued, the two world wars represent two stages of a modern "Thirty Years War" (1914–45). As the *Protocols* revealed, the world conspiracy for global conquest now approached its final stages. Who would strike first?

The Germans Needed a Messianic Führer

It is one thing to convince people that they are in apocalyptic times; it is another to convince them that you know the apocalyptic scenario whereby they will come out

---

[7] Rudolf Hess, "Wie wird der Mann beschaffen sein, der Deutschland wieder zur Höheführt," typescript in *NSDAPHauptarchiv*, roll 35, folder 689. Cited in David Redles, *Hitler's Millennial Reich: Apocalyptic Belief and the Search for Salvation* (New York: New York University Press, 2005), chap. 5.

[8] "This war is not the end, it is only the call to power. It is the forge into which the world will be beaten into new forms and new associations." Ernst Jünger, a hardened war veteran, in *In Stahlgewittern: Ein Kriegstagebuch* (Berlin: E. S. Mittler, 1926), cited in Waite, *Psychopathic God*, 307.

[9] Peter S. Fischer, *Fantasy and Politics: Visions of the Future in the Weimar Republic* (Madison, WI: University of Wisconsin Press, 1991), 26, 34; cited in Redles manuscript ("Racial Apocalypse: The Sources of Nazi Millennialism," 13) who compares "this mixture of apocalypticism, messianism, techno-utopianism, hyper-masculinity, and anti-Semitism" to that found in Andrew MacDonald's *The Turner Diaries* (Washington, D.C.: National Alliance, 1980), the inspiration for "Timothy McVeigh's attempt to induce the apocalypse at Oklahoma City." I thank Professor Redles for sharing his manuscript with me, and since the published version (*Hitler's Millennial Reich*) is significantly abridged, I must, until his further publications cite these passages from the manuscript.

triumphant. Theories about massive conspiracies most often induce resignation. How does one convince a demoralized people to fight back against such massive forces arrayed against them? Hitler's "solution" had a particularly powerful logic. It differed from the other revolutionary solutions by highlighting the importance of hierarchy as the key to both the apocalyptic transition and the millennial kingdom. For Hitler and the Nazis, and more broadly for fascists, the *Will to Power* was the key to every lock: the strongest ruled and the Germans (Aryans) were the strongest race.

He combined Nietzsche's "magnificent blond beast, roaming wantonly in search of prey and victory," with Wagner's mythical heroes, and presented them as a moral and behavioral model to the modernity-sickened German *Volk*. And in the process, he illustrated the characteristics of the "man of *ressentiment*" that Nietzsche so mordantly denounced.[10] If Marx turned Hegel on his head, then Hitler turned Nietzsche on his: "Nietzsche, more than any other thinker understood the situation which Hitler exploited. In response to this situation Hitler's messianic image came into being, embodying the religiosity Nietzsche despised."[11] Such subtleties, however, were lost on a generation in search of restoring past glory, including Nietzsche's sister, who gave her brother's walking stick to Hitler in a symbolic translation of the mantle of prophet.[12] This hierarchical and authoritarian vision centered on the charismatic leader, a man of iron will who could demand complete obedience. Only such a leader could translate that sacrifice into a national/racial omnipotence that could impose its stamp upon history.

The history of messianic emperors and imperial millennialism has a long and problematic history for Germans, beginning at least with Charlemagne's over-ambitious imperial coronation in the year 6000 from the creation of the world (801 CE), followed rapidly by collapse, followed by a disastrous cycle of once or future last emperors repeating throughout the next millennium.[13] And when Germans were not actually suffering the catastrophic results of these megalomanic pretensions and their inevitable disappointments, they were dreaming of dead messianic emperors, sitting in caves and volcanoes, awaiting the time to return.[14] In the case of Paul Anton Lagarde, the millennial stew included a strong dose of racism and anti-Semitism that identified the enemies of a "new religion of mystical

---

[10] See Walter Kaufmann, introduction to Nietzsche's *Genealogy of Morals* (New York: Vintage Books, 1989).

[11] J. P. Stern, *Hitler: The Führer and the People* (Berkeley and Los Angeles: University of California Press, 1975), 95.

[12] Carol Diethe, *Nietzsche's Sister and the Will to Power: A Biography of Eilsabeth Förster-Nietzsche* (Urbana: University of Illinois Press, 2003), 151.

[13] Landes, "Lest the Millennium Be Fulfilled"; Hannes Möhring, *Weltkaiser der Endzeit: Entstehung Wandel und Wirkun geiner tausendjährigen Weissagung*, Mittelalter-Forschungen 3 (Stuttgart: Thorbecke, 2000), who only deals with the Middle Ages.

[14] Möhring, *Weltkaiser der Endzeit*, 223–28.

nationalism."[15] In 1878, he traced an apocalyptic scenario, dominated by the appearance of a coming *Führer*:

> Only the…strong will of a single Man can help us…not parliament nor statutes nor the ambition of powerless individuals…a Führer who would so completely represent the people that in him they would be united and his command would be their will…a new Barbarossa [waiting inside a mountain for his beard to fill the chamber], a great one…a leader of genius with artistic temperament…a Caesar-Artist…whose fire of spirit and strength of arm will fulfill our ancient victorious longings.[16]

By eliminating the forces holding back the German race—the Jews in particular— the *Führer* would thereby allow the German *Volk* to return to their rightful place "over all" and from there, reach new heights.

Without a single figure of towering will, one capable of arousing implacable hatreds and making ruthless decisions that contemplated the sacrifice of vast numbers of human lives for the sake of the goal of national and racial collective salvation, this argument could not work.[17] The preexistence of a *Führerprinzip*, having a leader who stood above any common morality and dominated a grateful nation, played a key role in Nazi success.[18]

Hitler Was Their Messiah

From an early age, Hitler believed he had a divine mission, that he was the German savior, the *Führer* for whom they had longed. According to one legend, it was a Wagner opera that first gave him a glimpse of his destiny. His best "friend" Kubizek recalls going with him in 1906—so Hitler was seventeen—to a minor Wagner opera in Vienna: *Rienzi; The Last of the Roman Tribunes*.[19] The hero is a man of the people, a visionary who sings: "and if you choose me as your protector of the people's rights, look at your ancestors and call me your Volk tribune!" The masses shout back, "Rienzi, Heil! Heil, Volk tribune!"[20] On the way back, Kubizek realized that the play had transported Hitler.

> Never before and never again have I heard Hitler speak as he did in that hour.…It was as if another being spoke out of his body, and moved him as much as it did me. It wasn't at all the case of a speaker being carried away by his own words. On the contrary; I rather felt as though he himself listened with astonishment and emotion to what burst

---

[15] Paul Anton Lagarde, *Deutsche Schriften: Gesammt ausgabe letzter Hand* (Göttingen: Dieterich, 1886). The expression is Waite's, *Psychopathic God*, 274.

[16] Waite, *Psychopathic God*, 275.

[17] See Waite, *Psychopathic God*, 342–43; Ian Kershaw, "Le 'mythe du Führer' et la dynamique de l'etat Nazi," *Annales* 43, no. 3 (1988): 593–614.

[18] See Kershaw, *Hitler: Hubris*, 180–85, 294–98, 483–86; Redles, *Hitler's Millennial Reich*, 98.

[19] For a more elaborate discussion, see Redles, *Hitler's Millennial Reich*, chap. 5.

[20] See John Deathridge, *Wagner's Rienzi: A Reappraisal Based on the Study of the Sketches and Drafts* (Oxford: Clarendon, 1977), 22–23. On the historical figure, see Ronald G. Musto, *Apocalypse in Rome: Cola di Rienzo and the Politics of the New Age* (Berkeley and Los Angeles: University of California Press, 2003).

forth from him with elementary force....It was a state of complete ecstasy and rapture....He was talking of a mandate which, one day, he would receive from the people, to lead them out of servitude to the heights of freedom...It was a state of complete ecstasy and rapture, in which he transferred the character of Rienzi, without even mentioning him as a model or example, with visionary power to the plane of his own ambitions...a special mission which one day would be entrusted to him.[21]

In 1939, Hitler looked back on that performance as decisive: "in that hour it began," he confided in the presence of both Kubizek and Winifred Wagner.[22] The incident is, of course, subject to criticism for being a retrospective account that projects back into the past a self-identity as messiah that only came later.[23] On the other hand, such youthful enthusiasm, such *transportation*, which his friend never saw before *or again*, is hardly dubious per se.[24]

But between the time messiahs receive their call, and the time that they seize the opportunity to fulfill their destiny, they typically try many less exalted and more tentative paths. Hitler's prewar experiences, among them the failure of an entry exam that he had expected to pass easily and a failed career, left him disoriented and depressed. (Like Hong Xiuquan, he believed he was a genius against whom a corrupt academic system conspired.)

Whatever his earlier activity, the war had an enormous impact on him, dashing his enthusiastic hopes for a triumphant Germany, but not his sense of mission. On the contrary, crippled and blinded by injuries and tormented by humiliation, Hitler claims—like so many other messiahs, including Hong Xiuquan—to have experienced visionary heights and received a divine mission to save his people. He later reported: "as I lay there [blinded by gas], it came over me that I would liberate the German people and make Germany great."[25] This incident would, like Hong's, become part of the movement's narrative.

The war and defeat also had an enormous impact on Hitler's audience. Redles remarks on a postwar shift in the impact of Hitler's compulsive logorrhea.

> [Previously, h]is audience, while at times captive, was not always receptive, and his talent went largely unnoticed. However, shortly after the war, the insignificant lance-corporal's gift for "drumming," for stirring up the masses, was recognized.... [T]his first occurred in the barracks in post-war Munich, where Hitler's diatribes against the Jewish-Bolsheviks,

---

[21] August Kubizek, *The Young Hitler I Knew*, trans. E. V. Anderson (Boston: Houghton Mifflin, 1955), 99–100.

[22] Ibid., 290.

[23] See Ian Kershaw: "highly fanciful, reading in mystical fashion back into the episode an early prophetic vision of Hitler's own future...a melodramatically absurd claim." Kershaw, *Hitler: Hubris*, 610 n. 128. This reading shows little understanding of the nature of messianic calling. Probably hundreds of thousands of people have experiences like this in every generation; only the tiniest fraction become acclaimed messianic pretenders.

[24] See below on Hitler as *Trummler* or *Führer pp. 361–63a*; also Redles, *Hitler's Millennial Reich*, chap. 5, esp. n. 11.

[25] Karl von Wiegand, "Hitler Foresees his End," *Cosmopolitan* (April 1939): 28, as found in Walter C. Langer, *The Mind of Adolf Hitler: The Secret Wartime Report* (New York: Basic Books, 1972), 490; cited and discussed by Redles, *Hitler's Millennial Reich*, chap. 5.

largely ignored when the war was going well, now with the loss began to find an audience. Hitler was elected to the soldier's soviet.[26]

Observers, both hostile and favorable, all remarked on the intense power of Hitler's oratory. Both he and his audiences were literally transformed by the experience of one of his speeches. As Scott has argued, charismatic figures articulate the hidden transcript that others have repressed and make them public.[27] Otto Strasser noted in detail:

> Hitler responds to the vibration of the human heart with the delicacy of a seismograph, or perhaps of a wireless receiving set, enabling him, with a certainty with which no conscious gift could endow him, to act as a loudspeaker proclaiming the most secret desires, the least admissible instincts, the sufferings and personal revolts of a whole nation....I have been asked many times what is the secret of Hitler's extraordinary power as a speaker. I can only attribute it to his uncanny intuition, which infallibly diagnoses the ills from which his audience is suffering. If he tries to bolster up his argument with theories or quotations from books he has only imperfectly understood, he scarcely rises above a very poor mediocrity. But let him throw away his crutches and step out boldly, speaking as the spirit moves him, and he is promptly transformed into one of the greatest speakers of the century....[28]

Regarding Hitler's subsequent speech, Müller pointedly asked himself, "Was it the crowd, which inspired him with this mysterious power? Was it floating from him to them?" He further noted his impression: "Fantasizing hysterical romanticism, with a brutal core of will." That same night an American reporter, Ludwell Denny, also attended, noting the crowd's view of Hitler: "he was a popular preacher turned savior."[29]

As chancellor, he had his performances down to an art, with staging and timing.

> A search light lays upon his lone figure as he slowly walks through the hall, never looking to the right or the left, his right hand raised in salute, his left hand at the buckle of his belt. He never smiles—it is a religious rite, this procession of the modern Messiah incarnate. Behind him are his adjutants and secret service men. But his figure alone is flooded with light. By the time Hitler has reached the rostrum, the masses have been so worked upon that they are ready to do his will. But the masses also effect a transformation in him. He becomes electrified. He appears to go into a trance. He is carried away by his own eloquence. He returns to his chancellery completely washed up physically but revived spiritually.[30]

Nor was this pure emotional manipulation. It arose out of a profound millennial discourse that gave cosmic promise to the emotions Hitler aroused. He gave peo-

---

[26] Redles, *Hitler's Millennial Reich*, chap. 6.

[27] Scott, *Domination*, 6–10.

[28] Otto Strasser, *Hitler and I*, trans. Gwenda David and Eric Mosbacher (Boston: Houghton Mifflin, 1940), 62–65; cited in Redles, *Hitler's Millennial Reich*, 136–37.

[29] Ludwell Denny, "France and the German Counter Revolution," *The Nation* 116 (March 14, 1923): 295; cited in Redles, *Hitler's Millennial Reich*, 146.

[30] Lochner, *What About Germany?* (New York: Dodd, Mead & Company, 1942), 99. Redles, *Hitler's Millennial Reich*, chap. 6.

ple who accepted his message a redemptive vision and mission. One disciple reminisces about the profound effect Hitler had on him:

> Whatever I did from that time on, I would do as the upholder of a deeper knowledge,
> which it seemed my life's mission to formulate. I felt myself committed to this knowledge
> for all time. It remains untouched by all that was to come, untouched also by my
> subsequent separation from Hitler. This knowledge had given birth in me to a world
> view that struggled for realization. And I felt, as Hitler had said, like the guardian of the
> grail that holds the secrets of that worldview.[31]

Indeed, Andreas Dees found the Hitler experience so transforming that his faith in
Hitler replaced his belief in traditional religion. He stated that "In religion I am a
Catholic. Then I heard the *Führer*. What occurred inside me, alas, I cannot describe.
Then I knew, however, the Man and his movement and nothing else."[32]

Outside observers noted the same dynamic, although with less admiration:

> Their leader, Hitler, had worked up these emotions by using the reactions to economic and
> spiritual distress that pervade the psychology of the German people today. Radical antipa-
> thies and religious motives are fused with dreams of a better day to come. Hitler asks that the
> German nation be cleansed of all non-Aryan elements and that it find renewal in a church of
> the people in which the belief in the nordic Wotan shall be merged with that in Christ. To the
> purified nation shall at the appointed time come forth a new German emperor-king who, as
> national messiah, shall free Germany from the bondage of her foreign taskmaster.[33]

Because of Nazism's racist, antimodern ideology, it has entered the public sphere in
the postwar West as crude and revolting. It is sometimes difficult to keep in one's
mind at once the base nature of Nazism's ideology (certainly from a modern perspective) and its exceptional appeal to some of the most advanced and brilliant
minds of the age: Heidegger, Schmitt, Jung. And yet, only by keeping these two in
mind can one appreciate the power of millennialism to turn even highly developed
and sophisticated minds. Jaspers characterized Heidegger to the de-Nazification
Commission after the war as a "child who got his finger stuck in the wheel of
history."[34] Rather, he caught his finger in the wheel of a millennial movement that
empowered him beyond his wildest dreams.

---

[31] Wagener, *Hitler: Memoirs of a Confidant*, ed. Henry Ashby Turner Jr., tr. Ruth Hein (New Haven:
Yale University Press, 1985), 151, 325, cited in Redles, *Hitler's Millennial Reich*, chap. 6.

[32] *Die alte Gardespricht* (a collection of short biographies of the early Nazi Party commissioned by
Hess, on which see Redles, *Hitler's Millennial Reich*, 210 n. 8), vol. 2, Andreas Dees, 2.

[33] Paul Gierasch, "The Bavarian Menace to German Unity," *Current History Magazine* 223 (1923): 226.

[34] Mark Lilla, *Reckless Minds: Intellectuals and Politics* (New York: New York Review of Books,
2001), 4–31. Emmanuel Faye argues that Heidegger's philosophy was structurally Nazi; *Heidegger: The
Introduction of Nazism into Philosophy in Light of the Unpublished Seminars of 1933–1935*, trans.
Michael Smith (New Haven, Conn.: Yale University Press, 2009). More broadly, see Richard Wolin, *The
Seduction of Unreason: The Intellectual Romance with Fascism from Nietzsche to Postmodernism*
(Princeton, NJ: Princeton University Press, 2004).

Hitler's Millennial Role: Herald or Messiah?

In the first stage of his political career (1919–24), whether from a concern not to show all his megalomanic cards too soon, or a still-unclear sense of what his specific destiny might be, Hitler presented himself as the "John the Baptist," the *Trummler* (drummer), awakening the people to look for their coming savior.

> What can save Germany is the dictatorship of national will and national resolution. From this emerges the question: is a suitable personality here? Our duty is not to search for such a person. He is either sent by heaven or not. Our duty is to furnish the sword which that person will need when he is here. Our duty to the dictator when he comes is to present a Volk which is ripe for him! German Volk wake up! The day is near![35]

Putzi Hanfstängl reminisced that,

> In the early days, however, he did not conceive himself as the chosen leader. Even in 1923 [after the salute *Heil Hitler* had been adopted] he still referred to himself in his meetings as the "drummer," marching ahead of a great movement of liberation which was to come. Even after this time, he frequently used the words of St. Matthew and referred to himself as a voice crying in the wilderness and describing his duty as hewing a path for him who was to come and lead the nation to power and glory.[36]

Hitler here modestly attributes to himself only the beginning of the apocalyptic scenario; he was an apocalyptic herald. There is good reason to believe, however, that this "modesty" only served to mask claims for which the public needed more time to prepare. And, of course, not all observers believed that he limited himself to that secondary role. Otto von Berchem, General von Lossow's chief of staff, referred to Hitler's "pronounced Napoleonic and messianic mannerisms."[37]

But after the failed Beer Hall Putsch of 1923, his behavior at the trial reflects a millennial prophet's style—passionate "moral" denunciation, rejection of the court's jurisdiction to try him, and open appeal to the passions of the gallery. It was a highly successful strategy. In addition to a vast outpouring of solidarity from "ordinary" Germans, many high-profile figures came to visit him in prison and show their admiration for him. Kersaw notes that after the trial Hitler was "almost deified," leading to a "self-belief transcending all normal bounds."[38] Upon release, he became openly messianic:

---

[35] Adolf Hitler, *Hitler: Sämtliche Aufzeichnungen 1905–1924*, ed. Eberhard Jäckel and Axel Kuhn (Stuttgart: Deutsche Verlagsanstalt, 1980), 924. Of course, Hitler may have simply been waiting for the populace to acclaim him as the "coming man," which, in time, many did.

[36] Langer, *Mind of Adolf Hitler*, 901.

[37] See *Hitler und Kahr: Die bayerischen Napoleonsgrössen von 1923. Einim Untersuchungsausschuss des Bayerischen Landtags auf gedeckter Justizs kandal*, ed. Landesausschuss der SPD in Bayern, 2 parts (Munich: 1928), 2:116–18; and *Der Hitler-Prozess vordem Volksgericht in München*, 2 parts (Glashüttenim Taunus: D. Auvermann, 1973), Ottov. Lossow, 1:163.

[38] Kershaw, *Hitler: Hubris*, 223; Georg Schott, *Das Volksbuch vom Hitler* (Munich: Hermann A. Wiechmann, 1924), 223–24; cited Redles, *Hitler's Millennial Reich*, chap. 5.

After his imprisonment, the "drummer" pattern dropped out very rapidly and he referred more and more to himself as the Führer. This may have been due in part to Hess who coined the term and did his utmost to build a cult around it. But outside of this there was more and more evidence that he was thinking of himself as the Messiah and it was he himself who was destined to lead Germany to glory. He used quotations from the Bible more frequently when referring to himself and separated himself from the others as though he were a special creation.[39]

All these signs indicate that Hitler now understood that he was the chosen one, a transformation of consciousness similar to what happened to Akhenaten when he finally realized his mission and turned his physical disabilities into marks of election.[40]

We have the record of that transformation chronicled in his "autobiography," *Mein Kampf*, written largely in prison. Here the attentive eye can literally follow the self-creation of a messianic identity.[41] "It [writing *Mein Kampf* in prison] also reinforced his unbounded, narcissistic self-belief. It gave him absolute conviction in his own near-messianic qualities and mission...."[42] Joseph Goebbels wrote Hitler in prison stating, "What you said there [in *Mein Kampf*] is the catechism of a new political creed coming to birth in the midst of a collapsing, secularized world....To you a god has given the tongue with which to express our sufferings. You formulated our agony in words that promise salvation."[43] One could not ask for a better description of a millennial creed in action.

It is more accurate to view Hitler, like many leaders of apocalyptic movements before and since, as assuming the roles of both prophet and messiah, identifying with one or the other at different times and with varying degrees of confidence.[44] As with so many messiahs, followers played a key role. One of his disciples noted that "...this unlimited, almost religious veneration, to which I contributed as did Goebbels, Göring, Hess, Ley and countless others, strengthened in Hitler the belief that he was in league with Providence."[45] In Hitler's case, while he may have envi-

[39] Putzi Hanfstängl, cited in Langer, *Mind of Adolf Hitler*, 901; and Redles, *Hitler's Millennial Reich*, chap. 6. Max Rothe (Langer, *Mind of Adolf Hitler*, 604) noted similarly that after the putsch "he was no longer the 'drummer'...he made himself into the 'coming Man.'" Twelfth-century churchmen who knew the story of the Breton "royal messiah" Eon of the Star would understand the threat (see Cohn, *Pursuit of the Millennium*, 44–51).

[40] See above, chapter 6.

[41] Redles, *Hitler's Millennial Reich*, 125–26.

[42] Kershaw, *Hitler: Hubris*, 224.

[43] Quoted in Joachim Fest, *Hitler*, trans. Richard and Clara Winston (New York: Harcourt Brace Jovanovich, 1974), 210.

[44] It is a common feature of medieval descriptions of "false," popular messiahs that they begin by claiming to be inspired (prophetic), then (and presumably in relationship to their popular success) claim to be the equal of the apostles, of John the Baptist, and finally to be the Jesus of the Second Coming; see, for example, Gregory of Tours' description of the False Christ of Bourges, *History of the Franks*, 10.25 (above, chapter 2, n. 7).

[45] Baldur von Schirach, *Ich Glaubte an Hitler* (Hamburg: Mosaik Verlag, 1967), 160.

sioned himself assuming a messianic position in German history as early as the *Rienzi* experience, it was only in time that his mounting successes convinced him of the reality of that vision.

The Third (*Drittes*), Millennial (*Tausendjährige*) Reich

The word *Reich* carries a host of rich associations in German.[46] It means at once kingdom, realm, empire, and also something else, something sacred, something that transcends material categories, something to do with "age" or "epoch." When Engels spoke of the *Reich der Freiheit*, he means the realm or "age" of freedom.[47] It is about both the political and the sacred, about the orderly exercise of power, about dominion, and about salvation. *Reich* is one of those words immediately recognizable in normative political discourse as the "state" (as in the *Reichsbahn*, the state railway), and also capable of triggering vast and complex meaning associations in mystical discourse. *Reich* means empire, but also holy empire (*sacrum imperium, erstes Reich*).[48] Reich also has a fully religious meaning: When Germans pray "zu uns kommed ein Reich" (Thy kingdom come), they refer to the Lord's kingdom.

Hence in the German language, *Tausendjähriges Reich* means literally "millennial kingdom," and all earlier uses of the term referred to Christian millennial movements, as in the considerable literature on "*chiliasmus*" at the turn of the nineteenth–twentieth centuries in Germany.[49] And when Nazi ideologues developed their notions of the Third Reich as a millennial kingdom, they knew precisely to what they referred. Moeller van den Bruck commented on the notion of a "Third Reich."

> It is an old and great German conception. It arose from the collapse of our first Reich. It was fused early on with expectations of a millennial Reich. Yet always there lived within it a political conception which aimed to the future, not so much upon the end of times, but upon the beginning of a German epoch in which the German *Volk* will fulfill its destiny on earth.[50]

And such imagery fired the imaginations of a nation. Erich Ebermayer had a conversation with one of the well-educated sons of his colleague, the art historian Wilhelm Pinder, probing the son's enthusiasm for Hitler. Ebermayer expressed (an

[46] Thomas Flanagan, "The Third Reich: Origins of a Millenarian Symbol," *History of European Ideas* 8 (1987): 283–95.

[47] "Socialism, Utopian and Scientific," *Karl Marx and Frederick Engels: Selected Works*, 2 vols. (Moscow: Foreign Languages Publishing House, 1951), 2:151.

[48] Alois Dempf, *Sacrum imperium, Geschichts- und Staatsphilosophie des Mittelalters und der politischen Renaissance* (München: Oldenberg, 1927).

[49] See Erich Voegelin, *The New Science of Politics: An Introduction* (Chicago: University of Chicago Press, 1952), chap. 4.

[50] Moeller van den Bruck, *Das Drittes Reich*, 3rd ed. (Hamburg: Hanseatische Verlagsanstalt, 1931), 6.

owl's) concern that the Nazi movement would destroy the culture of the last four hundred years. "And what if it does, my dear friend! This culture is really not so important! According to the word of the *Führer*, the *Tausendjähriges Reich* is already arising. And it will create a new culture for itself."[51]

This millennial German epoch was one of peace—as are all messianic ages. Van den Bruck, sounding like a good owl, acknowledged both the chiliastic nature of the belief in world peace, and its impossibility: "It is the essence of all utopias that they never will be realized. It is the essence of all chiliastic hopes that they are never fulfilled. And it is the essence of the millennial Reich that it forever exists only in prophecy, yet men will never partake of it." Playing on a paradox that Hitler would brutally resolve, Van den Bruck could pass effortlessly from this Augustinian agnosticism into a rooster's political Augustinianism: "The conception of the Third Reich, of which we cannot let go as our highest and last ideological conception, can only be fruitful as an actualized conception...[which] will not arise in a time of peace...The Third Reich will be a Reich of recapitulation which must succeed politically in a time of European tremors."[52] And, born of a war of good (might makes right, racial Darwinism) versus evil (egalitarianism, Jewish corruption of the blood and mind), the *Drittes Reich* was predictably not the demotic peace of freedom, but the hierarchical order of "free" masters and slaves.

This was a far cry from the demotic millennialism of Joachim of Fiore, but one can quite distinctly trace the threads that filtered those visions of Christian "heretics" into a world that embraced both imperial trappings and paranoid conspiracies.[53] Nonetheless, one of the magic elements of the title "Third Reich" was the way in which it grafted itself onto Joachim's three "Ages" or "Status" of world history. And just as Joachim's exegetic system identified the present day as the apocalyptic moment when the shift from the second (Church) to the third (Spiritual Man) would take place, and just as the dialectic of history had delivered into Marx's own times the turning point between capitalism and Communism, so did Ariosophy deliver up to the interwar "pause," the moment of transition into the *Drittes, Tausendjähriges Reich*.[54] The Nazi millennial vision actually combined all four elements of the millennial dream: it was hierarchical for Aryan superiority (*Nazionalismus*) and demotic among Aryans (*Sozialismus*);[55] it was progressive in

---

[51] Cited in George Mosse, *Nazi Culture: Intellectual, Cultural and Social Life in the Third Reich* (New York: Schocken Books, 1981), 385.

[52] Van den Bruck, *Drittes Reich*, 7.

[53] Cohn, *The Pursuit of the Millennium*; Redles, *Hitler's Millennial Reich*, introduction. On Voegelin, see n. 103.

[54] On this theme, see recently, Udo Leuchner, "Das Dritte Reich: Ein tausendjähriger Mythos zwischen Utopie und Nostalgie," in *Sehn-Sucht: 26 Studien zum Thema Nostalgie* (HTML-Fassungfürs Internet, 2000), 95–102, online: http://www.udo-leuschner.de/pdf/sehnsucht.pdf, April 13, 2010.

[55] Note the strong emphasis on the dignity of manual labor (e.g., the theme of the Nuremberg Rally, 1937).

that it envisioned Aryan rule over the entire world (reactionary modernism)[56] and restorative in that it invoked a past glory (Teutonic roots).[57]

Unlike Joachim's scenario, which emphasized the most transformational of processes (anything less and he could not have escaped conviction of heresy), however, this Aryan apocalyptic scenario is cataclysmic and active: we fight as the agents of history. "The Third Reich, which ends the discord, will not arise in a time of peace...the conception of eternal peace is certainly the conception of the Third Reich. However its realization must be fought for, and the Reich must be maintained."[58] It was a mad gamble, but worth it, if only for the glory of the battle: "For every people the hour comes in which they die by murder or suicide, and no more magnificent end could be conceived for a great *Volk*, than its destruction in a world war in which an entire world gathered arms to conquer a single country."[59] When prophecy fails, at least we will go down in an epic battle.[60]

▪ THE RELIGIOUS NATURE OF HITLER AND NAZISM

Historians' Approaches

Hitler's religiosity continues to constitute a major problem for historians. Most tend to view Hitler though a secular prism. Alan Bullock expressed it concisely: "Hitler was a rationalist and materialist...What interested Hitler was power, and his belief in Providence or Destiny was only a projection of his own sense of power."[61] In some senses this comes down to: Did Hitler believe in what he said or was he cynically manipulating the German people? Differently put: to what extent he delude even *himself*? Perhaps the most common approach sees Hitler as a shrewd manipulator, someone who began to fail precisely when he started to believe his own rantings.[62] As for alleged claims of occultism, Hitler may have had followers who dabbled, but, according to these historians, he did not take such nonsense seriously; nor did the men who ran the Nazi bureaucracy.

---

[56] Jeffrey Herf, *Reactionary Modernism: Technology, Culture, and Politics in Weimar and the Third Reich* (Cambridge: Cambridge University Press, 1986).

[57] Leuschner, "Das Dritte Reich," 95–101.

[58] Moeller van den Bruck, *Drittes Reich*, 241. Julius Petersen, *Die Sehnsucht nach dem Dritten Reich in deutscher Sage und Dichtung* (Stuttgart: J.B. Metzler, 1934).

[59] Van den Bruck, *Drittes Reich*, 231. This is a theme Hitler would return to repeatedly, in his early speeches during the Weimar chaos and again toward the end of the Second World War. In this case, Van den Bruck's romantic nihilism became dark prophecy.

[60] Ironically, this fate is also that which threatens Israel in biblical prophecy, where the armies of the North shall mass against her. Apparently, envy of messianic status involves even envy of a terrible fate. On the relationship of Nazi notions of "chosenness" to those of the Jews, see below, pp. 382–87.

[61] Alan Bullock, *Hitler: A Study in Tyranny* (New York: Smithmark, 1995), 389–90.

[62] Bullock, *Hitler*, 375–77; Klaus P. Fischer, *Nazi Germany: A New History* (New York: Continuum, 1995), 341.

More broadly, the Nazis are seen as *anti–religious*, and in this sense at least, modern. Most of the arguments emphasize the irreducible hostility of the Nazis to Christianity. Hitler treated the Church with more contempt than any other ruler in the previous 1500 years of European Christianity.[63] Indeed, according to this approach, if the Nazis showed any interest in religion, it was a fascination with the ancient Germanic gods, something easily dismissed as so much esoteric posturing and tacky if effective propaganda. Any Christian religious sentiments Nazis expressed were not sincere and not addressed to religious Germans, but were a "new religion" offered up to an apostate nation living in a Nietzschean world where God was dead: "new secular wine in old Christian bottles."[64]

Such approaches, while they may ignore profound aspects of Hitler's—and Germany's—religiosity,[65] have deep conceptual roots. On the one hand, we have the school of postwar historians imbued with Weberian secularization theory. On the other, we find their philosophical counterparts like Hannah Arendt who dismiss any link between Nazism and Christianity a priori: "Nazism owes nothing to any part of the Western tradition, be it German or not, Catholic or Protestant, Christian...."[66]

Overall, there seem to be four levels of resistance to thinking about the connections between Nazism and religion. First, the "empirical" or "materialist" school sees in Nazism a secular phenomenon, and does not even entertain the possibility that it has a religious dimension.[67] Second, some call Nazism an ersatz "political religion" that "replaced" Christianity, but deny any connection between Nazism and Christianity and any "real" religious content to the religion (pure "political" propaganda).[68] Third, some admit that Christians grew enthusiastic about Nazism, but to insist that this was "unrequited love," that Nazism was not enthusiastic about

[63] Richard Steigmann-Gall discusses this view in the introduction to his *The Holy Reich: Nazi Conceptions of Christianity, 1919–1945* (Cambridge: Cambridge University Press, 2003); see also John Conway, *The Nazi Persecution of the Churches* (New York: Basic Books, 1968).

[64] George Mosse, *Nationalization of the Masses: Political Symbolism and Mass Movements in Germany from the Napoleonic Wars through the Third Reich* (New York: New American Library, 1977), 80; see also similar sentiments in Stern, *Politics of Cultural Despair* ("most thoroughgoing secularization"), xxv.

[65] See Richard Steigmann-Gall, "Apostasy or Religiosity? The Cultural Meanings of the Protestant Vote for Hitler," *Social History* 25, no. 3 (October 2000): 269. On the profound role of anti-Semitism in the rural vote, see John Weiss, *The Ideology of Death: Why the Holocaust Happened in Germany* (Chicago: Elephant Books, 1996), 271–87.

[66] Hannah Arendt, "Approches to the German Problem," quoted in Steven Aschheim, *Culture and Catastrophe: Germans and Jewish Confrontations with National Socialism and Other Crises* (New York: Macmillan, 1996), 112, cited in Steigmann-Gall, "Apostasy," n. 11.

[67] Bullock emphasizes Hitler's rationalism, *Hitler*, 375–82, 388–90; for an emphasis on the rational (if immoral) bureaucracy of the Nazi party, see Dietrich Orlow, *The History of the Nazi Party* (Pittsburgh: University of Pittsburgh Press, 1969–73).

[68] On the question of "political religion," *Political Religions as a Characteristic of the 20th Century*, ed. Marina Cattaruzza, special edition of *Totalitarian Movements and Political Religions*, 6, no. 1 (2005).*

their Christianity.[69] And finally, some actually admit that Nazism had a Christian dimension, but show no interest in the millennial dimensions of that religiosity.[70] Then there are the rare few who go the distance, and acknowledge Nazism as a millennial religion.[71]

These readings seem remarkably resistant to the overall pattern of the evidence. The Nazi episode represents one of the most powerful connections between religious leader and following of the faithful in recorded history. And the leader (Führer, messiah), led his enthralled people to transgress every cultural principle they had once held to be sacred. In other words, Nazism is a religious phenomenon in its own right: a *political religion* that, whatever its content, appealed to the same critical issues and emotions that religion does: faith, ultimate meaning, redemption.[72] And among those links are some of the most powerful forms any religious movement can take—the apocalyptic and messianic traditions that date back to the earliest centuries of Christian-Germanic relations.[73]

Ariosophy and the Occult Origins of Nazism

The religious world out of which Hitler's particular millennialism arose was that of the theosophical trends circulating at the turn of the century (among them Madame Blavatsky, Annie Besant, and Rudolf Steiner). In Germany, it took a peculiar turn toward a racist mythology known as Ariosophy (Aryan Wisdom), a school which, among the multitude of organizations to which it gave birth, produced the Thule Society in 1917, which then produced a more activist variant, the German Worker's Party (whose publication was *Tat* [deed]), which, finally in 1921, became the NSDAP, the *Nationalsozialistische Deutsche Arbeiterpartei*.[74]

---

[69] Susannah Heschel, "When Jesus was an Aryan: The Protestant Church and Anti-Semitic Propaganda," in *Betrayal: German Churches and the Holocaust*, ed. Robert Ericksen and Susannah Heschel (Minneapolis: University of Minnesota Press, 1999), 81, cited in Steigmann-Gall, *Holy Reich*, 9.

[70] This is true even of Steigmann-Gall (*Holy Reich*, 7) and Doris Bergen (*Twisted Cross: The German Christian Movement in the Third Reich* [Chapel Hill: University of North Carolina Press, 1996], 8).

[71] James Rhodes, *The Hitler Movement: A Modern Millennial Revolution* (Stanford, Calif.: Hoover Institution Press, 1980). David Redles discusses the historiography in *Hitler's Millennial Reich*, 8–13. On the longer history of modern German millennial thinking (political theology), see also Klaus Vondung, *The Apocalypse in Germany* (London: University of Missouri Press, 2000); and survey of the discussion in Vondung, "National Socialism as a Political Religion: Potentials and Limits of an Analytical Concept," in *Political Religions as a Characteristic* (above, n. 68), 87–96.

[72] On the issue of Nazism and political religions, see Vondung, "National Socialism as a Political Religion"; Vondug, "What Insights Do We Gain from Interpreting National Socialism as a Political Religion?" in *The Sacred in Twentieth-Century Politics: Essays in Honour of Professor Stanley G. Payne*, ed. Roger Griffin, Robert Mallett, and John Tortorice (New York: Palgrave, 2008), 107–18. On the remarkable connections between anti-Semitic medieval German millennial movements like the Drummer of Nickelshausen and the *Book of a Hundred Chapters*, see Cohn, *Pursuit of the Millennium*, chap. 7 and 12.

[73] On the issues involved here, see R. Landes, "*Millenarismus absconditus*: L'historiographie augustinienne et l'An Mil," *Le Moyen Age* 98, no. 3–4 (1992): 355–77.

[74] Redles, *Hitler's Millennial Reich*, 46–76, esp. 52–56; Sickinger, "Hitler and the Occult."

These groups spun the details of their millennial interpretation of history around the theme of racial purity (Aryan, might makes right), and its contamination by the degradation of the race (by Jews, slave morality), using the conspiracist vision so sharply enunciated in the *Protocols of the Elders of Zion* as their guide to identify the apocalyptic players. For Alfred Rosenberg, Rudolf Hess, Dietrich Eckart, and the other members of the Thule Society, the "Great War" was only the opening act of the final drama; the end of the war in 1918 merely a pause in the fighting; and the Bolshevik victory in 1917 another victory in the climaxing power-grab of the Elders of Zion.[75]

When, in the aftermath of the war and the abdication of the emperor (end of *zweites Reich*), there arose a fledgling German "democracy" and a host of avant-garde cultural experiments, the racist Ariosophists saw it as the onset of the final apocalyptic battle. Writing about the establishment of the Weimar Republic, one of the Thule Society wrote:

> Yesterday we experienced the collapse of everything that was familiar, dear and valuable to us. In the place of our princes of Germanic blood, rules our deadly enemy: Judah. What will come of this chaos, we do not know yet. But we can guess. A time will come of struggle, the most bitter need, a time of danger…As long as I hold the iron hammer [a reference to his Master's hammer], I am determined to pledge the Thule to this struggle. Our Order is a Germanic Order, loyalty is also Germanic. Our God is *Walvater*, his rune is the *Ar*-rune. And the trinity: *Wotan, Wili, We* is the unity of the trinity. The *Ar*-rune signifies Aryan, primal fire, the sun and the eagle. And the eagle is the symbol of the Aryans. In order to depict the eagle's capacity for self-immolation by fire, it is colored red. From today on our symbol is the red eagle, which warns us that we must die in order to live.[76]

The interwar period was rife with apocalyptic publications.[77] Many if not most of them wove their narratives around certain key Ariosophist themes. And among them, the *Reich* held pride of place as the political salvation of the embattled master race.

Another theme picked up elements of some of the more disturbing Christian heresies of the Middle Ages, in which the human becomes divinized. "God is eternal, and consequently the God-soul in men must be eternal," wrote the Aryan millennial thinker Guido "von" List, in a book Hitler and other German soldiers could have read in the trenches along with their Nietzsche and Bible. List called on all Aryans to awaken and develop their divine soul, what he called the "divine voice" in one's "ego," developing one's *Ichheit* (I-ness), meaning not egoism but the

---

[75] See, in particular, Dietrich Eckart, *Bolshevism from Moses to Lenin: Dialogue between Hitler and Me* (1924), online: http://www.jrbooksonline.com/HTML-docs/Eckart.htm, April 13, 2010; Redles, *Hitler's Millennial Reich*, 59–63.

[76] Rudolf von Sebottendorff, *Bevor Hitler kam: Urkundliches aus der Frühzeit der nationalsozialistischen Bewegung* (Munich: Grassinger, 1933), 57–50, cited in Goodrick-Clarke, *Occult Roots of Nazism*, 145; see discussion in Redles, *Hitler's Millennial Reich*, chap. 3.

[77] See Redles, *Hitler's Millennial Reich*, chap. 1.

individuality which is the divine spark of God within.[78] Movements like the Hitler Youth emphasized these themes heavily…as a justification for the discipline and hierarchy they demanded.[79] In the millennial kingdom, every German had access to the joys of the blond beast, every redeemed Aryan became a god.

Historians tend to dismiss the occult origins of Nazism as irrelevant. They view occultism as a flakey set of beliefs that characterize people who are essentially marginal and ineffective in life. Thus, given Hitler's enormous success, he could not have done more than dabble in occult thinking. Hitler himself gives some credence to this. In 1938, for example, he excoriated Himmler and Goering for speaking of Nazism as a cult.[80] Hitler vociferously denounced anyone doing horoscopes of his or the Nazi party's lifespan and fate. Thus, historians conclude, while some of his "circle" may have fallen prey to occultist seduction, Hitler stood above that.[81]

But perhaps they do not take these ideas seriously enough. Perhaps Hitler's opposition came from an even more radically occultist position rather than a rationalist one. Hence, he may have denounced "normative" occultism (Tarot card divination, horoscopes, etc.) because he strode above these petty exercises, which demeaned his protean, indeed god-like, nature. Rather than project onto Hitler our secular/rational cognitive egocentrism and imagine that he, like us, had nothing to do with such nonsense, we need to consider that Hitler was profoundly committed to religious paradigms that escape even our normative notions of religiosity (a fortiori of Christianity).

Hitler's Religious Messianic Vocation

Hitler was suffused with a sense of destiny and mission. Hitler's "one dominant and dominating characteristic was that he felt himself appointed by Providence to do great things for the German people. This was his historic 'mission,' in which he believed completely."[82] In his memoirs, Albert Speer, Hitler's architect and, after

[78] Cited in Redles manuscript, "Racial Apocalypse: The Sources for Nazi Millennialism," 25 n. 91, where Redles notes that "this is strikingly similar to how he viewed his inner voice." See also Jackson Spielvogel and David Redles, "Hitler's Racial Ideology: Content and Occult Sources," *Simon Wiesenthal Center Annual* 3 (1986): 227–46.

[79] Guido von List, "Wer ist der Starke von Oben?" *Prana* 7 (1917), cited in Redles, "Racial Apocalypse," 36 n. 125.

[80] "National Socialism is not a cult-movement—a movement for worship; it is exclusively a "volkic" political doctrine based upon racial principles. In its purpose there is no mystic cult, only the care and leadership of a people defined by a common blood-relationship….We will not allow mystically-minded occult folk with a passion for exploring the secrets of the world beyond to steal into our Movement. Such folk are not National Socialists, but something else—in any case something which has nothing to do with us." Nuremberg Party Rally speech of September 6, 1938.

[81] For examples of authors (specifically Alan Bullock, John Toland, and Joachim Fest) dismissing the idea of Hitler as occultist, see Sickinger, "Hitler and the Occult," 107–08.

[82] Walter Schellenberg, *The Labyrinth: Memoirs*, trans. Louis Hagen (New York: Harper, 1956), 93, cited in Redles, *Hitler's Millennial Reich*, 131.

Hess's flight, his closest underling, explains that Hitler was comforted even during his final days in the bunker by belief in "his mission by divine Providence."

This profound continuity in Hitler's self-perception had a distinctly "Christian" formulation. In a conversation with Nietzsche's brother-in-law, reported by Rauschning, Hitler confided that he

> would not reveal his unique mission until later. He permitted glimpses of it only to a few. When the time came, however, Hitler would bring the world a new religion.... The blessed consciousness of eternal life in union with the great universal life, and in membership of an immortal people—that was the message he would impart to the world when the time came. Hitler would be the first to achieve what Christianity was meant to have been, a joyous message that liberated men from the things that burdened their life. We should no longer have any fear of death, and should lose the fear of a so-called bad conscience. Hitler would restore men to the self-confident divinity with which nature had endowed them. They would be able to trust their instincts, would no longer be citizens of two worlds, but would be rooted in the single, eternal life of this world.[83]

Although Rauschning is a questionable source in general, this passage seems probable. Indeed, it offers a formulation that could find a favorable reception among the occult groups (the Thule Society and the Armanen Brotherhood) as well as the German Christians. Indeed, it sounds a lot like a religion for Nietzsche's *blond beast*.[84]

Thus, he at once used a Christian idiom, as one raised in a Christian culture, but did so in a framework shorn of all "Christian" insistence on humility.[85] That shortcoming aside (which, as in the following quote, he was at pains to partially conceal), he took *his* Christianity seriously.

> The peace on earth Christ wanted to bring is the very socialism of nations! It is the new great religion, and it will come because it is divine! It awaits the Messiah! But I *am* not the Messiah. He will come after me. I only have the will to create for the German Volk the foundations of a true Volk community. And that is a political mission, though it encompasses the ideological as well as the economic. It cannot be otherwise, and everything in me points to the conviction that the German Volk has a divine mission. How many great prophets have foretold this![86]

---

[83] Hermann Rauschning, *Men of Chaos* (New York: G.P. Putnam's Sons, 1942), 97, cited in Sklar, *The Nazis and the Occult* (New York: Dorset Press, 1977), 54.

[84] See the interesting parallels between this ecstatically violent resolution of the conflict between the demands of a warrior culture and Christian teachings in the impact of Pope Urban II's preaching of the "First" Crusade: Marcus Bull, *Knightly Piety and the Lay Response to the First Crusade: The Limousin and Gascony, c.970-c.1130* (Oxford: Clarendon Press, 1993), 3–5.

[85] See Lukacs' contrast of Hitler and his mother's Jewish doctor, Eduard Bloch (featured in *Collier's Magazine*, March 15 and 22, 1941), cited in *The Hitler of History* (New York: Alfred A. Knopf, 1998), 196.

[86] Quoted in Wagener, *Hitler*, 170, 172. For a discussion of this passage and its implications for Hitler's Aryanized Christ, see Redles, *Hitler's Millennial Reich*, 126–27.

According to one recent study, he wanted to create a *Reichskirche* that would complete the unfinished Reformation that Luther had wrought.[87]

We can understand the difference between the more familiar forms of Christianity based on the Gospels—however multivocal—and Hitler's Christianity by grasping *which* Christ Hitler held in veneration. It was, as his early companion Hanfstängl noted, "not Jesus Christ the crucified, but Jesus Christ, the furious."[88] In other words, not the Jesus of the First Coming, of "turn the other cheek," who allowed himself to be crucified, but the Christ of the *Parousia*, the warrior on horseback with a sword issuing from his mouth, slaughtering the enemies of the Lord (Revelation 19). "In the Bible," Hitler noted in a speech in 1923, "we find the text, '*That which is neither hot nor cold will I spew out of my mouth.*' [Revelation 3:16] This utterance of the great Nazarene [*sic*] has kept its profound validity until the present day."[89] Like Clovis in the sixth century, Hitler believed that "my Lord and savior was a warrior…who, by God, was not his greatest as a sufferer, but rather, as a warrior!"[90]

Favoring Christ, the warrior at Armageddon, over the meek and passive Jesus, he rereads the Gospels for signs of "his" Christ:

> In boundless love I read as a Christian and a human being the place where it is proclaimed to us that the Lord finally summoned up the energy,[91] seized the whip and drove the money-lenders—that brood of vipers and adders—out of the Temple! His immense struggle for this world against the Jewish poison—which I still perceive today after 2,000 years with the deepest emotion as the most profound of matters—that he, because of it [the struggle] had to bleed to death on the cross.

This is triumphalist Christianity. It represents the same active cataclysmic apocalyptic urge that we find it the First Crusade, with its exterminationist anti-Semitism and its lust to avenge the crucifixion of the Lord in rivers of blood.[92]

With Hitler at the helm, the crucified Germany of postwar Weimar would leap from the cross and begin to set the world aright for the next thousand years.

---

[87] The year 1933 was the 450th anniversary of Luther's birth, marked by the Nazis with great pomp, as part of their accession to power; see Steigmann-Gall, *Holy Reich*, 134–40.

[88] Langer, *Mind of Adolf Hitler*, 903.

[89] Adolf Hitler, speech in Munich, April 10, 1923, online: *http://www.hitler.org/speeches/04-10-23. html*. Note that Hitler attributes to "the Nazarene" the words of the Angel of the Apocalypse who speaks to the visionary John of Patmos. On this passage as characteristic of the apocalyptic mentality, see above, chapter 1.

[90] When Clovis first heard the story of Jesus, he allegedly responded: "If I had been there with my Franks, we would have revenged this injury!" *Fourth Book of the Chronicle of Fredegar*, 3.21, ed. Wallace-Hadrill (London: Nelson, 1960), 108.

[91] Note this formulation, suggesting that Hitler had found Jesus' previous behavior frustratingly weak and passive. "Finally summoning up the energy"—that is, what *Hitler* has *finally* done. He liked the apocalyptic scenario, but, this incident aside, he despised the first *Parousia*.

[92] For the description of the rivers of blood the Crusaders waded through to enter Jerusalem, see *Anonymi Gesta Francorum et aliorum Hierosolymitanorum*, cited in Augsut C. Krey, *The First Crusade: The Accounts of Eye-Witnesses and Participants* (Princeton: Princeton University Press, 1921), 261.*

Concluding that Jesus died because he fought the Jews for control of the world, Hitler makes it his mission to continue the very same struggle:

> As a Christian...I have the obligation to be a fighter for the truth and for the right. And as a human being I have the obligation to see to it that human society will not suffer the same catastrophic collapse as did that ancient civilization [Roman Empire] around two millennia [sic] ago, one which was also driven to ruin by these Jewish people....[93]

And, having destroyed Rome in the West, the Jews were at it again, in the chaos of Weimar, they carried on the work of the very same vipers and adders:

> If anything whatever is proof to me of the correctness of our actions, it is the daily escalating misery. Therefore as a Christian I also am confronted with an obligation to my own people—when I see this Volk worked and worked, pained and tormented, and yet at the end of its week it has nothing but lamentation and misery; when I go out in the morning and see these men standing in line before the Free Bank and I look into their careworn faces—then I believe I would be no Christian, but rather a devil if I would not feel compassion and, as Christ did two thousand years ago, make a front against those who today plunder and exploit these poor people!

Having identified himself with the warrior Jesus sent to save the world from the evil chaos of the Jews, Hitler ended his speech with a declaration about the spiritual basis of his movement: "That is the powerful thing that our movement should create; a new faith for these vast searching and lost masses, one which in this time of chaos will not forsake them, which they can swear and depend on, from which they at last can find a place again which gives their hearts peace."

To the people to whom he offered this redemption, he spoke in profoundly religious language.

> Hitler almost always speaks in one of only two moods. One is a mood of mystical and semi-religious self-abasement. It is in this mood that he habitually appeals for the confidence and support of the German people. In it, he speaks of faith and destiny and miracles, of regeneration and martyrdom, and of his struggle for the souls of men. Often in this mood he uses purely religious terms: shame, sin and expiation. He is a redeemer, calling upon the people to lay their sins and suffering on his shoulders.[94]

As Speer realized in retrospect from prison, Hitler wanted to found a new and enduring, a *Tausendjährige* religion.[95]

The history of this unfortunate alliance is still in its infancy, largely because so many German Protestants wanted to believe about their churches what the French

---

[93] All quotes in this paragraph come from Hitler, *Adolf Hitlers Reden*, ed. Ernst Boepple (Munich: Deutscher Volksverlag, 1933), 20–21, cited in Redles, "Hitler as Messiah" manuscript, 30.

[94] Quoted in Wallace R. Deuel, *People under Hitler* (New York: Harcourt Brace, 1942), 81, as found in Langer, *Mind of Adolf Hitler*, 40.

[95] See below, n. 128.

wanted to believe about their *Résistance*—that they overwhelmingly rejected Hitler. And one of the more underdeveloped themes in this history of Nazi Christianity is its millennial dimension.[96] While the tide may have turned in recent years—and that is still to be seen—such a historiographical turn, seventy years after the events in question, and fifty since the work of Norman Cohen, seems long overdue.

■ NAZISM AS MILLENNIAL MOVEMENT

One of the key issues in any case of a millennial movement is: How does it move from the margins to the center of society? Messianic pretenders are far more frequent than messianic movements that actually break onto the stage of history. How did the bizarre theosophist ravings of the Thule Society become the center of a political program, the driver of a nation, the scourge of a continent? Why did Hitler's violent megalomania catch on?

A German farmer's memory of his first encounter with Hitler gives a sense of how the Führer could move to the center of German culture:

> In July [1932] the Führer came to Tilsit. I saw him for the first time. About 40,000 people from near and far had gathered to greet him. I wore the brown shirt from the first time I heard his voice. His words went straight to the heart. From now on my life and efforts were dedicated to the Führer. I wanted to be a true follower. The Führer spoke of the threatened ruin of the nation and of the resurrection under the Third Reich.[97]

Hitler's spirituality, therefore, belongs in the subset of millennialism we call messianic: he was a man with a calling, who would help his own people achieve their great destiny. "He believes what he says, that the awaited hour of the savior of the *Volk*, the renewer, the creator of new values has come. Through any of the early speeches he employs always the same sequence of ever wilder approbations, always the same spiritual self-elevation, in which in the act of speaking he felt and experienced his personal 'mission.'"[98]

Such millennial pretensions are naturally megalomanic, but normally held in check by the tepid or hostile responses of others. In Hitler's case, however, he received the opposite: wild approval. The dynamic led to a spiral of "self-elevation" that alienated even early supporters. Hitler's mentor, Dietrich Eckart, who had first promoted Hitler as the coming *völkisch* messiah, now began to worry that Hitler

---

[96] Neither Bergen nor Steigmann-Gall address millennialism directly.

[97] Theodore Abel, *Why Hitler Came to Power: An Answer Based on the Original Life Stories of Six Hundred of His Followers* (New York: Prentice-Hall, 1938), 298, cited in Redles, *Hitler's Millennial Reich*, chap. 6, who analyzes the nature of the appeal.

[98] Unnumbered memo from Edward Deuss to Crane Brinton, in Langer, *Mind of Adolf Hitler*, 955; William C. White, "Hail Hitler," *Scribner* 9 (1932): 229; Theodor Heuss, *Hitlers Weg* (Stuttgart: Union Deutsche Verlagsgesellschaft, 1932), 2. Another observer noted that "he has come to accept himself as a messiah." Quoted in *Time Magazine*'s infamous "Man of the Year" issue, number 33 (May 1, 1939): 23–24.

was taking the label too far: "When one gets to the point of identifying himself with Jesus Christ, then he is ripe for an insane asylum like Nietzsche was."[99]

Ripe he may have been, and one cannot help but wish the Germans would have sent him there before 1930. But they did not. They embraced him as their savior, and he, in turn, led them—and many others—to terrible destruction.[100] In millennial matters, the relative sanity of the messiah—none of them are "normal"—matters less than the audience they gather. The same person may end up in an insane asylum or at the head of armies of millions, depending on his or her cultural matrix.

The key to Hitler's millennial career came the moment he acceded to power. Like a true demagogue like the "Elders of Zion," he played by the parliamentary rules and downplayed his more radical notions (including his anti-Semitism) until he had power, then rapidly shifted into dictatorial mode. While there is nothing new in such behavior generally, the rapidity with which he shifted modes, the messianic claims he put forth, and the technological sophistication with which he did so, distinguish this particular demagogue from most of his predecessors. Starting with a vote granting him dictatorial powers, the Führer seized communications technology, stifled independent voices, and reshaped the nation.

Kershaw notes that Nazism differs from other forms of fascism and antimodernism in its spectacular dynamism, its revolutionary momentum, and its "cumulative radicalization,"[101] remarks quite similar to the point Arendt makes about *ideologies*.[102] The point of Hitler's accession to power was not "merely" to stabilize the nation under a "benign" dictatorship that counteracted the noxious impact of modernity. His program involved a complete transformation of life in Germany, from the curriculum in the schools, to the nature and style of political discourse, to the "training" of its youth, to the genetic engineering of the next generation. Indeed many historians point to this dynamic to underline the difference between Nazism and other forms of fascism.[103]

Perhaps one key to Hitler's success lay in the reception he received from Germany's Protestant community, in particular, the *Deutsche Christen*, the German Christians.[104] Here we find many of the major elements of the

---

[99] Hanfstängel, in Langer, *Mind of Adolf Hitler*, 903.

[100] "Thus Hitler's psychopathology…is less frightening than the fact that millions of people believed they had found in him a lost part of themselves." Arno Gruen, "The Hitler Myth," *Journal of Psychohistory* 19 (2002): 323.

[101] Kershaw, "Le mythe," 593; Kershaw, *The Hitler Myth: Image and Reality in the Third Reich* (Oxford: Oxford University Press, 1987).

[102] Hannah Arendt, *The Origins of Totalitarianism* (New York: Meridian Books, 1958), chap.13, discussed above, pp. 341–43.

[103] There is a large literature on whether Nazism is a form of fascism or a fundamentally different phenomenon; see the early summary in Wolfgang Sauer, "National Socialism: Totalitarianism or Fascism?" *American Historical Review* 73, no. 2 (1967): 404–24.

[104] Bergen, *Twisted Cross*; Steigmann-Gall, "Apostasy"; Steigmann-Gall, "'Furor Protestanticus': Nazi Conceptions of Luther, 1919–1933," *Kirchliche Zeitgeschichte* 12, no. 1 (1999): 274–86.

Ariosophist millennial brew—a Thrasymachan political ideology, a racist historiography, a Jewish conspiratorial enemy, and the worship of hardness, violence, and sacrifice—articulated in a Christian key by members of some of the evangelical churches.[105] *Deutsche Christen* systematically reread the Gospels as a justification for warfare against the enemies of God—above all the Jews—and a hierarchical political ideal. Throughout his speeches, Hitler, with his biblical intonations, uses the Christian texts to claim authority. Did he not believe what he said? Far more likely, he considered his new reading as having liberated the text from the prison in which it had been kept by the church(es).[106] In which case he would have been deeply committed to both the Christian texts and (his own notion) of the God that stood behind them.

In fact, the path that Hitler took to move the margins of German society (the occult, often but not exclusively anti-Christian circles where he got his apocalyptic millennial discourse) to the center was not by converting *post*-Christians, but *disappointed* Christians, people who felt that the world had betrayed their religion and sought a savior to set it right. This appeal comes out particularly clearly in the enthusiasm not just of the rank and file, but of Protestant ministers and theologians who inherited a Protestantism that had played a key role in shaping the Protestant language of the *zweites Kaiserreich* and its *Reichskirche*.[107] Indeed, voting patterns indicate that the workers "*most* immune to the Nazi appeal…also tended to be the *most* secularized," and those most receptive, the *kleine Leute* who found the traditional religion undermined by modernity.[108]

After Hitler's victory in 1933, the *Deutsche Christen* held a special service of thanksgiving on February 3, at Saint Mary's Church in the center of the old city of Berlin, draped with Nazi flags. In November, a capacity crowd of over twenty thousand attended a gathering at the Berlin Sports Palace to listen to speakers under a massive banner, surrounded by swastikas inscribed with *Das Deutsche Christ liest das "Evangeliumim Dritte Reich"* (The German Christian reads the **Gospels in the Third Reich**). It offered a nationalist version of iconic monotheism: *Ein Reich, ein Volk, eine Kirche!*[109] The Nazi one was still more distinctly messianic: *Ein Reich, ein Volk, ein Führer!*

[105] Manfred Gailus, "Overwhelmed by Their Own Fascination with the 'Ideas of 1933': Berlin's Protestant Social Milieu in the Third Reich," *German History* 20, no. 4 (2002): 463–93. On Hitler's use of Christian rhetoric, see "The Agitator of Truth," 1922 Speech, *Adolf Hitlers Reden*, 20–21; extensive quotations and discussion in Redles, *Hitler's Millennial Reich*, chap. 4.

[106] Manfred Gailus, "Overwhelmed by their own Fascination with the 'Ideas of 1933': Berlin's Protestant Social Milieu in the Third Reich," German History 20:4 (2002), pp. 463–493. This authority is the fundamental Nazi "Gnostic" claim, which Voegelin emphasized, for example, in *Die politischen Religion* [Political Religion](Munich: Fink, 1996) where he traces the lineage of Hitler's *christliche Reichs apokalypse* (41). In the terminology of this book, I would call this "Gnostic" dimension, a revelation of special knowledge (*gnosis*) about an active cataclysmic apocalyptic process leading to a hierarchical millennium.

[107] Helmut Walser Smith, *German Nationalism and Religious Conflict: Culture, Ideology and Politics, 1870-1914* (Princeton, N.J.: Princeton University Press, 1995); Steigmann-Gall, "Apostasy," 280 and n. 91.

[108] Vernon Lidtke, "Social Class and Secularization in Imperial Germany: The Working Classes," *Leo Baeck Institute Yearbook* 25 (1980): 25–26, 35–36, cited in Steigmann-Gall, "Apostasy," 273.

[109] See the "Guidelines for the Movement of German Christians (National Church Movement) in Thuringia (1933)," in Mosse, *Nazi Culture*, 241–42; comments in Bergen, *Twisted Cross*, 102–07.

Charisma and Popular Enthusiasm: The Nuremburg Party Rallies

Once Hitler took power, Germany became witness to the blossoming of a wildly enthusiastic popular movement, the advent of a public apocalyptic moment with few precedents in the history of millennialism. Unlike the French or Russian revolutions, the Nazis came to power through parliamentary means, not through violent takeover. They were given a wide berth by the other European countries—unlike the immediate hostility solicited by demotic revolutions, and therefore, *despite* their elective affinity for paranoid discourse, they did not "melt down" into coercive totalitarianism the way these other "modern" revolutions did.[110] On the contrary, for the first six years of Nazi rule, we find a remarkable and relatively pacific explosion of millennial enthusiasm, engineered by visionaries who used every medium available—architecture, film, light shows, mass rallies, and one of the most sophisticated and creative uses of new communications technology on record.

In particular, the *Reichsparteitage* (*Reich* Party Congresses), held in Nuremberg (Nürnberg) between 1927–38, constitute one of the most exceptional examples of millennial orchestration in recorded history. Here, with each annual rally revolving around a particular theme—Awakening (1927), Composure (1929), Victory (1933), Unity (1934), Freedom[111] (1935), Honor and Freedom (1936), Labor (1937), and Greater Germany (1938)—hundreds of thousands of party members and ancillary groups gathered for elaborate rallies, speeches, displays and performances. In particular, the brilliant use of time and setting, enhanced with modern technology—nighttime rallies, "a forest of fiery red flags with a black swastika on white ground" and myriad spotlights pointed skyward, creating a "cathedral of light"—brought out mass psychological reactions.[112]

Here the ideology of a German *Volk*, chosen by God, mobilized by its Führer, reached its apogee.[113] Participants behaved like they were at a religious revival meeting, tears streaming down the cheeks of people hoarse with shouting *Heil Hitler*, women trying desperately to touch the Führer.[114] Shirer describes how,

---

[110] On the wide berth, see Martin Gilbert and Richard Gott, *The Appeasers* (Boston: HoughtonMifflin, 1963).

[111] It was at these ceremonies that Hitler enacted the Nuremberg Laws restricting the freedom of Jews—and therefore in the zero-sum world, enhancing German freedom.

[112] Ironically, the nighttime procession that inspired the "cathedral of light" was initially planned to cloak the procession of party officials who had "converted their small prebends into considerable paunches...[and] could simply not be expected to line up in orderly ranks," Albert Speer, *Inside the Third Reich* (New York: Macmillan, 1970), 58; Joachim Fest, *Speer: The Final Verdict* (Orlando: Harcourt, Inc., 2000), 50. From the ridiculous to the sublime.

[113] Hitler brought to the 1934 rallies copies of all the imperial insignia of the "First Reich" from Aachen. From the early fifteenth to the early nineteenth centuries, the imperial regalia (*Reichskleinodien*) were kept in Nuremberg until the advance of Napoleon's armies in 1796 forced their removal.

[114] See the photographs of Heinrich Hoffmann, in Rudolf Herz, *Hoffmann & Hitler: Fotografie als Medium des Führer-Mythos* (Munich: Klinkhardt & Biermann, 1994).

caught in a crowd of ten thousand people outside Hitler's hotel in Nuremberg in 1934, he was "shocked at the faces, especially those of the women, when Hitler finally appeared at the balcony for a moment. They reminded me of the crazed expressions I saw once in the back country of Louisiana on the faces of some Holy Rollers...They looked up at him as if he were the messiah, their faces transformed into something positively inhuman."[115]

And at the core of this millennial pageant stood Adolf Hitler, for whose oratorical gifts the Nazi true believers had staged all these effects. One insider described his appeal during this period:

> Far beyond his electrifying rhetoric, this man seemed to possess the uncanny gift of coupling the Gnostic yearning of the era for a strong leader-figure with his own missionary claim and to suggest in this merging that every conceivable hope and expectation was capable of fulfillment—an astonishing spectacle of suggestive influence of the mass psyche.[116]

Among Hitler's admirers we find not only Germans but others (with a claim to Aryan lineage) like Major Francis Yeats-Brown, an Englishman, drawn by Hitler's messianic charisma:

> During the rhetorical passages his voice mounted to the pitch of delirium: he was a man transformed and possessed. We were in the presence of a miracle...the tension was almost unbearable until the passionate voice was drowned by the cries of the audience. The delirium was real—Hitler was in a frenzy at these moments—but he was able to release this infectious atmosphere of quasi-hysteria without losing his self-control: whatever his emotion, a steady fervor and a more-than-feminine intuition are harnessed to a cool brain and a strong will.[117]

As Hitler's speeches were emotionally and physically satisfying for his audience, he too seems to have had a satisfaction that bordered on the sexual. Walter Schellenberg, SS officer, recalled that "[d]uring his speeches he fell, or rather, worked himself into such orgiastic frenzies that he achieved through them complete emotional satisfaction."[118]

Nor was this mere public masturbation. Hitler seduced his audience fully: Karl Alexander von Müller wrote that "it took him a long time to screw himself up to the usual excitement. But there would never fail to be the orgiastic outbreak, and

---

[115] William Shirer, *Berlin Diary: The Journal of a Foreign Correspondent, 1934–1941* (New York: Knopf, 1941), 17–18.

[116] As quoted in Kershaw, *Hitler: Hubris*, 187.

[117] Francis Yeats-Brown, "A Tory Looks at Hitler," *Living Age* 354 (1938): 512. On the value of this testimony, see Redles, *Hitler's Millennial Reich*, who also notes the comparison with modern rock stars and the role of ego and Self in an age of mass communication.

[118] Schellenberg, *Labyrinth*, 94–95. In an interview with John Toland, Hanfstängl reported that Hitler told him that "[t]he mass, the Volk, is for me a wife," cited in Charles B. Flood, *Hitler: The Path to Power* (Boston: Houghton Mifflin, 1989), 615 n. 28.

the orgiastic response."[119] Kurt Lüdecke described Hitler's speaking ability as being not "conscious," but rather the "perfect co-ordination of impulse and expression."[120] "In other words," Redles concludes, "Hitler with his penchant for non-directed thinking felt the impulse of the apocalypse complex and gave voice to symbols that express it. The audience, having given up its ego-consciousness and immersed itself in non-rational-thinking, heard their innermost thoughts made audible and were enraptured."[121]

As contemporary writer Hanns Johst explained it, the party rallies enabled the individual to experience "in the community of equally minded, equally feeling, equally believing people the dream of salvation as displayed and envisioned truth."[122] Hitler's rhetoric and imagery enthralled Germans. Alfons Heck, who experienced the mass rallies as a boy, was impressed by the "pomp and mysticism" which had an effect "very close in feeling to religious rituals," a "gigantic revival meeting but without the repentance of one's sins…it was a jubilant Teutonic renaissance." He elaborated that "no one who ever attended a Nüremberg *Reichsparteitag* can forget the similarity to religious mass fervor it exuded. Its intensity frightened neutral observers but it inflamed the believers."[123] French scholar Pierre Sironneau noted that "a genuine sacred drama was performed [at the rallies], which only the resurgence in the twentieth century, of religious drives that were supposed to have disappeared can explain."[124]

On the other hand, as a foreshadowing of future historiographical directions in the West, the same mysticism that moved Hitler enthusiasts left a *New York Times* journalist, cold. Commenting on the second day of the 1934 rally, he wrote: "The chancellor apparently found the going a bit easier today, than during yesterday's excursion into the mystic and mystifying realms of Nazi *Weltanschauung* and metaphysics…."[125] In so "reducing" the event to (what the journalist found to be) recognizable behavior, the correspondent missed the story of the century.

---

[119] Karl Alexander von Müller, *Im Wandeleiner Welt, 1919–1932* (Munich: Süddeutscher Verlag, 1966), 149. Sometimes the experience was mutually stimulating. Müller remembered of Dietrich Eckart, that "after one of Hitler's orgiastic cascades he jumped onto the table with a fiery red face screaming his song, 'Deutschland Erwache!' frantically…while a brass band performed the music roaringly: it was the picture of a lunatic raging with frenzy." Ibid.

[120] Ludecke, *I Knew Hitler*, 489.

[121] Redles, *Hitler's Millennial Reich*, 139.

[122] Hanns Johst, *Ich glaube!* (Munich: A. Langen, 1928), 75, as quoted in Klaus Vondung, "Spiritual Revolution and Magic: Speculation and Political Action in National Socialism," *Modern Age* 23:4 (1979): 400.

[123] Alfons Heck, *A Child of Hitler: Germany in the Days When God Wore a Swastika* (Frederick, Colo.: Renaissance House, 1985), 18, 23.

[124] Jean-Pierre Sironneau, *Sécularisation et religions politiques* (The Hague: Mouton, 1982), 581–82.

[125] "Hitler Sees All in Labor Service," *New York Times*, Friday, September 7, 1934, 13, col. 1: "The journalist apparently found he understood better today…." The same correspondent had already engaged in wishful thinking on July 15, with an article entitled: "Hitler is Weaker, Observers Think; Speech Warning Foes Held to Be Sign That Chancellor Is on the Defensive. Leader Shows Less Fire; Reich's 'Strong Man' Reveals Effects of Killings of Traitors Among His Aides," *New York Times*, July 15, 1934, 14.

Empowered by his people, Hitler became the omnipotent historical actor capable of divine, millennial deeds. The 1934 rally, in particular, marked the full deployment of the millennial imagination, recorded in celluloid by Leni Riefenstahl in her monumental film, *Triumph des Willens* (Triumph of the Will). Here Hitler appears as a savior, landing from the heavens to fulfill his and Germany's destiny.[126] "Hitler is cast as a veritable German Messiah who will save the nation, if only the citizenry will put its destiny in his hands."[127] The film and the rally conclude with his famous *Tausendjähriges Reich* speech in which he promised that the Nazi regime would last for millennia.[128]

At the 1935 rally for *Freedom* (where the party enacted the Nüremberg Laws against the Jews) he declared the intimate relationship of *Führer und Volk*:

My will—that must be our total creed—is our belief; my belief is to me—exactly as to you—everything in this world! But the highest thing that God has given me in this world is my *Volk*! In it rests my faith. I serve it with my will, and I give it my life…Just as I am yours, so are you mine. So long as I live, I belong to you and you belong to me![129]

At the 1936 rally, dedicated to *Honor*, he proclaimed:

How deeply we feel once more in this hour the miracle that has brought us together! Once, you heard the voice of a man, and it spoke to your hearts; it awakened you and you followed that voice…Now that we meet here, we are all filled with the wonder of this gathering. Not every one of you can see me and I do not see each one of you. But I feel you, and you feel me! It is faith in our nation that has made us little people great…You come out of the little world of your daily struggle for life, and of your struggle for Germany and for our nation, to experience this feeling for once: Now we are together, we are with him and he is with us, and now we are Germany.[130]

These rallies were the mutual discovery and affirmation of a messiah and his people. "That is the miracle of our time, that you have found me—that among so many millions you have found me! And that I have found you! That is Germany's

---

[126] Note that Riefenstahl's previous film for the 1933 *Reichsparteitage* was *Seig des Glaubens* (Triumph of Belief).*

[127] Frank P. Tomasulo, "The Mass Psychology of Fascist Cinema: Leni Riefenstahl's Triumph of the Will," in *Documenting the Documentary: Close Reading of Documentary Film and Video*, ed. Barry Keith Grant and Jeannette Sloniowski (Detroit: Wayne State University Press, 1998), 104.

[128] On the theme of the *Tausendjähriges Reich*, see Speer's revealing remarks about how he took it as mere rhetoric at first, but realized in retrospect that Hitler meant it, even to the point of gradually retreating from the limelight in order to make the *ritual* aspects sufficiently fixed that they could survive after Hitler's own death: "It now seems to me more likely that he was deliberately giving up the smaller claim to the status of a celebrated popular hero in order to gain the far greater status of founder of a religion," Albert Speer, *Spandau: The Secret Diaries* (New York: Macmillan, 1976), 262.

[129] 1935 Wolfgang Hammer, *Adolf Hitler: Ein Deutscher Messias?* (Munich: Delp, 1970), p. 14.

[130] 1936 speech, *Hitler: Reden und Proklamationen 1932-1945*, ed. Max Domarus (Munich: Süddeutscher Verlag, 1965), p. 641; for an extensive analysis of the biblical—specifically messianic—resonances of this passage, see J. P. Stern, *Hitler: The Führer and the People* (Berkeley and Los Angeles: University of California Press, 1988), 90–91.

[and the world's mis-] fortune."[131] In the terms of this study, the rallies corre-spond to the *fêtes de la fédération* of the French Revolution or the Peace Assemblies of the Peace of God movement or the Great Allelulia of 1233—the same unforgettable experience of collective unity and liberation, love-fests, the height of Nazism as a demotic movement.[132] Hess called these rallies "the high mass of the Nazi Party." They presided over a time that at least one Nazi nostal-gically remembered after the war as a period of "sunshine, happiness, rejoicing and joy."[133]

The end of these *Reichsparteitage* illustrates an interesting apocalyptic dynamic. The astounding success of these rallies had inspired the Nazi party to prepare the 1939 rally in the grandest possible fashion, putting up new buildings and monu-ments, bringing the railway station into the very grounds of the rallies, setting up tent cities for 350,000 people, anticipating possibly a million attendees, preparing the detailed program for September 2–11.[134] But, in the year after the 1938 rallies, Hitler fomented crises in Czechoslovakia and Poland and then set off to war (undeclared) on September 1, 1939 against Poland, prompting France and England to declare war against him.

His choices in timing suggest bizarre and self-destructive behavior, even for a messiah. He could have waited till mid-September, held this long-planned, extremely expensive event, in which he could reaffirm the love his people had for him and go to war with his approval at its highest point. Instead, Hitler canceled the rally at the last second, in the most dismissive fashion—no explanations, no apologies. "According to the press office of the NSDAP, the planned party rally from September 2 to 11 this year will not take place. Whether the meeting will be held later depends on political circumstances."[135] The party never held another.[136]

---

[131] Hitler, *Der Parteitag der Ehre vom 8. bis 14. September 1936* (Munich: Zentralverlag der NSDAP, 1936), 246–47, in Max Domarus, ed. *Hitler: Reden und Proklamationen 1932-1945* (Würzburg: Gesamtherstellung und Auslieferung), 643; cited in Kershaw, *Hitler: Hubris*, 591.

[132] See Hans-Ulrich Thamer, "The Orchestration of the National Community: The Nuremberg Party Rallies of the NSDAP," in *Fascism and the Theatre*, ed. Gunther Berghaus (Providence: Berghahn Books, 1991), 173. On the French revolutionary festivals, the Great Allelulia and the Peace assemblies, see above, chapter 9, n. 32.

[133] "Uber alles lagen Sonne, Glück, Jubel und Freude..." Hans Frank, *Im Angesicht des Galgens* (Munich: F. A. Beck, 1953), 320; cited in Lukacs, *Hitler of History*, 96.

[134] Hamilton Burden, *The Nuremberg Party Rallies, 1923–39* (New York: Praeger, 1966), 161–65, see his Appendix for the actual program, 190–93. The cost of preparing this rally must have been exorbitant. The 1938 rally had run a deficit of 8 million DM.

[135] Ibid.

[136] The timing of the invasion of Poland and the canceling of the rally are extremely curious and deserve close attention. He initially gave orders for the invasion on August 25 at 3:02 PM (last second), and then canceled them that evening, without a clear idea of when he would give the new order to invade. And yet, he canceled the rally the following day. See Ian Kershaw's account in *Hitler, 1936–45: Nemesis* (New York: W.W. Norton, 2000), 197–230.

This bizarre behavior signals the first major split between Führer and *Volk*.[137] That split may even have been signaled by Hitler's idiosyncratic behavior during the previous summer. He spent most of it out of the public eye, even out of touch with his government and military commanders, traveling around to places from his childhood.[138]

Why cancel the rally? Perhaps because, in addition to the peculiarly violent and aggressive Nazi rhetoric so much in display, these party rallies had also deployed demotic millennial themes—freedom, dignity of manual labor, classlessness, and, for this last, aborted rally, of all things, *peace*. Like most messianic figures, Hitler wanted to be all things to all people (or at least all Germans) and had encouraged those who wanted to, to think of him as a bringer of peace.[139] His diplomacy in the 1930s had registered among most observers, German and foreign, as brilliant bluffing, not the recklessness of a man bent on war. It was in this ambiguous framework where the *Volk* could imagine themselves on the path to (an only slightly more modest) national salvation as the greatest nation on earth *among other nations*, that Hitler achieved his greatest popularity.

But Hitler's ambitions were for a Germany that ruled a *Jüdenrein* world. And once he decided to go that path, he instinctively knew that he would never again have the kind of loving enthusiasm he had gotten before from his German *Volk*. The American correspondent William Shirer wrote on August 31, "Everybody [is] against the war. How can a country go into a major war with a population so dead against it?"[140] The contrast between 1914 and 1939 was palpable: "Not a soul on the street took notice of this historic event: Hitler driving off to the war he had staged."[141] The party feared "widespread tendencies toward disengagement or passive resistance," if not open revolt.[142]

---

[137] It is noteworthy that some historians, even as they emphasize the sudden turn of events that left most party members in the dark, do not even mention this cancellation, for example, Bullock, *Hitler*; Orlow, *A History of the Nazi Party*, 263; Gerhard Weinberg, *A World at Arms: A Global History of World War II* (Cambridge: Cambridge University Press, 1994), 32–50.

[138] Kershaw, *Hitler: Nemesis*, 197–99; the meeting with his childhood friend August Kubizek at the Bayreuth Festival, where he reminisced about Wagner's *Rienzi*, took place at this time.

[139] On religion, see above, pp. 365–73. Speer reminisces that, at the Party Rally of 1938, he sat on the wall of Nuremberg Castle with Wilhelm Brückner, Hitler's adjutant, who remarked, "We may be seeing this peaceful scene for the last time. Probably we shall soon be at war," *Inside the Third Reich*, 111. "Hitler made every effort to replace the 'horror image' of the Nazi empire that was frantically rearming with the picture of a peaceful and reconciled nation, headed by a politician who saw his mission in the promotion of works of culture," Fest, *Speer*, 52–54.

[140] Cited in Kershaw, *Hitler: Nemesis*, 221. Kershaw also quotes a report from Franconia: "Trust in the *Führer* will now probably be subjected to its hardest acid test. The overwhelming proportion of people's comrades expects from him the prevention of the war, if otherwise impossible even at the cost of Danzig and the Corridor." (ibid., n. 283). See also Wolfram Wette, "Zur psychologischen Mobilmachung der deutschen Bevölkerung, 1933–1939," in *Der Zweite Weltkrieg. Analysen-Grudzüge-Forschungsbilanz*, ed. Wolfgang Michalka (Munich: Piper, 1989), 220.

[141] Speer, *Inside the Third Reich*, 166–67; "The streets were emptier than usual. Most of those who turned to watch the line of cars accompanying the *Führer* stared in silence," Bullock, *Hitler*, 547.

[142] Orlow, *Nazi Party*, 264–65.

Hitler rarely appeared in public from that point on: "While the *Führer* shut himself off from all spontaneous and most large-scale contact with the German people, he gave the party the responsibility of maintaining morale among the civilian population."[143] So, like a lover sated with his conquest, he dumped the *Volk* on the very eve of their annual celebration, *before* they might leave him. Instead, Hitler set off to rape other nations.[144] From transformative to cataclysmic apocalypse.

Hitler's Anti-Semitism

Hitler's anti-Semitism has puzzled historians. There seems to be little in his personal life to prepare one for the depth and passion of the hatred that suddenly emerged *after* the war. And there seems to be little in our understanding of human behavior that would suggest that a political leader, in time of war, would sacrifice himself, his rule, and his people to the irrelevant killing so many men, *women, and children* of a population that neither had weapons, nor had declared war on him.

And yet, Hitler's anti-Semitism was at once his most powerful, passionate, and least rational conviction—surviving his love affair with the German people and his belief in his own success. The Jews had neither sovereignty nor military power. Like the pope, they had no divisions; and unlike the church, they had no overt diplomatic power. On the contrary, the Jews proved to be incredibly docile citizens, obeying commands to go to their own death—even buying their own train tickets to the death camps. They resorted to resistance only after extraordinary provocation. And yet, he feared them the most.[145]

This issue brings us deep into Hitler's—and Germany's—millennial imagination. The Jews were not a "realistic" threat, in the sense of either reality or *Realpolitik*; they were an apocalyptic threat, in the sense that modernity—*their* conspiracy!—threatened the very existence of the German people. And this held true in two registers. Modernity threatened the traditional German *Gemeinschaft*, the rural community and its pious continuities with a past that reached back to the mists of time. It also threatened an authoritarian Germany in which an aristocratic class was accustomed to ruthlessly dominating the commoner population. As Goethe had written, a little more than a century earlier, "[t]he [German] peasant stands between the land and the princes like metal between hammer and anvil."[146] The

---

[143] Orlow, *Nazi Party*, 263. Bullock notes: "In the whole of 1940 [Hitler] made only seven speeches of any importance, even fewer in succeeding years, a fact of some importance when it is recalled how great a part Hitler's oratory played in the history of the years before the war" (*Hitler*, 631).

[144] His speech before the Reichstag and subsequent behavior suggests that he was aware, and defensive, about his betrayal: "I am asking of no German man more than I myself was ready to do throughout four years…my whole life belongs henceforth more than ever to my people…" Hitler, *My New Order*, ed. Raoul de Roussy de Sales (New York: Reynal & Hitchcock, 1941), 689, cited in Bullock, *Hitler*, 547.

[145] Lucy Dawidowicz, *The War Against the Jews: 1933–1945* (New York: Bantam Books, 1986).

[146] "Diesen Amboss vergleich ich dem Lande, den Hammer dem Fürsten, und dem Volke das Blech, das in der Mitte sich krümmt…" Goethe, *Epigramme* 14 [Venice, 1790], ed. Jochen Golz und Rosalinde Gothe (Frankfurt: Insel, 1999).

rules of modernity not only meant the end of a romanticized rural life, it meant the end of cruder forms of Thrasymachan "might makes right," especially in the urban, professional circles in which Jews excelled—learning, money-making, media, law, and medicine.

Historians have much discussed the rather sudden and puzzling emergence of Hitler's anti-Semitism.[147] Although he asserted in *Mein Kampf* that he had already adopted a remorseless hatred of Jews in Vienna, most of the reliable evidence suggests that it came quite late in his Munich career, that is, in 1919, and that it coincides with the remarkable surge of Hitler's oratorical power.[148] Indeed, Hitler's rise to power though demagoguery and his adoption of virulent anti-Semitism coincide with his first exposure to the fully articulated racist millennialism of Ariosophy and the Thule Society and to the *Protocols of the Elders of Zion*.[149] Hitler himself called the revelation of the *Protocols*—the Jewish virus—"revolutionary."[150]

The central role of antimodern Judeophobia in this racist theosophy, and the cosmic scale of its millennial vision, suggests that Hitler seized upon anti-Semitism as a key ingredient of his particular brand of the Ariosophical*Weltanschauung*. It permitted him to fuel active cataclysmic beliefs, in which hatred galvanized the troops for apocalyptic battle. If his hatred surpassed even the beliefs of other German anti-Semites (with the exception of such fanatics as Julius Streicher), that may be due to Hitler's unique understanding of the ways in which the apocalyptic puzzle fit together.

Historians have spilled much ink on the peculiar path of the Germans, for which they have coined the term *Sonderweg* (special path), and the painful lesson of the mid-twentieth century teaches that Germany was the only (first?) "civilized" (modernized) nation to engage in a determined genocide of a target people within its citizenry.[151] Among those rivers of ink, one in particular runs through the terrain of the *Sonderweg* of German anti-Semitism.[152] If asked at the beginning of the twentieth

---

[147] Lukacs dedicates a chapter to it, admitting that at some level "the sudden eruption of his anti-semitism into his principal obsession remains a mystery (*Hitler of History*, 185); Lukacs cites Percy Ernst Schramm: "in the end, all attempts to explain the unprecedented and immeasurable intensity of Hitler's anti-Semitism finally founder on the inexplicable," *Hitler the Man and the Military Leader* (Chicago: Quadrangle Books, 1971), 51.

[148] See Kershaw, *Hitler: Hubris*, 60–67, 149–52; Lukacs comes down on the Munich side of his question: "The Crystalization: Vienna or Munich," in the *Hitler of History*, 52–75.

[149] Goodrick-Clarke, *Occult Roots of Nazism*, 135–52. Lukacs does not even mention the Ariosophists in his discussion (neither of the Munich "crystallization" nor of the anti-Semitism problem).

[150] "The discovery of the Jewish virus is one of the greatest revolutions that has ever take place," from a conversation Hitler had with Himmler after the 1942 genocidal Wannsee Conference, cited in Waite, *Psychopathic God*, 24; Fest, *Hitler*, 212.

[151] Of course, the Armenian massacres by the Turks preceded the Holocaust, and may have inspired Hitler himself (particularly since the Turks paid no price for it internationally); but that could be considered a "premodern" jihad (see below, chap. 15).

[152] The floodgates of this particular current of discussion were most recently opened up by Daniel Goldhagen's *Hitler's Willing Executioners: Ordinary Germans and the Holocaust* (New York: Knopf, 1996).

century to predict which nation would try and wipe out the Jews, an observer would probably have picked anti-Dreyfusard France—far more open and virulent about its Jew-hatred than Germany. And certainly anti-Semitism was something that Germans shared with many peoples of the time; one might even say anti-Semitism was the most powerful ecumenical movement of the mid-twentieth century, crossing barriers separating aristocratic, constitutional, and Communist politics, between conquered and conqueror, between races, ethnicities, and languages.

So was there any specific characteristic to German anti-Semitism that made it more virulent than the many virulent variants all around them? The hostile reception of Daniel Goldhagen's book, in which he argued that the Germans had a particularly noxious strain, a *Vernichtungsantisemitismus* (exterminationist anti-Semitism), suggests that many historians try hard not to attribute something special to German anti-Semitism.[153] In a sense, this may well be the Nazi parallel to the French revolutionary debate: how predetermined was Hitler's Judeocide?

From a millennial perspective, however, there is something unusual—not unique by any means, but unusual—about German anti-Semitism. All antimodern manifestations of Jew hatred share many of the apocalyptic elements of Nazi ideology— the sense of urgency at the nearly complete conspiracy, the ferocious hatred of a cosmic enemy, the profoundly paranoid sense of being suffocated by Jewish success, the assumption that all the major developments of modernity (marriage of capital and technology, urbanization, constitutional governments, public media, and public atheism) stemmed from the Jews and threatened chaos and enslavement. But beyond those similarities, we find one aspect that the Germans pushed further than any other nation—the claim to be a "chosen people."[154]

Having played a role in German self-identity for almost a millennium, the reading of "chosen people" as an exclusive status that annulled all other (previous) claims had, as we have seen, gone through an agonizing experience in its century-long encounter with modernity, and come out the other side of the "War to End All Wars" in complete humiliation. And in this matrix was born the German *Sonderantisemitismus*. The unbearable loss of control, the impotence, the humiliation—all drove toward a virulently zero-sum dualism, and thereby created a mutation in German Judeophobia. As Pastor Leffler put it in his *Christ and the Third Reich*: "Choose between Israel and Germany."[155]

---

[153] Goldhagen deliberately challenged the tendency among historians to claim "it could have happened anywhere," e.g., Christopher Browning's *Ordinary Men: Reserve Police Battalion 101 and the Final Solution in Poland* (New York: Harper Perennial, 1992).*

[154] Hartmut Lehmann, "The Germans as a Chosen People: Old Testament Themes in German Nationalism," *German Studies Review* 14, no. 2 (1991): 261–73. There are similar manifestations in French and English nationalism (in the French case dating back to the Middle Ages), but none compare with the Nazis for pitiless competitive intensity.

[155] Siegfried Leffler, *Christus im Dritten Reich der Deutschen; Wesen, Weg und Ziel der Kirchenbewegung "Deutsche Christen"* (Weimar: Verlag "Deutsche Christian," 1935), cited in Pieter Viereck, *Metapolitics: The Roots of the Nazi Mind* (New York: Capricorn Books, 1961), 288.

Hitler was no multiculturalist. For him there could only be one chosen people, and—in true "Social Darwinian" style—that chosen people proved their status by exterminating the other claimant(s). Rather than the positive-sum notion of biblical chosenness—"through you all the nations of the world will be blessed…those who bless you will be blessed…"—the Nazis articulated a vision in which the very existence of the rival chosen people, the Jews, meant the certain death of the German people. They could only live by exterminating their rival for "election" and subjugating the other nations. And this mission was precisely what they accused the Jews of wanting to do.

Apocalyptic time took authoritarian German culture from the *dominating imperative* "rule or be ruled" to the *paranoid imperative*, "exterminate or be exterminated." There, the very presence of the Jew, especially the successful Jew of the modern world, had become unbearable. And since the seed of that modern Jew lay in every child born to that inexplicable people, all Jews had to die.[156] At last, the authors of the *Protocols* had a world-historical actor who listened to their message. In the paranoid apocalyptic world of German humiliation and rage at the indignities of modernity, it had become as Hitler put it: *Sein oder nicht sein.*[157]

Again, other cultures/peoples/nations may have experienced this sense of strangulation at the advent of (Jewish-inspired) modernity, and even blamed the Jews for their unhappiness. But none brought it into such explosive a spark as the man who brought upon his people a wave of passionate solidarity by giving them a sense of their messianic identity and identifying the Jews as their apocalyptic enemy. As Saul Friedlander has recently argued, Nazi anti-Semitism is peculiar because it is "redemptive."[158] It was part of an "apocalyptic" or "eschatological" worldview. In Nazi ideology, the Jewish people represented the collective identity of Antichrist.[159]

In this sense, it may be possible to make some remarks about the possibility of the Holocaust starting in other countries, in France, or England, or Russia. Not every people who claim the status of chosen people necessarily interpret it in the most irreducibly *and* aggressive, zero-sum manner. The English, for example, viewed themselves as God's chosen people, but their apocalyptic scenarios tended to be more *philo-* than *anti-*Semitic, their relationship to demotic modernity more

---

[156] For a particularly thoughtful exploration of some of these themes, see Zygmunt Bauman, *Modernity and the Holocaust* (Ithaca, N.Y.: Cornell University Press, 2000).

[157] These are precisely the terms of the *Protocols of the Elders of Zion.*

[158] Saul Friedländer, *Nazi Germany and the Jews*, vol. 1, *The Years of Persecution, 1933–1939* (New York: Harper Collins, 1997), 72–112; he uses the terms apocalyptic and eschatological interchangeably, for example on p. 87.

[159] Claus Bärsch, "Der Jude als Antichrist in der NS-Ideologie: Die Kollektive Identität der Deutschen und der Antisemitismus unter religionspolitischer Perspective," *Zeitschrift für Relgions- und Geistesgeschichte* [Netherlands], 47, no. 2 (1995): 160–88.*

positive.[160] The French, in their brief philo-Judaic moment set in motion by the Revolution, had emancipated the Jews.

One significant variable here seems to be elements of demotic versus popular religiosity with their varying appeal to questions of integrity/guilt or honor/shame. Germany lagged well behind the English and the French in meeting the modern challenge to alpha males. They ferociously refused to renounce their right to "honorable behavior"—including "becoming a man by killing one."[161] One sees clearly the role of "honor" and the sociopolitical world it embodied in the Dreyfus Affair's anti-Semitism at the turn of the century. By fin-de-siècle Paris, many in the French elite had come to rue their revolutionary ancestors' generosity to the Jews. Among other things at stake was the place of a Jew, from an effeminate culture that does not kill, in a (supposedly) virile army.[162]

On one level, the Dreyfus Affair might be characterized as the question of whether Jews are part of French identity (and hence worthy of justice), part of France's sense of chosenness. And here, by exonerating Dreyfus, the "intellectuals"—also a suspiciously effeminate group—won the day. But in its aftermath, French politics resounds with appeals to a modern notion of French chosenness as citizens of the world, and French cultural capaciousness included Jews. They had passed through the fires of a public humiliation of political authority—army and church—self-critically and emerged "modern." In the world of egalitarian meritocracy, their "honor" no longer demanded the subjection of the Jews.[163] Education makes us all equals: nurture over nature.

In Germany, the warriors won; and much to their shame, in the liberal world that now dominated the global community, even (some) German intellectuals joined the madness.[164] As a result, they chose racial categories with which to interpret the world—the most visible form of "us versus them." For them, the Jews *could not* be "German," because, under modern conditions, they humiliated Germany's manhood. No matter how accomplished the Jew, no matter how eager to help the Nazis, he could not live. On the contrary, like Dreyfus, the more accomplished, the more dangerous. Nature trumps nurture, and the law of the jungle rules in apocalyptic time.[165]

[160] On the English, especially during the religious revolution of the mid-seventeenth century, see Christopher Hill, *The World Turned Upside Down: Radical Ideas during the English Revolution* (New York: Penguin Books, 1991).

[161] For an excellent discussion of the problems of males with honor and shame in this period, in terms of "audience," see Thomas Strychacz, "Dramatizations of Manhood in Hemingway's *In Our Time* and *The Sun Also Rises*," *American Literature* 61, no. 2 (1989): 245–60.

[162] Christopher E. Forth, *The Dreyfus Affair and the Crisis of French Manhood* (Baltimore: Johns Hopkins University Press, 2004), esp. 21–61.

[163] For a discussion of the theme of honor, shame, and the Jews as part of modern identity in which modernity views depriving the Jews of sovereignty as "shameful" whereas premodern notions view that as a source of honor, see online appendix: Napoleon's Egyptian Campaign, Islam, and the Jews.

[164] Thomas Scheff, *Bloody Revenge: Emotions, Nationalism and War* (Lincoln, NE: iUniverse, 2000), 105–23.

[165] Nor can one argue this is primarily a function of political insecurity. After 1870, the Germans were triumphalists, the French, the defeated.

Alone, the Germans under Hitler responded to the crisis of modernity in the early twentieth century with this particularly passionate obsession with national honor. And they formulated it in terms of a claim to be the chosen people who had found their messiah. In this, they, more than any other European nation, entered into direct competition with (what they imagined to be) Jewish claims.

While I do not know the variables sufficiently well, my sense of the case I know the best—France—suggests that no matter how virulent and (self-) destructive French anti-Semitism was in the early twentieth century (and maybe today), the French were (and are) a culture far more resistant than the Germans to the kind of millennial politics that Hitler sparked among the Germans.[166] Some combination, perhaps, of Augustinianism and skepticism has made of the French a culture too self-conscious and too ironic to "convert" to the tribal millennialism of Hitler which, despite its crudity, eventually appealed to the highest levels of German culture. For the French to fall prey to self-destructive millennial ideologies, they cannot come clothed in crude, "honor-shame" garb. Rather, they will come from masters of irony and self-deception, like Sartre and Baudrillard, not from the crude rantings of an autodidact.[167]

■ CONCLUSION

The reluctance of many historians to explore Nazism in terms of millennial dynamics should not surprise the readers of this book. But it should puzzle and trouble them. It does seem encouraging that a significant number of German historians, as well as Redles in the United States, have begun to explore this dimension of Nazism, although it remains to be seen what the larger profession will do. To the degree that most post-Holocaust historians view Hitler as a *unicum* and emphasize the singular nature of his evil, they reject any framework in which he can be compared to any other movement. From this point of view, to claim Hitler is millennial at once tarnishes other millennial movements, and relativizes Nazi evil. Thus, historians would rather view Hitler as mad, than as a messianic pretender.

But such good intentions may indeed contribute to allowing similar movements to gain strength, precisely as Hitler's movement did during the period of appeasement. By failing to recognize well-known (if grotesquely exaggerated) patterns of active cataclysmic apocalyptic and hierarchical millennialism, observers can miss

---

[166] Lukacs asks if Hitler could have been a successful Viennese politician, implying no. Indeed, Hitler may have had a particular—and in the case of his teetotaling, ironic—success in Munich where "the extreme and hyperbolical character of his oratory echoed better in the raucous atmosphere of Munich than in the tighter-lipped north: the rough and beery, jocular South German virility..." *Hitler of History*, 66. See above, n. 119, on Eckart's behavior.

[167] Note that at least one French enthusiast for Nazism, on seeing the power of the *Parteitage* asked longingly, "Can we Frenchmen share in this someday?" Robert Brasillach, *Notre Avant Guerre* (Paris: Plon, 1941), 276. On Baudrillard, see below, chapter 15, n. 21.*

PART FIVE

Postmodern Millennialism

13 Narcissistic Millennialism

UFO Cults (1946–2012? CE)

One of the most telling blows the "reflexive school" of anthropology landed on the modern master narrative was to point out something of the obvious. We too have cargo cults every bit as silly (or unwittingly insightful) as the ones "we" Eurocentric modernists mocked so blithely among the stone-aged natives of Melanesia. The parallels between *kago* cults and UFO beliefs are striking, all clearly bearing the same millennial imprint.[1] Creatures from a civilization vastly superior in technology to ours will land on our planet and bring with them salvific *kago* that will take us from this current catastrophic world of violent self-indulgence to a millennial era of abundance and peace. The *kago* will consist of both hyper-technology and the kind of evolutionary wisdom that will enable us to overcome the insane hostilities and greed that currently seem to consume us. It constitutes a classic millennial narrative about how we get from this world destined for destruction to the perfect kingdom via extraterrestrial cargo ships. And, appropriately, most UFOlogy comes in the shadow of Hiroshima: now that humanity can destroy itself, superior aliens will intervene to save us from ourselves. These anticipated UFOS, then, are the modern (or hyper-modern) version of stone-age *kago* cults.[2]

The parallel between *kago* cults and UFOs is at once less and more of a comparison than some might think. On one level, the comparison is disturbingly appropriate: the Raelians believe that if they could build an embassy for the Elohim (extraterrestrials who created humans "in their own image") in the city of Jerusalem, then these Elohim will grace us with their redemptive presence. And with a message like this, the prophet Rael, French-born singer and race-car driver Claude Vorhilon has been able to launch a religious group marked by pan-sexuality and universal tolerance.[3]

On another level, the comparison is inadequate. UFO visions seem to have far more range than *kago* cults, where the dominant scenario holds that the *kago*

---

[1] Gary Trompf made the connection in "The Cargo and the Millennium on Both Sides of the Pacific," in *Cargo Cults and Millenarian Movements*, ed. Gary Trompf (Berlin: Mouton de Gruyter, 1990), 35–94, which he then pursued more systematically in "UFO Religions and Cargo Cults," in *UFO Religions*, ed. Christopher Partridge (London: Routledge, 2003), 221–38, where he mentions the mixed reception his first suggestion elicited (236 n. 35).

[2] The Unarians are probably one of the best examples of UFO-based cargo thinking. See Diana Tumminia and R. George Kirpatrick, "Unarius: Emergent Aspects of an American Flying Saucer Group," in *The Gods Have Landed: New Religions from Other Worlds*, ed. James R. Lewis (Albany: State University of New York Press, 1995), 85–104.

[3] See lengthy discussion below, pp. 408–17.

comes to reward the believer. The range of the UFO imagination runs far wider, and more darkly, than their stone-age counterparts. Creatures from other planets may serve as agents of redemption, but they also can acts as agents of cataclysm, of conquest, of annihilation.

Many consider UFO cults a bizarre, fringe phenomenon, inhabited by people who live far more in a fantasy universe than in the realities of hard science and hard life. The anthropologist might respond, "that is precisely how the Melanesians who don't join the *kago* cults feel about their cultists." Are the believers in *kago* more numerous than the believers in UFOs? The distribution of owls and roosters is difficult to estimate. According to an American poll taken in 2008, 33 percent of the people questioned believe that it was very or somewhat likely that aliens had visited Earth.[4]

Of course the above analysis has not yet factored in apocalyptic time. *Kago* cults explode into their bizarre rituals and possessions, and thousands join in, only when the feeling of imminence sweeps up believers. In that sense, UFOs are very different from *kago* cults. With the exception of Orson Welles' famous 1938 broadcast of *War of the Worlds*, we have yet to see an outbreak of mass behavior driven by the widespread anticipation of an imminent UFO landing. That may explain why so much UFO thinking gets played out in science fiction and movies rather than in religious activity. The Melanesians have seen the *kago*—it has arrived but they have yet to get it. UFOlogists must imagine both the *kago* and its arrival.

But just as *kago* cults challenge the anthropologist to take the postmodern reflexive turn, so do UFOs challenge the modern sociologist. Belief in UFOs drives a wedge between the modern, scientific narrative, feet firmly planted in "objective reality," and the postmodern world of plural narratives, each valid in its own way. And in our current culture wars, UFOs have a special place: thinkers as diverse as Carl Sagan and Wendy Kaminer view the spread of the kind of thinking represented by UFOlogy as worrisome signs of cultural weakness if not decline,[5] while others such as Susan Palmer and Roy Wagner consider these beliefs as signs of a vigorous and potentially constructive imagination.[6] Nothing quite puts us up against the horns of the modernist/postmodernist dilemma than the stone-age *kago* cults and postmodern UFOlogy.

[4] Scripps Poll, May 2008, online: http://www.scrippsnews.com/node/34761, March 25, 2010. A Yankelovitch poll of January 2000 found similar numbers: Cynthia Fox, "The Search for Extraterrestrial Life," *Life* (March 2000) 56. #2. Over 50 percent in both polls believe there is intelligent life on other planets. A Roper Poll done in August 2002 found that 20 percent of Americans believed that UFO abductions had taken place. "UFOs & Extraterrestrial Life: Americans' Beliefs and Personal Experiences," online: http://www.scifi.com/ufo/roper/, April 14, 2010.

[5] Wendy Kaminer, *Sleeping with Extra-Terrestrials: The Rise of Irrationalism and Perils of Piety* (New York: Pantheon, 1999); Carl Sagan, *The Demon-Haunted World: Science As a Candle in the Dark* (New York: Random House, 1996).

[6] Susan Palmer, *Aliens Adored: Raël's UFO Religion* (New Brunswick, N.J.: Rutgers University Press, 2004) and Roy Wagner, "Our Very Own Cargo Cult," *Oceania* (June 2000), online: http://findarticles.com/p/articles/mi_qa3654/is_200006/ai_n8899271/pg_1, April 14, 2010.

For Carl Jung, UFOs represent the thirst of modern, alienated people deprived of their ability to strive for wholeness—the function of religion—finding an acceptable idiom whereby the unconscious with all its repressed needs and desires can communicate with consciousness. For Jung, UFOs are not so much about objects "out there" in physical space communicating with people on Earth, as the content of the unconscious "out there" in psychic space.[7] For UFOlogists, however, Jung's approach condescends and rationalizes: it takes the believers seriously, but not the object of their belief.

Trompf distinguishes between cargoism and UFOlogy (a "UFO culture"), on the one hand, and cargo cults and UFO "religions" on the other, a distinction that replicates that proposed at the beginning of this book between millennial and apocalyptic beliefs. Cargoism and UFOlogy represent cases of millennial dreams, a complex of beliefs and narratives about the nature of the world/cosmos in which a dramatic transformation of this world is foreordained. The cults emerge in apocalyptic time, when "a leader announces the approaching prospect, if not the awesome imminence, of the Cargo."[8] As a phenomenon, millennialism and its specific variants, cargoism and UFOlogy, have a much wider audience than the apocalyptic movements they occasionally spawn.

■ UFOS AS A MILLENNIAL IDEOLOGY

The future hangs like a Rorschach screen before the present. In traditional societies, where the future should look like the present, the invitation to project radical difference onto that future may face natural resistance. But in modern societies, where technology changes constantly, the future will necessarily differ from the present. Here Rorschach reading—or informed conjecture—are necessary elements of any sound policy.[9] And given some of the worrisome trends—weapons of mega-death, global warming, chaotic family, gender, and social roles, demographic decline/explosion—the future seems so tumultuous, one can understand why some may think that only an evolutionary leap for humanity can avert catastrophe.[10] In this sense, the modern world encourages, if not *demands*, millennial thinking.

---

[7] C. G. Jung, *Flying Saucers: A Modern Myth of Things Seen in the Skies*, in *The Collected Works of C.G. Jung*, vol. 10, ed. Sir Herbert Read et al. (Princeton, N.J.: Princeton University Press, 1975), 307–433; see also Robert Segal, "Jung on UFOs," in *UFO Religions*, 314–28.

[8] Trompf, "UFO Religions," 226.

[9] "Futurology" or "future studies" wishes to claim status as an academic field. For an interesting example, see John Peterson, *Out of the Blue: How to Anticipate Wild Cards and Big Future Surprises* (Arlington, Va.: Arlington Institute, 1997).*

[10] Two of the earliest, highly influential, and millennial of those articulating this point of view are Teilhard de Chardin, *The Phenomenon of Man* (New York: Harper, 1959); and Sri Aurobindo, *Evolution* (Calcutta: Arya Publishing House, 1923). See Ernst Benz, *Evolution and Christian Hope: Man's Concept of the Future from the Early Fathers to Teilhard de Chardin* (Garden City, N.Y.: Doubleday, 1966), 190–220.

UFOs respond to this need in a number of ways with a plausible scenario. First, they provide a "grounded" or scientific ("scientistic") approach. If modern Westerners can blow the minds of stone-age tribes with their technology, born of millennia of evolution, why could not some intelligent life, on one of the innumerable planets in the universe, have evolved yet another dozen or hundreds of millennia beyond us, and come blow our minds? Certainly, when trains and planes first appeared, many believed them impossible, even imagined that people would die if they went at such inorganic speeds. Does that not correspond quite closely to the argument (belief) that undermines the basic plausibility of the UFO argument? After all, if going faster than the speed of light (warp speed in *Star Trek* parlance) is impossible (for all but subatomic particles), and even if it were, humans could not possibly survive the experience, then no matter how many life forms have progressed beyond our ken out there, they will not be able to reach us.

In some ways, UFO beliefs make at least as much sense as the kind of dogmatic scientism that says what we know delimits the possible. The "down-to-earth" types in this equation look like Newtonians incapable of even imagining the possibility of an Einstein. UFO believers agree with Blake: "What is now proved was once only imagined." And in the imaginative world of both science fiction and futurology, imagining extraterrestrials—ETs—of vastly superior technological cultures, seems not only self-evident, but an excellent exercise in reflecting on the human condition.[11] Something like this logic lies behind the willingness of over half the Americans (and 60 percent of those with a college education) to affirm their belief that there is intelligent life somewhere in the universe. This constitutes a large number of people who, whether they know it or not, have opened themselves up to the allure of a millennial, even an apocalyptic narrative.

Projecting ETs and UFOs onto the Rorschach of the future gives full rein to the millennial imagination. Here—elsewhere—one can imagine societies that have reached their millennial goals. In fact, the tradition of a spatial (as opposed to temporal) millennium goes back at least to the "Voyage of Saint Brendan" in early medieval Irish and continental lore, if not to Odysseus' visit to the land of the Lotus Eaters.[12] The tradition picks up notably in the utopian literature of the Renaissance.[13] By mirroring ourselves in these images of millennial coherence, we can try and surmount the limitations in our behavior that, at this point, threaten our very existence.

---

[11] Much of the greatest science fiction—Asimov, Herbert, Le Guin—involves ETs.

[12] W. R. J. Barron and Glyn S. Burgess, eds., *The Voyage of Saint Brendan: Representative Versions of the Legend in English Translation* (Exeter: University of Exeter Press, 2002); Annette Lucia Giesecke, "Mapping Utopia: Homer's Politics and the Birth of the Polis," *College Literature* 34, no. 2 (2007): 194–214.

[13] Thomas More, *Utopia*, ed. George M. Logan and Robert M. Adams (Cambridge: Cambridge University Press, 2002); see also Frank E. Manuel and Fritzie P. Manuel, *Utopian Thought in the Western World* (Cambridge MA: Bellknap, 1982).

One can, then, imagine that these vastly superior societies will come to our planet and help us with the evolutionary leap we so desperately need to take. One visionary, Sheldan Nidle, promised that a Galactic Federation would send 15 million spaceships to Earth. With their advanced technology and their "angels" (at least one per ship), they will be able neutralize and beam up our weapons, bring individuals to "full consciousness" within sixteen hours, replace our inferior political and communications systems, and transform Earth into a "galactic showcase" of ecological and sociological equilibrium.[14] This sounds like a passive transformative demotic millennial scenario—swords into plowshares, with a technologically superior ET race playing the "divine" role in the transformation.

UFOs in fact offer a substitute "deity" for those who (can) no longer believe in a "God who intervenes in history."[15] Indeed, there is a remarkable overlap between some UFO scenarios and the equally popular "Premillennial dispensationalists." On the one hand, the suicides at Heaven's Gate believed that a ship would take them off the earth before it was "plowed under" with all its inhabitants, while preachers like Jack Van Impe believe that God will "rapture" a chosen few (presumably including him and his wife Rexilla) before visiting a terrible Tribulation upon the world. A common apocalyptic archetype informs both these "prophecies."

As if to illustrate the point, one Christian talk-show host interviewed a number of UFOlogists, mocking their beliefs openly, then concluded: "…in these last days, instead of looking into the starry heavens for the landing of an extraterrestrial mothership you will be looking to the heavens because you know your redemption draws nigh and the return of Jesus Christ is near…"[16] Thus, the relatively high figure of 63 percent of conservative Christians who do not believe in intelligent life on other planets hardly means that they do not believe in scenarios most skeptics would find just as strange as UFOs.[17]

UFOs, New Age, and Millennial Historiography

UFOlogy offers a major venue for synthesizing various New-Age spiritualities. UFO culture easily incorporates much of the theosophical trends of the nineteenth and twentieth centuries. Ascended masters become ETs whose ancestors had descended to Earth. "Channeling" St. Germain slides easily for some into channeling Space Brothers.

[14] Andres Grünscloss, "When We Enter into My Father's Space Craft: Cargoistic Hopes and Millenarian Cosmologies in New Religious UFO Movements," *Marburg Journal of Religion* 3, no. 2 (December 1998): 3.

[15] On the difficulty in believing in a God who intervenes in history after the Holocaust, see Emil Fackenheim, *God's Presence in History: Jewish Affirmations and Philosophical Reflections* (New York: New York University Press, 1970); also by the same author, *The Jewish Return into History: Reflections on the Age of Auschwitz and a New Jerusalem* (New York: Schocken Books, 1978).

[16] Bob Larson, *UFOs and the Alien Agenda* (Nashville, TN: Thomas Nelson Inc., 1997) and his video, *UFOs and the End-Times Agenda* (Bob Larson Ministries Video Production, 1997).

[17] Sagan's *Demon-Haunted World* reflects precisely this more extensive disquiet.

[T]he vocabulary, cosmology, anthropology, and numinous personnel of esoteric/theo-sophic traditions often seem to reappear simply in a modern "space age" outfit (Jerome Clark calls them "angels in space-suits"). This is true of the esoteric version of Jesus named "Sananda" or other so-called "Ascended Masters" and the "great White Brotherhood," as well as the prominent enlightened being and star fleet commander "Ashtar"...But the spiritual teachings basically reformulate the faith patterns and common esoteric/theosophic views on reincarnation, ascension of the eternal soul and world-and-matter-renouncing orientation to higher "spiritual" spheres and "resonating frequencies," and they often incorporate the ideas of sunken continents (Atlantis, Mu) and sometimes apply Indian meditation techniques and concepts of the soul (atman) and its gradual liberation from earthly matter.[18]

New Age meets futuristic science.[19]

And science meets history. UFOlogy can reinterpret the record of humanity's past in remarkably coherent ways. UFOlogy offers a coherent, dramatically updated exegesis of the great ancient texts of all civilizations. Ancient mysteries preserved in archeological wonders the world over, from Easter Island to Machu Pichu, make sense as the products of ETs visiting our planet tens, even hundreds of thousands of years ago. Visionaries can speak in evolutionary time and explain polytheistic mythologies. For just as the Pacific Islanders imagined the Europeans they met for the first time were gods, so archaic peoples viewed the space visitors. Such tales offer rational explanations for the mysteries and "miracles" of the Bible, especially for the curious passage in Genesis 6 on the Nephilim.[20]

In a sense, UFOlogical history is the most "scientific" of faith systems; indeed it redeems religious and mythical texts from their irrational, supernatural elements.

It is characteristic of our time that, in contrast to its previous expressions, the [self] archetype should now take the form of an object, a technological construction, in order to avoid the odiousness of a mythological personification. Anything that looks techno-logical goes down without difficulty with modern man. The possibility of space travel makes the unpopular idea of a metaphysical [i.e., divine] intervention much more acceptable.[21]

The role of ETs in human evolution—both in triggering a dramatic leap for-ward at the dawn of time and returning in the near future to trigger the next great

---

[18] Andres Grünschloss, "Waiting for the 'Big Beam': UFO Religions and 'Ufological' Themes in New Religious Movements," in *The Oxford Handbook of New Religious Movements*, ed. James R. Lewis (Oxford: Oxford University Press, 2004), 423–24.

[19] For an early example of the marriage of New Age, history, and UFO science see Louis Pauwels and Jacques Bergier, *Le matin des magiciens* (Paris: Gallimard, 1960).

[20] See the site "Return of the Nephilim," online: http://www.returnofthenephilim.com/ReturnOfTheNephilim.html, April 14, 2010.

[21] Jung, *Flying Saucers*, 328–29, cited in Segal, "Jung on UFOs." In a similar fashion one of the Indian gurus of the 1960s commented that Americans are so materialistic that they could only meet God through a pill (LSD).

leap—offers the UFOlogical version of Joachim and Marx's dialectic of history: the pattern for dramatic social change has already occurred, and is *about to happen again*. This millennial reading of history found a powerful articulation in Arthur Clarke and Stanley Kubrick's *2001: A Space Odyssey*. Critics panned the movie for its length, obscurity, and interminable pace, but it became an instant hit and long-term cultural phenomenon.[22] The opening scene takes place 4 million years ago in the African savanna, where we see an ape pack's first contact with a giant black monolith. The boldest of the pack touches the stone, and is inspired thereby to later contemplate bones and see them as potential tools/weapons, all to the thundering sounds of Richard Strauss's *Thus Spoke Zarathustra*. The ape, in exultation at his first weapon-enabled kill, throws the bone skyward and the camera follows its path. There, in the heavens, it morphs into a spaceship headed for the moon, where excavations of recent earth visitors have revealed another monolith. Thus the film joined two key eras in human evolution—our first emergence from primate apes and our current exploration of space. (The moon landing occurred the following year.) We are ready for our next step in evolution.[23]

UFO Conspiracy

Despite the beams of love that the angels in space-suits beam down, channel, and bathe their believers in, UFOlogy has its dark side, both in its imagination for evil ETs and for the conspiracies whereby they secretly work to take humanity prisoner and use us for their purposes—destruction, food, sexual experimentation and breeding, exploitation and slavery. In some cases—*War of the Worlds, Independence Day*—the aliens are merciless destroyers, technologically endowed Attilas, invading and eliminating the human race. In others, the process is slower, more insidious.

One of the most devastating films in this latter genre—*The Body Snatchers*—first came out in 1956, a film many considered a reflection on the McCarthy period in the very recent American past.[24] It conveys a peculiarly disturbing paranoia because, unlike Wells's open invasion from Mars, this happens silently, behind our backs; it is difficult to even discuss. The 1955 book ends on a bland note: the

---

[22] See the extensive essay by George DeMet, "The Search for Meaning in *2001*," with sections on its cultural impact, online: http://www.palantir.net/2001/meanings/essay00.html, April 14, 2010. DeMet points out the ferociously hostile initial reaction of film critics, especially in New York where, among others, caffeinated Pauline Kael heaped abuse on a movie she did not have the modesty to admit she might not have understood. The youthful (and often stoned) audience of the late '60s made this interminable cult film with no sex scenes the third most profitable of the year (#1 being *The Graduate*).

[23] Arthur C. Clarke explored the same theme in *Childhood's End* (New York: Ballantine Books, 1953), when spaceships came to save Earth's children by taking them off our doomed planet. Adults, that is, everyone over 13, were deemed incapable of the evolutionary leap such an odyssey demanded.

[24] The movie can actually be read either as anti-McCarthy or anti-communist. Walther Mirisch makes it clear that the creators of the movie had nothing of the kind in mind: *I Thought We Were Making Movies, not History* (Madison, WI: University of Wisconsin Press, 2008), 43-44.*

invaders inexplicably leave Earth.[25] The movie, directed by Don Siegel, came out the next year, with humankind saved only at Hollywood's insistence.[26] In Philip Kaufman's 1978 version, perhaps for the first time in Hollywood's history, the aliens won.[27] The victim awakens to his dilemma like the proverbial frog in the pot that slowly heats to boiling—too late to do anything but succumb knowingly. "You will be assimilated; resistance is futile."

But the paranoid discourse concerns not just the intentions of the aliens. It suspects everyone—from family and neighbors (who would sooner send insistent believers to asylums than listen to them), to the government, or rogue agencies within (who have entered into an unholy alliance with these malevolent ETs).[28] Themes of paranoia and madness pervade the UFO terrain: Who has encountered these awesome and intrusive creatures? What government cover-ups disguise this? How can we stop the march of this conspiracy? Indeed, anyone who believes that ETs have landed but that we do not know about them yet most likely believes that the government (primarily but not exclusively the U.S. government), has been hiding the knowledge from us, and that there is some secret conspiracy afoot that will make humanity its victims. UFOlogy has produced some of the most compelling conspiracist master narratives of our allegedly "postmodern" age.[29]

■ UFO MILLENNIALISM AND APOCALYPTIC TIME

While UFO millennialism appeals to a wide range of people, apocalyptic outbreaks of people who leave their normal life to greet the about-to-land aliens are relatively rare. The real dilemma with UFO narratives lies in passing from fiction to fact, from "compelling story" to "actually happening." For UFO enthusiasts, the day the aliens finally appear in public represents the apocalyptic moment when all will be judged—the mockers shamed, the believers justified.

And that is precisely what has *not* happened. The imminent advent of aliens anticipated vainly after World War II gave way not to the abandonment of this scenario, but to a UFOlogical post-apocalyptic jazz that postulated a conspiratorial presence of hidden aliens and the human allies. As with so many millennial phenomena, when

---

[25] On Jack Finney's book *The Body Snatchers*, see online: http://homepage.ntlworld.com/m.hodder/invasion.html;www.stayfreemagazine.prg/archives/19/bodysnatchers/html; and J. Hoberman, "Paranoia and the Pods," *Sight and Sound*, new ser. 4 (May 1994): 28–31.

[26] The original script was placed in a "framing story" in which the paranoid-seeming doctor finally convinces people outside of his small California town that the threat is real, and the movie ends with a call to government forces to stop the pods.

[27] In the 1978 version, where the star of the original, Kevin McCarthy, plays the part of the man who runs around trying desperately to tell anyone he can before being run over, the scene is San Francisco, and the ending was the complete defeat for all the earthlings.

[28] Yankelovitch poll of January 2000, in Cynthia Fox, "The Search for Extraterrestrial Life," *Life* (March 2000): 56, #2. The Roper 2002 poll has the number up over 70 percent.

[29] Michael Barkun, *A Culture of Conspiracy: Apocalyptic Visions in Contemporary America* (Berkeley and Los Angeles: University of California Press, 2003), chap. 5; see also further discussion below.

the apocalypse is delayed, new scenarios emerge that preserve the narrative, and adjust the apocalyptic one to correspond more closely with the disappointing evidence of unlanded ships, of unredeemed reality.

As a result, most UFO discourse has appeared in imaginative literature and film. And, appropriately for a narrative born of hyper-technology, UFO discourse has found a particularly resonant medium in film. Here, in certain key movies and TV series, many of the major themes get popularized in particularly powerful ways—the Rorschach of modern (and postmodern) imagination.[30] Indeed, UFO movies have articulated a millennial meditation on human aggression and the future of war that currently plays a powerful role in both popular and strategic political thinking about peace and international relations.

Cataclysmic

Most UFOlogical millennial scenarios start with hostile aliens and imagine a massive cataclysmic encounter that either destroys the earth (unredeemed/secular eschatological) or provokes a redeeming unified reaction among earthlings, inspiring us to rise above our petty differences (redeemed/secular millennial). "Shall I tell you what I find beautiful about you?" says the visiting Starman about the human race, "You are at your very best when things are worst."[31] The victory at the end of *Independence Day* inspires even Israelis and Arabs to embrace, something that found little favor in the eyes of Arab censors.[32]

Echoing concerns of deep ecologists (a fellow "New Age" apocalyptic community), many UFOlogists warn prophetically about our self-destruction. Earth is a lost cause, and no human who has not been "taken up" on a spaceship can hope to survive. Some UFO scenarios offer a Rapture wrapped up in scientist Gnosticism. For them, the spiritual realm above this indelibly corrupt earth consists of an evolutionarily superior "race" that saves a chosen few by taking them onto their ships before the remaining billions on the planet get plowed under. An atheist's "Rapture."[33] In 1956, the same year as the release of the first *Body Snatchers*, Dorothy Martin made precisely these apocalyptic promises, with a specific date for the event, to her followers. Leon Festinger took notice and, as a result of studying

---

[30] Roy Wagner, "Our Very Own Cargo Cult," 362–72.

[31] *Starman* (1984); online: http://www.imdb.com/title/tt0088172/.

[32] The movie had to undergo extensive alteration in order to be shown in the Arab world, where there was widespread objection to presenting the hero as a Jew. One editorial opined: "This film polishes and presents the Jews as a very humane people. You are releasing false images about them." Among other things, the final scene of embrace had to be removed. See Bernard Lewis, "Muslim Anti-Semitism," *Middle East Quarterly*, 5, no. 2 (1998), online: http://www.meforum.org/396/muslim-anti-semitism, March 30, 2010.

[33] For an extensive treatment of this parallel between UFO conspiracy and Gnosticism, see Carol Matthews, "The Plate in my Head is a Government Plot: Visions of the *Eschaton* in UFO Conspiracy Theories," *Journal of Millennial Studies* (1999), online: http://www.mille.org/publications/winter2000/matthews.PDF, April 14, 2010; and Barkun, *Culture of Conspiracy*.

the passage of her date, coined the term "cognitive dissonance" in *When Prophecy Fails.*[34]

Of course cataclysmic UFO scenarios have so far failed to ignite, because the aliens have yet to come and destroy. In their cognitive dissonance, UFOlogists tend toward conspiracism.[35] Aliens are infiltrating to prepare the invasion. The apocalyptic process has begun, but is not yet public.[36] Soon it will surface. In the meantime, like the malignant archons of ancient Gnostic lore whose task was to prevent souls from escaping the earthly prison, aliens have imprisoned us in "a frequency 'net' thrown around the planet."[37]

The impact of this conspiracist narrative on the larger culture should not be dismissed lightly, since it undergirds a growing literature on abductions, which, with researchers like Pulitzer Prize–winning psychiatrist John Mack at Harvard,[38] and websites galore, has rising numbers of "believers." One "scientific" observer opined as early as 1989:

> Abductions point to the rise of a technological supernaturalism in UFO reports, where the possibilities of alien science sanction wonders once possible only in magic. In abductions we also reacquaint ourselves with some old enemies. They have always been with us, these creatures lurking in the dark. Once again we are helpless as they swoop down to capture, terrify, and harm us for their own purposes. Science may have evicted ghosts and witches from our beliefs [sic],[39] but it has just as quickly filled the vacancy with aliens having the same functions. Only the extraterrestrial outer trappings are new.[40]

And these stories, with their fascinatingly terrible grand narrative of our "not being alone," feed into a much broader "paranoid style."[41]

---

[34] Festinger, *When Prophecy Fails.* Similar beliefs played a central role in the career and suicide of the Heaven's Gate cult in southern California in 1997 (see below).

[35] Festinger did not detect conspiracy narratives as a major form of cognitive dissonance, and did little with "scapegoating" in his follow-up systematic study, *A Theory of Cognitive Dissonance* (Stanford: Stanford University Press, 1957), 86.

[36] In this, it resembles the generation-long apocalyptic buffer perennially present in medieval Christian apocalyptic narratives: Antichrist is born but not yet an adult.

[37] David Icke, *And the Truth Shall Set You Free* (Frankston, Tex.: Bridge of Love Publishing Co., 1995), 39, cited in Barkun, *Culture of Conspiracy*, 105.

[38] On John Mack see, for example, "The UFO Abduction Phenomenon: What Does It Mean for the Transformation of Human Consciousness?" Online: http://www.centerchange.org/passport/92ufotran sformconsciousness.html, April 14, 2010; *Passport to the Cosmos: Human Transformation and Alien Encounters* (New York: Crown Publishers, 1999); and "Blowing the Western Mind," online: http://www.centerchange.org/passport/blowingmind.html; as well as the website dedicated to his work: http://www.centerchange.org/passport/index.html.

[39] Probably comparable numbers now believe in witches as in abductions.

[40] Thomas E. Bullard, "UFO Abduction Reports: The Supernatural Kidnap Narrative Returns in Technological Guise," *Journal of American Folklore* 102 (1989): 168; see also Barkun, *Culture of Conspiracy*, chap. 5–6, 8–9 and discussion below.

[41] Richard Hofstadter, "The Paranoid Style in American Politics," in *The Paranoid Style in American Politics and Other Essays* (Cambridge, Mass.: Harvard University Press, 1996), 3–40.

Television shows and movies like the cult classic *X-Files* (TV show from 1993–2002; movie, 1998), in which each episode explored "inexplicable phenomena," while the long-term plot drew people into a world of UFO abductions and secret dealings between shadowy inter-government agencies and space aliens determined to create a new hybrid race of beings for their own purposes, mainstreamed the grand narrative. As the series became more popular, it familiarized many with the vocabulary of UFOlogy, made it acceptable at least to toy with such beliefs.

▪ TRANSFORMATIVE UFOLOGY AND THE POLITICS OF PARANOIA

One way for the science fiction imagination to marry the cataclysmic and transformative was to place the narrative in a future beyond the looming apocalypse. Thus, one could skip the manmade war that kills several hundred million people and focus on the millennial world that lies beyond it. In *Star Trek*'s universe, the denizens of the twenty-fourth century, men and women who consider their spaceship home live on the other side of World War III in a fine world. Guided by Vulcans with their positive-sum rationality, a race-blind, multinational confederation has built a world in which "money doesn't exist…and the acquisition of wealth is no longer the driving force in our lives. We work to better ourselves and the rest of humanity."[42]

In transformative UFOlogy, the very discovery that "we are not alone" can have a dramatic impact on humankind, shifting our consciousness and dwarfing the petty rivalries and egotistical concerns that have us trapped in our self-destructive patterns.[43] Often, the ETs come as friends and our paranoia creates the hostility. Transformative UFO millennialism appeals to meliorative (Christian post-)millennialism. Here, the storyline runs, our own paranoia creates enemies; our madness brings on wars, not only with each other, but with these aliens as well. UFO tales use a superior (i.e., dramatically more mature) life form to judge humankind's culpability for its own belligerent tradition.

In *The Day the Earth Stood Still* (1951), aliens came in response to our use of nuclear weapons, to see if we represented a threat to other (more mature) life in the cosmos, and therefore, whether we deserved to live or die.[44] Produced during Cold War paranoia, in the midst of the Korean War,[45] the movie serves as a

---

[42] Captain Picard to Lily Sloane, the later twenty-first-century woman who comes aboard their Borg-infested ship in *Star Trek: First Contact* (1996).

[43] One of the more sophisticated explorations of this theme, one that looked directly at the dilemma of science and faith in these matters, is Carl Sagan's *Contact* (New York: Simon & Schuster, 1985).

[44] On the impact, both chronologically and thematically, of Hiroshima on the UFOlogical imagination, see Grünschloß, "Waiting for the 'Big Beam,'" 422–23.

[45] The Washington Bureau of the War Department (soon, the Defense Department), rejected the filmmaker's request for equipment (uniforms, jeeps, tanks). Director Robert Wise: "They didn't approve of our message of peace, I guess…" online: http://globetrotter.berkeley.edu/conversations/Wise/wise-con7.html, April 14, 2010.

cosmic-eyed view of our petty rivalries.[46] The paranoid position of the American military (without discipline or considered leadership) and the grandstanding of a jealous suitor—"I don't care about the rest of the world," he says to the object of his desire, "you'll feel different once you see my face in the papers"—threaten humanity with destruction.

In the end, the space visitor, Klaatu, leaves mankind with a sermon:

The universe is growing smaller every day and the threat of aggression by any group anywhere can no longer be tolerated. There must be security for all or no one is secure. And this does not mean giving up any freedom, except the freedom to act irresponsibly…We have an organization for the mutual protection of all planets and for the complete elimination of aggression. The test of any such higher authority is of course the police force that supports it. For our policemen, we created a race of robots. Their function is to patrol the planets in spaceships like this one and preserve the peace. In matters of aggression, we have given them absolute power over us. This power cannot be revoked. At the first sign of violence they act automatically against the aggressor. The penalty for provoking their action is too terrible to risk. The result is we live in peace. Without arms, or armies, secure in the knowledge that we are free from aggression and war. Free to pursue more profitable enterprises…It is no concern of ours how you run your own planet, but if you threaten to extend your violence, this earth of yours will be reduced to a burned-out cinder. Your choice is simple: join us and live in peace, or pursue your present course and face obliteration. We shall be waiting for your answer, the decision rests with you.

The movie's "utopian" solution operates from the millennial premise that "if only we could get rid of aggression, everything would be fine: rational, peaceful."[47] As prophetic rebuke, the movie struck home, and continues to do so.[48]

[T]his is a richly textured, smartly written parable about the human condition at its best and at its worst. What's more, it speaks to our times as clearly, today as it did when it was released at the height of the Cold War in 1951. Then as now, governments conduct business with each other while showing the emotional maturity of three-year-olds, all

---

[46] When asked to meet the president of the United States, Klaatu responds: "I don't intend to add my contribution to your childish jealousies and suspicions." "Our problems are very complex, Mr. Klaatu," responds the president's "secretary," Mr. Harley. "Don't judge us too harshly." "I can judge only by what I see," responds Klaatu coldly. "Your impatience is quite understandable," Harley replies. "I'm impatient with stupidity, our people have learned to live without it," responds Klaatu. "My people haven't, I'm very sorry, I wish it were otherwise," responds Mr. Harley. On the Cold War contribution to this movie, see Gary Bates, *Alien Intrusion* (Green Forest, Ariz.: Master Books, 2004), 41–43.

[47] For a classic spoof of this hope, see *Mars Attacks!* (1996), discussed below.

[48] Wise insists that normally movie directors should not get on a soapbox, but that this movie was the one exception, with the ET as the moralizer; online: http://globetrotter.berkeley.edu/conversations/Wise/wise-con5.html, April 14, 2010. It apparently had an effect: it so impressed the five-year-old Michael Ghiglieri that he later wrote *The Dark Side of Man: Tracing the Origins of Violence* (New York: Perseus Publishing, 1999), ix–x.

the while threatening to end the world more because of petty bickering and paranoia than any real threat that might or might not exist.[49]

And yet, this stirring call to rise above our pettiness is only matched by its astonishingly superficial understanding of the sources of and solutions to human aggression. Who, without a "modernist" confidence in "objectivity," could imagine that the wisdom necessary for just judgment about who, in any given case, is the "aggressor" can be programmed into robot policemen?[50] Or, even if the robot could reasonably detect who provoked the violence, who could believe that somehow, this ferocious "absolute" and impersonal power—a tyrannical superego if ever there were one—could put an end to human aggression? Far more likely, people would go mad with fear and with unexpressed aggression.

Ironically, particularly as a critique of "Cold War" paranoia, its "solution" imposes a scientific Leviathan of terrifying power. This solution to the problem of aggression may appeal to a schoolboy fantasizing a playground without bullies, but as a means to solve disputes among societies, it is hopelessly simplistic. And yet, its message resonates so strongly with a pacific millennialism that most enthusiasts—including the author, director, and actors—do not even notice.[51]

Thus, the enlightened moviemakers look down on the American government from the vantage of the cosmos and an imagined race of superior beings: "O Man!" intones their character: "Introspect and reconsider your hubris!" From where he stands, our paranoia appears as the sole source of our belligerence. And yet, lurking in the background of Mr. Klaatu's serene presence is his only companion, the robot, with his absolute power to throttle any signs of violence and single-"handedly" destroy planet Earth. Thus the vision strangely marries the most pacifist (if shallow) ideals with an omnipotent and tyrannical superego, a configuration that sheds important light on the early twenty-first-century peace movement.[52]

[49] Andrea Chase, review of DVD (released 1993); online: http://www.killermoviereviews.com/main.php?nextlink=display&dId=218, April 14, 2010.

[50] One of the key dimensions of "self-help" justice sees only external deeds, and ignores motivation. See discussion in Charles Radding, *A World Made by Men: Cognition and Society, 400–1200* (Chapel Hill: University of North Carolina Press, 1985), 23–30.

[51] Note the excitement Wise felt when he first read the script (interview cited above, n. 49). Compare with Richard Dreyfus's comments on *Close Encounters*, below, n. 53. These movies embrace positions that combine a liberal distaste for violence and psychologically superficial notions of how to eliminate it (see, e.g., the discussion of "cooperation and communication" in Ghiglieri, *Dark Side of Man*, chap. 8).*

[52] See Nick Cohen, *What's Left? How Liberals Lost Their Way* (London: Fourth Estate, 2007). One can understand how such a figure, with his proto-totalitarian program for "peace on earth" through a world government that has no patience for "stupidity," might fit the description of Antichrist as a liberal "bringer of world peace" that haunts the fundamentalist Christian apocalyptic imagination. See the otherwise subtle review of Mark Bourne: "1970s fire-and-brimstone bestseller Hal Lindsay wrote that Satan might land in a flying saucer proclaiming a message of world peace to steal the worship that belonged to Jesus…I mean, really—that pleasant, well-spoken Michael Rennie is *the devil*? Twaddle!" DVD reviews (2003), online: http://www.dvdjournal.com/reviews/d/daytheearthstood_fsc.shtml, April 14, 2010. And Klaatu? Hard to miss the point with more self-confidence.

Steven Spielberg was the most prominent and skillful of the film school of peaceful transformation via UFOs, and first gave voice to a new generation of transformative millennialists with *Close Encounters of the Third Kind*. Here, the alien presence is at once uncanny—it drives those it touches slightly mad—and benign. Even the government investigators, the classic UFO symbol of conspiratorial evil, behave properly under the leadership of Lacombe, a French scientist with an artist's soul (played by François Truffaut). The protagonist, Ray Neery, is an honest man, driven by a vision no one else believes in to the locale encounter: a Blakean artist pursuing his destiny willy-nilly, even at the expense of his family.

When he and others, touched by the aliens in ways that none around them can understand, appear at the sealed-off landing site, Lacombe (who, artist that he is, envies "Monsieur Neery" his UFO calling), instructs the troops to let them enter: "They have been invited," he wisely observes. Guided by Lacombe, the U.S. team enters into a musical conversation with the aliens. These beings, masters of a technology we can only wonder at, emerge childlike, and choose Ray Neery alone from all the hopeful candidates for pilgrimage to the alien world. They lead him into the promised ship, clustering around him like children around a surrogate father, open, trusting, eager for affection.

Years later, Richard Dreyfus (Neery) recalled the film's spiritual message.

> We all felt that this particular project had a noble agenda. This was a big idea that Steven was talking about. It wasn't just a sci-fi movie, it wasn't about monsters from the *id*. It was that we are not only not alone, but that we have relatively little to fear. People don't realize, or it's hard for people to remember, that *Close Encounters* was truly the first cultural iconic moment that said, "Calm down we're okay. They can be our friends." That really was a huge statement that I and lots of other people wanted to participate in.[53]

Spielberg gives us this determinedly optimistic take in his two first UFO films: uncanny but adorable childlike aliens in *Close Encounters*, one of whom would return to visit six years later in the "saccharine movie *ET*...[where] a merely alien-looking entity...at heart is just like us"[54]—or rather, like our inner child. Here the generation gap between simple and good-hearted children and insensitive, conspiratorial, and destructive adults takes up where *Childhood's End* had left off. Pop psychology UFO style—we're okay (at least we youth), they're okay—tells us the monsters in our closet are of our own imagining...all we need to do is hug them. "We have seen the enemy," said Pogo in honor of the first Earth Day, "and he is us."[55]

Some of *Close Encounters* pushes the limits of self-parody and has been deservedly spoofed. Prof. Donald Kessler (played by Pierce Brosnan) in *Mars*

---

[53] Special Features of 2001 DVD edition.

[54] Segal, "Jung on UFOs," 316.

[55] Walt Kelly, creator of the comic strip *Pogo*, first used the line "We have met the enemy and he is us" on a poster for Earth Day in 1970; online: www.igopogo.com/we_have_met.htm, April 14, 2010.

Attacks incarnates the Spielbergian position. Asked by the media-hound president (played by Jack Nicholson) what to make of these Martians, who have just vaporized the general sent to welcome them, along with troops and standers-by, the professor responds: "Logic dictates that given their extremely high level of technological development they are an advanced culture, therefore peaceful and enlightened. The human race on the other hand is an aggressively dangerous species. I suspect they have more to fear from us, than we from them." Meanwhile the Martians read a message from the president filled with vapid wishes for understanding and laugh in derision as they plan their invasion.

■ APOCALYPTIC INCIDENTS OF UFO BELIEFS

Of course, all this science fiction, like the *Left Behind* series written by Tom Lahay and Jerry Jenkins, represents fiction to ease the roosters' frustration with their interminable wait for daybreak.[56] Actual UFO apocalyptic outbreaks are rare. As much as modern communications stimulate UFOism, they also rapidly dispel any panic that aliens have "actually" landed. UFO apocalyptic believers therefore need to deploy sophisticated strategies to sustain the communities they form in their imminent expectation.

The Great Embarrassment of 1938

The most famous example of an apocalyptic outbreak of UFO panic came on October 30, 1938, when the iconoclastic director Orson Welles broadcast a performance of H. G. Wells' novel, *War of the Worlds*, on the radio. Having adapted the English novel to the New Jersey landscape outside of New York and put it in the language of news reports, the performance hit many a listener not as fiction but fact. Panic broke out in a number of areas, involving thousands of people. Even being in Grovers Mills, where the aliens had allegedly landed, did not disprove the fantasy. One local woman shrieked: "You can't imagine the horror of it! It's hell!" Some locals had shot up a water tower with their rabbit-hunting guns. The next morning, they felt like fools. The owls won again, and the bad-boy cynic who panicked the barnyard roosters laughed all the way home.[57]

The incident came in the wake of Hitler's masterful use of radio to whip his people into a nationalist and racist frenzy, whose threats of war just the month before had English schoolchildren donning gas masks. The two phenomena easily elided in brains filled with fear: "Lolly Dey was praying too, and pondering what was causing

---

[56] *Left Behind: A Novel of the Earth's Last Days* (Wheaton, IL: Tyndale Publishers, 1995); see also Melani McAlister, "Prophecy, Politics and the Popular: The 'Left Behind' Series and Christian Fundamentalism's New World Order," *South Atlantic Quarterly* 102, no. 4 (Fall 2003): 773–98.

[57] For a contemporary example, see the joke played by a Jordanian newspaper that panicked a small town of 13,000 people: "Mayor Sends in Troops after Alien April Fool Panic," *Daily Telegraph*, April 5, 2010, online: http://tinyurl.com/yddaapf, April 16, 2010.

this great catastrophe. 'I had been learning in high school about Hitler and his plans to take over the world,' she said. 'And it just made sense that maybe these Martians were Hitler's allies.'"[58] The panic was short-lived but intense, and reflected a deeply disturbed and credulous public whose often-comic reactions made it the UFO cautionary equivalent of William Miller's "Great Disappointment."

Certainly the American media—largely contemptuous of the public's credulity—did not hesitate to comment on the way in which this radio program revealed the primitive level of both the radio audience and the "pitch" of some of its programming. One editorial even opined on how the incident helped us understand the ways in which fascist governments of the day whipped their publics into a frenzy with the radio.[59] Reportedly, Welles, told in the midst of the broadcast about the hysteria he had set off, replied: "Good, they should be scared."[60] Was this his way of inoculating the public to the kind of paranoia Nazis exploited? Was he looking for the kind of mini-catastrophe that would shake humans from their petty folly?[61] Or was he merely expressing his sense of superiority over these country bumpkins? If the Nazis exploited paranoia to demonize and warmonger, progressives tried to use it, by showing its folly, to de-demonize and peace-monger.

Heaven's Gate and the Do-It-Yourself Rapture

When UFO contactees can convince enough people, quasi-religious communities can form (sects, [new religious] movements, churches). Heaven's Gate consisted of a small group of believers in the millennial worldview and apocalyptic promises of Marshall Applegate and Bonnie Lu Nettles in the mid-seventies. Applegate, a gentle and talented teacher and singer, presented both Jesus and himself as human containers into which "crew members of the Kingdom of Heaven," coming from "the "Kingdom Level Above Human" had deemed worthy to receive "soul deposits." These souls, now incarnate in human bodies (a benign form of body-snatching, if you will), represent an "away team" on Earth, in which Nettles (also known as Bo) was the admiral, and Applegate (Peep) was the captain. Their theology, explicitly Christian and profoundly Gnostic, reviled all manifestations of the flesh. Applewhite and a number of members actually had themselves castrated for the sake of Heaven's Gate.[62]

---

[58] Jon Blackwell, "1938: Space Invaders," online: http://www.capitalcentury.com/1938.html, April 14, 2010.

[59] *Baltimore Sun*, November 1, 1938, p. 10, cited in G. Joseph Wolfe, "'War of the Worlds' and the Editors," *Journalism Quarterly* 57, no.1 (1980): 41.

[60] Blackwell, "1938: Space Invaders."

[61] In *The Day the Earth Stood Still*, Prof. Barnhardt convinces Klaatu that he should scare people before he made his announcement. When the uncanny power shortage began, he asked his secretary "Tell me Hilda does all of this frighten you? Does it make you feel insecure?" "Yes sir, it certainly does," she responds. "That's good Hilda, I'm glad." Note the same function attributed to the signs over Constantinople by both Augustine and John Chrysostom (above, chapter 2).

[62] Robert Glenn Howard, "Attitudes Toward the Tragic: A Not-So-Horribly-Biased Approach to the Heaven's Gate Email Campaign," *Journal of Millennial Studies* 1 (1998), online: http://www.mille.org/publications/summer98/rghoward.pdf, April 14, 2010.

Their promise was apocalyptic and eschatological. Soon the foreordained apoc-alyptic cataclysm would come: the earth, which was never anything more than a "stepping stone" in evolution,[63] would be "spaded under," ridding it of the "human 'weeds' [that] have taken over the garden and disturbed its usefulness beyond repair." Before that cataclysm will occur, however, the true believers who had received "a deposit of recognition"

> have nothing to fear, nor will they know *DEATH*—even if they lose their human body. That continued *belief* will one day find them a member in the Level Above Human, in a physical body belonging to the true Kingdom of God—the Evolutionary Level Above Human—leaving behind this temporal and perishable world for one that is everlasting and non-corruptible.[64]

In a sense implied by Spielberg's treatment of Neery, Bo and Peep urged their fol-lowers to consider these aliens their true family. In distinction to Spielberg's opti-mistic hopes for a long-term mutually beneficial relationship between the ETs and earth, they impressed upon their followers a deep contempt for "human weeds" and an earth damaged beyond repair. Their few and devoted followers thirsted for the UFO Gnostic's solution: "Beam me up Scotty, this planet sucks."

The Heaven's Gate suicide on March 26, 1997 was a grotesquely literal applica-tion of this motto, and a parody of Christian Rapture apocalyptic, driven to wit's end by the interminable delay of the great event. It would be hard to calculate how often, in the course of their two decades of acquiring and losing disciples, Bo and Peep used the apocalyptic card. Given their active effort to rewrite and "correct" the record, and the extensive period of seventeen years when they dropped off the screen of public note, almost certainly no one could count. But the language of "last days," "last calls," and "last chances" permeate their writings.[65]

The suicide, then, represents a despair of ever seeing the promised apocalypse. When comet Hale-Bop appeared in the sky in 1997, Applegate, who may have been dying of cancer, seized upon it to make one last—and apparently desperate—promise.[66] Behind the comet a spaceship was traveling, close enough to Earth so that it could beam them up. In the agony of a disappointment at even this last gasp of hope, members could no longer bear it, and they chose *to "rapture" themselves*

---

[63] "The human kingdom was designed (created) as a *stepping stone* between the animal kingdom and the Evolutionary Kingdom Level Above Human (the *true* Kingdom of God)"; online: http://www.rickross.com/reference/heavensgate/gate_lastchance.html, April 14, 2010. Note a contempt for humanity similar to Hong's first view from heaven (but without the anger).

[64] "From Heaven's Gate Web Site: Last Chance To Advance Beyond Human," online: http://www.rickross.com/reference/heavensgate/gate_lastchance.html, March 25, 2010.

[65] See Robert W. Balch, "Waiting for the Ships: Disillusionment and the Revitalization of Faith in Bo and Peep's UFO Cult" in *Gods Have Landed*, 137–66.

[66] Note that only two years before the finale, Bo and Peep deemed suicide inappropriate and "*a turn against the Next Level when it is being offered.*" Such reversals are common once believers enter apoca-lyptic time (see next chapter on suicide terror).

in a collective suicide. Far more disciplined and far fewer than the disciples of Jim Jones, who two decades previously had led his apocalyptic sect into an orgy of hysterical omnicide that including killing the relunctant,[67] all of this group went quietly into that dark night. Were they like ancient philosophers who had "learned to die"? Or were they delirious apocalyptic believers who acted as if they were on a *Star Trek* holodeck, rather than on an earth which, in the final analysis, they thought should not exist anyway?

■ RAEL: THE NARCISSIST'S MILLENNIUM

Perhaps the single most successful UFO "religion" comes from the mission of a French rock singer and racing-car driver, Claude Vorhilon.[68] In December 1973, in the Massif Centrale, Vorhilon came in close contact with an "Eloha" from a distant planet in our galaxy.[69] The Eloha explained to Vorhilon that humans were created neither by God, nor by evolution, but by scientists (named *Elohim*) who "cooked" Adam and Eve in a laboratory, using their own genetic material, hence "in their image." Now, after Hiroshima,[70] and on the verge of being able to clone, humans needed to learn from their creators. Rael, the name the aliens gave Vorhilon, published a book called *Le livre qui dit la vérité* (The Book that Tells the Truth; 1974). French media gave it airtime, and a pubic "in the throes of a flying-saucer fever by the early 1970s," made it an instant sensation.[71]

In October of 1975, Rael was transported up to the ship where he made love with six gorgeous robots, saw his double cloned in a vat (hence he was guaranteed immortality), and learned a sensual meditation technique for telepathic communication with the ETs. Vorhilon's message to humanity: the Elohim want to come to Earth to teach us in our moment of need how, primarily through enhancing our sexual experiences, to transcend our petty foibles that threaten to destroy us. Guided by their chosen one, Rael, we should build an embassy in Jerusalem, Israel and they will land and bring us their blessings. This is a classic UFO cargo cult with

---

[67] See Rebecca Moore, "'American as Cherry Pie': People's Temple and Violence in America" in *Millennialism, Persecution and Violence: Historical Cases*, ed. Catherine Wessinger (Syracuse, N.Y.: Syracuse University Press, 2000), 121–37.

[68] Most of the following discussion is based on Susan Palmer's book, *Aliens Adored*. She argues that by numbers, Rael's movement is significantly larger than any other UFO "community."

[69] Note the strong similarities with Erich von Däniken, *Chariots of the Gods? Unsolved Mysteries of the Past* (New York: G.P. Putnam and Sons, 1970); compare von Däniken's website (online: www.daniken.com) with H. E. Legrand and Wayne E. Boese, "Chariots of the Gods and All That: Pseudo-History in the Classroom," *History Teacher* 8, no. 3 (May 1975): 359–70; for a commerical application of von Däniken, see E. A. Powell, "Theme Park of the Gods?" *Archeology* 57, no.1 (2004): 62–64, 66–67.

[70] The Raelians begin their calendar with that nuclear explosion.

[71] Palmer, *Aliens Adored*, 26. Despite its self-proclaimed Cartesianism, France has a *faible* for UFOlogy. Louis Pauwels' and Jacques Berger's *Matin des magiciens* (Morning of the Magicians) (1960), almost a decade before von Däniken, proposed a theory of the ET origins of man, R. T. Gault, "The Quixotic Dialectical Metaphysical Manifesto: *Morning of the Magicians*," online: http://www.cafes.net/ditch/motm1.htm, April 14, 2010.)

a transformative apocalyptic scenario: we earthlings must set in motion with our pre-apocalyptic project (Jerusalem embassy, free love) and the salvific kago will come, leading to a supposedly demotic, progressive millennium.[72]

Soon Rael claimed to be the "last and fastest" prophet,[73] centralizing power in a hierarchy (ironically modeled on the much-despised Catholic Church, with bishops and priests[74]), and disciplining trouble-makers and heretics. In 1979, he further escalated his claims by revealing to his followers that he was the half-brother of Jesus and Muhammad, both also sons of the Eloha, Yahwe.[75]

The "religious" movement that Vorhilon thus launched has had unusual longevity and size for a "flying-saucer cult." Most others either fade quickly, or become loosely affiliated "New Age" theosophical societies like the Unarians or the Brotherhood of the Sun/Son. Raelians claim today, over thirty years after inception, 65,000 members worldwide. The movement has garnered a great deal of media attention (which they both crave and fear).

Sexual Charisma, the Communitarian Dynamic, and Millennial Narcissism

The movement's success has as much to do with Rael's sexual charisma as it does with the millennial culture that it taps into. Vorhilon comes across as a good-humored man, full of affection—spiritual and physical. One of his earliest and enduring disciples described his first meeting with Rael: "I found him to be very natural, simple down to earth. I felt here was a man full of sensitive feelings, a simple man. He was full of love, he reminded me of Jesus and his apostles."[76] Rael is a "scintillating performer. He tells jokes, he mimes, he dances and sings to his audiences. His presence on stage is similar to a rock star's or a comedian's."[77]

All those within the movement seem to adore him, especially the beautiful women with whom he likes to surround himself. Palmer refers to his "sexual mysticism."[78] The idea of sexual freedom and the value of sensuality play a central role in Rael's teachings, in particular at the free-wheeling summer-camp Rael calls "The Garden of the Prophet."[79] There, "awakening seminars" allegedly liberate participants from

---

[72] See Palmer's analysis with similar results, using the terminology of Wessinger and Melton, *Aliens Adored*, 88–103.

[73] An allusion, among other things, to his racing-car passion which he continued to indulge, funded by the donations of his followers.

[74] On Rael's hostility to the Church and his significant following among ex-Catholics, see Palmer, *Aliens Adored*, 90–92, 114–15.

[75] Ibid., 39–40.

[76] Ibid., 39 (from 1994 interview).

[77] Ibid., 47.

[78] Ibid., 152, 20, 137.

[79] Compare "the Baby Garden" of the Halhali movement, with subsequent prostitution (above, chapter 5, n. 58).

paralyzing guilt and, through "sensual meditation" techniques he learned from the sexy space robots, achieve true bodily fulfillment.[80]

The enterprise seems lifted from the pages of Christopher Lasch's *Culture of Narcissism*:[81] Follow the joy. Sex is wonderful. (Use condoms.)[82] Attachments to individuals? Watch out. Go with the flow of your feelings. Jealousy is for the weak, a form of oppression. If things start getting uncomfortable, leave while the getting out is good.

> You will love with the person of your choice for only as long as you feel good with them. When you no longer get on well together, do not remain together because your union would become hell....[If] the being whom you used to like, no longer pleases you because you (or he) have changed...you must part from each other while keeping a good memory of your union instead of spoiling it with useless bickering which gives way to aggression.[83]

The main cathexis here is to one's own libido, one's own "bodily fulfillment,"[84] in a sense the complementary opposite of Klaatu's solution to aggression: anything that might make you angry, avoid at all costs, including the price of any real intimacy.

One sees the problem most clearly in the Raelians' attitude toward procreation. Children too vanish into the melting pot of self-fulfillment. Have them if they are your delight. If they come to make you weary...give them to the society.

> Thus if you give birth to a child you desired but after his birth you...no longer desire the child, you will be able to entrust him to society so that he may be brought up in the harmony necessary for his fulfillment....A child is a mutual fulfillment. If the child becomes a nuisance, however slightly, *he* realizes it and *his fulfillment* is affected. He should therefore be kept near you only if his presence is felt as a fulfillment...If not, he should be put in establishments that society *must* build....[85]

Far from being cruel or heartless selfishness, Rael insists, this approach works for everyone's good—that is, "'bodily fulfillment' which leads to 'the blossoming of

---

[80] See Palmer, "Women in the Raelian Movement: New Religious Experiments in Gender and Authority," in *Gods Have Landed*, 120. The Ranters might have looked like this had seventeenth-century England been more permissive, on which see Christopher Hill, *The World Turned Upside Down: Radical Ideas during the English Revolution* (New York: Penguin Books, 1991), chap. 9–10.

[81] See John Hall, *The Ways Out: Utopian Communal Groups in the Age of Babylon* (London: Routledge & Kegan Paul, 1978). On Lasch, see below, n. 92.

[82] In November of 1992, Raelians distributed ten thousand condoms to students at a Catholic high school in Montreal, Canada. The distribution, called *Operation Condom* was a response to the Montreal Catholic School Commission's decision not to install condom vending machines in the schools. Palmer, "The Raelian Movement International," in *New Religions in the New Europe*, ed. Robert Towler (Denver, Colo.: Auhus University Press, 1995), 203.

[83] Rael, *Extraterrestrials Took Me to their Planet* (Brantome: L'Edition du Message, 1977), 240; see similar quotation in Palmer, *Aliens Adored*, 137.

[84] Palmer, *Aliens Adored*, 136–37.

[85] Rael, *Extraterrestrials Took Me to their Planet*, 238; partially cited in Palmer, *Aliens Adored*, 137. Italics mine.

the mind.'"[86] Send away the child for its own good, because "he realizes [that he is a nuisance] and *his* fulfillment is affected." And who picks up the pieces? Foster homes that society *must* build.

There is here no trace of family loyalty, no encouragement to make it through the hard times as a sign of commitment. Vorhilon set the pattern himself at the outset of his prophetic career, when he cavorted with lovers in his wife's presence. She, thereby saddened, became a drag on his charisma,[87] until, according to Christine Vorhilon, one day at family dinner in front of their two children, Rael renounced his family, telling them that, in his ex-wife's words, "we meant nothing to him. From then on, only the movement would count."[88]

Palmer, after over a decade of close proximity to the group, knows of only two Raelians who have had children. "Raelians," Palmer notes dryly, "are not senti-mental regarding the joys of parenthood."[89] They tend to "put off child-bearing indefinitely…[until], as Rael puts it succinctly, 'the individual is fulfilled.'"[90] We are all grease on the wheel of each other's joy—post-contraception, Gnostic, solip-sistic, sexually promiscuous Shakers.

Rael's blueprint of a utopia offers a world set up for maximum personal self-in-dulgence. He offers a combination of Eric von Däniken and Hugh Hefner. *Playboy* magazine, recognizing a kindred soul, featured the hotter angels, in its October 2004 issue.[91] Rael's cult worships physical beauty above all else.[92] Palmer quotes Rael:

> Beauty is not the body, it is the essence. We become beautiful when we live the Raelian philosophy. All our women [note, no comment on men] try to do their best, even if they are not beautiful. Like Brigitte here [nodding toward Dr. Boisselier…[93]], she does her best to look beautiful, but she is not so young anymore. But she does her best.[94]

And despite Rael's high-minded talk about beauty *and* intelligence,[95] it is pretty clear that when given the choice, he will take (young nubile) beauty. "Exrael," one of Rael's oldest and most dedicated followers subsequently become his most vocif-

---

[86] Palmer, *Aliens Adored*, 137.

[87] According to the Raelians, Christine Vorhilon, Rael's wife, was nice enough, but "lacked fervor and evinced little utopian enthusiasm. This put a damper on Rael's charisma" (ibid., 42).

[88] According to Christine, she left Vorhilon in 1985 after a decade of loyal service because "she was tired of being humiliated by her husband's mistresses." Emmanuelle Chantepie, "Le Passé secret de Raël dévoilé par sesproches," *Dermière Heure*, January 18, 2003, p. 12; cited in Palmer, *Aliens Adored*, 42.

[89] Palmer, *Aliens Adored*, 137.

[90] Ibid.

[91] "The Rael World," *Playboy* (October 2004): 77–81.

[92] See Christopher Lasch, *Culture of Narcissism: American Life in an Age of Diminishing Expectations* (New York: Norton, 1991), chap. 8, and his "apocalyptic" preface, xii–xviii. On the heavy use of plastic surgery among Raelians, see Palmer, *Aliens Adored*, 122.

[93] Brasselier's thick make-up and glitzy attire shocked the media before whom she was supposed to play the role of "serious scientist," in the cloning affair (below, pp. 414–15); Palmer, *Aliens Adored*, 187. See photos in Palmer's book.

[94] Cited in Palmer, *Aliens Adored*, 140.

[95] Ibid., 140–45 (discussion of Rael's women).

erous critic, recalls waiting for four days and eventually never seeing Rael, while "a very pretty girl who was new—she wasn't even a Raelian"—got an instant invitation.[96] Rael's lookism seems to be completely internalized; for him the worst insult is to call someone ugly. When an older women in the movement dared to question his claim that the Elohim had sent AIDS as a punishment for people who deserved to die, he exploded in public: "She's not beautiful! Some women, when they come into the movement are not beautiful, but after a while they begin to look nice. But not her."[97] QED: Objection refuted.

■ APOCALYPTIC JAZZ AT THE APPROACH OF THE MILLENNIUM: THE "ANGELS" AND CLONE-AID

To cover this libidinal indulgence with an intellectual patina, Vorhilon chose a millennial UFOlogy. When he first appeared as a charismatic visionary, he claimed to have seen the future and found out how to realize it on earth. He could, therefore, offer an apocalyptic *identity* to his followers. He was a privileged messenger from those entities which humans in their long foolishness, took to be some "unrepresentable" God. He offered his followers both a coherent vision of the world (science and Bible), and a glorious pre-apocalyptic project that combined the premillennialism of the Protestant Zionists and the cargoism of Yali: build their embassy in Jerusalem and the Elohim will land with salvific kago. Since the Jews in Israel have been so slow in building the Third Temple, much to many Protestants' frustration,[98] and showed even less interest in an embassy for the Elohim, Vorhilon simply sought permission to build the embassy and the Elohim could do the rest when they landed.

Of course—whether Vorhilon knew it or not—none of his promises would come true. And in dealing with his disciples' disappointments, he found that sexual fulfillment offered a powerful antidote to cognitive dissonance. The high level of sexual satisfaction seems to have made it possible for Rael to get away with a relatively shallow apocalyptic jazz. One follower offers a good insight into the mix of cognitive coherence and personal/sexual fulfillment Rael offers:

> For me there is only one prophet and that is Rael. He makes too much sense. The way I have improved my life, the happiness I have now, through all the things I learned from him, I'm far more productive and far more serene with myself than seven years ago. And this is, for me, even if the whole thing is not true, if Rael was not the real prophet, he gave me so much joy in my life that it doesn't matter if it's true or not...[99]

---

[96] Ibid., 173.

[97] Ibid. A number of people left with her mate Victor Legendre, "fed up with her mistreatment."

[98] See Gershom Gorenberg, *The End of Days: Fundamentalism and the Struggle for the Temple Mount* (New York: Free Press, 2000), and below, next chapter.

[99] Palmer, *Aliens Adored*, 163 (students' notes). See almost identical sentiments from one of Rael's angels, ibid., 99.

Not that the apocalyptic promises and their failures do not count. Palmer notes that Vorhilon leaves no paper trail of failed prophecies. The oral discourse overflows with apocalyptic innuendo that no one writes down.[100] But Rael clearly feels compelled to respond in some way to their failure. Thus, documents like the one on the creation of Rael's "Order of Angels," represent key insights into the movement's ways of handling "prophecy failed."[101]

Rael's Angels: Upping the Sexual Ante

In 1998, Rael received a revelation from the Elohim about how, "although they had not yet come, they would soon."[102] In the meantime, Rael should create the "Order of the Angels," a collection of the most beautiful women believers and prepare them to welcome the Elohim in sexual delight. As long as the Elohim still tarried, these specially dedicated women should make Rael happy. The pink angels, the highest rank of the order, are—pending the arrival of the Elohim—reserved entirely for Rael.[103] "For Rael's angels," reads the official document recording the will of the Elohim, "the Elohim and their messenger come before everything else. They must be ready to sacrifice their lives for their Creators and their Prophet."[104]

These women rapidly became an end in themselves, the sexual thrill offered to those who wished to participate in the cult. An observer recounted the celebration of Rael's birthday in October 2000. There was a cabaret and the "angels" all got up and danced.

> They were gyrating their bums and grinding their hips—It was the sexiest dance I've ever seen, sort of like strippers.... Then they all sort of collapsed on the floor and pretended that they were having a lesbian orgy! Everyone was clapping from the tables—they loved it. Suddenly, Rael stood up and made a beeline for the stage. He tore past me—actually I was in his way and he shoved me rudely so I fell in a heap!...[105] He leapt

[100] Palmer has some excellent reflections of the "oral" nature of most apocalyptic promises, ibid., 99–101.

[101] "Ordre des Anges de Rael," online: http://mypage.bluewin.ch/a-z/a.i.d.e.r/anges/o/image2.htm, April 14, 2010.

[102] Note the dilemma similar to Nonquawuse in explaining the ancestors' reasons for delay.

[103] "Pink Angels must reserve their sexuality for the Elohim, but they may have sex with Rael, since he is currently the only prophet and Elohim half-breed on Earth. They may also have sex with each other." Palmer, *Aliens Adored*, 144–45.

[104] "If an assassin tried to shoot [me], an angel would lunge forward to shield [me] with her body, taking the bullet in her bosom to die in [my] stead" (journalist paraphrase of Vorhilon's words, cited in ibid., 142).

[105] Nothing stands between him and his fulfillment. Previously, the same observer had noted that his simple thanks had brought the angel who organized the event to tears: "He's so humble!" (ibid.) All this combines a narcissist's ability to charm people, with a nearly divine status among followers, so that people find his occasional "just us folks" persona so moving. To be so treated by a god! On his claims to (semi-)divinity and immortality, see above, n. 75.

up onto the stage and dived into the middle of the orgy…and everyone was screaming with laughter and clapping and cheering.[106]

Palmer compares these "angels" to sacred prostitutes,[107] although just how sacred is another matter: when angels came to Montreal, they often earned extra cash by lap dancing at the local strip clubs.[108]

The Clone-Aid Farce

Rael's resources for keeping his movement lively go beyond sex. The announcement of "cloning Eve" at the turn of the millennium illustrates nicely the ways in which Rael has learned to exploit the scientistic themes of his millennial discourse and to manipulate the media.[109] By riding a frisson of millennial excitement at the cloning of Dolly the sheep in 1997,[110] Rael and a "scientist" named Brigitte Boisselier played the media masterfully, promoting themselves as a progressive, technologically cutting-edge movement, unhampered by the pitiful scruples of people still stuck on their literal reading of the Bible.[111] Human cloning represents a substitute for a landing of the Elohim (now put comfortably off to somewhere between 2025–35, when Rael will be an old man). Any day now we will have living proof of the Raelian's superior (alien-inspired) technology. Palmer notes: "This is a moment of hushed apocalyptic expectation. This cloned baby girl, Eve, represents an epiphany in Rael's oral prophetic tradition."[112]

It is certainly a hoax. Dr. Boisselier's science is as tacky as her style. The "secret lab" at which she was pushing the limits of science, by channeling ET technology, was actually an old high school science lab in a building now given to a day care center and a senior-citizens club. The lab was minimally equipped for show purposes. Boisselier, recalled Mr. Casto, the caretaker, came a few times, stayed briefly, and left.

When the FDA arrived, they found no evidence even suggestive of human cloning. Why? We have two "narratives." On the one hand, the Raelians assure us that the brilliant doctor had slipped everything out at the last second to a secret foreign lab where another set of experimentation had been conducted synchronically. On the other hand, Mr. Casto offers a more prosaic account: "I'm in the building every day of the week, I tell you, there was nothing going on."[113]

---

[106] Ibid., 146.

[107] Ibid., 145–55.

[108] Ibid., 146–47.

[109] "The Rael Deal," *Religion in the News* 4, no. 2 (2001); this piece got Palmer in trouble with Rael (*Aliens Adored*, 7–12). Apparently, it matters to Rael that outsiders believe him.

[110] Rael entered the cloning circus a month after Dolly's announcement; Palmer, *Aliens Adored*, 180.

[111] For an analysis of the episode, see ibid., 177–94.

[112] Ibid., 193.

[113] Ibid., 185; for the latest developments in Clone-aid, see the Raelian website, online: http://www.clonaid.com/news.php. Nothing appears since 2004.

Rael's own comments indicate he played both sides against the middle: "If it's not true," he commented on Dr. Boisselier's claims, "she's also making history with one of the biggest hoaxes in history, so in both ways it's wonderful. Because thanks to what she is doing now, the whole world knows about the Raelian movement. I'm happy with that…This event saved me twenty years of work."[114]

So Rael may well just be a naked emperor laughing at us for even wondering if he is naked, a twenty-first-century avatar of Ken Kesey and his Merry Pranksters.[115] As one elated guide told Susan Palmer in early 2003: "We're having so much fun right now. We are out there doing our missionary work, and when pretty girls stop on the street to talk to us, I lean forward and say, "Can I have one of your hairs, please?" holding out tweezers and a plastic bag. They freak out and run away. They think we can clone them on the spot!" Comments Palmer, "We all burst out laughing."[116]

And like the Merry Pranksters, these Raelians may well be holding up a mirror that shows us a parody of ourselves and "our unquestioning acceptance of global development, our anthropocentric urge to control and obliterate nature, our daily accumulation of fresh data via the media and the Web, our dizzying production of ever-new technologies…the universal, if unconscious, reign of the scientific zeitgeist."[117] Along these lines, Palmer suggests we read Rael as a "deliberate parody of a predominant faith of our age—'the religion of technology'…a strategy…similar to Jonathan Swift's in 'A Modest Proposal.'"[118] She notes: "What does become apparent is that Rael is taking the mickey out of his disapproving audience."[119] What Lindstrom would have us do with cargo cults, she would have us do with Rael.

But when all is said and done, however many of "us" believe in this technological millennium Palmer identifies as our *Zeitgeist*, it is the Raelians and other scientistic fundamentalists, believers in the millennial subculture of UFOlogy, whom Rael parodies. Raelians seem less "postmodern" (Palmer[120]), than neo-modern, with the same faith in science and technology that Marx had, expressed both in their millennial historiography—rereading the Bible as a ship's log of ET experimentation—and their unquestioning faith in the power of technology to solve all our woes. The parody here targets the narcissistic culture at which Lasch lashed out, where parents have no time for the children and children learn to feel entitled to everything but intimacy.

---

[114] Bates, *Alien Intrusion*, 15.

[115] See Tom Wolfe, *Electric Kool-Aid Acid Test* (New York: Bantam Books, 1999), 99–103 (on the pranksters and their mirror).

[116] Palmer, *Aliens Adored*, 192. Presumably the "we all," includes our sociologist.

[117] Ibid., 203.

[118] Ibid., 202; David Noble, *The Religion of Technology: The Divinity of Man and the Spirit of Invention* (New York: Alfred A. Knopf, 1998), chap. 10.

[119] Palmer, *Aliens Adored*, 202.

[120] Ibid., 201.

Assessing the Raelians: Dangerous? Or Harmless Fun?

Are Raelians dangerous? Might they self-destruct like Heaven's Gate, or the Order of the Solar Temple?[121] Or are they "just" harmless hedonists? Palmer seems confident that they are nothing like the suicidal UFO groups. They do not have narratives, mythical or apocalyptic, about demon forces; they do not have the vindictive tendencies that lead so many groups to revel in imagining all we human failures, incapable of seeing with their cosmic eye, getting "spaded under." They are "refreshingly upbeat, optimistic…secular humanists…[with a] message [that] is a call for the faithful to have faith in the inherent goodness and common sense [*sic*!] of the ordinary human being…[taking the Elohim] as our role model.…We too can make intelligent, rational choices that will overturn our urge to self-destruct and the paralyzing fatalism of nuclear theology.[122] This sounds strangely like Klaatu's speech at the end of *The Day the Earth Stood Still*, urged upon us with a sexual carrot rather than a robot's stick.

It seems a bit strange to read Rael's discourse as a Swiftian satire, in which his artistic life as a religious genius adds up to a "Modest Proposal." Swift did not dedicate his life to drawing in tens of thousands of true believers around his proposal that we cannibalize the dead Irish babies from the famine. If we want to read Rael as parody, it might be more appropriate to imagine John Stewart reading from Rael's "utopian" prescriptions for human relations, replete with grimaces of disbelief. As for the line between grotesque credulity and ironic sophistication, it should not be drawn between Rael and "we" outsiders, but between Rael and his followers with their scientistic religion who (mis)take "having a good time" for deep personal growth.

Rael displays the characteristics of megalomania. His "revelations" conveniently give him permission to indulge his sexual appetites. And he "sells" this alpha-male sexual monopoly to his audience with his claims to a divine status, which include immortality,[123] and which make grown women weep.[124] He bristles at criticism, especially within a community he controls, by humiliating and arbitrarily expelling anyone who challenges his judgment. He seems like a Hong Xiuquan lite: As Jesus' half-brother, *his* divine erotic delight bathes the entire community with its salvific joy.[125] But Rael neither demands sexual abstinence from his followers, nor engages in mass murder.

The issue, however, is more complex when viewed from the perspective of apocalyptic dynamics. UFOlogy represents a significant part of a much larger millennial stew that, like Vorhilon, started cooking in the '70s, during the "Big

---

[121] On Heaven's Gate, see above, pp. 406–08; on the Order of the Solar Temple, see Jean-François Mayer, *Les mythes du Temple solaire* (Geneva: Georg, 1996).

[122] Palmer, *Aliens Adored*, 157–60, 202.

[123] Ibid., 49.

[124] See comments at his birthday celebration in 2000, ibid., 146.

[125] Palmer has interesting remarks on the parallels with other millennial figures, ibid., 147–55.

Chill."[126] This larger "New Age" stew consists of a wide range of spiritual and (occasionally) political movements with Gnostic elements (theosophy and its branches, Wiccanism, neo-paganism, native spiritualities[127]), mythology (sci-fi or fantasy history), environmental concerns, and conspiracism, and, at the approach of the New Age apocalyptic date of 2012, finds semiotic proof in "crop circles."[128]

This subculture operates in a world greased by a postmodern license to erase the boundaries between "fact" and "fiction," between science fiction and religious faith.[129] And this then doubles back on us in the postmodern epistemological crisis, where we dare not judge another's narrative even if we reject it personally. Notes Palmer, "as a non-Raelian who does not 'believe' in the message, I have to admit that sometimes what he says *sounds* crazy, but what is truth, after all? What is reality? I approach Rael rather as a creative artist, as a religious genius."[130] Can we not—and should we not—distinguish between a Rael and a Blake? Should postmodern affirmative action grant laurels of genius to whoever can "play" many people? This dilemma appears most clearly in a discussion of UFOs and conspiracy discourse.

■ UFO MILLENNIALISM IN THE TWENTY-FIRST CENTURY: THE DANGERS OF CONSPIRACISM

The end of the twentieth century saw the intersection of UFO culture and conspiracism teeming at the margins, but not quite breaching into the public sphere. This may play out quite differently not in twenty-first century galactic space, but cyberspace. Cyberspace, like printing, represents a revolutionary innovation in communication. Whereas in the sixteenth century, the printing press played out its effects in Europe, primarily in northern Europe, among a burgeoning bourgeoisie of (often self-) educated commoners, cyberspace has in two decades permeated far more deeply and widely, not only into Western society, but throughout the world. We can, therefore, expect the Internet to contribute significantly to the shaping of religious, political, social, and cultural change in the twenty-first-century global community.

Cyberspace offers ideal conditions for spreading conspiracy narratives. A limited audience constrained earlier conspiracy theories. Deprived of access to public space as *proscribed knowledge*, conspiracies before the Internet tended to

---

[126] *The Big Chill*, dir. Lawrence Kasdan (1983). The title refers to the period after the openly millennial '60s faded. On the millennial '60s, see Mendel, *Vision and Violence*, 223–63.

[127] Siân Lee Reid and Shelly T'Sivia Rabinovitch, "Witches, Wiccans and Neo-Pagans: A Review of Current Academic Treatment of Neo-Paganism," *Oxford Handbook of New Religious Movements*, 514–33.

[128] "2012 Prophecy Revealed in Crop Circle," online: http://www.cropcircles.cc/2012-prophecy-revealed-in-crop-circle.html, March 25, 2010. With their insatiable desire for publicity, the Raelians also dabble in New Age politics.*

[129] On "stigmatized knowledge," see Barkun, *Culture of Conspiracy*, 26–29; see also Robert Goldberg, *Enemies Within: The Culture of Conspiracy in Modern America* (New Haven, Conn.: Yale University Press, 2001).

[130] Palmer, *Aliens Adored*, 49.

remain local. Now they can gather a momentum previously unattainable. "The internet is like a Petri dish in which memes multiply rapidly."[131]

In the culture of the 1990s, as the Internet went from the passion of computer geeks to the playground of most American households, the culture of conspiracism blossomed, indeed, began to go mainstream. This was not only because of the Internet, of course. Television and movies played to a popular culture whose appetite for conspiracies goes back to the very beginnings of American political culture, and which, since the Kennedy assassination, have become part of a strong counter-culture. Television shows like the *X-Files* and pseudo-documentary films like Oliver Stone's *JFK* (1991) impregnated the public with memes of conspiracy theories, sugar-coated in celluloid.

But behind the growing public interest in a good conspiracy yarn lay a whole range of people who, surfing cyberspace, linked up with other conspiracists, synthesizing a wide range of political and mythical conspiracies into sweeping mega-conspiracies that include the *Protocols of the Elders of Zion*, subterranean reptilian races, malevolent ETs, government organizations (Men in Black, FEMA) with their secret concentration camps, and international organizations like the Tri-Lateral Commission and the Bilderberg Group. Appropriately, as a projection screen, UFOs serve to relocate older apocalyptic struggles: Milton William Cooper, one of the most influential of UFO conspiracists, who concluded his best-selling book *A Pale Horse* with a full text of the *Protocols*, divides the space aliens into various races, one of which is dwarfish, grey, with large noses, and then the "Nordic types, tall blond Aryans." If in 1800, the conspirators were Masons, and in 1900, Jews, then in 2000, they are, among others, aliens (or alien Jews).

These theories come from the far right—Jim Keith and the Patriot movement— and the far left—David Icke, once the "Tony Blair of the Greens."[132] Take, for example, the central thesis of David Icke's third book in his foray into UFOlogy, *The Biggest Secret*:

> The extraterrestrials come from the constellation Dracco. They are reptilians who walk erect and may appear "humanoid" on casual inspection [shades of body snatchers!]. They live not only on the planets from which they came but under the earth itself, in a hidden world of caverns and tunnels. They may be, wrote Icke, both "native" reptilians and "outer space" reptilians on earth at the same time. They control the Global Elite and Brotherhood by a combination of methods. They have crossbred with human beings, creating creatures that look human but are inwardly reptilian. These "hybrids" are possessed' by their "full-blood" reptilian masters. The hybrid "bloodlines" continually interbreed, moreover, so

---

[131] Richard Thieme, "How to Build a UFO...Story," *Internet Underground* 1 (November 1996): 38; online: http://underground-online.troybrophy.com/iu/archive/issue12/ufo/, April 14, 2010; cited in Goldberg, *Enemies Within*, 238. See R. Landes, "Jews as Contested Ground in Post-Modern Conspiracy Theory, *Jewish Political Studies Review* 19, no. 3–4 (2007).

[132] Barkun, *Culture of Conspiracy*, chap 6.

that the Brotherhood is not simply nonhuman but is also the product of intentionally manipulated unions.[133]

All this is grafted onto a huge array of smaller conspiracies, each nesting in the other like Russian dolls and accommodating everything but the kitchen sink. These things seem fantastical to the reader of scholarly work. The endless collection seems the product of someone who has imbibed any and every plot, no matter how unlikely—indeed, the more unlikely, the more probable. Is Icke a dualist? Definitely. Gnostic? Probably. Apocalyptic? If he can convince enough people.

This stuff may seem harmless, but paranoia, along with its demonizing discourse is a deeply destructive force. When mild paranoia holds hegemony, you get prime-divider societies, enforcing their dominating imperative and proliferating their zero-sum games. When acute paranoia takes over, we get totalitarian regimes, unlimited wars, and genocidal drives. As funny as it may seem, it is not.[134] The point is not whether this is still marginal or not? When it goes mainstream, it is already too late. The point is what routes is it likely to travel along, and what do we do to protect ourselves from it?

The Intellectual and Emotional Appeal of Conspiracy Thinking

In order to understand how conspiracism can go mainstream, one must consider not only its pathways (the Internet), but also what makes these stories so appealing. Conspiracy theories have their poetry, both intellectual and emotional. Intellectually, they offer the immensely satisfying ability to point to widely disparate and seemingly incomprehensible anomalies and tie them together in compelling ways. Big conspiracies, in the works for centuries, become rousing historical yarns, as in the *Da Vinci Code*.[135]

The relationship between conspiracism and apocalyptic is particularly important in understanding its role in UFO movements. Conspiracy, because it is hidden until it is too late, serves as an ideal means to keep the apocalyptic pot at a slow simmer, ready to turn into a rolling boil, a perfect answer to the cognitive dissonance of the ETs' delayed arrival. Thus, in the space between prophecy and fulfillment, the ETs have already landed, but not yet revealed themselves.[136]

At an emotional level, conspiracy thinking projects evil intentions onto the "other." *We* are the good guys—well intentioned, innocent victims, who need to protect ourselves from outside aggression. *They* are the bad guys—malevolent,

---

[133] Summary, ibid., 103.

[134] Analysis by Chip Berlet in *The Public Eye*, online: http://www.publiceye.org/Icke/IckeBackgrounder.htm, April 14, 2010.

[135] Dan Brown, *The Da Vinci Code* (New York: Doubleday, 2003); the book's popularity has led to several critical "commentaries" such as Bart D. Ehrman, *Truth and Fiction in the Da Vinci Code: A Historian Reveals What We really Know about Jesus, Mary Magdalene and Constantine* (Oxford: Oxford University Press, 2004).

[136] Note the parallel with cargo cults: the cargo has already arrived, just gone to the wrong person.

ruthless, and will stop at nothing to get absolute power at the expense of the rest of the world. The logic attributed to the conspirators in these theories is uniformly inhuman—no crime against humans (and humanity) is beyond them. And, as we saw with the Nazis, such projections often come from people who want to do what they pretend to denounce. The readiness of people to adopt conspiracy theories, then, should alert us to a problem.[137]

By projecting evil, believers in conspiracies wash themselves of guilt and responsibility, hence the absence of self-criticism in such thinking. In a sense, by accepting the conspiratorial nature of the enemy, believers can free themselves from any need to introspect. Responsibility for the problem lies over there, with the evil "other." Ultimately, conspiracy theories are radical forms of dualism that turn morality into a weapon. As such ideas go mainstream, people increasingly see their opponents as ruthless and mendacious, eliminating rapprochement or dialogue as an option. A conspiracy is a narrative that justifies lashing out at the conspirators. Almost all forms of violent apocalyptic beliefs involve conspiracism, accompanied by high levels of paranoia.

We learned all this from World War II and Nazi and Communist paranoid madness, and supposedly our culture had developed immunities to conspiracism's siren song. In the early twenty-first century, however, the Internet has enabled the rapid spread of a cluster of the most elaborate and portentous conspiracy theories in the history of the genre: 9-11 "Truthers."[138] The remarkable success of this conspiracy theory shows just how vulnerable to conspiracy Westerners actually are.

And yet, 9-11 conspiracism differs from earlier forms in a significant way: unlike most earlier forms that demonized an external enemy for the sake of internal unity, this brand demonizes an inside force (the U.S. government and all those thousands involved in the cover-up) while insisting that the outside forces (e.g., global jihad) are of no significance.[139] Given the serious potential consequences of such thinking, we should not take these matters lightly. We shall return to this topic after examining one more apocalyptic millennial movement, now in its early stages, but potentially the greatest in the history of this bizarre phenomenon: global jihad.

---

[137] This of course does not mean that there are no malevolent people, or conspiracies with which we might legitimately concern ourselves. It is the *readiness* of some people to believe that others are plotting mercilessly that we need to consider. Nor does it mean all who believe in these theories are potential cold-blooded mega-murderers. It does mean that this venue will attract, among its many acolytes, those capable of such deeds.*

[138] See their own website: "9-11 Truth Movement," online: http://www.911truth.org/, March 28, 2010; and the response: "Debunking 9-11 Conspiracy Theories," online: http://www.debunking911.com/, March 28, 2010. Nor are these theories only the domain of marginal figures; for example, consider Richard Falk, Professor Emeritus of International Law at Princeton and UN Special Rapporteur: see discussion at Wikipedia with references, online: http://en.wikipedia.org/wiki/Richard_A._Falk#9.2F11_and_the_Bush_administration, March 28, 2010.

[139] E.g., Marc Sills, "The 'War on Terror' as a Political Invention," *Helium*, online: http://www.helium.com/items/557,682-the-war-on-terror-as-a-political-invention, April 14, 2010.

14 Enraged Millennialism

Global Jihad (1400–1500 AH / 1979–2076 CE)

> "My coming and that of the hour are concomitant,
> indeed the hour might have come before me."
> "My coming and the hour are separated the one from the other,
> as my thumb and my index finger."
>
> —Hadiths according to Makrizi, 19.[1]

At the approach of the year 2000, a large number of apocalyptic prophecies appeared in Muslim publications, largely in pamphlets and audio tapes, from writers and preachers who were not from the official mainstream and who broke with traditional forms of apocalyptic writing. Using a number of techniques picked up from Christian literature, these marginal writings, of which most Muslims in the world—and the vast majority of the non-Muslim world—were ignorant, articulated a formidable apocalyptic scenario.[2]

This new literature represented an innovation in Muslim apocalyptic in several ways, in both form and content, medium and message. First, it discarded the conventional mold of Islamic apocalyptic writing, which limited the writer's creativity to the selection and ordering of previous apocalyptic passages (mostly hadiths). Second, far more than earlier literature (but perhaps not earlier preaching), these books and pamphlets elaborated extensively on various apocalyptic themes, including detailed accounts of the war between the Dajjal (antichrist) and the Mahdi, of Islam's victories, and even discussion of what would come after Islam's world conquest and what a Muslim millennium would look like.

In order to do so, these writers drew from Western apocalyptic traditions, interpreting biblical texts in detail—a shocking novelty.[3] Drawing on Protestant millennialism in particular, the new writings began to mutate, to incorporate new apocalyptic literature, both religious (Bible) and secular (UFO and Nostradamus), even "New Age" (Jean Dixon and Edgar Cayce), and embellish traditions with new narratives. They borrowed not only the messages, but the medium—apocalyptic

---

[1] Paul Casanova, *Mohammed et la fin du monde: étude critique sur l'Islam primitive* (Paris: P. Geuthner, 1911), 17–18.

[2] David Cook has best researched this extraordinary development, which is only now becoming part of a larger academic discussion: David Cook, *Contemporary Muslim Apocalyptic Literature* (Syracuse: Syracuse University Press, 2005); see also Timothy Furnish, *Holiest Wars: Islamic Mahdis, Their Jihads, and Osama bin Laden* (Westport, Conn.: Praeger, 2005).

[3] See the extended interpretations of the Christian favorite, the book of Revelation, in Cook, *Contemporary Muslim Apocalyptic*, 37–44.

tropes and marketing strategies. These pamphlets resembled the output of Christian missionaries far more than it did other Islamic publications, both in cover-art and in layout. They used modern techniques of mass communication including pamphlets, audiocassettes, videos, and with the advent of the Internet, websites to propagate their messages.[4] To use an American idiom, this was a form of apocalyptic hip-hop: restless, radical, open to foreign influences. Moreover, this improvisation served a critically important goal: to read current global traumas to Islam as the signs of the coming endtime.

Among the more popular borrowings from Christian apocalyptic discourse was the trope of the *Year 2000* as a key date.[5] Islam, like Christianity and Judaism, has had a long tradition of apocalyptic calculators, whom the tradition calls "the exact people."[6] And now, at the approach of the second Christian millennium, some Muslims writers embraced its apocalyptic significance.

For most of these authors, the "Lesser [preliminary] Signs of the Hour"—all seventy-nine of them drawn from the hadiths and some added from novel Western sources like the book of Revelation and Nostradamus—had already been fulfilled.[7] The West, with its atheism, licentiousness, and arrogant technological superiority, had corrupted the entire world. Women had broken all bounds of decency. Wars (especially the first Gulf War), earthquakes, plagues, and disasters were raining down upon mankind. "Houses of demons" (in one version, cars, which give women independence) have appeared and spread the world over. The power of the West (Crusader states) has scattered and fragmented the Muslim world. The forces of the Dajjal/Antichrist (especially Israel) had reached unprecedented strength, and joined forces with the United States, the modern incarnation of Muhammad's early enemy, the 'Ad.[8] The consensus: soon, very soon, indeed, in the year 2000 CE, the final events would unravel: the "Earthquake of the Hour" would destroy the United States and the apocalyptic battle would obliterate Israel.

The choice of 2000 illustrates extensively how this Muslim apocalyptic discourse arose in response to Christian apocalyptic calculations.[9] In particular, these publications developed a theme of great contemporary concern: the Jews and the Christians had joined together in messianic project to rebuild the Temple on *Haram al Sharif* (the Noble Sanctuary, a.k.a., the Temple Mount)—perhaps the

[4] See Cook, *Contemporary Muslim Apocalyptic*; on the Internet, see Gabriel Weimann, *Terror on the Internet: The New Arena, the New Challenges* (Washington, D.C.: United States Institute of Peace Press, 2006); and Mark Sageman, *Leaderless Jihad: Terror Networks in the Twenty-First Century* (Philadelphia: University of Pennsylvania Press, 2008), 109–25.

[5] Cook, *Contemporary Muslim Apocalyptic*, 84–97; Furnish, *Holiest Wars*.

[6] David Cook, "Muslim Fears of the Year 2000," *Middle East Quarterly* 5, no. 2 (1998), online: http://www.meforum.org/article/397, April 14, 2010.

[7] Cook, *Contemporary Muslim Apocalyptic*, 49–58.

[8] Ibid., 150–70.

[9] See Cook, "Muslim Fears"; for the role the year 2000 played in the West, see Charles B. Strozier and Michael Flynn, eds., *The Year 2000: Essays on the End* (New York: New York University Press, 1997); Martyn Percy, ed., *Calling Time: Religion and Change at the Turn of the Millennium* (Sheffield: Sheffield Academic Press, 2000).

single most contested piece of apocalyptic real estate on the planet.[10] *One person's messiah is another's antichrist*—this "Judeo-Christian" messianic project registered on Muslim screens as the behavior of the Antichrist, or, as Muslims call this apocalyptic figure of ultimate evil, the Dajjal.

In a larger sense, this new Muslim apocalypticism reflects the intensity of globalization in the final decades of the twentieth century, with the ever-more-rapid diffusion *and penetration* of Western culture. On the one hand, such responses should not surprise us: "nativist" millennial responses to the global incursions of modernity have happened perhaps since the dawn of imperialism, and certainly throughout the nineteenth century—the Xhosa Cattle-Slaying, the Cargo Cults, the Taiping. But this particular version of apocalyptic reaction to modernity came in the final decades of the twentieth century, when globalization had reached an intensity, penetration, and extension greater than all previous processes, and when means of communication had transformed the playing field.

This apocalyptic response to the approach of the year 2000 was not, of course, limited to Islam. No one escaped the impact of hyper-modernity, and apocalyptic responses were common both in the West and in other cultures. Indeed, one might argue, the wave of optimism and generosity that moved a number of Western movements for global peace—including the Oslo Peace Process and the Third World Debt Amnesty Appeal—represented a kind of "soft" demotic millennialism.[11] From the Muslim point of view, however, their vision of globalization was diametrically opposed and absolutely zero sum. Everything Western—useful technology aside—was subversive, evil, to be eradicated.[12] *Occidens delenda est.*

This new apocalypticism was, accordingly, remorselessly cataclysmic and paranoid. The forces of evil that conspired against God's chosen were everywhere, and everywhere evil. Muslim apocalyptic writings embraced any and every conspiracy theory, every fevered dread of annihilation, every envy-ridden and rage-soaked hatred that millennial visions can, at their worst, produce. The enemy, these writers assumed, and assumed their audience would agree, was cosmically evil, inhuman, diabolical. They plot the castration and humiliation of the Muslims, their massacre and enslavement—their very extinction. Nothing was too base or too evil for this enemy—human sacrifice, demonic plots, genocide.

During its first decade, however, this material remained largely at the margins of the Islamic public sphere. American Muslims professed utter bewilderment when told of these apocalyptic traditions, which had apparently played no role in their American Muslim upbringing. When major figures even deigned to address

[10] Gershon Gorenberg, *The End of Days: Fundamentalism and the Struggle for the Temple Mount* (New York: Free Press, 2000); Dore Gold, *The Fight for Jerusalem: Radical Islam, the West and the Future of the Holy City* (Washington, D.C.: Regnery Publishers, 2007).

[11] See Appendix at website.

[12] On the correlate to Saïd's "Orientalism," we find the phenomenon of "Occidentalism," in which perceptions of the West are shaped far less by scholarship and far more by fantasy than is the case with Orientalism. On Islam and Occidentalism, see Ian Buruma and Avishai Margalit, *Occidentalism: The West in the Eyes of Its Enemies* (London: Penguin Group, 2005), 103–39.

the issue, they dismissed these roosters as raving, uneducated, self-taught men. Most people, Muslims and non-Muslims alike, did not take it seriously.

Understandably so. Apocalyptic warrior narratives are the very stuff of religious wars and theocracy (e.g., Afganistan, 1989–2001). They therefore do not sit well in either authoritarian societies ruled by paralyzing elites or in civil polities. These men's teachings circulated in tapes and pamphlets. They did not preach from the pulpits of great mosques to numerous people, nor have their sermons broadcast on TV.

And yet, the passage of their eschatological date—2000—even as it failed to bring on the apocalypse they predicted, marked the moment when this marginal discourse stepped into the public sphere. And, as rarely happens in apocalyptic history, they took hold at the center of a major religious culture. With the help of new information technologies, they reached many, often different, political entities. The beginning of the twenty-first century marks the stunning advances of an Islamic apocalyptic millennial movement, global jihad.

■ THE APOCALYPTIC ORIGINS OF ISLAMIC MILLENNIALISM

In order to understand how this apocalyptic could "take" in the early twenty-first century CE (early fifteenth century AH), it helps to know something about the apocalyptic dynamic imbedded in Islam, the original thrust of expectation and disappointment that both marked Muhammad's own career and set the pattern for so many subsequent such expressions.[13] The following briefly outlines key aspects of Islam's apocalyptic genealogy. It differs substantially from most scholars in the field who, if they mention Muhammad's initial apocalyptic beliefs at all, do so in passing, and do not return to the subject.[14]

Indeed, of all the monotheistic traditions steeped in millennial and apocalyptic traditions, and despite some excellent early studies that identified the issues quite lucidly,[15] Islam has had the least amount of scholarly attention paid to its apocalyptic origins.[16]

---

[13] For a more extended discussion of the next section with more citations and references, see appendix at website.

[14] The *New Encyclopedia of Islam*, ed. Cyril Glassé (New York: Rowman & Littlefield, 2008), has minimal references to apocalypticism, none to millennialism/chiliasm. The entry on al-Mahdi and Eschatology both focus on doctrine, not on historical movements.

[15] Casanova, *Mohammed et la fin du monde*.

[16] The major exceptions to this generalization that I know (in addition to Casanova, above n. 1) are Patricia Crone and Michael Cook, *Hagarism: The Making of the Islamic World* (Cambridge: Cambridge University Press, 1977); David Cook, *Studies in Muslim Apocalyptic* (Princeton, N.J.: Darwin Press, 2002); Suliman Bashear, "Muslim Apocalypses," *Israel Oriental Studies* 13 (1993): 75–99; and Said Amir Arjomand, "Messianism, Millennialism and Revolution in Early Islamic History," in *Imagining the End: Visions of Apocalypse from the Ancient Middle East to Modern America*, ed. Abbas Amanat and Magnus T. Bernhardsson (London: I.B. Tauris, 2002), 106–25; Furnish, *Holiest Wars*; Hayrettin Yücesoy, *Messianic Beliefs and Imperial Politics in Medieval Islam: The 'Abbāsid Caliphate in the Early Ninth Century* (Columbia SC: University of South Carolina Press, 2009); Fred Donner, *Muhammad and the Believers: at the origins of Islam* (Cambridge Mass: Harvard University Press, 2010); Jean-Pierre Filiu, *Apocalypse in Islam* (Berkeley and Los Angeles: University of California Press, 2011).

This predominance of vesperian scholars in the field, reflects at once the standard tendencies of most historiography,[17] sharpened by the hostility of the faithful to this kind of narrative, and a corresponding political sensitivity to not bruising Muslims' self-esteem. For if the "mistaken" apocalyptic Jesus remains an unwelcome presence in New Testament scholarship,[18] so much the more do Muslim scholars find such approaches to Muhammad unacceptable.

This has resulted in a field where few works consider apocalyptic dynamics. Thus, the most recent major reference work on the Qur'an contains no entry examining the layers of apocalyptic discourse that weave through its suras.[19] To most scholars, any "chiliasm," "millenarianism," or "messianism," represents a later import, a graft onto the tradition, largely among the Shiites. Sunnis, the scholars assure us, are largely without a messianic tradition.[20] In a sense, scholarship on apocalyptic Islam is about where the historiography of the "historical Jesus" (i.e., the mistaken apocalyptic prophet) was before Schweitzer a century ago.

By the definitions of this book, however, Islam presents us with a particularly interesting case of an apocalyptic *eschatological* episode that, because of its earthly success, became a millennial movement. In this particular case, prophecy's failure acted as a trip-switch from passive to active apocalyptic: Muhammad and the faithful shifted from *waiting* for Allah's punishment of the unrepentant, to *taking* on themselves the task of *executing* Allah's punishment on sinners and scoffers.

This shift, carried out with great military success, generated an apocalyptic war against the enemies of God—jihad—which brought Muhammad temporal power (Medina) and shifted many of the overt concerns of the community from their (frustrated, passive) apocalyptic origins toward the details of the theocratic rule they established wherever they took power. Thus, scholars of the early movement can reasonably focus on the role of creating *Dar al Islam*, a society governed by divine law (Sharia), rather than the more embarrassing details of the initial, clearly mistaken message of imminent Judgment.

In the following remarks, I want to emphasize three elements of this apocalyptic dynamic that bear directly on the rebirth of apocalyptic jihad in the

---

[17] See above, chapter 3.

[18] Paula Fredriksen, "What You See Is What You Get," *Theology Today* 52, no. 1 (1995): 75; see, for example, the effort of Stephen Patterson in the same volume to declare the "apocalyptic Jesus" a discarded paradigm: "The End of Apocalypse: Rethinking the Eschatological Jesus," 29–48.

[19] Andrew Rippen, ed., *The Blackwell Companion to the Qur'an* (Oxford: Wiley-Blackwell, 2006) has 576 pages and 32 chapters. The only chapter that deals substantively with apocalyptic issues concerns later interpretations of the Qur'anic text (Twelver Shiites), rather than the apocalyptic contents of the text.

[20] Ignaz Goldziher wrote at the end of the nineteenth century, "It is in the Imamite form of Shi'ism that we ought to study Islamic messianism, because only this school of Shi'ism continued to cherish chiliastic hope," cited in Cook, *Studies in Muslim Apocalyptic*, 30–31. Goldziher's perspective remains the scholarly consensus; see, for example, Douglas Crow, "Islamic Messianism," *Encyclopedia of Religions* (New York: Macmillan, 2005).

twenty-first century: (1) the demotic elements of the initial message; (2) the shame and aggression (military jihad) that emerged from the failure of apocalyptic expectation; and (3) the millennial movement that resulted from the exceptional success of that jihad.

Demotic Ethics and Apocalyptic Islam

Virtually everyone—scholar and Muslim alike—agrees: Muhammad announced the imminent resurrection of the dead (al-Qiyāma) and the Day of Judgment (Yawm al-Hisāb, Yawm al-din). And like most apocalyptic prophets, Muhammad began with no coercive authority. His only strength lay in his rhetorical power to move people's souls. He came to warn and his apocalyptic scenario was, in the terms of this book, passive cataclysmic.[21] Those who hear and believe can only prepare by repentance and good deeds. They cannot bring on the inexorable Judgment Day; they can neither judge, nor execute judgment.

As for the good deeds, they involve justice toward the oppressed and unfortunate. They reject selfish behavior; they call for atonement and repentance; they appeal to *voluntary* conviction and transformation through belief accepted wholeheartedly. Here an early sura links lack of faith—whether scoffing or hypocrisy—about the coming Judgment to those hard-hearted attitudes that offend man and God:

> Do you see him who calls the reckoning [i.e., Judgment Day] a lie
> He is the one who casts the orphan away
> Who fails to urge the feeding of one in need....
> [and] hold back the small kindness. (107, *The Small Kindness*)[22]

David Cook points to an early hadith cited by a number of sources that resembles the Sermon on the Mount: "You will never enter paradise until you believe, and you will never believe until you love one another (*tahabbu*) and make peace widespread between yourselves, loving one another, and not one of you will ever believe until his neighbor is secure from his injustices."[23] Peace, faith, and mutual love in the framework of a society free from injustices—a demotic millennium.

Indeed, in this context one could argue that submission to Allah—*Islam*—represents the voluntary acceptance of the yoke of the kingdom of heaven: believers

---

[21] See, for example, 6:47–49. I use the translation by Abdullah Yusuf Ali for most quotations from the Qur'an, except where noted: *The Qur'an: Text, Translation and Commentary* (Elmhurst, N.Y.: Tahreike Tarsile Qur'an Inc., 2001).

[22] For a sympathetic treatment of these earliest (and most apocalyptic of) suras, see Michael Sells, *Approaching the Koran: The Early Revelations* (Ashland, Ore.: White Cloud Press, 1999), especially suras 96–114 with commentary.

[23] David Cook, "The Beginnings of Islam as an Apocalyptic Movement," in *War in Heaven, Heaven on Earth: Theories of the Apocalyptic*, ed. Stephen O'Leary and Glen McGhee (London: Equinox Publishing, 2005), 79–94.

will not treat their neighbors unjustly, but rather will love their neighbors and live at peace with them. No king but God; and the general will as product of mutual respect. Here, *jihad* (lit., struggle) makes sense as *inner striving*: "in each man an act of pure understanding that reasons *in the silence of passions* about what man may demand of his neighbor and what his neighbor has a right to demand of him."[24]

At this stage, Muhammad's eschatology seems decisively moral—faith is measured in the reality of justice in this world, not adherence to a particular "Faith." Correspondingly, the message was ecumenical, not denominational. Whether Jew, Sabian, or Christian, believing in God and the Last Day, working righteousness, "on them shall be no fear."[25] The just, whatever their religious faith, will be saved at the Last Judgment.[26] Muhammad's initial apocalyptic teaching—like John the Baptist's, like Jesus', like most demotic apocalyptic prophets, involved a moral, not a creedal eschatology.

Such origins explain Muhammad's initially capacious attitude toward Judaism and Christianity, whose eschatological vision—the resurrection of the dead and the Day of Judgment—formed the basic grand narrative around which Muhammad wove his particular set of prophecies of imminence.[27] Muhammad articulated an egalitarian, iconoclastic message, and his following came (like Hong Xiuquan's) from his relatives, from the socially disadvantaged, from anyone else moved by an urgent call to show mercy to others less fortunate, in anticipation of God's imminent (and harsh) Judgment.

When Prophecy Failed: Shame and Aggression

Of course, such prophecies have always failed. So how did Muhammad and his faithful respond to that failure? When did they recognize that their initial expectations were wrong, that *al Qiyāma* was not happening imminently? How did they talk about it among themselves? How did they handle the taunts of owls, of unbelievers?

When he began his apocalyptic mission, Muhammad did—with great reluctance—begin a contest, a bet, between roosters and owls, where each taunted the other and God was the arbiter. In the opening stages, the solitary prophet can only threaten—perhaps with the help of some signs and wonders—in the name of a God *who will deliver*. Those in the opposition understandably resist accepting the heavy burden of belief in an imminent Judgment. Accordingly, they bet on God's nonintervention. They actively mock the prophet who so threatens

---

[24] See above, chapter 9, n. 87.

[25] Qur'an 5:69.

[26] On this critical issue, see Fred Donner, "From Believers to Muslims," *Al-Abhath* 50–51 (2002–2003): 9–53; Cook, "Beginnings of Islam," 79-83.

[27] For details. see Casanova, *Mohammed et la fin du monde*, 20–30.

them with his or her sound and fury. The Qur'an describes them: "The hour [of Judgment] is nigh...But if they see a sign, they turn away, and say, 'this is transient magic.' They reject [the warning] and follow their lusts...The Day that the Caller will call them to a terrible affair, they will come forth, their eyes humbled from graves, like locusts scattered abroad...'Hard is this day!' the unbelievers will say."[28]

One can well imagine that among Arab tribesmen, fierce practitioners of the warrior's world of honor and shame, losing this contest would be painful and humiliating.[29] How can those who believed with every fiber of their being that *"This Day indeed are the unbelievers covered with shame and misery"* (Qur'an 16:27), handle the reversal when *un*believers are vindicated and *believers* are covered in shame and misery? Muhammad faced the same problem as early Christians: they too had to deal with the mockers who said, "Where are the promises of His coming?" (2 Peter 3:1–4).[30] "They say 'When will this promise come to pass, if you are telling the truth?'...Mocked were (many) apostles before thee..." (Qur'an 26:29–30).[31]

Indeed, the Qur'an contains more emotionally charged passages that rail against the taunters and the mockers than any foundational religious text in world history.[32] In the first Meccan period, Muhammad suffered repeated if not constant jeering, humiliating gestures, and brazen confrontations. Poets taught mocking verses to prostitutes who sang derisively about Muhammad in the taverns. He was Mecca's laughing stock.[33]

Initially a model of forbearance, Muhammad seems to have turned the other cheek, as it were, awaiting the Lord's vengeance. But as Allah tarried, Muhammad's patience wore thin. Certainly by the Medina period, when Muhammad had the power to avenge, he responded violently to insult. So many biographical hadiths

---

[28] Qur'an 54:1–8. Note the apocalyptic buffer in this, a later sura, of imagining the mockers rising from their graves, rather than get struck down in life. The formulation has already conceded what in the first stages of the movement would have been considered unthinkable—that the scoffers might die without rebuke and need to be resurrected in order to get their just desserts.

[29] See the world of ferocious honor and shame depicted in Suzanne Pinckney Stetkevych, *The Mute Immortals Speak: Pre-Islamic Poetry and the Poetics of Ritual* (Ithaca, N.Y.: Cornell University Press, 1993).

[30] This line of argument is speculative, and no historian to my knowledge has made this case, probably because the texts are largely silent on the specifics of why people mocked Muhammad. Most of the recorded objections to Muhammad concern his attack on the faith and authority of the leaders of the Quraish. These are safe objections for Muslims to remember. But it seems inconceivable that Muhammad's enemies would not have attacked him as a false prophet of a Day of Judgment that failed to materialize. Far more likely, Muslim sources passed over such criticism *ex post defectu*.

[31] It might even be possible to plot Muhammad's iconoclastic activism and the incident of the "Satanic Verses" into Muhammad's apocalyptic curve; compare both Akhenaten's and Hong Xiuquan's iconoclasm coming at crisis moments in their own apocalyptic careers, above chapters 6 and 7.

[32] For example: Qur'an 6:7–10; 21:36–41.

[33] The death of his protector in 619 may have marked a turning point, allowing opponents to insult Muhammad more freely.

record the assassination—with his approval—of men and women who mocked his teachings, that one modern compiler of the list wrote sarcastically of "Muhammad's Dead Poets' Society."[34]

And in order to justify such responses, which violated some of the basic elements of demotic religiosity,[35] Muhammad shifted the meaning of both submission to Allah and of Allah's intervention into history. Here, Muhammad proposed an "honorable" solution to the humiliation of cognitive dissonance: Allah wants Muslims to preserve *His* honor by punishing the unbelievers. No longer merely a *harbinger* of God's imminent intervention in history, the believers become *weapons* of Allah's will, *agents* of His intervention: from awaiters of the endtime's vengeance to agents of its advent.[36]

Thus, in one of the last suras revealed (9 *Tauba*, ca. 630–31), famous for its belligerence and therefore a favorite of jihadis,[37] God tells Muhammad, and through him the believers, that they have the right, indeed the duty, to serve as God's weapon in the chastisement of those who "…taunt you for your Faith…Fight them, and God will punish them by your hands, cover them with shame, help you [to victory] over them, heal/soothe the breasts of the believers."[38] Their defeat, their shame, heals the wounded pride of the (disappointed) believers.

The place of war and political power as a way to impose unity and conformity became increasingly central to Muhammad's own leadership in the Medina period. Internally, the community maintained demotic principles of equality and fairness. But the "saved" community lived increasingly in a zero-sum relationship with the apocalyptic "other." Violence became a sacred tool. Unlike Christianity, where Jesus demanded that his followers "turn the other cheek" (Matthew 5:39) and that Peter "put up his sword" (Matthew 26:42, John 18:11), Muhammad promised heaven to those martyrs who died during battle.[39] In this sense, military jihad represents to Islam what the Pentecost does to Christians: it gives the key to what a believer must do in the "middle time" between *now* and an ever-receding doomsday, how to spread the

---

[34] James Alrandson, "Muhammad's Dead Poets Society," *American Thinker*, March 8, 2006, online: http://97.74.65.51/readArticle.aspx?ARTID=5219, April 11, 2010.

[35] Compare the return of Ren'gan to the Taiping after the hierarchical (and deadly) turn, and the disagreement he voiced with his cousin Hong Xiuquan's attitude toward human life (pp. 207–08). Islam adopted the Talmud's dictum that to kill a person is to destroy a universe: "Whoever destroys a soul, it is considered as if he destroyed an entire world. And whoever saves a life, it is considered as if he saved an entire world," Jerusalem Talmud, *Sanhedrin* 4:1, 22a. This appears in the Qur'an as "That if anyone slew a person—unless it be for murder or for spreading mischief in the land—it would be as if he slew the whole people: and if any one saved a life, it would be as if he saved the life of the whole people." Qur'an 5:32.

[36] This is the main thrust of sura 8, "The Spoils of War," which includes references to resistance Muhammad received when he made this shift to open warfare (Qur'an 8:5–8).

[37] Cook, *Understanding Jihad* (Berkeley and Los Angeles: University of California Press, 2005), 9-11.

[38] Qur'an 9:12–13.

[39] Michael Bonner, *Jihad in Islamic History* (Princeton, N.J.: Princeton University Press, 2006), 72–81.

word as far and wide as possible before the Day of the Lord.[40] One hadith recites: "Behold! God sent me [the Prophet Muhammad] with a sword, *just before the Hour [of Judgment]*, and placed my daily sustenance beneath the shadow of my spear, and humiliation and contempt upon those who oppose me.[41] This passage is most often cited to show the spirit of jihad, without necessarily remarking on the framework: these Jihadis are *apocalyptic* warriors. Indeed, they are the solution to the failure of the first (Meccan) wave of eschatological hope in an imminent Last Judgment, replete with resurrection of the dead, and the key to the second (Medinan) phase of millennial imperialism. This reorientation gave apocalyptic enthusiasm a new and longer life and, in each subsequent generation, a world scale on which to play it out.

This shift to military jihad did not mean abandoning the demotic dream. Muhammad's followers were Allah's warriors at the final battle, and their victory brought liberation, peace, and justice.[42] They destroyed the "evil" empires that then sat so crushingly on their peasant populations. These oppressors prevented people from accepting the salvific message of Muhammad, and so, ran the millennial premise, eliminating them in war would liberate God's people.[43] As the French revolutionary and Napoleonic slogan went, "War on castles; peace to cottages."[44] No more waiting passively for the unendurably tarrying Last Judgment. The choice of 622 as the beginning of Islamic history corresponds to the moment when this new approach became practice.

The Origins of Islamic Millennialism: *Dar al Islam* and *Dar al Harb*

The astounding success of jihad in the period after Muhammad's death—perhaps the most astonishing in global history—was itself the miracle that proved Allah's intervention in history, the affirmation of Muhammad's prophecy. Within a dozen years of the prophet's death, Islamic warriors had conquered one great empire (Sassanian) and much of the other (Byzantine); within a century, *Dar al Islam*, the house of submission, spanned from the Atlantic to the Pacific. Muhammad had adeptly directed the strength of demotic voluntary communities to the noble task of shaming infidels and destroying evil empires.[45]

---

[40] Cook takes this analogy one step further: "the practice of *jihad* was roughly the equivalent in its redemptive and salvific qualities for the early Muslim as the doctrine of the cross was for the Christian... "only the sword wipes away sin" ("Beginnings of Islam," 88).

[41] Ibn Al-Mubarak, *Kitab al-Jihad* (Beirut: Dar al-Nur, 1971), 89–90 (no. 105); cited in Cook, *Understanding Jihad*, 23, and "Beginnings of Islam," 88.

[42] Later Islamic tradition distinguishes between *Jihad* and *Fitan*, with the latter as the apocalyptic war. *Fitan*, the plural of *fitna* (strife, dissension, civil war), has a special apocalyptic meaning in contrast with jihad; see Cook, "Muslim Apocalyptic and Jihad," *Jerusalem Studies in Arabic and Islam* 20 (1996): 66–104 (who dates the development to the third century AH/ninth century CE); Bonner, *Jihad*, 9; Yücesoy, *Messianic Beliefs*, 71.

[43] Suras accuse these infidel elites of preventing the (naturally good) people from accepting the word (e.g., 9 "Repentance").

[44] Above, chapter 9, n. 166.

[45] Fred Donner, *The Early Islamic Conquests* (Princeton, N.J.: Princeton University Press, 1981), 251; Cook, "Beginnings of Islam."

But millennial endeavors—bringing heaven to earth—cannot succeed. As with all such apocalyptic scenarios, it failed, but only in terms of millennial perfection, not in *this*-worldly terms (i.e., in normal time, where the owls discourse). And, as so often with such failed scenarios, Muslims inherited the mistaken but consequential result: in this case, a vast empire, the Caliphate.[46]

Here Allah's honor and the Muslim's honor coincide. People obey Allah, submit to His rule, where Sharia presides. And those subjects who chose not to obey God, that is, not to become Muslims, must be covered with shame to prove Allah's dominion. Islam thus made the transition from "No king but God," to "One God, one Rule (Caliph, Sharia), one dominant religion (Islam)".[47] For recalcitrants, Muslim legislators created a legal class of people—*dhimmi* (protected)—whom Muslims were forbidden to threaten with death in order to convert. In exchange for this "protection," these unbelievers—initially Christians and Jews, subsequently Zoroastrians and Hindus—lived in a state of legal and economic disadvantage, even subjection.[48]

And one of the main purposes of that subjection was humiliation. The Qur'an specified that the *jizya*, the tax on all *dhimmi*, should be done so that the payers "feel themselves subdued."[49] The earliest surviving commentary notes: "... meaning that they are humiliated by virtue of the fact that they have to give it without any recompense, and that it is taken from them by force."[50] In Scott's terms, the *jizya* is a formal public transcript, a ceremony of disgraced status.[51] Just as the humiliated Jew offered medieval Christians reassurance about the truth of their own revelation,[52] so *dhimmi*s (especially Jews and Christians) as the humiliated "other" provided the Muslims with ontological reassurance.

[46] Efraim Karsh, *Islamic Imperialism: A History* (New Haven, Conn.: Yale University Press, 2006), 21–35. For an example of these dynamics at work in the founding of Islam's most consequential empire, see Moshe Sharon, *Black Banners from the East: The Establishment of the 'Abbāsid State* (Jerusalem: Magnes Press, 1983); Yücasoy, *Messianic Beliefs*.

[47] Compare the analyses of Fowden, *Empire to Commonwealth*, who starts from empire as the monotheistic "given."

[48] Uri Rubin and David J. Wasserstein, eds., *Dhimmis and Others: Jews and Christians and the World of Classical Islam*, Israel Oriental Studies 17 (Winona Lake, Ind.: Eisenbrauns, 1997); Bat Ye'or, *Islam and Dhimmitude: Where Civilizations Collide* (Madison, N.J.: Fairleigh Dickinson University Press, 2002), 89–103. Parallels with Christian supersessionism deserve attention, especially in terms of an invidious identity formation rooted in the humiliation of the monotheistic predecessor: "we are right *because* they are humiliated/we humiliate them."

[49] Qur'an 9:29.

[50] Muqatil b. Sulayman, *Tafsir*, ed. Mahmud Shihata (Cairo: al-Ha'iya al-Misriyya al-Àmma, 1983), 2:167. Thanks to David Cook for the reference.

[51] See discussion in Mark R. Cohen, *Under Crescent and Cross: The Jews in the Middle Ages* (Princeton, N.J.: Princeton University Press, 1995), 41–44.

[52] Christian efforts to humiliate Jews produced, among other traditions, the Easter ceremonies involving everything from a public slap in the Jew's face, to making him kiss a pig's anus: Jules Isaac, *The Teaching of Contempt: Christian Roots of Anti-Semitism* (New York: Holt, Reinhart & Winston, 1964). On these rites of humiliation and violence in action, see David Nirenberg, *Communities of Violence: Persecution of Minorities in the Middle Ages* (Princeton, N.J.: Princeton University Press, 1996), 200–31.

The overall framework for the normative legislation of Sharia, repeated with variations by all Muslim legal scholars, distinguished between *Dar al Islam* and *Dar al Harb*. In *Dar al Islam*, or the realm of submission, the *Ummah* (community, collective identity of Muslims) held power, Sharia applied, and *dhimmis* paid the *jizya* in humiliation. It was, in Islam's first centuries, a sphere of wondrous expansion, a tale of conquest and hegemony that beggars the accomplishments of both Greeks and Romans.

By contrast, *Dar al Harb*, or the realm of the sword, represented that world which (so far) had successfully resisted Islam. Here *kafir* (infidels) refused to recognize (lit.: "covered") the truth. That realm's persistence, the surprising resilience of Christendom, was the fly in the ointment of apocalyptic success.

Dar al Harb, accordingly, constituted a realm of perpetual war, punctuated by cease-fires, a realm to be terrorized. "Remember Thy Lord inspired the angels (with the message): 'I am with you: give firmness to the believers, I will instill terror into the hearts of the unbelievers. Smite above their necks and smite all their finger tips of them'" (Qur'an 8:12).[53] If for Freud, the formula was: "where there was Id there shall be Ego";[54] for Muslims it was: "Where there is *Jahaliyya* (the ignorance that prevailed before the prophet's coming), there shall be *Sharia*; where there is Dar al Harb there shall be Dar al Islam." This resulted in the millennial vision of a world submitted to Allah, a global *Dar al Islam*, which the possibilities of modern globalization have now reawakened in the breasts of some zealots.

Apocalyptic Traditions: The Once and Future Day of Judgment

As with all religions that begin in apocalyptic time and survive reentry into normal time, Islam has an extensive but problematic set of traditions around the once and future apocalyptic denouement, about that "middle age" between the prophecy and its fulfillment. Among the hadiths were numerous statements about the coming End, and over centuries, a literature developed of the little and big signs of the hour,[55] from the battle between the Dajjal and the Mahdi, to how Allah's Judgment will manifest itself. Here, I emphasize seven themes of variable importance in the early period, but that reappear with considerable

[53] This text is highly contentious. On the one hand, jihadi believers and their opponents in the West cite it and others like it, as normative; on the other, apologists insist they only refer to the specific circumstances, here the battle of Badr where the Muslims were allegedly outnumbered; see Islam 101, online: http://www.islam101.com/terror/verse8_12.htm, March 11, 2010.

[54] Sigmund Freud, "The Dissection of the Psychical Personality," Lecture 31 in *New Introductory Lectures on Psychoanalysis* (1932), trans. James Strachey (London & New York: Penguin Books, 1991), 112.

[55] Compare with the very popular tradition of the "Fifteen Signs before Doomsday," on Latin Christendom, William W. Heist, *The Fifteen Signs Before Doomsday* (E. Lansing, Mich., Michigan State College Press, 1952); on the way such traditions played out around the year 1000, see Johannes Fried, "Awaiting the End around the Year 1000," in *Apocalyptic Year 1000*, 27–67.

vigor in the final decades before 2000 and now play a central role in this current round of Muslim apocalyptic discourse:

1. *The Mahdi, Leader of the Final Jihad:* One of the earliest and most popular apocalyptic traditions anticipated the arrival of a "rightly guided" leader who corresponds roughly to the messiah in both Jewish and Christian traditions (for Christians, Jesus upon return). Early Islam had numerous moments when candidates for the role of Mahdi appeared, all of whom failed in their redemptive task. But, as with the once and future Christ (*Parousia*) and the once and future Emperor of the Last Days, there developed the once and future Mahdi, or, as it became known in Shiite Islam, the Hidden Imam, with variants including Fiver, Sevener, and Twelver Shiism.[56] Although scholars often consider both Mahdism and the millennial currents to which it gives voice a peculiarly *Shiite* phenomenon, in fact Sunnis have similarly vigorous and fecund traditions.[57]

2. *The Destruction of Corrupt Governments:* Imperial Islam inevitably failed to create the just society on earth, thus disappointing serious apocalyptic thinkers. The resulting literature foresaw an apocalyptic scenario that would put an end to corrupt governments, even those with Muslim rulers. Millennial discourse in Islam contained the same subversive elements as it did in Christianity: the passion for justice and, on occasion, the apocalyptic call to rebellion.[58] Not surprisingly, Muslim authorities tend to be owls and keep the apocalyptic traditions at the margins.

3. *The Centrality of Jerusalem:* If Mecca is the sacred center of Islam in "normal time," Jerusalem becomes the central focus of apocalyptic time. Not only do the key eschatological events occur there—the resurrection of the dead (*al Qiyāma*) and the Last Judgment (*Yawm al'din*)—but in one hadith, the very Ka'aba stone at the center of the Mecca pilgrimage will move to Jerusalem.[59] These traditions reflect the importance of Jerusalem in the earliest stages of Islam, when Muhammad anticipated Jewish "conversion" to

---

[56] Abdulaziz Abdulhussein Sachedina, *Islamic Messianism: The Idea of Mahdī in Twelver Shīism* (Albany: State University of New York Press, 1981).

[57] See above n. 20, and the most recent discussion in Furnish, *Holiest Wars*, 30–72, who focuses almost exclusively on Sunni "Mahdi" figures.

[58] Fowden's argument deals with this phenomenon of empires breaking apart, although, one foot-note aside, he seems to have little appreciation for the role of apocalyptic thinking in the process. See *Empire to Commonwealth*, 174 n. 10. Fowden refers to these apocalyptic thinkers as "voices in the wilderness," which they are indeed, until apocalyptic time comes.

[59] According to one tradition, the Ka'aba of Mecca on the Day of Judgment will be brought to Jerusalem as a bride to a groom. Then it will serve as an advocate in favor of the pilgrims. The second tradition says that the Ka'aba will visit Jerusalem on the Day of Judgment and both will be taken to paradise with their inhabitants. This is not a descent of a heavenly Jerusalem, but an ascent of the Ka'aba and Jerusalem to paradise: Ofer Livne-Kafri, "Muslim Traditions on Jerusalem between Judaism and Christianity," in *Jerusalem in Early Islam: Selected Essays* (Jerusalem: Yad Ben-Zvi Press, 2000 [in Hebrew]), 38–39. Thanks to Eran Tzidkiyahu for this source.

his teaching, and prayed, like the Jews, in the direction of Jerusalem. As with many unfinished apocalyptic scenarios, the "second" end resolves the buried problems of the first (unsuccessful) end.

4. *Conquest of the World, Submission to Sharia:* Jihad and the empire it creates are a post-apocalyptic millennial mutation. Notes Bonner, Muslims believed in "the propagation of the faith through combat, [which] must be brought to the entire world, as when the Prophet says, 'I have been sent to the human race in its entirety,' and 'I have been commanded to fight the people/unbelievers until they testify: "There is no God but God and Muhammad is the Messenger of God."' This fighting and spreading the faith will continue until the end of the world as we know it."[60]

5. *The Dajjal:* Like Christian apocalyptic scenarios from which they drew much of their material, Muslims developed the notion of the Dajjal, a super-villain who would lead the forces of evil at the end of time. Like the Christian Antichrist,[61] the Muslim Dajjal has no Qur'anic sources, but unlike in Christianity, the Dajjal was relatively slow in developing.[62]

6. *The Extermination of the Jews:* Most Muslim apocalyptic literature concerns the major military enemy of early Islam, the Christians. Indeed, in the modern period, when Israeli Jews have become a military enemy, writers had to search for apocalyptic material on the Jews in the hadiths and found few. But they have found one hadith, of the "Rocks and Trees" that foretells of an apocalyptic slaughter: "The time will not come until Muslims will fight the Jews; until the Jews hide behind rocks and trees, which will cry: 'O Muslim! O servant of Allah! there is a Jew hiding behind me, come on kill him! This will not apply to the Gharqad, a Jewish tree.'"[63]

7. *The Date of the End and the Mujaddid:* Like Christianity and Judaism, Islam had a host of traditions that dated the end of the world, and among them, one tradition that only grew with the passage of centuries concerned the advent and passing of the chronological century marker, known as the *Mujaddid*, or the "Renewer." Like "Protestant Reformation," this term names the phenomenon *ex post defectu*: looking backward, one identifies a "renewer" of the Islamic tradition at the end of each century, understood in conventional

---

[60] Bonner, *Jihad*, 49.

[61] There are two mentions of antichrists in the letters of John, but neither refers to a single, superpowerful figure; see Bernard McGinn, *Antichrist: Two Thousand Years of the Human Fascination with Evil* (New York: Columbia University Press, 2000), 33–56.

[62] One the origins of the Dajjal, see Cook, *Studies in Muslim Apocalyptic*, 92–136. On contemporary manifestations, which have mutated notably and taken on far great importance, see Cook, *Contemporary Muslim Apocalyptic*, 184–200.

[63] Sahih Muslim, *Kitab Al-Fitan wa Ashrat As-Saàh* [The Book Pertaining to the Turmoil and Portents of the Last Hour], Book 41:6981-85, online: http://www.usc.edu/schools/college/crcc/engagement/resources/texts/muslim/hadith/muslim/041.smt.html, January 7, 2011. See David Cook, *Contemporary Muslim Apocalyptic Literatutre*, 36, and on Hamas, below, n. 145.*

terms.[64] Roosters, however, at the *approach* of a century's end and *before* failure, view the Mujaddid as an apocalyptic time, when the Mahdi will at last make his appearance.[65]

A final note: Most historians of Islam do not use millennialism (or chiliasm) as common terms. Even more than Christian studies, whole books on the subject of Islam never once mention the term. When the terms are taken in their broad, "religious studies" sense (as in this book), the general consensus recognizes a significant element of millennialism—this-worldly salvation—among the the Shiites, while asserting that the Sunnis held more eschatological—otherworldly—beliefs.[66]

■ MODERNITY AND THE HUMILIATION OF ISLAM

Islam had the Christian West on the defensive for the greater part of four centuries. By the millennium marker of Christianity (1000, Y1K), around the year 400 since the Hejira (AH), Islam represented the height of the "first world."[67] Western Europe, at its nadir, was at the bottom of the "third world," exporting to the fabulously wealthy Muslim world their primary materials, including human slaves. Islam even had a large foothold in Spain. There, the Muslim city of Cordoba with a population of a half a million, dwarfed anything in Christian Europe, where except for Rome, no city exceeded ten thousand. Anyone viewing the world in 1000 would predict that the next millennium belonged to Islam.

And yet, around precisely that moment, Western European culture underwent a striking mutation that turned it from a repeated victim of invasion, to an aggressively expansive, technologically innovative, highly productive culture whose global penetration continues to this day.[68] Over succeeding centuries, Islam and

---

[64] See Ella Landau-Tasseron, "The 'Cyclical Reform': A Study of the *Mujaddid* Tradition," *Studia Islamica* 70 (1989): 79–118; E. van Donzel, "Mudjaddid," *The Encyclopedia of Islam*, new ed. (Leiden: Brill, 2007).

[65] On the Abassids in 200AH (803 CE), see Yücesoy, *Messianic Beliefs*, 116–35; on the Fathimids and 400 (1009), see Landes, *Relics*, 43–46; on 1300 (1882) and the Mahdi of Khartoum, see John Voll, "The Sudanese Mahdi: Frontier Fundamentalist," *International Journal of Middle East Studies* 10 (1979): 166. On Khomeini's and Qaradawi's use of this tradition in 1980/1400, see below.

[66] See above, n. 20.

[67] Recently, one historian argued that it would have been better for Europe if the Carolingians had lost at Poitiers and the Muslims, a far more advanced civilization at that time, had conquered Europe: David Levering Lewis, *God's Crucible: Islam and the Making of Europe, 570–1215* (New York: W.W. Norton, 2008), 160–84. Hitler also regretted the victory of Christianity over Islam since, he believed, the German race, converted to Islam's belligerent ways, would have conquered the world much faster than it did, saddled with Christianity's slave morality; see *Hitler's Table Talk, 1941–44: His Private Conversations*, trans. Norman Cameron (London: Oxford University Press, 2000), 33, 46, 667.

[68] On the big picture, see D. Landes, *Wealth and Poverty of Nations*; for a discussion of the dynamics circa 1000, see R. Landes, "Demotic Religiosity": and most recently, the excellent popular historical work by Tom Holland, *Millennium: The End of the World and the Forging of Christendom* (London: Little, Brown & Co., 2008).

Christendom carried on a seesaw battle. Napoleon, however, shattered any lingering illusions of parity in Egypt in 1798, where his army revealed the degree to which Western Europe had, over the period from 1500–1800, vastly surpassed Islam militarily.[69]

For Muslims, this Western dominance meant shame and humiliation. History had gone wrong, terribly wrong.[70] Iranian scholars Ladan and Roya Boroumand remarked:

> For the last several centuries, the Islamic world has been undergoing a traumatizing encounter with the West. Since this encounter began, our history has been a story of irreversible modernization, but also of utter domination on the one side, and humiliation and resentment on the other. To Muslim minds the West and its ways have become a powerful myth—evil, impenetrable, and incomprehensible.[71]

So far, every effort to "catch up" has failed to change the dynamics of Arab primedivider society. Authoritarianism remained the rule everywhere: in places with no oil (Syria, Jordan, Egypt) and with immense oil revenues (Iraq, Lybia, Saudi Arabia), Arab commoners remained uneducated and impoverished; elites retained control; the demotic West remained more dynamic and more powerful.[72]

For an Arab Muslim like Sayyid Qutb (1906–66), no price in poverty was too great to pay in order to avoid the "hideous schizophrenia" that the Europeans inflicted on peoples and cultures in every corner of the globe.[73] The disorientations of modernity become still more acute for Muslims when they concern the role of women. Demotic principles grant individuals, including subordinates and women, high levels of autonomy that constitute unbearable affronts to the machismo so characteristic of both Mediterranean and Arab culture.[74]

---

[69] Note the cultural dimension of this differential. Saïd complained about Napoleon's "Orientalist" project (*Orientalism*, [New York: Vintage, 1979], 76–94), but these érudits who accompanied him were passionately interested in the Egyptian past, in marked contrast to the country's Muslim inhabitants. *French scholars found Akhenaten's ruins; they broke the hieroglyphic code and figured out what had happened.*

[70] Bernard Lewis, *What Went Wrong? Western Impact and Middle Eastern Response* (Oxford: Oxford University Press, 2002); Thomas Idinopolous, *Weathered by Miracles: A History of Palestine from Bonaparte and Muhammad Ali to Ben-Gurion and the Mufti* (Chicago: Ivan R. Dee, 1998); D. Landes, *Wealth and Poverty of Nations*, 392–418; Tamim Ansary, *Destiny Disrupted: A History of the World through Islamic Eyes* (New York: Basic Books, 2009). For a meditation specifically on modern Indian Muslims, see Rafiq Zakaria, *Indian Muslims: Where Have They Gone Wrong?* (Mumbai: Silverpoint Press, 2004).

[71] Ladan and Roya Boroumand, "Terror, Islam, and Democracy," *Journal of Democracy* 13, no. 2 (April 2002): 16. On the Boroumands work on the French Revolution, see above, chapter 9, n. 146.

[72] For the historical case, see Lewis and D. Landes (above n. 71). For the continuance of the pattern into the twenty-first century, see the annual *UN Arab Human Development Reports* (2002–), online: http://arabstates.undp.org/subpage.php?spid=14, April 15, 2010.*

[73] Paul Berman, "The Philosopher of Islamic Terror," *New York Times*, March 23, 2003, online: http://select.nytimes.com/search/restricted/article?res=F00B16F83C550C708EDDAA0894DB404482, April 15, 2010.*

[74] On Mediterranean machismo, see J.G. Persistany, ed., *Honour and Shame: The Values of Mediterranean Society* (London: Weidenfeld & Nicolson, 1965); for the difficulty Muslim culture had with equality, see Lews, *What Went Wrong*, chap. 4.

No other subject highlights this gender problem more than the issue of honor-killings which continue to plague not only their countries of origin in the Arab and Muslim world (Turkey, Pakistan, Iran), but also those Western countries where Muslim immigrants, even highly successful ones, find themselves enraged by their loss of control over women who take advantage of the opportunities for autonomy they find there.[75] Ironically, the persistence of honor-killings in the Muslim world may well represent a failure of Muslims to tame a pre-Islamic tribal practice that Islamic ethics forbade, and yet now has become a mark of intensified Islamic commitment.[76] Rather than adopt an Islamic ethical standard in harmony with modernity, then, many Islamists insist on honor-killings as a sign of rejecting the corrosive influence of modernity.[77]

The Unbearable Humiliation of Zionism

People can live, unhappily but quietly, with disgrace as long as no one reminds them.[78] Most Muslims in most places in the world could ignore their (comparative) failures and live local lives as before. The success of Zionism, however, greatly intensified modernity's humiliation, especially for the Arabs.[79] Christian nations had always been "honorable" opponents, men of war. But in the entire history of Islam, Jews had never been a nation, always subalterns, a *dhimmi* people. Defeat at their hands was therefore especially unbearable. As Thucydides had the Athenians explain to the Melians: "One is not so much frightened of being conquered by a power that rules over others...as of what would happen if a ruling power is attacked and defeated by its own subjects."[80]

Thus Jewish success at creating an autonomous state in the heart of *Dar al Islam* constituted a catastrophe—*nakba*—for Arab and Muslim honor. A *dhimmi* people had successfully declared independence in the very heart of *Dar al Islam*. The 1967 War, which should have redressed so unbearable an insult by wiping out the

[75] See Dodd, "Family Honor" on the problem in the Arab world; Unni Wikan, *Generous Betrayal: Politics of Culture in the New Europe* (Chicago: University of Chicago Press, 2002), on its importation to Europe and the failure of Westerners to oppose it.*

[76] For two Muslim statements against honor-killings, see Imam Zaid, "Islam and Honor-Killings," *New Islamic Directions*, online: http://www.newislamicdirections.com/nid/notes/islam_and_honor_killings/, April 15, 2010; and "Honor Killings: A Crime Against Islam," Muslim Council of Britain, 2007, online: http://www.mcb.org.uk/downloads/honour_killings.pdf, April 15, 2010.

[77] Colin Nickerson, "For Muslim Women, A Deadly Defiance: Honor Killings on the Rise in Europe," *Boston Globe*, January 16, 2006, online: http://www.boston.com/news/world/articles/2006/01/16/for_muslim_women_a_deadly_defiance/, April 15, 2010.

[78] For a particularly powerful example, see Gregory of Tours, *History of the Franks*, 9:19, trans. Lewis Thorpe [London, Penguin, 1974], 502).*

[79] See the interesting meditations on Judeophobia and modernity in Hyam Maccoby, *Antisemitism and Modernity: Innovation and Continuity* (London: Routledge, 2004); on Israel and the Arabs, see 148–53; and Zygmunt Bauman, *Modernity and the Holocaust* (Ithaca, N.Y.: Cornell University Press, 2000).

[80] Athenians to the Melians, according to Thucidydes, *Peloponnesian War*, 5.91.

offending "Zionist entity," ended up making things infinitely worse—after months of promising the world a slaughter of historic proportions, the Arab armies suffered a devastating six-day defeat.[81]

The creation and continuation of the State of Israel has provoked a massive and ongoing crisis of identity for the Arab and Muslim world, in which Israel represents a particularly poignant incarnation of a larger Arab struggle with the demands of a modern, globalizing world community. In 2006, Ahmed Sheikh, editor in chief of Al Jazeera and a seemingly Westernized professional, commented on the persisting feeling of shame and inadequacy that results from always losing to Israel. "It gnaws at the people in the Middle East that such a small country as Israel, with only about 7 million inhabitants, can defeat the Arab nation with its 350 million. That hurts our collective ego. The Palestinian problem is in the genes of every Arab."[82]

And what disturbs this modern journalist, drives apocalyptic writers to frenzy. Cook notes that "the vast majority of modern Arab Muslim apocalyptic writers are obsessed with Israel."[83] Speaking of the existence of the "Zionist entity," one Syrian writer exclaimed:

> The Arabs and the Muslims have torment imposed upon them, and are enduring the subjection and humiliation of their enemies, who fight the Arabs and the Muslims, and kill them in their own homes, steal their possessions and make them into slaves. This we have witnessed with our own eyes, and we have witnessed the slaughter of our children, the violation of our honor and our holy places, and the rape of our homelands, while we are not able to protect ourselves. Even more than that, when we begin to beg our enemies to stop and leave off their trampling upon us, we do not find anything other than derision and contempt, in addition to the humiliation [of begging].[84]

The humiliation brought on by Israel is twofold: on the one hand, a tiny population of subalterns have managed to establish their freedom; on the other, they did so by imbibing all the most potent elements of secular modernity. Nothing demonstrated the power of demotic modern culture more than the military superiority of this tiny "fossilized" people over a much larger population of Muslims, over a proud warrior culture. In this sense, the fear that the near-unanimous voice of the Arab public sphere expressed toward Israeli independence should be understood as a particularly difficult encounter between prime-divider cultures and a demotic millennial

---

[81] Michael Oren, *Six Days of War* (Oxford: Oxford University Press, 2002).

[82] Pierre Heumann, "An Interview With Al-Jazeera Editor-in-Chief Ahmed Sheikh," *World Politics Watch*, December 7, 2006, online: http://www.worldpoliticswatch.com/article.aspx?id=395, April 15, 2010.

[83] Cook, *Contemporary Muslim Apocalyptic*, 21.

[84] Al-Shihabi, *Istratajiyat al-Qur'an fi muwajahat al-yahudiyya al-'alamiyya* (Damascus: Arab Writers Union, 1997), 132–33, cited in Cook, *Contemporary Muslim Apocalyptic*, 227. "Begging our enemies" refers to the Oslo Peace Process.*

revolution.[85] Israel's civil polity, with its freedoms for journalists, commoners, individuals, minorities (including Arabs), but most especially for women, continues to represent an existential threat to the very social fabric of Arab political culture.

Thus, Israel and emancipated Jews become the injection point of a massive assault on every aspect of life:

> In summary, the Jewish presence in occupied Palestine *constitutes a great danger to the culture of the Islamic community*, and this danger is typified by the *Jewish cultural invasion* which is infiltrating the countries of the area in accordance with a written plan [*The Protocols of the Elders of Zion*], whose originators took advantage of the experience of the Western cultural invasion of the Islamic community, and use different methods and media for the purposes of this invasion: universities, educational and scientific curricula for schools, fine literature, arts, different informational media, such as the newspaper, radio and television, research centers and cultural centers and other things as well. Thus the *Islamic community is threatened in its culture, and thus it is threatened in its identity and personality, which distinguishes it from other communities, and protects its existence and independence.* The meaning of this is a *sentence of dissolution into the [other, world] communities and then disappearance and inclusion.*[86]

To the articulators of the Islamic apocalyptic antimodern discourse, Israel's very existence, indeed modernity, threatens the destruction of Islam as a community of belief, the extinction of the *Ummah*. Only by wiping out this enemy, can Islam survive—in other words, the apocalyptic paranoid position: *exterminate or be exterminated.*[87]

It is not accidental, I think, that Zionism, by my definition, represents a secular demotic millennial movement (with a strong religious undercurrent).[88] And like most every case of regions dominated by prime-divider politics—Europe in the late eighteenth century, the Arab world in the twentieth—the appearance of a demotic millennial movement in their midst produces violent alarm. One people's redemption is another's Dajjal. Although apocalyptic jihad was not the only Arab response to Zionism—there were and remain pro-Zionist Arabs[89]—it was a particularly strong and eventually dominant one.

[85] For a particularly interesting discussion of these issues and their relationship to apocalyptic, see Laurent Murawiec, *Mind of Jihad*, Cambridge: Cambridge University Press, 2008), 232–68: "Manichaean Tribalism."

[86] Shabir (1992), cited in Cook, *Contemporary Muslim Apocalyptic*, 21–22.

[87] For an analysis of the relationship between this sense of humiliation and impotence and genocidal hatred, see Daphne Burdman, "Hatred of the Jews as a Psychological Phenomenon in Palestinian Society," *Jewish Political Studies Review* 18, no. 3-4 (Fall 2006), online: http://tinyurl.com/y6u2mqo, April 16, 2010.

[88] See the analysis of Aviezer Ravitsky, *Messianism, Zionism, and Jewish Religious Radicalism*, trans. Michael Swirsky and Jonathan Chipman (Chicago: University of Chicago Press, 1996).*

[89] See Neville Mandel, "Attempts at an Arab-Zionist Entente: 1913–1914," *Middle Eastern Studies* 1, no. 3 (1965): 238–67; and Hillel Cohen, *Palestinian Collaboration with Zionism, 1917–1948* (Berkeley and Los Angeles: University of California Press, 2008).

The Global Mirror and Constant Humiliation

If modernity and Israel were not enough, by the end of the twentieth century, Internet-driven globalization made the Arab predicament even worse. By the last decades of the twentieth century, with other third-world economies "taking off" and communications revolutions like satellite TV and cyberspace linking up the "global village," the whole world could see how extensive the Arabs' failure. Despite trillions of petro-dollars, Arabs preside over the least productive economic block in the world, worse in performance than even the sub-Saharan economies. Arabs (5 percent of the world population) and Muslims (20 percent of the world population) currently produce a tiny fraction of the world's manufactured goods, of internationally recognized scientific output, of Nobel Prize winners, of world-class universities. Their wealthy go to Western, even Israeli, hospitals.

And on December 31, 1999, as countries around the world celebrated the advent of the first global millennial passage before the cameras, some non-Western countries, like China, put on spectacular displays, while Arabs and Muslims had nothing to show. Under these conditions, with images international as well as local pumped into their living rooms, everything recalls, reactivates, galls the sense of humiliation. And the unbearable must be borne, since, infuriatingly, no effort to fight back works, not against the West, not even against tiny Israel.

■ APOCALYPTIC JIHAD: A MUSLIM RESPONSE TO MODERNITY

The modern imperial West, like the Greeks and Romans before them, challenged the very identity of those nations and cultures it invaded. And like Roman and Greek culture, it produced rebellions, some of them nativist, some millennial, some both (i.e., nativism infused with a sense of divine, cosmic mission). As early as 1945, H. A. R. Gibb warned that in addition to acculturating and rejecting Western culture, a "third alternative" was emerging in Islam's "intolerable" confrontation with the West: "a violent assertion of the supremacy of sacred law...the kernel of revolutionary Mahdism."[90]

Which way a given culture goes in its encounter with modernity depends on many factors. What I want to trace below—the Muslim apocalyptic millennial response to modernity—is not the only response in the Arab world. But it is at once an exciting, comprehensive, and effective response...certainly the most exciting and comprehensive, and possibly the most effective response to the four humiliations of modernity—Western superiority, Israel's existence, women's liberation, and globalization. In order to appreciate current trajectories, it pays to follow the trail of this response over several generations.

[90] H. A. R. Gibb, *Mohammedanism: A Historical Survey* (London: Oxford University Press, 1949), 113, 117–18.

Early Stirrings: Muslim Brotherhood and Sayyid Qutb

The history of *modern* jihad begins with the teachings of Jamal al-Din al Afghani (1838–97), a fascinating figure who managed to appear as all things to all men: Sunni, Shiite, progressive modernist, and Jihadi.[91] He conducted perhaps his most productive campaigns in Egypt, where he laid the groundwork for Hassan al Banna (1906–49), who founded the Muslim Brotherhood in 1928. The Brotherhood constitutes the single most successful modern Islamic movement of twentieth (and, so far, the twenty-first) century.[92]

Al Banna thought strategically and in the long-term. He laid down a generational plan of action for a jihad that anticipated preparatory stages culminating in a final "active stage out of which the perfected fruits of the mission of the Muslim Brotherhood will appear."[93] "The realities of today," wrote al Banna, "are the dreams of yesterday, and the dreams of today are the realities of tomorrow."[94] From the perspective of this book's terminology, the Muslim Brotherhood launched a premillennial project designed to nurture and shape a future active cataclysmic jihad that would restore a transnational Islamic state, first to what was formerly *Dar al Islam*, and then....

As long as the Muslim Brothers were too weak for direct confrontation, the violence remained subterranean. But it was an essential element of the religiosity they formulated:

> If the Muslim Brothers were more effectively violent than other groups on the Egyptian scene it was because militancy and martyrdom had been elevated to central virtues in the Society's ethos... Banna told members again and again that they were "the army of liberation... you are the battalions of salvation for this nation afflicted by calamity." They were "the troops of God."[95]

From the outset, al Banna understood jihad as violent physical struggle, necessary to deal with the calamity of a world overrun with secular modernity. Jihad stood in close relationship to death and martyrdom. Al Banna became famous for the expressions, *fann al-mawt* (the art of death) and *al-mawt fann* (death is art). "The Qur'an has commanded people to love death more than life. Unless the philosophy of the Qur'an on death replaces the love of life that has consumed Muslims, they will fail. Victory can only come with mastering the 'art of death.'"[96] Working within

---

[91] For a more extensive discussion of Al Afghani's role in modern Jihadi thought, see Murawiec, *Mind of Jihad*, 29–32, 95–97; and appendix at the book's website.

[92] For a discussion of the genealogy, see Richard Mitchell, *The Society of Muslim Brothers* (Oxford: Oxford University Press, 1969).

[93] Ibid., 13–14.

[94] Hassan al Banna, cited by his grandson Tariq Ramadan, *Aux sources du renouveau musulman d'Al Afgani à Hassan al Banna, un siècle de réformisme islamique* (Paris: Bayard Centurion, 1998), 229.

[95] Mitchell, *Society of Muslim Brothers*, 206–07.

[96] Ibid.

a committee that secretly condemned "apostates to death" and carried out the sentence, al Banna and his Muslim Brotherhood waged a "relentless war...against 'the heathen, the apostate, the deviant' who would, when judged dangerous, be put to death in the name of Allah."[97]

One of the more significant influences on al Banna came not from Islam, but from European fascism. A rising force in the 1920s Europe, fascism provided a powerful articulation of antimodern (in the sense of intolerant and antidemocratic) sentiments, wrapped up in a language of authenticity through violence that restored the troubled honor of the alpha male threatened by the inroads of egalitarian legislation. The links between al Banna and fascism became still more intense in the links between Haj Amin al Husseini and Hitler's *Nazionalsozialismus*.[98] And imbedded in this transfer of attitudes and ideologies, lay a profound paranoia about Judaism.[99]

Indeed, the Zionists provided Hassan al Banna with his greatest recruiting device. From 1928 to 1936, the Muslim Brotherhood managed to recruit fewer than one thousand members; by 1938, after two years of supporting the Palestinian revolt against the Zionists, they claimed over two hundred thousand.[100] And when the Arab war against an independent state of Israel began, he joined al-Azhar theologians in declaring a jihad, and called for ten thousand volunteers to join "battalions of Allah."[101] The U.N. decision to recognize Israel, Al Banna explained, was Allah's gift to the faithful: "A wind is blowing from Paradise, sweet with the smell of martyrdom."[102]

Sayyid Qutb, a brilliant Egyptian peasant boy who studied briefly in the postwar United States, took the Muslim Brotherhood's Jihadi ideology to a new level. For him, *Jahiliyya*—the state of ignorance before Islam—applied not only to non-Muslims, but to secular "Muslims," particularly to the rulers of Muslim nations

---

[97] Amir Taheri, *Holy Terror: The Inside Story of Islamic Terrorism* (London: Sphere Books, 1987), 43, cited in Murawiec, *Mind of Jihad*, 38.

[98] Philip Mattar, *The Mufti of Jerusalem: Al-Hajj Amin al-Husayni and the Palestinian National Movement* (New York: Columbia University Press, 1988), 99–107; David G. Dalin and John F. Rothmann, *Icon of Evil: Hitler's Mufti and the Rise of Radical Islam* (New York: Random House, 2008).

[99] Matthias Küntzel, *Jihad and Jew-Hatred: Islamism, Nazism and the Roots of 9/11* (New York: Telos Press, 2007).

[100] Abd Al-Fattah Muhammad El-Awaisi, *The Muslim Brothers and the Palestinian Question, 1928–1947* (London: Tauris Academic Studies, 1998), 98. On the importance of the Palestinian question to Hassan al Banna's ability to gain international support, see Haim Levenberg, *The Military Preparations of the Arab Community in Palestine, 1945–1948* (London: Frank Cass, 1993). For links between the anti-Judaism/anti-Zionism in the Islamism of the 1930s and that of the present day, see Küntzel, *Jihad and Jew-Hatred*.

[101] Thomas Mayer, "The Military Force of Islam: The Society of the Muslim Brethren and the Palestine Question, 1945–48," in *Zionism and Arabism in Palestine and Israel*, ed. Elie Kedourie and Sylvia Haim (London: Frank Cass, 1982), 100–17. See Matthias Küntzel, "National Socialism and Anti-Semitism in the Arab World," *Jewish Political Studies Review* 17, no. 1–2 (Spring 2005).

[102] Barry Rubin, *The Arab States and the Palestine Question* (Syracuse, N.Y.: Syracuse University Press, 1981), 175.

where Sharia did not rule (e.g., his native Egypt). In their efforts to mimic the secular West, Muslims had apostatized and, in principle, if not yet in action, deserved death.[103]

> In practice, the line was sharply drawn around 'believers' for whom it was necessary to be not merely a Muslim but a Muslim Brother. The consequence of this structuring of the social order was to generate within the Society a current of rigid intolerance which *transformed mundane political disputes into elemental social clashes.* Independents as well as political opponents became the objects of a violence inspired by a social and religious exclusiveness, which could brook no compromise with him who was not a Brother.[104]

This political polarization occurred under the sign of the apocalypse. For Qutb, living in the first generation of Muslims forced to live with an autonomous Jewish state in *Dar al Islam,* the terrifying advance of secularism threatened the extermination of Islam.[105] And these signs of the end called for jihad. He "read" both the Jews and Israel as part of a vast sacred history:

> For they [the Jews] returned to corruption and so God gave them into the power of the [first] Muslims and they expelled them [the Jews] from the Arabian Peninsula entirely. Then they returned to corruption and God gave them [the Jews] into the power of other servants, until in our own time He gave them into the power of Hitler. They have returned today to corruption in the form of "Israel," which has caused the Arabs…to taste woes, and God will give them into the power of someone who will impose upon them the worst of torments….[106]

One could still read this as a passive even non-apocalyptic scenario: Allah will find someone to punish the Jews—could be Muslims, could, like Hitler, be someone else, could be soon, could be eventually.

Egyptian president Gamal Abdul Nasser, the "Arab Nationalist," the very quintessence of Qutb's apostate in a state of *Jahiliyya,* executed his critic Qutb in 1966. The following year, however, Nasser presented himself to the world as a candidate to be the divine instrument that Qutb had anticipated, that "someone who will impose on the Israelis the worst of torments." He electrified the Arab and Muslim world, awakening the same unity and excitement in Arab capitals that marked the

---

[103] Sayyid Qutb, *Milestones,* trans. S. Badrul Hasan (Karachi: International Islamic Publishers, 1981), 49.

[104] Mitchell, *Society of Muslim Brothers,* 318–19. On Qutb's totalitarian tendencies, see Paul Berman, *Terror and Liberalism* (New York: W.W. Norton, 2003), 77–103; and Boroumand and Boroumand, "Terror, Islam, and Democracy," 7–9.

[105] Berman, *Terror and Liberalism,* 93. See also Luke Loboda, "The Thought of Sayyid Qutb," Ashbrook Statesman Thesis 1, online: http://www.ashbrook.org/publicat/thesis/loboda/loboda.pdf, March 11, 2010.

[106] Qutb, cited in Cook, *Contemporary Muslim Apocalyptic,* 108.

invasion of 1948. In anticipation of certain victory, huge crowds gathered in Arab capitals and chanted, "Drive the Jews into the Sea."[107]

The massive and lightning-fast Israeli defeat of Syria, Jordan, and Egypt in the Six Days' War proved a catastrophe for the "secular" model. "The Six Days' War of 1967 ... was the seminal event that reopened the Mahdist Pandora's box in the twentieth century: since the likes of Nasser had failed to reglorify Muslim societies, perhaps it was time for the Mahdi to come and do [so]."[108] So while Arafat and his PLO, dressed up in the secular clothes of "National Liberation," dominated the international stage, Muslim apocalyptic traditions took the relay from below.[109]

The most obvious task, for the apocalyptically minded, was to locate the horrific phenomenon of modern-day Israel in the apocalyptic scenario.[110] The difficulties they experienced illustrate the overwhelming *desire* to see Israel as an apocalyptic figure despite the lack of anything in the literature that could accommodate even a symbolic reading. And yet, each passing year in which Israel continued and prospered, while the Arab world remained mired in premodern impotence, was an insult to Allah:

> The Jews say: "Allah's hand is tied"; may their own hands be tied and may they be damned for what they say. His hands are rather outstretched; He grants freely as He pleases. And what has been sent down to you from your Lord will certainly increase many of them in arrogance and unbelief. We have cast in their midst animosity and hatred till the Day of Resurrection.[111]

In particular, the Jewish control of the Haram al Sharif (Noble Sanctuary/Temple Mount), captured in the 1967 war, is an unbearable shame, especially given the Muslims' immense numerical superiority: "If the Jews reach the al-Aqsa Mosque and put into action their plots in the midst of a generation of Muslims reaching a quarter of the inhabitants of the earth, may God help us for the shame ('ar) that would not be wiped away by time nor washed away by water."[112] No, only blood could wash away such a humiliation.

And millennial Islam held the torch that lighted the path forward to vindication:

> The *role of the Islamic stream is to keep the flame of hatred toward Zionism burning in their souls. This is because we are not ready to fight and use our military power, due to*

[107] Moshe Shemesh, "Did Shuqayri Call for 'Throwing the Jews into the Sea'?" *Israel Studies* 8, no. 2 (2003): 70–81, online: http://muse.jhu.edu/journals/israel_studies/v008/8.2shemesh.html, March 12, 2010.*

[108] Furnish, *Holiest Wars*, 88.

[109] See the discussion in Ansary, 329–94.

[110] Cook, *Contemporary Muslim Apocalyptic*, 232–33.

[111] Qur'an 5:64. See the discussion of this passage by Mughniyya in Cook, *Contemporary Muslim Apocalyptic*, 108.*

[112] Àbd al-Àziz Mustafa, *Qabla an yuhdam al-Aqsa* (Cairo: Dar al-Tawziwa-l-Nashr al-Islamiyya, 1990), 284, cited in Cook, *Contemporary Muslim Apocalyptic*, 23.

the limitations forced on us. We are not capable of conducting daily confrontations with Israel in the battlefield, because it is not in our hand, but rather in the hands of others [meaning, the Palestinian Authority]. Nevertheless, *we are capable of cultivating the flame of hatred to this enemy in the souls of our sons, daughters, and grandchildren.* We can make hatred burn among the public. If we manage to do so, *in our homes and with the help of our schools and media,* our efforts will be successful. The fighting will come one of these days and *if by that time the ideology of hatred has faded, we will be defeated; on the other hand, if on this day we will still hate [Israel], victory will be ours, with the help of Allah.*[113]

And the more apocalyptic the hatred, the better.

Over the years since the 1967 disaster for Arab (secular) nationalism, the religious dimension, always a key player on the ground,[114] became increasingly prominent. But in order to understand how that played out, we must turn from the Arab-Israeli conflict to Iran and Afghanistan in order to observe the first breaches not only into the public sphere, but into power, of full-fledged apocalyptic Islam. They coincided with the advent of the Mujaddid in AH 1400.

■ RENEWAL OF JIHAD FROM 1979/1400 ONWARD

Shiites

The year 1979 proved a critical moment in the rebirth of Muslim apocalyptic for both Shiites and Sunnis. On the one hand, it marks the victory of Khomeini over the shah of Iran and the revolutionary launch of the first Islamic (Sharia-based) society of the modern world. On the other, the year marks the invasion of the Soviets into Afghanistan and the birth to the *Mujehaddin* in response. Ten years later, the Mujehaddin expelled the Soviets, giving birth simultaneously to a second experiment in Mahdist Sharia, this time in Sunni Taliban Afghanistan (1996), and, still more consequently, to bin Laden's global jihad.

In the mid-1980s, a sociologist remarked: "1979 marks the death of modern sociology, because in 1979 the juggernaut of Weberian secularization was reversed by Khomeini in Iran."[115] Of course, for Khomeini and his enthusiasts, the year was AH 1400—a potentially apocalyptic year.[116] What had upended the Westerner's

---

[113] Interview with Salim Al-'Awa, Islamic intellectual close to Sheikh Qaradawi, published in *Al-Istiqlal*, August 28, 1998, trans. MEMRI, Special Dispatch Series, no. 5, August 31, 1998, online: http://memri.org/bin/articles.cgi?Page=archives&Area=sd&ID=SP0598, April 15, 2010.

[114] Benny Morris, *1948: The First Arab-Israeli War* (New Haven, Conn.: Yale University Press, 2008), 393–96.

[115] Reinhold Kant, University of Pittsburgh, personal communication, Fall 1986.

[116] On the Mujaddid tradition see above, n. 64; on Khomeini's turn to "totalitarian" Islamism and terror in the period before AH 1400, see Boroumand and Boroumand, "Terror, Islam, and Democracy," who attribute his turn away from the more traditional views of his colleagues to the influence of both Mawdudi and Qutb (9–12).

expectations of secular triumphalism, had less to do with religion broadly speaking, as it did with apocalyptic religion.

Still worse, it had to do with the most dangerous of all variants—one with a millennial agenda of dominion (Muslim over infidel), and a violent apocalyptic scenario. Khomeini wrote:

> [I]f we kill infidels in order to put a stop to their [corrupting] activities, we have indeed done them a service...To allow the infidels to stay alive means to let them do more corrupting [activities]. [To kill them] is a surgical operation commanded by Allah... *War is a blessing for the world and for every nation.* It is Allah himself who commands men to wage war and kill... *The wars that our Prophet... waged* against the infidels were *divine gifts to humanity...* We have to wage war until all corruption, all disobedience of Islamic law ceases...The Quran commands: "War! War until victory!" *A religion without war is a crippled religion...* It is war that purifies the earth... *to kill the infidels is one of the noblest missions Allah has reserved for mankind.*[117]

Nor did Khomeini and other ideologues merely consider infidels (*kafir*) legitimate targets, but even Muslims deemed insufficiently observant (*jahali*).[118] Indeed, readiness to kill enemies of Allah constituted a crucial characteristic of an Islamic revolutionary:

> Our own Prophet...was even more of a revolutionary... *A people that is not prepared to kill and to die* in order to create a just society cannot expect any support from Allah...that day [of Islam ruling over the entire world] must be hastened through our *jihad*, through our readiness to offer our lives *and to shed the unclean blood of those who do not see the light brought from the Heavens by Muhammad...It is Allah who puts the gun in our hand. But we cannot expect Him to pull the trigger as well, simply because we are faint-hearted.*"[119]

The ideologues of the French revolutionary terror would have found themselves fully at home in such activist "logic."

Indeed, Michel Foucault's reaction to Khomeini's takeover almost perfectly mirrored Marx's response to the Taiping. "[A]n Islamic movement can set the entire region afire, overturn the most unstable regimes, and disturb the most solid. Islam—which is not simply a religion, but an entire way of life, an adherence to a

---

[117] Cited in Amir Taheri, *The Spirit of Allah: Khomeini and the Islamic Revolution* (Chevy Chase, MD.: Adler and Adler, 1986), 113.

[118] David Zeidan, "The Islamic Fundamentalist View of Life as a Perennial Battle," *Middle East Review of International Affairs* 5, no. 4 (December 2001): 239. Khomeini here invoked the groundbreaking work of Sayyid Qutb who extended *takfir* (declaring someone an apostate) to secular Muslims; Kepel, *Jihad*, 31–32. Ömer Çaha identifies this as one of the main reasons for the failure of democracy in the Arab world, "The Deficiency of Democracy in the Arab World," in *Islam and the West: Critical Perspectives on Modernity*, Logos: Perspectives on Modern Society and Culture, ed. Michael Thompson (Oxford: Rowman & Littlefield, 2003), 44–45.

[119] Muhammad Taqi Partovi Samzevari, *Future of the Islamic Movement* (1986), cited in Amir Taheri, *Khomeini*, 239.

history and civilization—has a good chance to become a gigantic powder keg, at the level of hundreds of millions of men."[120] Like a pyromaniac cheering on a forest fire, he thereby illustrated a peculiar Western intellectual disease we have already seen at work in the case of Communism, and see again in response to 9-11: a fascination with conflagration and mega-death.

And Foucault got more than he imagined. From 1980–88, Iraq and Iran engaged in a war that killed millions. When, in 1982, a chastened Saddam Hussein offered a resolution, Khomeini, responded, "The road to Jerusalem goes through Karbala." And he cleared the way with waves of young and old martyrs with plastic keys to heaven (purchased in bulk from China) around their necks, urged on by a man dressed as Imam Hussein, the great Shiite martyr killed in 680 (played, among others, by Ahmadinejad).[121] Khomeini did not relent until 1988, by which time more than a million people had been killed.[122]

Nor did Khomeini stand alone in response to the advent of AH 1400. The Mujaddid tradition encouraged a number of candidates and uprisings, including a rebellion in Nigeria led by *Maitatsine* ("he who damns") that resulted in thousands of deaths,[123] and a Wahabi attempt to seize the Great Mosque at Mecca from the hands of the infidel Saudi government on the first day of the year 1400.[124] A classic example of the power of apocalyptic dates, this minefield in sacred time—Islam's fin de siècle—caught the West, both its academic and intelligence communities, by surprise. It continues to do so.

Indeed, perhaps the most significant (and least remarked) case of invoking the Mujaddid in 1980/1400 came from one of the most influential Muslim preachers in the last two decades, the "global Mufti" Yusuf al-Qaradawi, who argued that the hadith in question could refer not only to a single individual (the "renewer") but a collective movement: "This is what I prefer in understanding this noble hadith and its implementation in our century which we parted from [the fourteenth Hijri century which ended in 1980] in order to receive a new century, in which we ask Allah to make our today better than our yesterday, and our tomorrow better than

[120] Michel Foucault, "A Powder Keg Called Islam," *Corriere della sera*, February 13, 1979, reproduced in *Foucault and the Iranian Revolution: Gender and the Seductions of Islamism*, ed. Janet Afary and Kevin Anderson (Chicago: University of Chicago Press, 2005), 241; see also Nick Cohen, *What's Left? How Liberals Lost their Way* (London: Fourth Estate, 2007), 107–08. See also, Richard Falk, "Trusting Khomeini," *New York Review of Books*, February 16, 1979. On Marx and the Taiping, see above, chapter 10, n. 79.

[121] Matthias Küntzel, "Ahmadinejad's Demons: A Child of the Revolution Takes Over," *The New Republic*, April 24, 2006, online: http://www.matthiaskuentzel.de/contents/ahmadinejads-demons, April 11, 2010.

[122] Farhang Rajaee, *The Iran-Iraq War: The Politics of Aggression* (Gainesville: University Press of Florida, 1993); Efraim Karsh, *The Iran-Iraq War, 1980–1988* (Oxford: Osprey Publishing, 2002).

[123] Rosalind Hackett, "Theorizing Radical Islam in Northern Nigeria," in McGhee and O'Leary, *War in Heaven/Heaven on Earth*.

[124] See J. Ketchichan, "Islamic Revivalism in Saudi Arabia: Juhayman al-'Utaybi's 'Letters' to the Saudi People," *Muslim World* 80 (1990): 1–16.

our today."[125] Qaradawi embodies the new, activist, technologically empowered, Islamic revivalism of the early fifteenth century AH.

The early stages in the launching of a global jihad aiming at world conquest began at the century mark.[126] Initially, Iran provided the only enduring case of a successful political movement launched in AH 1400, and for the first decade of the new century, the Shiites monopolized the Islamic apocalyptic podium. In their effort to spread their message, they began as early as 1982 to appeal not only to other Shiites but to Sunnis as well. The Palestinian Sunni, Fathi Shqaqi, dissatisfied with the "quiescence" of the Palestinian Muslim Brotherhood, wrote an encomium entitled *Khomeini: The Islamic Alternative* in 1979, which praised Khomeini and Hassan al Banna as "the two men of the century." He went on to found the Palestinian movement Islamic jihad and "Islamiz[e] the Palestinian question."[127] Muslim Brotherhood members who assassinated Anwar Sadat in October 1981 "were inspired by the Iranian model, and expected the death of Sadat to trigger a mass uprising that would replay in Cairo the same sort of events which had taken place two years earlier in Teheran."[128]

But despite the initial flush of enthusiasm, the Iranian revolution hardly triggered the kind of instantaneous domino effect that apocalyptic believers expect. The wave of Islamic triumphalism that surrounded AH 1400 broke its teeth on hard realities: Khomeini on Iraqi armies, Muslim Brotherhood on the state crackdown after the assassination of Sadat. Generally Arab "secular" dictatorships managed to hold the line.[129]

Indeed, even within Islam a reaction against "Mahdism" developed in the early 1980s/1400s;[130] and by the 1990s/1410s, many observers declared imperialist Islamism was on the wane.[131] As we have seen with apocalyptic hopes, however, "wrong does not mean inconsequential," and cognitive dissonance does not necessarily lead to the waning of the apocalyptic impulse, certainly not one so deeply rooted in the historical experience of the believers. On all fronts, the millennial dream continued to operate, to find projects that could prepare for the dreamed-of wave of conquest to succeed.[132]

---

[125] Yusuf al-Qaradawi, *Awalawiyyat al-Haraka al-Islamiyya fi al-Marhala al-Qadima* [The preferences of the Islamic movement in the next stage] (Cairo: Maktabat Wahaba, 6th ed., 2005 [originally 1990]), 13–14; translation provided by Shammai Fishman, whom I thank for pointing out this text. Note that the text was composed *ex post defectu*, a decade after the passage of the Mujaddid in 1979.

[126] Gilles Kepel, whose book, *Jihad: Expansion et déclin de l'islamisme* (Paris, Gallimard, 2000), focuses precisely on the renewal starting in 1979, has no mention of the Mujaddid tradition.

[127] Kepel, *Jihad: The Trail of Political Islam* (Cambridge, Mass.: Harvard University Press, 2002), 122. Shqaqi was expelled from Egypt after the assassination of Sadat.

[128] Boroumand and Boroumand, "Terror, Islam, and Democracy", 10.

[129] Martin Kramer addresses the resilience of Arab dictatorships in the last few decades, something that surprised both Islamists and post-Orientalist Western scholars, *Ivory Towers on Sand: The Failure of Middle Eastern Studies in America* (Washington, DC: The Washington Institute for Near East Policy, 2001), chap. 4.

[130] Furnish, *Holiest Wars*, chap. 5.

[131] Gilles Kepel's subtitle: *L'expansion et déclin de l'islamisme*, was changed in its English translation two years later: *The Trail of Political Islam*.

[132] Karsh, *Islamic Imperialism*, 220–22.

Sunnis

Sunnis soon developed their own apocalyptic ideologies. The Russian invasion of Afghanistan in 1979 offered the opportunity to rally the vanguard of the revolution. One of the most prominent figures to respond was Abdallah Yusuf Azzam, a West Bank Palestinian who fled the Israeli conquest in 1967, joined the Qutb-inspired Brotherhood in Egypt, and set up a recruiting and training station in Pakistan for Jihadis. Azzam formulated the contemporary radical [apocalyptic] theories of how warfare should be waged and became Osama bin Laden's spiritual mentor.[133] He promised the Mahdi: "…the black banners will rise from the east, and they will kill a number of you the like of which has never been seen previously… when you see him [coming] swear allegiance to him, even if you have to crawl on the snow, for he is the caliph of God, the Mahdi."[134] Nor did Azzam forget his Palestinian origins. Afghanistan, in his apocalyptic scenario, was the prologue, the precursor to the destruction of Israel. His book, *From Kabul to al-Quds*, views liberating Kabul as a necessary precursor to liberating Jerusalem.[135] For apocalyptic Sunnis and Shiites, apparently, all roads lead to Jerusalem.

In 1989, when the Mujehaddin chased the Russians from Afghanistan and the Soviet Union fell shortly thereafter, the Sunnis had an even more dramatic victory than the Shiites a decade earlier. Whatever Westerners may have thought, Osama bin Laden and his fellow warriors believed that they, and they alone, had brought down the Eastern empire—just as the earliest followers of Muhammad had taken down one of the two superpowers of the seventh century, the Sassanian Empire.[136] The other empire, the West, with at its head, America, the second 'Ad, was next. The auguries seemed favorable: the same year Khomeini issued his fatwa against Salman Rushdie, sending the author—previously a supporter of the Iranian revolution—into hiding, and thereby showing that Sharia could be extended to *Dar al Harb* even without military conquest.[137]

---

[133] Cook, *Understanding Jihad*, 128–31.

[134] Muhammad b. Yazid Ibn Maja, *Sunan* (Beirut: Dar al-Fikr, n.d.), 2:1367, no. 4084; cited in Cook, *Contemporary Muslim Apocalyptic*, 173.

[135] *Min Kabul ila al-Quds* (1989, 1991) cited in ibid., 174. Compare Khomeini's response to Saddam Hussein's peace offers of 1982, "The Road to Jerusalem goes through Karbala!" discussed in Christiane Gruber, "Jerusalem in the Visual Propaganda of Post-Revolutionary Iran," in *Jerusalem: Idea and Reality*, ed. Tamar Mayer and Suleiman Ali Mourad (New York: Routledge, 2008), 172–73.

[136] This perspective is not only apocalyptic: Sorbonne-educated Hassan Hanafi describes the dream even before the fall of the USSR:

> In the past Islam found its way between two falling empires, the Persian and the Roman. Both were exhausted by wars. Both suffered moral and spiritual crises. Islam, as a new world order, was able to expand as a substitute to the old regimes. Nowadays Islam finds itself again as a new power, marking its way between two superpowers in crisis. Islam is regenerating, the two superpowers, degenerating. Islam is the power of the future, inheriting the two superpowers in the present.

Hassan Hanfi, "The Origins of Modern Conservatism and Islamic Fundamentalism," in *Islamic Dilemmas: Reformers, Nationalists, and Industrialization*, ed. Ernst Gellner (Berlin: Mouton, 1985), 103.

[137] On the Rushdie affair and the stakes, see Daniel Pipes, *The Rushdie Affair: The Novel, the Ayatollah, and the West* (New York: Birch Lane, 1990), 155–78 (on the timorous Western response both political and intellectual); 179–93 (on Iran's long shadow).

From this point on, Muslim ambitions for global conquest ceased to be a pipe dream and entered a new, "realistic" phase. The Mujehaddin scanned the world for conflicts to which they could profitably contribute—Chechnya, the Balkans, Palestine. Osama declared war on the "Great Satan," America.[138] From 1989 onward, both Shiite and Sunni Islam produced global Jihadi warriors, intent on fulfilling the original millennial vision of Islam: establish the caliphate and transform the whole world into *Dar al Islam*.

Hamas: Genocidal Apocalyptic Phase of the Muslim Brotherhood

In 1987 (AH 1408), Palestinians Islamists created *Hamas* as branch of the Muslim Brotherhood. Their charter, issued the following year, illustrates the combination of current events, apocalyptic worldview, and cataclysmic violence that characterizes fifteenth-century AH Muslim activism. The charter makes the "religio-national" stakes in the fight with Zionism abundantly clear.[139] It offers jihad as the only legitimate Muslim response to the existence of a non-Muslim entity inside *Dar al Islam* (para. 11), and considers itself the latest avatar of a jihad against the Jews in Palestine that dates back to 1939, 1948, and 1968:

> The Islamic Resistance Movement believes that the land of Palestine has been an Islamic Waqf throughout the generations and until the Day of Resurrection, no one can renounce it or part of it, or abandon it or part of it. No Arab country nor the aggregate of all Arab countries, and no Arab King or President nor all of them in the aggregate, have that right, nor has that right any organization or the aggregate of all organizations, be they Palestinian or Arab.…(para. 11).

Hamas repeatedly states that no Muslim can "negotiate" with non-Muslims over Palestine and that anyone who dares is a traitor worthy of their hatred. "There is no solution for the Palestinian question except through Jihad" (para. 13).[140]

Perhaps more significantly, Hamas viewed itself as representing the next stage in the premillennial project of the Muslim Brotherhood. Its founding document invokes Hassan al Banna's millennial dream of a global Muslim community (para. 5), and then invokes the apocalyptic hadith of "Rocks and Trees" as a goal:

> The Hamas has been looking forward to implement Allah's promise whatever time it might take. The prophet, prayer and peace be upon him, said: "The time will not come

---

[138] For the text of the *World Islamic Front's* declaration of jihad against the West (February 23, 1998), see *Messages to the World: The Statements of Osama Bin Laden*, ed. Bruce Lawrence (New York: Verso, 2005), 58–61.

[139] Hamas Charter (1988); online: http://www.yale.edu/lawweb/avalon/mideast/hamas.htm, April 15, 2010.

[140] Clearly jihad here does not mean "inner struggle."

until Muslims will fight the Jews (and kill them); until the Jews hide behind rocks and trees, which will cry: "O Muslim! there is a Jew hiding behind me, come on and kill him! This will not apply to the Gharqad, which is a Jewish tree" (para. 7).[140a]

Accompanying these repeated appeals to a sacred history now approaching its culminating phases, we find many of the paranoid themes of cataclysmic apocalyptic expressed unapologetically: the antimodern conspiracy narrative so popular among Nazis and other fascists of the early twentieth century, including the Muslim Brotherhood (para. 22); the *Protocols of the Elders of Zion* as a key to understanding contemporary history; and the belief that the two blue stripes on the Israeli flag signal their ambitions to rule from the "Nile to the Euphrates" (para. 32).

In 1998, one scholar noted that the overall impact of conspiracy thinking in the Arab Muslim world produced passive responses to the perceived power of an overwhelming enemy.[141] Furnish notes a similar quietist impact of "waiting for the Mahdi."[142] But Hamas's charter represents an attempt to radically reverse the fatalism on a global scale, and in this shares with Osama bin Laden the sense that all of Islam begins to awaken.[143]

> By virtue of the distribution of Muslims, who *pursue the cause* of the Hamas, *all over the globe*, and strive for its victory, for the reinforcement of its positions and for the encouragement of its Jihad, *the Movement is a universal one*... Whoever denigrates its worth, or *avoids supporting it*, or is so blind as to *dismiss its role*, is *challenging Fate itself*. Whoever closes his eyes from seeing the facts, whether intentionally or not, *will wake up to find himself overtaken by events*, and will find no excuses to justify his position. *Priority is reserved to the early comers* (para. 7).

Owls beware, the text announces: the juggernaut of jihad is about to spew out the tepid. Khosrokhavar described jihad the way Michelet wrote about the French Revolution: "*Jihad* operates as a substitute to an Apocalypse that is too long in the coming."[144] Hamas, like the Mujehaddin, represents a dramatic shift from passive to active cataclysmic apocalyptic.

[140a] On this hadith, see above n.63.*

[141] Daniel Pipes, *The Hidden Hand: Middle East Fears of Conspiracy* (New York: St. Martins Press, 1996), 26.

[142] Furnish, *Holiest Wars*, 80–129.

[143] "[Infidels] massacring Muslims... sent shivers in the body and shook the conscience. All of that happened and the world watched and heard, and not only did not respond to these atrocities, but also with a clear conspiracy between America and its allies prevented the weaklings [Muslims] from acquiring arms to defend themselves by using the United Nations as a cover. Muslims became aware that they were the main targets of the Jewish-Crusader alliance of aggression," Osama bin Laden, *Declaration of Jihad against the Americans*, online: http://en.wikisource.org/wiki/Osama_bin_Laden's_Declaration_of_War, April 1, 2010.

[144] Farhad Khosrokhavar, *Les Nouveaux martyrs d'Allah* (Paris: Flammarion, 2002), 315. On Michelet, see above, chapter 9, n. 12.

■ MAINSTREAMING JIHAD: THE IMPACT OF 2000 ON MUSLIM APOCALYPTIC EXPECTATIONS

Of course, such chest-thumping among active apocalyptic writers is fairly common in any culture. These ambitions, however, rarely "take." And even Hamas and bin Laden labored for over a decade to make any real headway in the public sphere. At the turn of the millennium, however, apocalyptic global jihad quite suddenly went from the margins to the center of the Arab and Muslim public sphere. In the first decade of the twenty-first century, the paranoid apocalyptic and imperialist millennial discourse that informs the Hamas charter and the writings of Osama bin Laden became one of the dominant forms of religious *and* political discourse in much of the Arab and Muslim world. Using the new technology of the Internet, and exciting isolated believers the world over, drawing many in to this vast transformative project, this discourse made inroads everywhere. And such novel boldness spilled out into the Western public sphere: jihadis publicly announced their intentions to infidels—Islam will dominate the world—in ways that only a few brief years earlier would have been unthinkable.

And who could have imagined how successful Muslims would be in openly asserting this millennial agenda right in the heart of the target population? How many people in the 1990s—even those who knew how much these ideas circulated in "student" movements—imagined that in 2006, they would see angry Muslims demonstrating in London streets with signs announcing Islam's rule over Britain/Europe/the world, and promising Europeans their very own Holocaust?[145] Who among the founders of Hamas in 1988, as they penned their genocidal charter, would imagine that Christian pacifists would come to their defense,[146] and crowds of infidels would march with *their* banners in the streets of European capitals in 2009 shouting "Allahu Akhbar" and carry signs reading "We are Hamas"?[147]

In order to understand how this all happened, let us return to the bizarre street-level apocalyptic literature that sprouted so vigorously among Israel's "neighbors" (Egypt, Jordan, Palestinian territories, Lebanon), with its borrowings from

---

[145] Juan Jose Escobar Stemmann, "Middle East Salafism's Influence and the Radicalization of Muslim Communities In Europe," *MERIA Journal* 10, no. 3 (September 2006), online: http://openpdf. com/viewer?url=http://www.e-prism.org/images/MIDDLE_EAST_SALAFISM_-_1-9-06.pdf, April 20, 2010. More recently, Roel Meijer, ed., *Global Salafism: Islam's New Religious Movement* (New York: Columbia University Press, 2009).

[146] Among two of the more prominent ones to do so, see Jimmy Carter, *Palestine: Peace not Apartheid* (New York: Simon & Schuster, 2007); and Helen Cobban, "Hamas's Next Steps," *Boston Review*, May/June 2006, online: http://bostonreview.net/BR31.3/cobban.php.*

[147] For footage of a rally in Germany attended by members of Die Linke party, see online: http://tinyurl.com/5szlppm (footage taken by Sebastien Meskes, provided by Sebastien Voigt); for coverage of the pro-Hamas rally in London, see Ben Cohen, "Gaza Protests: Fanatics and Fading Celebs Take to the Streets," online: http://blog.z-word.com/2009/01/gaza-protests-fanatics-and-fading-celebs-take-to-the-streets/.

Protestant apocalyptic, its innovations in Muslim apocalyptic, and its curious date of AD 2000.[148]

The New Apocalyptic Literature and Y2K

The literature, no matter how bizarre and even heretical it might appear—to Muslims and Westerners alike—hit on every theme of grievance traced in this chapter. For example, the following passage on UFOs, the Bermuda Triangle as the "throne of Satan," and the location of the Dajjal, may sound fanciful, but it also reveals a great deal, and intersects repeatedly with political and media "realities."[149] Here the author identifies the 5 percent of UFO sightings that are "real," as actually being the work of the Dajjal who kidnaps the unfortunate travelers who happen to stray into his lair, the Triangle, and then possesses their minds and turns them into a secret army that he keeps hidden under the Dome of the Rock:

> He is training a gigantic army (I still do not know their number) under the earth. Where? Under the al-Aqsa Mosque and [the area] nearby to it. Why has the messiah of error chosen this unique place? Because it became available after the Jewish occupation of Palestine…The kidnapped are very young and are given a military education…Male and female look alike, like animals. They are educated to hate [male] Muslims and to love the women of the Muslims and the Arabs…[They are told that soon] they will have a life above when the great king, god [the Antichrist] comes to take them out and give them spoils and women…. The Jewish call for the destruction of the al-Aqsa Mosque is nothing more than sand in the eyes, since the Jews know that the Mosque cannot be destroyed, while the hidden hands dig in secret for other reasons.[150]

Note the clear link between Antichrist's army and Israeli/Jewish activity—the Jews pray constantly in the area nearby the Mount, tunnel under it, and have men and women in their army. Note also the characteristic projection involved: hating the enemy men and desiring their women, promises of spoils and women, standing ready "for the hour"—these are all classic promises to the Jihadi warrior who succeeds on earth.[151] And note that the tunnel riots that exploded in 1996 reflect precisely these anxieties about what goes on "under the Temple Mount."[152]

---

[148] See discussion above, beginning of chapter. Most recently, see Filiu, *Apocalypse in Islam*.

[149] M. Da'ud, *Warning: The Antichrist Is Invading the World from the Bermuda Triangle* (Cairo, 1992), adds exciting new elements to the narrative popularized by Ayyub (cited in Cook, *Contemporary Muslim Apocalyptic*, 79).

[150] M. Da'ud, *Warning*, 126–27, cited in Cook, *Contemporary Muslim Apocalyptic*, 80.

[151] On the tradition of booty and jihad, see Karsh's account of Muhammad's rise to power, *Islamic Imperialism*, chap. 1; one of the demonstrators in London during the Muhammad Cartoon affair (November 2005) invoked raping the women of the defeated infidel Europeans, on which see "Muslims March in Cartoons Protest," online: http://news.bbc.co.uk/2/hi/uk_news/4726472.stm, April 15, 2010.

[152] For an extensive discussion of this incident, see Gorenberg, *End of Days*, 181–96. Note that the French news media (among others) reported as accurate the false accusations of tunneling under the Dome of the Rock and al-Aqsa that inspired the rioting (as dealt with in the film *Decyrptage* [Paris, 2003]).

In an unprecedented move, semiotically aroused Muslim apocalyptic writers interpret biblical texts. One commentator offers a Muslim's view of the Christian apocalyptic favorite, the "little horn" of Daniel 7:8:

[The little horn is] none other than America, since America has appeared on the world scene as a great power after World War II... and the little horn is a hint at world Zionism, which manages America, and rules through it, and it is also a hint at the Antichrist, just as the Christians interpret it, because world Zionism manages it [the world] and moves it from behind the veil of the Antichrist, as we have noted previously. There is a perfect correlation between the little horn and Zionist America, since this Zionist state has waged many wars against the Muslims (the saints), and the Zionists have humiliated the Muslims with the aid of America that persecutes them, imposes an economic and military siege [upon them] and forbids them from weaponry and supplies.[153]

Invoking Revelation, another writer pursues the issue of imminent Western destruction:

God's punishment falls on the evilest of His creation, and the more evil, the more intense the punishment. Since America is now the chief and first Zionist power (the dragon [of Revelation 12]), and the strong arm of the Antichrist (the false prophet), and the first head of the beast which leads the other six heads, so the punishment will be more intense upon it than upon others. Since in New York especially there are more Jews than in other places, and in it is their wealth, their banks, their political foundations which control the entire world (the U.N., the Security Council, the International Monetary Fund, the World Bank, and the principal media networks), so there is no evil greater than in New York in any other place on the inhabited earth, and for this reason their portion of the punishment will be greater in measure and it will be a total uprooting.[154]

This apocalyptic language unleashes a conspiratorial imagination that projects evil, fantasizes omnipotence, and embraces cataclysm.[155] And in these matters, nothing, not even Revelation, competes with the *Protocols of the Elders of Zion*. Cook notes:

The use of the *Protocols of the Elders of Zion* is a predominant feature of the contemporary Arabic-language Muslim apocalyptic scenario. It is the lens the apocalyptic writers view the world and interpret everyday events occurring in the political, religious, economic and cultural arenas. One can see how and why they have focused upon the concept of freedom as being the enemy, because for them it is the *true* enemy, denying

---

[153] Àbd al-Hamid (Cairo, 1997), cited in Cook, *Contemporary Muslim Apocalyptic*, 45–46. Note that the author is already in debate with Muhammad 'Abdullah, whose extensive exegesis of Revelation represents the cornerstone of the Muslim apocalyptic revision of Christian texts (ibid, 39–45).

[154] Àbdallah, *Zilzal al-ard al-'azim* (Cairo, 1994), 395–96, cited in Cook, *Contemporary Muslim Apocalyptic*, 164.

[155] Above, chapter 13; see in particular, Michael Barkun, *A Culture of Conspiracy: Apocalyptic Visions in Contemporary America* (Berkeley and Los Angeles: University of California Press, 2003).

them their power over their audience. Many...describe it as a Jewish plot to cause chaos...the basic theme of the *Protocols*.[156]

The Jews have plotted modernity and its freedoms in order to destroy Islam.[157] Accordingly, strong, independent-*minded* women terrify these writers and their audiences. Since some of the earliest apocalyptic hadiths hold that women's disobedience is one of the signs of the coming Day of Judgment, misogyny and antimodern Muslim apocalyptic expectation go hand in hand.

> The woman, by her going to work, has ripped every veil, and has taken every calumny and sin. The issue is, as the Messenger of God said, "I went into Heaven and saw that most of its people were poor people, and I went into Hell and I saw that most of its people were women." The sad thing is that the woman by her disobedience of this drags with her everyone who has guardianship or authority over her—husband, or father or brother who manages her affairs, or even lord, judge and ruler (*sultan*).[158]

Even if sexuality does not come into play, the woman's very desire to live independently (i.e., to Westernize) drags her men into hell with her. The pervasive gynophobia of Muslim apocalyptic resonates closely with many less obviously apocalyptic elements of Arab and Muslim culture the world over, in particular, honor-killings. The Islamists' deep fears of women, embodied in their ferocious desire to hide them behind the veil/burqa/*niqab*—to the point of throwing acid on the faces of women who refuse to cover them—makes these men particularly susceptible to the most ferocious of apocalyptic transcripts.[159]

We have already seen the profoundly paranoid apocalyptic vision at the heart of the *Protocols* work on the Nazi mind, feeding its cataclysmic fears, its deepest resentments and rage at humiliation, and its overweening ambitions with a perfect mirror of projection: *the Jews* want to do to us what we must do to them.[160] But whereas back then, Hitler thought the Jews *secretly* controlled the world, *now* it is clear to Muslim apocalyptic writers that they *openly* control the world:

> There cannot be the slightest doubt that the Jews have reached this great arrogance now [Qur'an 17:4] through the world Zionist government, which rules the world, and through the blind support that the Zionist American government gives them in thought and in tendency, and through the United Nations and the Security Council which are both under the control of the American government and the Zionist world government

[156] Cook, *Contemporary Muslim Apocalyptic*, 33–34.

[157] Muhammad 'Izzat Àrif, *Nihayat al-Yahud* (Cairo: Dar al-I'tisam, 1996), 157, cited in Cook, *Contemporary Muslim Apocalyptic*, 34.

[158] Amin Jamal al-Din, *Al-Qawl al-mubin fi ashrat al-sa'a al-sughra li-Yawm al-Din* (Cairo: Maktaba al-Tawfiqiyya, 1997), 59, also 75, cited in Cook, *Contemporary Muslim Apocalyptic*, 52.

[159] Shamita Das Dasgupta, "Acid Attacks," in *Encyclopedia of Interpersonal Violence*, ed. C. Renzetti and J. Edleson (Thousand Oaks, Calif.: Sage Publications, 2008), 5–6.

[160] For a confessional discussion of Muslim attitudes toward Jews and Israel, see the remarks of a former Muslim, the Egyptian-born Mark A. Gabriel's *The Unfinished Battle: Islam and the Jews* (Lake Mary, Fla.: Charisma House, 2003).

[sic!], which are managed from behind the curtain by the Antichrist and Satan, just as the book of Revelation points out.[161]

Here the Muslims rejoin the far-right racists in the United States: they both consider the U.S. government to be ZOG: Zionist Occupied Government.[162] As Cook notes, the discovery of this European anti-Semitic literature, especially the *Protocols*, sparked the emergence of modern (contemporary) Islamic apocalyptic exegesis.[163]

Muslims, especially apocalyptic ones, view modernity as an elaborate humiliation inflicted on proud and manly cultures by effeminate Jews. Civil polities, egalitarian law codes, and human rights are all forms of castration. Here the Christians are the first victims (hence first to modernize), and the Muslims know that they are the next target.

> Thus the Jewish slap on the faces of the Christians continues, who apparently enjoy and allow this sort of humiliation and attack, and give them their other cheek so that the Jew can continue to slap the Christians—just as we see—ruling them in Europe through the Masons who dig the grave of Western civilization through corruption and promiscuity. The Crusader West continues like a whore who is screwed sadistically, and does not derive any pleasure from the act until after she is struck and humiliated, even by her pimps—the Jews in Christian Europe. Soon they will be under the rubble as a result of the Jewish conspiracy.[164]

Given this perfidy, Muslim apocalyptic thinkers come to the same millennial conclusion as the Nazis: *genocide*. In the Muslim version of Armageddon, the Antichrist (Dajjal), is a Jewish "messiah." And, as the hadith promises, when the hour comes, Muslims will wipe out all of them.[165]

The extermination of the Jewish enemy represents a part of a larger claim: the entire West with its (Jewish-inspired) corruptions will fall: "Islam is the final word of God, and the final word of God to His creatures is the Qur'an, and His final word should be generally [accepted] throughout the globe. War is the final solution, but he will send ambassadors to all the non-Muslim countries of Europe [to persuade them to accept Islam peacefully]."[166] Meantime, the proleptic joys of

---

[161] Hisham Kamul Àbd al-Hamid, *Iqtaraba khuruj al-masih al-Dajjal* (Cairo: Dar al-Bashir, 1996), 64; cited in Cook, *Contemporary Muslim Apocalyptic*, 119–20.

[162] On ZOG, see Barkun, *Culture of Conspiracy*; Chip Berlet, *Right Wing Populism in America: Too Close for Comfort* (New York: Guildford Press, 2000). For an example of ZOG thinking, see "Jew Watch," online: http://www.jewwatch.com/jew-occupiedgovernments-usa.html, April 15, 2010. Now, after 9-11, the Left has become increasingly susceptible to this kind of thinking; see Robert Wistrich, *Lethal Obsession: Anti-Semitism from Antiquity to the Global Jihad* (New York: Random House, 2010), 274–435.

[163] See Cook, *Contemporary Muslim Apocalyptic*, 18–35.

[164] Àrif, *Nihayat al-Yahud*, 85, cited in Cook, *Contemporary Muslim Apocalyptic*, 220.

[165] See above, nn. 63, 144. Despite variants that include Christians, only versions mentioning the Jews are cited in modern Muslim apocalyptic literature (Cook, *Contemporary Muslim Apocalyptic*, 36). The original hadith can be read only as the extermination of a Jewish army, not the entire people, but most contemporary Jihadi readings involve the entire population of Jews the world over (see below, p. 462).

[166] Muhammad 'Isa Da'ud, *Al-Mahdi al-muntazar 'ala al-abwab* (Cairo: Dar Randa Amun, 1997) 241, cited in Cook, *Contemporary Muslim Apocalyptic*, 143.

imagining the West's destruction occupy an important part of these apocalyptic writings:

> The 24 hours has passed, and only minutes remain before the terrifying explosions will reverberate in the three capitals, which have turned to ruins: Paris, with its iron Eiffel Tower turned to a heap of destruction and ruin everywhere. London, the capital of whoredom, and hypocrisy vis-a-vis America, has been wiped out. The miserable and antiquated crown [of England] will fall in the mud and ruin that swallow the city. Washington, the city of the White House, where the policies of Satan [are laid out], and the cursed Congress, whose decisions are led by the devil, and are carried out by the Antichrist, will be swallowed by fires and will become past tense.[167]

Except for the Eiffel Tower, which was in fact a (failed) target, these apocalyptic promises from the mid-1990s all produced deeds in the course of the early twenty-first century.

In some of the scenarios we find a messianic figure, the Mahdi, whose arrival brings on a complete reversal in which the last shall become first and the first, last: "The Mahdi's power with all of its trappings will dazzle the West, even before they comprehend the particulars of the orthodox law of God [i.e., before they convert to Islam], just as previously the Arabs would gaze dazzled towards the West."[168] As a result, all the world will turn with one mind to Islam, and all the technology of the world will find its fulfillment in the advent of Muslim globalization.

> European and American youth will come immigrating to see the Mahdi, dazzled by his personality, and will come to Jerusalem to meet him, and the meetings will be safe-havens in which there will be discussions at a high level of thought. Thought is the most important weapon and the thinker is the greatest doctor for the spirit, and the engineer for the mind, and the artist for the personality and its reformation. Not a single one of the delegations will leave these discussions without converting to Islam.... the United States of America will never be able to do anything, because the Mahdi will rule the entire world, and the technology is the main thing. Most of his miracles that he will accomplish will not be divine miracles, but very advanced scientific miracles that stupefy the people and make them happy at the same time. The youth will work with him to make the world into a vision which he sees—those sciences of Islam which make the people happy and not make them frightened as happened at Hiroshima and Nagasaki.[169]

Of course, should any resistance appear, the Mahdi knows what to do: "He will not allow anyone to stop the propagation of Islam, and war will be for anyone who attempts to put out the light of this great faith or tries to stop it."[170]

---

[167] Da'ud, *Al-Mahdi al-muntazar*, 273, cited in Cook, *Contemporary Muslim Apocalyptic*, 144.

[168] Da'ud, *Al-Mahdi al-muntazar*, 272, cited in Cook, *Contemporary Muslim Apocalyptic*, 144.

[169] Da'ud, *Al-Mahdi al-muntazar*, 237, cited in Cook, *Contemporary Muslim Apocalyptic*, 146.

[170] Da'ud, *Al-Mahdi al-muntazar*, 284–85, cited in Cook, *Contemporary Muslim Apocalyptic*, 148. The Mahdi here plays the same role as the technologically advanced ET's in UFO transformational millennial scenarios.

David Cook notes that degree of wish fulfillment in the fantasy, a "magical" millennium:

> This is strikingly similar to the Qur'anic fiat of creation: "Indeed, when We want a thing to be, We just say to it: Be, and it comes to be" [16:40]. There are no practical insights about how humanity will change, nor how exactly Islam could do a better job at ruling (supposedly) than the West has done. It is simply that it is Islam's place to rule, not the West's place, and so once this rule is returned to its rightful possessors, then human civilization will be rectified and the messianic age will be achieved.[171]

But when will such events occur? Khomeini left a powerful legacy, but few call him the [now, once-again hidden] Imam. Afghanistan's Mullah Omar may have worn the mantle of the prophet, but the American army and allies swept him and his caliphate aside in weeks. Muslim writers faced the same apocalyptic problem all believers do: how to make those magnificent dreams "take" and how to deal with their failure even in success.

Among the most common such efforts, we find the proliferation of dating systems. As noted above, among the most popular borrowings from Christian apocalyptic discourse in the 1990s was the year 2000 as a key date. Numerous pamphlets feature the Christian date on the cover. So pervasively did the Western dating system enter into Muslim apocalyptic calculations that "[w]hen predicting the end of Israel, Jirrar chooses not to write the Muslim year (1443), but the year 2022 in his title and on his cover. 'Abdallah even mixes the Christian and Islamic systems, dating his earthquake with a Muslim month (Dhu al-Hijja) and a Christian year (1997)—a completely unheard of blend."[172] Jirrar was one of the founding intellectuals of Hamas, head of an institute dedicated to using computer technology to prove the truth of the Qur'an. His exegeses appeared in a number of the earliest Hamas pamphlets. And he was only one of an unofficial battalion of "exact men" who searched the Qur'an and the Bible and current events, for a date.

The year 2000, the Christian date that started the trend, derives its explicit apocalyptic meaning for Muslims from the expectation that in that year the Jews will begin rebuilding the Temple."[173] For Muslims, 2000 signaled the arrival of the Dajjal who would trample the Haram al Sharif (the Noble Sanctuary/Temple Mount) with an army, desecrate the sacred mosque, and begin construction of the Temple. The scenario was classically paranoid, belligerent, apocalyptic: enemies marshaled their forces for final battle; Muslims had to respond.[174] Perhaps they could prove worthy of the Qur'an's promises of Israel's destruction.[175]

---

[171] Cook, *Contemporary Muslim Apocalyptic*, 149.

[172] Cook, "Muslim Fears of the Year 2000," 60. Note that Hamas uses AD dates in its charter.

[173] Cook, *Contemporary Muslim Apocalyptic*, 84–97, 113.

[174] Gorenberg, *End of Days*, 187–90.

[175] Sheikh Abu Al-Waleed Al-Ansari, online: http://www.missionislam.com/nwo/termination.htm, April 15, 2010.

One person's messiah is another's dajjal. Semiotically aroused Muslim apocalyptic writers paid close attention to Christian and Jewish enthusiasm for rebuilding the Third Temple on the very site where the Dome of the Rock, Islam's earliest monumental structure, stood.[176] Any remark about 2000 by Israelis, no matter how anodyne, had apocalyptic echoes for Muslims caught up in this calculus.[177] Anything that remotely resembled these plans, like the opening of an exit from a tunnel alongside the Temple Mount in 1996, provoked a ferocious response.

Who Believed? Apocalyptic Hamas

It is hard to say who actually believed in these scenarios in the 1990s. The texts came not from the elite, but from the "street," freelance writers publishing in pamphlets and tapes. Judging from the increasing number of publications over the decade, it struck a popular chord.

> The books analyzed here are not obscure studies but popular and visible tracts, every one of which has gone through multiple editions. During times of apocalyptic expectancy (like the Kuwait war) it was difficult to keep them on the shelf. In many cases... stacks of these books are available at bookstores near the entrances of mosques, where they sell for a minimal price. I have seen all but one of them in Jerusalem, Cairo, and 'Amman. Ayyub is continually sold out in Jerusalem; Jirrar is one of the best-sellers in the West Bank, Jordan, and Lebanon.[178]

The movement seems to have had remarkable success from the beginning, due to a significant degree to its apocalyptic rhetoric. Researchers living in the Gaza Strip during the first Intifada (1987–92) note:

> At first glance, the ideas of clerics like Jarrar, Sabri and at-Tamimi might seem dense and esoteric, but by the end of the first Intifada, they had gained enormous popularity. The title of at-Tamimi's book—*The Disappearance of the State of Israel is a Qur'anic Inevitability*—became a major slogan and was spray-painted on walls throughout the West Bank and Gaza. Cooks in Jericho, taxi-drivers in Rafah, and video salesmen in Ramallah could all tell you something about the end-time ideas of Jirrar. Indeed, great interest was shown in all things apocalyptic, which served to endow the figures and events of the uprising with teleological purpose and sacred import.[179]

[176] In addition to Cook, see Gorenberg, *End of Days*; Gold, *Fight for Jerusalem*, 231–54.

[177] David Cook notes how apocalyptic writers like Da'ud followed the speeches of Israeli officials, interpreting seemingly random comments as clues to Israel's apocalyptic designs ("Muslim Fears," 58). Here, Da'ud took the comments of a former Israeli chief of staff made about the growth of new leadership in the year 2000, to signal the coming of the Dajjal and the building of the Third Temple.

[178] Cook, "Muslim Fears," 61.

[179] See Anne Marie Oliver and Paul Steinberg *The Road to Martyrs' Square: A Journey into the World of the Suicide Bomber* (New York: Oxford University Press, 2005), 110.

But this popular success was lost on most observers and scholars who, unlike Cook, Steinberg, and Oliver, conformed to the owlish academic training they received and therefore dismissed apocalyptic discourse as fringe material.[180] Islamic scholars did the same and encouraged Westerners to follow suit.[181] To this day, few commentators on Hamas and its intentions or ideology mention this apocalyptic genealogy.[182] Indeed, even as this literature flourished and suicide bombing proliferated, accentuating how seriously Hamas and its target public took the apocalyptic passages in the covenant's clauses, Israeli policy-makers, including experts on religious violence, advised that Hamas might offer a viable alternative to the PLO.[183] The same is true for Hizbullah, and, despite the openly and—to us— absurdly apocalyptic dimensions of Ahmadenijad's religiosity, for Iran as well.[184]

The First Apocalyptic Movement of the Twenty-First Century: Global Jihad

Millennial historians looking back at the early twenty-first century will note that the year 2000 marked a new and more vigorous stage in the apocalyptic wave of global jihad. Although the role of Muslims who invoked apocalyptic language may not have registered much on the awareness of Westerners before the turn of the millennium (how many people knew anything of al Qaeda before 9-11?), never- theless, their spectacular successes in Central Asia had won the attention of Muslims the world over. But even then, the dominant anti-apocalyptic tradition within Islam continued to dominate the public sphere. How much the less, were Westerners aware of this phenomenon.[185]

---

[180] "None of the fissiparous groups that participated in the violent struggles within Sunni Islam ever raised a messianic banner, not even during the... the first and second intifadas in Palestine/Israel," Gabriel Almond, R. Scott Appleby, and Emmanuel Sivan, *The Rise of Fundamentalisms around the World* (Chicago: University of Chicago Press, 2003), 65.

[181] One searches in vain among the publications of the anti-Orientalists and the conferences at MESA in the 1990s and even in the early years of 2000 for papers or discussions of current Islamic apocalyptic beliefs; for an analysis of some of the political trends that led to this neglect, see Martin Kramer, *Ivory Towers on Sand*.

[182] In a book widely acclaimed for "de-demonizing" Hamas, two Israeli scholars have no discussion of Hamas's anti-Semitism: Shaul Mishal and Avraham Sela, *The Palestinian Hamas: Vision, Violence, and Coexistence* (New York: Columbia University Press, [2000] 2006). Note that the BBC has a special page dedicated to Hamas, in which none of this gets mentioned: "Who are Hamas," online: http://news. bbc.co.uk/2/hi/1654510.stm, April 12, 2010.

[183] See Ehud Sprinzak, "How Israel Misjudges Hamas and Its Terrorism," *Washington Post*, October 19, 1997, C1, cited in Ken Levin, *The Oslo Syndrome: Delusions of a People Under Siege* (Hanover, N.H.: Smith & Kraus, 2005), 396.

[184] On Hizbullah, see for example the book by Augustus Richard Norton, *Hezbollah: A Short History* (Princeton, N.J.: Princeton University Press, 2007); on Iran, see the approach of Juan Cole, *Engaging the Muslim World* (New York: Palgrave Macmillan, 2009), 193–237.

[185] Note that Brenda Brasher's discussion of the apocalyptic Internet, published on the eve of 9-11, did not discuss the Islamic phenomenon at all, *Give Me that Online Religion* (San Francisco: Jossey Bass, 2001), 160–83.

As a result, the radical agenda—conquer the world—and its strange and paranoid apocalyptic language remained largely at the margins of the global Muslim public sphere, even if certain areas (like those surrounding Israel: West Bank, Gaza, Jordan, Egypt, Lebanon) teemed with the literature. Mainstream Muslim theologians disapproved of such writings and even condemned suicide terrorism, which originated in the most apocalyptic circles of Hamas in the mid-1990s.[186] Similarly, bin Laden's demand that the "honorable and righteous scholars" of Islam rise up and proclaim jihad against the West that will "go on until the Day of Judgment," fell largely on deaf ears.[187]

In the first years of the '00s (aughts), however, the apocalyptic dynamic turned upside down: almost every apocalyptic trend went mainstream in the Muslim world, including the most transgressive of them—suicide terrorism. The key event was the outbreak of the Al-Aqsa Intifada in October of 2000. This at once broke the back of hopes for the "civil" global millennium, heavily invested in the "Oslo Peace Process," and gave a new dynamic and direction to both Islamic jihad and Muslim media, including the news media.

In particular, the picture of Muhammad al Durah, allegedly slain "in cold blood" by Israeli soldiers on September 30, 2000, which went around the world at lightning speed, awakened a global Muslim rage against an apocalyptic enemy and a deep sympathy for that rage among Westerners, especially Europeans and the radical "left."[188] Bin Laden, who used the footage to great effect in a recruiting video he produced in the months after its appearance, considered that this story revealed the signature of the apocalyptic enemy: "It is as if Israel—and those backing it in America—have killed all the children in the world."[189] Images from the Intifada flooded the homes of people the world over, and Muslims, in particular, found what they saw unbearable. Suddenly, the Jihadi roosters found favor, while the moderate owls looked like rich, ugly, old maids, courted by incapacity.

The public sphere in the Muslim world saw a dramatic rise in discourse that, while not necessarily explicitly eschatological—predicting or dating the end, proclaiming a Mahdi—articulated the most troubling forms of cataclysmic apocalyptic rhetoric and action. Always present in the Arab and Muslim world, sometimes lively, this discourse made major strides from the margins toward the center, its path amply assisted by mutations created by the new possibilities of television and the Internet. The demonstrators outside the Danish Embassy in London in 2006, protesting the publication of mostly anodyne cartoons featuring the prophet Muhammad, held signs and gave speeches revealing these active

---

[186] On the context of the development of suicide terrorism (suicide attacks on civilians rather than on military or political targets) in the apocalyptic circles of the Palestinian branch of the Muslim Brotherhood, Hamas, see Oliver and Steinberg, *Road to Martyrs Square, and appendix at website.*

[187] See his *Declaration of Jihad against the Americans*, (ca. 1995/6), in *Messages to the World*, 15–19; online: http://en.wikisource.org/wiki/Osama_bin_Laden's_Declaration_of_War, April 1, 2010.

[188] On Al Durah, see the website: "Muhammad al Durah and Global Jihad."

[189] *Messages to the World*, 147–48.

cataclysmic ambitions at world conquest to the Western public in quite startling terms.[190]

- **Conspiratorial Genocidal Anti-Semitism:** In the late twentieth century, Muslim anti-Semitism still seemed like a European import of limited significance.[191] In the years after 2000, however, the most delirious and apocalyptic of these memes—blood libels, *Protocols*, child-murder—gained an intensity and originality that both revived indigenous Islamic strains and fused with the worst of European strains.[192] The *Protocols of the Elders of Zion*, along with a cascade of blood libels old and new, were turned into immensely popular serialized television shows in both Egypt and Syria, and featured in the news Arabs and Muslims consumed. The passive impact of conspiracy theories in the Arab world before 2000, more often inspired violent actions after it.[193] This has joined together with the genocidal hadith of the "Rocks and Trees" in most disturbing forms.[194] Nor were Jews the only target; demonstrators in London promised Europe its very own holocaust.

- **Suicide Terrorism,** which in its Hamas-generated forms has a strong apocalyptic genealogy, went from the fringes to the center of Palestinian and Muslim society.[195] Before 2000, Muslim theologians universally condemned "martyrdom operations," and even Palestinians gave limited (20–25 percent) approval. But once the "Second Intifada" broke out in October 2000, suicide terror became the weapon of choice for global jihad, suddenly and widely praised by theologians and achieving over 80 percent approval rates among Palestinians. Competition set in so strongly that "secular" Fatah tried to one-up Hamas and Islamic Jihad by sending off the first *female* suicide

[190] "Butcher/behead/slay those who insult/mock Islam"; "Europe you will pay, your extermination/demolition/holocaust is on its way." For images of the protestors, see online: http://en.wikipedia.org/wiki/Islamist_demonstration_outside_Danish_Embassy_in_London_in_2006, April 15, 2010.

[191] Bernard Lewis, *Semites and Anti-Semites: An Inquiry into Conflict and Prejudice* (New York: Norton, 1986, 1999).

[192] Cook, *Contemporary Muslim Apocalyptic*, 18–35; Küntzel, *Jihad and Jew Hatred*; Andrew Bostom, *The Legacy of Islamic Antisemitism: From Sacred Texts to Solemn History* (New York: Prometheus Books, 2008). Bostom insists on a native Muslim anti-Semitic tradition that predates any Western imports. See also Rivka Yadlin, "Anti-Semitic Imagery in the Contemporary Arab-Muslim World," in *Demonizing the Other: Antisemitism, Racism and Xenophobia*, ed. Robert S. Wistrich (London: Francis & Taylor, 1999), 311–22; Wistrich, *Lethal Obsession*, 600–927.

[193] Itamar Marcus and Barbara Crook, "*The Protocols of the Elders of Zion*: An Authentic Document in Palestinian Authority Ideology," in *The Paranoid Apocalypse*, chap. 11.

[194] On the astonishingly profuse culture of genocidal hatred against the Jews, see "Anatomy of Hate," Palestinian Media Watch, online: http://www.palwatch.org/main.aspx?fi=113; and "Anti-Semitism Documentation Project," MEMRI, online: http://www.memri.org/subject/en/51.htm, April 19, 2010.

[195] For a discussion of the apocalyptic issues involved in Muslim suicide bombing, see book's website: "The Apocalyptic Genealogy of the Suicide Terror."

terrorist, followed soon by Hamas. The difference between Islamic insurgencies before and after 2000, as in the first and second Chechen war, illustrate how powerful the impact of the Intifada on legitimating suicide terrorism as a weapon of global jihad. Osama bin Laden's attack on the United States on 9-11—itself a suicide operation that caught Western intelligence by surprise[196]—changed the dynamic of the century. It provoked powerful emotions on a global scale, and gained many recruits to both global jihad and to a Western "crusade"—"the war on terror." It has inspired copycat actions, some of which—Madrid and London—succeeded.[197]

- *Global Jihad:* Before 2000, military jihad with the millennial goal of world conquest operated not only at the margins of Muslim discourse, but also well below the radar screen of the Western cultures that were the target. Indeed anyone speaking of these millennial ambitions in the West became, like roosters, the immediate target of attempts to marginalize their discourse as paranoid, absurd, and Islamophobic. Nor was jihad limited to the most violent expressions like 9-11 or the London or Madrid bombings. A wide range of aggressive attitudes emerged in Western countries with large immigrant populations from the Muslim world. Worldwide protests, as in the case of the Danish cartoon affair, gave increasingly full-throated voice to the most aggressive and openly defiant millennial ambitions to rule the world.

- *Culture of Death:* The apocalyptic trope so characteristic of active cataclysmic scenarios, the *embrace of death and killing as salvific,* has a long history in Islam as well as a prominent role in the apocalyptic revival that first breaks the surface in 1979.[198] From 2000, Jihadis have used it as a way to contrast Islamic culture with their Western target: "We tell them [Jews and Christians]: 'in as much as you love life—the Muslim loves death and martyrdom. There is a great difference between he who loves the hereafter and he who loves this world. The Muslim loves death and martyrdom.'"[199] While these sentiments can be found in Jihadi circles since the time of Maududi and Hassan al Bana, in no society have the religious and political elites more deeply immersed the entire population in this culture of death than the Palestinian territories created by the Oslo Process in 1993.[200] Here the media and the education

---

[196] On the difficulty of anticipating such matters (as, also, Khomeini in 1979), see Joel Fishman, "The Need for Imagination in Global Affairs," *Israel Journal of Foreign Affairs* 3, no. 3 (2009): 95–108.

[197] Assaf Moghadam, *The Globalization of Martyrdom: Al Qaeda, Salafi Jihad, and the Diffusion of Suicide Attacks* (Baltimore: Johns Hopkins University Press, 2008).

[198] From "God is dead; everything is permitted," to "Allah wills it; everything is permitted." Muraviec, *Mind of Jihad,* 5–59. Anna Geifman compares the terrorism of Russian revolutionaries circa 1900 with those of Muslims, circa 2000 in *Death Orders.*

[199] Palestinian Mufti Sheikh Ikrimeh Sabri on May 25, 2001 at the Al-Aqsa Mosque in Jerusalem.

[200] The process has been documented in detail by Itamar Marcus and Palestinian Media Watch, online: http://www.pmw.org.il/, and http://www.palwatch.org/, April 20, 2010.

system teach children at the earliest ages to eagerly seek death in killing the enemy.[201]

- **Internet Jihad** exploits the new technological revolution in pervasive and often highly innovative fashion much as apocalyptic Christian movements used printing in the early sixteenth century.[202] This has created a worldwide presence for Salafi Islam, a neo-Islamic, reactionary modern identity that at once separates youth from their more traditional (and less apocalyptic) Islam (especially in Western countries) and unites zealous new Muslim identities across a wide range of cultures, ethnicities, languages, and customs.[203] One of the major themes to find innovative expression on the Internet is the culture of death, which, with the execution of Dan Pearl against the background picture of Muhammad al Durah, entered a new phase with the launching of "execution videos," downloaded by millions in moments.

The year 2000 inaugurated the century—if not the millennium—of an unprecedentedly connected global culture. For decades the question had been: just how "civil" the global public sphere would be. In the late twentieth century, with the collapse of the Soviet Union and the fall of the Berlin Wall in 1989, the sudden multiple successes of the Asian economic tigers, and the spectacular and pervasive spread of the Internet the world over—a communications revolution without precedent in human history—it seemed like civic prosperity in liberal democracies might preside over the new global century.[204] Others warned that history (understood as the warring world of the *saeculum*) was far from over.[205] But at the very turn of the millennium, a new force crashed the optimistic Western-inspired party—the first truly global, active cataclysmic millennial movement in the history of the phenomenon.

Nor is this phenomenon restricted to any single movement. The Al-Aqsa Intifada might have inspired those who launched to believe it was the decisive

[201] "'Ask for Death!' The Indoctrination of Palestinian Children to Seek Death for Allah—Shahada" at Palestinian Media Watch, online: http://www.pmw.org.il/ASK%20FOR%20DEATH.htm, April 16, 2010.

[202] On the apocalyptic, millennial dimension of early Protestantism, see R. Landes, "Millenarianism and Millennialism," in *Encyclopedia of Protestantism*, ed. Hans Hillerbrand (New York: Routledge, 2004), vol. 3; on the role of printing in Protestantism's success, see Elizabeth Eisenstein, *The Printing Press as an Agent of Change* (Cambridge: Cambridge University Press, 1979), 303–450.

[203] On the uses of the Internet, see Gabriel Weimann, *Terror on the Internet*: on new identities, see Daniel Benjamin and Steven Simon, *The Next Attack: The Failure of the War on Terror and a Strategy for Getting It Right* (New York: Macmillan, 2006); Moghadam, *Globalization of Martyrdom*; and *Global Salafism*.

[204] The most articulate version of this vision was Francis Fukuyama, *The End of History and the Last Man* (New York: Free Press, 1992).

[205] Samuel Huntington, *The Clash of Civilizations and the Remaking of World Order* (New York: Simon & Schuster, 1998) was written in direct response to Fukuyama's book. For most of the decade (and beyond) Huntington's work was dismissed as Islamophobic war-mongering.

"shaking off" of the Zionist entity. And for the first days, months, and years, as Israelis cowered in their homes, and tourists cease to come to the terror-stricken land, it might have seemed so. But by 2005, it was clear that, at least this round, for all its successes, was not the apocalyptic round.

Taliban rule in Afghanistan, with its mantle-of-the-prophet-bearing leader, and the spectacular success of 9-11 might have seemed, briefly, like the beginning of an irresistible restoration of the caliphate around the world. And to such apocalyptic hopefuls, the Americans who invaded 2002 had made a fatal error, the onset of the destruction "other empire," the crusading empire. But within months of landing, Americans had dispatched the caliphate and chased bin Laden into mountain caves. Similarly, it might have seemed to the suicide "martyrs" of the Iraqi "insurgency" that they were on the verge of driving a humiliated American out of the Middle East with its tail between its legs. But with startling rapidity, their hopes were dashed by the "surge," which, crucially, recruited other Muslims against the "insurgents."

But we must beware of imagining that such dashed hopes will turn into a long-range trend away from the apocalyptic hopes of destroying the West and creating a global caliphate. Already, one of the most prominent architects of this millennial Muslim revival, Hassan al Banna, had laid out *long-term strategies* that make partial success part of a larger pattern of inevitable, total success. Premature reports of its demise will be premature for quite some time. On the contrary, old hopes return quickly: Hamas has sovereignty in Gaza if not yet Jerusalem; the Taliban have spread through both Afghanistan and Pakistan; and once the Americans leave Iraq or any place they have troops, all bets are off.

What we have seen, beginning with 2000, was the "take off" of an Islamic apocalyptic discourse in the public sphere. Although it has not set the entire population of over a billion Muslims afire, it burns ardently in significant areas, and continues to start new conflagrations, as well as to revive older ones. The resonance of this Muslim millennial dream for world dominance has a broad appeal, even with people unwilling to burn bridges. The attacks of 9-11 stirred many a heart with pride and joy in people—Muslim and infidel—who would rue the day the Jihadis took over. But that stirring, felt by some more passionately, by others more distantly, marks a paradigmatic shift in how Muslims think of their identity in the new global millennium, and this paradigm's products, destructive and creative, will remain unusually dynamic for decades to come. Many a Muslim feels that "the twenty-first century, is the century of Islam."[206]

In such an atmosphere, every failure in apocalyptic terms—the Al-Aqsa Intifada, Taliban Afghanistan—becomes part of a vast millennial pattern, and every decade brings us closer to the next great chronological millennial moment in Islam: AH

---

[206] "The 21st Century Is the Century of Islam," online: http://www.youtube.com/watch?v=7DJ2gfNKTUY.

1500, or 2076 CE.[207] Given how prominent the role played by the advent of the year AH 1400 (1979/80 CE) in starting this current wave of apocalypticism in Islam, and the consistent history of messianic movements around the century marker in the Mujaddid tradition, one can certainly anticipate that the next, even more "round" number of 1500, will inspire its share of millennial hope and action.

If millennial studies has something to offer our current understanding, it is the power of these discourses, the significance of moments when they enter the public sphere with such power, gaining rather than losing momentum when their outrageous, violent hopes become public. Medieval and late antique historians can sail their ships through the iceberg-laden waters of millennial discourse and not know that their ship has sunk. We, today, ignore these phenomena at our own peril. Neither the *Titanic*, nor Western civilization, was or is invulnerable: neither can survive, sailing full speed and blind through such laden waters. Perhaps we should start to think strategically, and pick out the long and difficult road that leads to the millennium-and-a-half marker of Islam and the three hundreth anniversary of the first declaration of a modern democracy in 2076. And, at the risk of sounding like a demotic millennialist, may pluralism and tolerance prevail over the cataclysmic apocalyptic voices on both sides.

---

[207] Jalal al-Din al-Suyuti in the tenth century AH (fifteenth century CE) invoked AH 1500 as an end-term apocalyptic date, a pattern which replicates closely the calculations involved in the year 6000, with its origins among owls (Al-Suyuti) when the date is half a millennium off, and its appropriation by roosters (the Egyptian apocalyptic writer Jamal al-Din) in the final, fourteenth century, on which see Cook, *Contemporary Muslim Apocalyptic*, 90–96.

Conclusion

Assessing Apocalyptic Threats in the New Millennium

If I am not for me, who will be?
If I am only for me, who am I?

■ CONCLUSION

The first decade of the twenty-first century offers a number of apocalyptic prophecies. Some are based in various kinds of fantasy, like the links between 2012 as the end of the Mayan Calendar and extraterrestrial crop-circle communications, some, for example the Rapture beliefs held by tens of millions of Christians, based on particular readings of scripture. These scenarios thereby interest Hollywood just as similar date-based apocalyptic prophecies drew out the skills other masters of narrative in previous eras. Currently, the most popular is the prediction of a catastrophic apocalypse at the end of the Mayan calendar on December 21, 2012. Indeed, a small village in the French Massif Central has already in 2010, begun to draw believers who believe that a spaceship will land and take them off the planet before the doomsdate.[1]

Hopefully, we moderns have developed our capacity to distinguish between reality and fantasy, in our ability to just say "no" to the semiotic intoxication of apocalyptic fantasies. Granted some alarmed business executives spent some $600 billion on preventing a Y2K computer catastrophe when it seems to have been a dud,[2] but at least the whole culture did not melt down into a full-blown panic, as might have occurred in yesteryear.[3]

But some apocalyptic prophecies are not based on dates, or revealed texts, or crop circles, or any of those matters that appeal exclusively to the semiotically aroused (William Blake would say "imaginative") mind. Some are based more on empirical evidence, and thereby demand the attention of the most hardened modern owl. There are predictions afoot in the new century/millennium that, purely on the basis of empirical data, warn of catastrophic scenarios so great that they mean "the end of the world as we know it" (TEOTWAWKI). Thus, one need not be a religious person to find such apocalyptic prophecies compelling, to enter into apocalyptic time at the dawn of the third millennium CE. The two most

---

[1] Bugarach (population, 189): Henry Samuel, "French village which will 'survive 2012 Armageddon' plagued by visitors," *The Telegraph*, December 21, 2010.

[2] I went on record before the fateful second, "Millennialism Now and Then."*

[3] Gustave le Bon, *The Crowd: A Study of the Popular Mind* (London: T. Fisher Unwin, 1895).

credible such apocalyptic prophecies are *anthropogenic global [climate] warming (AGW)* and *global jihad warming (GJW)*. Both have their roosters sounding (quasi-)apocalyptic alarms; both use concrete evidence; both demand massive response. While there are obviously significant differences between these two prophecies, it may offer some valuable insights to consider them together as apocalyptic phenomena.

In the case of global climate warming, we confront a natural phenomenon. Thus, on the social-psychological plane, we only find one set of roosters predicting catastrophe, with variants along a spectrum from passive (nothing we can do) to highly active. Depending on how much of the change seems anthropogenic, i.e., the product of human technology, one can either take a passive approach—there is nothing we can do about it—or call for massive reallocations of funding and efforts. This latter approach, AGW, constitutes one of the most powerful activist apocalyptic voices in this generation. Roosters of the anthropogenic school use apocalyptic discourse to mobilize and exercise our civilization's collective will. Owls, on the other hand, oppose massive reallocation of technological and financial resources to solve an anticipated problem they do not consider real.

In the case of global jihad warming (GJW), we find a markedly different configuration. Since both sides of the equation are human, two sets of owls and roosters operate: on the Islamic side, the Jihadi roosters who embrace an apocalyptic reading of Islamic millennial ambitions (above, chapter 14), and the conservative or traditional owls who, for a variety of reasons, dismiss or oppose the apocalyptic stirrings in their midst. On the outside, among apocalyptic "others" we find roosters who, as jihadis gain in strength, warn against the attack on what these jihadis consider Dar al Harb, and owls who reject the alarms sounded by observers of apocalyptic Islam's progress.

Ironically, these two "rational," empirically based apocalyptic fears have produced a radical, a seemingly incongruous combination of rooster and owl rhetoric *from the same people* (at least in the West): most roosters on AGW are owls on GJW and vice-versa. The irony here is particularly biting since the same issue—the West's addiction to oil—feeds both of these looming anthropogenic catastrophes. One might have expected at least some analysts to consider these two mutually reinforcing concerns in a larger, uniting framework. Instead, an almost universally consistent split seems to override any such analysis. From this angle, it seems like apocalyptic rhetoric from both sides participates in the culture war.

◼ THE APOCALYPTIC "OTHER" AND THE "RIGHT-LEFT" CONTINUUM

This remarkable (and one might argue counter-empirical) split between the AGW and the GJW apocalyptic camps may have something to do with a fundamental clash between a modern, civic mentality/ethical systems and premodern ones. In premodern modes ("right-wing," authoritarian along a democratic political spectrum), the "other" is the enemy and our relationship to that "other" is zero-sum; one can—indeed must—fight against "them," even at the cost of commitment to higher ethics. Us versus them; our side, right or wrong; we only win if they lose. Such premoderns in apocalyptic mode favor active cataclysmic scenarios: the Battle of Armageddon.

Modern, and even more so, postmodern modes of interpretation emphasize both self-criticism and empathy with the "other." Whoever is right, my side or not; us *and* them; win-win; war is *not* the answer. "We can work it out..." Western progressives favor this essentially active transformational apocalyptic mode. I have argued that this perspective animated much of the demotic millennialism and the egalitarian revolutions of the eighteenth century with their attempts to dismantle the prime divider. Indeed one might argue that it defines the most dynamic and creative dimensions of modernity. Its positive-sum attitude makes possible institutions like the United States, the United Nations, and the European Union—all pipe dreams from the perspective of prime divider societies. Not surprisingly, most of the intellectual and principled players in the modern West today take this approach as a given, the moral imperative. There is even a postmodern, postcolonial school of *alterity* that gives epistemological priority to the "other's" narrative. In its most extreme form it starts from the position: "their side right or wrong."[4]

Westerners generally find the "AGW" apocalyptic scenario much more appealing, not only because of the powerful empirical evidence, but also because it "suits" self-critical, modern and postmodern, psychological orientations. Saving the earth is a noble progressive cause: Earth is the victim of our own assaults, the last and most disastrous "conquests" that Western, Promethean hubris has achieved over its various rivals. Because *we* are at fault, because the "other" is a beneficent victim, because repenting means ceasing to rape (our mother nature!), AGW registers positively with all our progressive priorities: paying attention to the "other," self-criticism, self-restraint.

These self-critical attitudes and the lively conversations they enable play a central role in many of the most creative aspects of our culture, especially global, Internet-driven interactions, itself hailed as one of the most powerful *progressive* forces of the new millennium.[5] In the same way that the printing press transformed sixteenth-century Europe, the Internet constitutes a communication revolution that will transform global culture.[6] For such believers in "soft power,"

---

[4] The approach was adumbrated in a series of essays published in 1970 by Emmanuel Levinas: *Alterity and Transcendence*, trans. Michael B. Smith (New York: Columbia University Press, 1990). See also Jeffrey Thomas Nealon, *Alterity Politics: Ethics and Performative Subjectivity* (Durham, N.C.: Duke University Press, 1998). For a critique of the more extreme tendencies of this school, see Stephen Hicks, *Explaining Postmodernism: Skepticism and Socialism from Rousseau to Foucault* (Tempe Arizona: Scholargy Publishing, 2004). See below, n. 11.

[5] See Rick Levine, Christopher Locke, Doc Searls, and David Weinberger, *The Cluetrain Manifesto* (New York: Basic Books, [2000] 2009).

[6] Richard Landes, "Printing and the 16th Century, Cyberspace and the 21st—Lessons from the Past, Thoughts on the Future," online: http://worldcat.org:80/arcviewer/1/OCC/2007/09/28/0000073852/viewer/file683.html, September 13, 2010.

AGW is the perfect apocalyptic narrative for a guilt-integrity culture: our hubris has brought upon us our suffering. "We have met the enemy, and he is us."[7] At the very least, we need to go on an energy diet; in more drastic versions, most of us need to die.

The owls on AGW, on the other hand, tend to congregate on the "right." Taking a nineteenth- and twentieth-century definition of industrial modernity as the Promethean *hero*, they establish the "tradition" that, as "conservatives," they protect: productivity, competition, wealth. No global diets at a time like this; on the contrary, full-speed ahead on the *Titanic* of modernity and damn the (melting) icebergs.

Of the two apocalyptic prophecies under consideration, AGW is the older one. The solitary "voices in the wilderness" warning of global climate change appeared in the first half of the twentieth century, when the impact of human technological activity was only beginning to make itself felt. By the 1970s, when apocalyptic prophecies of environmental damage first began to make headway, it was not clear whether the future would bring global warming or global cooling. But the apocalyptic stakes in terms of audience were clear: one witness to the first Earth Day in Greenwich Village commented "Why did I waste my time preaching Marx?" he said. "This works much better."[8]

But by the 1980s, based on an ever-widening base of data produced by ever-more-sophisticated instruments, global *warming* was coming to dominate scientific discourse on climate change. By the 1990s, it became a near-international consensus, first at the Earth Summit in Rio in 1992, then with incipient legislative force in Kyoto in 1997. By 2006, Al Gore's *Inconvenient Truth* had swept away all but the most dogged skeptics. A new dominant consensus emerged in the public sphere, consecrated by the joint Nobel Peace Prize given to Gore and the *Intergovernmental Panel on Climate Change*.[9] The discourse was apocalyptic, even if the will to act decisively is still slow in coming. The now-marginalized owls, sensing the danger, seized at any chink—like the email scandal—to attack the armor of the new "grand narrative."[10]

---

[7] Walt Kelly, on a poster for Earth Day in 1970; see above, chapter 13, n. 55.

[8] Testimony of Clark Whelton, email correspondence, January 23, 2011.

[9] See their site online: http://www.ipcc.ch/.

[10] Art Horn analyzes the response of AGW roosters to what the owls call "Climategate," specifically in terms of cognitive dissonance and apocalyptic expectations, "Wounded Warmists Attack: It's What Happens 'When Prophecy Fails,'" *Pajamas Media*, May 16, 2010, online: http://pajamasmedia .com/blog/wounded-warmists-attack-its-what-happens-when-prophecy-fails/?singlepage=true. See also Christopher Booker, "Climate Change: This is the Worst Scientific Scandal of Our Generation," *Telegraph*, November 28, 2009, online: http://www.telegraph.co.uk/comment/columnists/ christopherbooker/6679082/Climate-change-this-is-the-worst-scientific-scandal-of-our-generation. html; and the extensive coverage at *Pajamas Media*, online: http://pajamasmedia.com/?s=climategate. For a systematic study of the issue that does not consider the implications of the email affair serious for the AGW hypothesis, see *The Independent Climate Change Email Review*, headed by Sir Muir Russell, http://www.cce-review.org/; all sites accessed August 11, 2010.

In the case of *global jihad warming* (GJW), on the other hand, the timetable and dynamics differ significantly. First, the phenomenon itself has emerged much more recently, first visible (if not recognizable to the West) in 1979, and a pervasive global phenomenon only in the last decade—since the Al-Aqsa Intifada and 9-11 at the dawn of this century. Muslim roosters successfully entered and have come to dominate much of the global public sphere in the Muslim world over the course of the last generation. At the same time, Western intellectuals, committed to a worldview that rejects the idea of zero-sum enemies (and certainly of apocalyptic ones), have responded more slowly. Even as AGW roosters become the main public voice of authorities and experts, GJW roosters remained largely marginalized.

This raises the second significant difference between the two. In AGW, only one side of the equation is anthropogenic: the global climate system is a force of nature, responding to various natural and man-made influences. Neglecting AGW can make things worse, but nature does not "react" to our failures by accelerating the process even more.

Global jihad, on the other hand, is not a natural juggernaut that might crush us in its inexorable but supremely indifferent inertia. Rather it represents an entirely *human*, if premodern apocalyptic movement, steeped in "us-them" political attitudes. Jihadis have engaged in an (outrageously hopeful) asymmetric war with the West, which, to most observers, even Muslims, seems ludicrous. But it is only a ludicrous fantasy if the opponents of such a dream act decisively to discourage it. Failure to acknowledge the threat and respond appropriately can have direct consequences on jihad itself. For apocalyptic warriors, perceived weakness on the part of "the enemy" encourages aggression and wins over fence-sitters. Neglect not only *allows*, but *encourages* the apocalyptic movement to grow.

And yet, paradoxically, we seem more disoriented, more reluctant to confront the problem, perhaps precisely because it is a human one. Ferocious apocalyptic movements inevitably trigger "us-them" instincts among their enemies, indeed, as one of the "laws" of apocalyptic dynamics states, often with a matching apocalyptic dualism: one person's messiah is another's antichrist. The Western public sphere, steeped as it is in progressive principles, finds such reactions deeply troubling, reminders of the kind of atavistic fascism that brought such catastrophe to Europe in the mid-twentieth century.

Thus, even "secular" thinkers, arguing on the basis not of "our" revelatory (apocalyptic) texts (Daniel, Revelation, Nostradamus), but of empirical data (including "their" religious texts), find themselves facing a determined opposition which prefers accusing "us" (the West) than "them" (the Muslim world).[11] In its early stages

---

[11] An interesting case of those who regret the West's ability to defend itself is the Pakistani-born English writer Ibn Warraq, *Defending the West* (Amherst, N.Y.: Prometheus Books, 2007), an ardent patriot for Western-style (reciprocal) freedoms, much dismayed by the cowardly folly of the Western response to the Danish Cartoon Affair. Notes Warraq: "many leftists are not just self-critical, they are inverted nationalists. They identify with their nations' enemies: just as Whig radicals empathized with Napoleon, Kim Philby and his cohorts made the Soviet Union their adopted homeland, and hard left Israeli academic Han Pappe identifies with Hezbollah" (p. 278). Roger Scruton has coined the term *Oikophobia* for this default suspicion of one's own side: Roger Scruton, *England and the Need for Nations* (London: Civitas, 2004), 33–38, online: http://www.civitas.org.uk/pdf/cs49-8.pdf, August 11, 2010.

(1979–2000), when the conflict seemed absurdly asymmetrical—"What, Islam take over the West? Don't be absurd!"—early-warners registered as fringe paranoids, warmongers, racists, Islamophobes. In the 1990s, such figures—Samuel Huntington, Dan Pipes, Steve Emerson—were marginalized, certainly by the punditocracy.[12] And yet, in the *aughts* ('00s), as more empirical data became available on the rapid expansion of Jihadism, some observers have not only confirmed their concerns, but chartered an even-more-dire prognosis.[13] From unthinkable to inevitable.

One can readily see how Western progressives would find this brand of rooster's apocalyptic scenario far less attractive than AGW: sounding the alarm about the apocalyptic threat of the Islamic "enemy" carries none of the generous and self-critical emotions associated with warning about our own excesses destroying our planet.[14] On the contrary, it seems to demand that we retreat into tribal, "us-them" thinking; that we view the "other" as an enemy, not a potential friend; that we protect ourselves, rather than open up and share; that we accuse and not self-criticize.

Such sentiments make us understandably uneasy. Western progressives are committed to avoiding violence and seeking positive-sum solutions to conflicts whenever possible. Our core values, those that have permitted us to dismantle the prime divider as much as we have, demand that we avoid demonizing and stereotyping. Thus, we much prefer the rhetoric of the owl in terms of the danger posed by Islam, and the rhetoric of the transformative rooster (dialogue and peace-building) as the solution to whatever cultural problems might exist.

Those who persist in sounding the alarm strike most as somehow tainted with the very millennial zeal against which they warn. Unlike with AGW, the roosters warning about GJW continue to face a widely negative consensus of owls who denounce the their strident language as a attempt to "other" Muslims, to smear

---

[12] The most resounding of the warnings came from Samuel Huntington in 1994: *Clash of Civilizations and the Remaking of the World Order* (New York: Simon & Schuster, 1996). The book elicited a great deal of criticism, including a book-length refutation from Amartya Sen, *Identity and Violence: The Illusion of Destiny* (New York: W.W. Norton, 2006). Edward Saïd attacked Huntington's thesis in the immediate aftermath of 9-11: "The Clash of Ignorance," *The Nation*, October 22, 2001, online: http://www.thenation.com/article/clash-ignorance?page=full.

[13] Thus, the response to Bat-Ye'or's *Eurabia: The Euro-Arab Axis* (Madison, N.J.: Farleigh Dickinson University Press, 2005) was either to ignore it or to denounce it as conspiracy- and fear-mongering Islamophobia. "What began as an outlandish conspiracy theory has become a dangerous Islamophobic fantasy that has moved ever closer toward mainstream respectability," Matt Carr, "You Are Now Entering Eurabia," *Race and Class* 48, no. 1 (2006): 1–22; "Tales from Eurabia," *The Economist*, June 22, 2006, online: http://www.economist.com/node/7086222?Story_ID=7086222, August 11, 2010. In quick succession a small cottage industry of books and articles, often by major academics, have reiterated Bat Ye'or's thesis.*

[14] It should be noted that Westernized Muslims and ex-Muslims like Irshad Manji and Ibn Warraq warn that the first and worst victims of Jihadi and Islamist movements are Muslims.

them.[15] Some express legitimate concerns that efforts to use the law against Islamic radicals endangers free speech.[16] Others want the law to actually repress what they term "Islamophobia."[17]

And yet, unlike mother nature, people—more precisely active cataclysmic apocalyptic believers waging an asymmetrical war against far more powerful forces—respond directly to their enemy's actions. This is particularly true if the same sense of capacious tolerance that makes us so determined to silence the tribal, hate-mongering voices in our own midst, also compels us, in the name of self-criticism and inter-civilizational dialogue, to allow our apocalyptic enemies to broadcast their lethal narratives even as we take the blame for their hatreds.[18] With such a marriage of premodern sadism and postmodern masochism,[19] we pour oil, not water, on the fire.

Osama bin Laden invoked the old Arab proverb about the "strong horse" in his exultation over 9-11: people will side not with the stronger, but with the one they think will be the winner, the one with momentum.[20] If the West looks stupid and ineffective, not by its own standards, but by those of our enemies, and those looking on the sidelines (which includes "moderates" on all sides) have to decide, then we will look like the "weak horse." If Europeans out of an irresistible anti-Americanism cheer on Bin Laden,[21] then they at once strengthen the forces of a regressive apocalyptic rage aimed at them, and confirm their folly in the eyes of those foes. When the French attacked Bush for his desire to invade Iraq in 2003, they saw themselves as heroes. "The brave are those who attack the strongest," said one journalist.[22] But in Arab countries they were viewed as weak: "They attack their friends and side with their enemies."[23]

---

[15] On the prohibition of "othering" the "Orient" (by which he meant primarily the Arab world), the most powerful voice was that of Edward Saïd, *Orientalism* (New York: Vintage, [1978] 1994).*

[16] Shawn Marie Boyne, "Free Speech, Terrorism, and European Security: Defining and Defending the Political Community," *Pace Law Review* 30 (2010): 417–83.

[17] For a review of legal efforts to silence hate speech directed at Muslims, see Brooke Goldstein and Aaron Eitan Meyer, "'Legal Jihad': How Islamist Lawfare Tactics Are Targeting Free Speech," *ILSA Journal of International & Comparative Law* 15:2 (2009): 395–410.

[18] For one of the better-known authors who blamed the West for 9-11, see Noam Chomsky, *9-11* (New York: Seven Stories Press, 2001).

[19] Bruckner, *Tyranny of Guilt.*

[20] See the analysis of Lee Smith, *The Strong Horse: Power, Politics, and the Clash of Arab Civilizations* (New York: Doubleday, 2010).

[21] "That *we have dreamed of this event*, that *everybody without exception has dreamt of it*, because *everybody must dream of the destruction of any power hegemonic to that degree*,—this is unacceptable for Western moral conscience, but it is still a fact, and one which is justly measured by the *pathetic violence of all those discourses which attempt to erase it.*In the end, they did it, but *we wanted it.*" Jean Baudrillard, "The Spirit of Terrorism," *Le Monde*, November 2, 2001.*

[22] Richard Landes, "Chiraq-Iraq: Sailing Full-Speed in Iceberg-Laden Waters," *The Augean Stables*, March 2003, online: http://www.theaugeanstables.com/essays-on-france/paris-notes-spring-2003/.

[23] Communication from a friend in Morocco at the time.

On Being an Honest Rooster in the Early Twenty-First Century

Now granted, these remarks apparently giving apocalyptic status to both global warming and global jihad make me something of a rooster, something of an alarmist about the direction of Western civilization. On one level, this is only natural: Western culture is the ultimate "hot" culture. Unlike traditional cultures, it does not replicate the past. On the contrary, it embraces cumulative change; it is constantly in motion, indeed in mutation. And much of this Western dynamic is—whether we are conscious of it or not—driven by demotic millennial dreams and apocalyptic moments, both cataclysmic (the Communists) and transformative (the '60s).[24]

On another level, even the most superficial glance at the course of the aughts of the twenty-first century suggests that Western elites are thoroughly disoriented by the challenges of the new, global millennium, that our "traditional" political choices, including our "right-left" political spectrum, seem increasingly inadequate to the task. Indeed, rather than lead to deeper and richer discussion, our internal political conflicts have produced a superficial, ever-widening and hostile culture war symbolized by the self-defeating split between roosters and owls on GJW and AGW. The end of the Mayan Calendar and the completion of President Barack Obama's (first?) term as president within ten days of each other in 2012/13 will likely stimulate rich undercurrent of apocalyptic speculation among a population in the United States and abroad who see enormous problems and few leaders who inspire confidence. The thirst for an explanatory "grand narrative" grows in proportion to the sense of danger and distrust.[25]

Those of us who are committed to the demotic principles of modern society—equality before the law, productive labor, self-criticism, merit, mutually granted freedom, compassion for the disadvantaged—owe an enormous debt to the nation-states that, from the late eighteenth century onward, have created constitutional societies based on the principle of equality before the law. We thus owe to this culture and its progressive commitments the wit to discern and the courage to sound the trumpet when a major (apocalyptic?) threat arises against "us."

As Zeng Guofan, a scholar who bewailed the advances of the (demotic) Taiping put it: "How can all those who study books and know the ideograms sit comfortably with hands in sleeves without thinking of doing something about it?"[26] If we do not assess these two threats—AGW and GJW—accurately, if we do not make sound judgments about their strength, identifying their causes, and developing appropriate responses, this demotic experiment of the last 250 years could, indeed,

---

[24] On both communism and the '60s as millennial movements, see Arthur Mendel, *Vision and Violence*, chap. 4 and 6.

[25] On the troubling growth of "magical" thinking among a public bombarded via the Internet with alternative "narratives, see Damian Thompson, *Counterknowledge* (New York: Norton, 2008).

[26] Jonathan Spence, *God's Chinese Son* (New York: W.W. Norton, 1996), 227–28.

fail, and fail spectacularly. Historically speaking, societies based on equality before the law and granting all their citizens freedom of speech are the anomaly, not the rule. There is no reason to believe that our experiment is immortal.

The issues of the twenty-first century will be the subject of one of my next books. Here let me just say that the future stands before us as a Rorschach, and, especially we in a now-global "hot" society, must think about the future and gauge present behavior in terms of what we anticipate as larger and longer term trends. The anticipated computer disaster of Y2K may have been a dud, but it was only the first in an endless stream of apocalyptic prophecies about runaway technology that will populate the future as long as "technology-driven" civilization continues.

In the matter of the two empirically based apocalyptic prophecies that face us, I would argue that we must learn to discipline our emotions in assessing empirical evidence about these threats in every sense. Recent studies in cognitive psychology have emphasized the profound effect of emotions on the cognitive process and its interference in our "rational" decision-making processes.[27] The ability to absorb information that assaults our sense of identity and of security is very difficult, and often one must wait until it is too late before accepting the evidence one wants to deny.

Just studying apocalyptic thinking, one inevitably gets drawn into its trademark style—semiotic arousal. Everything becomes meaningful or, in abreaction, meaningless. For the roosters, things take on a grander symbolic sense that may not accord with empirical reality; for owls, even serious evidence can, *must* be dismissed. The student of apocalyptic beliefs is like Odysseus listening to the Sirens' song, and only by being tied to the mast of reliable empirical evidence and sober assessment, can we hope not to get drawn into the swift, rocky currents that beckon. And yet, when dealing with secular apocalyptic prophecies—that is, ones that predict TEOTWAWKI rather than cosmic Apocalypse—such sober analysis does not mean always siding with the owl: it is just as easy to get inebriated with denial as with affirmation.

At the approach of Y2K, with its host of things we knew we did not know and, still more disconcerting, those things we did not know we did not know, many observed that *someone* has predicted the outcome exactly right, we just could not know who that was until afterward. We can only do the best we can. The problem is, can we do much better? As one researcher put it, not only are there problems (or factors) that we do not know we do not know, but also solutions:

> Unknown unknown solutions haunt the mediocre without their knowledge. The average detective does not realize the clues he or she neglects. The mediocre doctor is not aware of the diagnostic possibilities or treatments never considered. The run-of-the-mill lawyer fails to recognize the winning legal argument that is out there. People fail to reach

[27] Justin Kruger and David Dunning, "Unskilled and Unaware of It: How Difficulties of Recognizing One's Own Incompetence Lead to Inflated Self-Assessments," *Journal of Personality and Social Psychology* 77, no. 6 (1999): 1121–34.

their potential as professionals, lovers, parents and people simply because they are not aware of the possible.[28]

This is the psychologists' version of what the literature critic Northrop Frye warned about when he spoke of critics having "too little imagination."[29] And if it is hard to ask individuals to rise to the challenge; how can we possibly expect that a whole generation do so?

Historians can afford to be wrong, very wrong about the apocalyptic discourse of the past. After all, we are dealing with matters that occurred decades if not centuries and millennia ago. Historians can afford, along with Virgil, to smile and say: *Olim et haec meminisse iuvabit* [Someday we will even look back on this and smile]. For our own times, however, we cannot afford such detachment. Whereas historically, the rule "apocalyptic prophecies are always wrong" holds, it does not hold about the future, especially a future in which humankind has the ability to self-destruct or, short of that, inflict cataclysmic damage on itself and the miraculous and crowded planet on which we live. We cannot afford to misread the signs and to take counter-indicated action too long.

If the third millennium is to be one of global civil polities living in even relative harmony and prosperity—a thrash rather than a clash of civilizations—then we have a massive task before us. We must at once find some constructive and reasonably reliable ways for the large majority of "traditional" societies and cultures to make the political transition from rapacious, prime-divider structures to the productive, civil polities that characterize—indeed, define—modernity. At the same time, we must find ways for successful civil polities to harness their technological prowess in ways that discipline appetites, and bring under control the addictions that inevitably multiply in a culture of abundance.

These two challenges, to premodern and to modern societies, not only do not mutually exclude each other, they may well be two aspects of the same problem. And I respectfully submit that we will do better in the face of this immense challenge if we understand the varieties and dynamics of the most protean belief in human history: millennialism.

---

[28] Erroll Morris interviewing Prof. David Dunning, "The Anosognosic's Dilemma: Something's Wrong but You'll Never Know What It Is (Part 1)," online: http://opinionator.blogs.nytimes.com/2010/06/20/the-anosognosics-dilemma-1/?emc=eta1, July 21, 2010.

[29] Northrop Frye, *Fearful Symmetry,* 422; quoted above, chapter 2, n. 42.

■ BIBLIOGRAPHY

Blake, William. *The Complete Poetry and Prose of William Blake.* Edited by David Erdman. New York: Anchor Books, 1997.

Brandes, Wolfram. "'Tempora periculosa sunt.' Eschatologisches im Vorfeld der Kaiserkrönung Karls des Großen." In *Das Frankfurter Konzil von 794. Kristallisationspunkt karolingischer Kultur,* ed. R. Berndt. Vol. 1, *Politik und Kirche,* 49–79. Mainz: Gesellschaft für mittelrheinische Kirchengeschichte, 1997.

Burridge, Kenelm. *New Heaven, New Earth: A Study of Millenarian Activities.* New York: Schocken Books, 1969.

Cohn, Norman. *The Pursuit of the Millennium: Revolutionary Millenarians and Mystical Anarchists of the Middle Ages.* New York: Oxford University Press, 1970.

Daniels, Ted. *Millennialism: An International Bibliography.* New York: Garland, 1992.

Desroche, Henri. *The Sociology of Hope.* Translated by Carol Martin-Sperry. Routledge & Kegan Paul, 1979.

Festinger, Leon, Henry W. Riecken, and Stanley Schachter. *When Prophecy Fails: A Social and Psychological Study of a Modern Group that Predicted the Destruction of the World.* Harper Torchbooks, 1956.

Fowden, Garth. *Empire to Commonwealth: Consequences of Monotheism in Late Antiquity.* Princeton, N.J.: Princeton University Press, 1993.

Glaber, Roduflus. Five Books of Histories, ed. John France, Niethard Bulst and Paul Reynolds (Oxford: Clarendon Press, 1993).

Gregory of Tours. *History of the Franks.* Translated by Lewis Thorpe. London: Penguin, 1972.

Gutierrez, Cathy, and Hillel Schwartz, eds. *The End That Does: Art, Science And Millennial Accomplishment.* London: Equinox Publications, 2006.

Karsh, Efraim. *Islamic Imperialism: A History.* New Haven, Conn.: Yale University Press, 2006.

Katz, David, and Richard Popkin. *Messianic Revolution: Radical Religious Politics to the End of the Second Millennium.* London: Penguin Press, 1999.

Landes, David S. *The Wealth and Poverty of Nations: Why Some Are So Rich and Some Are So Poor.* New York: Norton, 1998.

Landes, Richard. *Relics, Apocalypse, and the Deceits of History: Ademar of Chabannes, 989–1034.* Cambridge, Mass.: Harvard University Press, 1995.

———. "The Massacres of 1010: On the Origins of Popular Anti-Jewish Violence in Western Europe." In *From Witness to Witchcraft: Jews and Judaism in Medieval Christian Thought,* edited by Jeremy Cohen, 79–112. Wolfenbüttel: Wolfenbüttler Mittelalterlichen-Studien, 1996.

———. "Lest the Millennium be Fulfilled: Apocalyptic Expectations and the Pattern of Western Chronography, 100–800 CE." In *The Use and Abuse of Eschatology in the Middle Ages,* edited by Werner Verbeke, Daniel Verhelst and Andries Welkenhuysen, 178–203. Leuven: Katholieke University, 1988.

———. "The Historiographical Fear of an Apocalyptic Year 1000: Augustinian History Medieval and Modern." *Speculum* 75 (2000): 97–145.

———. "Millennialism Now and Then." In *Calling Time: Religion and Change at the Turn of the Millennium,* edited by Martyn Percy, 233–61. Sheffield: Sheffield Academic Press, 2000.

———. "Economic Development and Demotic Religiosity: Reflections on the Eleventh-Century Takeoff." In *History in the Comic Mode: The New Medieval Cultural History,* edited by Rachel Fulton and Bruce Holsinger, 101–16. New York: Columbia University Press, 2007.

———, Andrew Gow, and David Van Meter, eds. *The Apocalyptic Year 1000: Religious Expectation and Social Change,* 950–1050. New York: Oxford University Press, 2003.

———, and Steven Katz. *The Paranoid Apocalypse A Hundred Year Retrospective on the Protocols of the Elders of Zion.* New York: New York University Press, 2011.

Lifton, Robert J. *Destroying the World to Save It: Aum Shinrikyo, Apocalyptic Violence, and the New Global Terrorism.* New York: Henry Holt, 1999.

Mannheim, Karl, and Louis Wirth. *Ideology and Utopia: An Introduction to the Sociology of Knowledge,* tr. Louis Wirth and Edward Shils (New York: Harcourt, Brace and World, 1965).

Markus, Robert A. *Saeculum: History and Society in the Theology of St Augustine.* Cambridge: Cambridge University Press, 1989.

McGhee, Glen S., and Stephen D. O'Leary, eds. *War in Heaven/Heaven on Earth: Theories of the Apocalyptic.* Millennialism and Society 2. London: Equinox, 2005.

Mendel, Arthur. *Vision and Violence.* Ann Arbor: University of Michigan Press, 1999.

Middlefort, Erik. "Madness and the Millennium of Münster, 1534–1535." In *Fearful Hope,* edited by C. Kleinhenz and F. J. Lemoine, 115–34. Madison: University of Wisconsin Press, 1999.

Nietzsche, Friedrich. *On the Genealogy of Morals and Ecco Homo.* Translated by Walter Kaufman and R. J. Hollingdale. New York: Random House, 1989.

Noble, David. *The Religion of Technology: The Divinity of Man and the Spirit of Invention.* New York: Penguin Books, 1999.

O'Leary, Stephen D. *Arguing the Apocalypse: A Theory of Millennial Rhetoric.* New York: Oxford University Press, 1994.

Sagan, Eli. *The Honey and the Hemlock: Democracy and Paranoia in Ancient Athens and Modern America.* Princeton, N.J.: Princeton University Press, 1991.

Saïd, Edward. *Orientalism.* New York: Vintage, 1979.

Scholem, Gershom. *Sabbatai Sevi: The Mystical Messiah,* 1626–76. Translated by R. J. Zvi Werblowski. Princeton, N.J.: Princeton University Press, 1973.

Scott, James C. *Domination and the Arts of Resistance: Hidden Transcripts.* New Haven, Conn.: Yale University Press, 1992.

Talmon, Jacob. *The Rise of Totalitarian Democracy.* New York: Praeger, 1960.

Thucydides. *The Peloponnesian War.* Translated by Aubrey de Selincourt. New York: Penguin, 1972.

Trevett, Christine. *Montanism: Gender, Authority and the New Prophecy.* Cambridge: Cambridge University Press, 1996.

Weber, Eugen. *Apocalypses: Prophecies, Cults, and Millennial Beliefs through the Ages.* Cambridge, Mass.: Harvard University Press, 2000.

Wilson, Bryan R. *Magic and the Millennium: A Sociological Study of Religious Movements of Protest among Tribal and Third-World Peoples.* New York: Harper & Row, 1973.

■ SUBJECT INDEX